MW01630014

An Italian Journey

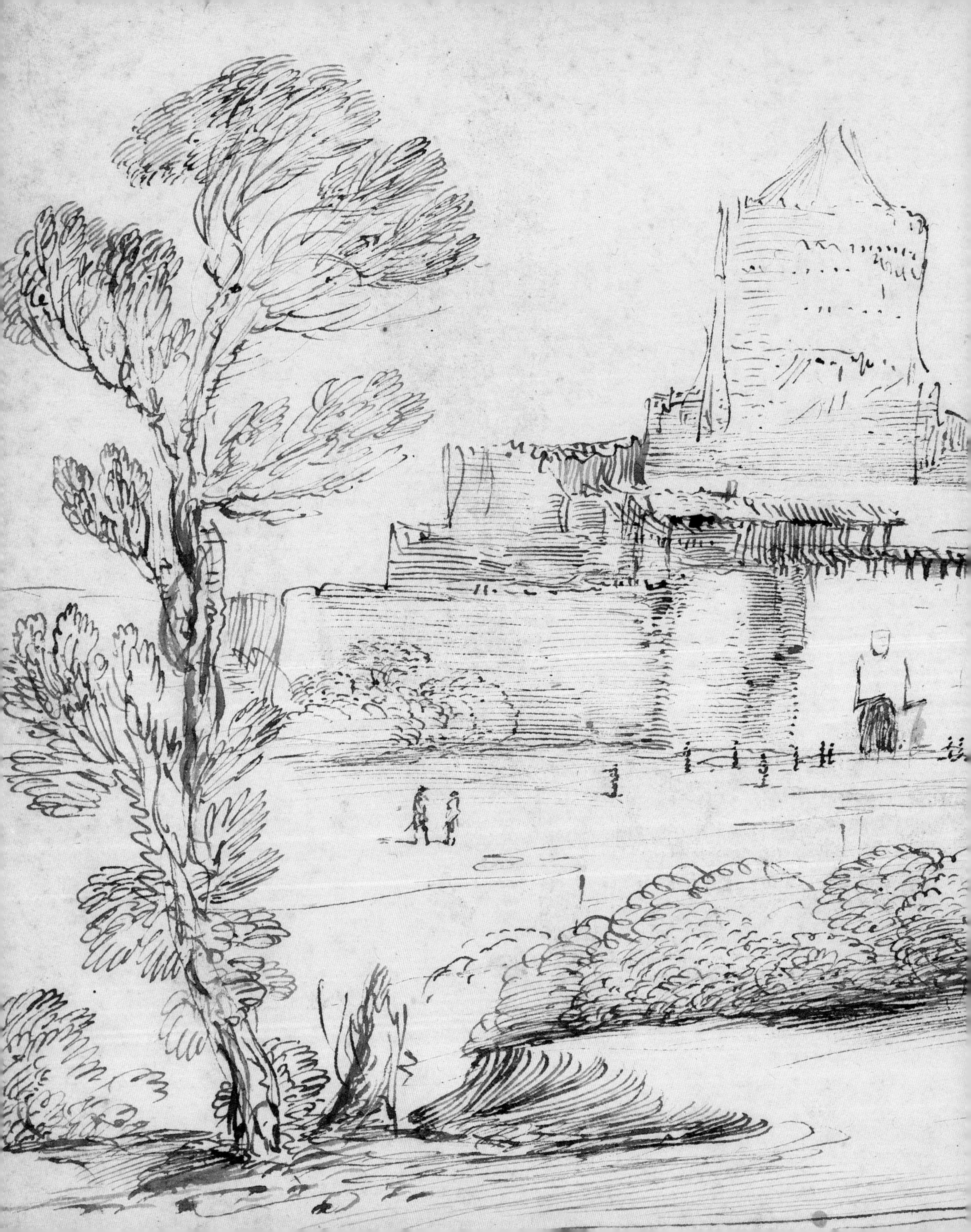

An Italian Journey

Drawings from the Tobey Collection: Correggio to Tiepolo

Linda Wolk-Simon and Carmen C. Bambach

With contributions by Stijn Alsteens, George R. Goldner,
Perrin Stein, and Mary Vaccaro

The Metropolitan Museum of Art, New York

Yale University Press, New Haven and London

This catalogue is published in conjunction with the exhibition
"An Italian Journey: Drawings from the Tobey Collection, Correggio to Tiepolo,"
on view at The Metropolitan Museum of Art, New York, May 12–August 15, 2010.

Published by The Metropolitan Museum of Art, New York

Gwen Roginsky, General Manager of Publications
Margaret Rennolds Chace, Managing Editor
Peter Antony, Chief Production Manager
Elizabeth L. Block, Editor
Bruce Campbell, Designer
Robert Weisberg, Assistant Managing Editor
Salvatore Destro, Production Manager
Penny Jones, Bibliographer

Separations by Professional Graphics, Inc., Rockford, Illinois
Printed and bound by Mondadori Printing, S.p.A., Verona, Italy
Printed on 135gsm Gardapat Kiara
Typeset in Bembo Std

Jacket illustration: Andrea del Sarto, *Study for the Head of Julius Caesar*,
ca. 1520–21 (cat. no. 3, recto)

Frontispiece: Guercino, Detail of *A Wooded Landscape with Figures outside the
Gate of a Castle* (cat. no. 45)

Cataloging-in-Publication Data is available from the Library of Congress.
ISBN 978-1-58839-379-1 (hc: The Metropolitan Museum of Art)
ISBN 978-0-300-15524-2 (hc: Yale University Press)

Contents

Director's Foreword

It has been said that the sixteenth-century Tuscan painter, architect, and biographer Giorgio Vasari invented the concept of Renaissance art when he composed his incomparable *Lives of the Most Eminent Painters, Sculptors, and Architects*, first published in 1550. It may also be said that he invented the practice of collecting Italian drawings—or was at least one of its first and most enthusiastic adherents—when he assembled his *Libro dei disegni*, a volume comprising examples by many of the artists about whom he wrote. From Vasari's time until the present, Italian old master drawings have continued to exercise a seductive aesthetic allure and intellectual appeal for collectors.

The storied days of happening upon two drawings by the likes of the brilliant sixteenth-century draftsman Polidoro da Caravaggio for £10 are long gone (the great British scholar and connoisseur John Gere liked to recount having scored such a coup in the early 1960s), but for a discerning eye opportunities to alight on exceedingly fine examples by historically important draftsmen still abound. Ample testimony exists in the marvelous and richly varied collection of old master drawings, principally by Italian masters but also by artists whose careers brought them south of the Alps, assembled over the last quarter century by David M. and Julie Tobey. We are honored to have the opportunity to present the wonderful and diverse array of figure and composition studies, landscapes, portraits, copies after the antique, botanical specimens, and other types of drawings—works by the likes of Andrea del Sarto, Parmigianino, Bernini, Poussin, Guercino, Tiepolo, and their contemporaries—that they have so assiduously and intelligently acquired and forged into one of the premier private collections of its kind.

The exhibition catalogue is a collaborative effort on the part of a number of authors. I thank Linda Wolk-Simon, curator in the Department of Drawings and Prints and the exhibition's organizer; George R. Goldner, Drue Heinz Chairman; Carmen C. Bambach and Perrin Stein, curators; and Stijn Alsteens, associate curator, all of the Department of Drawings and Prints; as well as Mary Vaccaro, professor of Art History at the University of Texas at Arlington. The exhibition and its catalogue also provide a fitting occasion to acknowledge with deep gratitude the generosity of David M. and Julie Tobey as benefactors of the Metropolitan Museum: David Tobey's role as Honorary Trustee and Co-Chairman of the Visiting Committee of the Department of Paper Conservation; his and Julie Tobey's dedicated support of the Department of Drawings and Prints in myriad ways, including as members of that Visiting Committee; and their past and promised gifts of drawings that have greatly enriched the holdings of this institution.

Thomas P. Campbell
Director, The Metropolitan Museum of Art

Acknowledgments

The authors acknowledge the many colleagues whose kind assistance and scholarly expertise contributed to the content of this catalogue, among them Alessandra Baroni, Rhea Blok, Jonathan Bober, Babette Bohn, Maurizio Boni, Suzanne Boorsch, Julian Brooks, Hans Buijs, Hugo Chapman, Rhoda Eitel-Porter and the staff of the Morgan Library and Museum, Marzia Faietti, Suzanne Greenawalt, William M. Griswold, Ann Sutherland Harris, Andrée Hayum, Eric Löffler, Anne-Marie Logan, Michael McAuliffe, Mark McDonald, Giorgio Marini, Tobias Nickel, Andrew Robison, Cristiana Romalli, Nathalie Strasser, Fabrizio Tonelli, Carel van Tuyll van Seeroskerken, Louis A. Waldman, and Jon Whiteley.

At The Metropolitan Museum of Art we are grateful to Kit Basquin, Michael Batista, Andrea Bayer, David Bressler, Barbara Bridgers, Meryl Cohen, David del Gaizo, Catherine Jenkins, Ricky Luna, Emil Micha, Mark Morosse, Rachel Mustalish, Nadine M. Orenstein, Marjorie N. Shelley, Linda Sylling, Elizabeth Zanis, and Mary Zuber. Invaluable administrative and research assistance was carried out by Eveline Basseggio, Margaret Bordonaro, Elizabeth Eisenberg, and Rachel Stern. For the impeccable design and production of the catalogue, as well as editorial assistance, we are indebted to the late John P. O'Neill, Gwen Roginsky, Peter Antony, Bruce Campbell, Salvatore Destro, Penny Jones, Alexandra Bonfante-Warren, Jane S. Tai, and foremost our gifted editor, Elizabeth L. Block, who gracefully, patiently, and skillfully ushered this book into existence. Finally, we thank David M. and Julie Tobey for the rewarding opportunity to immerse ourselves in the study of their exceptional collection.

Contributors to the Catalogue

SA   Stijn Alsteens, Associate Curator, Department of Drawings and Prints,
The Metropolitan Museum of Art

CCB   Carmen C. Bambach, Curator, Department of Drawings and Prints,
The Metropolitan Museum of Art

GRG   George R. Goldner, Drue Heinz Chairman, Department of Drawings and Prints,
The Metropolitan Museum of Art

PS   Perrin Stein, Curator, Department of Drawings and Prints,
The Metropolitan Museum of Art

MV   Mary Vaccaro, Professor, Department of Art and Art History,
The University of Texas at Arlington

LWS   Linda Wolk-Simon, Curator, Department of Drawings and Prints,
The Metropolitan Museum of Art

All artist biographies were written by Linda Wolk-Simon, with the exception of the
following: Johannes Stradanus (Jan van der Straet) and Master of the Egmont Albums (SA);
Callot and Poussin (PS); Correggio, Parmigianino, and Bedoli (MV).

PREFACE

Each collector is brought to pursue the challenging activities of selection and acquisition through a different set of experiences. David M. Tobey grew up with parents who were both prominent graphic artists, thereby gaining an instinctive appreciation of the special qualities that pertain to the drawn line and the image rendered on paper. His father, Barney Tobey (1906–1989), was a well-known cartoonist for the *New Yorker*, while his mother, Beatrice Szanton Tobey (1907–1993), designed covers for the same magazine. Barney Tobey's cartoons include a delightful example showing a pair of children walking toward the Metropolitan Museum.

After beginning a successful business career, David M. Tobey lived for several years in Singapore, where he acquired Asian art, with objects of Japanese, Philippine, and Thai origin. From about 1970 he also started a collection of Precolumbian art, which was later donated to a university museum. The collecting of drawings commenced after David married Julie Tobey, and it has remained a joint enterprise. Though they both had some grounding in art history, their initial interest was in finding works that would be suitable in the context of antique furniture, and they began with a decorative drawing by Clérisseau. However, they soon focused their collecting almost entirely on Italian drawings dating from the beginning of the sixteenth to the end of the eighteenth century. This was in part due to their friendship with Julien Stock, then head of the Drawings Department at Sotheby's, London. The first work acquired is a lively and expressive sheet of studies of a horse's head by Perino del Vaga (cat. no. 10).

The Tobeys have always shown a wide-ranging taste within the specialty of Italian drawings. Further early purchases include a splendid Guercino landscape from Holkham Hall and a richly executed allegory by Giovanni David (cat. nos. 45, 72), which differ from one another in subject, as well as medium and expressive character.

By the early 1990s the Tobeys became more closely associated with The Metropolitan Museum of Art through their friendship with William M. Griswold, then assistant curator at the Museum and now director of the Morgan Library and Museum. By the time I arrived at the Metropolitan in 1993, they were already members of our Visiting Committee and actively involved with the Department of Drawings and Prints. Since then they have expanded their interests in Italian drawings and their dedication to forming a collection of real distinction. The result is one of the finest such private holdings, with examples

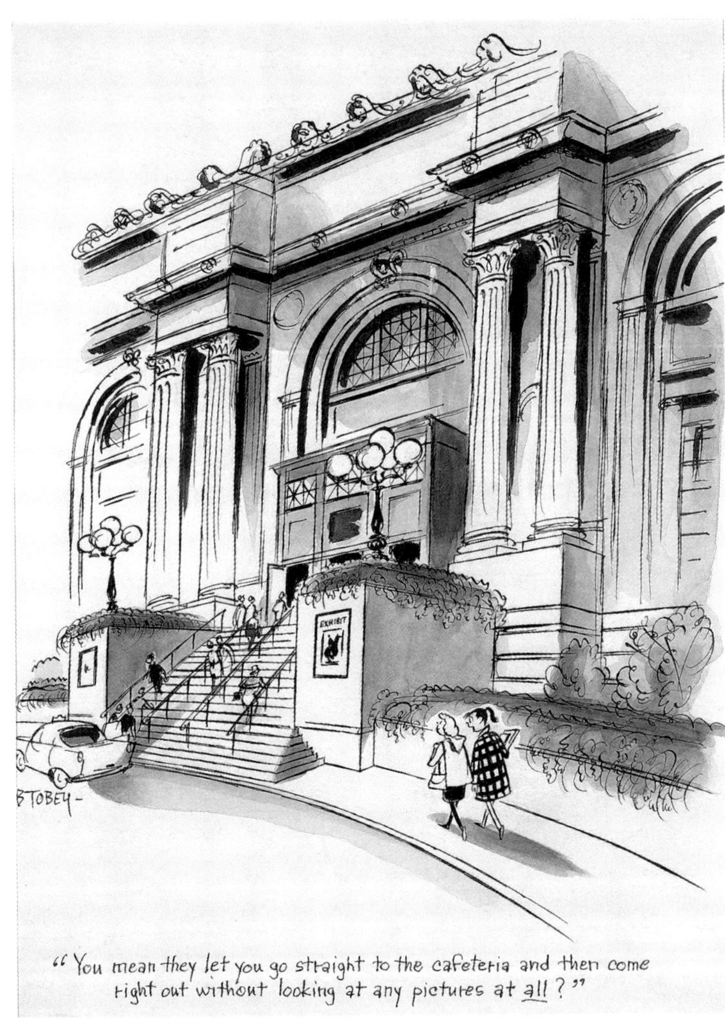

Barney Tobey. "*You mean they let you go straight to the cafeteria and then come right out without looking at any pictures at all?*" December 12, 1964. © *The New Yorker*

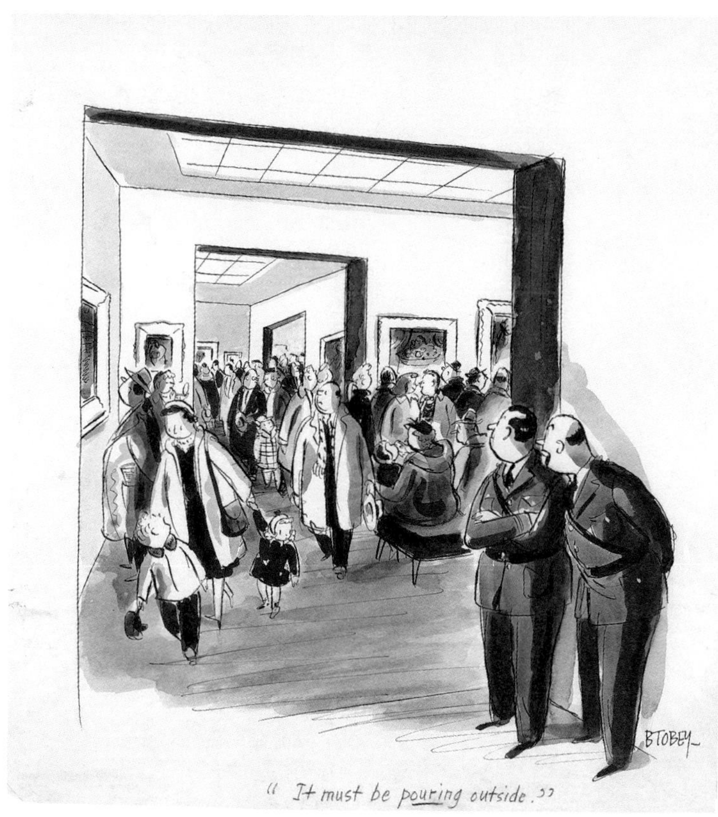

Barney Tobey. "*It must be <u>pouring</u> outside.*" February 27, 1954.
© *The New Yorker*

by Correggio and Andrea del Sarto, as well as outstanding works by less famous figures like Salimbeni and the aforementioned Giovanni David. The main focus has been on figure drawings, but there are also landscapes and views, animals, and even an important study for a ceremonial ship by Algardi.

All of us who collect have different approaches to the moment of decision. The Tobeys' has been one of growing meticulousness, with careful consultation and due consideration of attribution, condition, aesthetic merit, and art historical importance. No drawing has been bought without much reflection, and there have been some that involved spirited debate, as this is a collection formed by two individuals with similar but not identical taste. Having been a party to many of these discussions, I can testify to the thoughtfulness and integrity with which these choices have been made.

This brief preface to the catalogue celebrating their collection is a fitting place to recognize the great contributions that the Tobeys have made to the Department of Drawings and Prints, and to the Metropolitan Museum in general. They have been among the most loyal and devoted supporters of our program, for which we are deeply grateful.

George R. Goldner
Drue Heinz Chairman, Department of Drawings and Prints
The Metropolitan Museum of Art

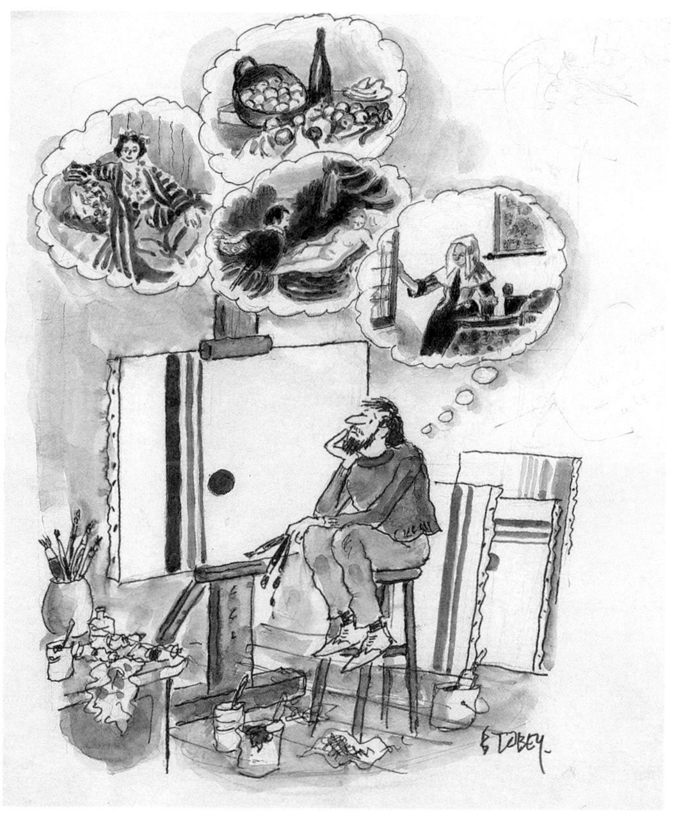

Barney Tobey. *Artist in His Studio*

NOTE TO THE READER

Drawings in the catalogue are reproduced as close as possible to actual size. Height precedes width in dimensions. Exact or approximate dates are given when known. Information on watermarks is included in instances where it is significant for the dating or attribution of the work in question. The provenance of each drawing concludes with the date acquired by David M. and Julie Tobey. References are cited in abbreviated form in each entry. The corresponding full citations are provided in the Bibliography. In cases where the sources are numerous, the authors have provided selected references.

An Italian Journey

Drawings from the Tobey Collection: Correggio to Tiepolo

Lorenzo Costa began his career in Ferrara, where he trained with Ercole de' Roberti. He moved to Bologna, working for the ruling Bentivoglio family and other prominent patrons for whom he painted frescoes, altarpieces, and portraits. Costa succeeded Andrea Mantegna as court artist to the Gonzaga in Mantua; in keeping with the sophisticated taste and antiquarian culture that prevailed there, he produced a number of mythological scenes. Drawings by Costa are rare.

1. Recto: *A Meeting of Notable Personages and Their Courts: A Cleric and Noblemen*, ca. 1520–35
Verso: *Fragmentary Head of a Man in Profile; Incidental Sketches*

Recto: Pen and brown ink; verso: black chalk; pen and brown ink, 4⅟₁₆ x 8¾ in. (10.3 x 22.3 cm)

Provenance: Giuseppe Vallardi (Milan, 1784–1863) (Lugt 1223); Schwarz Collection; sale, Sotheby's, New York, January 16, 1986, lot 33; acquired in 1986

Reference: Sotheby's, New York 1986, no. 33

The vigorous composition sketch on the recto of the Tobey double-sided sheet was attributed to Lorenzo Costa at the time of its sale in 1986, a proposal of authorship that is cautiously endorsed by the present author, in view of the state of research on the still-undefined corpus of works that can be connected to the artist. Evident here and in the painted oeuvre of Costa after 1500 in general are the expressive and highly inflected outlines of forms from Ercole de' Roberti (ca. 1455/56–1496) and the Ferrarese tradition of drawing and painting in which Costa was trained, but they are much softened by an attention to naturalistic detail and an expansive conception of space, together with an elegant daintiness of the figure that are typical of the Bolognese masters at the end of the century, particularly Francesco Francia (ca. 1450–1517), with whom Costa became an artistic partner in Bologna.

A probable stylistic companion for the recto of the Tobey sheet is a quick sketch in pen and brown ink without wash at Christ Church, Oxford, depicting the *Raising of the Cross* (fig. 1.1), which was tentatively attributed to Costa, and dated after the artist's arrival in Mantua in 1506, by James Byam Shaw in 1976.[1] The manners of composition, drawing, and figural anatomy in the Tobey sheet also resemble those of two other pen-and-ink drawings attributed to the artist, both of which were formerly in the Carl Robert Rudolf Collection, London, *A Procession of Soldiers and Other Figures by the Seaside* and *A Procession of Soldiers on Horseback with a Chariot* (figs. 1.2, 1.3).[2] According to Giorgio Vasari's biography of Costa in the 1568 edition of *Le vite de' più eccellenti pittori, scultori e architettori (The Lives of the Most Eminent Painters, Sculptors, and Architects)*, the Ferrarese artist produced various paintings for Francesco II Gonzaga (1466–1519), marquess of Mantua, including a cycle dedicated to the glorification of the Gonzaga family for the

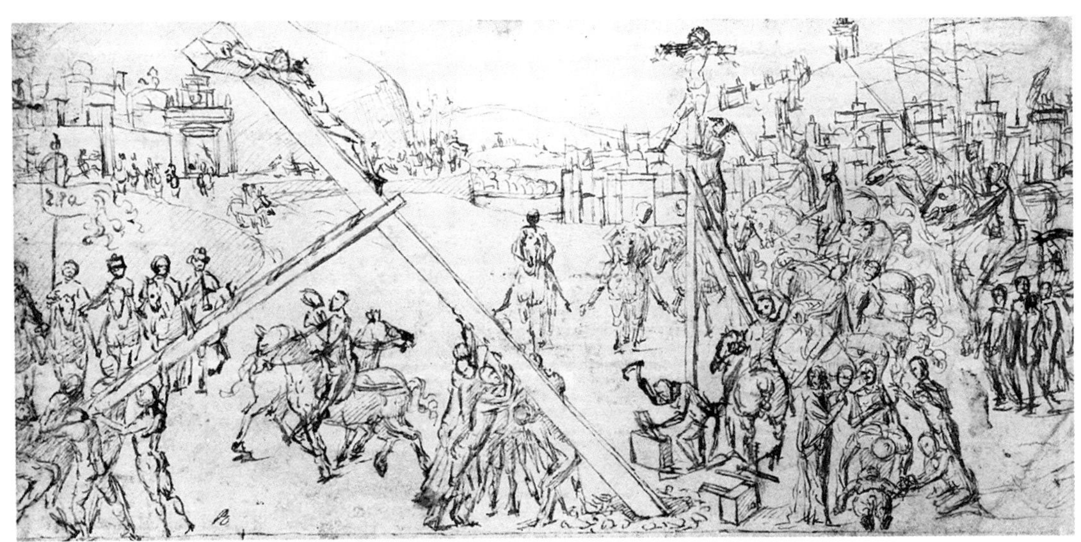

Fig. 1.1. Attributed to Lorenzo Costa. *Raising of the Cross*, after 1506. Pen and brown ink, 5⁹⁄₁₆ x 11 in. (14.2 x 28 cm). Christ Church, Oxford (0281; JBS 862)

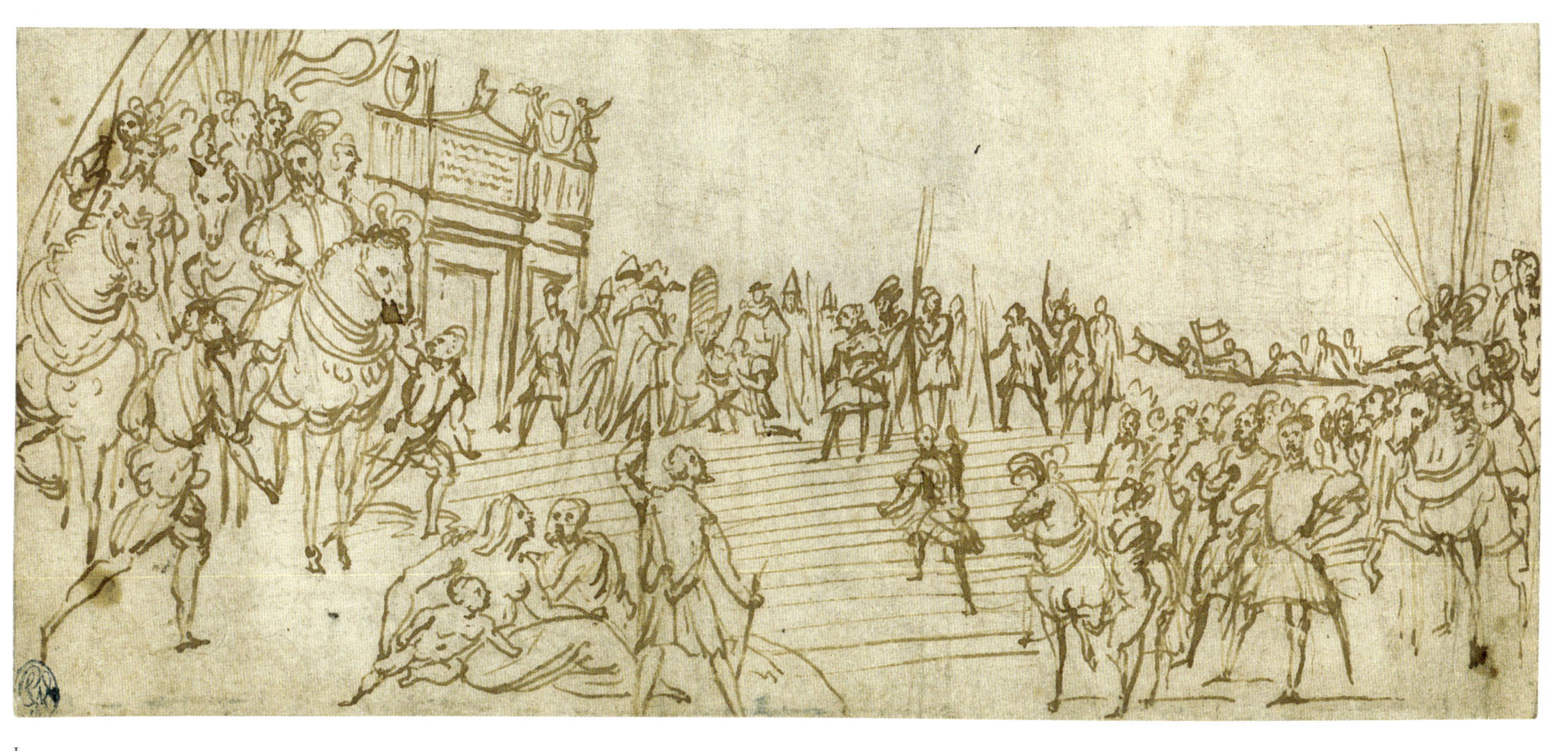

1

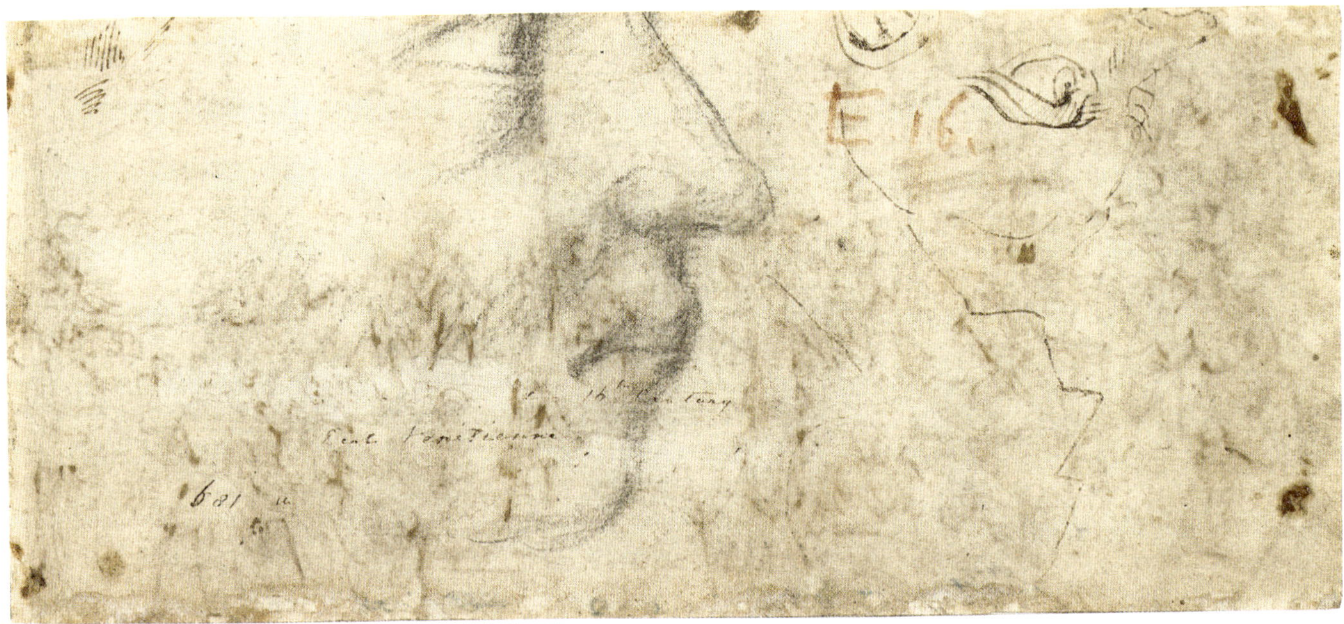

1 verso

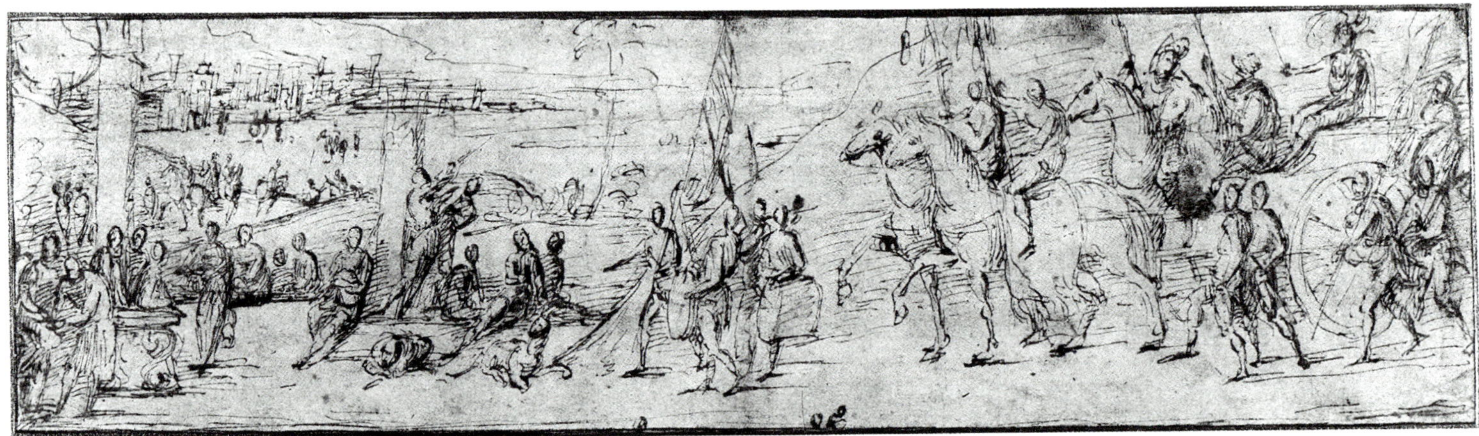

Fig. 1.2. Attributed to Lorenzo Costa. *A Procession of Soldiers and Other Figures by the Seaside*, after 1506 (ca. 1515–25?). Pen and brown ink, 3⁵⁄₁₆ x 11⁵⁄₈ in. (8.4 x 29.6 cm). Formerly Carl Robert Rudolf Collection, London

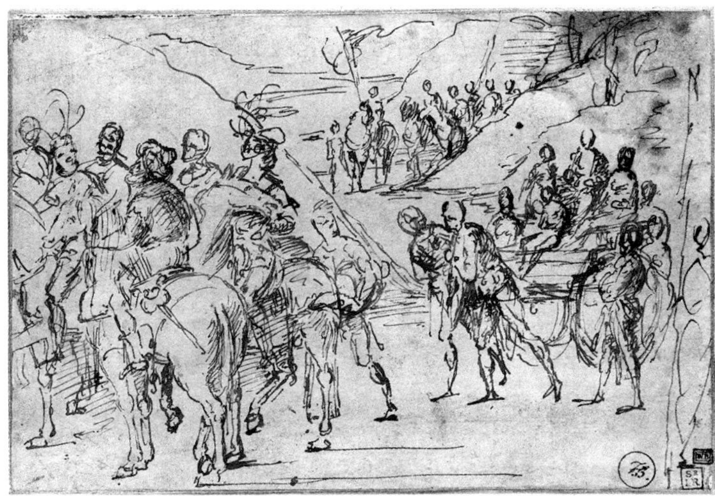

Fig. 1.3. Lorenzo Costa. *A Procession of Soldiers on Horseback with a Chariot*, 1515–25. Pen and brown ink, 7½ x 11⅛ in. (19.5 x 28.3 cm). Formerly Carl Robert Rudolf Collection, London

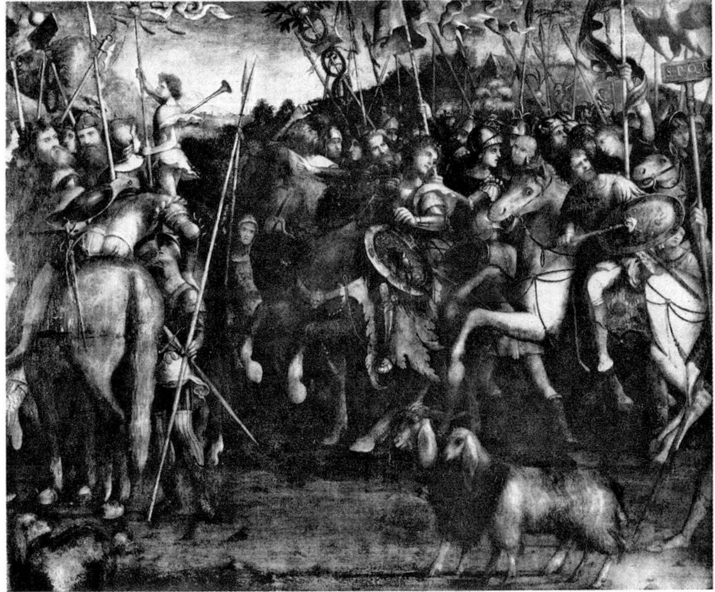

Fig. 1.4. Lorenzo Costa. Detail of *The Investiture of Federico Gonzaga as Captain of the Church*, 1522. Oil on canvas, 105⅛ in. x 21 ft. (267 x 639 cm). Národní Galerie v Praze (O 8274)

great hall (*sala grande*) of the Palazzo San Sebastiano, Mantua.[3] Of this project, the detail of the extant painting at the Národní Galerie in Prague, dated 1522 (fig. 1.4), exhibits figures of similar proportions and nearly toylike horses, as in the Tobey sheet.[4] Given Costa's long employment at the Gonzaga court in Mantua—between 1509 and 1535, he drew an annual salary of 669 lire, 10 soldi[5]—it is likely that he produced more secular decorations connected with his princely patrons than were recorded by his somewhat unsympathetic Tuscan biographer, Vasari, and one possibly to which the Tobey sheet may have been preparatory. Among the family honors, Pope Leo X de' Medici named Francesco's son, Federico Gonzaga, *Gonfaloniere* (Standard-Bearer) and Captain General of the Church in 1521.

Drawn with bold summary strokes, the scene of a triumphal entry on the recto of the Tobey sheet is yet to be precisely identified, although the long poles for standards are seen on the left and right sides. The commanding figure of a princely ruler on horseback is portrayed at extreme left, and next to him in an oblique perspective rises a triumphal arch adorned with heraldic devices and trophies, none drawn distinctly enough to provide a clue as to the protagonist family or event. Nearby, almost at the center, an enthroned cleric (a pope or bishop) and his court receive a kneeling dignitary. This momentous encounter takes place by the landing of a monumental staircase that spreads commandingly within the space of the composition to occupy much of the foreground and middle ground. At extreme right, a cortege of noblemen—some on foot, others on horseback—arrives upon the scene, among them a gesturing rider wearing a plumed hat. In the foreground near the center, a soldier stands watch as a witness to the event, and by his side the reclining figures of a mother and father with their child allude to tranquility and plenty; their poses are unmistakably meant to evoke those of a Holy Family at the Rest on the Flight into Egypt. The possibility may not be discounted that the scene alludes to the meeting of Emperor Charles V and Pope Clement VII de' Medici at Bologna in 1533.[6]

The large fragmentary sketch of a man's profile on the verso seems portraitlike, although not easily connected to a project by Costa. ccb

1. Byam Shaw 1976, vol. 1, pp. 231–32, no. 862.
2. Ibid., under no. 862.
3. Vasari ed. 1966–87, vol. 3 (text), pp. 416–17.
4. Berenson ed. 1968, vol. 3, no. 1636.
5. The document was published by Gaetano Milanesi in Vasari–Milanesi ed. 1906, vol. 3, p. 134 n. 2.
6. On the historical details of this event, see especially Francesco Guicciardini's *Historia d' Italia* written in the 1530s and 1540s but published posthumously in Florence in 1561 (Guicciardini ed. 1984, pp. 438–39).

AMICO ASPERTINI

Bologna, 1474/75–Bologna, 1552

Painter, sculptor, draftsman, illuminator, printmaker, and antiquarian, Amico Aspertini developed an eccentric, expressive style that prompted the biographer Giorgio Vasari to portray him, unsympathetically, as mentally disturbed. His manner was indebted, on the one hand, to contemporary Emilian artists such as Ercole de' Roberti and Francesco Francia and, on the other, to the works of Michelangelo and Raphael that he had seen during his two trips to Rome. Aspertini's profound interest in antiquity is reflected in his sketchbooks, in which he recorded details of many of the city's most celebrated ancient monuments. The stocky, inflated, often overwrought figures seen in works of his maturity frequently echo the classical sources he assiduously studied, but are transformed by his idiosyncratic and highly personal idiom.

2. *The Mourning of a Classical Warrior*, ca. 1503–10

Pen and brown ink, brush with gray, brown, and white gouache, on light brown paper, 10⅛ x 14⁹⁄₁₆ in. (25.7 x 37 cm)
The Metropolitan Museum of Art, New York, Promised Gift of David M. Tobey

Provenance: Carl Robert Rudolf (London, ca. 1884–1974); sale, Sotheby's, London, July 4, 1977, lot 62; P. & D. Colnaghi, London, June 19–August 3, 1979, no. 43; sale, Christie's, London, July 7, 1981, lot 6; Private Collection, London; acquired in 2006

References: London 1962, no. 9; Scaglietti 1963–64, p. 330; Cosmo 1984, p. 36; Daniela Scaglietti in Bologna 1988, pp. 284–85, no. 79; Angelelli and De Marchi 1991, p. 79, no. 136; Kügelgen 1992, p. 443; Faietti and Scaglietti Kelescian 1995, pp. 250–51, no. 35 (discussed from a photograph when in the Rudolf collection, London); Elena Rossoni in Bologna 2008–9, p. 274, fig. 3 (as whereabouts unknown)

This finished composition of an enigmatic subject is among the finest early Italian drawings in the Tobey Collection. Although it has been known as a major autograph work by Amico Aspertini since at least 1962, it has rarely been exhibited, or studied by scholars in the original. The muted lighting, relieflike composition, delicately proportioned figures, and refined modeling are all typical of the artist's drawings from the first decade of the sixteenth century. The painterly style in a monochrome palette of warm, brown hues (*en brunaille*) with white gouache highlights, and some passages of fine ink-hatching in the shadows, together with the overall specificity of line and detail, indicate that it may have been intended as a study for a fresco decoration on a palace facade or courtyard. The technique of facade fresco painting in monochrome was a specialty of Aspertini, but few such decorations by him have survived the ravages of time and climate. In the *Vite*, his biographer Giorgio Vasari mentioned in the *Vita* of Bartolomeo Bagnacavallo (in both the 1550 and 1568 editions) that Aspertini painted numerous front exteriors of buildings in Bologna.[1] The decorations on the Casa Cortelli in the Via San Donato, Casa Schiappa, Scuderie dei Marsili, the houses near the Porta San Mamolo and on the Via San Pratello, as well as others, have all disappeared. It is also possible that the present sheet served another, entirely different purpose, as a preparatory design for a small-scale decorative ensemble of a much more intimate nature—a scene for a panel on a chest, or a frieze. A pair of such small, painted panels *en brunaille* by Aspertini, datable to the same period in his career, passed through the art market in 1993, one an *Amazonomachia*, and the other a *Battle of Romans against Barbarians*.[2] The figures are of similar scale, while the mood and classical themes are also comparable.

Although the precise subject remains to be identified, visual clues in the Tobey composition suggest that it combines complex and imaginative levels of allegorical content, undoubtedly inspired by antique literary sources. An ingenious use of iconography is typical of the erudite Aspertini's work, but it was often misunderstood by some of his contemporaries, and especially by Vasari, who, as a good Tuscan, felt no fondness for Bolognese artists and disparagingly called Aspertini "a capricious man of bizarre mindset," who "produced figures, all over Italy, that can even be called crazy."[3] While Giulia Cosmo

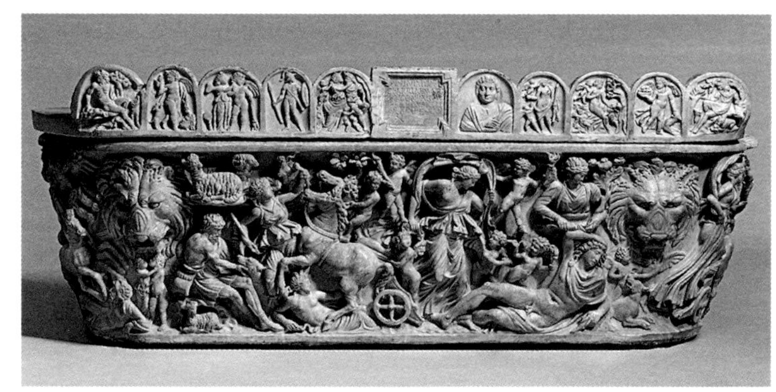

Fig. 2.1. *Endymion Sarcophagus*, early 3rd century A.D. Roman. Marble, H. 28½ in. (72.4 cm). The Metropolitan Museum of Art, New York, Rogers Fund, 1947 (47.100.4a, b)

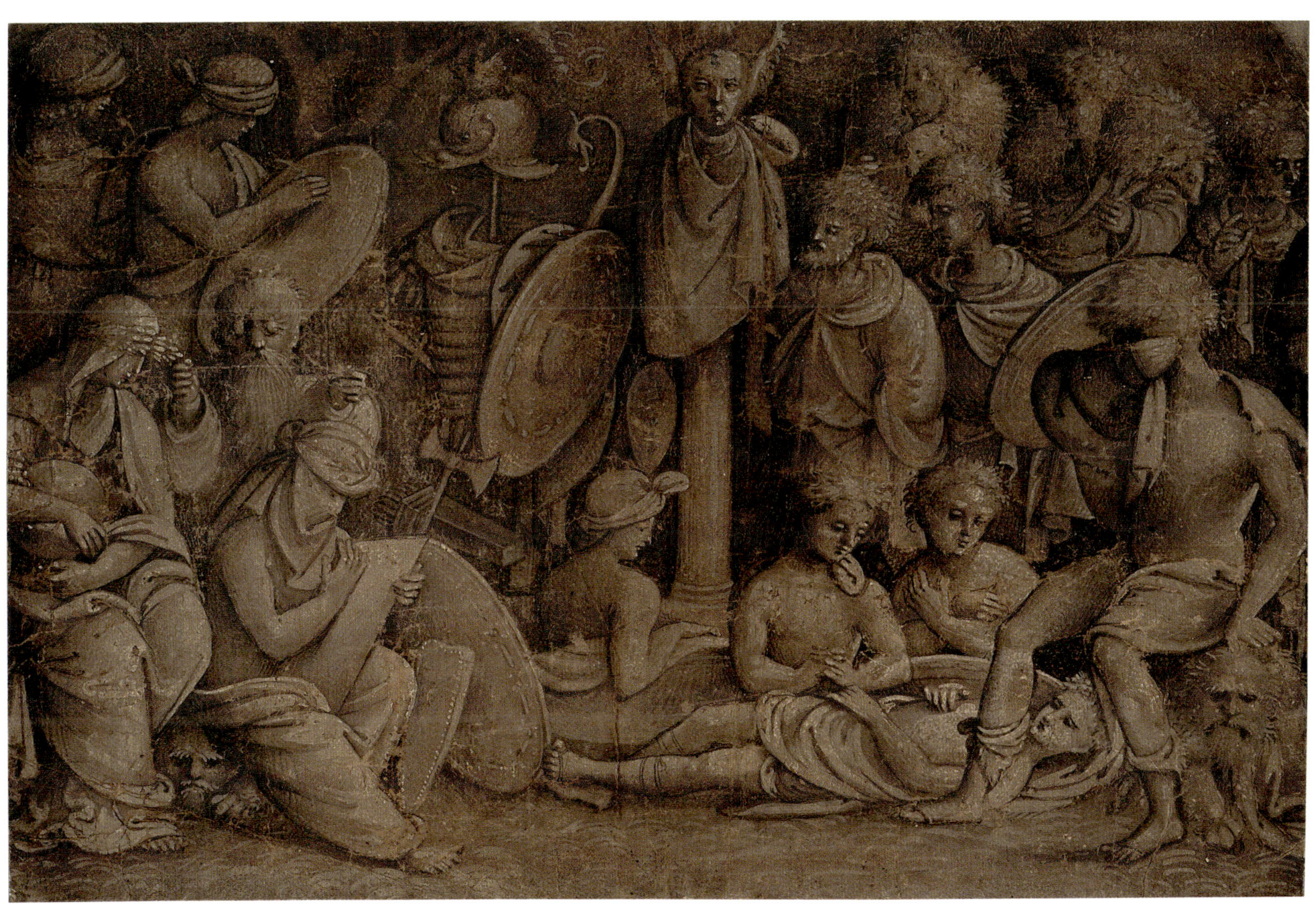

2

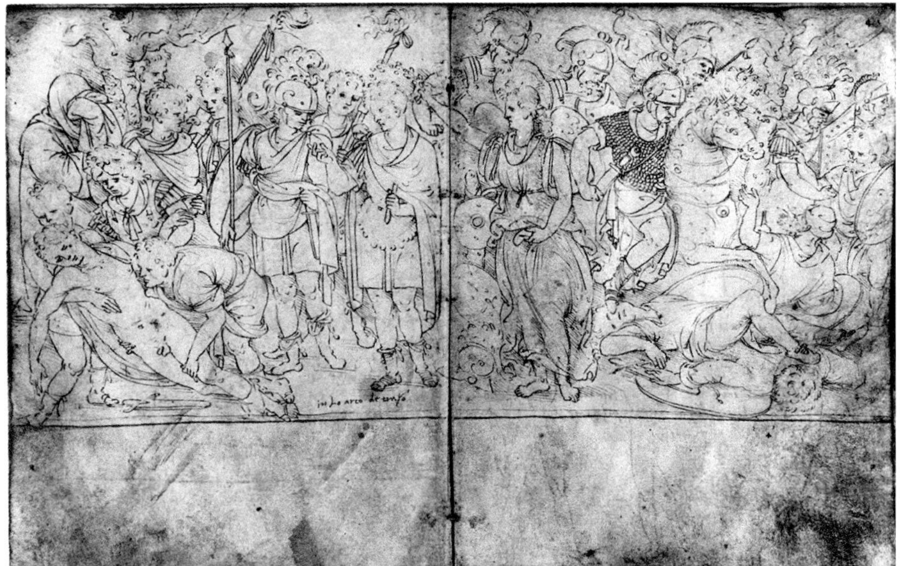

Fig. 2.2. Amico Aspertini. Wolfegg Codex, fols. 40v and 41r, ca. 1500–1503. Pen and brown ink, 8⅞ x 6¹¹⁄₁₆ in. (22.5 x 17 cm) (approx.). Collection of Count Max Willibald von Waldburg, Schloss Wolfegg, Württemberg

has read the composition as the mourning of Achilles over the dead corpse of his friend Patroclus, an episode of the Trojan War narrated in book XVIII of Homer's *Iliad*, several details do not agree with such an interpretation.[4] The mysterious scene is set amid trees suggesting a forest, and at upper right, two men bear sheep on their shoulders, much like shepherds who provide a sacrificial offering. In the foreground, the seated man at lower right is perched upon the head of a bearded captive and shrouds his face in a classical gesture of mourning. On the ground before him lies a dead, partly nude boy of placid countenance, contemplated by numerous attendants. The seated youth covering his head at extreme right has been said to derive from the grieving young matron in the Roman relief of the *Nova Nupta* (The New Bride), which is itself based on a late Hellenistic prototype, but the similarity is that of a generic pose.[5] Likewise, the deceased figure in the foreground has been thought to be based on a sculpture of the dying Niobid, once in the Maffei Collection in Rome, and which Aspertini

himself copied in a line drawing about 1500–1503 (Wolfegg Codex, fol. 33v),[6] but the resemblance of motifs in the Tobey drawing and the Wolfegg copy after the antique, again, is not especially satisfying.

Rather, the composition with the dead boy generally recalls portrayals in Roman sarcophagi of Endymion (fig. 2.1), the beautiful youth who fell into eternal sleep, as told in Lucian's *Dialogues of the Gods*, even though this is not the actual subject of the Tobey drawing. The motif closely relates to that of another outline-drawing in Aspertini's Wolfegg Codex (fols. 40v and 41r; fig. 2.2), but which renders the mourning figures in agitated movement.[7] In any case, the cautiously drawn Wolfegg model book, which belongs in Aspertini's Roman years, about 1500 to 1503 (his return to Bologna in March 1503 is documented),[8] scrupulously adheres to the ancient originals[9] and markedly contrasts in technique and figural vocabulary.

The array of military paraphernalia immediately to the

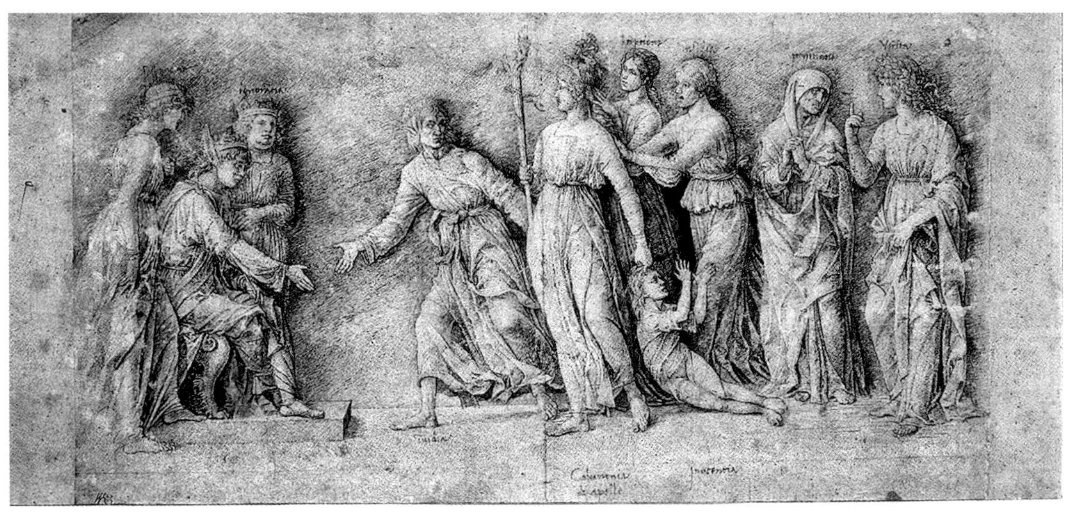

Fig. 2.3. Andrea Mantegna. *The Calumny of Apelles*, ca. 1504–6. Pen and brown ink, highlighted with white gouache, 8⅛ x 14¹⁵⁄₁₆ in. (20.6 x 37.9 cm). British Museum, London (1860-6-16-85)

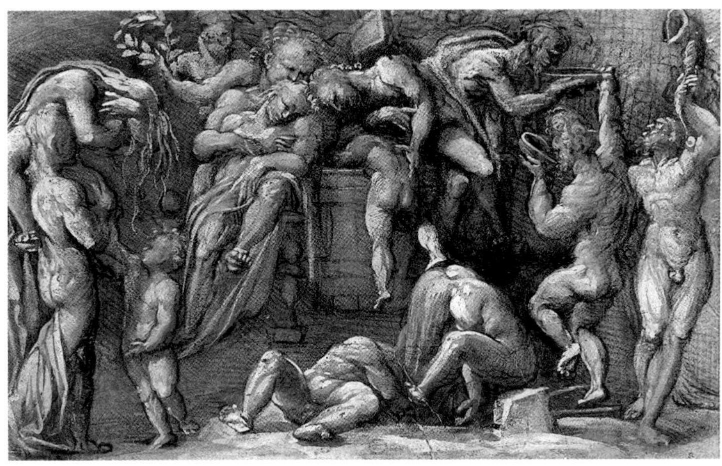

Fig. 2.4. Amico Aspertini. *Bacchanalian Scene*, ca. 1525–35. Black chalk, highlighted with white gouache on brown-washed paper, 10⅞ x 16¾ in. (27.6 x 42.5 cm). The Metropolitan Museum of Art, New York, Rogers Fund, 1908 (08.227.27)

left of center in the Tobey sheet is reminiscent of the *Trophies of Marius* in the Piazza del Campidoglio, Rome, another ancient monument that Aspertini freely reprised in his Wolfegg Codex (fol. 18r),[10] a relationship that identifies the scene in the present drawing as the death of a classical warrior. Adding a moralizing tone, at center, the bust of a balding man is prominently placed high atop a column with his breast draped by a tuniclike apron. His head exhibits large protrusions, but the details seem somewhat indistinct.[11] While these could be wings, possibly alluding to Inspiration or the *furor poetico* (as described in some early iconographic dictionaries),[12] they more likely are pointy animal ears, like those of King Midas, who was bestowed the ears of an ass for offending Apollo in a musical contest, according to Ovid's *Metamorphoses* (XI:146–93).[13] The figures on the left in Aspertini's composition are more puzzling. Seated there, in the foreground, a man wearing a turban and shroud holds an ax and tablet to his breast, while behind him a bearded, bareheaded man looks down attentively at a thread stretched between his hands, possibly the "thread of life."[14] In the extreme left foreground, a veiled woman crowned in laurels (perhaps a personification of Poetry) sits clutching a shield, and behind her, one of the two turbaned half-figures on the upper left may or may not be blindfolded, as he or she appears to be writing on a shield.

The symbolic qualities of the figures and abstruse references to historical literary sources recall those in the late allegories by Andrea Mantegna (1430/31–1506) and his followers. Indeed, the present work has often been compared to Mantegna's pen-and-ink drawing *The Calumny of Apelles*. A late work dating to about 1504–6, and now in the British Museum (fig. 2.3), it is based on the description by Lucian of a painting

by Apelles.[15] But the similarities are not precisely iconographic, beyond the fact that Mantegna's seated Midas and the present central figure on a column both display long ears. Aspertini's close study of Mantegna, however, is evident in his work throughout more than three decades, from about 1500 until 1535.[16] A late example is his *Bacchanalian Scene* in The Metropolitan Museum of Art, New York (fig. 2.4), from about 1525–35, in which the composition more or less paraphrases Mantegna's engraving of the *Bacchanal with a Wine Press*.[17] The Tobey drawing is, in contrast, minutely executed and considerably less monumental in its conception of the figure than the Metropolitan *Bacchanalian Scene*, in keeping with its much earlier date, but it already represents the full command of antique sources seen in the artist's maturity and a creative ownership with respect to the ancient past.   CCB

1. See references to Aspertini's facade decorations in Vasari ed. 1966–87, vol. 4 (text), p. 497: "Fece costui, una facciata in chiaro scuro in sulla piazza de' Marsigli . . . un'altra facciata dipinse alla Porta di San Mammolo; . . . insomma non è chiesa né strada in Bologna che non abbia qualche imbratto di mano di costui." (He made a facade in monochrome [on a building] facing the Piazza de' Marsigli . . . he painted another on the gate of San Mammolo; . . . In sum, there is no church or street in Bologna that has not something by his hand.)

2. This relationship has gone previously unnoticed. See sale, Sotheby's, London 1993, lots 6 and 7 (color ills.), said to be from the Galleria Colonna, Rome, according to an old inscription on the reverse of both panels. The height dimension of each of the two panels is extremely close to those of the Tobey drawing (both panels measure 9⅞ x 26 in. [25 x 66 cm]).

3. See the *Vita* of Bagnacavallo in Vasari ed. 1966–87, vol. 4 (text), pp. 496–99 (p. 496: "Uomo capriccioso e di bizzarro cervello, come sono anco pazze, per dir così, e capricciose le figure da lui fatte per tutta Italia e particolarmente in Bologna").

4. Cosmo 1984, p. 36.

5. As suggested by Daniela Scaglietti in Bologna 1988, pp. 284–85. On the *Nova Nupta* relief, see Bober and Rubinstein 1986, pp. 231–32, no. 198 (ill.). This sculpture, however, does not appear to be recorded in any of Aspertini's drawings and consequently may not have been known to him.

6. As suggested by Daniela Scaglietti in Bologna 1988, p. 284. The motif in the Wolfegg Codex, fol. 33v, is discussed and illustrated in Schweikhart 1986, pp. 84–85, fig. 17.

7. The scene in the Wolfegg Codex, fol. 40v, is discussed and illustrated in Schweikhart 1986, pp. 93–95, fig. 24.

8. See the document of March 4, 1503, regarding the division of property of Aspertini's father-in-law, transcribed by Manuela Iodici in Faietti and Scaglietti Kelescian 1995, p. 344.

9. On the issues of authorship and dating of the Wolfegg Codex, see Schweikhart 1986, pp. 24–28.

10. Discussed and illustrated in Schweikhart 1986, pp. 58–59, fig. 3.

11. The condition of the drawing surface here and elsewhere in the composition is generally very good, although there are some small losses of support, stains, craquelure of thickly applied medium, and darkening of the paper.

12. For example, see Ripa ed. 1976, pp. 191–92.

13. See the passages from Ovid's *Metamorphoses* in Ovid ed. 1916, vol. 2, pp. 130–33.

14. The tentative proposal that this is the "thread of life" is from Scaglietti in Bologna 1988, p. 285.

15. This point was most recently discussed in Faietti and Scaglietti Kelescian 1995, pp. 284–85, no. 79. On Mantegna's drawing at the British Museum, see David Ekserdjian in London and New York 1992, pp. 467–68, no. 154.

16. Michele Danieli emphasizes this point in Bologna 2008–9, p. 311.

17. Aspertini's drawing in The Metropolitan Museum of Art has been variously dated, from 1520 to 1535. Compare Bean and Turčić 1982, p. 27, no. 13; Danieli in Bologna 2008–9, pp. 310–11, no. 125.

ANDREA DEL SARTO

Florence, 1486–Florence, 1530

Andrea del Sarto was the leading painter in Florence in the early decades of the sixteenth century until his death in 1530. With the exception of an early trip to Rome and an unhappy stint in France at the behest of King Francis I, he spent his entire career in his native city. He became an independent master in 1508 following a period in the workshop of Piero di Cosimo. His most important early works were painted for Santissima Annunziata, the Servite conventual church in Florence that continued to patronize him throughout his career; he also had an enduring association with the Compagnia dello Scalzo, in whose cloister he executed an impressive cycle of monochrome frescoes illustrating the life of Saint John the Baptist. In addition to frescoes, Sarto also painted serenely balanced altarpieces, touching images of the Madonna and Child and the Holy Family, and the occasional portrait, receiving commissions from Florentine patricians such as the Borgherini and the Panciatichi, and from Cardinal Giulio de' Medici, de facto ruler of Florence during the pontificate of his cousin Pope Leo X. Mythological subject matter seldom figured into his repertoire. Andrea del Sarto worked closely with the painter Franciabigio and the sculptor Jacopo Sansovino, and was an influential teacher and mentor to a younger generation of Florentine Mannerists, notably Jacopo Pontormo, Rosso Fiorentino, Francesco Salviati, and Giorgio Vasari.

3. Recto: *Study for the Head of Julius Caesar*, ca. 1520–21
Verso: *Profile Sketch of a Man's Head*

Red chalk, 8⅞₁₆ x 7¼ in. (21. 5 x 18.4 cm)
Annotated at upper left, in red chalk: *64*
Verso not reproduced

The Metropolitan Museum of Art, New York, Partial and Promised Gift of
Mr. and Mrs. David M. Tobey, 2008 (2008.367)

Provenance: Sale, Galerie Koller, Zurich, March 23, 2007, lot 3413 (as Florentine
School); acquired by The Metropolitan Museum of Art, 2008

Reference: New York 2008–9 (entry by Carmen C. Bambach), http://www.
metmuseum.org/special/philippe_de_montebello_years/exhibition/view.
aspx?vt=lv&pg=15&an=2008.367 (February 12, 2010)

*T*he *Tribute Presented to Julius Caesar in Egypt* is the largest and most complex composition of Andrea del Sarto's career (figs. 3.1, 3.2). It is part of the decoration of the *salone* in the Medici villa at Poggio a Caiano, near Florence, devised by Paolo Giovio, and commissioned by Pope Leo X and Cardinal Giulio de' Medici about 1520, shortly after the artist's return from France. The scene is a historical allegory, aiming to liken the giving of gifts by the Egyptian sultan to Lorenzo the Magnificent in 1487 to an ancient Roman precedent.[1] The elaborate composition and grandeur of setting and expression are due not only to the nature of the subject but also to the artist's experience of contemporary Roman painting, especially Raphael's frescoes in the Vatican. Vasari relates that Sarto visited Rome at this time; the impact of Raphael's work is evident in *The Tribute Presented to Julius Caesar in Egypt*, as is well explained by John Shearman.[2]

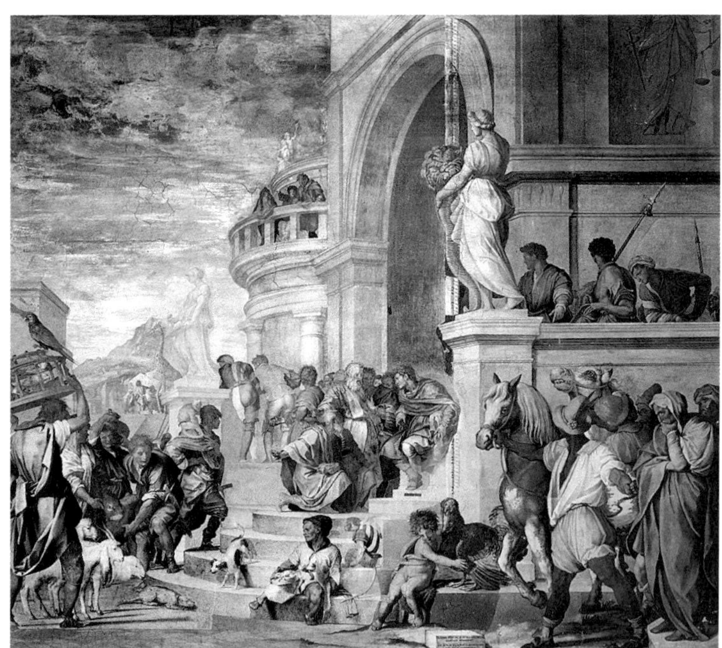

Fig. 3.1. Andrea del Sarto. *The Tribute Presented to Julius Caesar in Egypt*, 1521. Fresco. Medici villa at Poggio a Caiano

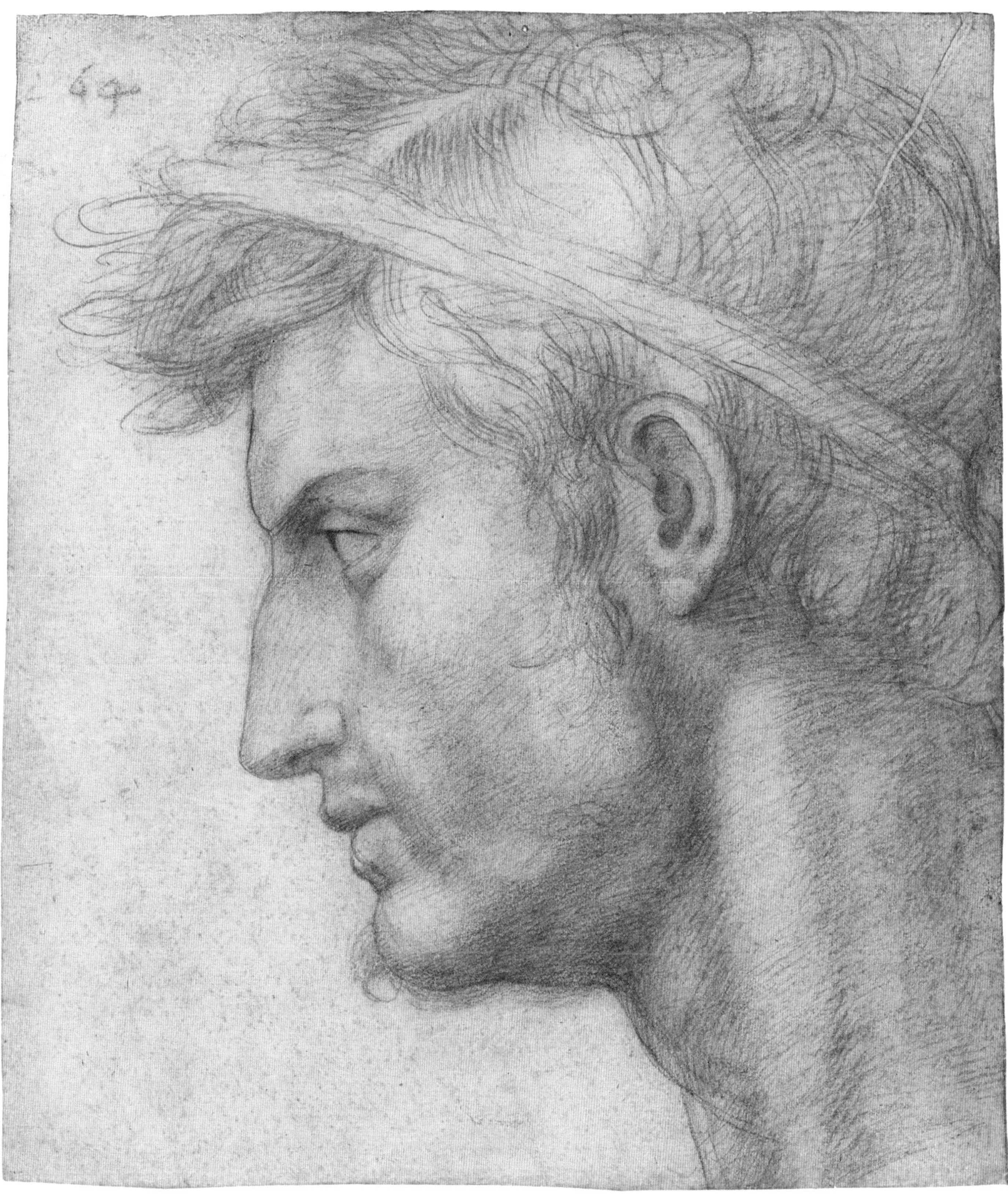

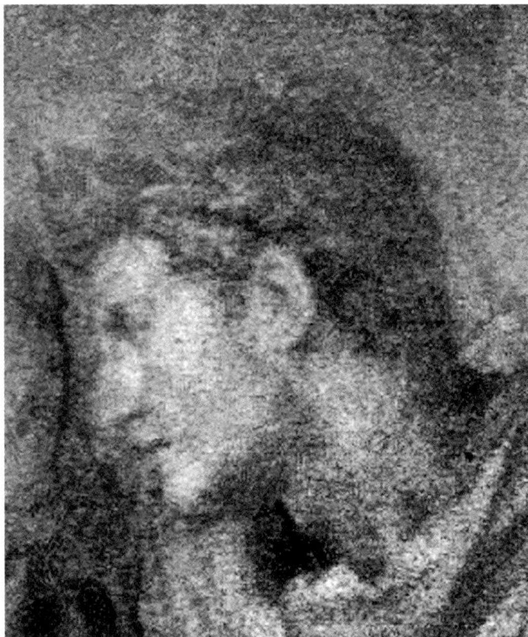

Fig. 3.2. Andrea del Sarto. *Head of Caesar*. Detail of fig. 3.1

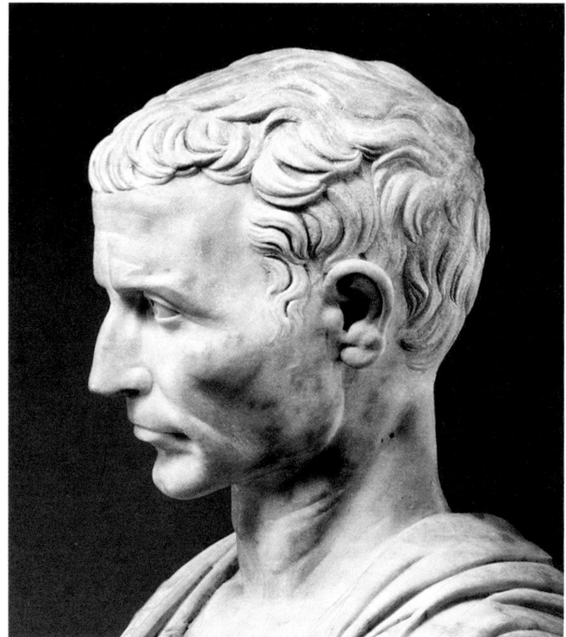

Fig. 3.3. Andrea di Pietro di Marco Ferrucci. *Julius Caesar*, ca. 1512–14. Marble, H. 27 in. (68.6 cm). The Metropolitan Museum of Art, New York, Bequest of Benjamin Altman, 1913 (14.40.676)

The recto of this drawing is a study for the head of Julius Caesar. It is close to the final work in most respects, though the painted version departs from it in the angle at which the head is set and in the absence of the laurel in the drawing. As would be expected, the rendering of details such as the hair is looser in the preparatory sketch. The execution is characteristic of Sarto, with a firm outline, subtle interior modeling, and a number of flourishes of free draftsmanship in the hair and other areas.

The portrayal of Caesar may well have been based on a portrait sculpture or coin (figs. 3.3, 3.4), given that it bears some resemblance to his actual appearance—for example, in the long, aquiline nose that shows a break at the bridge. This recourse to an ancient source is in keeping with Sarto's response to his Roman experience, as one of the other figures in the fresco was based on a bust of Homer. Lastly, it is most telling that the dimensions of the drawn head are almost precisely those of the painted image. This fact and the closeness of the two works suggest that the drawing was made as an auxiliary cartoon. The creation of such drawings was central to Raphael's practice, as Andrea del Sarto, newly returned from Rome, would have been keenly aware.

The verso consists of a summary outline sketch of a man in profile. It has been plausibly suggested by Philippe Costamagna that it represents a preliminary study for the man seen prominently walking up the steps toward Caesar in the fresco.[3] It, too, is imbued with the classicism and gravitas of the recto.

GRG

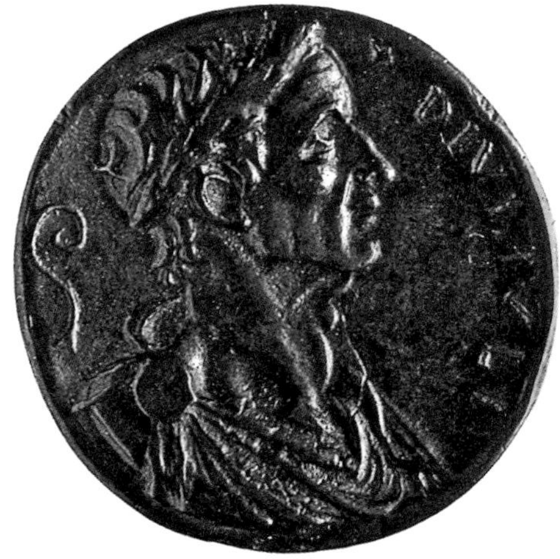

Fig. 3.4. *Draped Bust of Julius Caesar Crowned with Laurel Wreath*. Florence, 15th century. Plaquette. Bronze, Diam. 1⅝ in. (4.1 cm). British Museum, London (1915,1216.165)

1. For an excellent discussion of the project and its iconography, see Shearman 1965, vol. 1, pp. 78–89.
2. Ibid.
3. In discussion with the present author.

GIOVANNI DA UDINE

Udine, 1487–Rome, 1564

If Giorgio Vasari's vague account of his artistic beginnings is to be believed, Giovanni da Udine trained with Giorgione in Venice before removing to Rome and entering Raphael's workshop about 1515. A brilliant specialist in still life and archaeologically accurate, highly sophisticated re-creations of ancient Roman stucco and wall painting, he collaborated with Raphael on a number of important commissions, including the designs for the Acts of the Apostles *tapestries for the Sistine Chapel, the Vatican Logge, the fresco decorations of the Villa Farnesina, and the interior and gardens of the Villa Madama. After Raphael's death he carried out various decorative projects for Pope Clement VII (r. 1523–34), before eventually returning to his native Udine, where he was active as a painter and architect, with an intermezzo in Venice working for the Grimani in 1539–40. He traveled back to Rome at the end of his life and was once again engaged in carrying out decorations in one of the Logge of the Vatican Palace. Relatively few drawings by Giovanni da Udine survive; among the most notable are a group of highly naturalistic watercolor studies of birds, which may well be fragments of a sketchbook of such drawings by the artist mentioned by Vasari.*

4. Recto: *Designs for Saint Jerome in His Study, Landscapes, and the Decoration of an Interior Wall*, ca. 1527–30
Verso: *Studies for Grotteschi Decoration: Naturalistic and Fantastic Animals, Birds, and a Sphinx*

Recto and verso: Pen and brown ink, 10½ x 8 in. (26.7 x 20.3 cm)
Annotated on recto in pen and brown ink at lower left by a sixteenth-century hand: *Giouanni da Udine*; annotated on verso in pen and brown ink at lower left by a sixteenth-century hand: *Giouannj da Udine*

Provenance: R. E. A. Wilson, London, 1934; Richard and Trude Krautheimer, New York; sale, Christie's, New York, January 10, 1996, lot 5; acquired in 1996

References: Poughkeepsie 1963, no. 1; Nesselrath 1989, pp. 270–71, nos. 24 and 25

The author of this double-sided sheet with important compositional sketches on the recto and more meditated decorative motifs on the verso can be securely identified on the basis of iconography, style, and technique as Giovanni da Udine, the gifted specialist of nature studies from the eponymous town in the Friuli region, who received various artistic training in northern Italy before his arrival in Raphael's workshop in Rome about 1515.[1] Few firmly attributable drawings by this painter from Udine have survived, and figural sketches of the type seen on the recto of the Tobey sheet are rarer still. Shown here are three small initial ideas for a composition of Saint Jerome seated in his study, a painting that was meant to be part of a larger decoration of a wall punctuated by a tall arched niche or window, if not in the interior of a chapel (possibly as an altarpiece), then in the private space of an ecclesiastical building. Three different solutions are depicted, with that at upper left being the most schematic. The design at left center

portrays the scene of Saint Jerome flanked by rectangular fields of antique-style *grotteschi* motifs, in a program that is especially reminiscent of the Stufetta of Pope Clement VII at the Castel Sant'Angelo, Rome, frescoed about 1525–27 and 1530–32 by Polidoro da Caravaggio, Giovanni da Udine,[2] and the assistants of Giulio Romano, whereas the design at right center presents the intended figural scene (although here it is left blank) as set within a luscious vista, at either side, containing ancient buildings in the background. The style of decoration with a verdant landscape generally evokes that of the frescoes in the Chapel of San Mariano by Polidoro at San Silvestro al Quirinale, Rome, of about 1524–27.[3] Of the two further sketches on the lower part of the Tobey recto, the most advanced in design is that at lower right, in which the detailed architectural interior also includes the crouching lion (one of the attributes of Saint Jerome), but no known painting of this subject by our artist seems to have survived.

As is true of almost all of Giovanni da Udine's drawings, the task of dating the Tobey sheet is not straightforward. An archival note on an early photograph of this work—when it was in the Krautheimer Collection—indicates that according to Nicole Dacos (who published a monographic study of our artist's drawings in 1987), the recto sketches were done in the artist's native town of Udine, after he was forced to leave Rome in 1522. The owners of the sheet, Richard and Trude Krautheimer,

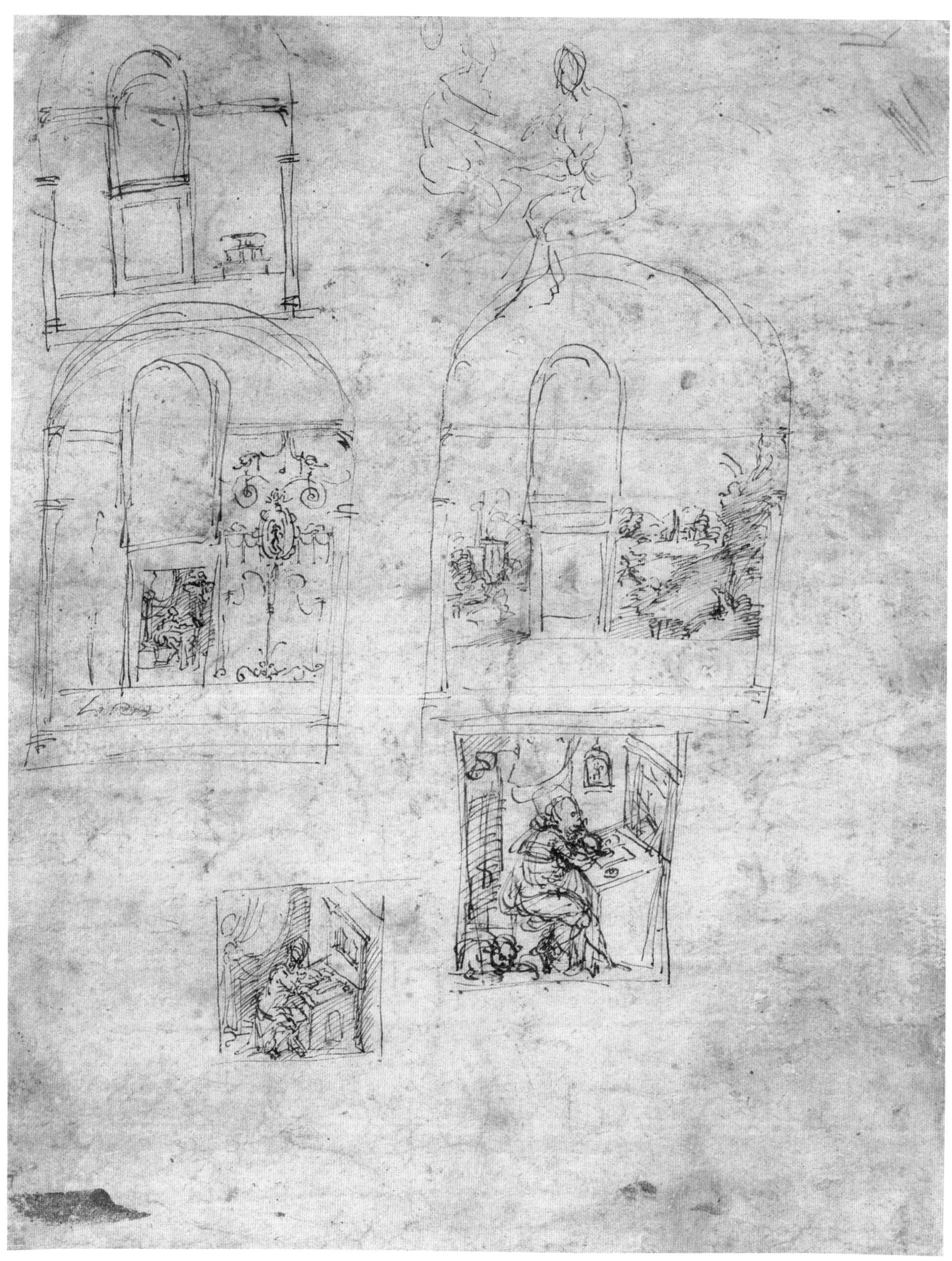

4

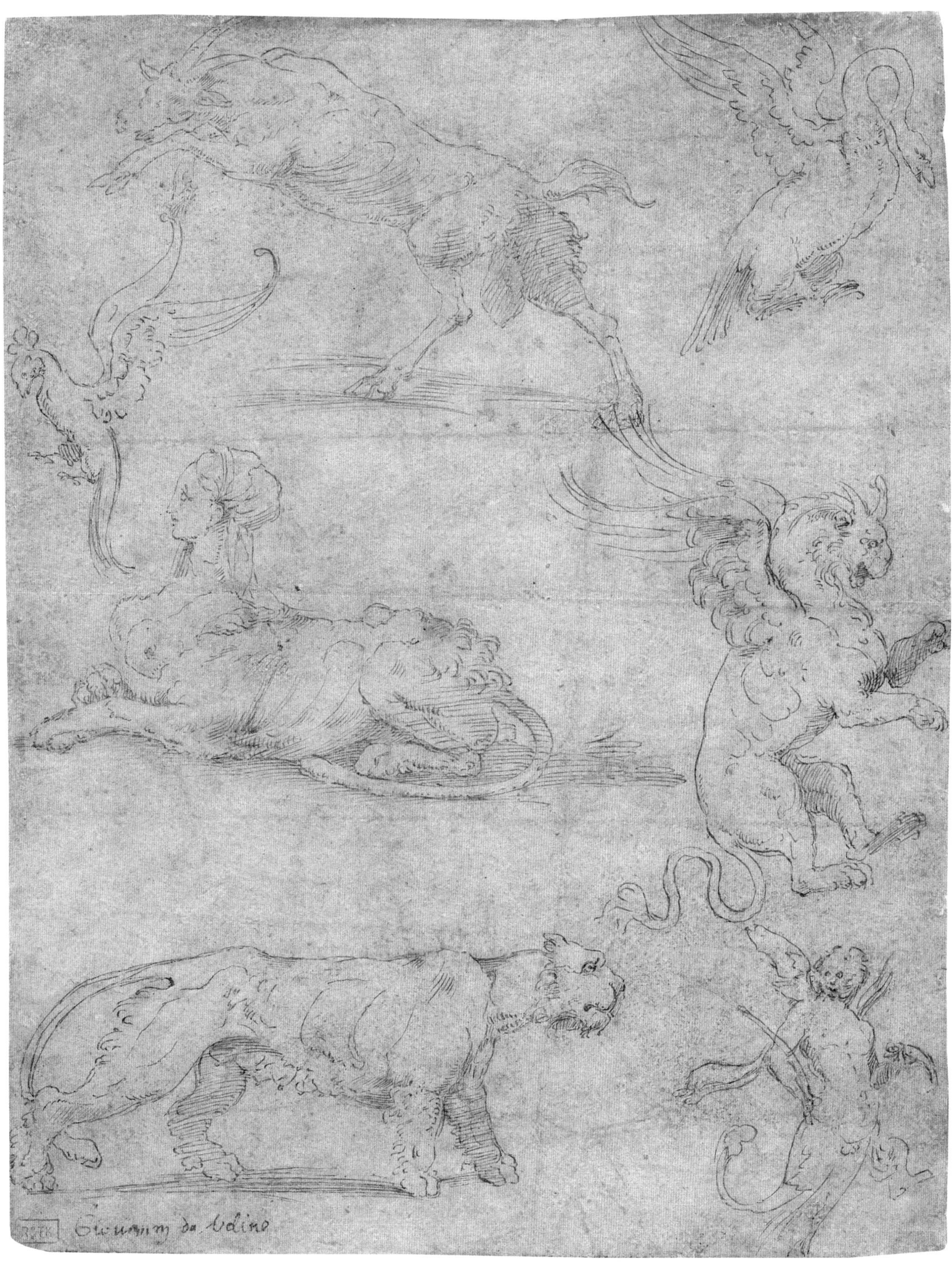

Giovanni da Udine

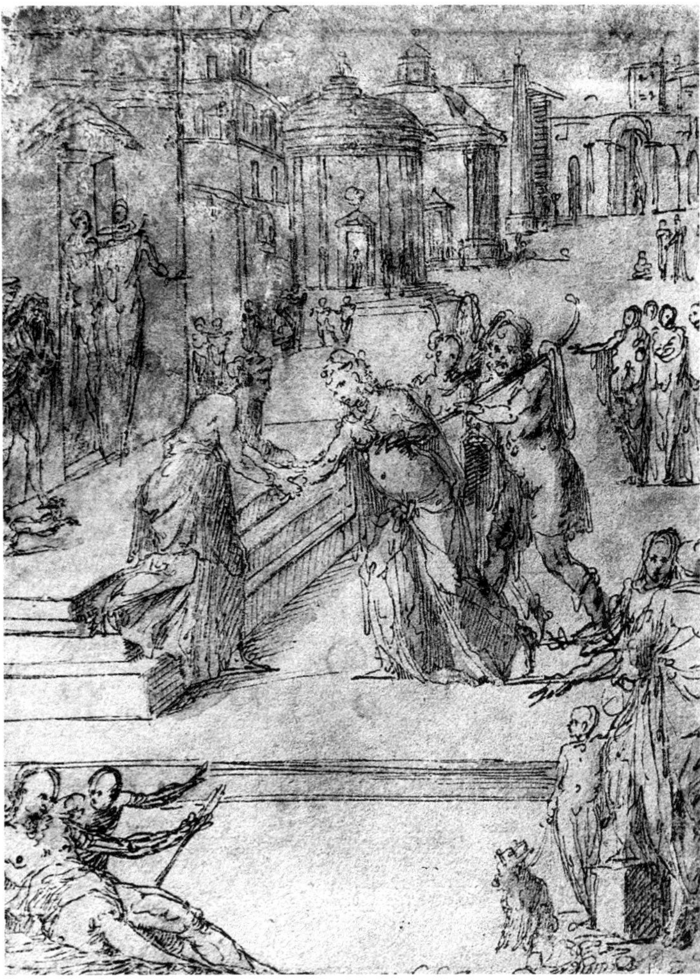

Fig. 4.1. Giovanni da Udine. *Visitation*, 1520s–30s. Pen and brown ink, 6½ x 4¾ in. (16.5 x 12.1 cm). Crocker Art Museum, E. B. Crocker Art Collection, Sacramento (1871.226)

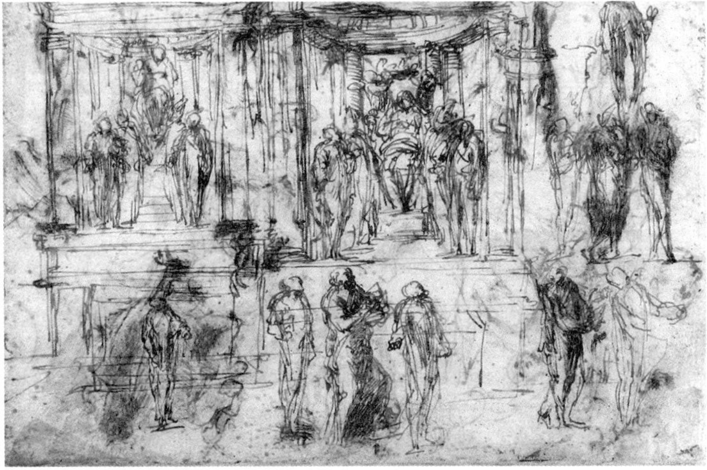

Fig. 4.2. Polidoro da Caravaggio. *Studies for an Altarpiece with the Virgin Enthroned, Attended by Four Saints* (recto), early 1530s. Pen and brown ink, some brush and brown wash, 7¹⁵⁄₁₆ x 11¾ in. (20.2 x 29.8 cm). The Metropolitan Museum of Art, New York, Bequest of Walter C. Baker, 1971 (1972.118.270)

however, considered the recto to date late in the artist's first Roman period (ca. 1516/17–1522),[4] a positing that was more or less endorsed in Arnold Nesselrath's essay of 1989.[5] Both the drawing technique and figural vocabulary on the recto appear to the present author to postdate Raphael's death in 1520, perhaps almost by a decade (hence, in greater agreement with Dacos). The verso of the sheet offers antique-style motifs of *grotteschi* that our artist began developing about 1516–18, but which he continued to reprise for some time afterward, inspired by the fresco and stucco decorations of ancient Roman buildings. The classical restraint and choices of iconographic motifs on both the recto and verso of the Tobey sheet almost certainly indicate one of Giovanni da Udine's various Roman periods (when away from the Eternal City, his decorative designs seem much more exuberantly naturalistic), probably in the late 1520s, or even about 1531–34. He was in Rome from about 1515 until 1521/22, in late 1522 until the Sack of Rome in 1527, then on and off in 1531–34, and again in 1560.

To this author's eye, and not noticed before, Giovanni da Udine's sketchy drawing style on the recto of the Tobey sheet is particularly reminiscent of Polidoro da Caravaggio's inventive, nervous, delightfully free pen-and-ink technique of the mid- to late 1520s,[6] a time in which the two artists, having come out from under the shadow of their master Raphael, closely collaborated. Their formative pen-and-ink styles continued to exhibit similarity later in their careers even when they no longer worked in the same city. One may compare the *Visitation* of the 1520s–30s by Giovanni da Udine (fig. 4.1) and a sheet of figural sketches by Polidoro of the early 1530s (fig. 4.2).[7] In the typical style of Giovanni da Udine's drawings of the first and second Roman periods, the motifs on both sides of the Tobey sheet are all drawn with the same scratchily thin, reinforced outlines full of energy, together with a sparing use of diagonal parallel-hatching to deepen some shadows, in which the short diagonal strokes exhibit hook returns. To the present author's eye, the different modes of execution of his drawings on the recto with respect to those on the verso are solely due to the speed of execution. Closely comparable to the Tobey sheet for their style and technique are our artist's two securely attributed drawings in the Staatliche Graphische Sammlung, Munich.[8] Of these, the double-sided Munich sheet depicting architectural studies, a putto driving two deer, and various sketches for *grotteschi* designs, is inscribed on the verso with the word, "Ricamator" (embroiderer), alluding to the early alternative name of our artist, given to him after his father's profession—Giovanni da Udine himself at times signed "io Zuan Ricamador pitor" (see figs. 4.3, 4.4).[9]

Although the verso of the Tobey sheet depicts motifs that typically recur in Giovanni da Udine's first Roman fresco and

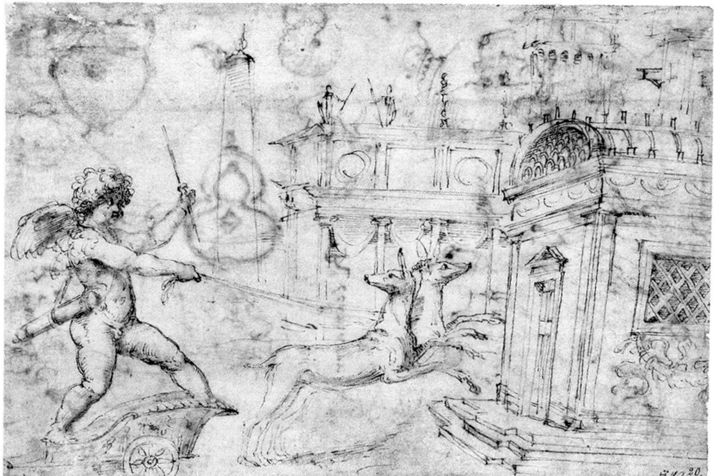

Fig. 4.3. Giovanni da Udine. *A Cupid Driving a Chariot and Other Motifs*, 1520s. Pen and brown ink, 7¹⁄₁₆ x 10⁵⁄₁₆ in. (18 x 26.2 cm). Staatliche Graphische Sammlung, Munich (2520r)

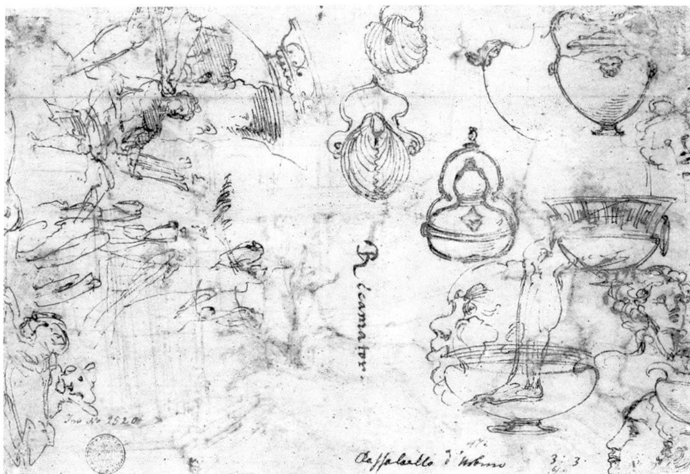

Fig. 4.4. Giovanni da Udine. *Studies of Figures, Animals, and Ornaments*, 1520s. Pen and brown ink, 7¹⁄₁₆ x 10⁵⁄₁₆ in. (18 x 26.2 cm). Staatliche Graphische Sammlung, Munich (2520v)

stucco decorations, it is worth emphasizing that they also became types in his later works, continuing to appear in his fresco decorations, for instance, into the 1530s. As has been previously observed, the sphinx at left center served for a detail in the Stufetta of Cardinal Bibbiena (Vatican Palace) of about 1516, and the griffin at right center and the springing goat at upper left appear in the Loggetta of Cardinal Bibbiena also in the Vatican; the winged swan appears twice, as a mirroring pair, on the cupola of the first Vatican Loggia of about 1517–19.[10] The winged swan on the Tobey verso is also drawn in reverse design orientation on another sheet by the artist in the Ashmolean Museum of Art and Archaeology, Oxford,[11] and a closely similar detail of this bird was frescoed in the 1520s by Perino del Vaga's workshop on the vault of the Sala dei Pontefici (Vatican Palace). An exact reprise of the lioness at lower left exists in a drawing of unknown date by Giovanni da Udine (Staatliche Graphische Sammlung, Munich).[12] Similar versions of the sphinx, griffin, and grotesque winged creature at lower right also occur on the walls and vault of the Stufetta of Pope Clement VII, frescoed about 1525–27 and 1530–32.[13]

CCB

1. On Giovanni da Udine's various apprenticeships in northern Italy, see Bartolini 1987, pp. 19–34.
2. This project is discussed and illustrated with different points of view on the questions of attribution in Dacos and Furlan 1987, pp. 138–48; Leone de Castris 2001, pp. 190–96.
3. This project is discussed and illustrated in Leone de Castris 2001, pp. 212–47.
4. According to their annotation on the back of a photograph (L34223), Archive of the Department of Drawings and Prints, The Metropolitan Museum of Art, New York.
5. Nesselrath 1989, pp. 267–69.
6. See, for example, the drawings by Polidoro da Caravaggio (Musée du Louvre, Paris, inv. no. 4339; Gabinetto Disegni e Stampe degli Uffizi, Florence, inv. no. 12127 F); illustrated and catalogued in Leone de Castris 2001, pp. 474, 485, nos. D86, D206, figs. 43, 53.
7. On the drawing by Giovanni da Udine mentioned above, see Dacos and Furlan 1987, p. 248, no. 15. On the drawing by Polidoro da Caravaggio, see Bean and Turčić 1982, pp. 192–94, no. 188; Leone de Castris 2001, p. 482, no. 175, dating it about 1530–35.
8. Inv. nos. 2489, 2520. On these two sheets, compare Dacos and Furlan 1987, pp. 244–46, nos. 10–12; Nesselrath 1989, pp. 278–82, figs. 37–38.
9. This form of Giovanni da Udine's signature appears in his *Libro dei Conti* (Bartolini 1987, p. 3); Nesselrath 1989.
10. As first pointed out in Nesselrath 1989, pp. 267–69.
11. Discussed and illustrated in Parker 1956, p. 389, no. 727, pl. 161.
12. Inv. no. 2259. Discussed and illustrated in Nesselrath 1989, pp. 274–75, fig. 32.
13. For these motifs in the Stufetta of Pope Clement VII at Castel Sant'Angelo, see illustrations in Rome 1984, figs. 48, 49, 85, 102, 103, 104.

CORREGGIO

Correggio, ca. 1489–Correggio, 1534

Hailed by Giorgio Vasari as the first Lombard artist to paint in the modern style, Correggio worked in northern Italian towns such as his native Correggio and nearby Parma, rather than in the main artistic centers. He presumably learned the rudiments from his uncle, a minor painter, but found his first true inspiration in the art of Mantegna and Leonardo da Vinci. Throughout his career, Correggio painted easel pictures of religious and mythological themes, but apparently few portraits. He was also responsible for major and highly innovative fresco cycles in Parma, for example, in the cupola of the town's cathedral. The theatrical illusionism and affective charge of Correggio's imagery were so widely imitated in the seventeenth century that he is often considered to be a precursor to the Baroque.

5. *Eve and Other Figures*, ca. 1525–30

Red chalk, 6¾ x 7⅞ in. (17.1 x 20 cm)

The Metropolitan Museum of Art, New York, Promised Gift of David M. Tobey

Provenance: Private Collection, Europe; acquired in 1999

References: Ekserdjian 1997, p. 247; London and New York 2000–2001, p. 71, no. 30 (entry by George R. Goldner); Di Giampaolo 2001, p. 76, no. 31

Executed in Correggio's favorite medium of red chalk, this recently discovered sheet is a preparatory design for one of his most important commissions. In November 1522, the artist signed a contract to decorate the cupola of the cathedral in Parma.[1] The document does not specify the intended subject matter, but the general iconographic scheme almost certainly involved from the beginning the Assumption of the Virgin Mary, the feast day to which the town's cathedral is dedicated. Correggio painted the large dome with a dazzling scene of the Virgin's ascent amid clouds and music-making angels. She is welcomed into heaven by biblical figures, male to the left and female to the right. Immediately to either side of her are Adam and Eve, the first parents whose sin the Virgin Mary, known as the new Eve, was believed to have reversed (fig. 5.1). The Tobey sheet shows Eve, who holds, as she does in the fresco, the attribute of an apple, along with several attendant figures.

Although it has recently come to light that he only began to paint the frescoes in 1530 (four years later than scholars had previously assumed),[2] Correggio undoubtedly devoted much

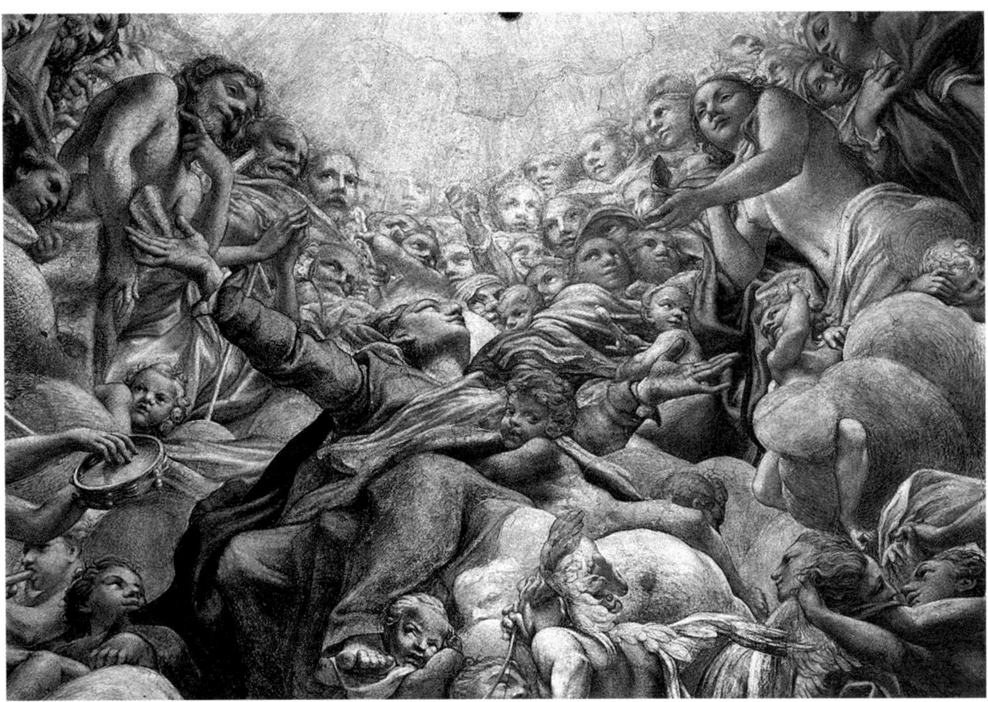

Fig. 5.1. Correggio. *The Virgin between Adam and Eve and the Angels*. Detail of the *Assumption*, ca. 1530. Fresco. Parma Cathedral

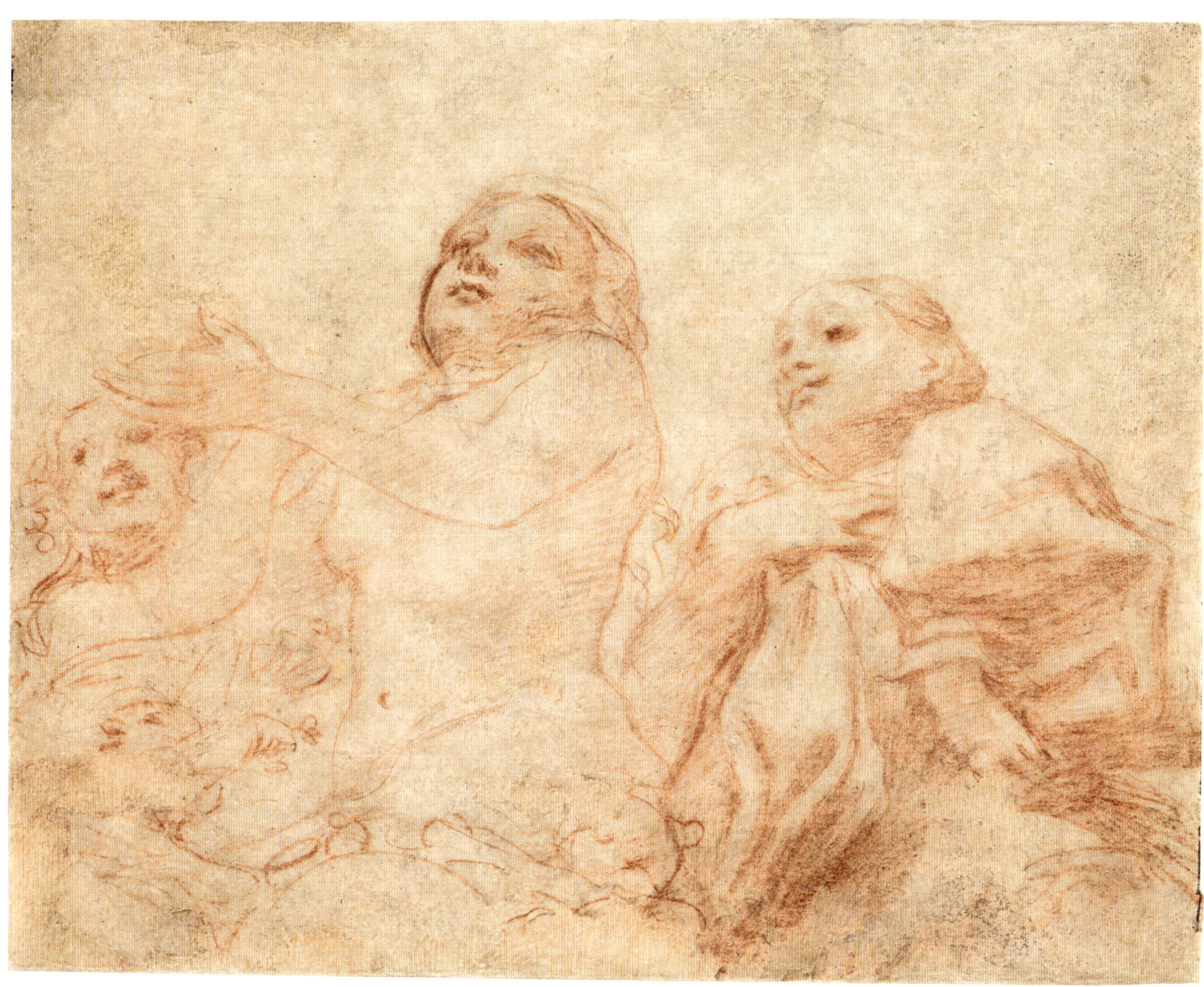

5

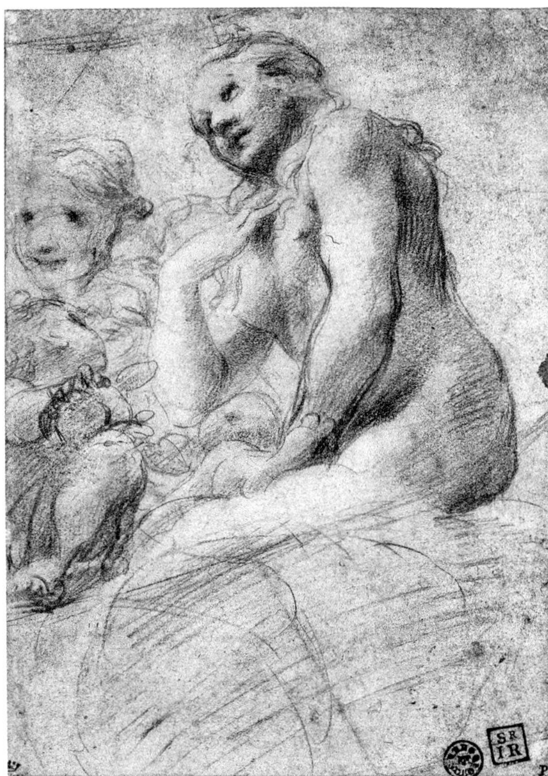

Fig. 5.2. Correggio. *Study of Eve*, ca. 1524. Red chalk, 7³⁄₁₆ x 5⅛ in. (18.3 x 13 cm). British Museum, London (PD 1895-9-15-738)

time in advance to the planning of the project. The illusionistic tour de force must have required hundreds, even thousands of graphic preliminaries, relatively few of which survive. The only known designs that reveal anything of the early stages of his objectives involve sketches for the base of the cupola and its drum. What have mainly come down to us are instead studies for individual figures, or for groups of figures, as in the case of the Tobey sheet, which closely correspond to the frescoes and therefore belong to the later stages of the design process. These works nonetheless elucidate key aspects of Correggio's fastidious method.

For instance, no fewer than five studies for Eve, including that in the Tobey collection, are known.[3] In the earliest of these, a design in the Teyler Museum, Haarlem, Correggio used red chalk to sketch Eve with a putto and then fixed the

contours in pen. The putto is depicted holding the apple. With red chalk, the artist traced the pen outlines of these two figures on to another sheet, now in the British Museum (fig. 5.2).[4] He added a smiling face to the left of Eve and slightly adjusted the placement of the apple that the putto holds, but otherwise made no compositional changes. The British Museum drawing was presumably intended to investigate the effects of light and shade on Eve's body.

In the Tobey sheet, Correggio subsequently modified Eve's pose so that she proffers the apple. The design reveals, furthermore, that he retained the self-referential gesture of her right arm and hand that can be seen in the earlier drawings, if now partly obscured by her raised left arm, and used it as well for the woman, probably the Old Testament heroine Rebecca,[5] to the immediate right. The handling of chalk—such as the summary marks used to denote the accompanying putti—is confident and free, with only a minor adjustment to the profile of Eve's head. A single-figure study for Eve in the Louvre essentially repeats the pose found in the Tobey sheet and must have been made, like that in the British Museum, to clarify the fall of light on her body. Yet another drawing for Eve and her attendants (Städelsches Kunstinstitut, Frankfurt), which is squared for transfer and calibrated to accommodate the curvature of the dome, represents a final stage in the preparation.

The chance survival of such closely related studies for Eve and nearby figures—and none (or relatively few) for the hundreds of others that Correggio painted on the cupola, or for the different intervals of its overall planning—suggests that merely a fraction of the original graphic preliminaries has survived. The loss is all the more regrettable when one considers the inventive energy and delicacy of touch that Correggio could and did achieve as a draftsman in works such as the Tobey design.   MV

1. On the commission, see Ekserdjian 1997, pp. 241–63, with bibliography.
2. Per newly discovered archival documents that were discussed by Cristina Cecchinelli in her lecture at the Convegno Internazionale di Studi sul Correggio, held in Parma, Italy, on November 28, 2009 (publication forthcoming).
3. For the five studies (ill.), as well as the other drawings related to the project, see Ekserdjian 1997, especially pp. 246–47.
4. London and New York 2000–2001, p. 70 (entry by Hugo Chapman).
5. On the identification of this figure, and the iconography of the fresco cycle in general, see Smyth 1997, especially pp. 62–64.

BACCIO BANDINELLI

Gaiole in Chianti, 1493–Florence, 1560

The self-styled rival of Michelangelo and antagonist of Benvenuto Cellini, Baccio Bandinelli produced marble sculptures of both sacred and secular subjects, as well as portrait busts and funerary monuments. Throughout his career he enjoyed the patronage of the Medici, who commissioned some of his most important works, primarily in Florence, but also in Rome. His early style reflects the influence of Leonardo da Vinci, who was the friend of his teacher, Giovanni Francesco Rustici. Bandinelli oversaw a large studio. Among his pupils were Giorgio Vasari and Francesco Salviati; until recently many of the latter's drawings in both red chalk and pen and ink were often confused with the work of Bandinelli.

6. *Studies of Nude Male Warriors*, ca. 1525–30

Pen and brown ink, brush and brown wash, over black chalk, 16⅝ x 11 in. (42.3 x 28 cm)
Annotated in pen and brown ink at upper left: *63*; and at lower left: *4.B.*

Provenance: Unidentified collector's mark HF (not in Lugt); Private Collection, Switzerland; sale, Christie's, London, July 3, 2007, lot 17; acquired in 2007

Reference: Christie's, London 2007, pp. 28–29, no. 17

Full of energetic exploratory outlines, this large composition sketch of three heroic intertwined male nudes is executed with a boldness of outline and chiseled planes of shading that are typical of a Renaissance sculptor's drawing, being first blocked out by the artist over a tentative undersketch in black chalk. He then more carefully searched for the essential contours of the forms by drawing lightly on the paper with a fine-tipped pen and brown ink. He defined the final contours of the figures with thick pen-and-brown-ink outlines. The unusually great extent to which he employed pale layers of brown wash in freely modeling the anatomy of the figures, but with a minimal amount of diagonal parallel-hatching, only to deepen areas of shadows, and in which the hatched strokes exhibit hook returns, are all stylistic elements identifying this large, little published drawing as a work of the mid- to late 1520s by Baccio Bandinelli. It may be perhaps regarded as a fragment of a *modello*, or demonstration drawing, as *modelli* and comprehensive composition sketches were the drawing types of the 1520s by our artist that most frequently exhibited an extensive use of wash combined with hatching.[1] A similarly thorough technique of wash modeling within firmly reinforced outlines occurs in two of Bandinelli's most securely datable composition drawings in the Louvre, *The Martyrdom of Saint Lawrence* of 1526 (fig. 6.1)

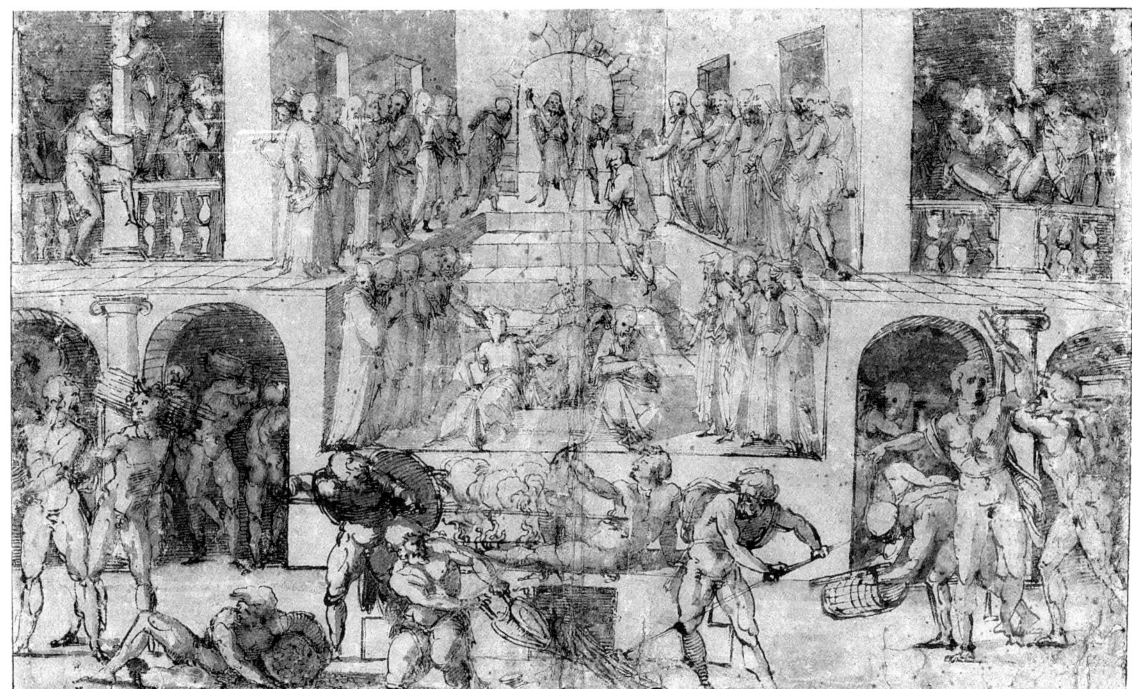

Fig. 6.1. Baccio Bandinelli. *The Martyrdom of Saint Lawrence*, 1526. Pen and brown ink, brush and brown wash, 13¹⁵⁄₁₆ x 22⅜ in. (35.4 x 56.8 cm). Département des Arts Graphiques, Musée du Louvre, Paris (99)

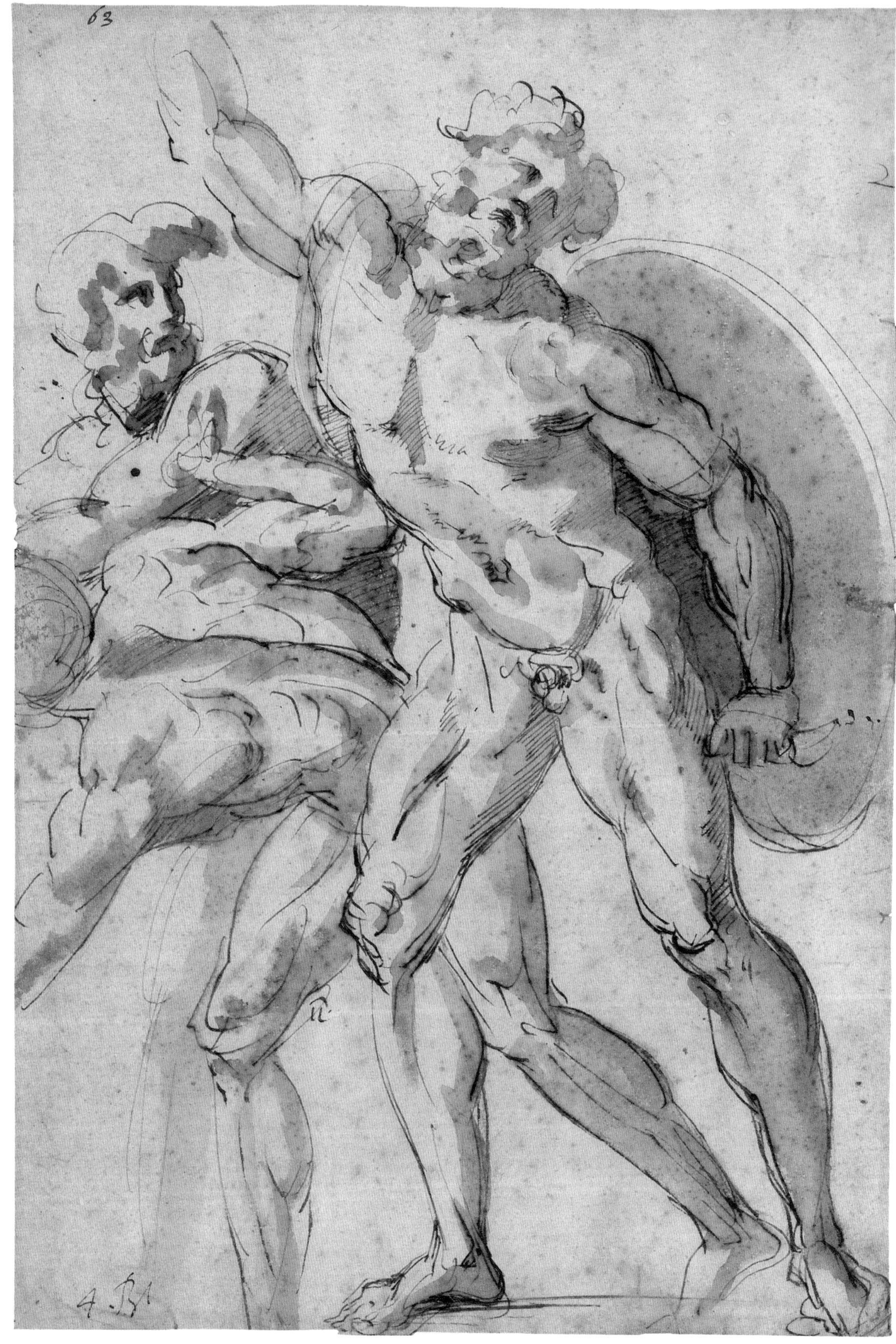

6

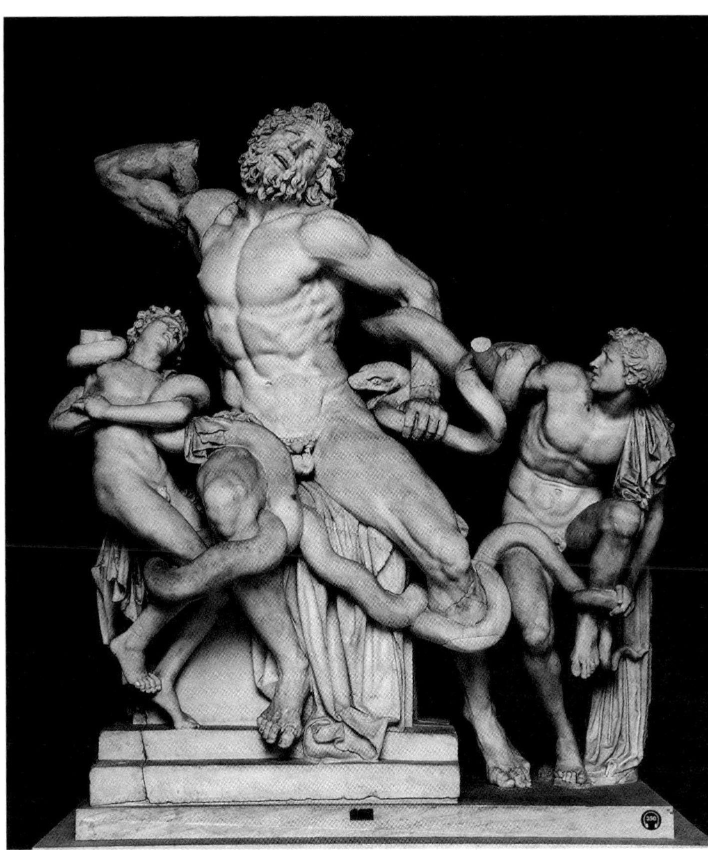

Fig. 6.2. Athenodoros, Hagesandros, and Polydoros of Rhodes. *Laocoön and His Sons*, early 1st century B.C. Marble, H. 72⁷⁄₁₆ in. (184 cm). Vatican Museums, Vatican City

Considering Bandinelli's thorough acquaintance with the Hellenistic masterpiece in his role as frequent copyist and restorer of the original statue (discussed below), it is not surprising that he took ample opportunities to explore variations on the arrangement of the secondary figures in works of his own. The detail of the Roman soldiers at lower right in the engraving *The Martyrdom of Saint Lawrence*, produced by Marcantonio Raimondi after Bandinelli's design for a never-executed fresco of this subject on the side walls of the church of San Lorenzo, Florence, offers commensurate nudes in action as the Tobey sheet (fig. 6.4).[4] Similar figures also occur in another monumental engraving after Bandinelli's design, Marco Dente's *Massacre of the Innocents*, printed before April 10, 1526.[5]

The most famous ancient sculpture known in the Renaissance before the discovery of the Farnese *Hercules*, the *Laocoön* was unearthed on January 14, 1506, near the Basilica of Santa Maria Maggiore in Rome, within the property of Felice de' Freddi, and was soon afterward purchased by Pope Julius II.[6]

and the *Resurrection of Lazarus* of about 1525–27.[2] In contrast, Bandinelli's most familiar kinds of drawings from the 1520s and later tend to rely primarily on parallel- and cross-hatching, done firmly and in a highly disciplined manner with the pen, almost entirely forgoing the use of wash.

The heroic nude at center foreground of doleful expression and raised right arm in the Tobey sheet is boldly drawn, with reinforced, beautifully dynamic contours. His figure derives from the monumental Hellenistic marble sculpture *Laocoön and His Sons* (fig. 6.2), of the early first century B.C., carved by Athenodoros, Hagesandros, and Polydoros of Rhodes. Two precisely rendered drawings by Bandinelli of Laocoön's torso, datable to about 1520–22, are in the Gabinetto Disegni e Stampe degli Uffizi, Florence,[3] of which one is especially softly modeled in red and black chalks, a technique that our artist virtually abandoned after the early 1520s (fig. 6.3), and the tight handling of which contrasts with the great freedom of the present sheet. The two leaning male nudes on the left of the Tobey drawing are not based on the poses of the sons in the *Laocoön* group.

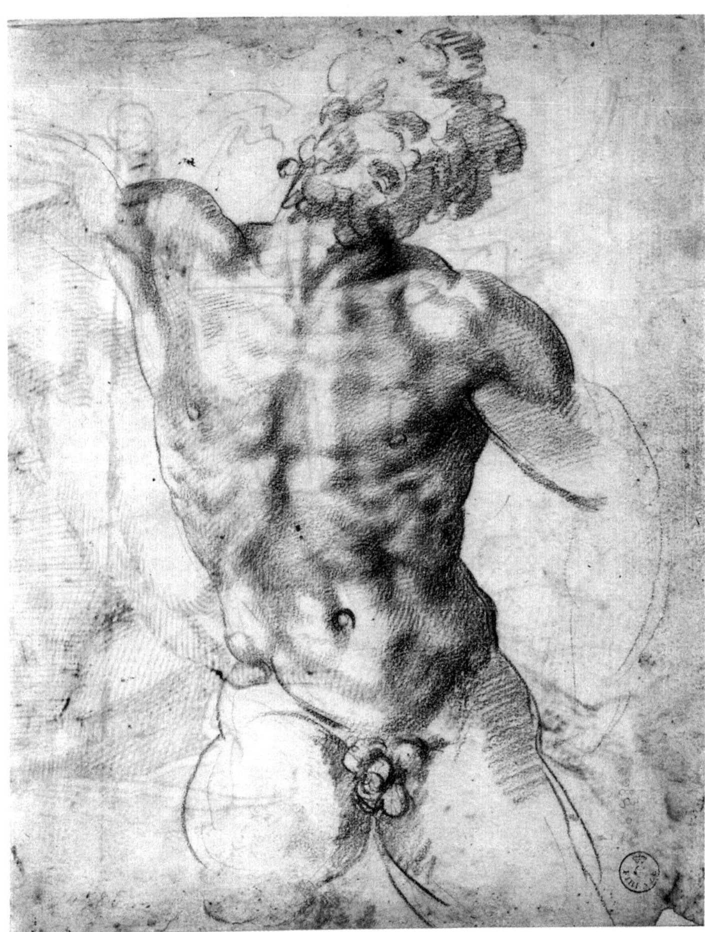

Fig. 6.3. Baccio Bandinelli. *Study after Laocoön*, ca. 1520–22. Red and black chalk, 11 x 8⁷⁄₁₆ in. (27.9 x 21.4 cm). Gabinetto Disegni e Stampe degli Uffizi, Florence (14785F)

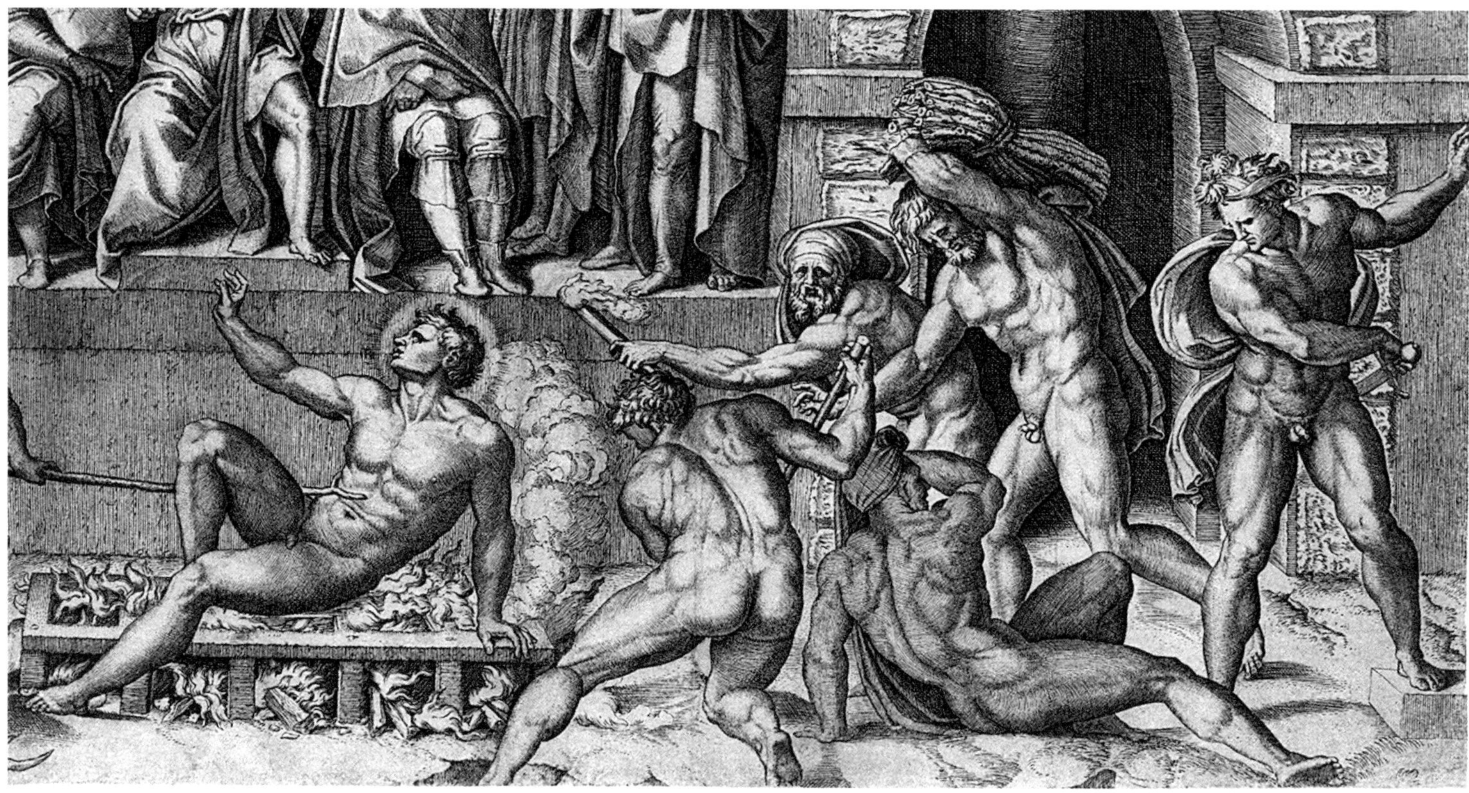

Fig. 6.4. Marcantonio Raimondi, after Baccio Bandinelli. Detail of the saint and the nudes at right in *The Martyrdom of Saint Lawrence*, 1526. Engraving, 16¹⁵⁄₁₆ x 22⅝ in. (43.1 x 57.5 cm). The Metropolitan Museum of Art, New York, Harris Brisbane Dick Fund, 1917 (17.3.3496)

It was immediately identified as the lost sculpture described by Pliny and was admired by Michelangelo soon after its discovery, but it was Bandinelli's career that became especially closely allied with the famous sculpture between 1520 and 1531, further reinforcing the dating in the late 1520s proposed here for the Tobey sheet. For most of our artist's lifetime, as it is today, the *Laocoön* was displayed inside a niche in the Belvedere Courtyard, the Cortile delle Statue, of the Vatican Palace. It appears recorded as a small motif in this location in the background at left, in a drawing in pen and brown ink with wash by Maarten van Heemskerck (1498–1574), datable to the Flemish painter's sojourn in Rome in 1532–36/37.[7] None too kind to Bandinelli, the biography of him in Vasari's *Vite* mentions that two ambassadors of King Francis I of France admired the collection of antiquities in the Vatican Palace during a state visit to the court of Pope Leo X de' Medici, and the *Laocoön* in particular, which prompted Cardinal Giulio de' Medici (the future Pope Clement VII) and Bernardo Dovizi da Bibbiena, Cardinal of Santa Maria in Portico, to offer that "this work or a facsimile will be sent to His Majesty, and there will be no difference [between the original and the copy]."[8] According to Vasari, Bandinelli was then commissioned to make the large

reproduction, and he also produced a model sculpted in wax ("uno di cera"), as well as a full-scale drawing in white gouache and charcoal in the size of the original statue ("un cartone di biacca e carbone della grandezza di quello di marmo").[9] The meeting of the cardinals with the French ambassadors must have occurred in the winter of 1520 (although November or December 1519 is also possible), and the circumstances of Bandinelli's involvement in the project of the *Laocoön* copy can be independently ascertained from recently discovered documentary evidence.[10] Two letters of January 29 and February 11, 1520, exchanged by Leonardo Sellaio in Rome and his friend and employer, Michelangelo Buonarroti in Florence, incidentally allude that there was talk in the papal court that a "bronze copy" of the *Laocoön* was apparently desired by the king of France, that Baccio Bandinelli appeared to be the artist to whom this could be entrusted, and that within the month he had produced a *chartone* (cartoon, or full-scale drawing) of the *Laocoön*.[11]

Dated September 21, 1520, a contract from Cardinal Bibbiena was awarded to Bandinelli to carve a marble copy in the full size of the original *Laocoön* group in the Cortile del Belvedere ("uno Laocoonte di marmo, della grandezza dell'antico che è a Belvedere, con li figlioli"), and it also notes that our artist was to finish the sculpture by the end of September 1521 ("per tutto el mese di settembre proximo futuro"); his compensation was to be 900 cameral ducats ("ducati 900 d'oro di camera").[12] In 1523, a report to the Venetian Senate by its ambassador at the papal court (perhaps Piero Pesaro) confirms that Bandinelli was still carving the *Laocoön* marble and that only the two figures of the high priest's sons were finished, "but even if the master lived five-hundred years, and had made one hundred copies of it, he would never be able to make something equal [to the original]."[13] The sculptor's work on the full-scale marble copy of the *Laocoön* lasted through the reigns of three popes, Leo X (r. 1513–21), Hadrian VI (r. 1522–23), and Clement VII (r. 1523–34), to whom it was consigned before August 31, 1531.[14] According to Vasari's *Vite*, Bandinelli also restored the missing right arm of the original antique statue, and this prosthesis of *Laocoön*'s right arm was in an extended pose (it was removed in the 1960s), as is seen in the Tobey drawing.

CCB

1. In addition to the examples of drawings with wash modeling by Bandinelli discussed here, see those illustrated and discussed in Ward 1988, nos. 25, 31, 44; and by Louis A. Waldman in Franklin et al. 2005, nos. 90, 92, 93.

2. Musée du Louvre, Paris (inv. nos. 99 and 100, respectively). See Waldman in Franklin et al. 2005, pp. 258–59, no. 90; and Van Tuyll van Serooskerken 2008, pp. 73–74, nos. 16–17. The convincing proposal of dating *The Martyrdom of Saint Lawrence* to 1526 is due to Waldman in Franklin et al. 2005, pp. 258–61, nos. 90–91.

3. Inv. no. 14785F and inv. no. 14786F. See Julian Brooks in Los Angeles 2007–8, fig. 6; Nathaniel Silver in Los Angeles 2007–8, pp. 86–87, no. 72.

4. On the print by Marcantonio Raimondi after Bandinelli (Bartsch XIV.89.104) and the related project for the never-realized fresco in San Lorenzo, Florence, see especially Waldman in Franklin et al. 2005, pp. 260–61, no. 91.

5. The print by Marco Dente is Bartsch XIV.24.21 (an impression is at The Metropolitan Museum of Art, New York [49.97.618]). See the document confirming April 10, 1526 as the *ante quem* date of the publication of Dente's print after Bandinelli's design, *The Massacre of the Innocents*, in Waldman 2004, pp. 84–85, no. 156.

6. Haskell and Penny 1981, pp. 243–47, no. 52.

7. This drawing by Heemskerck is British Museum, London, inv. no. 1946-7-13-639.

8. The present author's translation of Vasari ed. 1966–87, vol. 5 (text), p. 246: "Allora il cardinale gli disse: 'A Sua Maestà si manderà o questo o un simile, che non ci sarà differenza.'"

9. Ibid.

10. Waldman 2004, p. xvi, and following discussion.

11. Transcribed in ibid., pp. 55–56, doc. nos. 109–110.

12. Transcribed in ibid., pp. 56–57, doc. no. 113.

13. Quoted here in the present author's translation of an ambiguous phrasing in the original report. See Waldman 2004, pp. xvi, 69, no. 133 ("ma il maestro, se anche vivesse cinquecento anni, e ne avesse fatti cento, non potria mai far cosa eguale").

14. See documents in ibid., pp. xvii, 113–15, nos. 208–10.

SCHOOL OF RAPHAEL:
TOMMASO VINCIDOR

Bologna, ca. 1495(?)–Breda, 1534/36

OR

GIANFRANCESCO PENNI

Florence, ca. 1496–Naples, after 1528

One of Raphael's first pupils was Gianfrancesco Penni, whose role in the industrious workshop was primarily that of executant of the master's designs, both frescoes and panel paintings. Unlike Raphael's other followers, Penni (whose nickname "il Fattore" suggests an administrative role) did not forge a distinctive style or successful independent career. Discerning the hand of this rather nebulous personality in paintings and drawings emanating from the workshop has proven difficult, and attribution questions persist. The enigmatic Tommaso Vincidor was a later entrant into Raphael's circle. Vasari lists him among the assistants who worked on the Vatican Logge decorations, and he was dispatched to Flanders to help oversee the weaving of tapestries designed by Raphael and his pupils. From 1527 until his death, he worked as an architect in Breda. A small corpus of drawings and cartoon fragments has been ascribed to Vincidor, as have a few Raphaelesque paintings. On their evidence his style appears close to that of Raphael's principal disciple, Giulio Romano.

7. *The Silhouetted Head of a Bearded Man in Profile Facing Left (fragment of a tapestry cartoon, The Adoration of the Magi)*, ca. 1521–30

Brush with brown ink and wash; red, brown, and white gouache; over black chalk or charcoal; on two glued sheets of paper with overlapping seams. Silhouetted: 12³⁄₁₆ x 10⁷⁄₁₆ in. (31 x 26.5 cm) maximum

Provenance: Possibly Govaert Flinck (1615–1660); possibly Nicholaes Anthoni Flinck (Rotterdam, 1646–1723); Brophy Collection (his notes on the verso of the mount); Private Collection, England; Pandora Old Masters, 1998–99; acquired in 1999

"I have great patience with foreign barbarians when they are far away" ("Io ho gran patientia con barbari strani luntani").[1] So said Tommaso Vincidor, one of the proposed authors of this work, in his letter of 1521 to Pope Leo X de' Medici, when explaining his activity as a tapestry designer working with the Flemish weavers entrusted to follow his cartoons (full-scale drawings). The Bolognese painter, a pupil of Raphael's, appears to have been sent to Brussels specifically to supervise the weavers producing a tapestry series. Although Vasari noted in the *Vita* of Gianfrancesco Penni that this artist helped Raphael paint many of the cartoons for the tapestries in "the Chapel of the Pope and the Consistory,"[2] Vincidor, rather than Penni or Giulio Romano, has often come to be considered the maker of some of the tapestry cartoons for the series on the Life of Christ, or *Scuola Nuova*. The name *Scuola Nuova* was intended to distinguish the tapestry set from that of the earlier *Acts of the Apostles* (*Scuola Vecchia*) by Raphael and his workshop, commissioned by Pope Leo X in 1515 to decorate the lower register of the walls of the Sistine Chapel on ceremonial occasions. The

Scuola Nuova series consists of twelve tapestries, each dedicated to a scene from the Life of Christ, apparently woven between about 1521 and early 1531, and meant to hang during the Christmas and Easter seasons in a room that documents of the period called the "sala del Consistoro secreto" (Chamber of the Secret Consistory) and that was perhaps the space in the Vatican Palace today occupied by the Sala Regia.[3] The tapestries appear to have been commissioned not long after the death of Pope Leo X on December 1, 1521, probably by his cousin Pope Clement VII (r. 1523–34), and were delivered to the papal court in Rome as a completed project before June 1531. Eleven pieces of the set survive today in the Vatican Museums (the twelfth was probably lost in the Napoleonic lootings of 1798).[4]

An unpublished cartoon fragment related to this series, the large, silhouetted man's head in the Tobey Collection was carried out in a painterly technique in colored gouaches, of opaque consistency, over a bold, summary underdrawing in black chalk or charcoal, that became typical of cartoons for tapestries by Italian artists from this period. This style of execution was essentially pioneered by Raphael and his workshop in producing the seven *Acts of the Apostles* cartoons, or *Scuola Vecchia* (Royal Collection, Windsor Castle, on permanent loan to the Victoria and Albert Museum, London).[5] The drawing surface of the Tobey fragment exhibits mended creases, as well as some tears and abrasions, all of which are signs that it was a highly utilitarian object in the artist's and weavers' workshops; the cartoon's

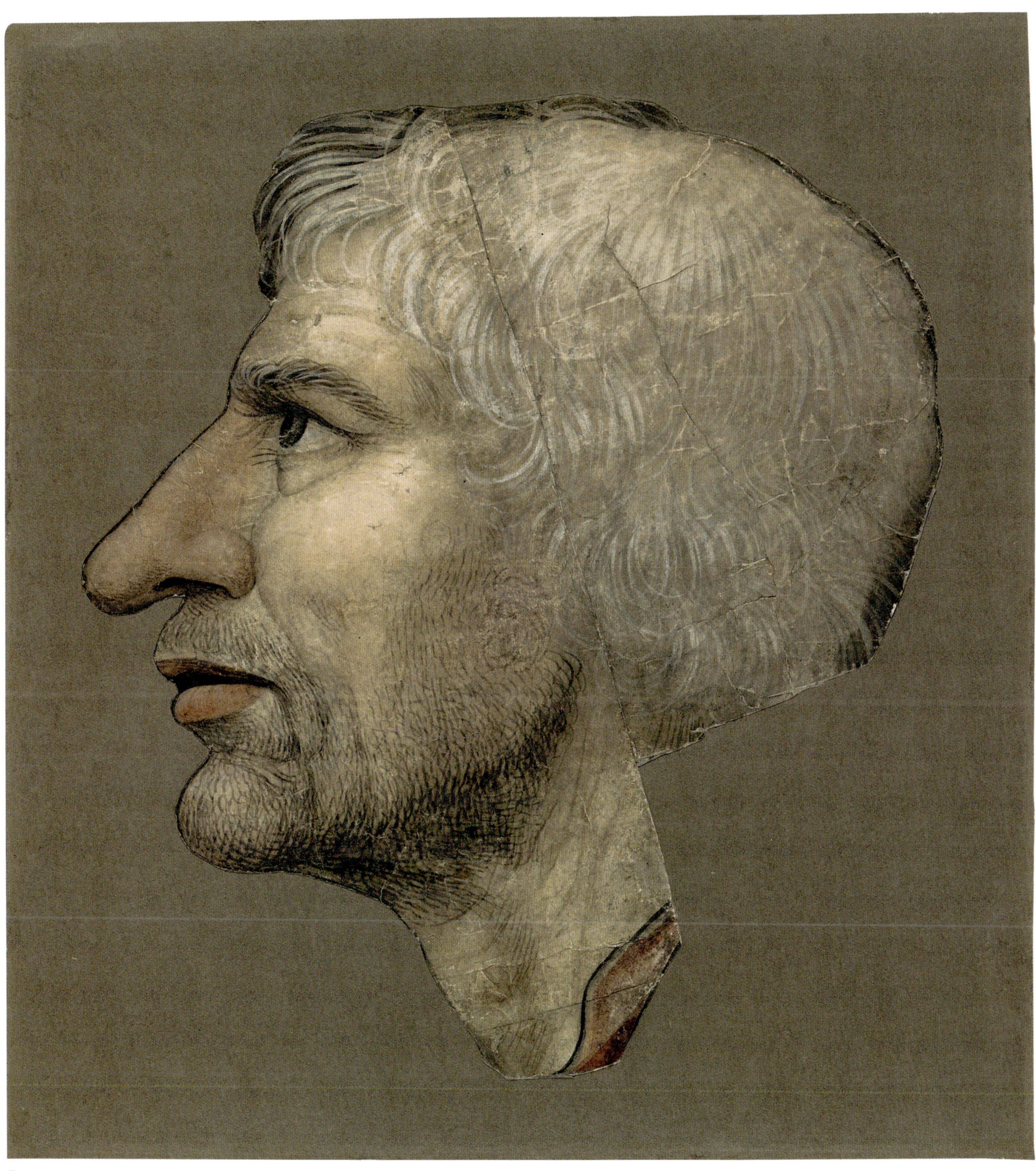

7

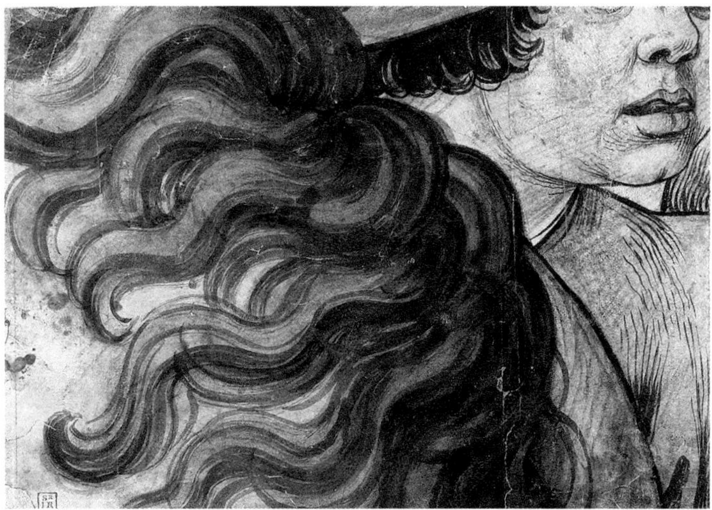

Fig. 7.1. School of Raphael. *Head of a Youth and Portion of Horse's Mane*, 1521–30. Cartoon fragment for *The Adoration of the Magi*. Brush with brown and red gouache over black chalk, 15⅝ x 8⅞ in. (39.6 x 22.5 cm). The Metropolitan Museum of Art, New York, Gift of John W. Lisle, in memory of his father, Joseph William Lisle, 1922 (22.72.2)

design was probably cut up into strips or smaller portions by the weavers.[6] The silhouetting around the man's head was almost certainly done by a later collector in an attempt to remove damage on the paper, owing to the vicissitudes of time.

Only one set of tapestries was woven based on the *Scuola Nuova* cartoons. A vast number of the original, related tapestry cartoon fragments from this series exist, dispersed among various public and private collections, none a repetition or a copy of a given motif in the designs; the largest group (twenty) is at the Ashmolean Museum of Art and Archaeology, Oxford.[7] The *Scuola Nuova* cartoons seem to have survived more or less intact until well into the seventeenth century, before being dismembered into pieces.[8] Many fragments were owned by Govaert Flinck (1615–1660), Rembrandt's pupil in the early to mid-1630s, and then by his son Nicholaes Anthoni Flinck (1646–1723), and probably through the younger Flinck, either directly or indirectly, Nicolas Dorigny (1658–1746) obtained "104 fragments, chiefly of hands and feet." A group of "not less than fifty pieces" consisting of heads, hands, and feet made its way to Jonathan Richardson, Sr. (1665–1745).[9]

According to Giorgio Vasari's biography of Raphael, Vincidor was Raphael's pupil and assisted him with the series of tapestry cartoons for the Vatican Palace. He was sent to Flanders in 1520 by Pope Leo X to oversee the production of cartoons and tapestries to be woven in Brussels for the Vatican's Sala di Costantino and Sala del Consistoro. The Tobey cartoon fragment was preparatory for the head of one of the male onlookers appearing on the left half, at center, in the tapestry *The Adoration of the Magi* (fig. 7.3), woven in the workshop of Pieter van Aelst in Brussels. As is typical of such cartoon designs, the man's head

here faces left, in the mirror orientation of the textile (tapestries are woven from the back, in reverse of the cartoon), and is detailed in color, with clear black outlines to provide the weavers with an exact guide. The finished tapestry by the Flemish craftsmen retained the great precision in the man's features. Two cartoon fragments relating to details on the right half of the same tapestry are in the Metropolitan Museum (figs. 7.1, 7.2).[10] Four further fragments for figures in *The Adoration of the Magi* are in the Ashmolean Museum of Art and Archaeology, Oxford.[11]

The present author, however, prefers to leave the vexed question of the authorship of this and the other *Scuola Nuova* tapestry cartoon fragments somewhat open. Two tentative attributions, to Tommaso Vincidor or Gianfrancesco Penni, seem to have the most merit, for the notion that these drawings carefully executed in brush and colored goauches are by the School of Raphael seems most commensurate, given the historical details of how the Raphael workshop was directed after the great master's death in 1520 by his two artistic heirs,

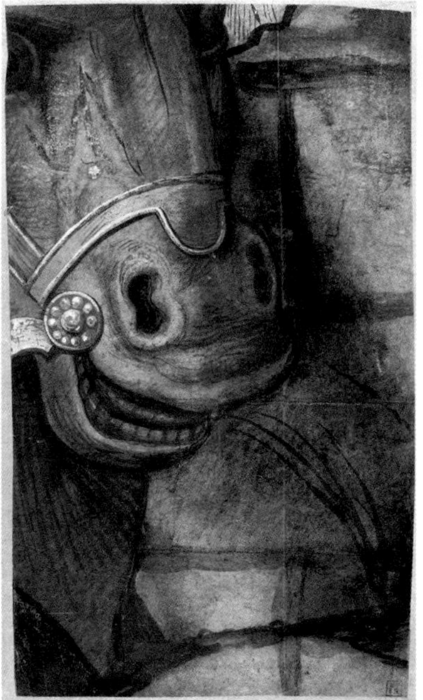

Fig. 7.2. School of Raphael. *Muzzle of a Horse*, 1521–30. Cartoon fragment for *The Adoration of the Magi*. Brush, brown, red, green, yellow, and white gouache, over black chalk, 9⁷⁄₁₆ x 13¹⁄₁₆ in. (24 x 33.2 cm). The Metropolitan Museum of Art, New York, Gift of John W. Lisle, in memory of his father, Joseph William Lisle, 1922 (22.72.1)

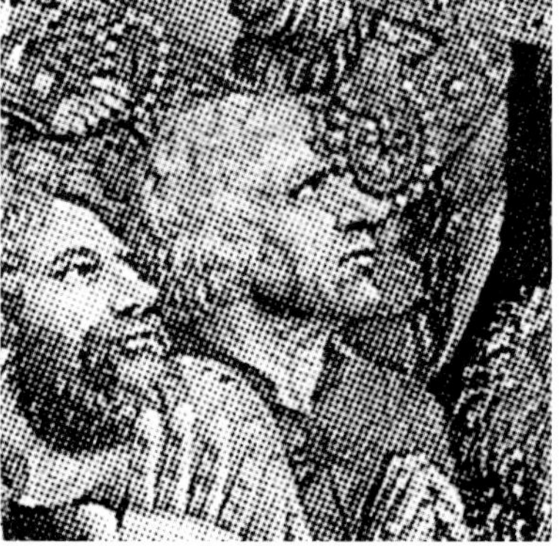

Fig. 7.3. Tapestry designed by School of Raphael, woven in the workshop of Pieter van Aelst, Brussels. Detail of *The Adoration of the Magi*, ca. 1521–30. Wool, silk, and gilt-metal-wrapped thread, 18 ft. 6½ in. x 31 ft. 5¹⁄₁₆ in. (567 x 958 cm). Vatican Museums, Vatican City

Giulio Romano and Penni. Vasari's *Vita* of Giulio states: "after the death of Raphael, Giulio and Giovanfrancesco called *il Fattore* became his heirs entrusted with the duty of finishing the works left incomplete by the said Raphael, and they honorably executed the greatest part of these with perfection."[12] The wording in Vasari's *Vita* of Penni is somewhat different, although also alluding to the fact that the two artists had been Raphael's "disciples" and that on his death, "they worked together for a long time, and in partnership finished the works left incomplete by Raphael."[13]

James Byam Shaw rejected the attribution of the *Scuola Nuova* tapestry cartoon fragments to Giulio himself, instead assigning the surviving examples at Christ Church, Oxford to the "Studio of Giulio Romano."[14] When they catalogued the two examples in the British Museum, London, Philip Pouncey and John A. Gere attributed them to Penni, working under Giulio's supervision, not only emphasizing the weight of Vasari's testimony in the *Vita* of Penni but also accounting for the stylistic evidence of many of the preparatory studies connected with the project.[15] In the Metropolitan Museum's 2002 exhibition *Tapestry in the Renaissance: Art and Magnificence*, the designs of the *Scuola Nuova* series and the related cartoon fragments were presented as "by Giovanni Francesco Penni and others."[16] Reattribution of most of the *Scuola Nuova* tapestry cartoon fragments to Tommaso Vincidor rests primarily with Nicole Dacos, on the strength of some visual comparisons, but mostly because of the documented fact of this artist's direct involvement with the weavers in Brussels in 1521.[17]

CCB

1. The present author's translation, as quoted from Dacos et al. 1980, p. 94.
2. Vasari ed. 1966–87, vol. 4 (text), p. 332 ("onde fu di grande aiuto a Raffaello a dipignere gran parte de' cartoni dei panni d'arazzo della cappella del Papa e del Concistoro").
3. This and what immediately follows is based on Campbell et al. 2002, pp. 237–41, which provides an up-to-date, documented summary on the project of the *Scuola Nuova* tapestry series.
4. The lost tapestry, *The Descent to Hell*, is known from various engravings (Campbell et al. 2002, p. 237).
5. For different points of view, compare Shearman 1972; Fermor 1996; and Campbell et al. 2002, pp. 187–218, no. 23.
6. On the dismemberment of the Sistine tapestry cartoons by Raphael and his workshop, see Fermor 1996, pp. 54–57. On the destructive working procedures in the use of cartoons, including those for tapestries, see Bambach 1999 (especially pp. 283–95).
7. Compare Pouncey and Gere 1962, vol. 1, pp. 80–81; Parker 1956, pp. 326–30, nos. 599–619; and Byam Shaw 1976, vol. 1, pp. 135–37, nos. 457–60.
8. Compare Parker 1956, p. 326; and Byam Shaw 1976, vol. 1, pp. 135–37, nos. 457–60, for an account of this dispersion.
9. Compare Parker 1956, pp. 326–30, nos. 599–619, quoting Gunn 1831, pp. 25–27, as the source for these often quoted facts, without attribution.
10. Bean and Turčić 1982, pp. 216–17, nos. 213–14.
11. Parker 1956, pp. 327–28, nos. 605–8.
12. The present author's translation of Vasari ed. 1966–87, vol. 5 (text), p. 57: "morto Raffaello, e rimasi eredi di lui Giulio e Giovanfrancesco detto il Fattore, con carico di finire l'opere da esso Raffaello incominciate, condussero onoratamente la maggior parte a perfezzione." See Shearman 2003, vol. 1, pp. 672–73, 700–1, 706–7, nos. 1521/6, 1521/30, and 1521/37, for references in documents from 1521 to Giulio Romano and Giovanfrancesco Penni as executing works in Raphael's studio after his death.
13. The present author's translation of Vasari ed. 1966–87, vol. 4 (text), p. 333: "Intanto venuto a morte Raffaello, Giulio Romano e Giovan Francesco, stati suoi discepoli, stettono molto tempo insieme e finirono di compagnia l'opere che di Raffaello erano rimase imperfette."
14. Byam Shaw 1976, vol. 1, pp. 135–37, nos. 457–60.
15. See Vasari ed. 1966–87, vol. 4 (text), p. 332; and Pouncey and Gere 1962, vol. 1, pp. 80–81, nos. 137–38, vol. 2, pl. 111.
16. See discussion and captions identifying the tapestries in Campbell et al. 2002, pp. 237–41, figs. 98–100.
17. See especially Dacos 1987, vol. 1, pp. 611–23; and Nicole Dacos in Brussels and Rome 1995, pp. 388–92 (with other bibliography). The present work has not been published, but Professor Dacos has accepted an attribution to Vincidor based on a photograph (letter to David M. Tobey, November 20, 2002).

GIULIO ROMANO

Rome, ca. 1499–Mantua, 1546

Giulio Romano was Raphael's principal pupil and artistic heir. Working with the master's drawings he had a significant hand in the execution of a number of the most important frescoes, altarpieces, portraits, and private devotional images from Raphael's later career. Like Raphael, he also worked as an architect in Rome and later in Mantua, where he relocated in 1524 in order to become court artist to the Gonzaga. Assuming there the role of artistic impresario, he turned his boundless energy and inventive talent to myriad undertakings, large and small, designing frescoes, stucco reliefs, religious images, secular architecture, tapestries, metalwork, and ephemeral structures. According to Vasari, who visited him in Mantua, Giulio intended to return to Rome, the city of his birth, but that plan was thwarted by his death. Like his paintings, Giulio's early drawings in both chalk and pen and ink reflect his thorough command of a Raphaelesque manner, an aptitude that underlies the ongoing debate over matters of attribution.

8. *Allegory of the Regency of Cardinal Ercole Gonzaga: Study for a Lost Tapestry*, ca. 1540–45

Pen and brown ink, brush and brown wash, over black chalk; some traces of red chalk at lower border, 16¹³⁄₁₆ x 11⁵⁄₁₆ in. (42.7 x 28.8 cm)

The Metropolitan Museum of Art, New York, Promised Gift of David M. Tobey

Provenance: Sir Peter Lely (London, 1618–1680) (Lugt 2092); Nicholaes Anthoni Flinck (Rotterdam, 1646–1723) (Lugt 959); William, 2nd Duke of Devonshire (Chatsworth, 1672–1739) (Lugt 718); by descent to the eleventh duke; The Trustees of the Chatsworth Settlement, inv. no. 105; sale, Christie's, London, July 3, 1984, lot 18; Private Collection; sale, Christie's, New York, January 10, 1996, lot 99; acquired in 1996

References: London 1953, no. 59; Hartt 1958, vol. 1, pp. 252–53, 308, no. 362, vol. 2, fig. 518; London 1960, no. 571; Popham 1962–63, p. 21, no. 27; Viale Ferrero 1963, p. 19; Popham 1969, no. 27; Van Regteren Altena and Ward-Jackson 1970, under no. 81; Tokyo 1975, no. 27; Jerusalem 1977, no. 27; Jane Martineau in London 1981–82, p. 204, no. 204; Meijer and van Tuyll 1983–84, under no. 66; Delmarcel and Brown 1988, p. 112; Konrad Oberhuber in Mantua 1989, p. 166; Nello Forti Grazzini in Mantua 1989, pp. 478–80; Jaffé 1994, p. 110, no. 222; Brown and Delmarcel 1996, pp. 69, 181–82; Delmarcel 1997, pp. 383–92 (pp. 388–89, listing the location of this drawing as still in Chatsworth); M. Schwartz in Cox-Rearick et al. 1999, no. 16; Linda Wolk-Simon in Mantua 2001, p. 96, no. 4; Van Tuyll van Serooskerken 2000, pp. 209–10 (under no. 152); Nello Forti Grazzini in Campbell et al. 2002, pp. 506–13 (under no. 59), fig. 224

This well-preserved drawing once formed part of the fabled art collections of the dukes of Devonshire, Chatsworth, by which provenance it is best known in the literature. The correct attribution to Giulio Romano was given by Frederick Hartt in 1958, who also identified the drawing as a probable design for a tapestry.[1] A celebrated late work by the artist, this charged, elaborately detailed scene depicts a political allegory extolling the virtues of Cardinal Ercole Gonzaga (1505–1563). Ercole had been appointed bishop of Mantua on March 10, 1521, and on the premature death of his brother, Duke Federico II, in 1540, became regent for his young nephew, Duke Francesco III

(1533–1550). He was the only cardinal of the Gonzaga family during the last years of Giulio's life in Mantua, and is said to have told Giorgio Vasari that "Giulio was more the head of the state than he was," so great was the cardinal's esteem for him.[2]

As in his other very late drawings, the artist used the brush freely here for the application of the wash in a thick, painterly manner, even relying on it to achieve the curved parallel-hatching in the modeling of the figures, instead of doing this finely with the pen. As is also typical, the overall tonal scale of the composition is dramatic, tending toward dark shadows. He arranged the scene within an arched trellis, formed on the sides by trees, their branches interlaced with fruit-laden vines. Beyond it, a putto, possibly Cupid, drives a quadriga (chariot of state) of eagles, the ancient heraldic emblems of the Gonzaga family; fortunately, the eagles were also the imperial device of ancient Rome and of Charles V, from whom Mantua sought political protection. The putto is poised to throw his lance (the tip is barely indicated in very light pen-and-ink outlines). Above him hover two winged genii triumphantly holding a cardinal's hat and the oval shield—*lions rampant* quartering *barry of eight*—of the Gonzaga family. The landscape is reminiscent of the flat marshy terrain of Mantua, which is enclosed by mountains in the distance.

The detailed Tobey sheet likely served as the *modello*, or *petit patron*, for a lost tapestry—Giulio's proficiency as a designer for such textiles is mentioned in Vasari's *Vite*[3]—commissioned by Cardinal Ercole between 1540 and 1545, presumably a por-tiere (an overdoor piece), based on the strong vertical format of the composition, as proposed by Nello Forti Grazzini.[4] Some early scholars thought that the tapestry may have been woven in either Ferrara or Mantua.[5] It could have been part of a set of twelve lost pieces called the *Spalliere della Fortuna*,

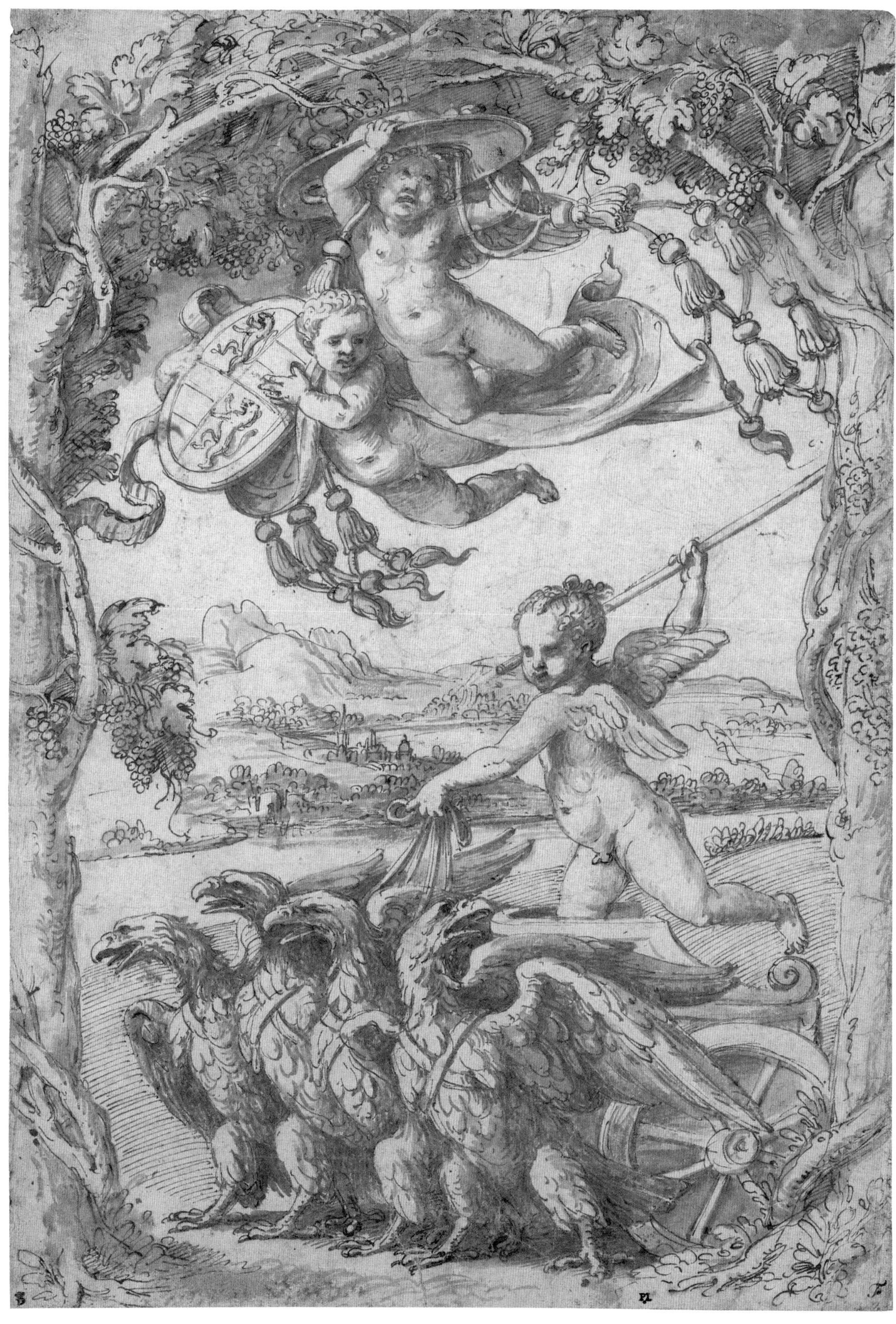

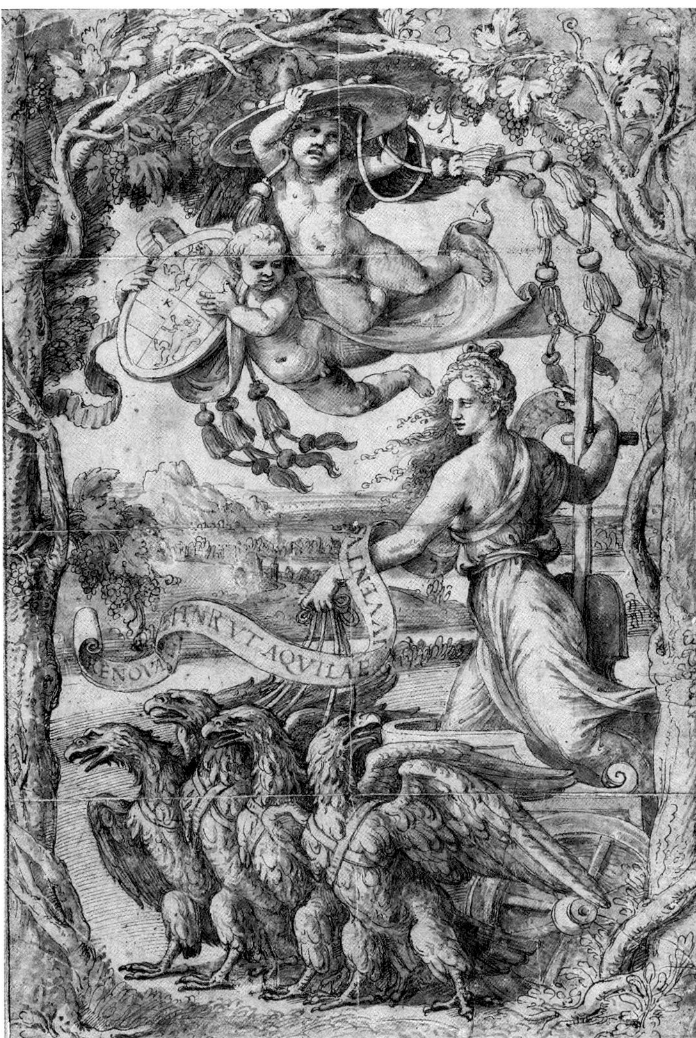

Fig. 8.1. Giulio Romano. *Fortune in a Chariot Drawn by Eagles (Allegory of the Regency of Cardinal Ercole Gonzaga)*, ca. 1540–45. Design for a tapestry. Pen and dark gray ink, brush and gray wash, 16⅝ x 11⅛ in. (42.2 x 28.3 cm). Teyler Museum, Haarlem (A*64)

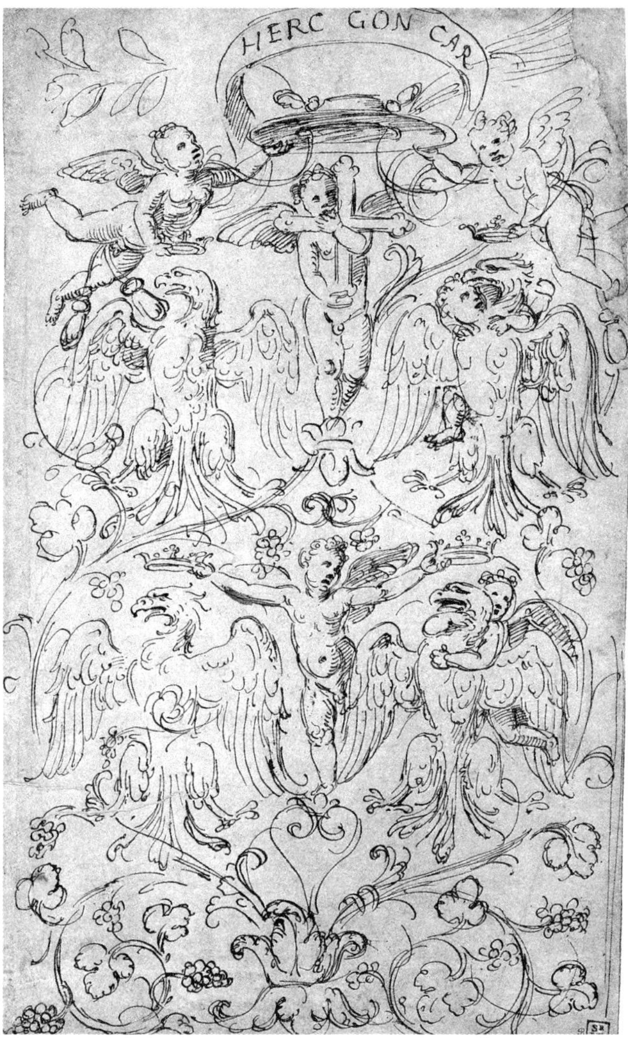

Fig. 8.2. Giulio Romano. *The Arms of Cardinal Ercole Gonzaga*, ca. 1538–40. Pen and brown ink, over black chalk, 15⁹⁄₁₆ x 9¼ in. (39.5 x 23.5 cm). The Morgan Library and Museum, New York (IV.16)

owned by Cardinal Ercole Gonzaga, which were realized in the Netherlands based on designs sent from Mantua.[6] Alternatively, it seems more probable that the tapestry from Giulio's Tobey drawing was produced in 1545 in Mantua by the Flemish weaver Nicolas Karcher (who died there in 1562), to complete a fourteen-piece set of *Puttini* or *Giochi di Putti*, which had been begun for Federico II and continued by his brother, Cardinal Ercole.[7]

A closely related variation of the drawing in the Tobey Collection exists in the Teyler Museum, Haarlem (fig. 8.1),[8] made in nearly the exact size and technique, although of slightly more inert execution, for it exhibits little if any underdrawing in black chalk. It was probably produced by Giulio as an alternative design, at the request of his patron after he had made the Tobey drawing,[9] given that the putto at center was substituted by an allegorical female figure of Fortune in the Teyler Museum sheet. She holds a twirling scroll inscribed "RENOVABITUR VT AQUILAE IUVENTUS" (thy youth is renewed like the eagle's), a quotation from Psalm 103 (5–6): "Who satisfieth thy mouth with good things, so that thy youth is renewed like the eagle's. The Lord executeth righteousness and judgment for all that are oppressed."[10] Curiously, in the Tobey sheet, the energetic preliminary strokes of the black-chalk underdrawing at center, directly above Cupid's head, were never finally outlined in pen and ink with wash, but they depict a version of the scroll with lettering seen in the Haarlem composition. This hitherto unnoticed evidence would seem to confirm that the two drawings represent two successive stages of design for the same project. In the Teyler Museum drawing, the striding female figure—as noble a classical matron as Giulio ever produced—appears to embody specifically Fortuna Pacifica (Peaceful Fortune), for she holds in her right arm a long rudder, according to the personification described in the 1603 edition of Cesare Ripa's *Iconologia*.[11] Hence, the message of the final composition was to leave no doubt in proclaiming the beneficent regency of Cardinal Ercole.

Another sheet worthy of comparison with the Tobey drawing is Giulio's earlier rapidly done pen-and-ink sketch *The Arms of Cardinal Ercole Gonzaga* in the Morgan Library and Museum (fig. 8.2), datable to about 1538–40,[12] because, like many of his drawings of these years, it entirely omits the use of wash. It displays all the political power of certain emblems— the cross, cardinal's hat and name, Gonzaga eagles, and ducal coronets—but in a considerably less narrative way than in the Tobey sheet.   CCB

1. Hartt 1958, vol. 1, pp. 252–53, 308, no. 362.
2. The present author's translation of Vasari ed. 1966–87, vol. 5 (text), pp. 78–79 ("a che rispose il cardinale Giulio essere più padrone di quello Stato che non era egli").

3. Vasari ed. 1966–87, vol. 5 (text), p. 77 ("fece al Duca di Ferrara molti disegni per panni d'arazzo").
4. Nello Forti Grazzini in Mantua 1989, pp. 478–80. Delmarcel and Brown 1988, p. 112, thought that this drawing and its companion in the Teyler Museum, Haarlem, were both woven as tapestries as part of a *spalliera*, but this proposal is unconvincing as both drawings are of a decisively vertical format.
5. As suggested in Viale Ferrero 1963, p. 19.
6. Compare Delmarcel and Brown 1988; Brown and Delmarcel 1996; and Forti Grazzini in Campbell et al. 2002, pp. 512–13.
7. Forti Grazzini in Mantua 1989, p. 479; Forti Grazzini in Campbell et al. 2002, pp. 506–13.
8. On this drawing, compare Meijer and van Tuyll 1983–84, no. 66; Forti Grazzini in Mantua 1989, p. 478.
9. The proposal that the Teyler Museum sheet might represent an alternative was first made in Hartt 1958, vol. 1, p. 253.
10. Compare Jane Martineau in London 1981–82, p. 204, no. 204; Meijer and van Tuyll 1983–84, no. 66; Forti Grazzini in Campbell et al. 2002, pp. 512–13.
11. Ripa 1603, p. 170.
12. On the sheet (Morgan Library and Museum, New York, inv. no. IV.16), compare Bean and Stampfle 1965–66, pp. 53–54, no. 79.

DOMENICO CAMPAGNOLA

Venice(?), 1500–Padua, 1564

Domenico Campagnola was the adopted son of the artist Giulio Campagnola, to whom he was apprenticed in Venice about 1507. As a painter, draftsman, and printmaker he was profoundly influenced by Titian; the poetic, evocative, pastoral pen-and-ink landscape drawings for which he is most celebrated have in the past often been ascribed to the great Venetian master, and some may even have been deliberately executed as forgeries. Domenico Campagnola's woodcuts are his most important and innovative contributions; in a virtuoso display, he appears to have cut his own blocks rather than delegating this manual translation of his designs to a specialized professional.

9. *Roman Soldier Galloping on Horseback and Holding a Banner*, ca. 1517–25

Pen and brown ink, 8⅞ x 7¹⁄₁₆ in. (22.5 x 18 cm)
Annotated on recto in pen and brown ink at lower right: *campagnola*

Provenance: Private Collection, France; Galerie de Bayser, Paris; acquired in 2007

Reference: Tobias Nickel, unpublished catalogue-entry typescript, ca. December 2006, pp. 1–7

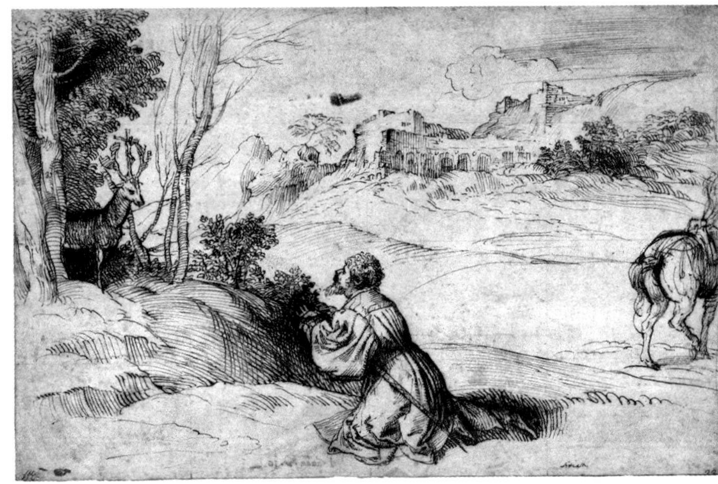

Fig. 9.1. Titian. *Vision of Saint Eustace*, ca. 1515–20. Pen and brown ink, lightly squared for transfer, 8½ x 12⁷⁄₁₆ in. (21.6 x 31.6 cm). British Museum, London (1895-9-15-818; JCR 371)

As a major printmaker active in the circle of Titian, Domenico Campagnola rendered drawings into woodcuts, and in his own draftsmanship in pen and ink he was influenced by the great Venetian master's graphic style especially during the crucial years from about 1515 to 1525, but also later. Campagnola left Venice (where he was trained in the workshop of Giulio Campagnola) for Padua about 1520 and was a great deal younger than Titian (ca. 1485/90?–1576).[1] For all these reasons, the attribution of drawings in pen and ink to Domenico Campagnola and to Titian (who was not a prolific draftsman, according to early sixteenth-century sources[2]) have occasioned heated dispute among art historians. While the authorship of the Tobey sheet by the young Domenico Campagnola is clear, the impact of Titian's pen-and-ink drawing style is undeniable, evident here in the pictorial handling of the medium, as well as the expressive manner of cross-hatching and lively, firm contours. The kinships of style and technique in the work of the two masters may be assessed by comparing the present sheet by Campagnola to securely attributed pen-and-ink drawings by Titian, such as the *Vision of Saint Eustace* of about 1515–20 in the British Museum (fig. 9.1).[3]

Although hitherto unpublished, the exuberant Tobey drawing was first thoroughly studied from a photograph by art historian Tobias Nickel, who also pointed out the connection to the woodcut designed in 1517 by Campagnola, *Massacre of the Innocents*, in which the image of a similar galloping Roman soldier occurs at left and faces in a mirror orientation (fig. 9.2).[4] It may be recalled that the design of a preparatory drawing is reversed in the process of printmaking. In the Tobey sheet, the motif of the soldier is presented as an autonomous composition, on a groundline indicating a landscape, rather than as a rider and rearing horse who are part of a complex, semiurban setting. Nevertheless, the figure in both works wears armor, cape, and boots in the ancient Roman style (*all'antica*), a type that was also emulated by sixteenth-century Paduan bronze sculptors,[5] but in the woodcut, as opposed to the present drawing, the head of the soldier is seen foreshortened and gazing upward, and the head of the horse is bent to the side and in a full frontal position.

In contrast to the print, the Tobey drawing exhibits a much subtler tonal control together with a greatly more expressive quality in the curved parallel- and cross-hatching of the modeling (in some passages, the pooling ink from the densely hatched strokes heavily impregnates the paper). For these reasons,

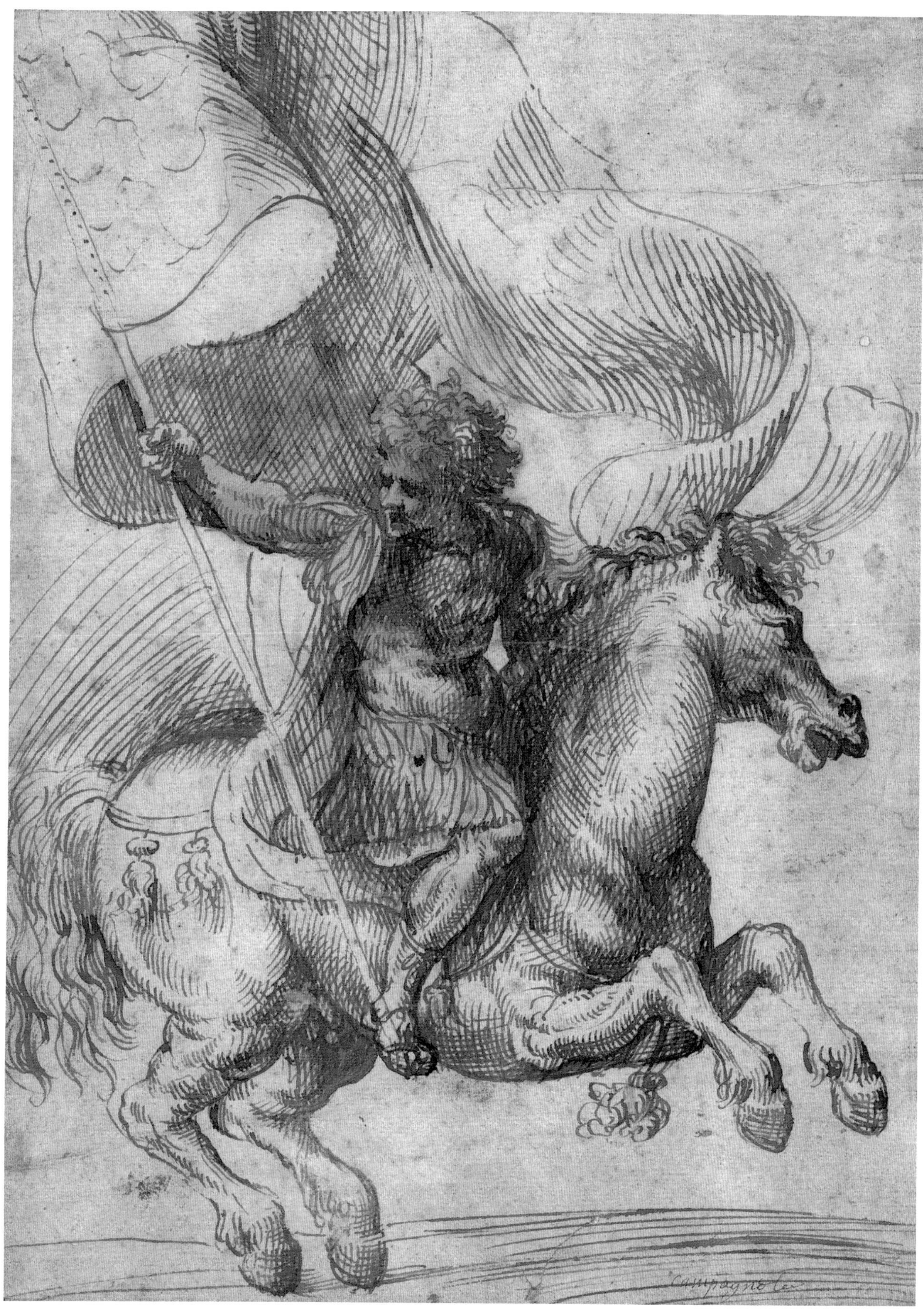

the study has been dated a few years later than the print, to the early 1520s.[6] The drawing style and technique of the Tobey sheet have been most closely compared to two pen-and-ink studies, one for a standing young woman in three-quarter length in the Teyler Museum, Haarlem, and another for the *Resurrection* in the British Museum (figs. 9.3, 9.4).[7] In the present author's opinion, some caution is necessary when considering the finer points of chronology in Campagnola's early graphic oeuvre, in that, generally speaking, the translation of a pen-and-ink drawing into the cruder medium of woodcut (in which lines are indicated as forms carved in relief on a wood surface) results in a design in which freely drawn contours and strokes of hatching are much hardened by the subtractive technique, also causing a loss in tonal modulation. Therefore it is plausible that the Tobey drawing and the *Massacre of the Innocents* date from a similar time, as the designs of the horsemen in both works seem too closely connected to be overlooked, even though the Tobey drawing may not have been directly preparatory for the woodcut, given the differences of details. While considering a prudent range of about 1517 to 1525, a dating of Campagnola's Tobey sheet to about 1517–20 may also be justified by the echoes of Titian's early pen-and-ink style.

That Campagnola undertook a thorough process of study and drawing in executing the *Massacre of the Innocents* may be intuited from the complexity of the composition, as this is the largest and most ambitious woodcut associated with him, having been printed from two separate woodblocks. The traditional attribution of both the design and execution of the woodcut has been to Campagnola himself, as his name and the date 1517 are inscribed in the tablet on the lower left corner of the composition.[8] However, all the extant impressions of this woodcut seem to date to the late seventeenth century, as they also include an inscription below the lower border of the composition at left, "IN VENETIA.IL.VIECERI," apparently alluding to the Venetian family of publishers, the Vieceri, of whom Lunardo and Felice Vieceri are documented in 1676 and 1683,[9] leading to some doubts regarding Campagnola's actual execution of the print.[10] In a recent catalogue, Gert Jan van der Sman, for instance, preferred to publish the woodcut of the *Massacre* as by an anonymous printmaker after Campagnola.[11]   CCB

1. I am grateful to Tobias Nickel, author of a PhD dissertation in progress, "The Drawings of Domenico Campagnola," Universität Wien, Institut für Kunstgeschichte, who has helpfully shared his observations on the documentary aspects of Campagnola's career. The artist is at the latest documented as "pictor(. . .)habitator Paduae" in 1523 (see Sambin 1973–74, pp. 381–88).

2. Of the immense literature on the draftsmanship of Titian, compare especially Rearick 1976; Wethey 1987; and Konrad Oberhuber in Paris 1993, pp. 483–502 (with entries by various other authors, pp. 503–38, nos. 86–152).

3. On this drawing attributed to Titian (British Museum, London, inv. no. 1895-9-15-818), see especially W. R. Rearick in Paris 1993, p. 618, no. 208.

4. My thanks to Tobias Nickel for his observations on this drawing, and for providing his unpublished catalogue-entry typescript, ca. 2006 (correspondence, January 2010).

5. Ibid.

6. Ibid.

7. On these sheets (Teyler Museum, Haarlem, inv. no. A 46; and British Museum, London, inv. no. 1895-9-15-837), see Nickel, as above. For the drawings of the early 1520s, see Saccomani 1991, pp. 31–36, especially p. 35, figs. 3, 10.

8. That Domenico Campagnola executed woodcuts himself is discussed in Rosand and Muraro 1976–77, p. 124. On the *Massacre of the Innocents* (Bartsch XIII.384.1), see ibid., pp. 136–37, no. 20.

9. For the citation of the documents regarding Lunardo and Felice Vieceri, see ibid., pp. 124–25 n. 10.

10. Compare the contrasting opinions in Rosand and Muraro 1976–77, pp. 124, 136; Van der Sman and Sellink 2002–3, p. 116, no. III.8. Hans Tietze and Erika Tietze-Conrat identified a sheet in the British Museum, London, inv. no. 1892-4-11-3, as a preparatory drawing for the *Massacre of the Innocents*, but it must be a copy rather than an exploratory study (see Tietze and Tietze-Conrat 1944, p. 128, no. A 485).

11. Van der Sman and Sellink 2002–3, p. 116, no. III.8 ("graveur sur bois anonyme d'après Domenico Campagnola").

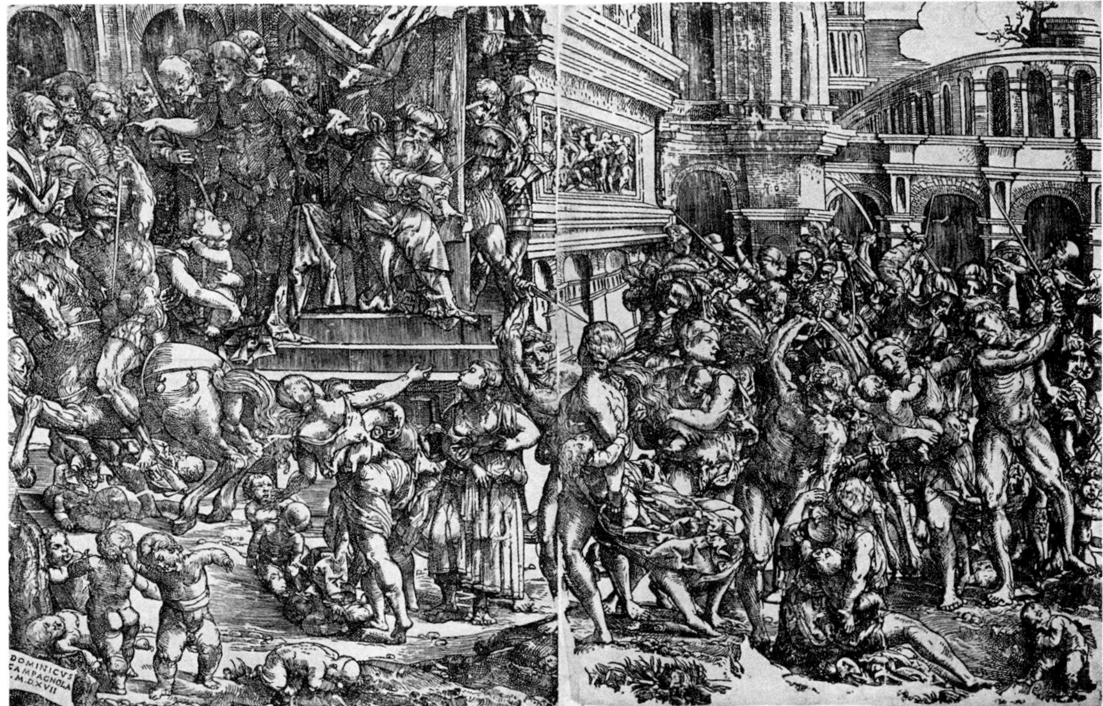

Fig. 9.2. Domenico Campagnola. *Massacre of the Innocents*, 1517. Woodcut, 20¹³⁄₁₆ x 32³⁄₁₆ in. (52.8 x 81.8 cm). Boijmans Van Beuningen Museum, Rotterdam (BDH 14474)

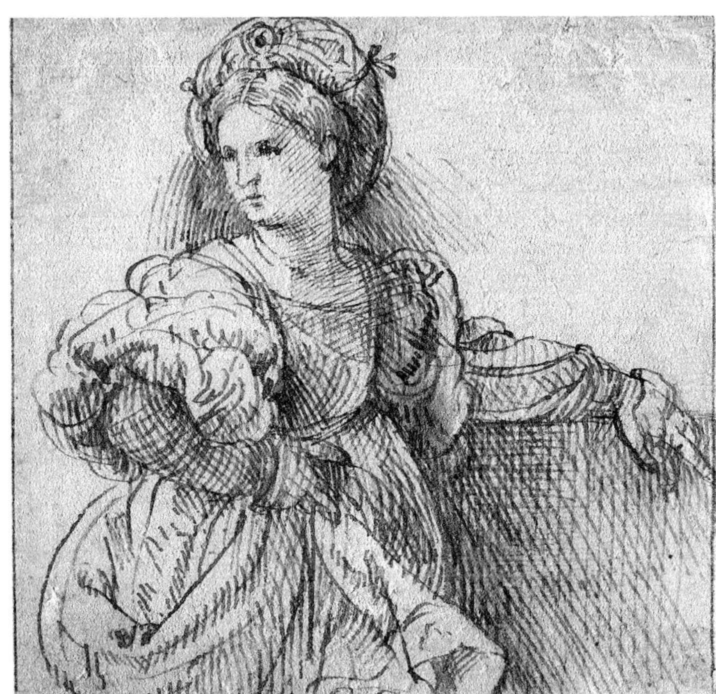

Fig. 9.3. Domenico Campagnola. *Young Woman with Balzo*, ca. 1520–25. Pen and brown ink, 4⅞ x 4¹⁵⁄₁₆ in. (12.4 x 12.5 cm). Teyler Museum, Haarlem (A 46)

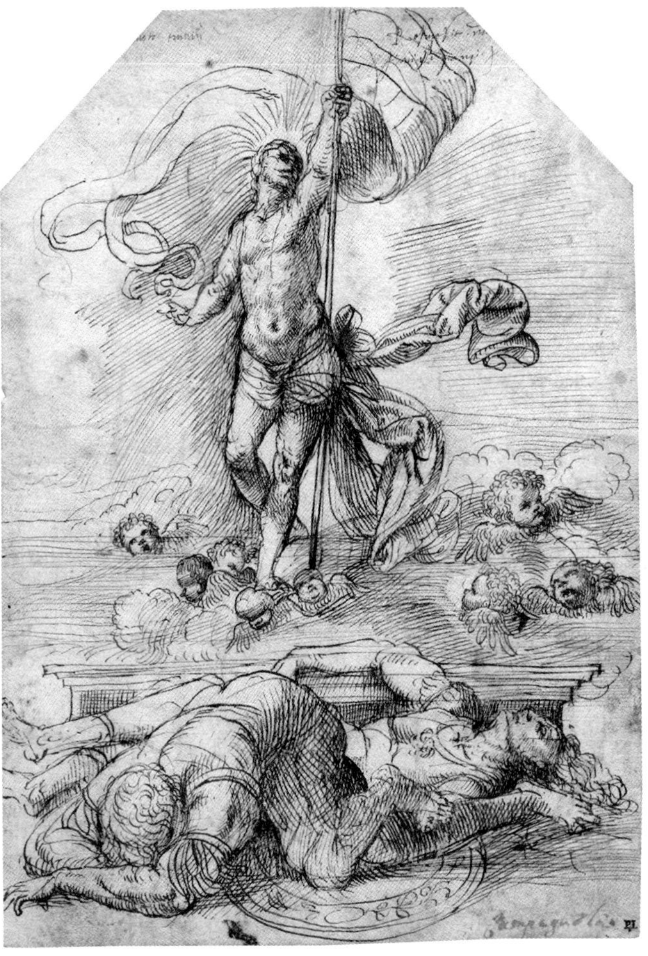

Fig. 9.4. Domenico Campagnola. *Resurrection*, 1520s. Pen and brown ink, 11¼ x 7¹¹⁄₁₆ in. (28.6 x 19.6 cm) (upper corners cut). British Museum, London (1895-9-15-837)

PERINO DEL VAGA

Carmignano (near Florence), 1501–Rome, 1547

A pupil of Ridolfo Ghirlandaio in Florence, Perino del Vaga entered Raphael's workshop in Rome about 1517, working on various decorations in the Vatican Palace, and became the preeminent mural painter in the city in the 1520s, following Raphael's death. In the aftermath of the Sack of Rome in 1527 he removed to Genoa, where he was engaged as court artist to Admiral-Prince Andrea Doria, at work for many years on the decorations of the Palazzo Doria on the outskirts of the city. He returned to Rome in the late 1530s and soon entered the service of Pope Paul III Farnese, in whose employ he remained until his death. A prolific and gifted draftsman, Perino designed frescoes, stuccos, tapestries, embroidery, medals, and rock crystals. He also executed a small number of altarpieces and private devotional images over the course of his thirty-year career. His graceful, elegant, and inventive style, in which formal and compositional elements culled from Raphael, Michelangelo, and the antique were synthesized, exercised a profound influence on artists working in Rome in the middle and late sixteenth century.

10. *Studies of a Horse's Head and Upraised Arms*, ca. 1530–31

Pen and brown ink, 7¼ x 5¾ in. (18.5 x 14.5 cm)

Annotated in a contemporary hand at lower right: *la soma fac-/ ▽ -123-/35/bartolomeo orefi[ce]/12/m[ae]s[tro] gia[n]pietro crivell[i]/20/perino————/26/————————— 25/li debiti mo[n]tano ▽ 84;*[1] at the bottom edge of the sheet, in a later hand, *1520; Raffaello* (cropped)

Provenance: Prince de Ligne; Donadieu Collection of Autographs; Donadieu sale, Paris, 1861; Federico Gentili di Giuseppe; unidentified collector's mark; sale, Sotheby's, London, December 7, 1976, no. 7 (as Perino del Vaga); sale, Sotheby's, New York, January 16, 1986, lot 25; acquired in 1986

References: Blanc 1870, p. 40 (as Raphael); Ruland 1876, p. 273, no. 7 (as "probably by Perino del Vaga"); Fischel 1912, pp. 300–301, no. 23, ill. (as Raphael); Gentili di Giuseppe 1933, p. 37 (as Raphael); Pouncey and Gere 1962, vol. I, p. 100, under no. 169 (as Perino del Vaga); Wolk-Simon 1987; Widauer 1991, pp. 50, 54, fig. 2; Griswold and Wolk-Simon 1994, pp. 72–73, 207, no. 65; New York 1996, p. 93; Widauer 1997, under no. 1; Mantua 2001, no. 110

Perino del Vaga entered the service of Andrea Doria, newly proclaimed ruler of Genoa, in 1528, and was engaged during the ensuing several years in the decoration of the admiral-prince's suburban residence on the outskirts of the city, the Palazzo Doria, then under construction. One of the principal rooms of the palace is the Loggia degli Eroi, decorated in 1530–31, where Perino portrayed the noble seafaring ancestors of Andrea Doria (fig. 10.1). Deployed around the walls on a shallow stage before *all'antica* marble panels in a friezelike arrangement, the monumental seated figures are outfitted in ancient Roman military garb. Exemplars of the *vita activa*, they twist and posture restively, displaying an array of martial and maritime trappings, including batons, shields, rudders, and swords. Although none is identified by name, the animated cast undoubtedly includes the Doria heroes whose celebrated naval exploits and res gestae are commemorated in a series of inscriptions on the facade of San Matteo, the Doria family

church in Genoa.[2] Battle scenes from ancient Roman history, the protagonists upheld as models of heroism and civic virtue, occupy octagonal fields in the center of each bay of the richly stuccoed ceiling.

Numerous drawings by Perino for the Loggia degli Eroi survive.[3] A fairly new addition to the group is this sheet in the Tobey Collection. (Known in the nineteenth century, when it was ascribed to Raphael and attached to a fragmentary page inscribed with his purported signature, it essentially vanished from the literature until resurfacing at auction in 1976, minus the autograph and with the correct attribution to Perino, although its function was at that time unrecognized.) The horse's head seen in left profile is preparatory for one of the ceiling narratives, *Marcus Curtius Throwing Himself into the Chasm of the Roman Forum* (fig. 10.2), and the upraised arms are studies for the Doria heroes.[4] A similar and undoubtedly contemporaneous pen-and-ink drawing by Perino for the Loggia degli Eroi in the Stadtmuseum Linz-Nordico, likewise identified in recent years, contains virtually identical sketches of upraised arms as well as studies for some of the seated figures (fig. 10.3).

Although Perino worked in Genoa for nearly a decade and was employed as court artist by Andrea Doria for almost that entire time, virtually no documents relating to his artistic activity in this period have been discovered. The annotations at the lower right of the Tobey drawing are therefore of particular interest because they mitigate (however slightly) this lacuna: made in the form of account book entries, they record payments to a number of recipients, among them Perino, who received 25 *ducati* (or possibly *scudi*) for unspecified labor—perhaps his work in the Loggia degli Eroi.[5]   LWS

1. As in Wolk-Simon 1987, p. 413 n. 7.
2. Wolk-Simon 1992, p. 167.

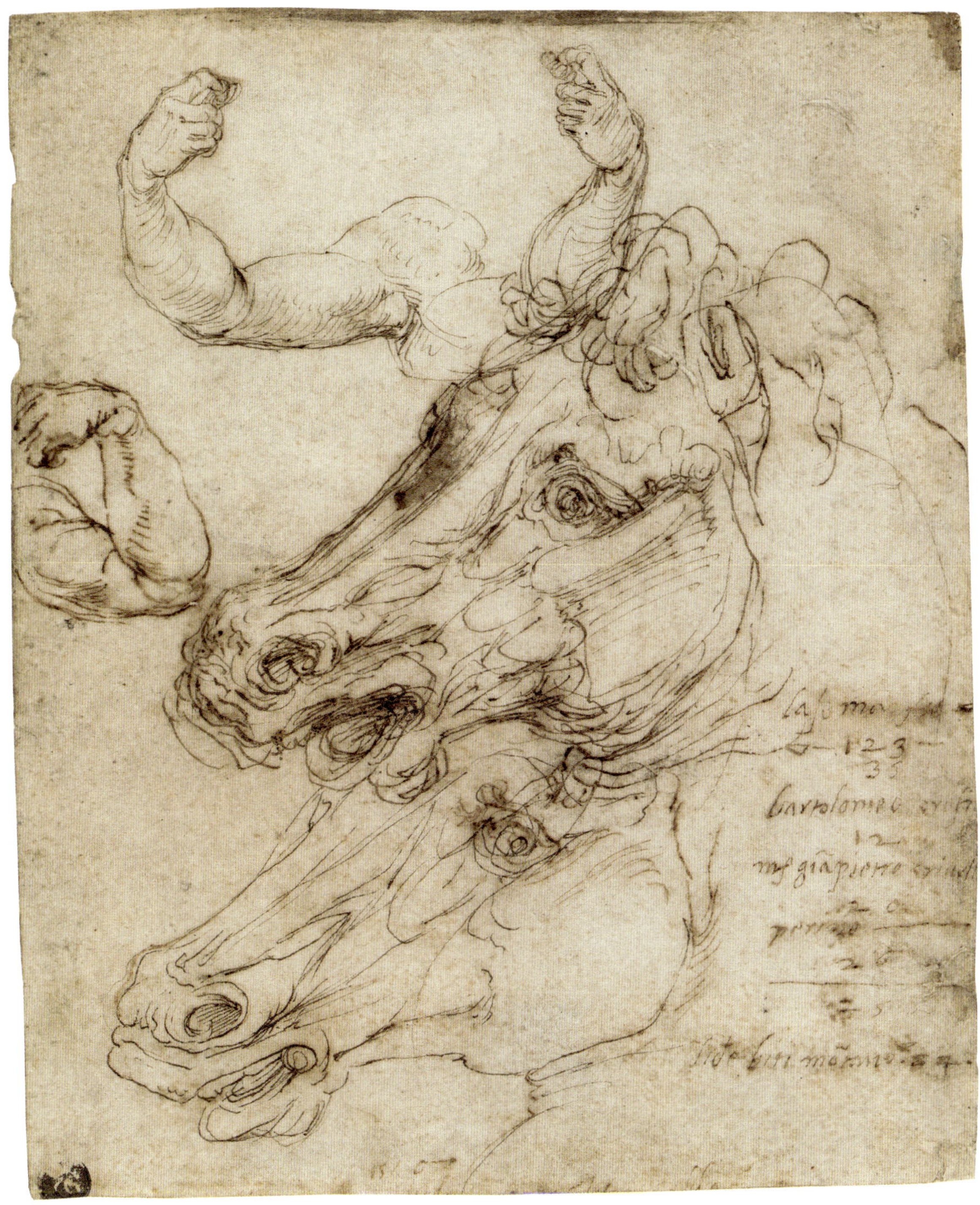

10

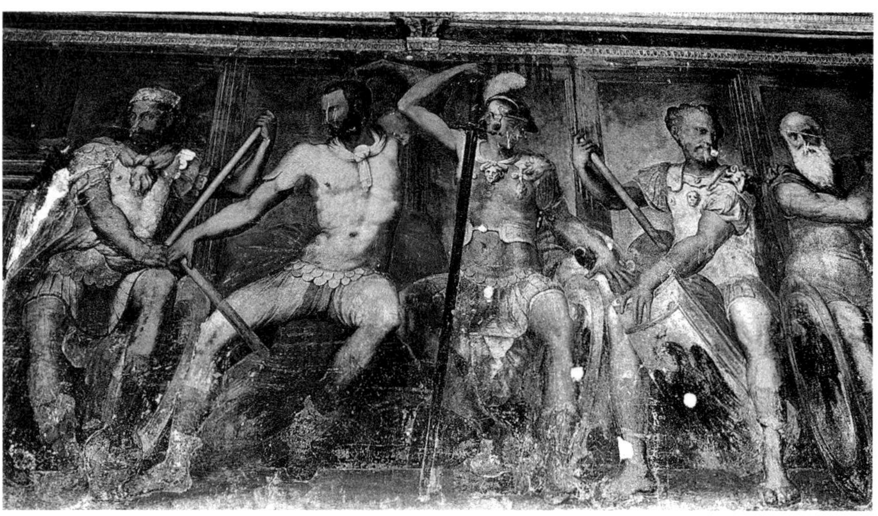

Fig. 10.1. Perino del Vaga. *Seated Doria Heroes*, 1530–31. Fresco. Wall, Loggia degli Eroi, Palazzo Doria, Genoa

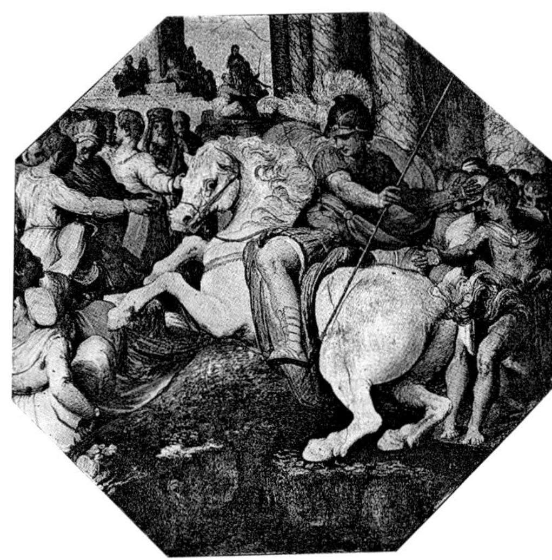

Fig. 10.2. Perino del Vaga. *Marcus Curtius Throwing Himself into the Chasm of the Roman Forum*, 1530–31. Fresco. Ceiling, Loggia degli Eroi, Palazzo Doria, Genoa

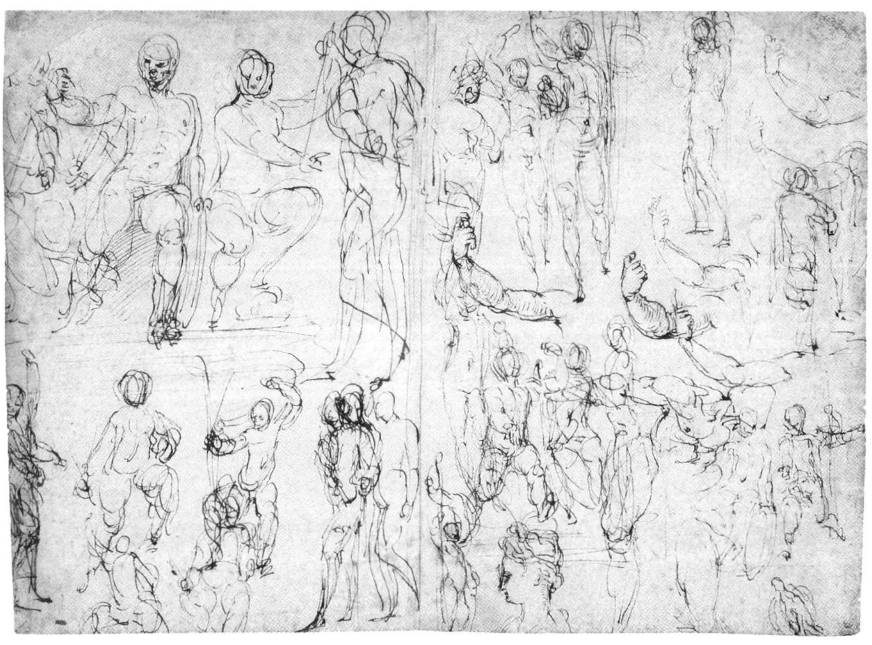

Fig. 10.3. Perino del Vaga. *Sheet of Studies*, ca. 1530. Pen and brown ink, 11 ⅛ x 15 ¹⁄₁₆ in. (28.3 x 38.3 cm). Stadtmuseum Linz-Nordico, Graphischen Sammlung des Nordico (SV/248)

3. See Davidson 1959, especially pp. 318–21.

4. Wolk-Simon 1987; Griswold and Wolk-Simon 1994, pp. 72–73, 207, no. 65.

5. Wolk-Simon 1987, pp. 412, 413 n. 7. The suggestion of Bambach in New York 1996, p. 93, that this sheet instead relates to Perino's activity in Rome in the 1540s is unlikely given the tight connection with the Loggia degli Eroi decorations of the early 1530s and the fact that the unit of payment specified here is as likely to be *ducati* as *scudi*. The currencies were comparable and were both denoted by the inverted triangle symbol. The former was widely used across Italy in the sixteenth century.

11. *The Raising of Lazarus*, ca. 1537–38

Pen and black ink, gray wash, over black chalk, with indications of a squaring
grid along the lower edge; 11¼ x 8⅛ in. (28.6 x 20.7 cm)
Annotated at lower left in brown ink: Raphal Sanzio [ ]

The Metropolitan Museum of Art, New York, Promised Gift of David M. Tobey

Provenance: John Barnard (Lugt 1419); Mr. and Mrs. Hugh Squire, London; sale,
Sotheby's, London, June 28, 1979, lot 58; Thomas Williams Fine Arts, London;
acquired in 2003

References: Gere 1960, p. 13, fig. 9; Parma Armani 1986, p. 183, fig. 219, pp. 186–87,
286, under no. A.XIII; Mantua 2001, no. 73

One of Perino del Vaga's first commissions following his
return to Rome in 1537 after a ten-year absence was the
decoration of the Massimi Chapel in the church of The Trinità
dei Monti (fig. 11.1). The patron, Angelo Massimi, was ceded
jus patronatus (patronage rights) to the chapel on October 3,
1537—the terminus post quem for Perino's activity there. Work
was completed by July 29, 1539, when the gem engraver
Giovanni Bernardi penned a letter referring to rock crystals
based on Perino's then-finished wall paintings that he was
about to execute for Cardinal Alessandro Farnese. Preexisting
decoration carried out for a prior patron in the early 1520s by
Giulio Romano and Gianfrancesco Penni, who executed frescoes in the lunettes and the vault as well as an altarpiece, was
retained; Perino's intervention of the late 1530s was thus limited to the lateral walls. Destroyed in the mid-nineteenth century, it consisted of two large and four small frescoed narrative
scenes illustrating the miracles of Christ surrounded by elaborate *all'antica* stucco reliefs and richly ornamented decorative
fields. Some idea of Perino's scheme may be gleaned from a
beautiful finished drawing in the Szépművészeti Múzeum,
Budapest, for the chapel's south wall (fig. 11.1).[1]

The Tobey sheet is a composition study for one of the two
large narrative scenes that formed the centerpiece of each side
wall. It depicts the Raising of Lazarus from the Dead, one of
Jesus's first miracles (John 11:41–44). The corresponding fresco,
which adheres to the design established in this drawing, was
formerly on the north wall of the Massimi Chapel; removed
during the nineteenth-century renovation, it is preserved,
in damaged condition, in the Victoria and Albert Museum,
London (fig. 11.2). Paradigmatic of Perino's late graphic style
are the trembling, wiry line, delicate veils of wash, and dense,
planar composition, as well as the figures' elongated torsos,
small heads, and inflated, weightless aspect—features that become
increasingly pronounced in his drawings of the 1540s.

The elaborate composition of *The Raising of Lazarus* reprises
a number of favorite pictorial motifs culled from Raphael and
employed by Perino in works executed a decade and a half
earlier, during his first Roman period. Descended from the

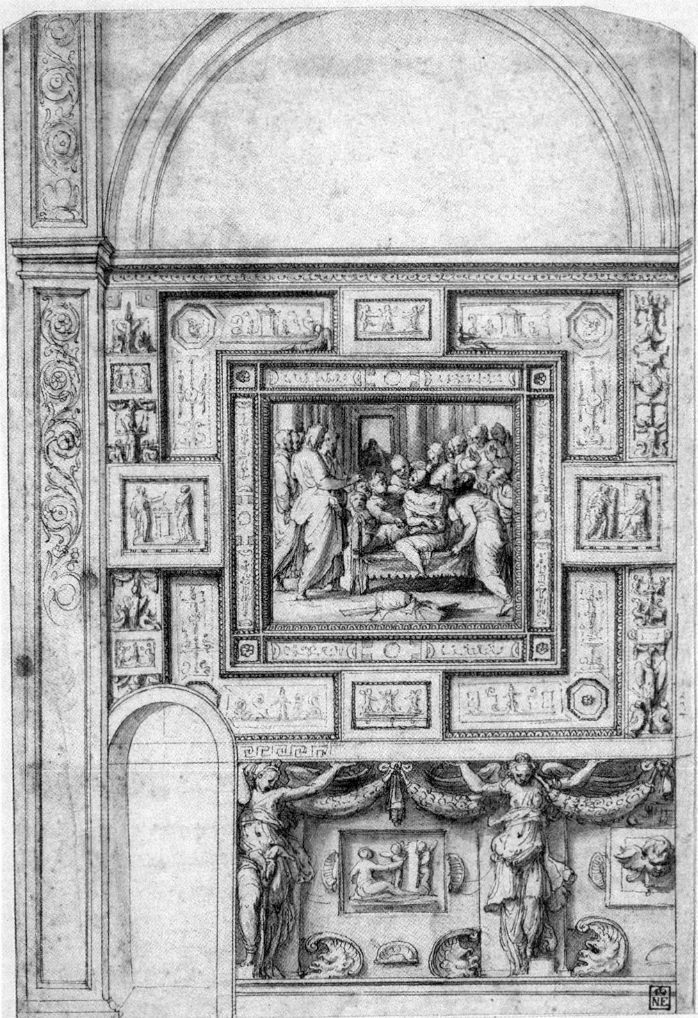

Fig. 11.1. Perino del Vaga. *Design for the Decoration of a Chapel* (recto),
ca. 1537. Black chalk, pen and brown ink, with brown and gray washes,
16½ x 11⁷⁄₁₆ in. (41.9 x 29 cm). Szépművészeti Múzeum, Budapest (1838)

bound captive in the left foreground of Raphael's *Battle at
Ostia* in the Stanza dell'Incendio, the kneeling *repoussoir* figure
at the lower left occurs, in a varied iteration, at the lower
right of Perino's celebrated design of *The Martyrdom of the Ten
Thousand* (1522–23).[2] The spectator clutching the column at
the far right who is grasped around the waist by another
onlooker quotes in reverse an identical spiraling pair seen at
the left of Raphael's *Expulsion of Heliodorus* and recalls Perino's
earlier adoption of this rhetorical device in one of the narrative
scenes from the *salone* of the Palazzo Baldassini (ca. 1520–22).[3]
Even the architectural setting, with the monumental, proscenium-
like archway opening on to an architectural backdrop in the
distance is indebted to canonical inventions of Raphael, evok-
ing the *School of Athens*, the *Expulsion of Heliodorus*, and the

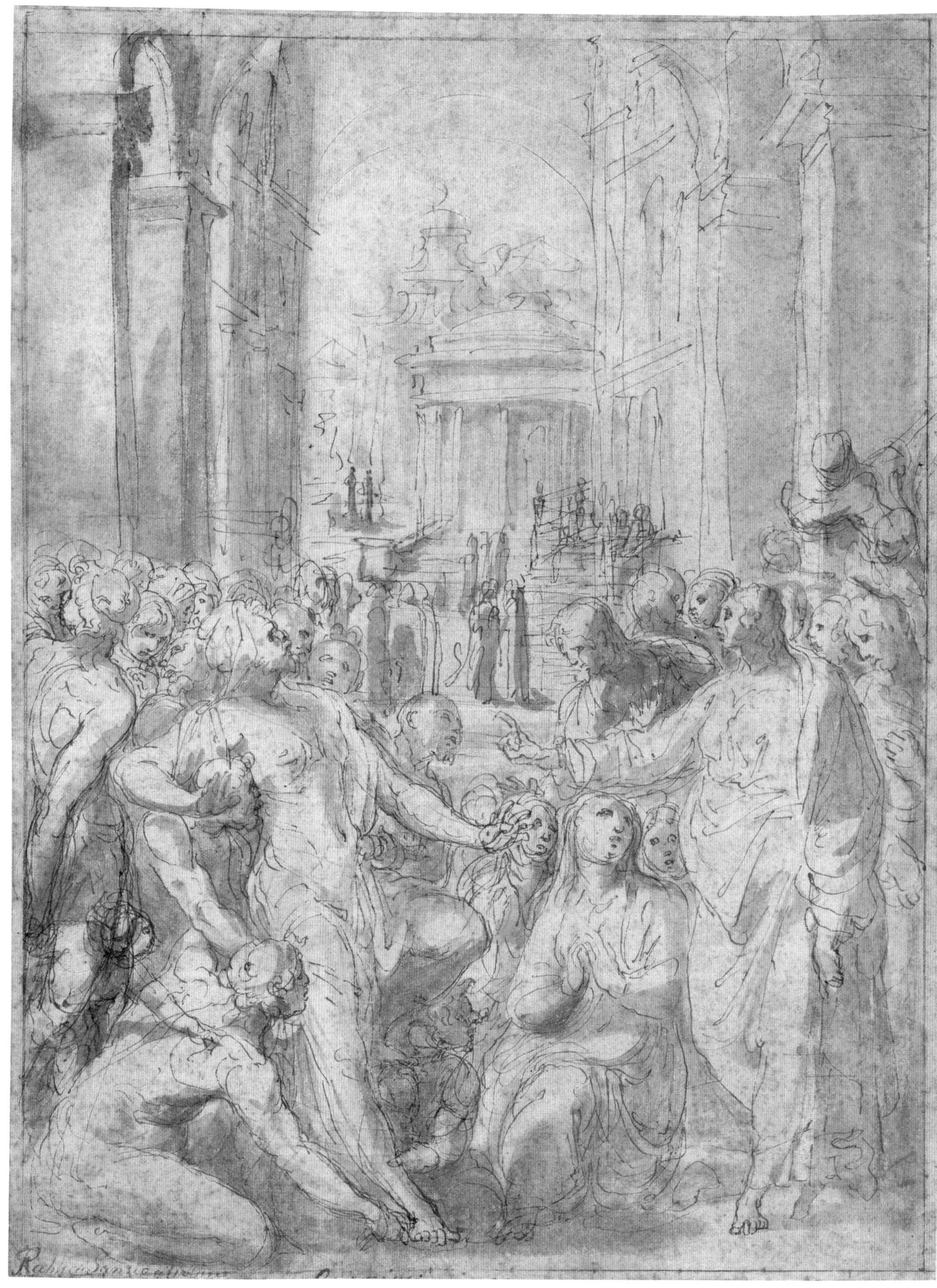

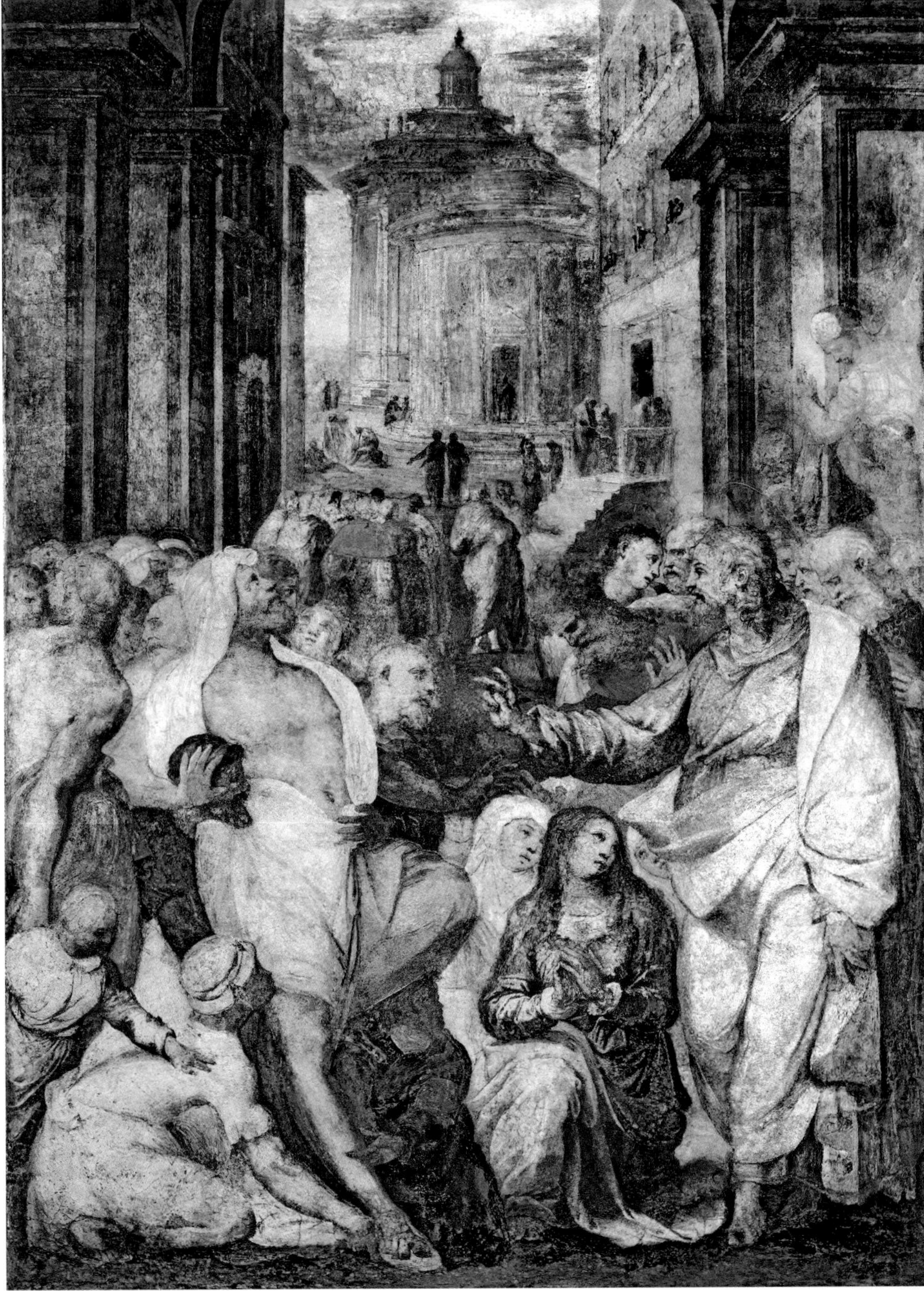

Fig. 11.2. Perino del Vaga. *The Raising of Lazarus*, ca. 1538. Detached fresco from the Massimi Chapel, Trinità dei Monti, Rome, transferred to canvas, 64⁷⁄₁₆ x 45¼ in. (163.6 x 114.9 cm). Victoria and Albert Museum, London (362-1876)

Fire in the Borgo. Through such obvious appropriations, Perino—newly returned to Rome after a protracted absence and fearful that he had been all but forgotten—announced his status as Raphael's heir. That claim carried considerable weight in the Eternal City, whose artistic culture, devastated by the sack by imperial troops a decade earlier, was slowly reawakening. Indeed, Vasari reported that it was Perino's work in the Massimi Chapel that attracted the admiring attention of "il Gran Cardinale," Alessandro Farnese, the powerful grandson of the artist's future patron, Pope Paul III, thus fatefully paving the way for his future success and preeminence at the papal court.

LWS

1. On this drawing and the Massimi Chapel commission, see Gere 1960 and, most recently, Linda Wolk-Simon in Ottawa 2009, under no. 47, pp. 201–3, with earlier references.
2. Vienna, Albertina, inv. no. 2933 SL384; see Mantua 2001, no. 20.
3. *The Augur Attius Cleaving a Whetstone in Two*, a detached fresco now in the Uffizi; see Mantua 2001, no. 15. See also Wolk-Simon 2002, p. 13, where the correct identification of the obscure subject matter is made.

AGNOLO BRONZINO

Monticelli, 1503–Florence, 1572

The preeminent Florentine painter of the mid-sixteenth century as well as a gifted poet, Agnolo Bronzino was the pupil, follower, and adopted son of the brilliant, eccentric Mannerist artist Jacopo Pontormo. For much of his career he was court painter to the Medici duke Cosimo I, ruler of Florence, and his wife, Eleonora of Toledo, producing portraits, altarpieces, frescoes, private devotional images, and arcane, often erotic, secular scenes for members of the Medici circle. For Cosimo he also designed a sumptuous series of tapestries illustrating the Old Testament story of Joseph, and for Eleonora he frescoed a chapel in the Palazzo Vecchio with another Old Testament subject, the story of Moses. Bronzino's drawings, executed primarily in chalk with an emphasis on the sculptural modeling of forms, reveal a debt to Pontormo and also to Michelangelo.

12. *Study of a Left Leg and Drapery*, ca. 1549–53

Black chalk, 15⅜ x 10 in. (39.1 x 25.4 cm)
Annotated on recto in pen and brown ink at upper right: *di michel angelo / Bonarotta*; on verso in pen and brown ink at center: *Michelangelo*

The Metropolitan Museum of Art, New York, Promised Gift of David M. Tobey, and Purchase, several members of The Chairman's Council Gifts and Joseph Pulitzer Bequest, 2006 (2006.449)

Provenance: Private Collection, Belgium; W. M. Brady and Co., New York; acquired by The Metropolitan Museum of Art, 2006

References: Bambach 2007, ill.; George R. Goldner in New York 2010, p. 186, no. 45

This exceptionally well-preserved study of a single leg is a recent discovery. The attribution to Agnolo Bronzino, first proposed by Philippe Costamagna,[1] has gained general acceptance. With its firm, highly refined outlines and subtly graduated shading, the drawing exemplifies Bronzino's technique about 1550. The old attribution to Michelangelo, recorded in an early inscription of about 1600 on the recto, is fully understandable, as Bronzino's draftsmanship here owes a great deal to that master's highly finished presentation drawings.

The leg depicted in this study was probably drawn from a studio model in preparation for a painting or tapestry. The figure of Joseph in the *Joseph Fleeing Potiphar's Wife* tapestry, a work that was delivered as a finished piece on August 3, 1549,[2] displays a similar leg (fig. 12.1), as does the Risen Christ in Bronzino's *Resurrection* altarpiece in the Guadagni Chapel in Santissima Annunziata, Florence, of 1549–52.

GRG

1. Oral communication to W. M. Brady and Co., New York, summer 2006.
2. See Adelson 1990, pp. 371–72, no. 15.

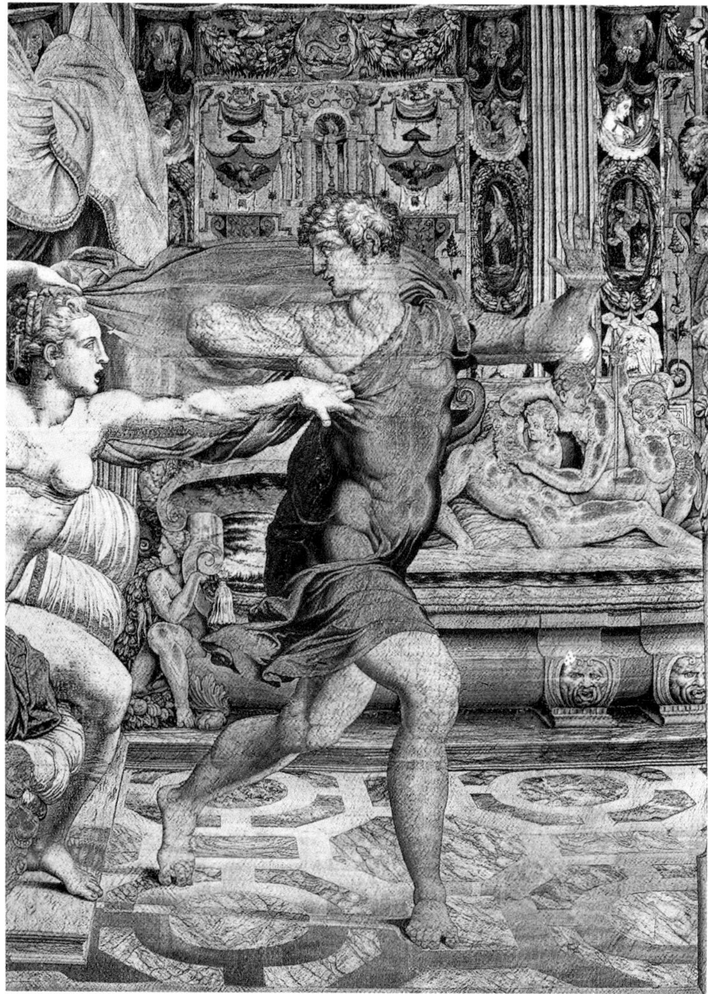

Fig. 12.1. Nicolas Karcher and workshop, after design by Agnolo Bronzino. Detail of Joseph in *Joseph Fleeing Potiphar's Wife*, 1549. Tapestry of wool, silk, silver threads, and gilded silver threads. Palazzo Vecchio, Salone delle Bandiere, Laboratorio di Restauro, Florence (IA 1912-25 no. 729)

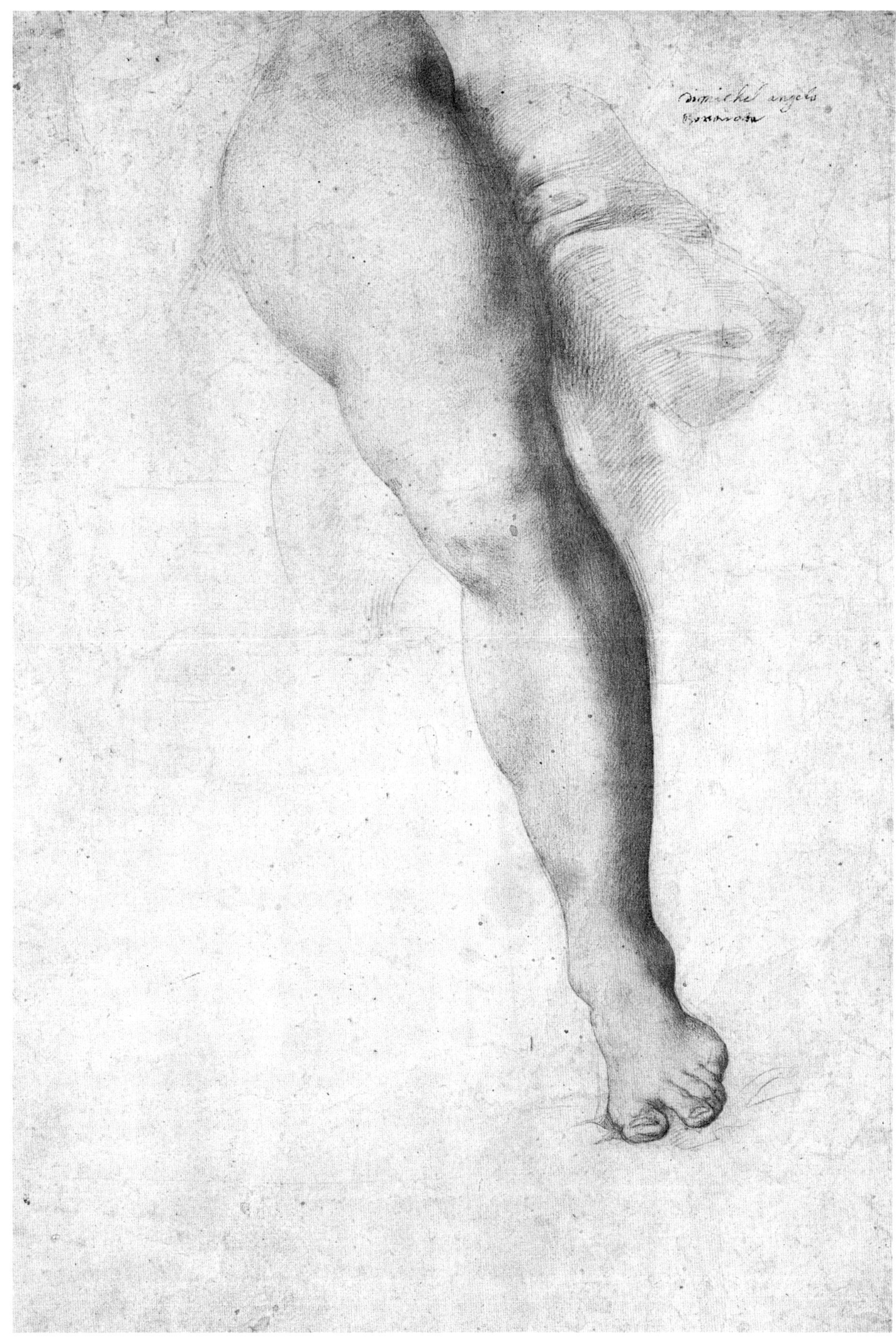

di michel angelo
Bonaroti

PARMIGIANINO

Parma, 1503–Casalmaggiore, 1540

Born in Parma to a family of minor painters, the young Parmigianino quickly distinguished himself, and his early work reveals a profound debt to Correggio. In 1524 he left for Rome to study the art of Raphael and Michelangelo, as well as antiquities. Although he had hoped to secure the patronage of the newly elected Pope Clement VII, the Sack of 1527 soon forced the artist to flee the city. He settled temporarily in Bologna, but by 1531 he returned to Parma, where he began (but never completed) both his most famous altarpiece (the so-called Madonna of the Long Neck) *and a fresco cycle in the church of Santa Maria della Steccata. Parmigianino was a prolific and versatile draftsman, as well as a pioneer printmaker. His drawings have been continuously prized for their invention and refinement.*

13. Recto: *Studies of a Female Head, a Winged Lion, and Finials*, ca. 1523
Verso: *Study of a Man and a Woman with Foliage*

Recto: Red chalk, pen and brown ink; verso: pen and brown ink, 7¼ x 5¾ in. (18.5 x 14.5 cm)

Inscriptions on recto: pen trials, mostly indecipherable; lower left: *a amor quando fioriva*; upper center: *. . . tempo del mio . . .* (?); center right: *ra l'arbato/del sole*

The Metropolitan Museum of Art, New York, Promised Gift of David M. Tobey

Provenance: Sir Peter Lely (Lugt 2092); J. Richardson, Sr. (Lugt 2184); T. Hudson (Lugt 2432); B. West (Lugt 419); J. Malcolm and by descent to the Hon. R. Gathorne-Hardy (sale, Sotheby's, London, April 28, 1976, lot 20); British Rail Pension Fund; Private Collection, Europe; acquired in 1997

References: Popham 1971, vol. 1, p.215, no. 748; London and New York 2000–2001, p. 90, no. 47 (entry by George R. Goldner); Ekserdjian 2001, p. 44; Vaccaro 2001, pp. 244, 255; Parma and Vienna 2003, pp. 257–58, no. 2.3.11a/b (entry by Hugo Chapman); Franklin and Ekserdjian 2003–4, pp. 90–95, no. 13; Gnann 2007, vol. 1, pp. 62, 71–72, 82, 371, no. 136, vol. 2, p. 151; Rubin 2007, pp. 23–25

This beautiful double-sided design can be connected to two projects on which Parmigianino was at work for the Sanvitale family in Fontanellato, a feudal stronghold near Parma, in the years immediately prior to his departure for Rome. The verso depicts two figures in a landscape setting: a bearded man, who is seated in a Savonarola-type chair, twists around to address a woman behind him.[1] The exuberant and varied pen-work, such as the curvilinear notations used to denote foliage, accords with the artist's graphic style about 1524. In another design in the Louvre (fig. 13.1), Parmigianino first carefully drew the chair and then quickly rendered the same man.[2] Although without a female companion, the sitter looks to his side, and seems to hold an object in his left hand, as if he were engaged in casual conversation. Presumably taken from life, these studies relate to a panel portrait of Count Galeazzo Sanvitale (fig. 13.2) and reveal the degree to which the artist modified his initial ideas for its composition. As in the drawings, the chair is used in the painting as a device to establish the foreground of the pictorial plane. The foliage in the Tobey sheet occupies only part of the background in the picture, as if seen through a window, balanced to the left by a display of armor. The painting employs a strictly frontal view of Count Sanvitale's face and upper torso to achieve an altogether more hieratic effect: alone, he gazes with probing intensity at the (intended) spectator to whom he presents a medal.[3] The Tobey drawing offers insight into the portrait's genesis and points to the artist's broader capacity to transpose everyday experiences—for example, a convivial dialogue between a man and a woman—to a complex key.

The sheet relates as well to the so-called Camerino, a small rectangular room in Count Sanvitale's residence at Fontanellato, which the young Parmigianino frescoed. A rich decorative scheme includes scenes from the classical myth of Diana and Actaeon in lunettes on the walls. The ceiling is painted to resemble a verdant rose-filled pergola, which is open to the sky, and the spandrels of its vault terminate in four corner finials interspersed with ten gesso reliefs of snake-haired women (fig. 13.3). As Arthur Ewart Popham recognized, the four ornamental sketches in pen on the recto of the Tobey design are variations for the finials at the angles of the Camerino. The second from the left is closest to the solution that Parmigianino adopted in the room. Popham further surmised that the red chalk studies of a female head on the same page were preliminaries for the Medusalike masks that also serve as finials. The fact that this lovely head is studied from two points of view in the drawing supports the possibility that it was made with a sculptural purpose in mind.

On the lower half of the sheet, also drawn in red chalk, is a winged lion in profile, next to a partial sketch of the same. This creature bears no obvious link to the decoration at Fontanellato.

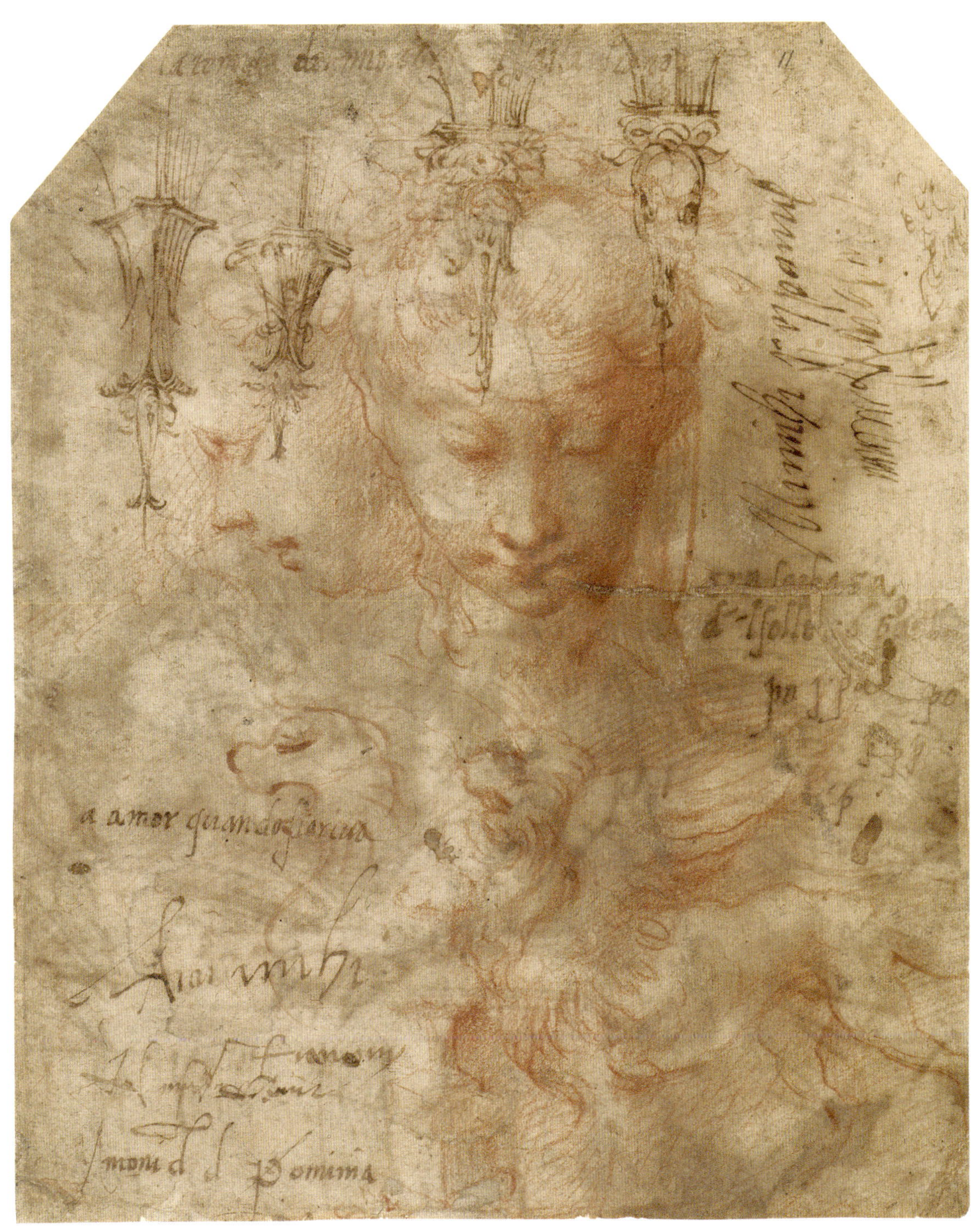

13

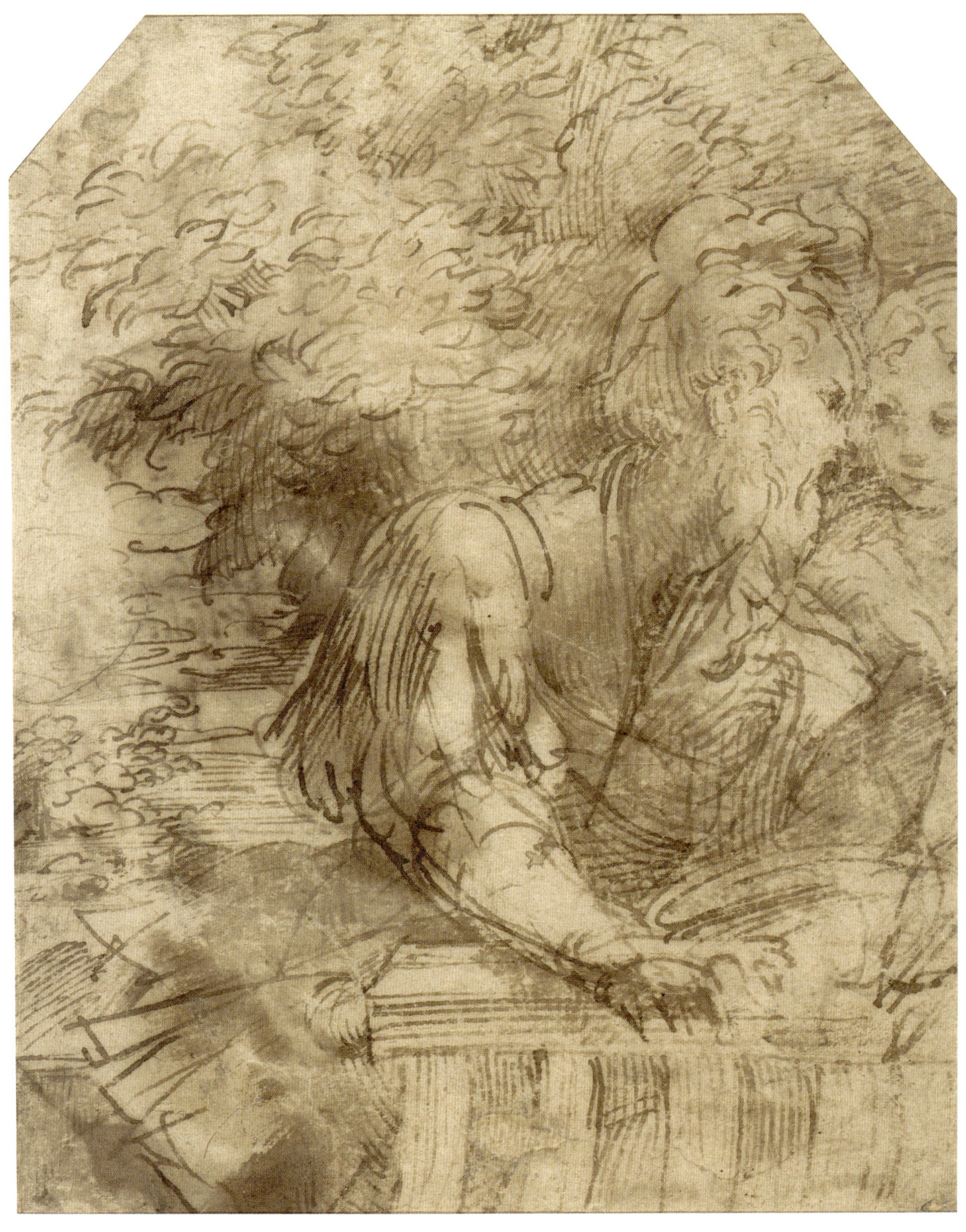

13 verso

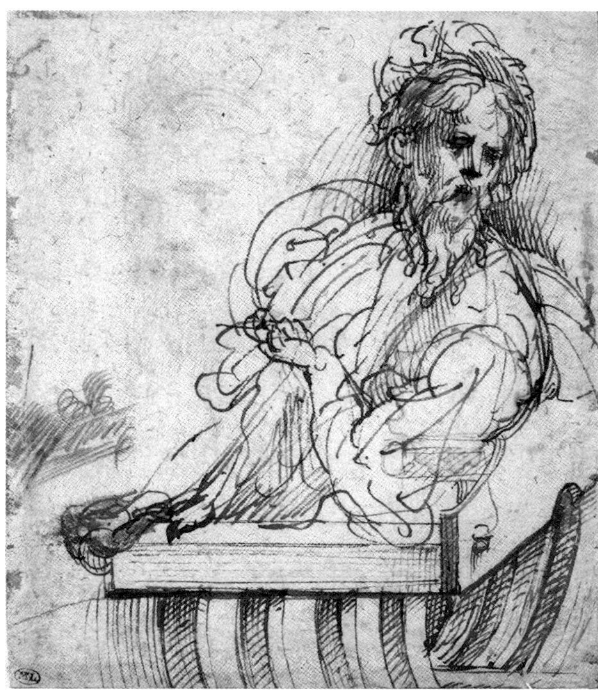

Fig. 13.1. Parmigianino. *Study of a Man (Study of Count Galeazzo Sanvitale)*, ca. 1524. Pen and brown ink, traces of red chalk, 5½ x 4⅝ in. (14 x 11.8 cm). Département des Arts Graphiques, Musée du Louvre, Paris (6472r)

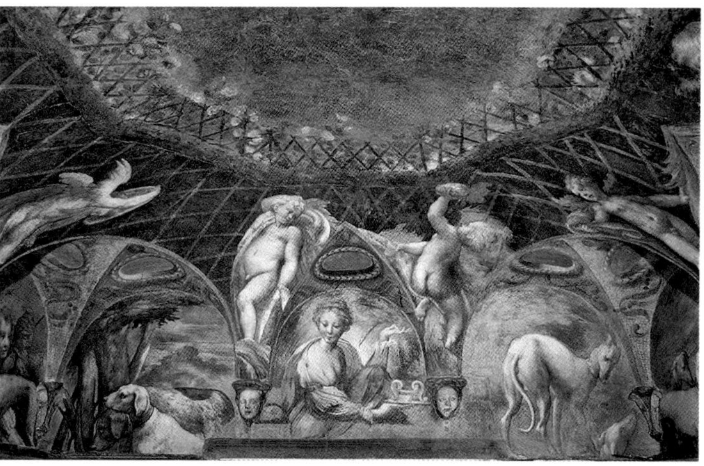

Fig. 13.3. Parmigianino. *Dogs and Cup-bearing Maiden*, ca. 1523–24. Fresco. Hall of Diana and Actaeon, Camerino at Rocca Sanvitale, Fontanellato

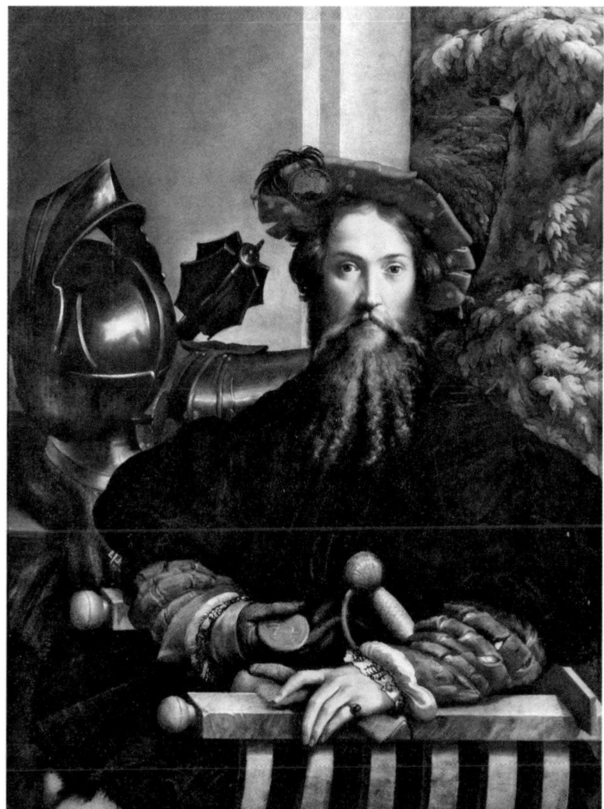

Fig. 13.2. Parmigianino. *Portrait of Count Galeazzo Sanvitale*, ca. 1524. Oil on panel, 42⅞ x 31½ in. (109 x 80 cm). Museo e Gallerie Nazionali di Capodimonte, Naples (111)

It recalls an ancient relief, which Parmigianino might have known directly or through the intermediary of Correggio, who adapted the motif for his nearly contemporaneous frescoes in the Parmesan church of San Giovanni Evangelista.[4] Written text scattered about the page consists of largely insignificant and indecipherable pen trials in Parmigianino's hand. Nevertheless, the words "amor quando fioriva" can be traced to a poem by Petrarch.[5] During the Renaissance, Petrarch's verses offered an important model of lyrical subjectivity in the creation and reception of beauty for visual artists as well as writers. The Tobey drawing attests to the fact that, even as a young artist, Parmigianino was interested in such poetry.

MV

1. This woman has been tentatively identified as Count Galeazzo Sanvitale's wife, Paola Gonzaga, but no secure likeness of her is known to exist. Augusta Ghidiglia Quintavalle seems to have been the first to identify the sitter as Paola Gonzaga, an idea that Popham repeated with considerable caution.
2. Gnann 2007, vol. 1, p. 372, no. 144, vol. 2, p. 157, with bibliography. The verso (ill.) is another study of Sanvitale's head.
3. The medal is emblazoned with "72," which, as Ute Davitt-Asmus first observed, refers to the Kabbalistic number for the name of God. For more on the portrait and its interpretation, see Rubin 2007, pp. 24–36, with bibliography.
4. The common source is a frieze in the Forum of Trajan; for which see Ekserdjian 2001, p. 44, ill. As Parmigianino had not yet been to Rome at the time he made the Tobey design, he may have known the relief from a (lost) copy after it by his older colleague Correggio.
5. The words begin Petrarch's poem number 324 in the *Rime sparse*, as noted in Vaccaro 2001, p. 244, with discussion of the broader significance of Parmigianino's poetic interests throughout his career.

14. *Studies for the Maidens in Santa Maria della Steccata,* ca. 1535

Red chalk, 10¾ x 8 in. (27.2 by 20.2 cm)

Provenance: J. Richardson, Jr. (Lugt 2170); Brian Sewell, London; acquired in 1998

References: Ekserdjian 1999, pp. 35–36, no. 61; Mario Di Giampaolo in Béguin, Di Giampaolo, and Vaccaro 2000, no. 119; London and New York 2000–2001, p. 160, no. 106 (entry by George R. Goldner); Turner 2002, p. 229 (as Simone Cantarini); DeGrazia 2003, p. 390 (as Simone Cantarini); Gnann 2007, vol. 1, pp. 269, 482, no. 820, vol. 2, p. 607

This drawing is one of the many extant graphic preliminaries for Parmigianino's notoriously protracted project in the church of Santa Maria della Steccata in Parma.[1] In May 1531, the confraternity of the church officially enlisted the artist to paint the eastern apse and its coffered barrel vault. Although Parmigianino optimistically promised to complete all the work within eighteen months, eight years later, he had still not painted the apse. The earliest known document for the commission establishes that the apse was to contain a scene of the Coronation of the Virgin, for which Parmigianino supplied a drawing at the time, but no mention is made of the subject matter of the other areas to be decorated. Extant preparatory designs—close to one hundred sheets for the vault and soffits—suggest that the artist may have been, at least in part, responsible for the development of its iconographic program. Painted at the base of the vault, to either side, is a triad of young women in the act of exchanging lamps, unlit on the north wall and lit on the south, the so-called Wise and Foolish Virgins.

The basic compositional concept of three standing maidens with outstretched arms to either side of the vault (fig. 14.1) appears to have evolved slowly over the course of numerous designs. Although they cannot be placed in any definitive chronological sequence, the drawings explore changes in movement and stance for the women, either singly, or in groups of two or three. Parmigianino entertained the possibility of baskets atop their heads (effecting them as *canephori*) but decided on amphorae, filled with lilies, a visual metaphor for their lovely bodies. At evidently some late stage in the graphic preliminaries, he introduced the lamps that are seen in the painting, an attribute that permitted an association with the biblical parable of the Wise and Foolish Virgins (Matthew 25:1–13).[2]

The Tobey sheet represents a woman whose face is shown in profile, but in a pose that otherwise corresponds to that of the center maiden painted on the vault. With an economy of rectilinear marks, the artist indicated the coffers of the intended architectural setting around the figure. He added further ideas, notably a maiden in full profile to the left in a reserve area of the paper that would have been impossible to paint on the actual vault. An alternative profile for the central maiden and faint notations for other heads, shown frontally, between the two full-length figures may also be discerned (fig. 14.2). The presence of a (burning) lamp, as well as the amphorae atop the maidens' heads, suggests that

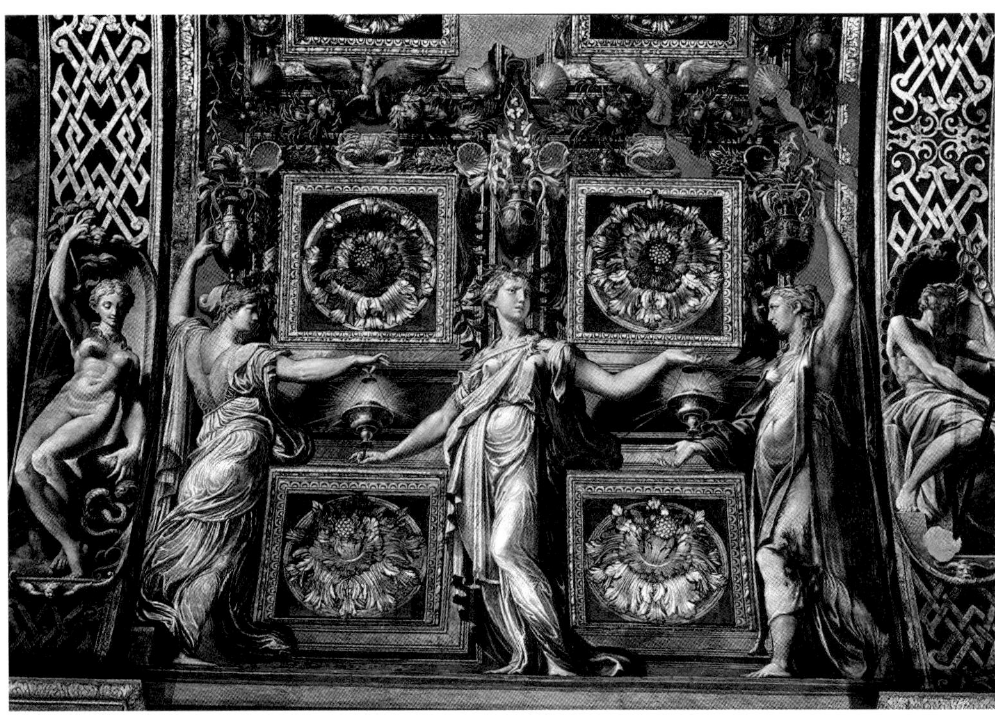

Fig. 14.1. Parmigianino. *The Wise Virgins,* ca. 1535–39. Fresco. Eastern vault, Santa Maria della Steccata, Parma

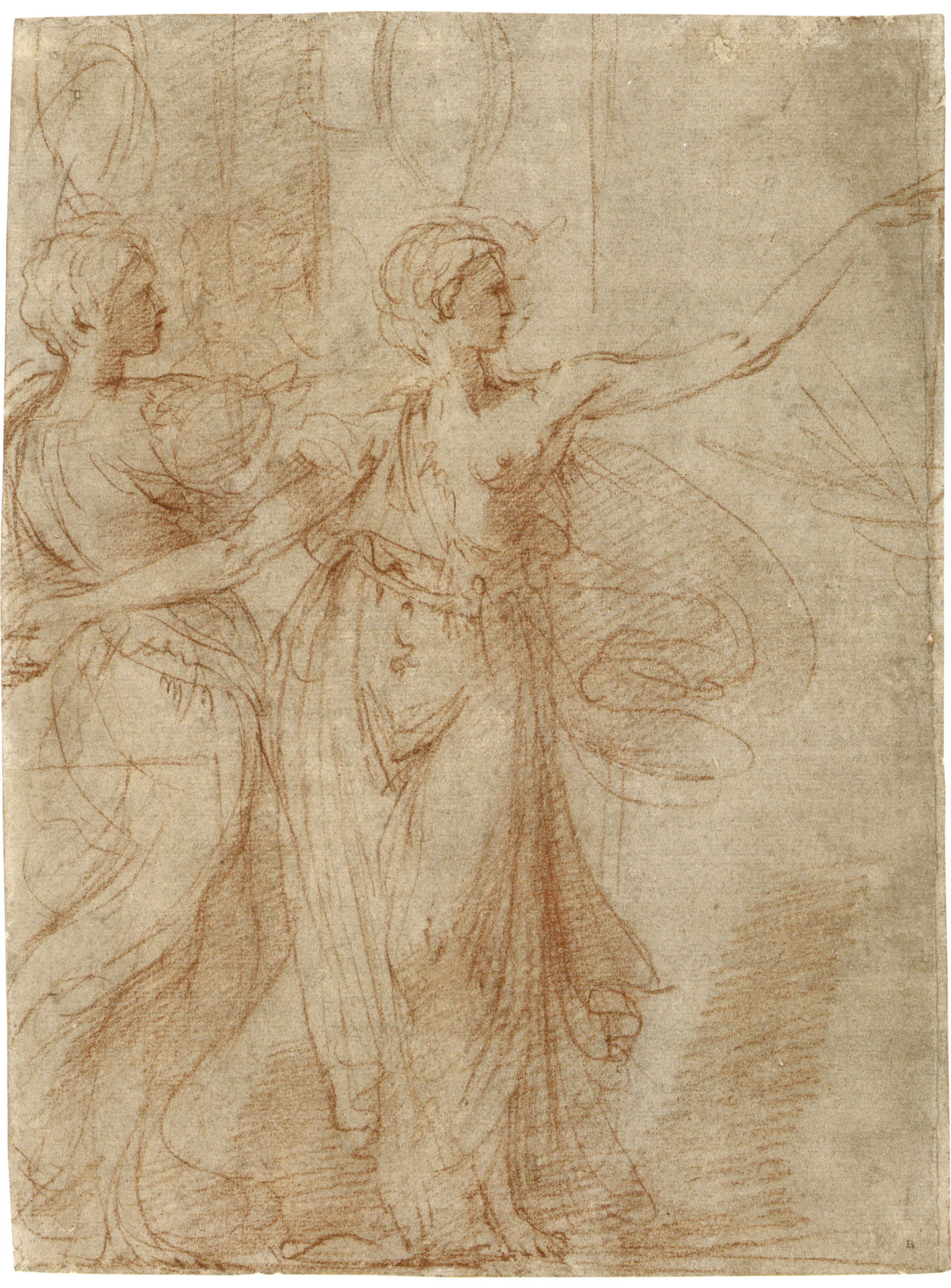

the design belongs to a relatively late phase in the planning of the decorative scheme.

Although its attribution has been recently questioned,[3] the drawing exhibits clear parallels with others in the same medium by Parmigianino, for example, a double-sided study for the portrait of Charles V (fig. 14.3).[4] The handling of the chalk and the morphologies, such as the broad diagonal hatching and the spidery notations used to describe the hands, are identical. The changes, or pentimenti, in the Tobey sheet further argue in favor of its status as an autograph preparatory design rather than a copy after the frescoes, and the sequence of variant heads recalls an exercise (almost automatic or free drawing of variations in heads and profiles) that frequently occurs in the

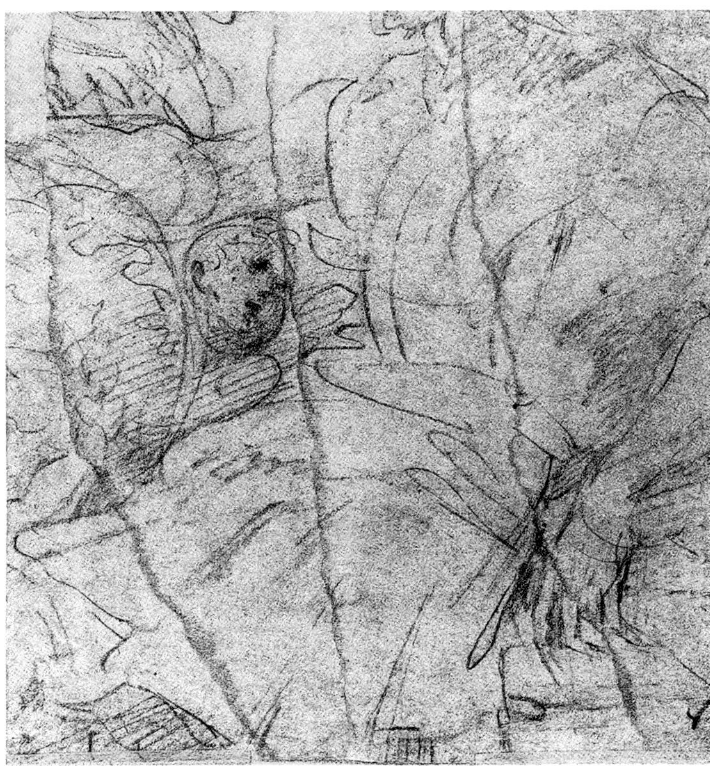

Fig. 14.3. Parmigianino. *Study for a Portrait of Charles V*, ca. 1530. Red chalk, over stylus indentations, 5⅝ x 5⅛ in. (14.3 x 13 cm). The Morgan Library and Museum, New York (IV, 43)

artist's graphic corpus.[5] In its grace and freedom of execution, the drawing fully captures the spirit of the elegant dance that Parmigianino sought to choreograph and paint in the Steccata church. MV

1. For the commission and Parmigianino's related drawings, see Ekserdjian 2006, pp. 59–66, with bibliography.
2. For more on the iconography, see Vaccaro 2005.
3. Turner 2002, p. 229, proposed the sheet to be a copy after Parmigianino's frescoes by Simone Cantarini (1612–1648), a suggestion with which DeGrazia (2003) agreed. Yet the drawing departs from the painted version, for example, in the costume of the central figure, in ways that are inconsistent with a copy. The technique, although similar to Cantarini's use of red chalk, can also be found in designs by Parmigianino.
4. Gnann 2007, vol. 1, p. 466, no. 720, vol. 2, p. 560 (both sides, ill., but plates reversed). I thank George R. Goldner for bringing this example to my attention. In May 2008, Julie Tobey kindly brought her drawing to the Morgan Library and Museum, where we were able to compare directly the two sheets and resolve any doubts regarding Parmigianino's authorship.
5. See Popham 1971, vol. 3, pls. 423–24, for examples of such studies of heads. See Popham 1971, vol. 1, p. 200, no. 668, pl. 423 (Royal Collection, Windsor Castle), which represents four slightly different women's heads in profile, and dates to the time of the Steccata project.

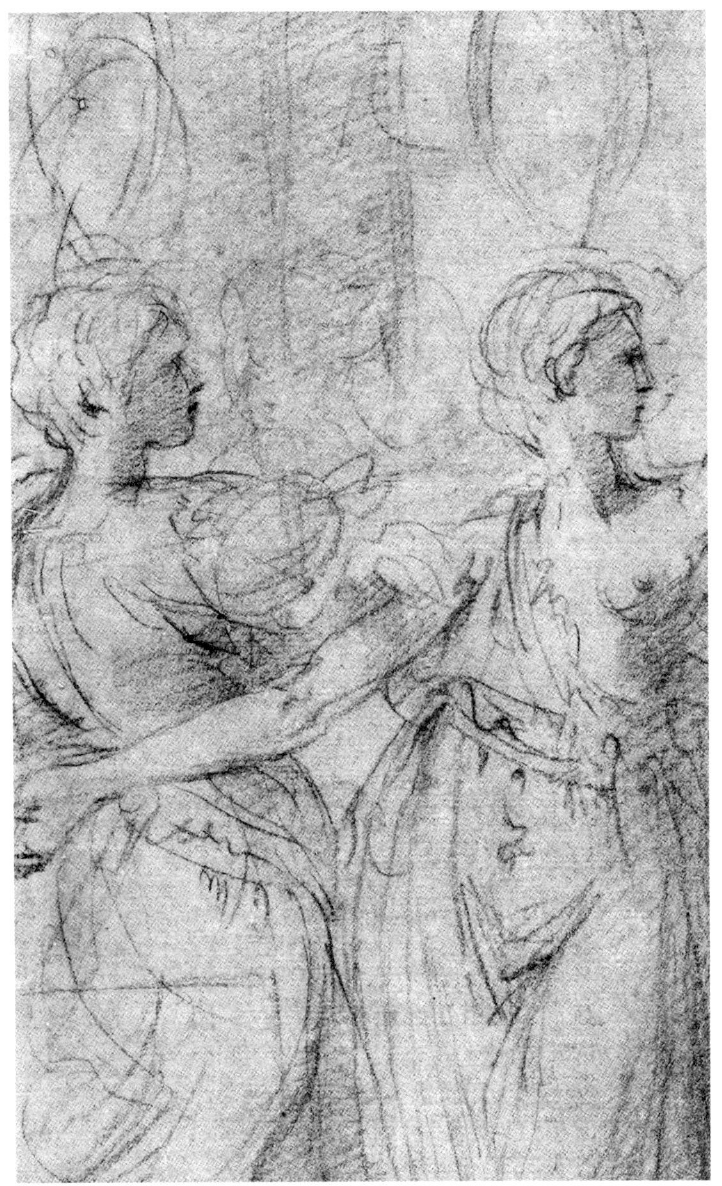

Fig. 14.2. Parmigianino. Detail of cat. no. 14 (area left of the head of the center maiden)

FRANCESCO PRIMATICCIO

Bologna, 1504/5–Paris, 1570

Following a period of training in his native Bologna with two local High Renaissance painters, Innocenzo da Imola and Bartolomeo Bagnacavallo, Francesco Primaticcio assisted Giulio Romano in the mid-1520s on the decorations of the Palazzo Tè in Mantua. That inventive Mannerist confection, in which vibrant frescoes of secular, predominantly mythological subjects are combined with equally rich and elaborate stucco ornament, became the model for his own later work in the palace of King Francis I at Fontainebleau, where the artist worked, at the invitation of the king, in the company of Rosso Fiorentino, beginning in 1532. Together with Rosso, whom he succeeded upon the latter's death in 1540, and his Italian collaborator Niccolò dell'Abate, Primaticcio was responsible for introducing Italian Mannerism to France, spawning what became known as the School of Fontainebleau. Much of the palace's sixteenth-century decorations—an ornate combination of fresco and stucco notable for its pictorial illusionism, all'antica *vocabulary, and inventiveness—was heavily restored or destroyed; Primaticcio's refined drawings for the Galerie d'Ulysse and other parts of the interior provide an important record of the brilliance of his original design.*

15. *Standing Male Draped Figure; The Head of Another Draped Figure,* ca. 1545–50

Red chalk, highlighted with white gouache (in small passages oxidized), on off-white paper washed light brown, 9⅛ x 4⅛ in. (23.2 x 10.5 cm)

Provenance: Sir Peter Lely (London, 1618–1680) (Lugt 2092); William Gibson (his attribution "Primaticcio" and price codes "1.4/3.3"); H. Barderou; Galerie Aubry 1971, no. 86; sale, Christie's, London, July 6, 1999, lot 132; acquired in 1999

References: Paris 1971, no. 86; Christie's, London 1999, no. 132

At center in this vigorously drawn small sheet, a bearded man in hood or cap standing in a frontal pose exhibits a small head and large hands and wears heavy drapery; he entirely overpowers the beautiful, expertly drawn motif at upper right, depicting a woman in bust-length and near profile, whose veil artfully falls over her shoulder.[1] The isolated fragmentary motif of a right hand in the act of clutching an object is rendered at lower left, about three-quarters of the way down the border of the sheet. Some lightly drawn, red-chalk outlines of mildly purpler hue than the majority of the drawing of the man lie over the layers of white gouache highlights. The main male figure on the sheet has suffered from abrasion to the drawing surface, while the motif of the woman at upper right is better preserved, its tonal subtleties and linear rhythms nearly intact.

Although the Tobey sheet offers a main figure of admittedly clumsy bodily proportions with a somewhat overly bold application of highlights, it was reasonably published in 1976 and 1999 as by Francesco Primaticcio rather than his workshop when it passed through the art market, an attribution that is maintained here. The principal drawing resembles the style and technique of numerous other mature studies by the artist depicting single or paired figures, which exhibit similarly small heads and voluminous draperies, and in which the white

gouache highlights on the red-chalk modeling are applied very broadly with the brush in parallel-hatching or in thick, single strokes. Many of these examples are in the Louvre (see fig. 15.1), and have been convincingly dated to about 1541–46, based on the projects to which they loosely relate.[2] The connection of the main figure in the Tobey drawing to Primaticcio's designs for the series of enamels of the twelve apostles, executed by Léonard Limosin in 1547 on the commission of King Francis I (1494–1547), and taken over at his death by Henry II (1519–1559),[3] seems particularly noteworthy. The individual figure studies for these holy men, most of which belong to the Louvre (Département des Arts Graphiques), nearly exactly resemble the man in the Tobey sheet in their awkward bodily proportions, static poses, and drawing technique. While the bearded man in the present drawing stands with arms crossed and wears a hood or cap, he greatly approximates the figural types in the two different enamels portraying Saint Paul, one being the version based on the portrait of Jacques Galiot de Genouillac (1465–1546; Département des Objets d'art, Louvre, inv. no. MR 210, N 1246), and the other the figure from the series in Chartres (Musée des Beaux-Arts, inv. no. D.50.2.2).[4]

That the Tobey sheet is an autograph Primaticcio can be judged further by comparing its expressive quality to that of the more stilted renderings in copies by his workshop or followers, often done with pen-and-ink reworking of the red chalk and white chalk. Examples of the latter are a contemporary sheet of copies of three figures after lost drawings for the Chartres enamels by Primaticcio, identified by Catherine Jenkins among the anonymous French sixteenth-century drawings of The Metropolitan Museum of Art, New York

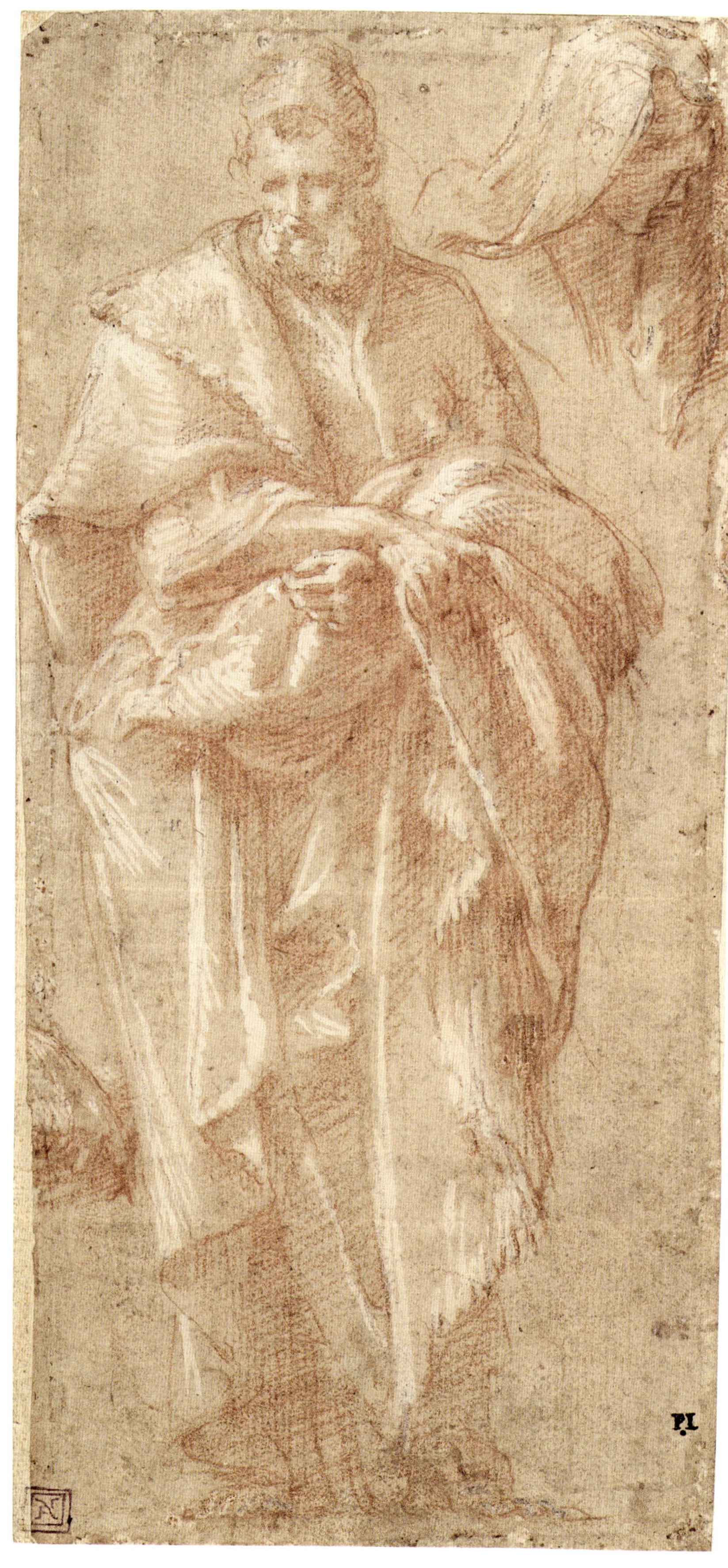

15

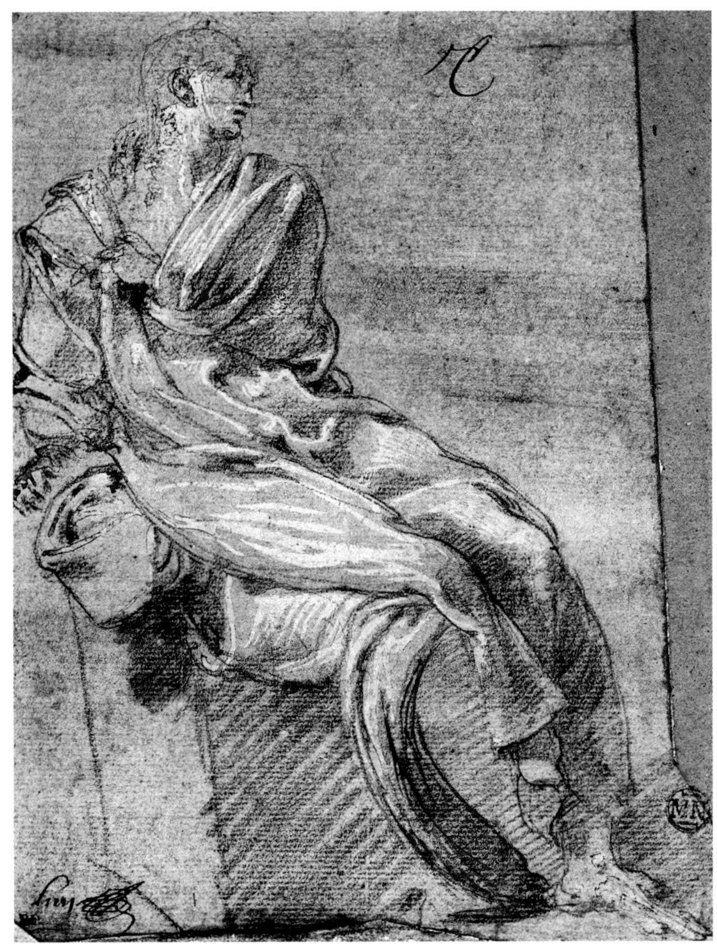

Fig. 15.1. Francesco Primaticcio. *Seated Figure*, ca. 1541–46. Red chalk, highlighted with white gouache, over stylus underdrawing, 8³⁄₁₆ x 6 in. (20.8 x 15.3 cm), maximum; sheet with irregular borders. Département des Arts Graphiques, Musée du Louvre, Paris (8598)

(fig. 15.2);[5] and another workshop copy after Primaticcio's Chartres Saint John the Evangelist attributed by Dominique Cordellier to "Michel Rochetel (?)," which is in pen and ink with leadwhite (Département des Arts Graphiques, Louvre, Paris, inv. no. 33648).[6] The Tobey sheet can therefore be dated with some confidence to the late 1540s, perhaps even about 1547, at a time in the mature artist's career of particularly busy activity and close collaboration with craftsmen engaged in royal projects.

CCB

1. I am indebted to Catherine Jenkins, assistant curator, Department of Drawings and Prints, The Metropolitan Museum of Art, New York, for fruitful discussion of this drawing.
2. Inv. nos. 8589, 8590, 8593, 8595, 8598. These examples are illustrated and catalogued by Dominique Cordellier in Paris 2004–5, pp. 230, 261, 284–85, nos. 94, 115, 130, 131; Cordellier in Bologna 2005, pp. 182–83, 190–91, nos. 53, 55.
3. On this project, compare Sophie Baratte in Paris 1993, p. 84, nos. 15 and 16; Baratte and Cordellier in Paris 2004–5, pp. 283–85.
4. Both are illustrated and catalogued by Baratte in Paris 2004–5, pp. 288–89, nos. 133, 135.
5. I am grateful to Catherine Jenkins for permitting me to publish her discovery here.
6. Cordellier in Paris 2004–5, p. 285, no. 132.

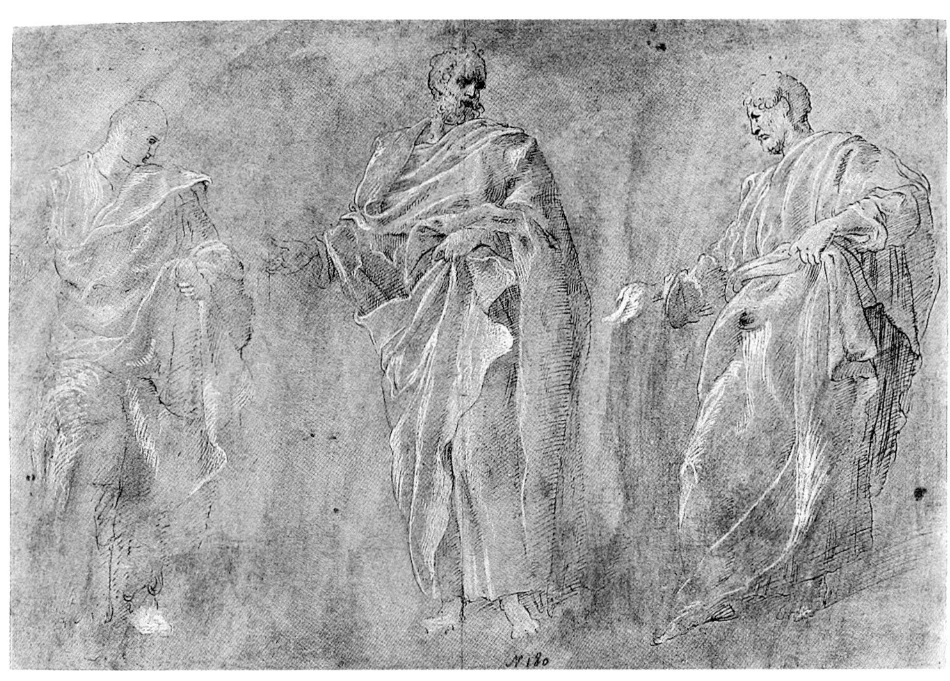

Fig. 15.2. Copy after Francesco Primaticcio. *Three Standing Figures*, ca. 1540s–50s. Pen and brown ink highlighted with white gouache, over traces of black chalk, on paper washed gray, 17⅛ x 12 in. (43.5 x 30.5 cm). The Metropolitan Museum of Art, New York, Purchase, Mr. and Mrs. David M. Tobey and Howard G. Lepow Gifts 1996 (1996.22)

GIROLAMO MAZZOLA BEDOLI

Viadana, ca. 1505–Parma, ca. 1569/70

Probably trained by Parmigianino's uncle Pier Ilario Mazzola, whose daughter he married in 1529, and whose surname he added to his own name, Girolamo Mazzola Bedoli emerged as one of the leading painters in Parma after the death of Parmigianino in 1540. He produced numerous easel pictures, including altarpieces for churches in Parma, as well as in his native Viadana and Mantua, and portraits. He was also in great demand as a fresco painter, working extensively in Parma Cathedral and the nearby church of Santa Maria della Steccata. His art relies, to varying degrees, on the examples of Correggio, Giulio Romano, and especially Parmigianino. Close parallels between Bedoli's elegant style and that of his cousin have led to confusion over the attribution of their respective oeuvres.

16. *Female Figure (Fortitude?)*, ca. 1553–55

Pen and ink and wash, over traces of black chalk, heightened in white, 7⅞ x 3⅝ in. (20 x 9.3 cm)

Provenance: Private Collection, France; Thomas Le Claire, Hamburg; acquired in 2006

This heretofore unpublished sheet relates to frescoes by Girolamo Mazzola Bedoli in Santa Maria della Steccata, the church in Parma where his cousin Parmigianino had earlier been commissioned to paint the eastern apse and vault (see cat. no. 14). Soon after Parmigianino's death in 1540, other mural decorations in the church were assigned to local artists, including Bedoli, who painted the northern apse and vault (documented, 1546–53), followed by the southern apse and vault (documented, 1553–67).[1] The choice of Bedoli, who was considered to be his kinsman's artistic heir, was probably motivated by a desire to maintain stylistic coherence in the decorative program. Both of the related contracts stipulate that Bedoli was expected to follow his cousin's prototype: for example, the respective vaults were to contain six colored figures similar to, yet varied from, those previously painted. Bedoli depicted a triad of women at the base on either side of each vault, as had Parmigianino, but with different and far-ranging attributes.[2]

The Tobey sheet is an early idea for the female figure, perhaps a personification of Fortitude,[3] at the far end of the southeast vault (figs. 16.1, 16.2). With black chalk, Bedoli sketched the woman next to two coffers of the vault and then elaborated her form in pen, wash, and heightening. She holds a small book in her extended right hand and a baton in her left hand, and her upper body turns more to one side than it does in the fresco. Another, presumably later drawing (fig. 16.3) more closely corresponds to the fresco: she holds the baton in her right hand, along with a large book that is propped against her hip, and places her left hand atop the hilt of her sword.[4]

To what extent Bedoli or his assistants, notably his son Alessandro, painted the frescoes in the south arm of Santa

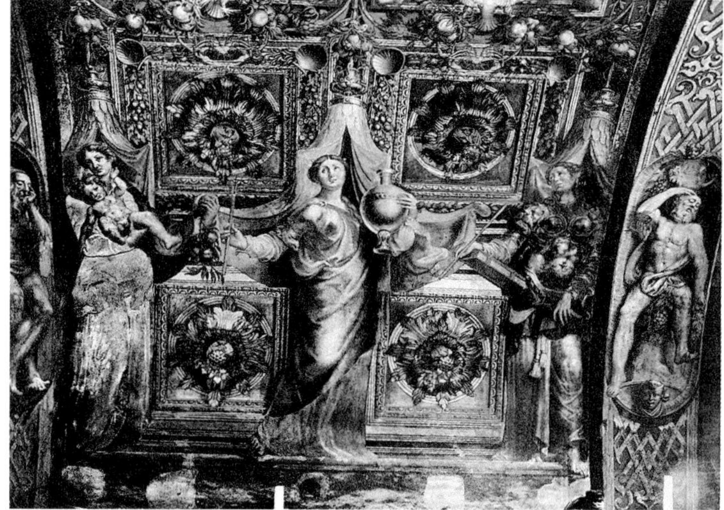

Fig. 16.1. Girolamo Mazzola Bedoli. Fresco, ca. 1555–67. Southeast vault, Santa Maria della Steccata, Parma

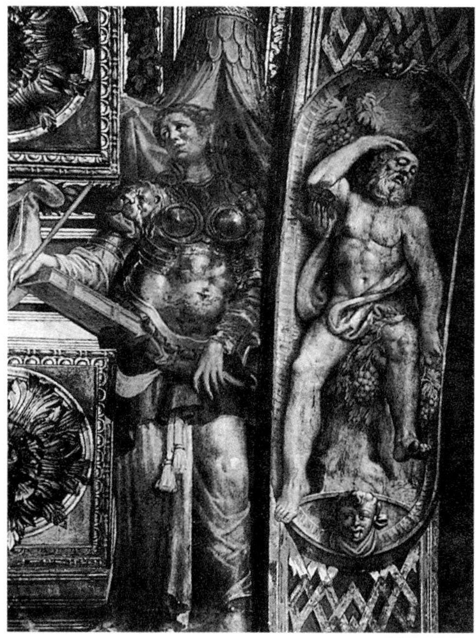

Fig. 16.2. Girolamo Mazzola Bedoli. Detail of fig. 16.1

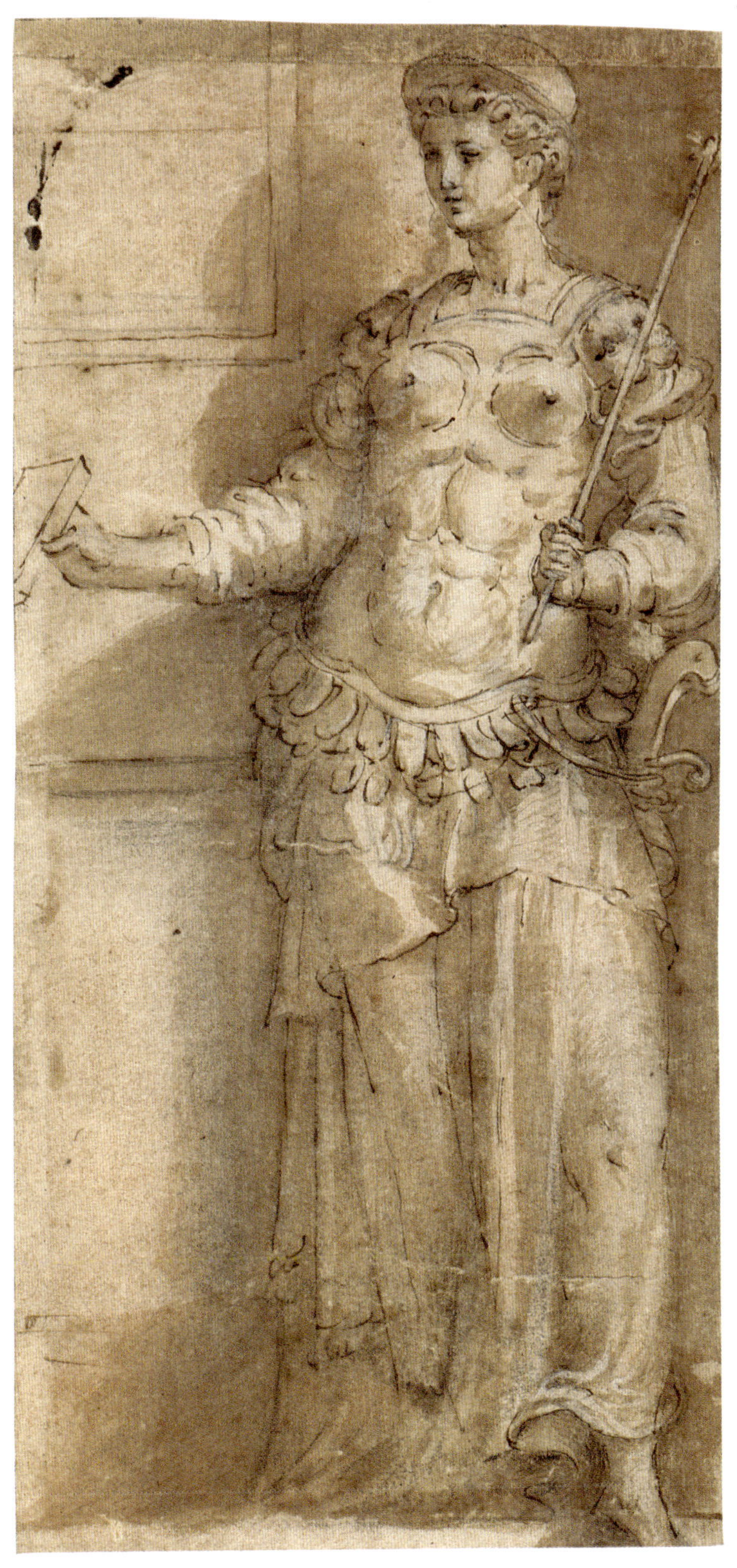

16

Maria della Steccata is a matter of debate.[5] Bedoli is nonetheless believed to have been responsible for the planning of the cycle. The Tobey drawing confirms his involvement, and its technique is typical of his mature graphic style. Contours are likewise described with gentle, broken pen marks over initial chalk indications in a study, now in the Uffizi, for a scene of the Adoration of the Shepherds in the southern apse of the church.[6] The delicate handling and attenuated figural proportions in the Tobey sheet testify to Bedoli's abiding interest in Parmigianino's draftsmanship.

MV

1. For Bedoli's frescoes in the Steccata church, see Milstein 1978, pp. 188–92, 221–26, ill.
2. Parmigianino's maidens hold lamps that evoke the biblical parable of the Wise and Foolish Virgins (see cat. no. 14). Only a few of the corresponding figures painted by Bedoli, such as the Old Testament heroine Judith with the head of Holofernes (north vault), can be clearly identified. The iconographic program merits further study. See Fornari Schianchi 2008, pp. 224–30, for preliminary remarks.
3. Fortitude, one of the four cardinal virtues, is typically represented as a warrior in armor.
4. Ex-Finarte auction, Milan, first attributed to Bedoli by Giovanni Godi. See Di Giampaolo 1997, pp. 180–81, no. 99.
5. See Milstein 1978, p. 225, for Alessandro Bedoli's possible execution of the six female figures on the vault preceding the southern apse, based on his father's cartoons.
6. For this drawing, see Di Giampaolo 1997, p. 163, no. 75, ill.

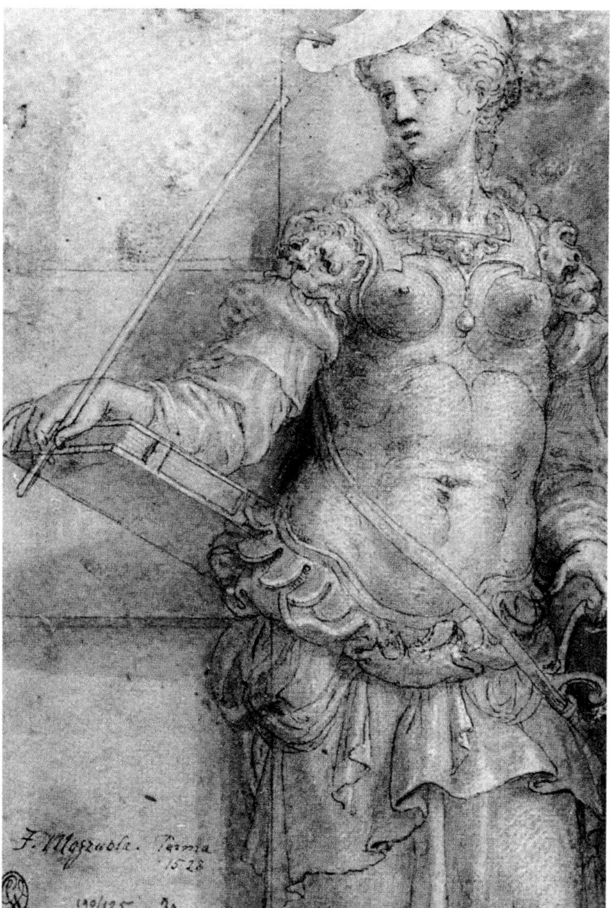

Fig. 16.3. Girolamo Mazzola Bedoli. *Female Figure (Fortitude?)*, ca. 1555. Pen and ink, brush and brown wash, 7½ x 4¹⁵⁄₁₆ in. (19 x 12.5 cm). Whereabouts unknown (Milan art market, 1975, as Pirro Ligorio)

NICCOLÒ DELL'ABATE

Modena, 1509(?)–Fontainebleau(?), 1571

Niccolò dell'Abate spent the first part of his career working in and around his native Modena in Emilia, where he absorbed influences from Correggio and Dosso Dossi, and the second in France at the royal court at Fontainebleau, where he collaborated with the Bolognese painter Primaticcio. His Italian paintings frequently depict concerts set in lyrical, idealized landscapes and other pastoral subjects. He also executed altarpieces and secular fresco cycles illustrating scenes from ancient history and Renaissance poetry, working for prominent patrons in Bologna. His activity in France took place mostly in the royal palace at Fontainebleau, where he served as Primaticcio's assistant and executant, painting frescoes after that master's designs, most notably the destroyed decorations of the Galerie d'Ulysse.

17. *Scenes from Livy's* Roman History, ca. 1547

Recto: *King Tarquin the Proud Orders Lucius Junius Brutus to Accompany His Sons Titus and Arruns to the Oracle of Delphi* (left); and *The Embarkation for Greece* (right)
Verso: *The Visit to the Oracle of Delphi* (left); and *The Return to Rome* (right)

Recto and verso: pen and brown ink, 7⅛ x 10½ in. (18.1 x 26.7 cm)
The scene at left on the recto is inscribed with the same brown ink as the drawing, *Prima parte*; at right: *Seconda parte*. The scene at left on the verso is inscribed with the same brown ink as the drawing, *Terzza parte* [*sic*]; at right: *Qarta parte* [*sic*]. Annotated on recto in pen and nearly black, brown ink at upper right by an early collector: "no. 366."

Provenance: Katherine Canaday; her estate sale, Christie's, New York, January 13, 1993, lot 8; acquired in 1993

References: Béguin 1983–84; Béguin 2001, pp. 73–74, fig. 5; Sylvie Béguin in Modena 2005, pp. 335–36, no. 112a

As Sylvie Béguin first recognized in 2001, the composition sketches on this important, vibrantly drawn double-sided sheet were intended for the first four scenes from the *Story of Tarquin and Lucretia* in a lost fresco cycle on the frieze of the *salone* in the Palazzo Torfanini on the Via Galliera in Bologna, executed about 1547.[1] The subject was closely based on Livy's *Roman History* (Book I, chapters 56–59), from which Niccolò dell'Abate painted fourteen episodes; he numbered each of the preliminary drawings, permitting a precise reconstruction of their sequence (see the inscriptions mentioned above). Other companion sheets for the Palazzo Torfanini fresco cycle, all similarly inscribed and quickly sketched, are in the Biblioteca Marucelliana, Florence (figs. 17.1–17.4); these were preparatory for the fifth to the eleventh episode.[2] The sheet of preliminary sketches for the last segments of the program has not yet come to light. The entire group of known drawings for the Palazzo Torfanini frescoes were exhibited together for the first time in 2005, confirming their consistent drawing technique and scale of the figures.[3] The lost fresco cycle was described in Pietro Lamo's *Graticola di Bologna* (manuscript, ca. 1560; published in

1844) but was not completely understood as a monument until Béguin's first publication on the subject in 1983–84. With regard to their unfortunate history, author Giovan Pietro Zanotti explains that before the interior of the Palazzo Torfanini was renovated, Domenico Fratta was asked in 1735 by Giacomo Bartolomeo Beccari to copy the frieze and the scenes in the adjoining room of the palace as a keepsake, but these drawings by Fratta (bequeathed to the Istituto delle Scienze, Bologna) were themselves stolen, though fortunately not before they were copied for G. B. Venturi (for independent reasons) and were also reproduced in engravings. Hence, the copies after the copies of the Venturi set enabled the subsequent reconstruction of the cycle and the eventual identification of Niccolò dell'Abate's preparatory drawings for the project. The drawn copies after copies of the Venturi set, preserved in a manuscript in the Biblioteca Panizzi (Comunale) of Reggio Emilia, were discovered and published in 1929 by Guido Zucchini.[4]

Especially on the recto of the Tobey sheet, the artist achieved a sense of immediacy and continuous narrative, in that as the telling of episodes one and two ("Prima parte" and "Seconda parte") merge almost seamlessly together, the second framed sketch superimposed on the first, focusing the viewer's attention on the more monumental scene of *The Embarkation for Greece* at right. On the verso at left, the third scene ("Terzza parte" [*sic*]) depicts *The Visit to the Oracle of Delphi*, in which Arruns kneels on the ground and kisses the earth, thereby showing that he was to be the chosen future king of Rome. Next to Arruns, Lucius Junius Brutus and Titus with their entourage, not having understood the words of the Oracle in answer to their question of who should be king ("he who first kisses his mother"), stand by the statue of Apollo. Behind the

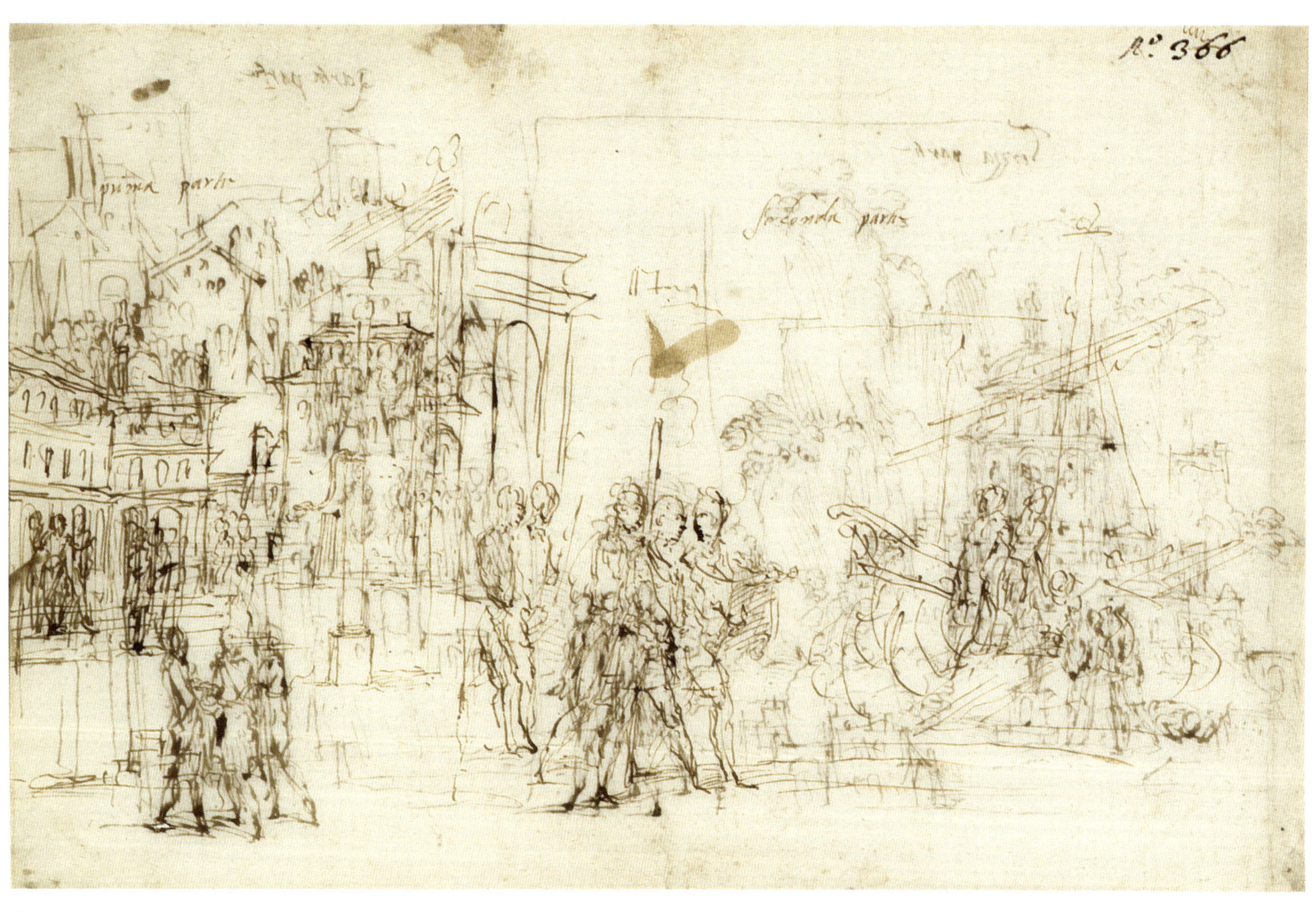

17

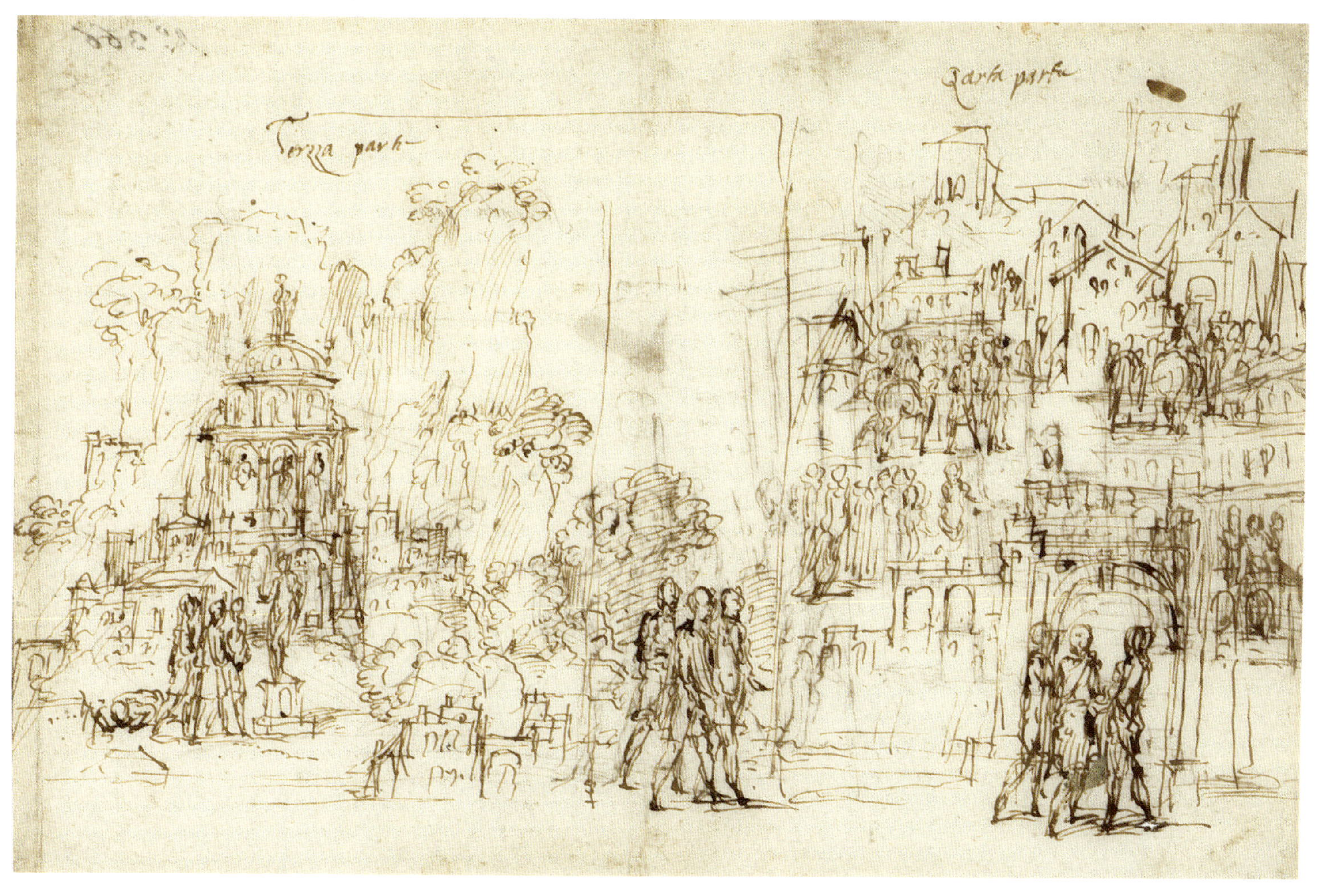

17 verso

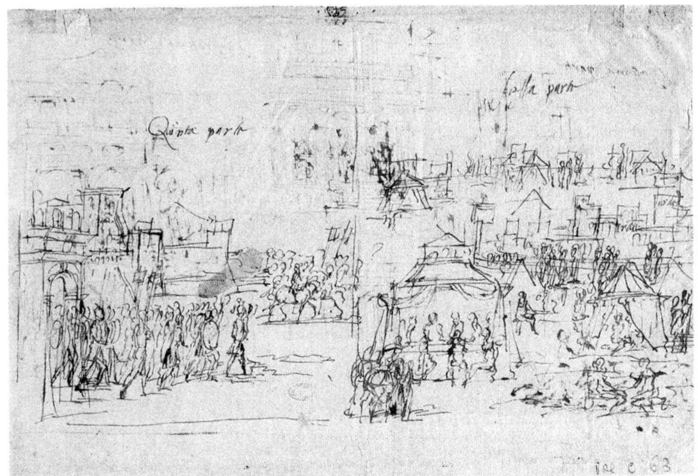

Fig. 17.1. Niccolò dell'Abate. *Story of Tarquin and Lucretia*, ca. 1547. Pen and brown ink, 10¹⁵⁄₁₆ x 7½ in. (27.8 x 19 cm). Biblioteca Marucelliana, Florence (Dis. C 63v)

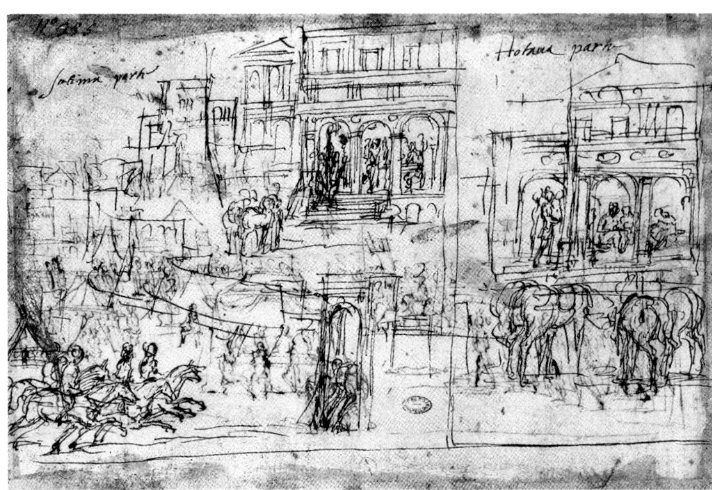

Fig. 17.2. Niccolò dell'Abate. *Story of Tarquin and Lucretia*, ca. 1547. Pen and brown ink, 10¹⁵⁄₁₆ x 7½ in. (27.8 x 19 cm). Biblioteca Marucelliana, Florence (Dis. C 63r)

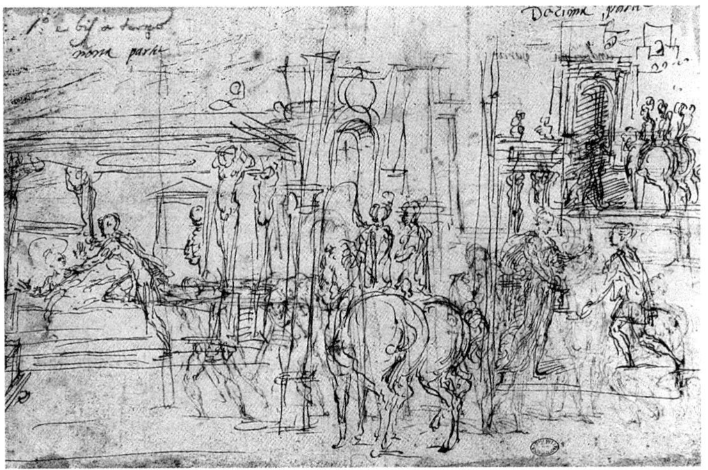

Fig. 17.3. Niccolò dell'Abate. *Story of Tarquin and Lucretia*, ca. 1547. Pen and brown ink, 11 x 7½ in. (28 x 19 cm). Biblioteca Marucelliana, Florence (Dis. B 19r)

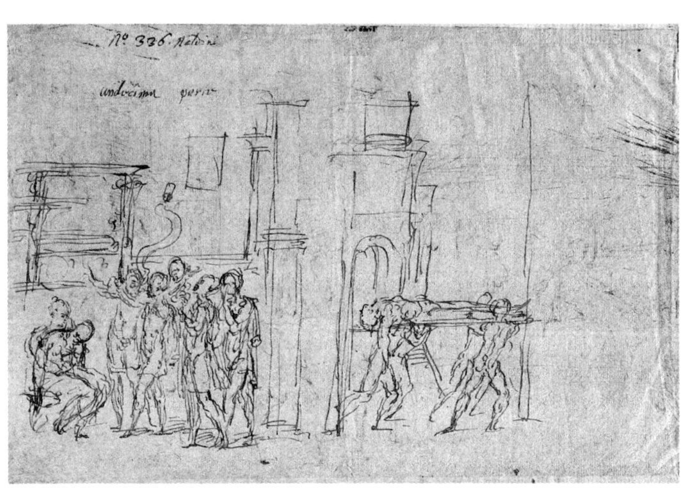

Fig. 17.4. Niccolò dell'Abate. *Story of Tarquin and Lucretia*, ca. 1547. Pen and brown ink, 11 x 7½ in. (28 x 19 cm). Biblioteca Marucelliana, Florence (Dis. B 19v)

figures rises the great edifice of Apollo's temple. The fourth episode, *The Return to Rome* ("Qarta parte" [*sic*]), renders a complex amalgamation of buildings and vignettes of history, one on top of the other, which have not yet been completely unified as a composition. Béguin reasonably proposed that the upper reaches of this design portray Tarquin Calling the Rutuli to War.[5]

CCB

1. Béguin 1983–84, pp. 183–84; Béguin 2001, pp. 73–74, fig. 5; Sylvie Béguin in Modena 2005, pp. 335–36, no. 112a.
2. Béguin 1983–4; Di Giampaolo et al. 1989, nos. 72–73; Béguin 2001, pp. 73–74.
3. See Sylvie Béguin in Modena 2005, p. 335, nos. 112a–112c.
4. See Biblioteca Communale di Reggio Emilia, Ms. Venturi, cart. XXI, G.12. Béguin 1983–84; Béguin 2001, pp. 73–74.
5. Béguin 2001, p. 74.

FRANCESCO SALVIATI

Florence, 1510–Rome, 1563

A prolific draftsman and versatile painter, Francesco Salviati is the paradigmatic Mannerist artist, renowned for his refined artifice, inventive fantasy, and all'antica decorative vocabulary. He divided his career between Florence and Rome. Among his early teachers in Florence were Giuliano Bugiardini, Baccio Bandinelli, and Andrea del Sarto; he was also deeply influenced by the art of Perino del Vaga in Rome, where, together with his friend Giorgio Vasari, he assiduously studied the work of Raphael and Michelangelo as well as the antique. Salviati took his name from his important early patron, Cardinal Giovanni Salviati, scion of a prominent Florentine family, for whom he executed a number of works. He also received notable commissions from other members of the Florentine community in Rome as well as from the powerful Farnese family; from Duke Cosimo I de' Medici in Florence; and from the Grimani in Venice. He also spent a brief period in France. In addition to frescoes and altarpieces, Salviati painted portraits, devotional images, and secular allegories; designed tapestries, prints, and metal work; and produced hundreds of drawings in which his boundless capacity for invention is abundantly revealed.

18. Recto: *Two Designs for Table Flatware (Knife Handles?): A Man Intertwined with a Serpent*; and *A Couple Embracing*, ca. 1550–60
Verso: *Fragmentary Figural Composition for* Samson Breaking the Lion's Jaw (attributed to Peter Paul Rubens), ca. 1615–28

Pen and brown ink, brush and gray-brown wash, highlighted with white gouache (partly oxidized), over black chalk, on buff-light brown paper (recto); pen and brown ink, brush and brown wash (verso), 7¾ x 6 in. (19.8 x 15.3 cm)
Annotated on recto in pen and brown ink along bottom border by a seventeenth-century hand: *Anibal Fontana. Milanse. Beelthouver.*
Engraved: *Cornelius Bos*, in reverse (the left knife handle only)

Provenance: Peter Paul Rubens (1577–1640); by bequest to his son; Valerius Röver (1686–1739) (Lugt 2884 a–c), his numbers "32/26"; Hendrik de Leth; Jonkheer Johann Goll van Franckenstein, Sr. (1722–1785) (Lugt 2987), his number "N 3123" on the verso; sale, Christie's, New York, January 28, 1999, lot 96; acquired in 1999

References: Christie's, New York 1999, no. 96; Gerszi 2005, pp. 252–54, under no. 248 (when at Christie's, New York, in 1999); Belkin 2009, vol. 1, p. 182, vol. 2, pl. 243 (as whereabouts unknown)

On the recto of this double-sided sheet, the two precisely drawn figural designs for the handles of knives (in fact, they seem no less suitable for other flatware, such as forks or spoons) depict at left a standing nude youth coiled by a serpent and at right a pair of kissing nude lovers. The latter motif at left is evidently based on one of the figures of the sons in the famous Hellenistic marble sculpture from the early first century B.C., *Laocoön and His Sons* (see fig. 6.2, p. 23), a quotation that in the small scale of an object for the table was playfully meant to stimulate the imagination of the viewer and banquet participant. Although the two designs are worked up to a full finish with highlights in leadwhite gouache and rendering in brown wash, they are done over a generous quantity of searching black-chalk underdrawing (overlooked in previous publications), and this fact establishes the deeply purposeful exploratory nature of the work. A closely comparable study by Francesco Salviati in the same media, degree of finish, and type of underdrawing is a design for a ewer, now in the Ashmolean Museum of Art and Archaeology, Oxford (fig. 18.1); it exhibits a standing nude woman for a handle, and two seated nude nymphs around the neck.[1] Salviati's authorship of that work is widely accepted, and together with the motifs on the Tobey sheet, the two drawings give credence to the words of Salviati's earliest biographer and friendly rival, Giorgio Vasari. According to Vasari's 1568 edition of the *Vite*, Salviati received his first artistic training as a silversmith, excelling in this craft at a young age as a draftsman of fantastic creations.[2] Salviati also appears to have entertained the ambitions of being a sculptor (at least, in small scale) until the very end of his life: "he cast some small figures in bronze, which were in the possession of Duke Alessandro de' Medici, which were extremely witty and graceful" ("gittò alcune figurette di bronzo, le quali ebbe il duca Alessandro, che furono graziosissime").[3] He is known to have designed the types of knife handles seen in the Tobey recto, with intricately intertwined figurative details. Four such works are recorded in two engravings of 1583 by Cherubino Alberti (1553–1615), which are inscribed with our artist's name, "*Frac' Salviati · In ·*" (figs. 18.2, 18.3), and were then reproduced in reverse in 1605 by Aegidius Sadeler.[4]

The double-sided Tobey sheet with Salviati's exquisite designs on the recto was once owned by the celebrated Flemish painter

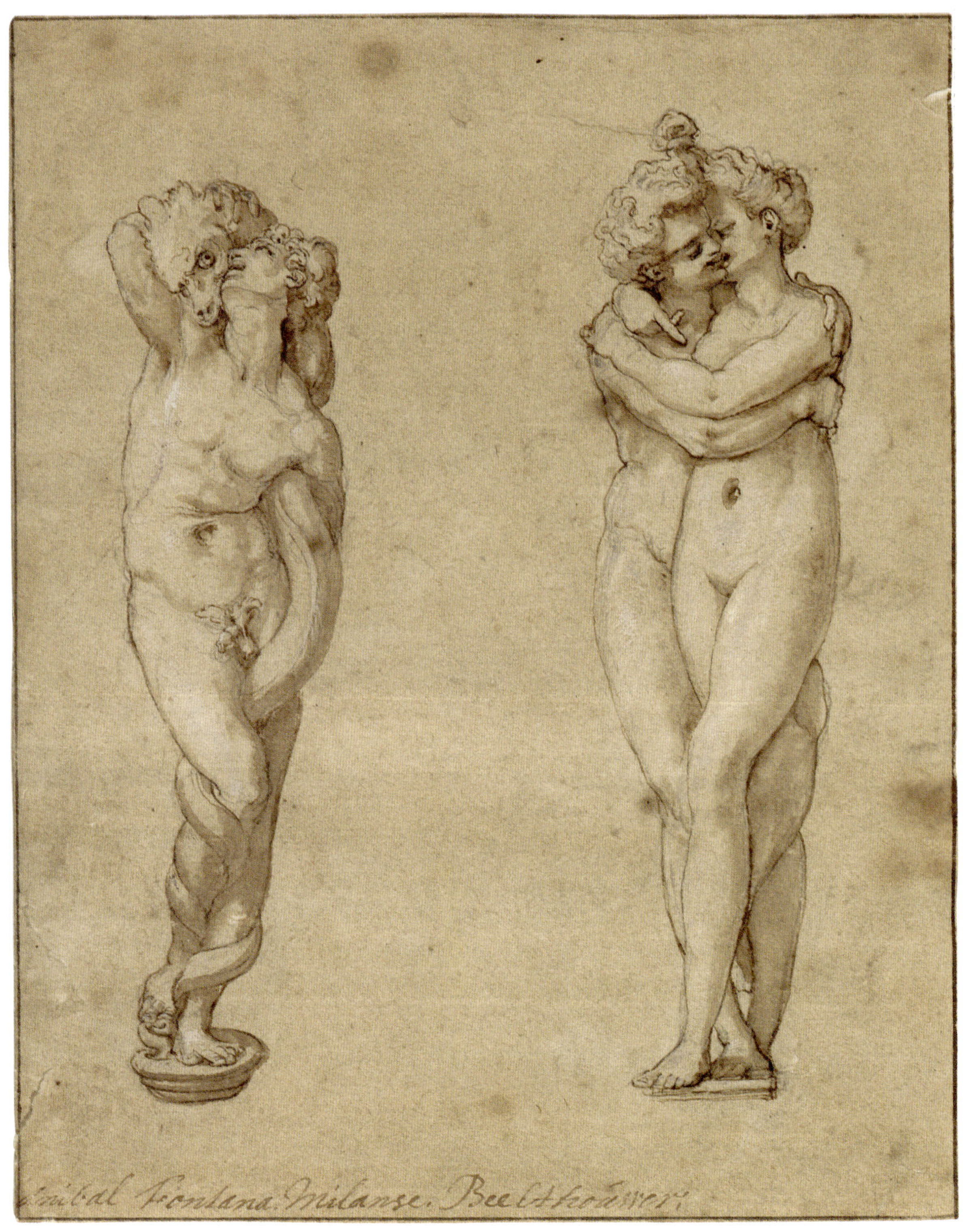

18

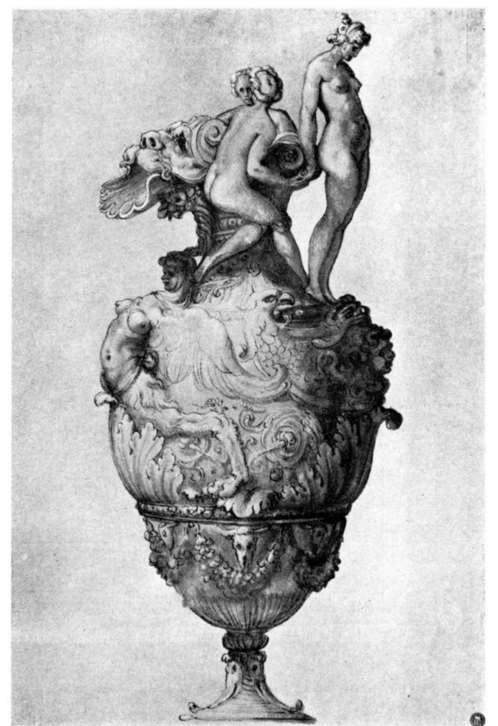

Fig. 18.1. Francesco Salviati. *Design for a Ewer*, 1530s–40s. Pen and brown ink, brush with gray and brown ink, highlighted with white gouache, over black chalk, 16³⁄₁₆ x 10⅞ in. (41.1 x 27.6 cm). Ashmolean Museum of Art and Archaeology, Oxford (WA 1863.675)

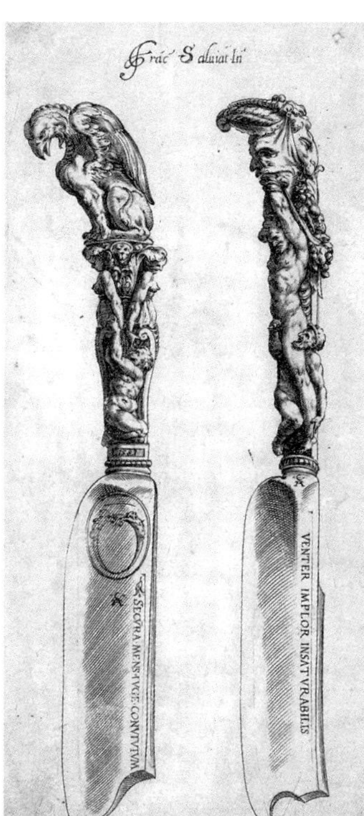

Fig. 18.2. Cherubino Alberti, after Francesco Salviati. *Designs of Knives*, 1583. Engraving, 10¹⁄₁₆ x 4¾ in. (25.6 x 12 cm) (plate). The Metropolitan Museum of Art, New York, Harris Brisbane Dick Fund, 1925 (25.24.56)

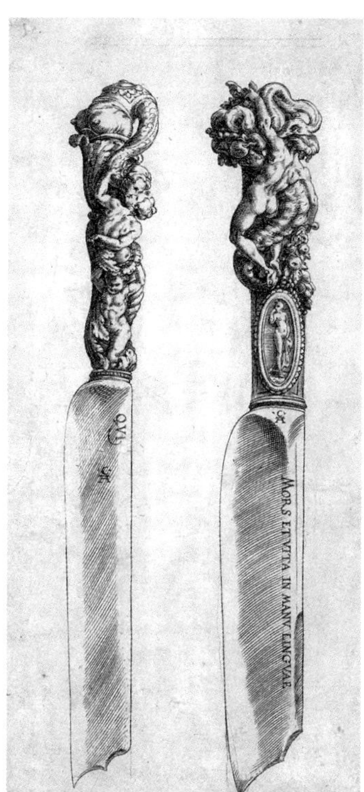

Fig. 18.3. Cherubino Alberti, after Francesco Salviati. *Designs of Knives*, 1583. Engraving, 10 x 4⅝ in. (25.4 x 11.8 cm) (plate). The Metropolitan Museum of Art, New York, Harris Brisbane Dick Fund, 1925 (25.24.57)

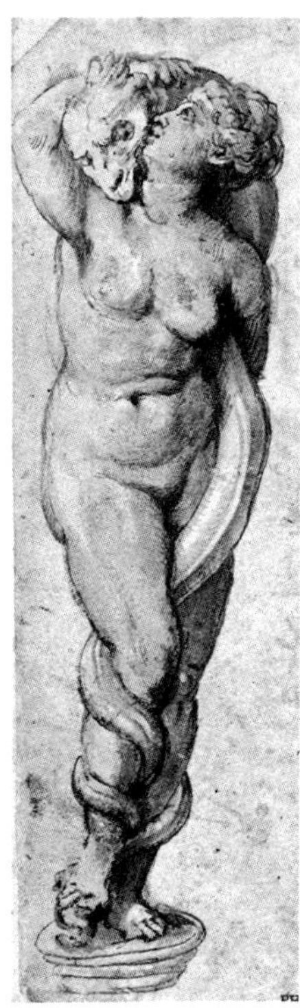

Fig. 18.4. Attributed to Peter Paul Rubens (correcting Cornelis Bos). *Decorative Figure: Eve with the Serpent*. Pen and brown ink, brush and brown wash, over black chalk, highlighted with white oil-color, 7⅛ x 2¹⁄₁₆ in. (18.1 x 5.2 cm). Christ Church, Oxford (1089; JBS 1376b)

Peter Paul Rubens (1577–1640), who was also an erudite collector of drawings and who may have drawn the sketch on the verso. The motif by Salviati at left on the recto appears in a drawing now in Christ Church, Oxford (fig. 18.4), which a number of scholars have reasonably attributed to Rubens himself, but in which the figure is obviously female.[5] An early specialist of Northern art had previously thought the Christ Church sheet to be by Cornelis Bos (1510[?]–1566), who engraved this and the related designs.[6] The motif by Salviati at right on the recto appears in a drawing now in the Szépművészeti Múzeum, Budapest (inv. no. 1658), attributed to Bos and retouched by Rubens.[7] The drawing now in the Tobey Collection was eventually acquired by the Dutch collector Valerius Röver (1686–1739), who thought Salviati's two recto designs to be by the Milanese sculptor and medalist Annibale Fontana (1540–1587) and catalogued them as such in 1711: "Annibal Fontana. 2 staande beeltjes, malkander omhelzende en een ander met een slang, getekent voor hegten tot messen van Annibal Fontana, met de pen gewassen en gehoo[c]ht op geel pap[ier]" ("Annibale Fontana. 2 standing small figures

embracing each other and another with a serpent, drawn for the hafts of knives by Annibale Fontana, with pen and wash and heightened on yellow paper. sold for f 1 :10").[8] Röver's collection was bought from his widow in 1761 by the dealer Hendrik de Leth, who sold forty-two albums of drawings to Goll van Franckenstein, although the present drawing is not recorded in Goll's sales of 1819 and 1833.[9]

The verso sketch, drawn as preparation for a composition of *Samson Breaking the Lion's Jaw*, was unknown in the literature before its discovery at the Christie's auction in New York in 1999. The attribution to Rubens was proposed in the auction catalogue; it has been accepted by Stijn Alsteens, and the present author is inclined to agree, although it has been doubted by Anne-Marie Logan.[10] The beautifully energetic, summary scrawls depict a portion of the biblical giant's figure—his head, arms, large hands, and bent left knee—wrestling open the jaw of the lion, while the limp paw of the beast along the bottom border suggests that the struggle is over. The fragmentary nature of the verso sketch indicates that the sheet with Salviati's detailed drawings on the recto was greatly cut down, that it

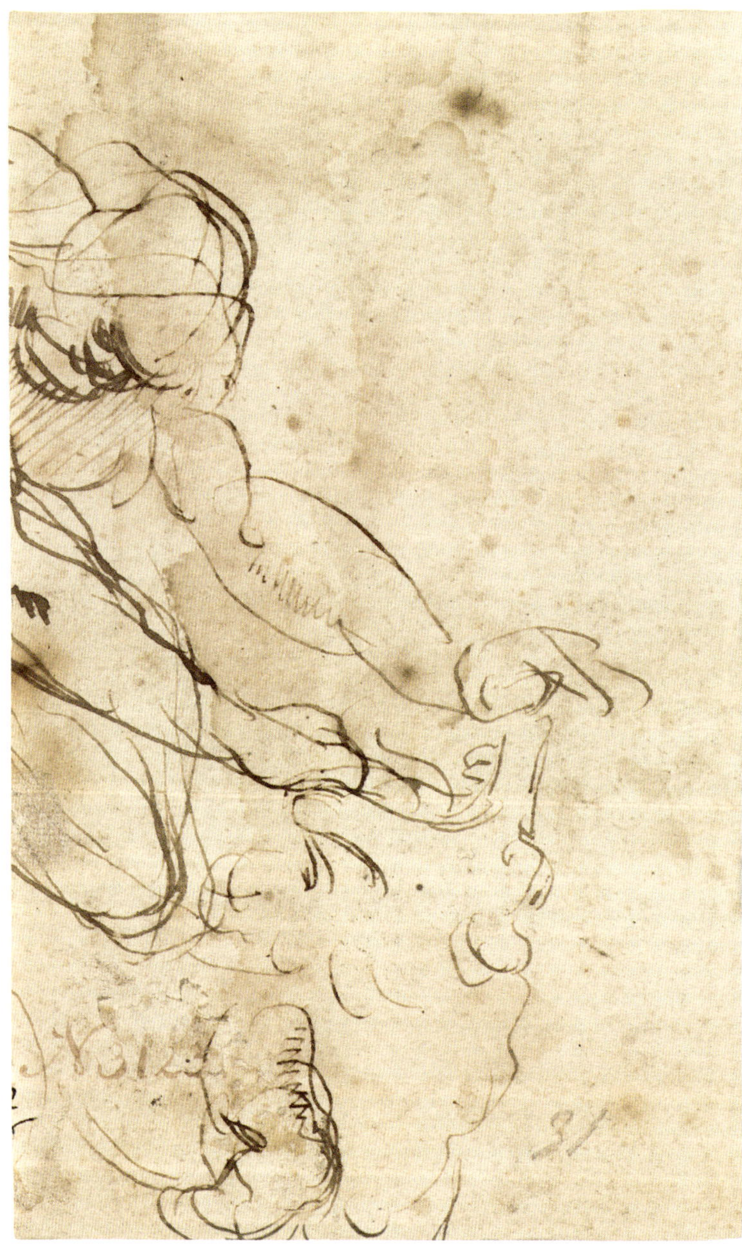

18 verso

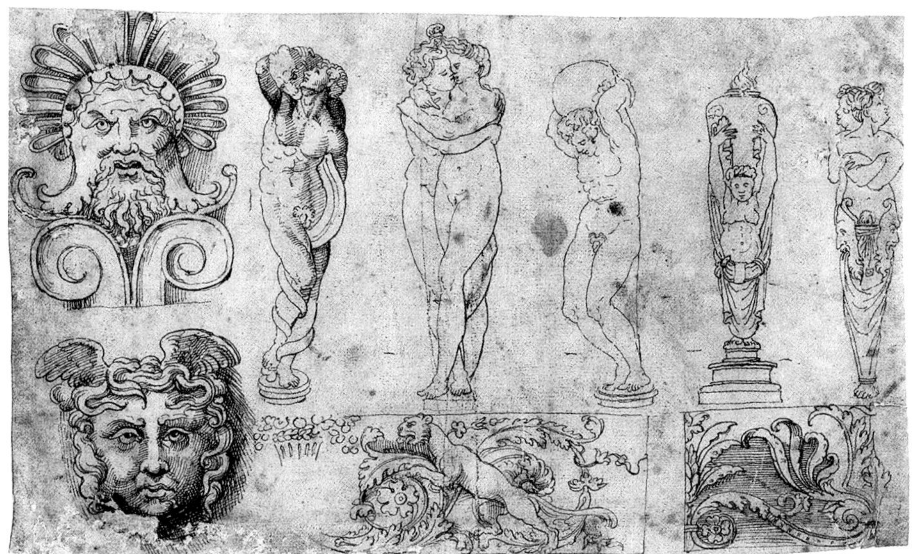

Fig. 18.5. Cornelis Bos. *Studies of Sculptural Figures and Ornament; with Two Masks at Left and a Lion amongst Acanthus Scroll Below*. Pen and brown ink, 9½ x 15⅛ in. (24.1 x 38.4 cm). British Museum, London (1933,1205.4)

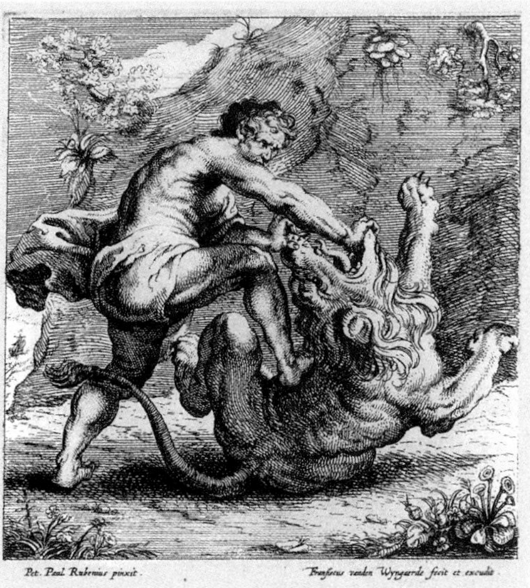

Fig. 18.6. Frans van den Wijngaarde, after Peter Paul Rubens. *Samson Breaking the Lion's Jaw*. Engraving, 5¼ x 4⅝ in. (13.1 x 11.8 cm). British Museum, London (1859-5-14-263)

was originally a little higher and perhaps twice as wide. The dismemberment must have occurred after Rubens's possession, as the original size is suggested by a drawing relating to Salviati's designs attributed to Cornelis Bos, now in the British Museum, London (fig. 18.5), which seems to record five figural handles, together with two antique-style masks and two fragments of friezes.[11] Another closely linked variant also firmly attributed to Bos is in the Boijmans Van Beuningen Museum, Rotterdam.[12] The verso sketch attributed to Rubens has been connected to a large canvas executed mostly by the artist's workshop (Duque de Hernani Collection, Madrid) that was documented in the Alcázar of Madrid in 1636,[13] the creation of which has been variously dated by scholars, about 1615–16,[14] alternatively about 1618–20,[15] or, most probably, in this author's opinion, about 1628.[16] The composition of the Madrid picture and of the extant copies after Rubens's oil sketch in Stockholm, Munich, and Besançon[17] is in reverse orientation with respect to what is seen in the Tobey sheet. The vigorous Tobey sketch, however, is drawn in the same direction as the engraving executed by Frans van den Wijngaarde after Rubens (fig. 18.6),[18] suggesting the possibility that Rubens perhaps created the present drawing, presumably along with other preparatory studies, in order to rehearse the composition for the printmaker. Apparently a companion, the double-sided sheet of sketches for *Samson and the Philistines* in Amsterdam closely resembles the Tobey verso sketch in execution.[19]   CCB

1. On the sheet in the Ashmolean Museum of Art and Archaeology, Oxford (inv. no. WA 1863.675), compare Parker 1956, pp. 367–68, no. 683, pl. 152; and Macandrew 1980, App. 2, no. 284. I am indebted to Stijn Alsteens and Hans Buijs for their assistance in preparing this entry.

2. Vasari ed. 1966–87, vol. 5 (text), p. 511.

3. Quoted from ibid., p. 534.

4. On Cherubino Alberti's and Aegidius Sadeler's prints of knife-handle designs after Salviati, compare Buffa 1982, pp. 302–3, no. 172 (III); New York 1997a, pp. 91–93, no. 20; and Catherine Monbeig Goguel in Rome and Paris 1998, pp. 276–77, no. 109.

5. The attribution to Rubens of this sheet is apparently due to Jaffé 1956, fig. 7; and was endorsed in Byam Shaw 1976, vol. 1, p. 334, under no. 1376, vol. 2, pl. 813.

6. Buschmann 1916, pl. 1D; Schéle 1965, no. 47.

7. Discussed and illustrated in Belkin 2009, vol. 1, pp. 180–81, no. 85, vol. 2, pl. 239.

8. Quoted from the catalogue of the art collection of Valerius Röver, Universiteitsbibliotheek Amsterdam, ms.II A 18, p. 158. The identification of the present drawing in Valerius Röver's catalogue of 1711 is due to Hans-Ulrich Beck, as quoted in Christie's, New York 1999, no. 96.

9. Hans-Ulrich Beck, as quoted in ibid.

10. Communications by Stijn Alsteens to the present author, February 2010; communication by Anne-Marie Logan to the present author, February 26, 2010. Belkin 2009, vol. 1, p. 182, published the verso sketch as "plausibly attributed to Rubens."

11. The sheet in the British Museum, London (inv. no. 1933.1205.4), was published and illustrated in Byam Shaw 1976, vol. 1, p. 334, under no. 1376, fig. 103. This drawing had been previously thought to be by an anonymous artist (see Schéle 1965, p. 195, no. 217).

12. The sheet in the Boijmans Van Beuningen Museum, Rotterdam, was discussed and illustrated in Jaffé 1956, fig. 6; Schéle 1965, p. 195, no. 216; Byam Shaw 1976, vol. 1, p. 334, under no. 1376, fig. 102.

13. See Arnout Balis in Antwerp 1993, pp. 174–79, nos. 81–84; D'Hulst and Vandenven 1989, pp. 96–99, no. 26.

14. This is the view of Jaffé 1989, p. 211, no. 334.

15. This is the view of Held 1980, vol. 1, pp. 429–30, no. 311; and Jaffé 1989, p. 211, no. 334.

16. The date of about 1628 is in agreement with the view of Arnout Balis, as stated in Antwerp 1993, p. 175; and D'Hulst and Vandenven 1989, p. 98, no. 26.

17. These copies are all catalogued in Held 1980, vol. 1, pp. 429–30, under no. 311; and D'Hulst and Vandenven 1989, pp. 96–104, nos. 26–28.

18. Catalogued by Arnout Balis in Antwerp 1993, p. 179, no. 85.

19. As noted in Christie's, New York 1999, under no. 96.

GIORGIO VASARI

Arezzo, 1511–Florence, 1574

Giorgio Vasari, author of the magisterial Le vite de' più eccellenti pittori, scultori e archittettori (The Lives of the Most Eminent Painters, Sculptors, and Architects)—*a vast compendium of biographies of fourteenth-, fifteenth-, and sixteenth-century painters, sculptors, architects, goldsmiths, and printmakers—was himself a painter and architect, as well as one of the earliest collectors of drawings. He traveled across much of the Italian peninsula, painting frescoes and altarpieces in Venice, Bologna, Rome, Naples, and elsewhere, but his career was most closely tied to Florence and the Medici, who employed him as court artist and from whom he received some of his most important commissions, including the charge to decorate a number of rooms in the Palazzo Vecchio and to design the duchy's administrative offices (the Uffizi). He was equally successful in Rome, where he was employed by the Farnese and by Pope Julius III. Vasari was closely connected with Francesco Salviati—in their youth the two had feverishly studied the artistic marvels of Rome—and oversaw a large corps of assistants, who helped him carry out his many large-scale commissions. In the writing of the* Vite, *in which he championed Michelangelo as the supreme practitioner of the arts, he relied on the guidance and literary contributions of Vincenzo Borghini. A competent painter and talented draftsman, Vasari absorbed the inventions of Michelangelo, Raphael, Perino del Vaga, Rosso Fiorentino, and other eminent artists of the day.*

19. *Saint Jerome Pulling the Thorn from a Lion before a Monastic Community*, ca. 1572

Pen and brown ink, brush and brown wash, over soft black chalk (with some traces of squaring in soft black chalk?); glued onto secondary paper support, 13 x 9 in. (33 x 22.9 cm)
Annotated on recto in pen and brown ink at lower right by a sixteenth-century hand: *m. Giorgio Vasarj*; on the backing in red chalk: *N. 670*.

Provenance: Sale, Sotheby's, New York, January 25, 2002, lot 5; acquired in 2002

Reference: Sotheby's, New York 2002, p. 14, no. 5

Inspired by the thirteenth-century account in the *Golden Legend*, written by Jacobus de Voragine, this composition depicts Saint Jerome (ca. A.D. 347–419/420), seated in profile at left foreground, in the act of extracting the thorn(s) from the wounded lion's paw, while four monks contemplate him.[1] The setting is a rural monastic community, with farm buildings at left and a series of vignettes depicted in the background as a continuous narrative with various figures and animals—monks, laborers, merchants, horses, mules, a donkey, and the lion. Although carefully finished in pen and ink with washes, this composition was developed over a vigorous and extensive underdrawing in soft black chalk. The technique of firm, somewhat jagged outlines and diagonal parallel-hatching over the wash layers is typical of Giorgio Vasari's mature and late drawings (his numerous workshop assistants rarely used the technique of copious hatching over the wash modeling in their drawings).

The Tobey sheet remains little known in the literature, despite being an autograph work that is connected with a documented project. As was first recognized by Florian Härb, it was preparatory for a now lost painting on panel executed during the time that the Aretine artist was attempting to finish the frescoes of the Sala Regia in the Vatican Palace in 1572–73, a project that had been begun by various painters under the patronage of Pope Paul III Farnese in 1549.[2] A letter written by Vasari from Rome to Francesco de' Medici (the future Grand Duke of Tuscany, who ruled as Francesco I from 1574 to 1587) in Florence, dated February 23, 1572, explains that Pope Pius V of the Ghislieri family had commissioned Vasari to finish the decorations of the Sala Regia and also to paint *Saint Jerome with the Lion* and a companion *Ascension of Saint Mary Magdalene* for him, two paintings that the artist had just begun sketching on the respective wood panels ("ho atteso, Signor mio, a bozzar duo tauole").[3] The survival of this letter is fortunate, given that it and the works described postdate the publication of the second edition of Vasari's *Vite* (Florence, 1568), the usual source of informative particulars on his projects.

Although providing much less detail than Jacobus de Voragine's account of Saint Jerome in the *Golden Legend*, Vasari's letter to Francesco de' Medici nevertheless explains at some length the subject of the painting with which the Tobey drawing is connected, and his words clarify the meaning of the various vignettes seen here in the background: "In the other panel, I have done [the scene] when Saint Jerome extracts the thorn of the lion, who never left him because of this good deed, and the friars make [the lion] guard [the donkey] of the convent, and when [the lion] was asleep the donkey was stolen, and the friars doubting that the lion had not eaten the donkey,

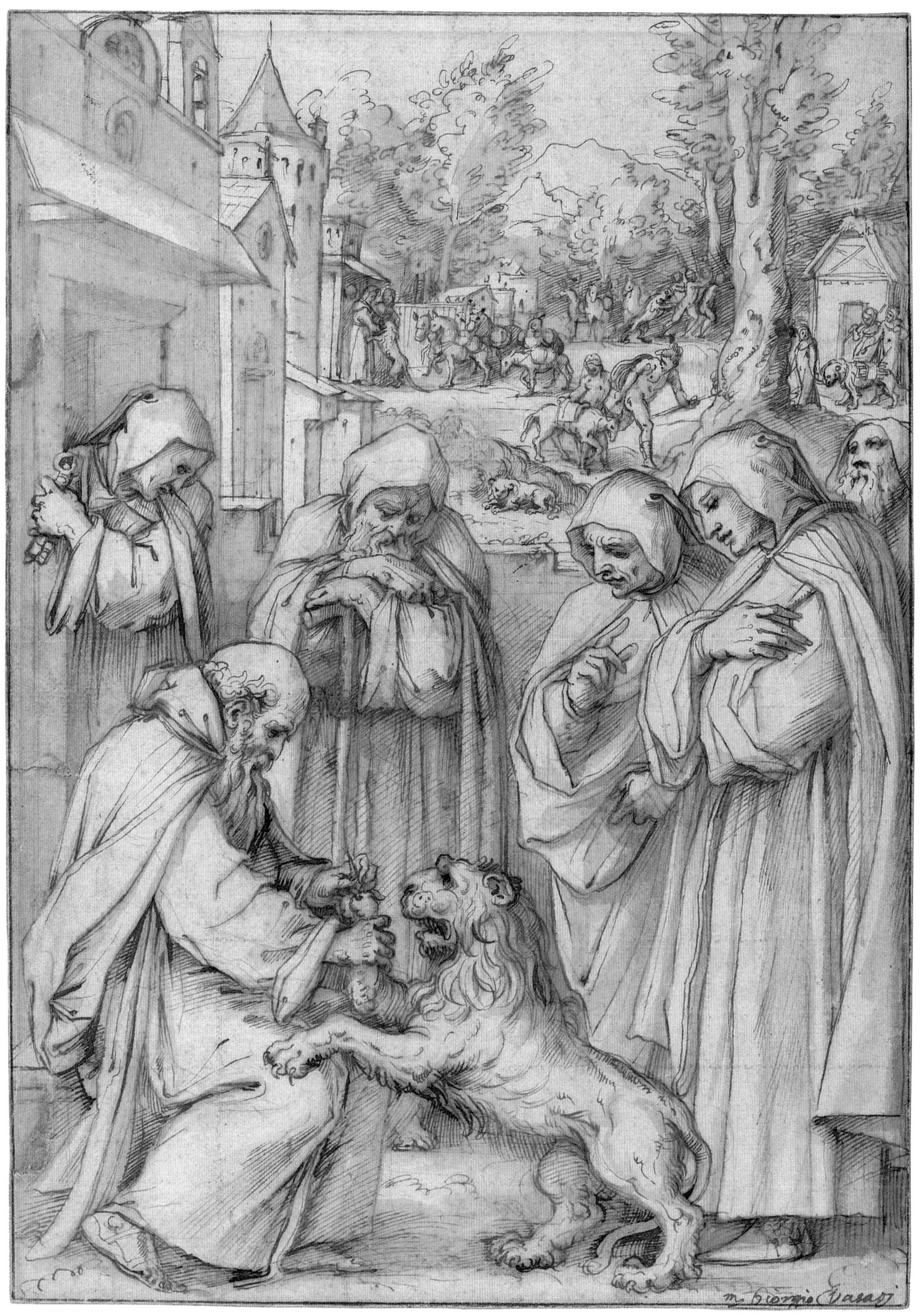

make the lion carry the wood; then, having discovered the drivers of carts loaded with the goods stolen from the donkey, [the lion] makes them flee and guides the mules and the donkey to the convent loaded with the provisions of which the friars had been deprived, and prepared them to feast."[4]

CCB

1. Voragine ed. 1993, vol. 2, pp. 211–16.
2. Florian Härb's identification is acknowledged in Sotheby's, New York 2002, p. 14, no. 5.

3. This letter is fully transcribed in Frey 1923–30, vol. 2, pp. 647–50, no. DCCCLXIII (with an original, archaeologically precise phrasing); and Vasari–Milanesi ed. 1906, vol. 8, pp. 466–68 (with a modernized orthography); quoted above from Frey 1923–30, vol. 2, p. 648.
4. Present author's translation of Vasari's letter, as transcribed in Frey 1923–30, vol. 2, p. 648: "Nell altra tauola ci o fatto, quando San Ieronimo caua la spina al leone, il quale per quel benefitio maj si partj da quello; ecj quando i fratj gli fan guardar l asino del conuento, che dormendo il leone gli e tolto, et che dubitando i frati che non lauessin mangiato, fan portar le legnie al leone; poi auendo ritrouato certi vetturalj che aueuon carico frumento, che gli aueuon rubato l asino, gli fa fuggire et conducie i mulj et l asino al conuento carichj dj vettouaglia, che i fratj non aueuon piu, et egli fa festa loro." I have taken the liberty of substituting the subjects in brackets for certain pronouns, in order to clarify the otherwise ambiguous narrative.

PIRRO LIGORIO

Naples, ca. 1513–Ferrara, 1583

Painter, architect, antiquarian, and archaeologist, Pirro Ligorio worked in Rome and Ferrara. He succeeded Michelangelo as architect of Saint Peter's and designed the Casino of Pius IV in the Vatican gardens and the celebrated Villa d'Este at Tivoli, the latter for his major patron, Cardinal Ippolito d'Este. After frescoing one of the narrative scenes in the Oratory of San Giovanni Decollato in the mid-1550s, he all but abandoned painting. Drawing after the antique was a lifelong undertaking for Ligorio, whose magnum opus, unfinished at the time of his death, was a magisterial encyclopedia of antiquities. Many of his manuscripts relating to this supremely ambitious, unrealized project survive.

20. *Female Winged Figure Drawing in the Company of a Putto (Study for an Allegory of Painting)*, 1550s

Red chalk, 7⁵⁄₁₆ x 4¹⁵⁄₁₆ in. (18.5 x 12.5 cm)

Provenance: Sir Joshua Reynolds (Plympton and London, 1723–1792) (Lugt 2364); N. F. Haym (Lugt 1970); Sir John and Lady Witt (?), London; their sale, Sotheby's, London, February 19, 1987, lot 237; acquired in 1987

Reference: Bohn 1988, pp. 120–21 n. 15, fig. 68

Seen in profile, the seated winged woman here wears an elaborate, antique-style coiffure and tunic and is bent over, intently drawing figures on a panel or sheet of paper. She is attended by a standing putto at her right, holding a small inscribed tablet, undoubtedly alluding to the genius of inspiration. The exquisitely refined study in red chalk in the Tobey Collection attests to Pirro Ligorio's consummate technique as a draftsman and his great literary sensibilities as an artist, displaying a vocabulary of the figure of classical monumentality and a learned mode of allegory. In many of its details the personification conforms to the description of "Pittura" in Cesare Ripa's *Iconologia*.[1] The sheet may be compared to a large number of other such composition drawings in this medium on white paper from Ligorio's Roman years, in the late 1550s or early 1560s (he probably arrived in the Eternal City in 1534), black chalk being another favorite medium of the artist's early-to-mature period.[2] His biographer Giovanni Baglione, who only cared about the artist's Roman career (from about 1534 to 1569), noted in 1642 that "many beautiful drawings by Ligorio are here in Rome in the possession of those who are knowledgeable about great virtuosos, which because of their execution and age give worthy testimony of his accomplishment" ("molti belli disegni del Ligorio sono qui in Roma appresso quelli, che delle opere de' gran Virtuosi hanno buon conoscimento; e per l'esperienza, e per l'età son degni di far fede della virtù di lui").[3] Ligorio spent the last fourteen years of his life in Ferrara, and the drawings from this late phase are almost exclusively in pen and ink with wash. Falling primarily in the early-to-mature part of his career, many of his red-chalk composition studies represent mythological subjects and are now dispersed in various collections, including the Louvre (inv. nos. 9692, 9685, 9695), the British Museum, London (inv. no. 1910-2-12-36), and in the pages of the *Libro dei disegni* at the Archivio di Stato, Turin, the latter a work that has been thoroughly analyzed only recently.[4] A carefully rendered study of a sibyl in red chalk, with an attendant genius, at The Metropolitan Museum of Art, New York (fig. 20.1), also demonstrates Ligorio's often Michelangelesque amplitude of form in his later Roman years.[5]

The Tobey drawing was used by the Bolognese painter and printmaker Bartolomeo Passerotti (see cat. no. 25) to produce the etching *Allegory of Painting* (fig. 20.2), which is signed with his monogram.[6] Various were the personifications of Painting

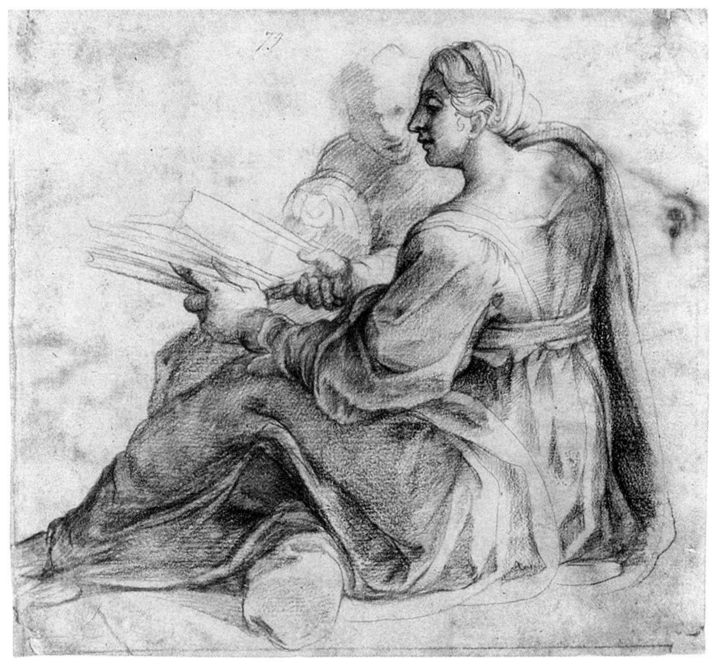

Fig. 20.1. Pirro Ligorio. *Seated Sibyl and Attendant Genius* (recto), 1550s. Red chalk, 9⁵⁄₈ x 10⁷⁄₁₆ in. (24.5 x 26.5 cm). The Metropolitan Museum of Art, New York, Pfeiffer Fund, 1962 (62.120.7)

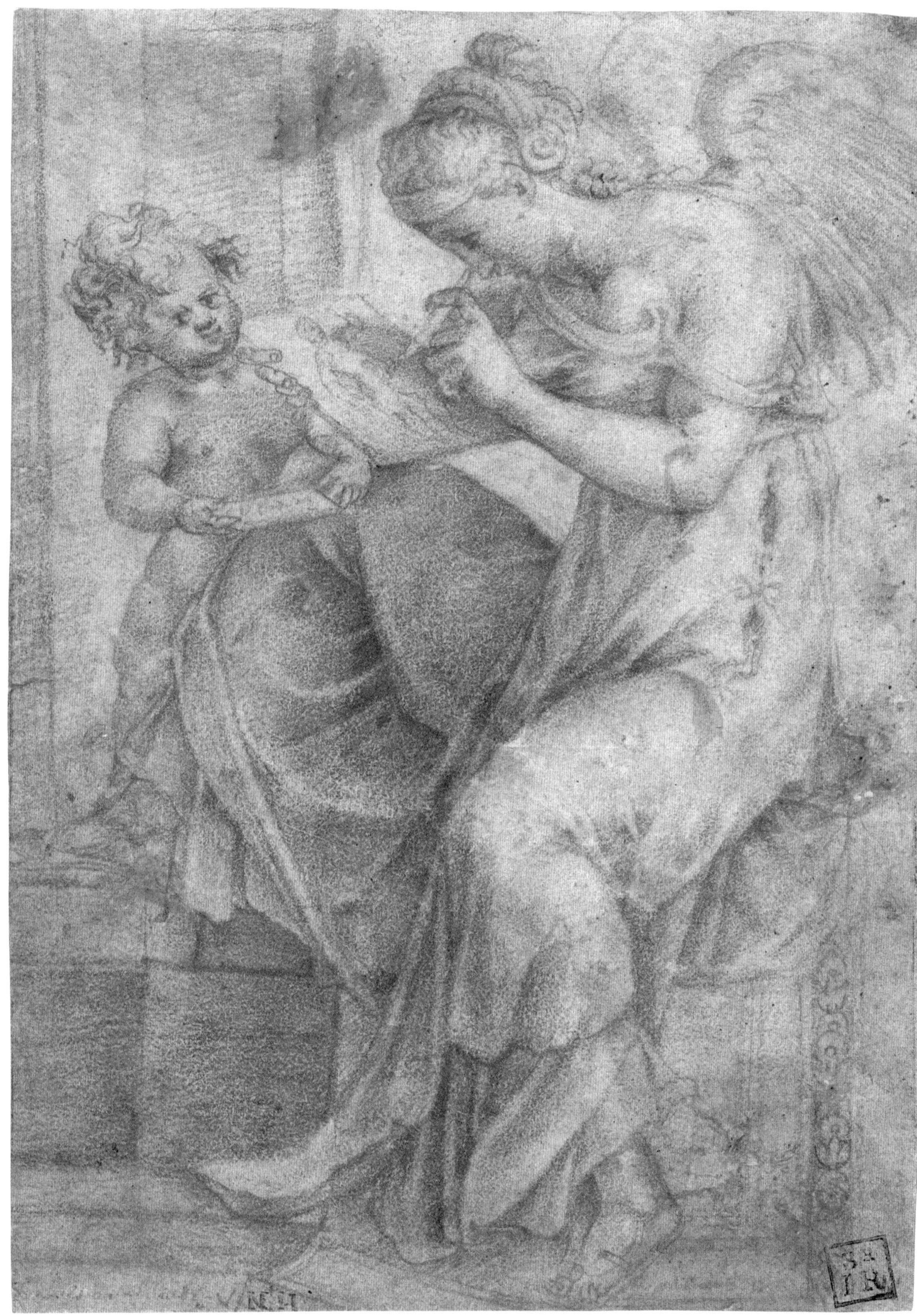

20

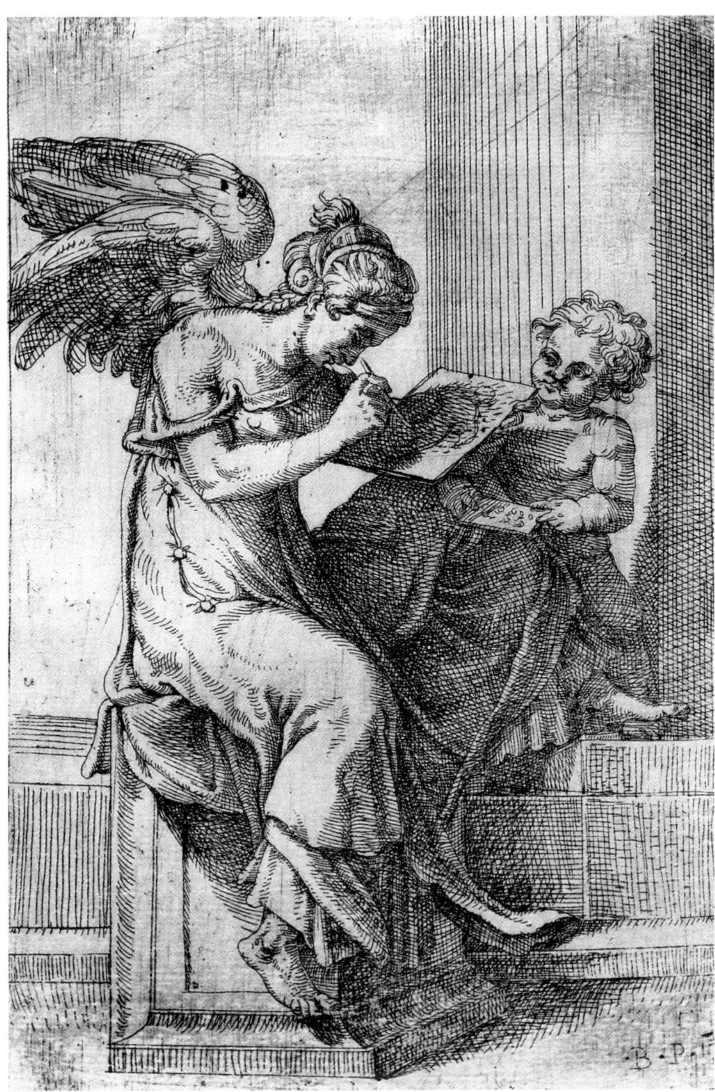

Fig. 20.2. Bartolomeo Passerotti. *Allegory of Painting*, 1550s. Etching, 11 ¹/₁₆ x 7³/₁₆ in. (28.1 x 18.2 cm). Graphische Sammlung Albertina, Vienna (It III 17, fol. 010 bottom; Bartsch XVIII.6.13)

proposed by authors of the period.[7] Passerotti seems to have made prints from a number of works by other artists that he studied in Rome in the 1550s (he is documented in the Eternal City in 1551, but by 1560 he had settled in Bologna), and it has been suggested that he may have even collaborated in person with Ligorio in producing his etching *Allegory of Painting*, after the present drawing.[8] As is most often true of drawings used in the production of prints, the design in the vigorously drawn Tobey study is in a mirror-orientation to the print (the process of printing from a plate reverses the design), and the etching omits the ornamental border relief around the block on which the woman sits.

CCB

1. See Ripa ed. 1976, under "Pittura."
2. See the fundamental publication on the drawings by Ligorio, Gere 1971.
3. The present author's translation of Baglione 1642, p. 9.
4. On the Turin *Libro dei disegni* (vol. 30, Ja.II.17, Archivio di Stato, Turin), see Volpi et al. 1994.
5. On this drawing, see Gere 1971, p. 244, pl. 15; Bean and Turčić 1982, p. 123, no. 114 and Linda Wolk-Simon, in Griswold and Wolk-Simon 1994, no. 68.
6. Compare DeGrazia Bohlin 1980, p. 23, no. 13 (6); Bohn 1988, pp. 120–21 (figs. 67, 68).
7. Compare Ripa ed. 1976, pp. 429–30.
8. Bohn 1988, p. 120.

JACOPO TINTORETTO

Venice, 1518–Venice, 1594

Tintoretto's entire career was tied to the Venetian state, which, save for a brief trip to Mantua to carry out work for the Gonzaga, he appears never to have left. His artistic beginnings are unrecorded and a number of different artists, among them Paris Bordone and Schiavone, have been posited as his master. Influences from central Italian Mannerism, transmitted to Venice by artists like Battista Franco and Francesco Salviati and also through the small-scale replicas of Michelangelo's sculptures that Tintoretto assiduously studied, shaped his style, as did the looming example of Titian. Although Tintoretto never achieved the same success with artistocratic and royal patrons as the older master, he procured prestigious commissions for vast series of canvases in Venetian churches and scuole and in the Palazzo Ducale. He also executed many altarpieces and portraits. Tintoretto's paintings are notable for their sure-handed rapidity of execution; expressive, flickering light; energetically posturing and dramatically foreshortened figures; naturalistic landscape passages; and high-pitched drama. By Venetian standards he was a prolific draftsman: roughly 130 drawings, mostly figure studies, ascribed to him survive.

21. *Study after Michelangelo's* Samson and Two Philistines (recto and verso), ca. 1550–55

Recto and verso: soft black chalk, highlighted with white gouache, on blue paper, 15³⁄₁₆ x 6⁷⁄₁₆ in. (38.6 x 16.4 cm)

Verso not reproduced

Provenance: Katrin Bellinger Kunsthandel, 1992; Trinity Fine Art Ltd., 1995; acquired in 1995

References: London 1992a, no. 10; New York 1995a, pp. 14–15, no. 4

As a painter and draftsman, Jacopo Tintoretto grappled with the influence of Michelangelo (1475–1564) for more than forty years, although he never traveled to Florence, or Rome, where the final part of the great Tuscan master's career unfolded.[1] Full of feral vigor, the Tobey drawing reprises the main view of a celebrated lost sketch-model in clay, wax, or plaster by Michelangelo, *Samson and Two Philistines*. The marble sculpture of *Samson* was intended as a pendant to Michelangelo's colossal *David* on the Piazza della Signoria, Florence, but was never executed. The great master's sketch-model (also lost), however, was much copied in bronze in the 1550s, during his lifetime.[2] While Michelangelo's first ideas for the *Samson* probably originated in 1508 or so, he seems to have developed the clay models of the statue only in the early 1530s. The actual source for Tintoretto's drawing was a copy after Michelangelo's original, as the Venetian painter apparently owned several small reproduction models (probably sent to him in Venice by Daniele da Volterra, as the early biographer Carlo Ridolfi stated).[3] Tintoretto seems to have studied especially closely the replicas of Michelangelo's sculptures in the New Sacristy (Medici Chapel) of San Lorenzo in Florence, adapting the designs of *L'Aurora* (Dawn) and *Crepuscolo* (Dusk) for his lost frescoes on the facade of Ca' Gussoni in Venice, about 1550–52, which are recorded in engravings by Anton Maria Zanetti of about 1760.[4]

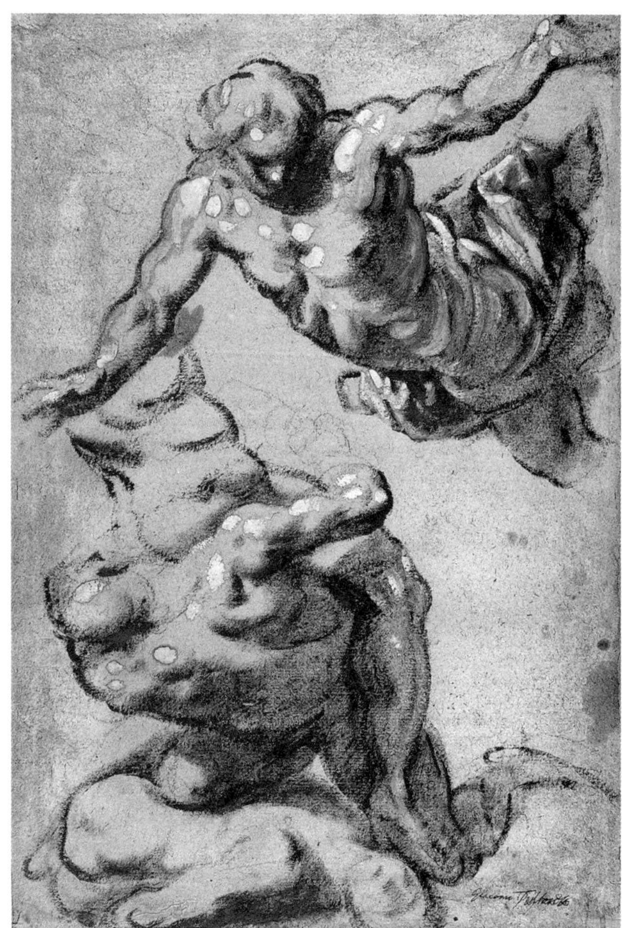

Fig. 21.1. Palma Il Giovane. *Studies for Christ the Redeemer and Samson and Two Philistines* (recto), ca. 1600–20. Brush with brown and white oil paint, over black chalk, on light brown paper, 16 x 10⁵⁄₁₆ in. (40.6 x 26.1 cm), maximum; sheet with irregular borders. The Metropolitan Museum of Art, New York, Purchase, Florence B. Selden Bequest, 1998 (1998.32a)

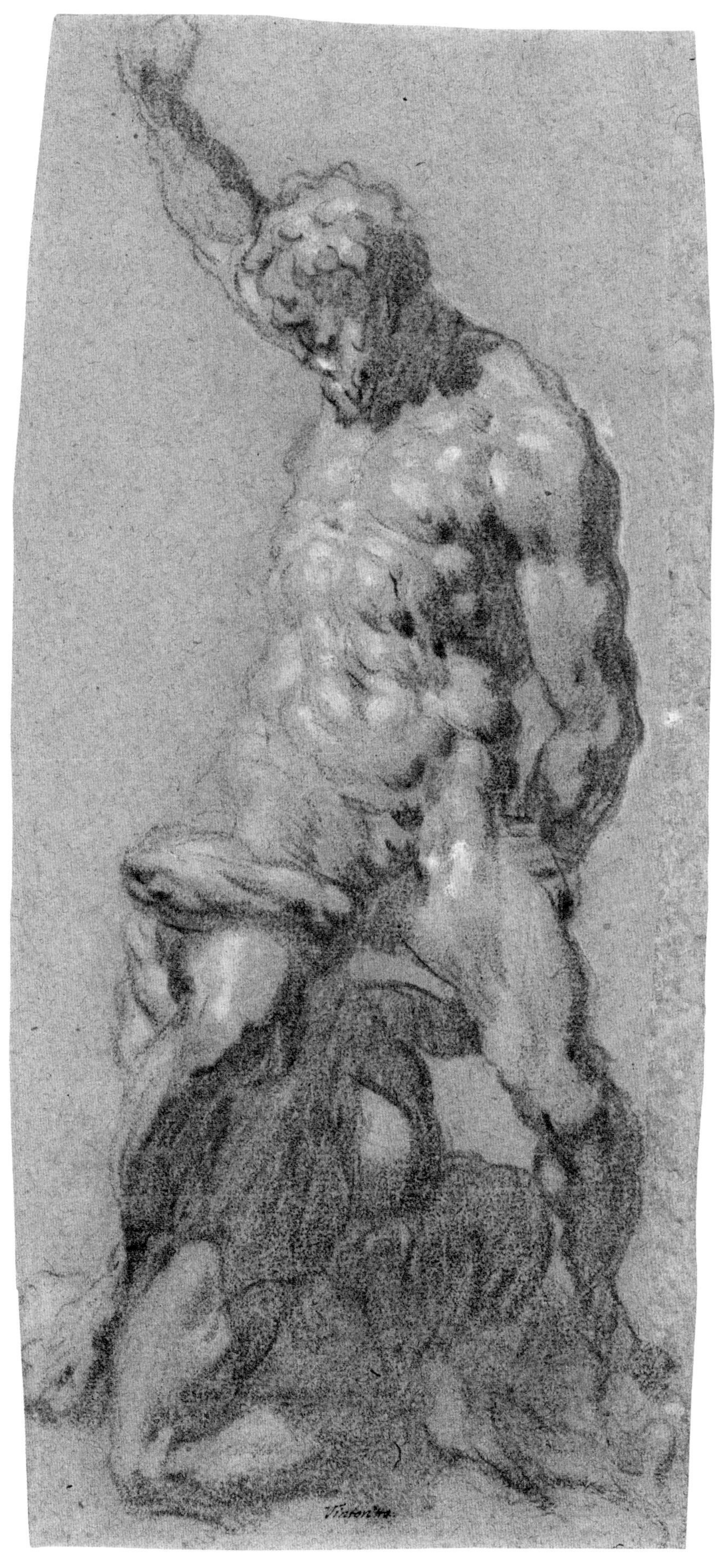

21

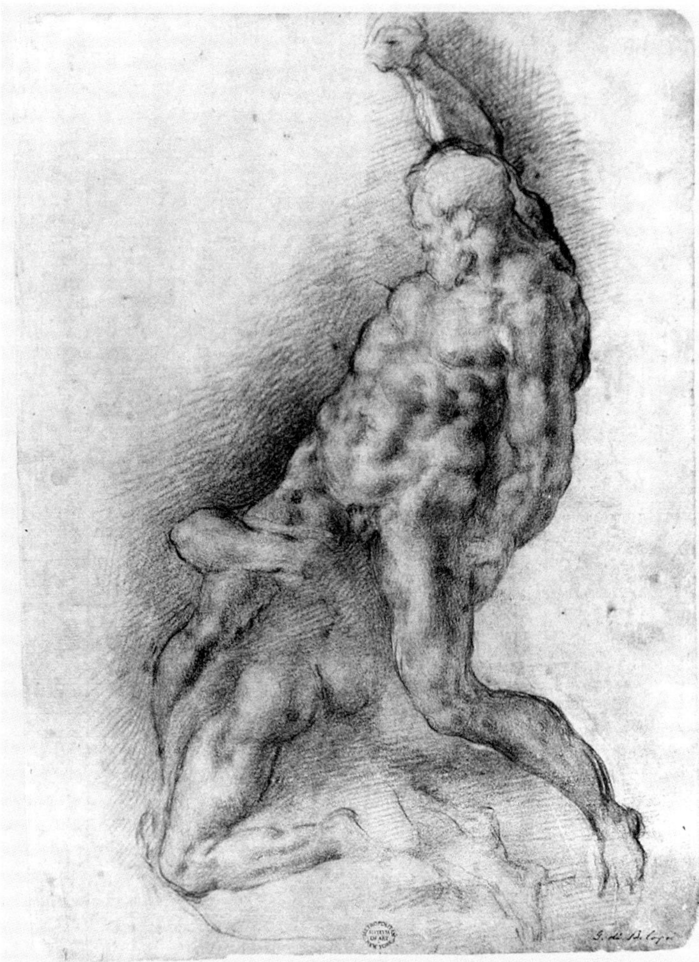

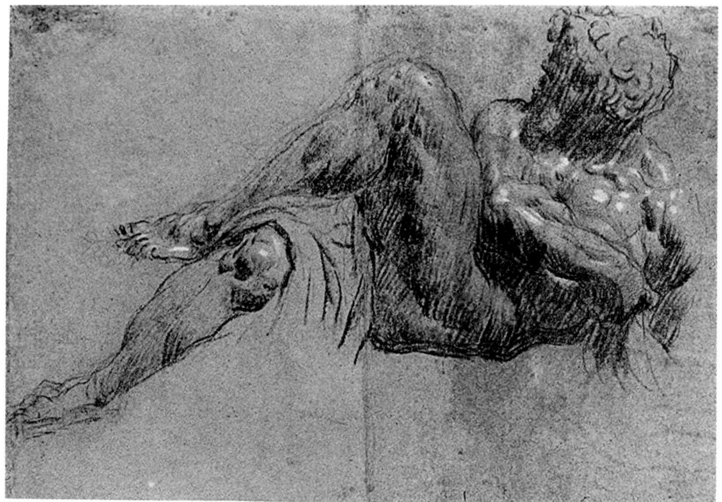

Fig. 21.3. Tintoretto, after Michelangelo. *Study after* Il Giorno *(Day) in the San Lorenzo New Sacristy*, ca. 1550–55. Black and white chalk on blue paper, 13¾ x 19⅞ in. (35 x 50.5 cm). The Metropolitan Museum of Art, New York, Rogers Fund, 1954 (54.125)

Fig. 21.2. Giovanni Battista Naldini, after Michelangelo. *Samson Slaying the Philistine*, 1550s. Red chalk on paper, 13⅛ x 9⅛ in. (33.4 x 23.2 cm). The Metropolitan Museum of Art, New York, Gift of Cornelius Vanderbilt, 1880 (80.3.301)

More than thirty drawings after the statuette of *Samson and Two Philistines* by Tintoretto and his workshop have been claimed to exist,[5] and they vary in quality of execution. Certain groups of them portray the sculpture from different angles. The best examples are at the Ashmolean Museum of Art and Archaeology, Oxford;[6] Musée Bonnat, Bayonne;[7] Musée des Beaux-Arts et d'Archéologie, Besançon; Harvard University Art Museums, Cambridge, Massachusetts; Christ Church, Oxford (JBS 763);[8] Kupferstichkabinett, Staatliche Museen zu Berlin;[9] in a private collection, New York;[10] and one formerly in the Kurt Meissner Collection, Zurich.[11] The pose of the statuette of *Samson and Two Philistines* in the Tobey drawing, which is without doubt autograph, is closest to that in the sheets in Berlin, Cambridge, and that formerly in the Kurt Meissner Collection.

Drawn in red chalk, a more detailed copy by the Florentine painter Giovanni Battista Naldini (ca. 1537–1591), who was an equally ardent admirer of Michelangelo, at The Metropolitan Museum of Art, New York, renders the same statue type but from a slightly different angle (fig. 21.2).[12] Naldini's rendition of the subject likely dates to a similar time as the Tobey drawing by Tintoretto. A large sheet in the Metropolitan by Palma Il Giovane, who was Tintoretto's younger contemporary in Venice, renders at lower left an expressive copy after Michelangelo's lost statue, probably also derived from a replica (fig. 21.1). Tintoretto produced a number of compelling drawings after three-dimensional copies of Michelangelo's sculptures, as this was a frequent exercise in draftsmanship for him. A monumental example is represented in a double-sided sheet done in the same technique as the Tobey drawing and which portrays the back view of a replica of the figure of *Il Giorno* (Day) in the New Sacristy of San Lorenzo (fig. 21.3).[13]

CCB

1. See especially Ilchman and Saywell 2007.
2. On Michelangelo's lost sketch-model, compare De Tolnay 1948, p. 102, figs. 277–78; Pope-Hennessy and Radcliffe 1970, pp. 186–95.
3. Ridolfi 1648, vol. 2, p. 6.
4. Nichols 1996.
5. Edward Saywell in Madrid 2007, p. 403 n. 3.
6. Inv. no. KP II 714. Rome 1991, p. 48, no. 21.
7. Bean 1960, no. 170.
8. There are two double-sided sheets with drawn versions after copies of Michelangelo's *Samson and Two Philistines* at Christ Church, Oxford (inv. nos. 0359 [JBS 763] and 0360 [JBS 764]), of which the first is the better drawing. See Byam Shaw 1976, vol. 1, pp. 205–6, nos. 763, 764.
9. Regarding the Berlin sheet (inv. no. KdZ 5228), see Edward Saywell in Madrid 2007, pp. 402–5, nos. 55–56.
10. Linda Wolk-Simon in Griswold and Wolk-Simon 1994, p. 130, no. 116.
11. Sumowski 1967, p. 50, no. 73.
12. Bean and Turčić 1982, p. 146, no. 138.
13. Ibid., pp. 242–43, no. 248.

MARCO PINO

Siena, 1521–Naples, 1583

A native of Siena, Marco Pino was active in Rome and Naples for most of his long career. The early influence of Domenico Beccafumi, his Sienese master, was eclipsed by that of Perino del Vaga, whose workshop in Rome he joined in 1544, assisting in the decorations of the Sala Paolina in Castel Sant'Angelo. Following Perino's death in 1547, he collaborated with two other former disciples of that artist, Pellegrino Tibaldi and Daniele da Volterra, in Rome. In the mid-1550s, he went to Naples, executing a number of altarpieces for churches in the city. During the last two decades of his life he returned intermittently to Rome, where he participated with a number of other painters in one of the most important artistic commissions of the second half of the sixteenth century, the decorations of the Oratory of the Gonfalone. In addition to Beccafumi, Perino, and Tibaldi, other artists who shaped Marco Pino's style as both a draftsman and a painter include Taddeo Zuccaro, Francesco Salviati, and Michelangelo.

22. *Saint John the Evangelist Immersed in a Cauldron of Boiling Oil*, 1568–69

Pen and brown ink, brown wash, heightened with white, over black chalk, on gray-green paper, 16 x 10¾ in. (40.8 x 27.3 cm)
Annotated in brown ink at lower right: *Barocci*

Provenance: Sale, Paris, Nouveau Drouot, October 10–11, 1983, no. 79 bis, ill. (as attributed to Trometta); Anna Maria Edelstein, London, 1985; Jeffrey Horvitz, Cambridge, Mass.; sale, Sotheby's, New York, January 23, 2008, no. 21; acquired in 2008

References: Wolk-Simon 1991–93, pp. 36–39, no. 9; Leone de Castris 1994, p. 85 n. 33; Zezza 1994, p. 152, fig. 18, and p. 155 n. 12; Rome 1995, pp. 35–36, 342 (under no. 196), 435 n. 32; Zezza 1995, p. 115; Leone de Castris 1996, p. 198; Zezza 2003, p. 152, pl. 24, p. 163, fig. IV.I, and p. 315, no. C3

In August 1568, Giovanni Battista Capogalli commissioned Marco Pino to paint an altarpiece for his chapel in the church of Santi Apostoli in Rome. The contract stipulated that the painting was to be executed in oil, that it was to be completed by the Feast of the Nativity the following year, and that it was to depict Saint John the Evangelist, to whom the chapel was dedicated, in a cauldron of boiling oil.[1] The subject was culled from the *Golden Legend*, a thirteenth-century compendium of hagiographic apocrypha: "The Emperor Domitian, hearing of his fame, summoned him to Rome, and had him plunged into a cauldron of boiling oil which was set up before the gate called the Porta Latina; but the saint came forth untouched."[2] Described in the early seventeenth century by the biographer Giovanni Baglione, who praised the artist's "buona maniera" and "gran diligenza,"[3] Marco Pino's painting vanished during an early eighteenth-century renovation of the church, but its appearance is recorded in the Tobey drawing—undoubtedly a *modello* for this important lost work. Here, the artist faithfully records the salient elements of the narrative, setting the scene before a colonnade meant to suggest the Porta

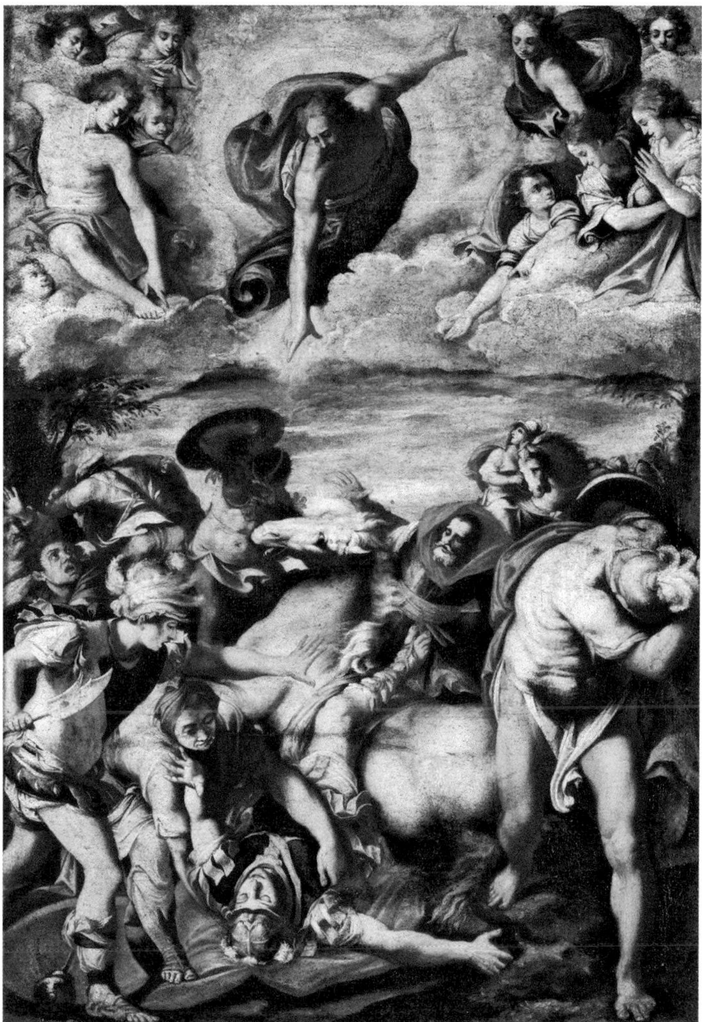

Fig. 22.1. Taddeo Zuccaro. *Conversion of Saint Paul*, ca. 1560–65. Fresco. Frangipani Chapel, San Marcello al Corso, Rome

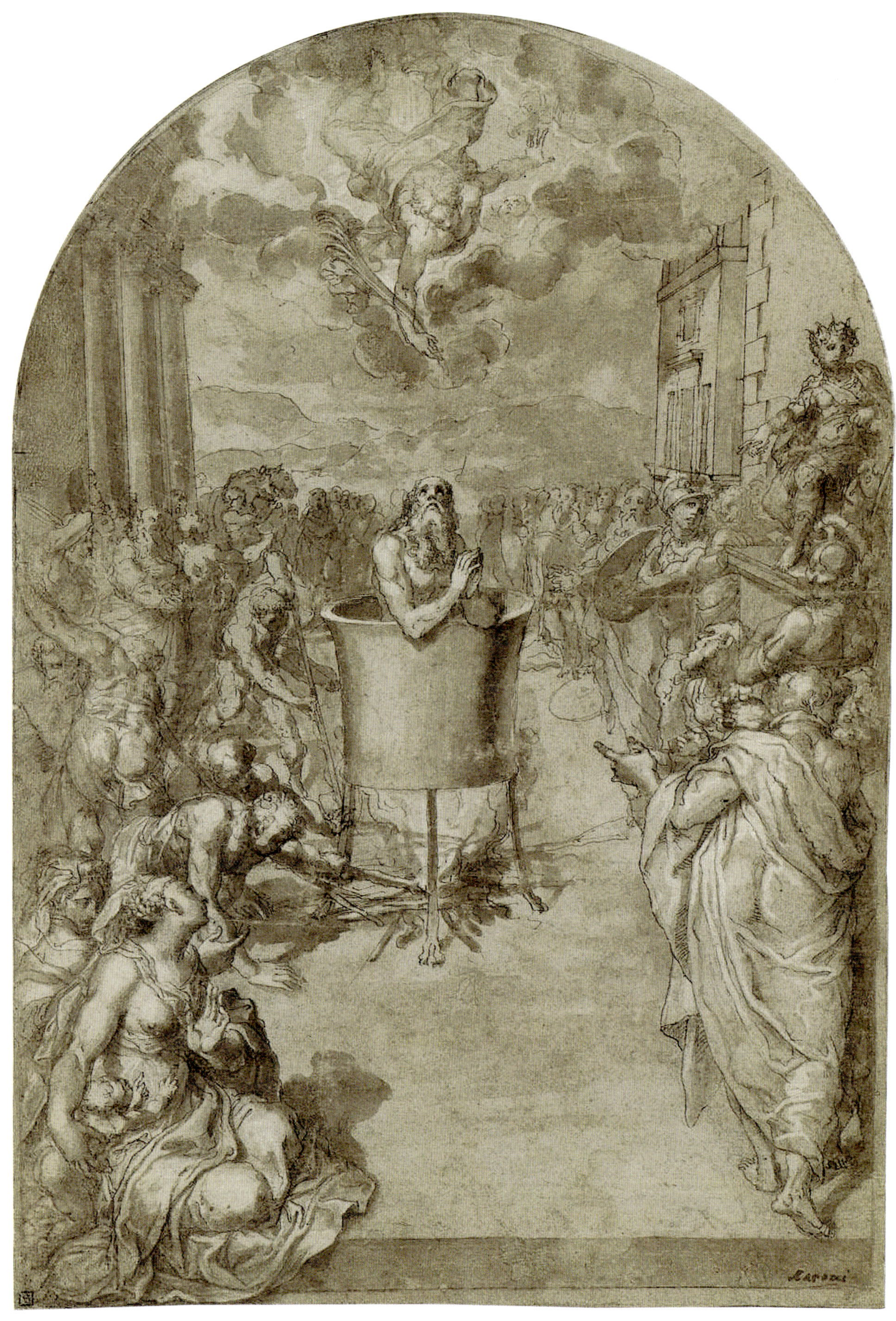

22

Latina and showing the emperor Domitian enthroned at the right, gesturing at the brutal tableau he commanded take place.

The rich, painterly combination of media and the rhetorically posturing figures cloaked in ample draperies that characterize this sheet are hallmarks of Marco Pino's graphic style. The artist gathered inspiration from a number of painters active in Rome in the mid-sixteenth century, above all Pellegrino Tibaldi, with whom he collaborated in the 1550s, and Taddeo Zuccaro. The influence of both artists may be discerned here— Tibaldi's in the muscular, extravagantly contorted figures, and Taddeo's in the particular types, characterized by elongated proportions and swollen hips. A specific homage to Taddeo is the angel emerging from the clouds, which is based on the

Christ descending from heaven in that artist's *Conversion of Saint Paul* in the Frangipani Chapel in San Marcello al Corso (fig. 22.1).[4] A drawing by Marco Pino of angels floating on clouds in an arched field, executed in the identical technique as the *Saint John the Evangelist* modello, may be a study for the upper part of the composition.[5]   LWS

1. Wolk-Simon 1992, no. 9. The contract is transcribed in Masetti Zannini 1974, pp. 83–84.
2. Voragine ed. 1969, p. 58.
3. Baglione 1642, p. 31.
4. The stylistic and compositional sources are elaborated at length in Wolk-Simon 1992, no. 9. The annotation at the lower right records an old attribution to the painter Federico Barocci, who worked in Rome with Taddeo Zuccaro in the 1550s.
5. Sotheby's, Monaco, June 20, 1987, no. 15, ill., present whereabouts unknown.

JOHANNES STRADANUS (JAN VAN DER STRAET)

Netherlandish, 1523–1605

Known best by his latinized name, Jan van der Straet was born in Bruges, but left his native Flanders about 1545 to pursue a career in Italy. He worked as a designer of tapestries and as a painter, mainly assisting Giorgio Vasari on major commissions in Florence, but is most remembered for his innumerable, and successful, print designs, which combine Mannerist grace and anecdotal detail in an attractive style that never belies his Northern origin. All of his prints were published in Antwerp, although he appears to have spent only two years outside Italy after his move.

23. *Theagenes Conquering a Stray Sacrificial Bull*, 1602

Pen and brown ink, brown wash, heightened with white gouache, over a sketch in black chalk, on pale brown tinted paper, 7¹³⁄₁₆ x 11⁵⁄₁₆ in. (19.9 x 28.7 cm) Framing line in pen and gray ink; inscribed on recto in pen and brown ink at lower right: *ioan Stradanus 1602*; inscribed on verso in graphite at upper left: *Aukt. Oct 1928 / Coll. Six / Coll. Welcker, Amsterdam*; at lower left, collector's mark of Welcker (Lugt 2793ᶜ), and below, his inventory number *Inv. Nᵉ 698* in pen and black ink; to the right, the collector's mark of Witt (Lugt 646ᵃ)

Provenance: Gerard Leembruggen Jz. (The Hague and Hillegom, 1801–1865); his sale, Amsterdam, March 5–8, 1866, lot 617 (to Six for 3 guilders); Jan Pieter Six (Amsterdam, 1857–1926), and his sale, Frederik Muller & Cie, Amsterdam, October 17–18, 1928, perhaps from lot 503 or 504 (to Brandt for 310 or 80 guilders, respectively);[1] Albert Welcker (Amsterdam, 1884–1957); W. R. Jeudwine, London, in 1955 or 1956 (?); P. & D. Colnaghi, London, in 1956; John Clermont Witt (London, 1907–1982); sale, Christie's, London, December 9, 1980, lot 203; acquired in 2005

References: London n.d., no. 59; London 1956b, no. 11; London 1963, no. 13; Boon 1992, vol. 1, p. 352, under no. 200; Baroni Vannucci 1997, no. 584, ill.; Van Sasse van Ysselt 2003, p. 8 n. 5; Van Sasse van Ysselt 2009; Marjolein Leesberg in Bruges 2008–9

Although Stradanus's work is remarkably diverse, a considerable part is devoted to depictions of hunts. Apart from an extensive set of tapestries for the Medici villa at Poggio a Caiano near Florence (1567–77), which seems to have been at the origin of his interest in the theme, five print series of a total of more than 120 hunting scenes have been made after his drawings.[2] As indicated by its title, the largest and most exotic of these series takes as its subject not only *Venationes ferarum, avium, piscium* (Hunts of wild animals, birds, and fishes) but also a few *Pugnae bestiariorum & mutuae bestiarum* (Fights of gladiators and beasts among each other), such as the one reproduced here in figure 23.1.[3]

Engraved by Netherlandish printmakers and published in Antwerp, the *Venationes* were aimed at an international audience, addressed in the Latin verses. Many of the subjects are based on ancient literature and may have been suggested by the Florentine humanist Luigi Alamanni, who worked with Stradanus on some of his series of drawings and prints.[4] Several of the prints in the *Venationes* refer directly to Pliny the Elder's

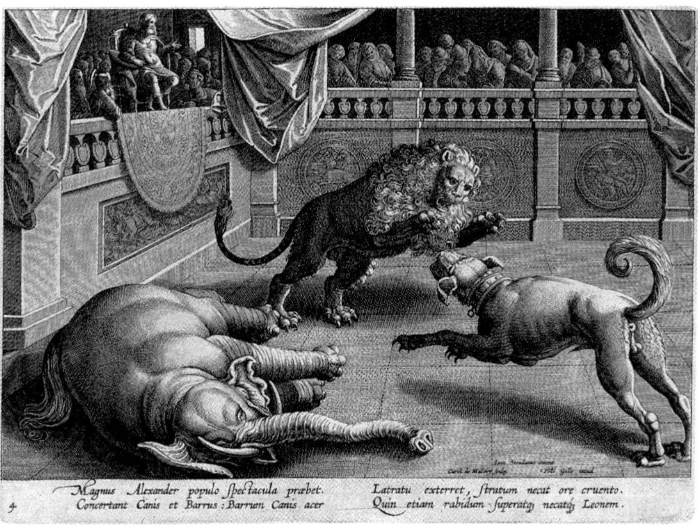

Fig. 23.1. Karel de Mallery, after Johannes Stradanus. *Alexander the Great Watching a Fight between an Elephant, a Lion, and a Dog*, ca. 1596. Engraving, 14½ x 11 in. (36.8 x 27.9 cm). The Metropolitan Museum of Art, New York, Harris Brisbane Dick Fund, 1945 (45.68, pl. 4)

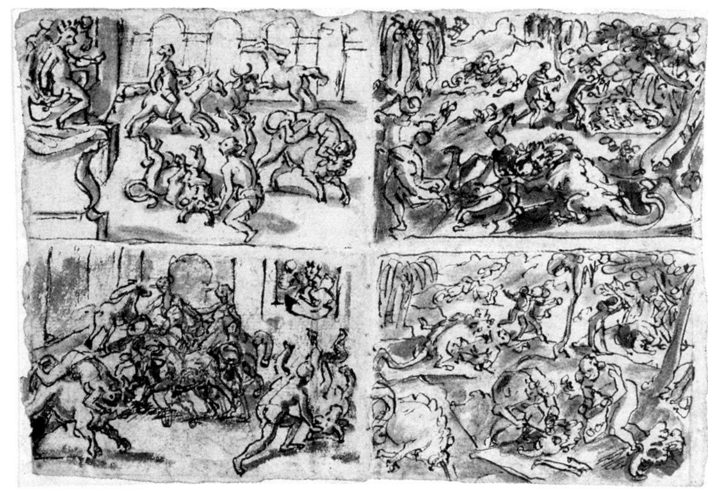

Fig. 23.2. Johannes Stradanus. *Study Sheet with Sketches of Theagenes Conquering a Stray Sacrificial Bull and of an Indian Dragon Hunt* (recto), 1602 or before. Pen and brown ink, corrected with white gouache(?), over a sketch in black chalk, 6⅛ x 8⅞ in. (15.5 x 22.5 cm). Cooper-Hewitt, National Design Museum, Smithsonian Institution, New York (1901-39-154)

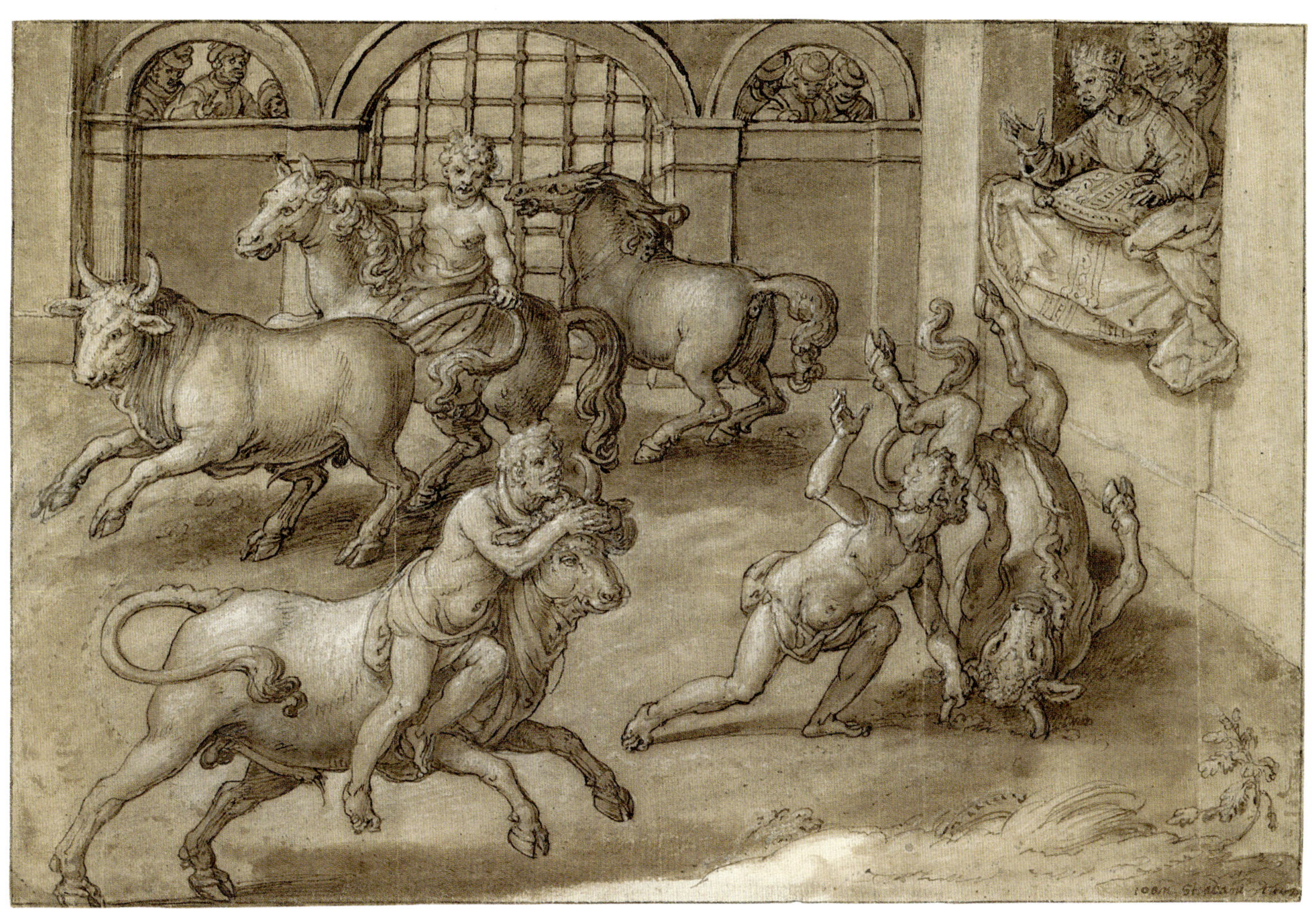

23

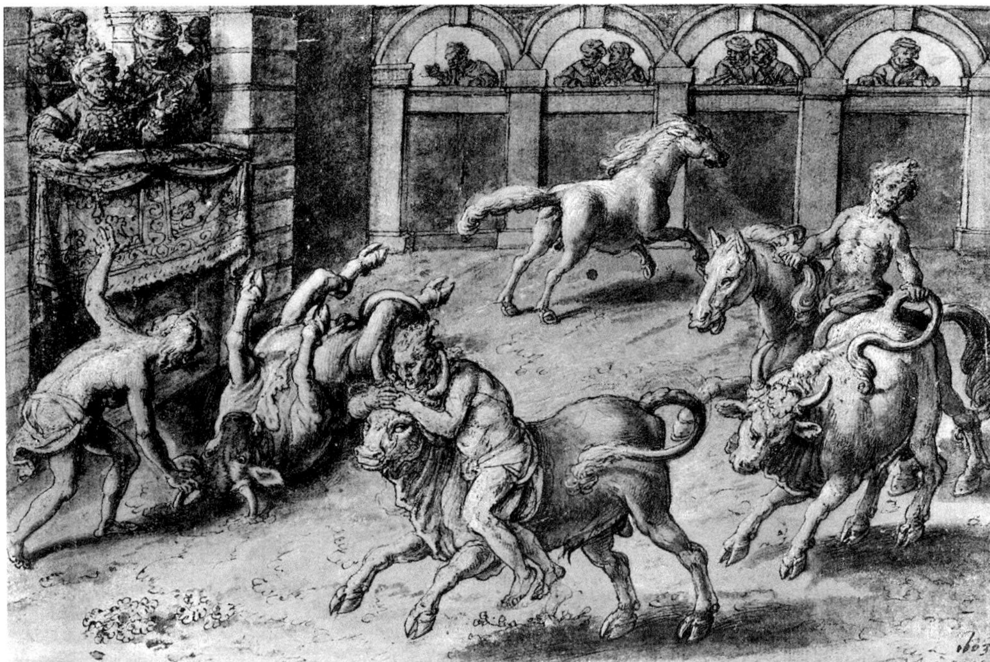

Fig. 23.3. Johannes Stradanus. *Theagenes Conquering a Stray Sacrificial Bull*, 1603. Pen and brown ink, heightened with white gouache, 6¹⁵⁄₁₆ x 11 in. (17.7 x 28 cm). Whereabouts unknown

Natural History, as proven by the artist's own inscriptions on a few sheets in a unique, albeit dismembered, sketchbook preserved at the Cooper-Hewitt, National Design Museum.[5] No print after the drawing in the Tobey collection is known;[6] dated 1602, it probably was made only after the publication of the first edition of the series, shortly after 1596.[7] The artist seems to have been fascinated by this peculiar bull-fight, or to have struggled with its depiction, for at least two studies for the composition can be found in the Cooper-Hewitt sketchbook. One of these, at lower left on a sheet containing four sketches (fig. 23.2),[8] must have directly preceded the Tobey drawing, notwithstanding differences in the architecture and the grouping of the figures and animals in the background.

The sketches contain no reference as to the literary source of the scene depicted but have been connected with a passage from Book VIII, chapter 70 of *Natural History*, where Pliny describes that "it is a device of the Thessalian race to kill bulls by galloping a horse beside them and twisting back the neck by the horn."[9] More recently, Dorine van Sasse van Ysselt convincingly linked the drawing with the story of one particular Thessalian, Theagenes, described in Book X, chapters 28–30, of the Greek novel *Aethiopica* by Heliodorus of Emesa, who lived in the third century A.D.[10] The scene takes place near the end of the novel, when Chariclea's lover Theagenes, a noble from Thessaly (north of Athens), is held in captivity by the former's father, the Ethiopian king Hydaspes,[11] who plans to sacrifice him with other captives and animals. Three of these, a bull and two horses, are suddenly startled by a "camelopard" (camel, leopard, lion, and swan in one) and break away, provoking great

fear among the king and other onlookers. Theagenes is seen three times in the Tobey drawing: once galloping on the white horse "side by side with [the bull] so that the flesh of the animals touched and the horse's breath and sweat mingled with the bull's"; then, having leaped from the horse onto the bull, at the moment when he "put his head between the bull's horns, placed his arms around them like a crown, and laced his fingers together over the bull's forehead"; and finally, after the bull "stumbled, fell head first, and rolled over his shoulders and back" and we see "his horns fixed in the ground and his rooted head immovable, while his legs thrashed about in vain," while Theagenes "used only his left hand to hold him down; his right, he held up to the sky and waved repeatedly."[12]

The sketch at upper left in the Cooper-Hewitt *taccuino* is a variation illustrating the same passage, but it is unrelated to any known completed drawing by Stradanus; it may be an earlier, rejected version of the Tobey composition. A third sketch, on the back of the sheet, does relate to a finished sheet of the same subject (fig. 23.3),[13] the last known work by the artist, dated one year after the Tobey drawing. This second version of the composition was also not engraved, but there are some indications that Stradanus was intending to continue the success of his earlier sets of hunting scenes with a new one, and he may have planned to include one of the two depictions from the story of Theagenes, as has been suggested by Alessandra Baroni.[14] They have approximately the same size and technique as the print models for the earlier series.[15] A design for a frontispiece, dated 1599 and inscribed with the name of the Antwerp engraver and publisher Philips Galle, also not engraved, could well have been meant for this new series.[16] Stradanus's death in 1605 may have been the reason why it was eventually aborted.[17]

SA

1. There is no reason to assume (as does Van Sasse van Ysselt 2009, p. 60 n. 1) that the drawing was in album 5 of the collection of works on paper owned by Jan Six I (sale, Amsterdam, April 6, 1702); the mention of the Six collection on the verso of the drawing undoubtedly refers to that of Jan Pieter Six.
2. For Stradanus's hunting scenes in different media, see Bok-van Kammen 1977; for the tapestries, see Baroni Vannucci 1997, nos. 683.1–683.12, ill.; for the prints, see Leesberg 2008, vol. 3, nos. 403–526, ill.; and Marjolein Leesberg in Bruges 2008–9. I thank the authors of the forthcoming exhibition catalogue *Stradanus (1523–1605): Court Artist of the Medici* (Groeningemuseum, Bruges), referred to here as Bruges 2008–9, for kindly providing manuscripts of their essays to me.
3. Leesberg 2008, vol. 3, no. 469, ill. For the other prints of the *Venationes*, see ibid., nos. 465–68, 470–526.
4. On Alamanni, see Gert Jan van der Sman in Bruges 2008–9.
5. Notably on 1901-39-114, 1901-39-124, 1901-39-153, 1901-39-157, 1901-39-158, and 1901-39-2501 (Baroni Vannucci 1997, nos. 630, 617, 590, 615, 640, 616, ill.).
6. The drawing is not incised for transfer (*pace* Van Sasse van Ysselt 2009, pp. 59, 60 n. 1).
7. The dating of the series is based on some of the preparatory drawings, inscribed "1596" (see Baroni Vannucci 1997, nos. 472, 474, 479, 492–93, 497, ill.).
8. Ibid., no. 609, ill. For the preliminary sketches on the verso of the sheet, see note 13, below.
9. Translation by Harris Rackham in Pliny ed. 1938–62, vol. 3, p. 127; for the original text, see ibid., p. 126: "Thessalorum gentis inventum est equo iuxta quadripedante cornu intorta cervice tauros necare." The connection with this passage in Pliny was already made in an inscription on the mount of the drawing reproduced here as fig. 23.2. For the Thessalian bull-fights, see also Heliodorus ed. 1960, vol. 3, p. 112 n. 1; and Van Sasse van Ysselt 2009, pp. 57–58.
10. Van Sasse van Ysselt 2009. Stradanus seems to have been the first to depict a scene from the novel, apart from a few medieval manuscripts; for these and later depictions, most of which appear to be by Northern artists, see Bonger-van der Borch van Verwolde 1941; Stechow 1953; Pigler 1974, vol. 2, pp. 343–44; and Brugerolles and Guillet 1994–95, pp. 364–67, under no. 85.
11. Well before the identification of the exact subject of the scene, the similarly crowned onlooker in the drawing reproduced in fig. 23.3 had already been described as "a negro potentate" (Reitlinger 1922, p. 136). In his sketch for this drawing at the Cooper-Hewitt, National Design Museum, Smithsonian Institution, New York (see note 13, below), Stradanus himself denotes him with the word "moro"; and both this sheet and the Tobey drawing, which were briefly brought together by the London dealer W. R. Jeudwine in or before 1956, were catalogued by him as "Bull-fight at a Moorisch court" (London n.d., nos. 58–59).
12. Heliodorus ed. 1960, vol. 3, pp. 109–13; the translation is from Heliodorus ed. 1957, pp. 267, 268.
13. Present whereabouts unknown, formerly in the collection of Henry Scipio Reitlinger, and following his death, sold at auction at Sotheby's, London, June 23, 1954, lot 791, where it was acquired by W. R. Jeudwine (Reitlinger 1922, no. 27, ill.; W. R. Jeudwine in London 1956a, no. 43; Baroni Vannucci 1997, no. 585, ill.). For the preliminary sketch on the verso of the sheet in the Cooper-Hewitt sketchbook reproduced here in fig. 23.2, see Baroni Vannucci 1997, no. 610. The sketchbook also contains a quick study of the bull with the man on its back at center (1901-39-126 verso; ibid., no. 634, ill.), with Stradanus's inscription "a stare col vise tra le corne e co[n] le mane sula fronte che/il toro vede lume corendo" (to remain with the head between the horns, and with the hands on the forehead, so that the bull sees the light when it runs).
14. Baroni Vannucci 1997, p. 316, under no. 585; see also ibid., p. 320, under no. 586, pp. 320–21, under nos. 605 and 608, and p. 327, under no. 641; see also Marjolein Leesberg in Bruges 2008–9.
15. All known drawings for the earlier series are mentioned throughout Leesberg 2008. For the definitive drawn model for the frontispiece of the *Venationes* in the print room of the Warsaw University Library (inv. no. zb. d. 7535), see Jerzy Wojciechowski in Łódź and Warsaw 2007, no. 158, ill.
16. Rijksmuseum, Rijksprentenkabinet, Amsterdam, inv. no. RP-T-1997-33 (Fuhring 1989, vol. 1, no. 94, ill.; Schapelhouman 1998, pp. 370–71, no. 3, fig. 2; Marjolein Leesberg in Bruges 2008–9).
17. At least two other finished drawings of a hunting scene were also not engraved: one in the Rijksmuseum, Rijksprentenkabinet, Amsterdam, inv. no. RP-T-1961-91 (Baroni Vannucci 1997, no. 581, ill., where it is related—without reason, it seems—to a work from one of the earlier print series, described in Leesberg 2008, vol. 3, no. 443, ill.); the second is at the Lyman Allyn Art Museum, New London, Connecticut, 1977.10 (Van Sasse van Ysselt 2003, pp. 2–3, fig. 2). There are several preliminary sketches in the Cooper-Hewitt sketchbook for which no corresponding prints or finished drawings exist: 1901-30-122, 1901-39-128, 1901-39-166, 1901-39-167, 1901-39-594, 1901-39-597 recto and verso, and 1901-39-159 (Baroni Vannucci 1997, nos. 594, 608, 607, 605, 606, 641, ill.; for the subject of the first drawing, see Bruges 2008–9). Of course, as none of these can be dated securely, they may also be compositional ideas that were rejected, either by Stradanus himself or by Galle, before the publication of the *Venationes*. It is interesting to note that the Tobey drawing once was folded in four, perhaps when it was sent by Stradanus from Florence to Galle in Antwerp.

PELLEGRINO TIBALDI

Puria di Valsolda, 1527–Milan, 1596

Pellegrino Tibaldi was a painter and architect who worked principally in Rome, Bologna, Milan, and Madrid. His formative years were spent in Bologna, although nothing is known about his artistic training and early activity before his appearance in Rome in the mid-1540s, when he joined the group of artists working with Perino del Vaga on the decorations of the papal apartments in Castel Sant'Angelo. In the years following Perino's death, he collaborated with two members of that circle, Daniele da Volterra and Marco Pino, in chapels in the Trinità dei Monti and San Luigi dei Francesi, and also carried out frescoes for Pope Julius III in the Vatican Palace and elsewhere. In 1555, Tibaldi returned to Bologna, where his major patron, Cardinal Giovanni Poggi, commissioned him to execute frescoes in his palace and in his family chapel in San Giacomo Maggiore. The muscular, posturing figures, pictorial illusionism, and narrative structure of the Palazzo Poggi frescoes—Tibaldi's masterpiece—abound with references to Perino, Michelangelo, and other Roman prototypes, while bearing the distinctive imprint of the artist's fanciful, witty, and prodigious imagination. Tibaldi's later years were given over primarily to architecture. Cardinal Carlo Borromeo engaged him on a number of building projects in Milan; he also designed a series of magnificent windows for the cathedral. In 1586, Tibaldi moved to Spain at the invitation of Philip II, succeeding Federico Zuccaro in the decorations of the Escorial and resuming his career as a painter. He returned to Milan shortly before his death in 1596. Tibaldi was an important conduit for introducing the Roman maniera to Bologna, influencing such artists as Prospero Fontana, Orazio Samachini, Bartolomeo Passerotti, and Annibale Carracci.

24. *The Avenging Archangel Saint Michael with Other Figures*, ca. 1554–56

Pen and brown ink, brush with gray and brown wash, over black chalk, highlighted with white gouache on beige paper; some outlines stylus-incised, 6⁷⁄₁₆ x 7¹³⁄₁₆ in. (16.3 x 19.8 cm)
The Metropolitan Museum of Art, New York, Promised Gift of David M. Tobey

Provenance: Sir Joshua Reynolds (Plympton and London, 1723–1792) (Lugt 2364); T. Banks (Lugt 2423); sale, Christie's, Monaco, June 20, 1994, lot 13; acquired in 1994

Reference: Christie's, Monaco 1994, no. 13

As is evident from its repeatedly reinforced, vibrantly kinetic outlines, the Tobey composition sketch by Pellegrino Tibaldi still bears some echoes of Perino del Vaga's late pen-and-ink drawing style, which is not altogether surprising, given that Tibaldi had assisted Perino in 1545–47 in the fresco and stucco decorations of the apartments of Pope Paul III at the Castel Sant'Angelo, Rome (see cat. nos. 10 and 11), and that Tibaldi took over the project after Perino's death in 1547, completing it in 1549. By the early 1550s, however, Tibaldi's dazzling gifts as a draftsman and painter of complex illusionistic compositions with the human figure had fully matured in highly original work for Roman and Bolognese patrons. The present drawing, dating to about 1554–56, vividly illustrates his dynamic new manner.

The pen-and-ink outline of the arched top of the intended composition is faintly evident here, an indication of the correct orientation of the Tobey drawing with respect to the related final work. In this luminous, exuberant evocation, the nude figure of the Archangel Saint Michael is seen in a horizontal pinwheel pose of flight, in the act of vanquishing Lucifer by the hair with the rebellious angels falling, while the good angels witness the scene amid the clouds of heaven (Revelation, 12:7–9). The horizontal pose of Saint Michael exudes action with a crystalline elegance. Some of the earliest owners of the Tobey composition, however, among them the great British painter and collector Sir Joshua Reynolds (1723–1792), preferred to view the drawing in a vertical orientation, as evidenced by the placement of their stamps on the sheet.

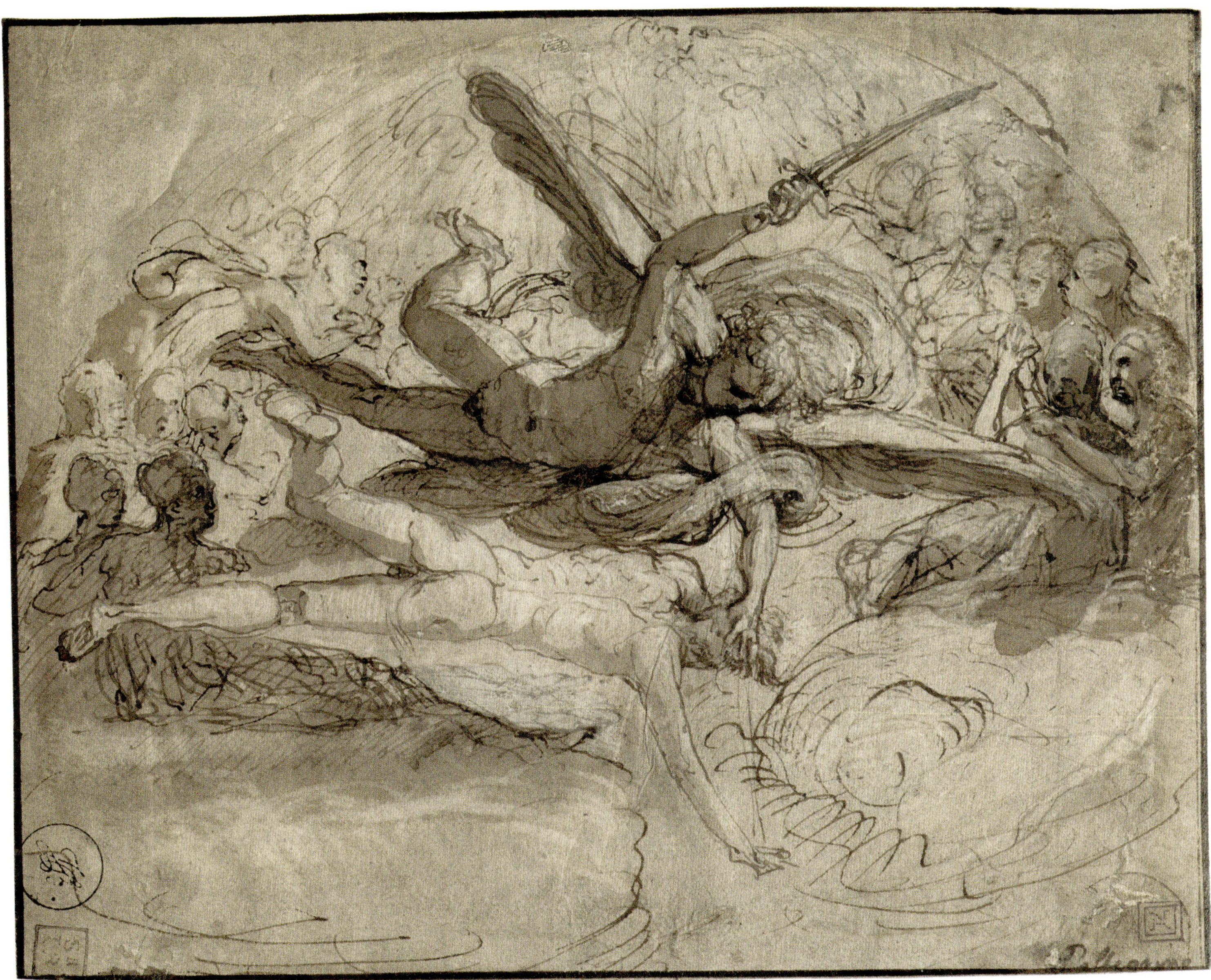

24

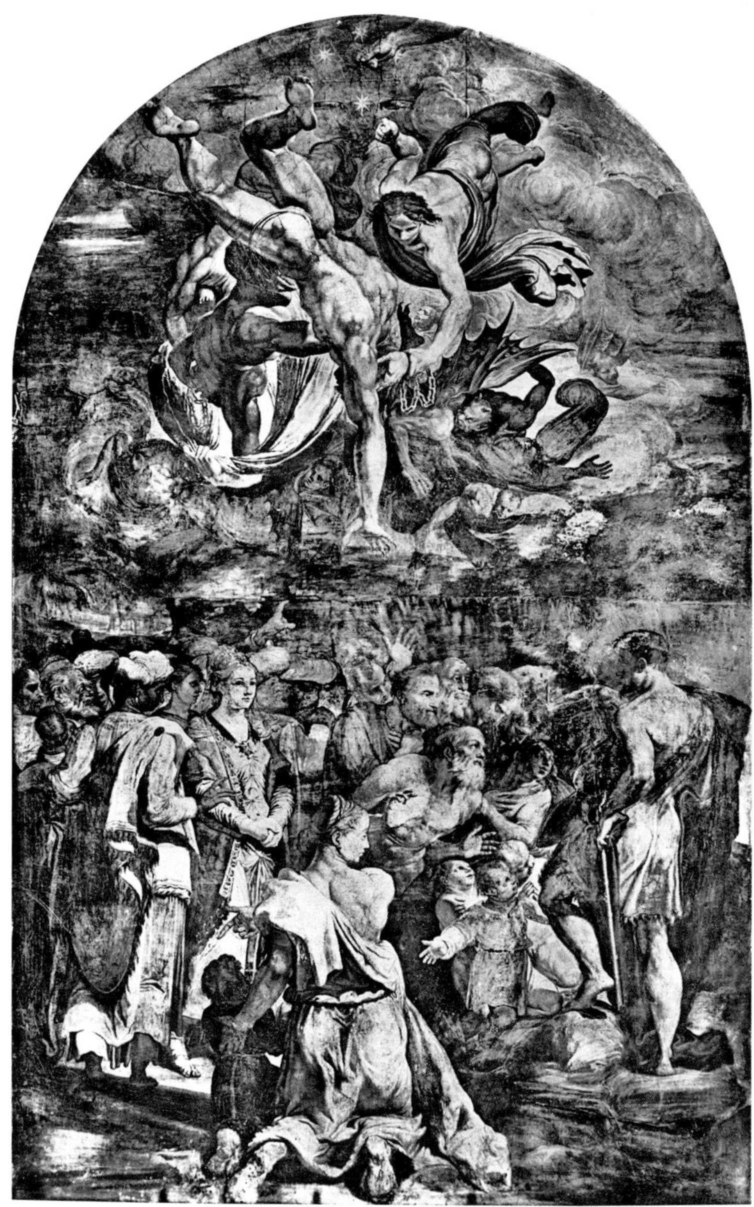

Fig. 24.1. Pellegrino Tibaldi. *Saint John the Baptist Baptizing the Multitude*,
ca. 1554–56. Fresco. Left wall, Poggi Chapel in San Giacomo Maggiore, Bologna

The Tobey composition sketch was intended for the upper portion of Tibaldi's fresco *Saint John the Baptist Baptizing the Multitude*, on the left wall of the Poggi Chapel in the church of San Giacomo Maggiore, Bologna (fig. 24.1), probably executed in 1554–56[1] for Cardinal Giovanni Poggi, who died in February 1556 and was buried in this sacred space. The composition is part of a program in which each frescoed scene on a wall is conceived as an extension of the actual architecture of the chapel and is intended to be seen from the entrance to the altar.[2]

Portrayed in the Tobey composition are the combined episodes of the victory of the Archangel Michael over Lucifer and the fall of the rebel angels. In the fresco, the figure of Michael, who is ethereal and of slender, nearly wiry bodily proportions in the present drawing, would be rendered monumental, with an imposing display of Michelangelesque musculature.

Pellegrino Tibaldi's composition sketch for the lower part of the scene of *Saint John the Baptist Baptizing the Multitude* at The Metropolitan Museum of Art, New York (fig. 24.2),[3] is done

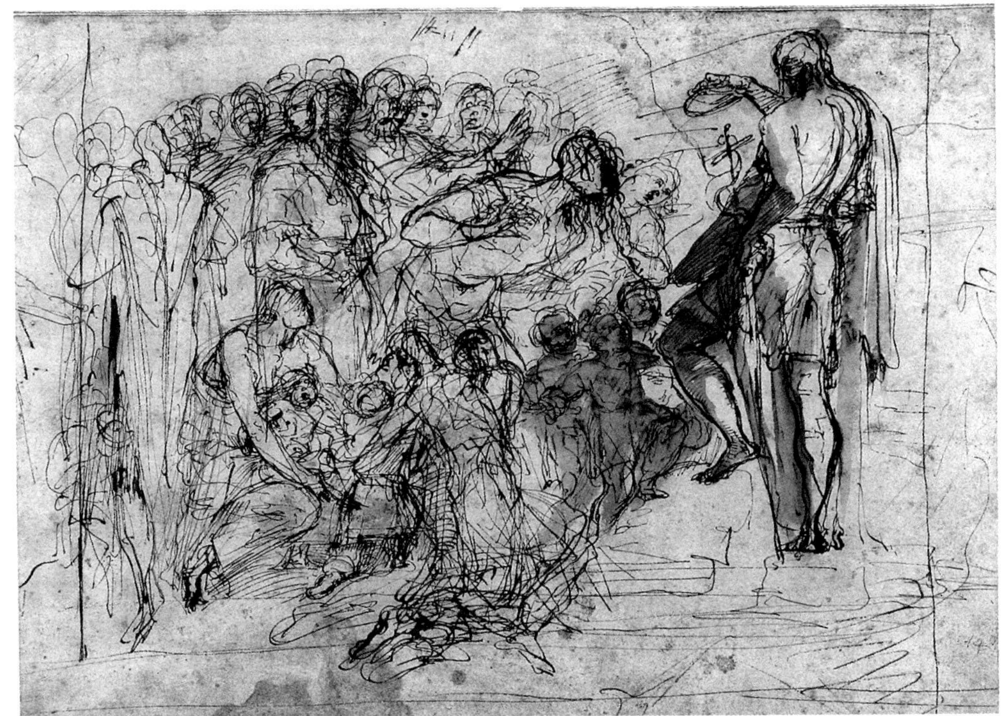

Fig. 24.2. Pellegrino Tibaldi. Sketch for the lower portion of *Saint John the Baptist Baptizing the Multitude*, ca. 1554–56. Pen and brown ink, brush and brown wash, 9⁵⁄₁₆ x 12¹¹⁄₁₆ in. (23.7 x 32.3 cm). The Metropolitan Museum of Art, New York, Bequest of Walter C. Baker, 1971 (1972.118.272)

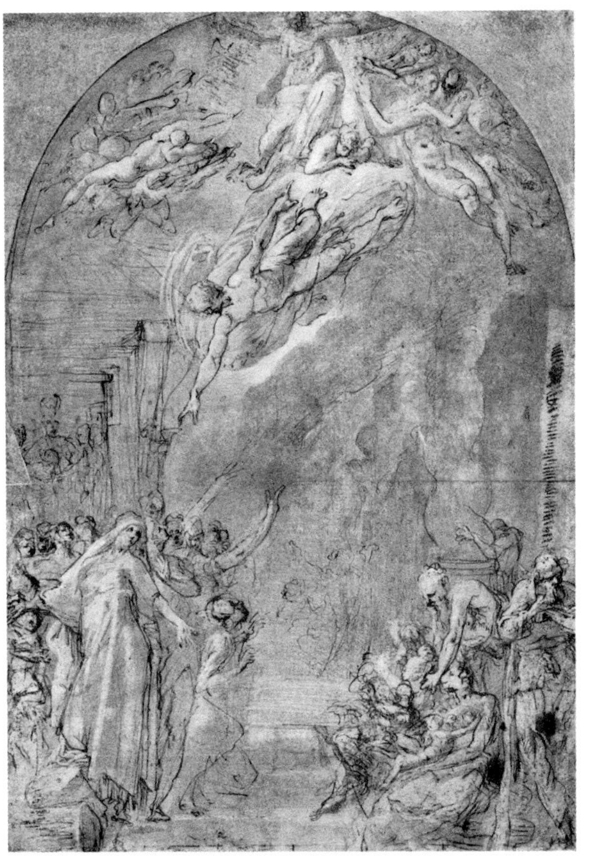

Fig. 24.3. Pellegrino Tibaldi. *The Conception of Saint John the Baptist* (*The Annunciation of the Coming of Saint John the Baptist*), ca. 1554–56. Pen and brown ink, brush and brown wash, over red chalk, highlighted with white gouache, 16⅝ x 11¼ in. (42.3 x 28.6 cm). The Royal Collection. © Her Majesty Queen Elizabeth II (RL 5965)

with a very similar, if less individualized figural style, a slightly freer pen technique, and only a selective use of wash. The two drawings were undoubtedly made at the same moment in the creative process, but it is unlikely that they were originally portions of the same sheet, given their subtle physical differences, as one scholar has rightly noted.[4] While the scale of the figures is nearly the same in the two drawings, the dimensions of the Metropolitan Museum sheet are substantially larger (even accounting for the fact that collectors often cropped sheets of paper).[5] The Tobey work is also executed in a more complex, painterly technique with extensive black-chalk underdrawing and white-gouache highlights, with a more careful attention to the overall final effects of lighting in the composition. The style and elaborate media of the Tobey sheet further resemble one of the preparatory studies for the composition on the opposite wall of the Poggi Chapel, *The Conception of Saint John the Baptist* (a scene also sometimes identified as *The Annunciation of the Coming of Saint John the Baptist*), now in the Royal Library, Windsor (fig. 24.3).   CCB

1. This is the dating proposed by Jürgen Winkelmann in Fortunati Pietrantonio et al. 1986, vol. 2, pp. 486–87.
2. See Vittoria Romani in Bologna, Washington, D.C., and New York 1986–87, pp. 204–6, under no. 77.
3. Bean and Turčić 1982, p. 241, no. 246.
4. William M. Griswold in a letter to the owners, dated November 17, 1994.
5. The Metropolitan Museum of Art sheet measures 9⁵⁄₁₆ x 12¹¹⁄₁₆ in. (23.7 x 32.3 cm), whereas the Tobey sheet is 6⁷⁄₁₆ x 7¹³⁄₁₆ in. (16.3 x 19.8 cm).

BARTOLOMEO PASSEROTTI

Bologna, 1529–Bologna, 1592

One of the leading artists in Bologna in the later sixteenth century, Bartolomeo Passerotti was connected to the city's most elevated cultural and intellectual circles. Correggio, Parmigianino, and Pellegrino Tibaldi were important formative influences; his style also reflects his absorption of elements of Venetian and Lombard painting, and of mannerist tendencies from local Bolognese artists such as Prospero Fontana. Active as a painter, draftsman, and engraver, Passerotti executed a number of altarpieces, portraits, and genre scenes. The last of these, often satiric and ribald in character, were greatly admired by the Carracci. He was also famous as a collector of antiquities—an interest that may have been nurtured during early trips to Rome—establishing a much-frequented museum in Bologna. Some of Passerotti's portraits depict fellow antiquarians.

25. *The Boncompagni Dragon*

Pen and brown ink over black chalk; left side made up, 14¼ x 17⅜ in. (36.1 x 44 cm)

Provenance: Philip Pouncey, London; sale, Sotheby's, New York, January 12, 1994, lot 38; acquired in 1994

References: Höper 1987, vol. 2, no. A 200 (as attributed to Passerotti); Llewellyn and Romalli 1992, no. 42

This study of a fantastic dragon, its scaly wings outstretched as it bursts from a heraldic shield like a blossom exploding from the calyx of some monstrous botanical specimen, exhibits the hard, incisive line characteristic of Bartolomeo Passerotti's draftsmanship. In both style and subject matter, it is akin to a small group of drawings of dragons' heads by the artist, including an example in the Palazzo Rosso, Genoa (fig. 25.1).[1] That sheet has been linked to a portrait drawing by Passerotti in the Uffizi of his Bolognese compatriot, Pope Gregory XIII Boncompagni (r. 1572–85)—whose family emblem was a dragon—which was probably executed during a trip the artist is believed to have made to Rome in 1572 following the papal election (fig. 25.2).[2] In a biography of 1584, Raffaele Borghini recorded that Passerotti painted a portrait of Gregory XIII; the Uffizi study may have been executed in connection with this important commission.[3]

The Uffizi drawing shows the pope seated, raising his right hand in blessing, and resting his left hand on a celestial globe that is embraced in the batlike wing of a Boncompagni dragon. Beside him stands a personification of Prudence, whose mirror-attribute (in which the pope's profile is reflected) is adorned with two more of these ubiquitous Boncompagni heraldic beasts. Although the Tobey sheet has not been connected with a specific work, the particular subject matter points to a Boncompagni patron, as has long been recognized: the drawing presumably relates to a commission Passerotti received from the pope or a member of his family in Bologna, where the artist spent most of his career. Exactly what this design was for is uncertain, however. It might be an idea for a small-scale object such as a furniture mount or other decorative element, or for a bronze, marble, or stucco relief. The indications of vertical framing elements or supports suggest a wall or other surface to which the dragon was meant to be attached. Dragons similar to the one in Passerotti's drawing populate the late sixteenth-century fountain in the Piazza Grande in Modena; perhaps a similar setting was envisioned for this Boncompagni beast.

LWS

1. See Höper 1987, vol. 2, no. Z 115 and pl. 44a; other examples are published in ibid., nos. Z 109 and Z 259.
2. Another version, formerly in the collection of Kurt Meissner, Zurich, was sold at Christie's, London, July 3, 1998, lot 7 (see Höper 1987, vol. 2, no. Z 345, pl. 30a). It is accepted as autograph by Höper and by Angela Ghirardi in Ghirardi 1990, under no. 25, pp. 179–81. Babette Bohn raises the possibility that the ex-Meissner drawing is instead by Domenico Tibaldi, who executed a print after Passerotti's portrait drawing. See Bohn 1996, under no. 011 [B.7 (16)]; Bohn 1994, p. 166.
3. At least two portraits of Gregory XIII by Passerotti have been identified, and both have been related to the Uffizi study. See Ghirardi 1990, pp. 179–81, no. 25 (Museen der Stadt, Gotha); and Höper 1987, vol. 2, p. 109, no. G 208 (Casa Sacchetti, Rome). Passerotti also executed a drawing after the monumental bronze sculpture of Gregory XIII by Alessandro Menganti on the facade of the Palazzo Comunale, Bologna; see Llewellyn and Romalli 1992, no. 41.

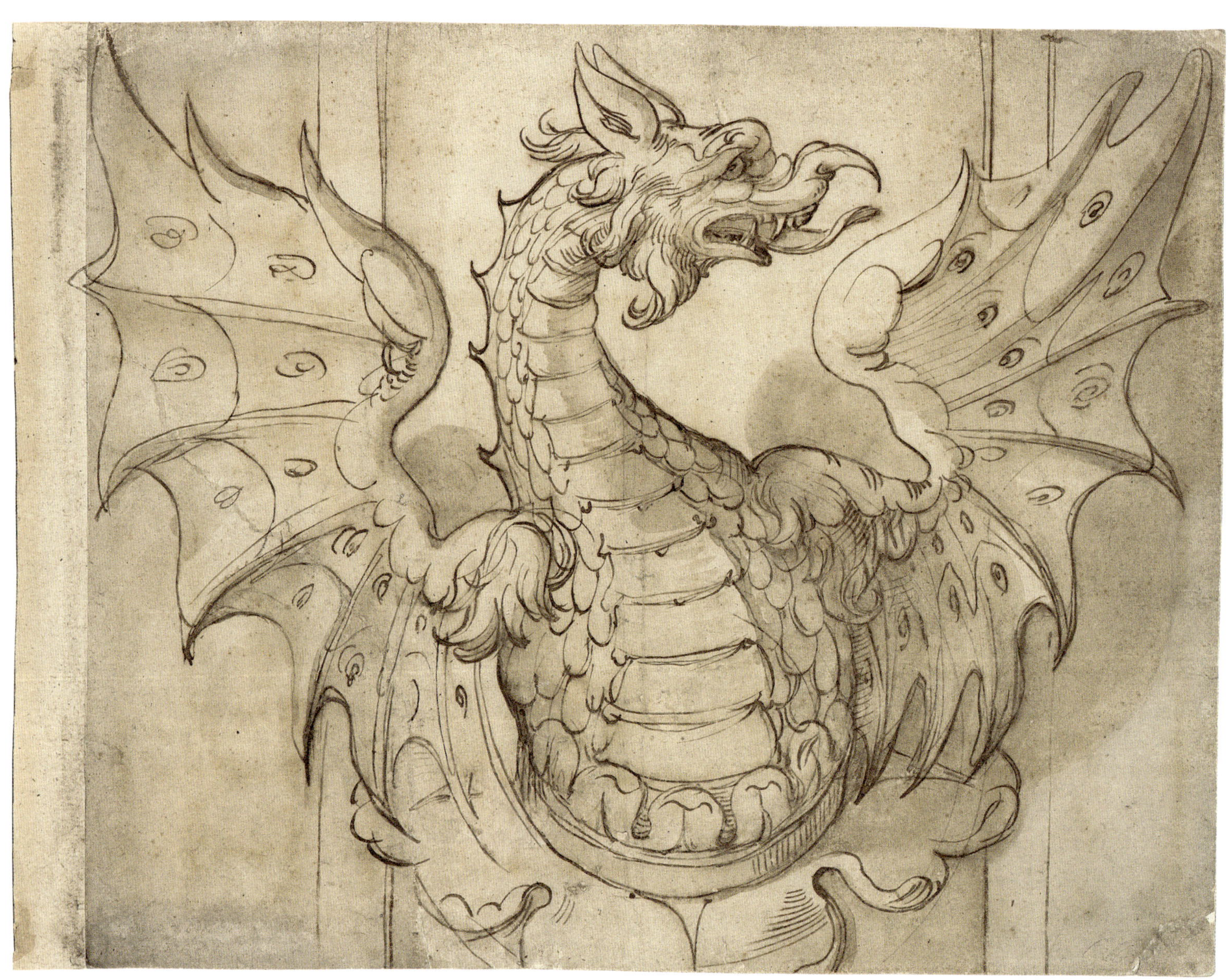

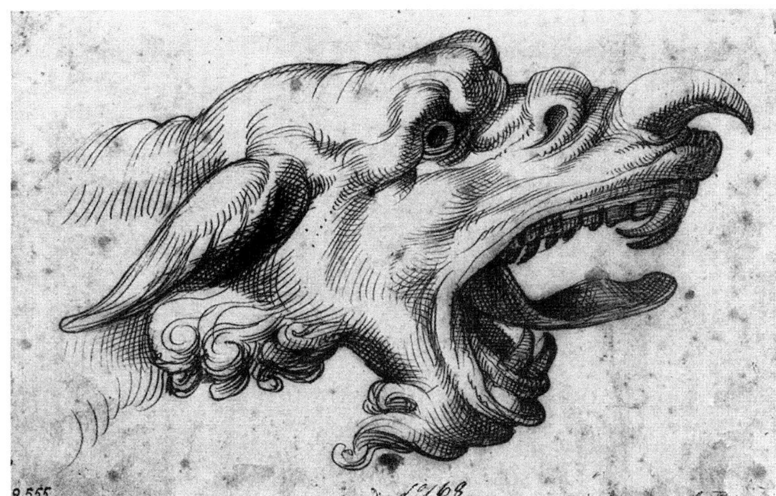

Fig. 25.1. Bartolomeo Passerotti. *Dragon Head*. Pen and brown ink. Collezione Disegni di Palazzo Rosso, Genoa (2555)

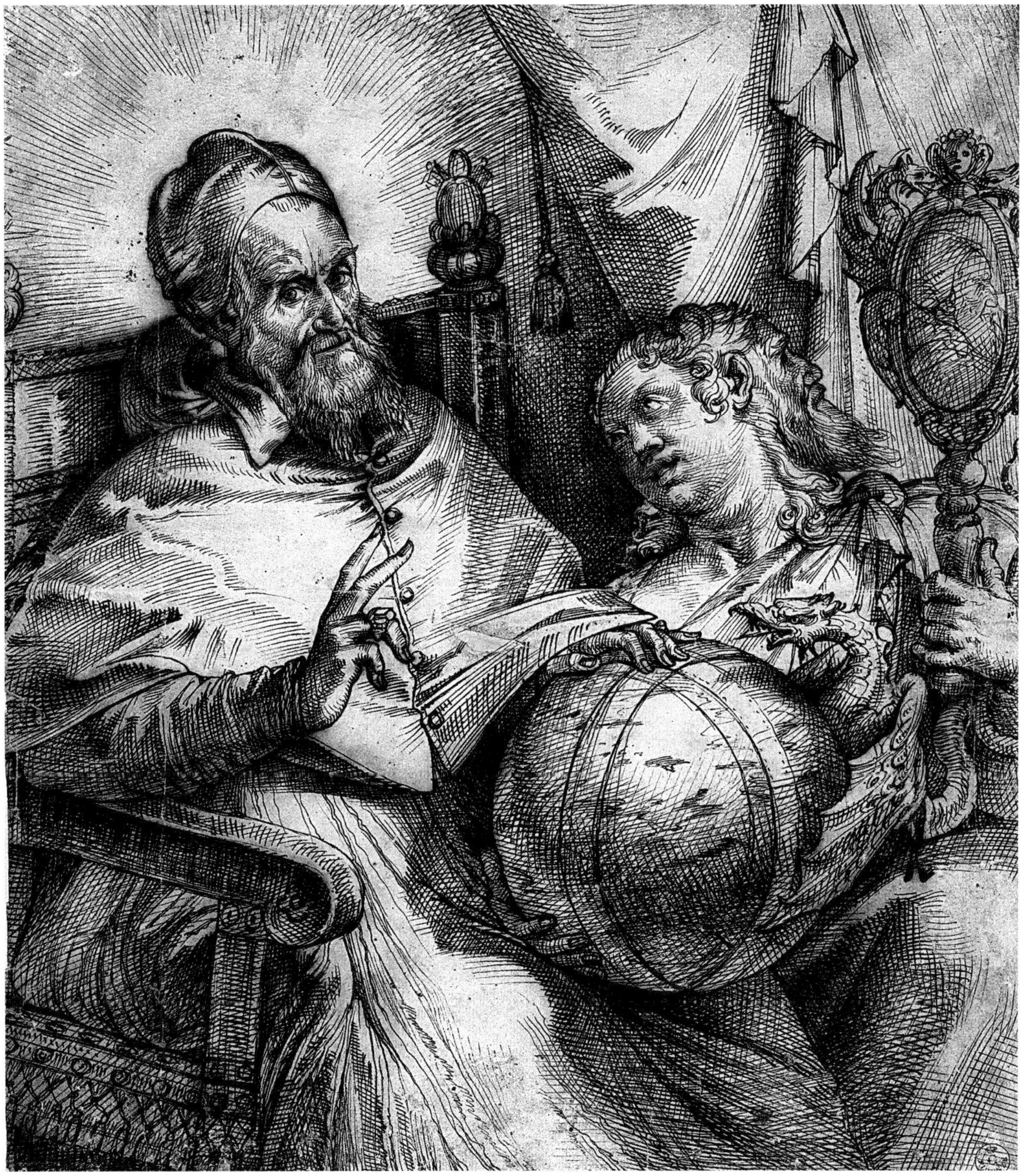

Fig. 25.2. Bartolomeo Passerotti. *Portrait of Pope Gregory XIII Boncompagni*, 1572. Pen and brown ink, 18⅜ x 15¹¹⁄₁₆ in. (46.7 x 39.8 cm). Galleria degli Uffizi, Florence (6157F)

TADDEO ZUCCARO

Sant'Angelo in Vado (the Marche), 1529–Rome, 1566

As the epitaph on his tomb in the Pantheon recounts, Taddeo Zuccaro was viewed by contemporaries as the spirit of Raphael reborn. At the age of fourteen he went to Rome, where he executed painted facades in the manner of Polidoro da Caravaggio—work that earned him the admiring attention of Michelangelo, according to accounts of the time—as well as altarpieces and fresco cycles in chapels, palaces, and villas. He collaborated with Federico Barocci at the Casino of Pius IV in the Vatican, and was employed by Cardinal Alessandro Farnese to decorate his palaces in Rome and nearby Caprarola. A fluent decorator, he also designed an elaborate majolica service for the Duke of Urbino. Taddeo's perfect fusion of the grace of Raphael, the stylized artifice of Perino del Vaga, and the grandeur of Michelangelo—evident in his effortlessly posturing figures and complex narrative compositions—makes him a consummate exemplar of the Roman maniera, *although his religious imagery, like some of his drawings, reveals strains of an affecting piety and expressive naturalism.*

26. *Battle Scene (Emperor Charles V Fighting against the Lutherans?)*, ca. 1563–66

Pen and brown ink, brush and brown wash, highlighted with white gouache (oxidized in some passages), over traces of black chalk; squared in black chalk; some outlines of the figures at left are stylus-incised, 9½ x 16$\frac{5}{16}$ in. (24.2 x 41.5 cm)
Annotated on recto in pen and brown ink at lower right: *polidoro del*
Watermark: a cardinal's hat similar to Briquet 3395 (found in documents in Siena and Rome, ca. 1560–62)

Provenance: Nicholas Lanier (London, 1588–1666) (Lugt 2886); William Mayor, London (Lugt 2799); Private Collection, Germany; Colnaghi 1990, no. 7; sale, Christie's, London, July 4, 1995, lot 102; acquired in 1995

References: London 1875, p. 28, no. 131; New York 1990, no. 7; Christie's, London 1995, no. 102

At his death on November 11, 1563, the Florentine painter Francesco Salviati (see cat. no. 18) had left unfinished the fresco cycle in the Sala dei Fasti Farnesiani on the second story (piano nobile), spanning behind the main facade, of the Palazzo Farnese in Rome. The task of completing the project for the long-suffering Cardinal Ranuccio I Farnese (Salviati had begun it in 1549) fell on Taddeo Zuccaro, who had been employed since 1559 by Ranuccio's elder brother, Cardinal Alessandro Farnese (the future Pope Paul III), for the fresco decorations of Alessandro's villa at Caprarola.

Executed by Taddeo about 1563–66, the fresco for which the dynamic Tobey composition sketch was preparatory is prominently sited in the interior of the Sala dei Fasti Farnesiani, above the main window on the piano nobile, which opens toward the Piazza Farnese (fig. 26.1). The fresco is painted illusionistically to imitate a tapestry, complete with suspension gear, decorative borders, and flaps, although none of this is indicated in the drawing. Rediscovered at the time of its exhibition by Colnaghi's in New York in 1990, the Tobey sketch shows all the signs of an animated, undoubtedly creative study, executed in pen and ink with wash, over traces of black chalk, and squared in soft black chalk, much like many of the artist's other autograph drawings for the Sala dei Fasti Farnesiani frescoes. Examples include *The Foundation of Orbetello* at the Morgan Library and Museum, New York (fig. 26.2), *A Group of Warriors* also at the Morgan, and *Cardinal Albornoz Giving the Keys of Valentano to the Farnese* in the J. Paul Getty Museum, Los Angeles.[1]

The subject of the Tobey drawing, a major battle scene before the gates of a city, was somewhat plausibly identified in the 1875 catalogue of the William Mayor Collection, London, as "Constantine Defeating the Army of Maxentius under the Walls of Rome,"[2] but such a theme does not accord with the fact that much more modern, directly relevant episodes in the history of the Farnese family are celebrated in the decorations of the Sala dei Fasti Farnesiani. The subject of the scene was identified as Emperor Charles V fighting against the Lutherans in the early photograph by the Anderson Studio of the fresco, and it is here retained with a measure of doubt. An early copy of the Tobey sheet at the Gabinetto Disegni e Stampe degli Uffizi, Florence (fig. 26.3), exhibits a greater level of detail but a rather more mechanical-looking approach to the outlines and use of the wash. Not knowing the work now in the Tobey Collection, John A. Gere illustrated the Uffizi sheet and published it tentatively as the autograph preparatory drawing for the fresco by Taddeo Zuccaro.[3] The Uffizi drawing, like the fresco, depicts the fleur-de-lis of the Farnese family on the standard held by the main soldier on horseback at left in the composition. The Mayor catalogue of 1875, however, was the first to publish a correct attribution to Taddeo Zuccaro of the sheet now in the Tobey Collection.

The composition was reproduced in an engraving (with etching) by an anonymous French seventeenth-century artist (Bibliothèque Nationale, Paris).[4] The Tobey drawing reveals several changes with respect to the Sala dei Fasti Farnesiani fresco, principally that the two phalanges of fighting soldiers at

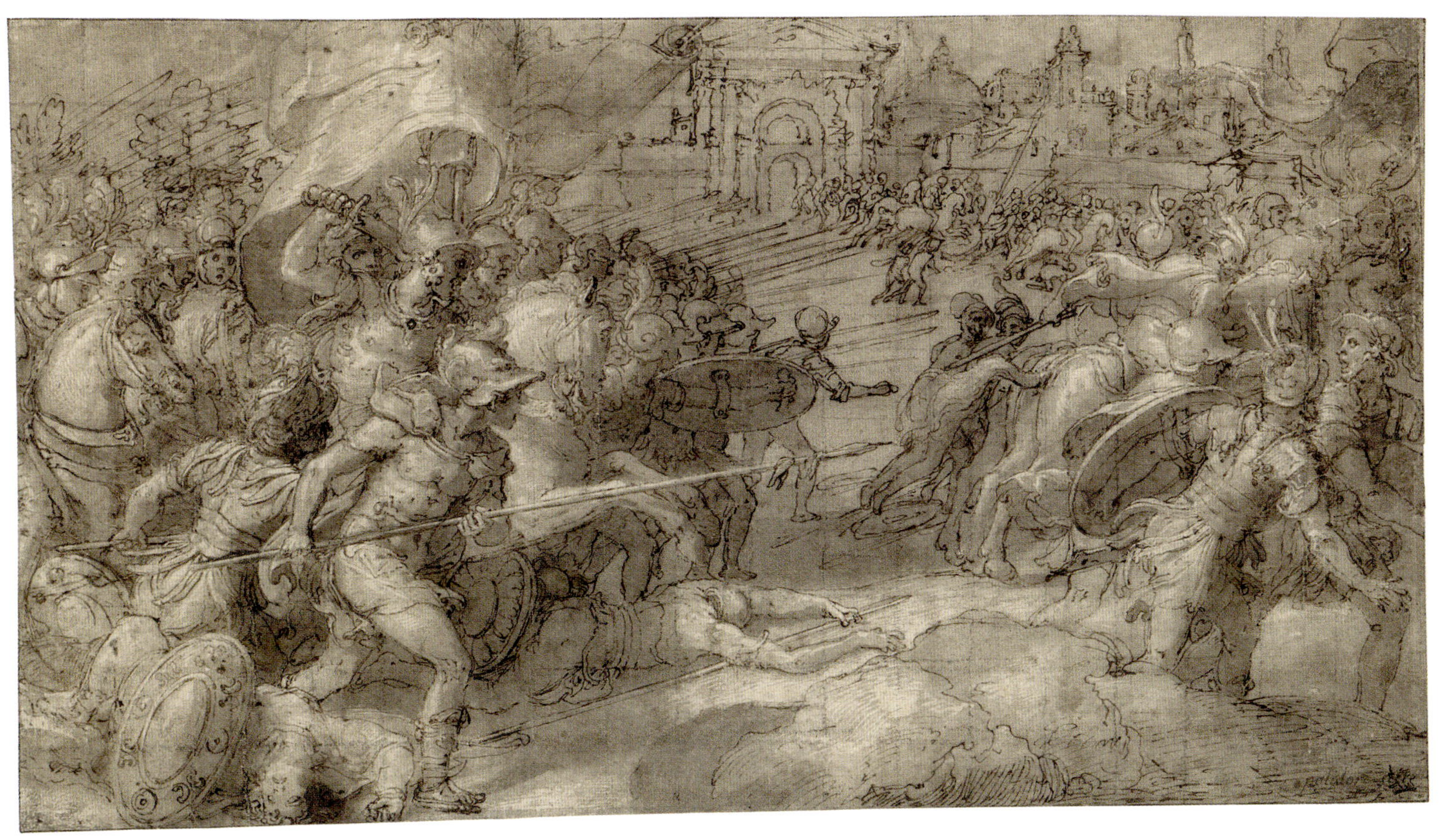

26

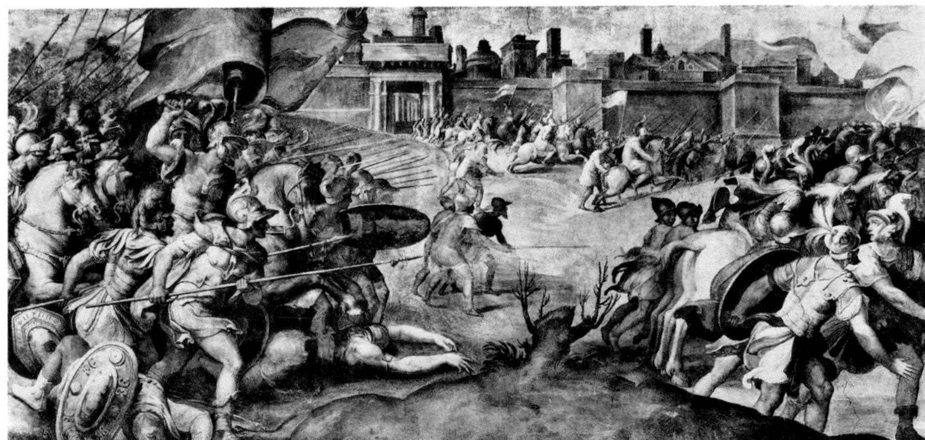

Fig. 26.1. Taddeo Zuccaro. *Charles V Fighting against the Lutherans*(?), ca. 1563–66. Fresco. Sala dei Fasti Farnesiani, Palazzo Farnese, Rome

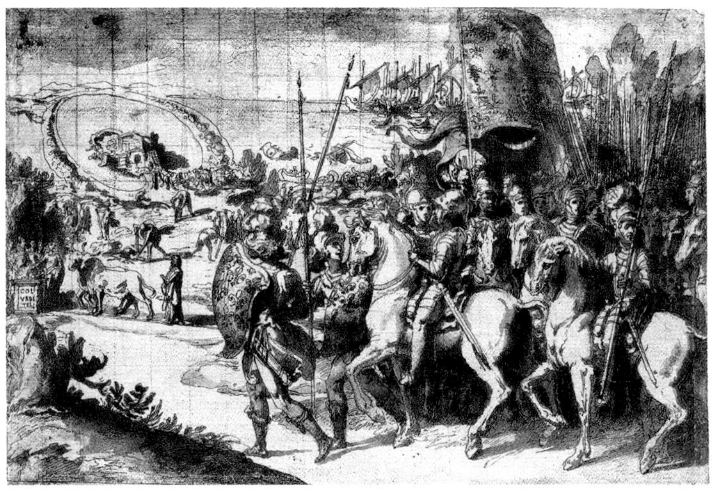

Fig. 26.2. Taddeo Zuccaro. *The Foundation of Orbetello*, ca. 1563–66. Pen and brown ink, with brown wash, over black chalk, lightly squared for transfer in black chalk, 10⅜ x 15⁵⁄₁₆ in. (26.4 x 39.2 cm). The Morgan Library and Museum, New York (1973.28)

left and right are seen much farther apart in the final painting, and the initial idea of a rusticated gate by the city wall was turned into a robustly classical structure with an enormous entablature. The alternative attributions that have been proposed for the present sheet have all been unconvincing, for it was once assigned to the workshop of Taddeo Zuccaro (which raises the question of why assistants rather than the master himself would invent the squared *modello* design for an important fresco commissioned by one of the most eminent Roman families) and to Cesare Nebbia (ca. 1536–1614), the painter and draftsman from Orvieto whose drawing style falls far short of the quality seen here.[5]

CCB

1. *A Group of Warriors* at the Morgan Library and Museum is inv. no. 1978.1 (not illustrated here). The sheet at the Getty is inv. no. 87.GG.52. See Mundy 1989–90, pp. 128–41, nos. 34, 35, 36.
2. London 1875, p. 28, no. 131.
3. See Gere 1969, p. 143, no. 39, pl. 166.
4. Inv. no. H 103085. Massari 1993, pl. 33.
5. As stated in New York 1990, no. 7.

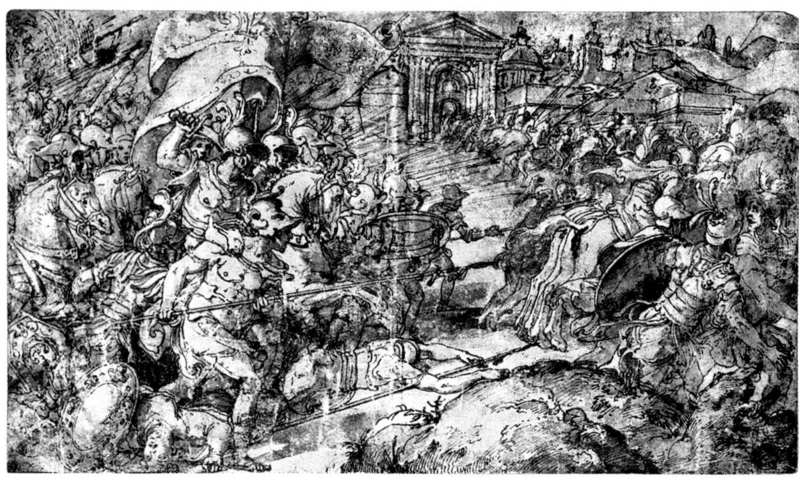

Fig. 26.3. Taddeo Zuccaro. *Battle Scene*, 1563–66. Pen and brown wash, 9⁷⁄₁₆ x 16¼ in. (24 x 41.3 cm). Gabinetto Disegni e Stampe degli Uffizi, Florence (632F)

FEDERICO BAROCCI

Urbino, ca. 1535–Urbino, 1612

Other than two relatively brief, early stints in Rome, Federico Barocci spent his entire career in his native Urbino. His early Mannerist style, absorbed from his teacher, Battista Franco, and from Taddeo Zuccaro, was displaced by an affecting and naturalistic idiom—greatly admired by the Carracci—that synthesized influences from Raphael, Correggio, and contemporary Venetian painting. The many altarpieces that Barocci painted for churches in Umbria, the Marche, and elsewhere exemplify his dramatic and expressive yet accessible devotional style. The act of painting was physically difficult for Barocci, who suffered from lifelong stomach ailments (possibly ulcers, although he believed his affliction was the result of having been poisoned by jealous rivals), and the complex compositions of his altarpieces were typically preceded by a lengthy and elaborate preparatory process that included the production of numerous figure, drapery, and composition studies and modelli, *as well as individual heads, often executed in color.*

27. *Head of an Infant in Three-Quarter View Facing Right (Study for the Perdono di San Francesco d'Assisi,* ca. 1574–76

Pastel, black chalk, and traces of white chalk with stumping, on light brown paper (originally blue?), 8⁷⁄₁₆ x 7¹¹⁄₁₆ in. (21.5 x 19.5 cm)
Annotated in pen and dark brown ink at lower left, by an early eighteenth-century hand: *Barotius*

Provenance: Jonathan Richardson, Sr. (London, 1665–1745) (Lugt 2184); Sir Joshua Reynolds (Plympton and London, 1723–1792) (Lugt 2364); Private Collection, Sweden; Thomas Williams Fine Art Ltd., London; acquired in 1998

The medium of pastel (fabricated colored chalks), applied in this unpublished drawing with stunning mastery, became closely associated with the work of Federico Barocci in the region of the Marche in central Italy during the late sixteenth century. The biography of Barocci published in 1672 by Giovanni Pietro Bellori (who closely based his narrative on the artist's family papers as directly gathered by Pompilio Bruni) rightly or wrongly states that the young artist first began to use this technique upon being shown examples of monumental pastel drawings of *teste divinissime* (most divine heads) by Correggio—a Renaissance artist, however, by whom no pastel drawings are extant.[1] The works by Correggio were said to have been brought back to Barocci's native town of Urbino by an unnamed painter who had visited Parma.[2]

Fresh and well preserved, this luminous study after life in pastel evidences Barocci's command of the medium long after the biographical events narrated in Bellori's anecdote, in the artist's full maturity, for with pastels he achieved the *sfumazione e soavità del colore* (the smokiness and softness of color), which Bellori so praised in his work.[3] A virtual painting in dry media, the Tobey drawing was intended for the head of the flying putto at upper left in Barocci's famous altarpiece portraying the *Perdono di San Francesco d'Assisi* (Pardon of Saint Francis of Assisi), which is still in situ in the choir of the church of San

Francesco, Urbino (figs. 27.1, 27.2).[4] A closely related study for a child's head in the *Perdono* is in the collection of Christ Church, Oxford (fig. 27.3), there facing left rather than right, as in the Tobey sheet, but both drawings are of similarly square dimensions, with framing outlines in pen and dark brown ink, and were executed in pastel. Both are also annotated by the same early eighteenth-century hand, "Barotius," which attests to a common early provenance.[5] The altarpiece of the *Perdono* was finished in 1574–76, although according to Bellori, "it consumed more than seven years" of the artist's life.[6] It represents a rare subject, an allegorical vision of Saint Francis in which the Virgin appears interceding with Christ to grant a plenary indulgence for all those who pray to the saint of Assisi at his shrine of the Porziuncola.[7] Saint Francis is, therefore, seen in mystical adoration of this holy vision,[8] and the representation of light is symbolic of the divine.

The Tobey and Christ Church pastel drawings, as well as the altarpiece, depict the forms of the children in softly graded colors bathed by radiant light, but the Tobey drawing is greatly more detailed and lifelike than the final painting. In this, the study appears to confirm Bellori's statement that Barocci "always turned to the live model, and he did not allow himself to paint even a small stroke without having first observed it."[9] The artist built up the highlights here with a high density of pink and white pastel pigments, leaving the rest thinly in shadows, quickly drawn and unfinished. The strokes of parallel-hatching course daringly across the face, and a few well-placed accents of saturated color animate the child's features, touched by "the light which is diffused everywhere between the splendid clouds of cherubim."[10]

An oil sketch by Barocci, today at the Galleria Nazionale delle Marche (Palazzo Ducale, Urbino), portrays the full compo-

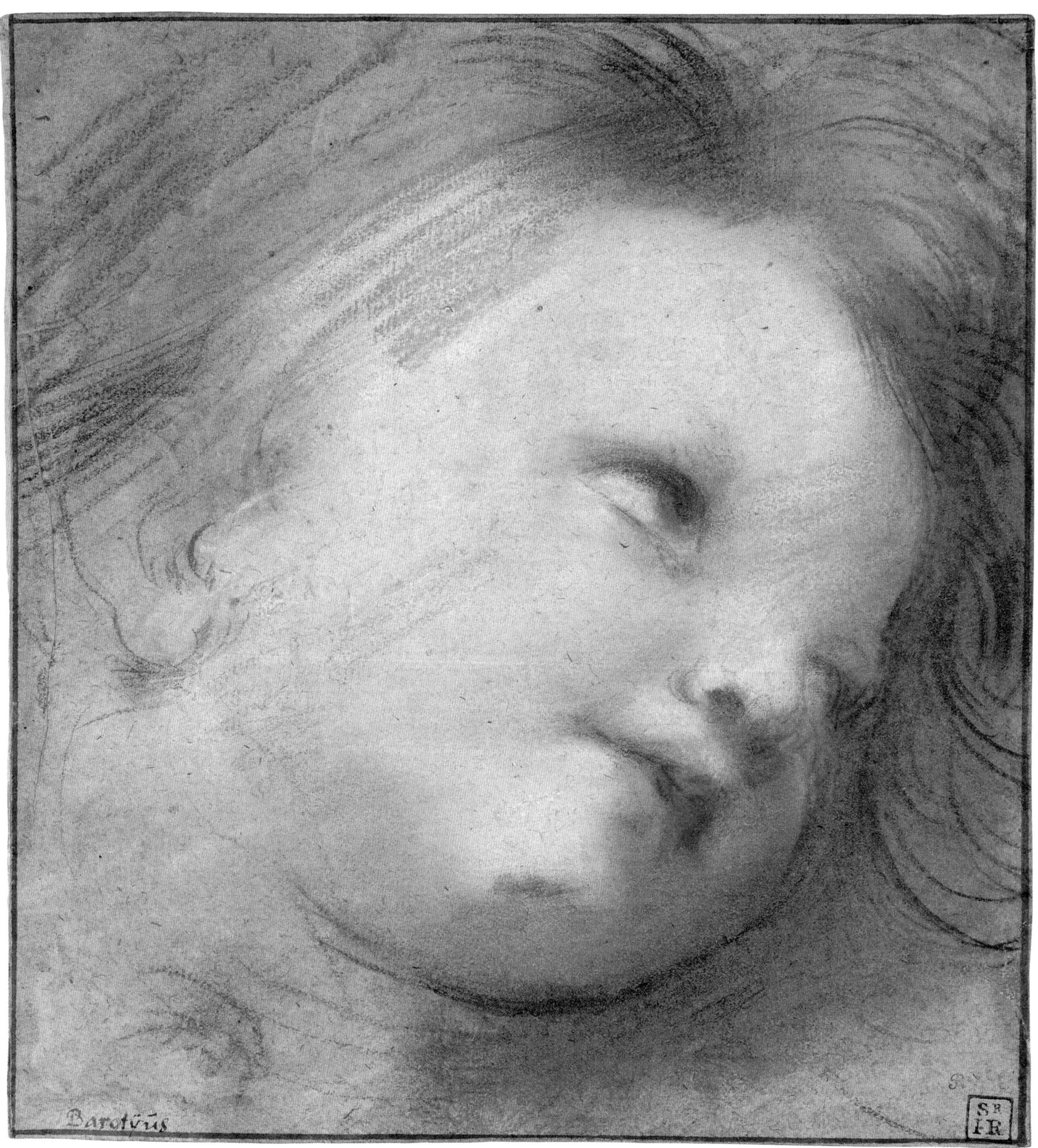

27

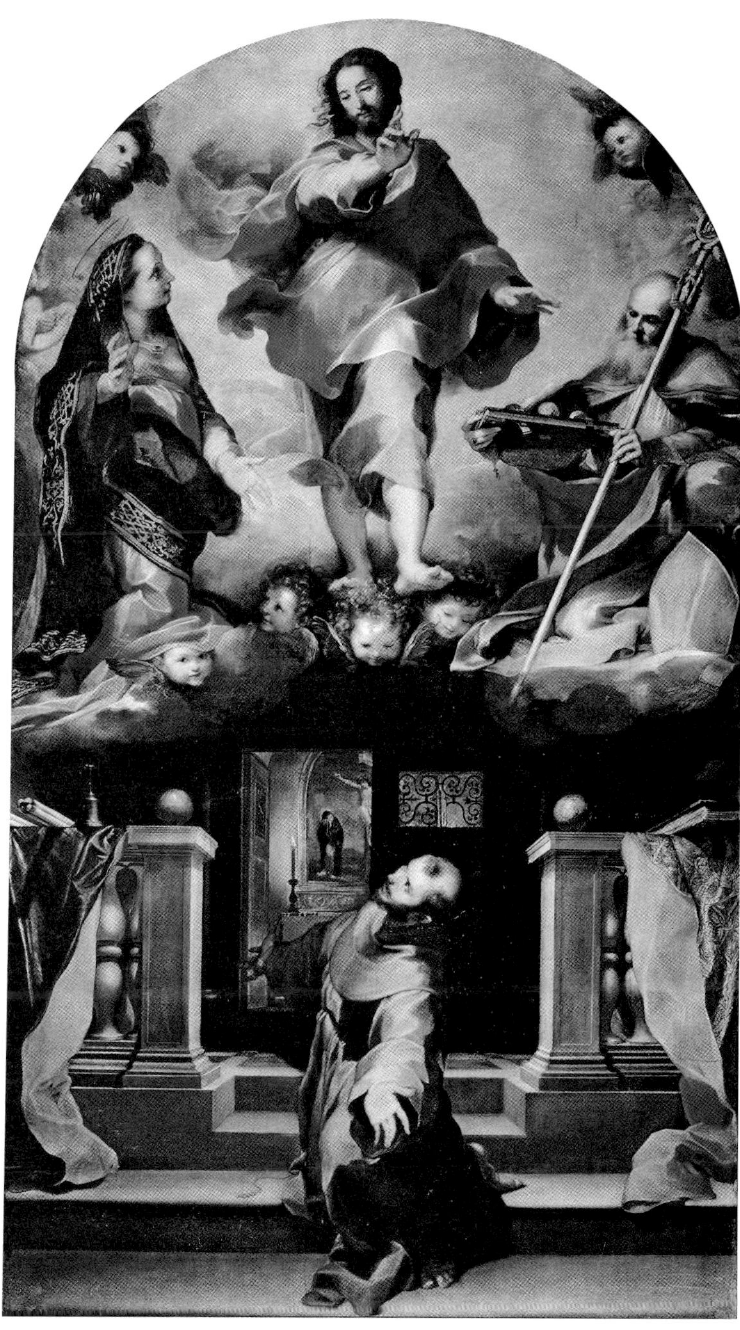

Fig. 27.1. Federico Barocci. *Perdono di San Francesco d'Assisi*, ca. 1574–76. Oil on canvas, 168½ x 92¹⁵⁄₁₆ in. (427 x 236 cm). Choir of the church of San Francesco, Urbino

sition of the altarpiece in almost final form, but exhibits a rectangular rather than arched top. The child's head at upper left corresponding to the Tobey drawing is, therefore, rendered complete. In the Tobey pastel, the upper left portion of the infant's head was reworked by the artist with bold, diagonal parallel-hatching in soft black chalk, and these stiff strokes relate to the abrupt cropping of the angel's head by the actual border of the arched canvas in the final painting (fig. 27.1). Although the area

below the infant's chin in the pastel drawing is seen as nearly blank, with only minor curved outlines, in the ultimate painting this passage is fully covered by the angel's overlapping wings.

Barocci prepared numerous drawings for the composition of the altarpiece of the *Perdono*, of which several are also in pastel. While a drawing now in the Royal Library, Windsor (inv. no. 105), has been related as a preparatory work for the same putto in the painting of the *Perdono*, its different anatomical

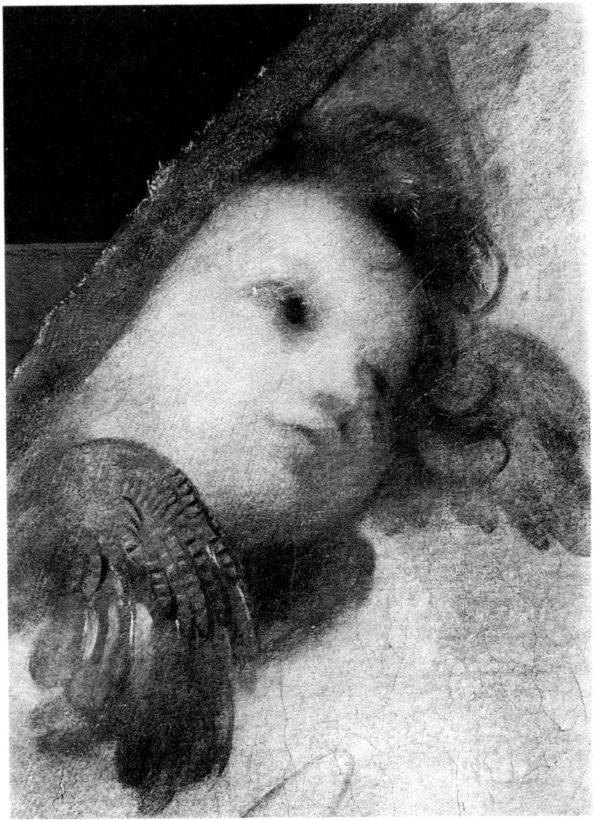

Fig. 27.2. Federico Barocci. *Head of a Cherub*. Detail of fig. 27.1

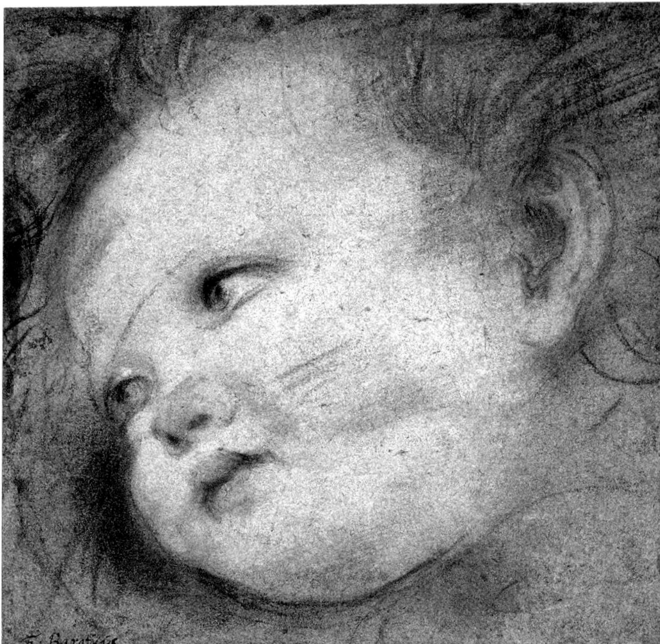

Fig. 27.3. Federico Barocci. *Study for the Head of a Child* in the *Perdono di San Francesco d'Assisi*, ca. 1574–76. Pastel on greenish-blue paper, 7³⁄₁₆ x 7³⁄₁₆ in. (18.3 x 18.3 cm). Christ Church, Oxford (1172; JBS 325)

type and more pronounced sculptural qualities than both the final painting and the Tobey drawing rule it out as a study at least for the painting of this infant. Rather, the deeply sculptural articulation of tone in the Windsor drawing connects, in the present author's view, with the various reproductive prints done after Barocci's altarpiece, executed as etchings by Barocci himself, and as engravings by other artists.   CCB

1. See especially DeGrazia et al. 1984, pp. 36–37.
2. Bellori ed. 1976, p. 183:"nel qual tempo capitando in Urbino un pittore, che tornava da Parma con alcuni pezzi di cartoni e teste divinissime a pastelli di mano del Correggio, Federico restò preso da quella maniera, la quale si conformava del tutto al suo genio."
3. Ibid.
4. Emiliani 1985, vol. 1, pp. 104–19; Turner 2000, pp. 58–63.
5. Byam Shaw 1976, vol. 1, p. 109, no. 325.
6. Bellori ed. 1976, p. 188:"e vi consumò sopra sette anni."
7. The Porziuncola began as a very small church in the surroundings of Assisi where Saint Francis received his vocation on February 24, 1208. It is now commemorated by a shrine, placed within the church of Santa Maria degli Angeli, below the town of Assisi.
8. Bellori ed. 1976, pp. 187–88, for a description of the iconography of Barocci's *Perdono*.
9. Ibid., p. 205:"Li modi tenuti da Federico Barocci nel suo dipingere, non ostante il mal suo, furono di molto esercizio ed applicazione; egli operando ricorreva sempre al naturale, né permetteva un minimo segno senza vederlo."
10. Bellori ed. 1976, p. 187:"diffondendosi per tutto il chiarore in giro fra splendide nuvolette di Cherubini."

FEDERICO ZUCCARO

Sant'Angelo in Vado (the Marche), 1540/42–Ancona, 1609

Federico Zuccaro was the younger brother and artistic follower of Taddeo Zuccaro, whose style he closely imitated. He collaborated with Taddeo in Rome on various commissions, including frescoes in the church of the Trinità dei Monti, the Villa Farnese at Caprarola, and the Sala Regia in the Vatican, interrupting his activity there with a trip to Venice and Lombardy in 1564. Later in his career he ventured to England, the Netherlands, and Spain, and to numerous cities in Italy, always returning to Rome, where he continued to receive important commissions for frescoes. His later religious imagery—didactic, unembellished, and straightforward—conforms to the decrees of the Council of Trent and the overall sensibility of the Counter-Reformation. Federico was a tireless draftsman and a leader of the Accademia di San Luca, the painters' academy in Rome. Toward the end of his life he devoted considerable energy to teaching and to theoretical writings on art.

28. *Modello for the Votive Procession of Pope Saint Gregory against the Plague*, ca. 1580

Pen and brown ink, brush and brown wash, over black chalk; the arch at the top was drawn with a compass, of which the center point is at the foot of Saint Michael
18½ x 10¼ in. (47 x 26.1 cm)
Watermark: the dove of the Holy Spirit in a cartouche

Provenance: Sir Thomas Lawrence (London, 1769–1830) (Lugt 2445); Samuel Woodburn (London, 1786–1853); his sale, Christie's, London, June 4, 1860, p. 79, part of lot 1074 (63 guineas to Sir Thomas Phillipps); Sir Thomas Phillipps (London, 1792–1872); by descent to his grandson, T. Fitzroy Fenwick (London, 1856–1938); Dr. A. S. W. Rosenbach (Philadelphia, 1876–1952); Philip H. and A. S. W. Rosenbach Foundation, Philadelphia (as inv. no. RF 472/22, no. 23); The British Rail Pension Fund; sale, Sotheby's, New York, January 11, 1990, lot 36; sale, Christie's, London, July 2, 1996, lot 96; acquired in 1996

References: London 1836; Gere 1970, no. 17, pl. 17; Mundy 1989–90, pp. 252–55, under no. 85, fig. 42; Birke and Kertész 1992–97, vol. 2, p. 1183, under no. 2258; Acidini Luchinat 1999, vol. 2, p. 127, fig. 13 (as in "Londra, mercato antiquario")

An altarpiece, *The Votive Procession of Pope Saint Gregory against the Plague*, was commissioned by Paolo Ghiselli, the steward of Pope Gregory XIII (r. 1572–85), to adorn his family chapel in the church of Santa Maria del Baraccano in Bologna.[1] The project became a cause célèbre, and for some time stained Federico Zuccaro's career. The historical circumstances—at least with regard to the preparatory drawings—are difficult to reconstruct, given that Zuccaro's painting was lost at some point after 1776. The design of the altarpiece is known from an engraving published in Rome in 1581 by Aliprando Caprioli (doc. Rome 1574–1599), according to the inscription along the bottom margin of the print (fig. 28.1).[2] Zuccaro's altarpiece was to be installed in the right transept of the church, in a prominently visible place. Pope Gregory XIII was himself a native of Bologna, hailing from the powerful Boncompagni family, and this played an important part in the subsequent scandal regarding the project. The subject of the

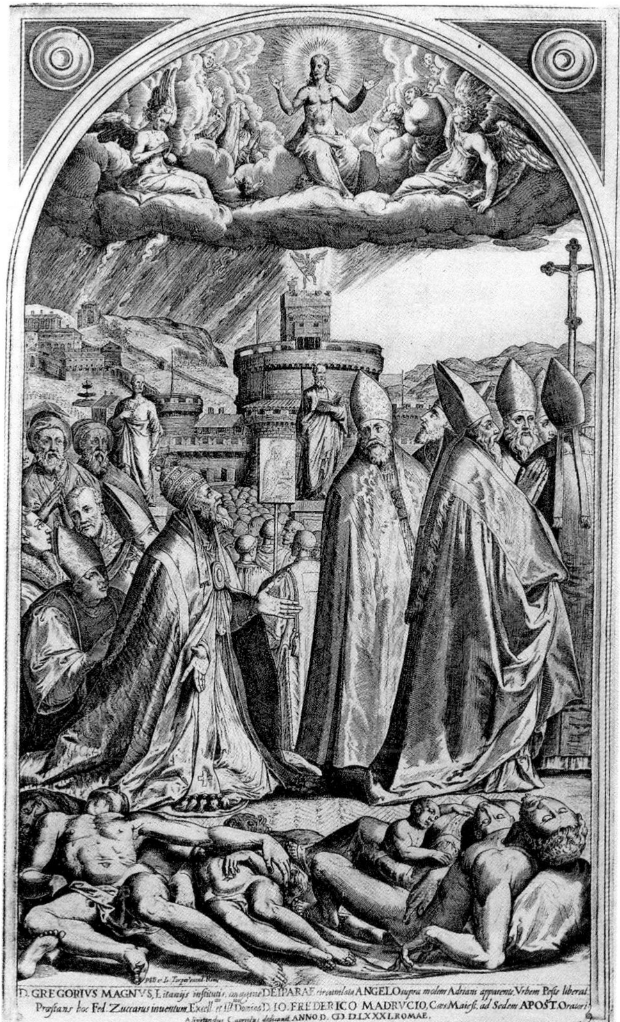

Fig. 28.1. Aliprando Caprioli, after Federico Zuccaro. *The Votive Procession of Pope Saint Gregory against the Plague*, 1581. Engraving. Graphische Sammlung Albertina, Vienna (HB 014, fol. 054,060)

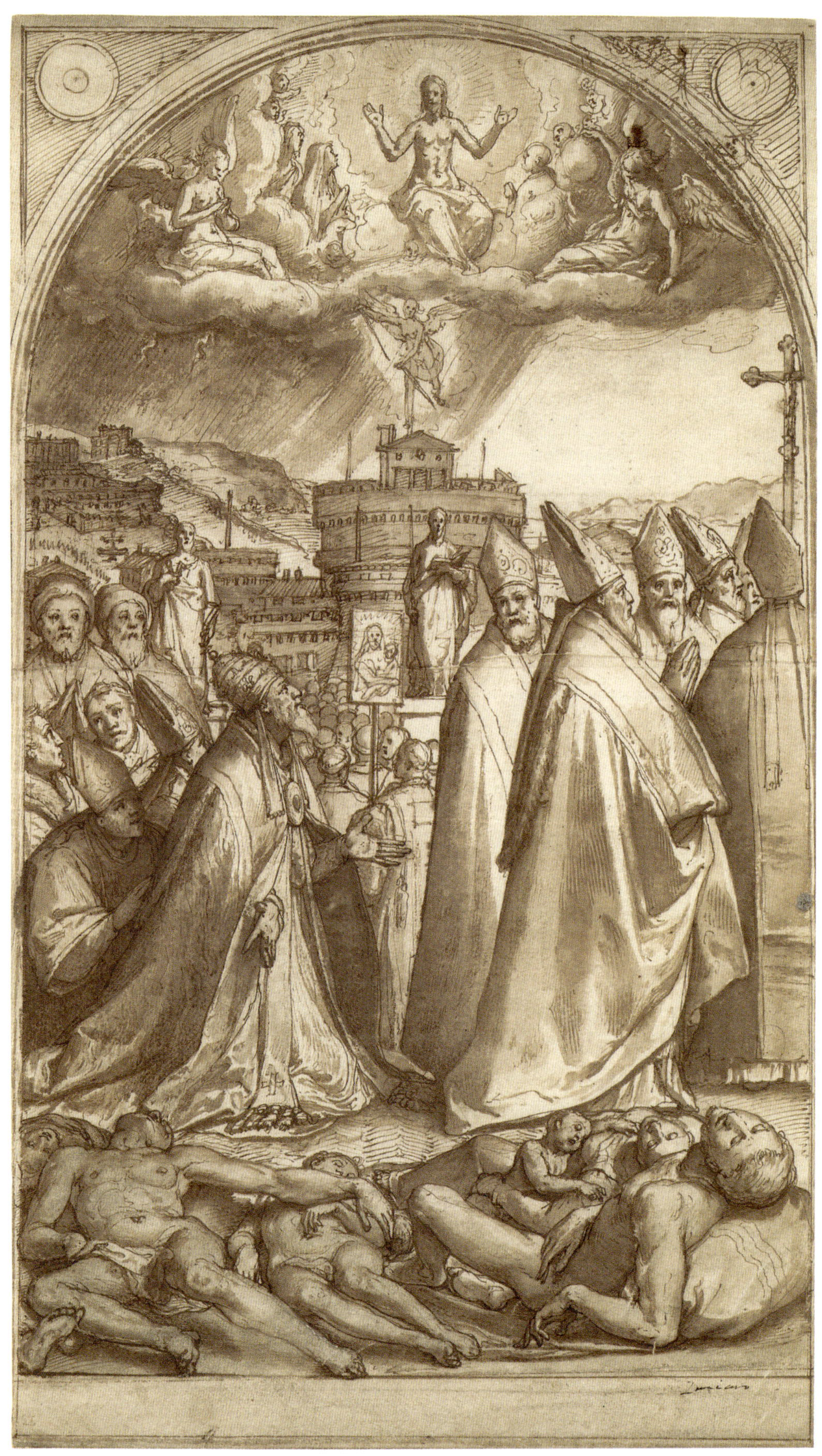

100   FEDERICO ZUCCARO

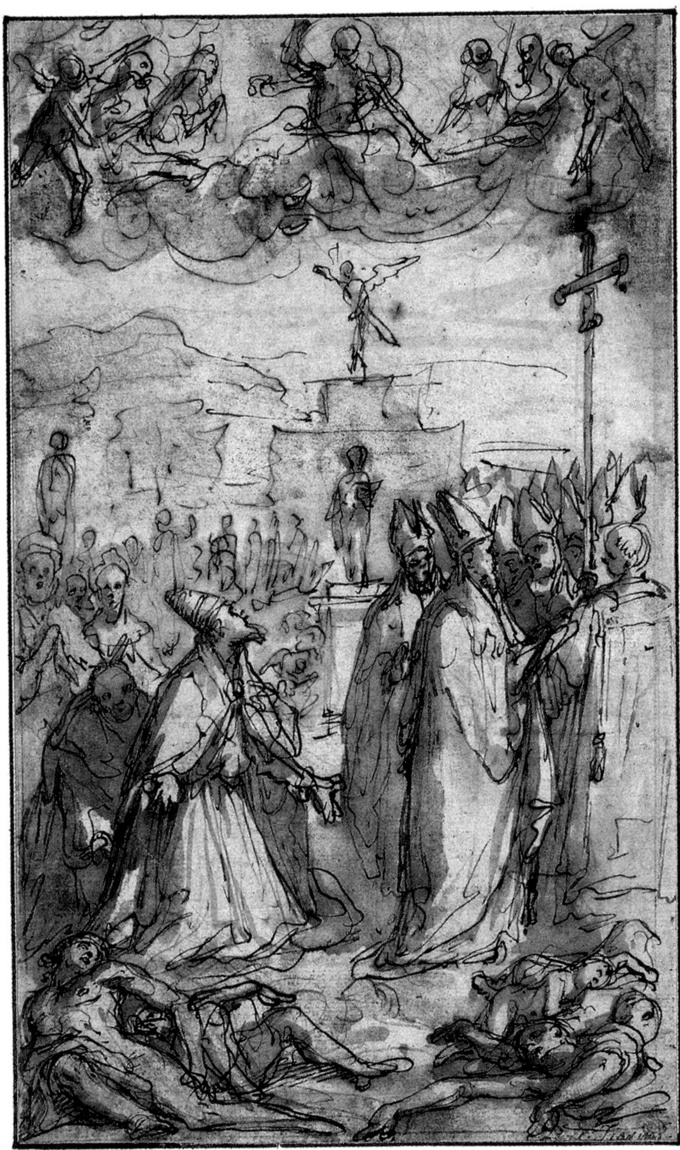

Fig. 28.2. Federico Zuccaro. *Sketch for the Votive Procession of Pope Saint Gregory against the Plague*, ca. 1580. Pen and brown ink, brush and brown wash, over red chalk, 10¹³⁄₁₆ x 5⅝ in. (27.4 x 14.3 cm). Graphische Sammlung Albertina, Vienna (2258)

Tobey drawing and altarpiece alludes to the Boncompagni pontiff in depicting a miracle performed by the intercession of Pope Saint Gregory "The Great," his namesake; his facial features were also said to have been given to the saint. Zuccaro completed the altarpiece in Rome (he had just arrived there, after long residing in Florence from 1574 to 1580) and sent it to Bologna shortly before Christmas of 1580. His picture was so viciously criticized by the community of local artists that Ghiselli (the patron) rejected it and even turned down Zuccaro's offer to paint another altarpiece in its place. The embittered artist took revenge by producing the satirical portraits of his detractors in the *Porta Virtutis* (Gate of Virtue), a composition rendering Virtue as triumphant over the Ignorant People—

a thinly veiled allegory. He had this canvas (it is called a *cartone*, or large-scale drawing, in the documents) placed on the facade at San Luca, the confraternity church of painters, on October 18, 1581, the feast day of Saint Luke, patron of painters; that work is lost, although several preparatory drawings survive.[3] Zuccaro was sued for slander and expelled from Rome.[4] He offered the rejected altarpiece of *The Votive Procession of Pope Saint Gregory against the Plague* to the doctors of the Collegio del Gesù in Rome, who in turn passed it to the church of Santa Lucia in Bologna, where it was last mentioned in 1776.[5] The altarpiece of this subject today in situ at Santa Maria del Baraccano is by Cesare Aretusi and displays the same arched shape at the top as the Tobey drawing and the lost altarpiece.[6]

The design of Aliprando Caprioli's engraving is in the same direction as that of the Tobey sheet and Zuccaro's other related sketches (see figs. 28.2, 28.3). It has been suggested that Zuccaro himself supervised Caprioli in the making of the reproductive print, and that the Tobey drawing may have been preparatory for the print rather than for the lost Bolognese altarpiece.[7] The latter part of this hypothesis does not seem convincing, for the carefully finished Tobey composition displays vigorous underdrawing in black chalk and a spirited technique of modeling (at first lightly done with wash, then reworked with hatching, and then again reinforced with darker wash). The design corresponds closely to Caprioli's engraving,[8] but it is not exactly the same. The five bishops' heads at extreme right are arranged in different poses, and in the drawing the heads at left are not yet entirely individualized as portraits, as in the print. Caprioli's engraving reproduces the medallions on the upper corners of the composition, and the blank rectangle at the very bottom of the sheet. Had the Tobey drawing always been intended as a *modello* (demonstration drawing) for the print, one would have expected that its outlines would be incised for transfer and that the design would be in reverse orientation— the printing process reverses the image—but this is not the case. Close examination of the Tobey drawing also reveals that Zuccaro at first envisioned the composition of the upper register as a rectangle, rather than as an arched shape. The vivid pen-and-ink contours of the quickly sketched angels at the upper corners continue much beyond the framing outlines, to the borders of the paper. On the upper right corner of the drawn frame, the bold outlines of figures and their wings are especially evident underneath the final layers of drawing. The much looser composition sketch in the Graphische Sammlung Albertina, Vienna (see fig. 28.2), evidently preceded the Tobey sheet, and depicts the composition plainly as a rectangular field, without afterthought.[9] The composition sketch at the Staatliche Graphische Sammlung, Munich (fig. 28.3), represents the cleanly outlined, final arched shape of Caprioli's print, and includes the arms of the Zuccaro family at the bottom.[10]

In this author's view, therefore, it is likely that the Tobey composition and the sheet in Vienna were originally conceived as drawings for the painting (fig. 28.2), while it is possible that the Munich sketch represents Zuccaro's initial attempt in thinking about the print (figs. 28.3, 28.1). It appears that the Tobey sheet, which is the most detailed and finished of the designs, was later reworked by Zuccaro in order to adapt it for use in Caprioli's engraving of 1581 (the final working drawing for the print is presumably lost). In certain passages of the Tobey drawing, the fluently applied shadows seem quite deepened with wash, and, on the extreme left, they exceed the drawn frame. From the later stage in the Tobey drawing's use resulted the additions of the arched framing outlines at the top and the emphatic outlines at the bottom. The bold lines on this bottom border seem to reprise partly, more lightly done preliminary strokes.

The altarpiece by Aretusi that finally replaced Zuccaro's at the church of Santa Maria del Baraccano retains many important features from the iconography of the earlier work, as they are represented in the Tobey drawing and Caprioli's print, but omits the icon of the Virgin Mary and the corpses of the plague victims strewn in the foreground.[11] The church of Santa Maria del Baraccano was known for the cult of the image of the Blessed Virgin. It was founded in 1403, at first as a chapel to protect a *Madonna and Child* painted by Lippo di Dalmasio, and was commissioned by Giovanni I Bentivoglio, ruler of the city. Various miracles were attributed to this fifteenth-century picture. Zuccaro's composition therefore seems to allude to this historical tradition and highlights the importance of an early miracle in the cult of Marian iconography. According to the *Golden Legend* of Jacobus de Voragine, Saint Gregory, who was Pope Gregory I (ca. A.D. 540–606), stopped the outbreak of a plague in Rome by ordering that on Easter Day a procession should march around the city, bearing the picture of the Blessed Virgin kept in the Basilica of Santa Maria Maggiore, which was thought to have been painted by Saint Luke.[12] "And all at once the sacred image cleansed the air of infection, as if the pestilence could not withstand its presence . . . and it is told that the voices of angels were heard around the picture singing, *Regina coeli laetare, alleluja*." The plague was understood to have ended when Saint Michael, "a mighty angel wip[ed] a bloody sword and put it back into its sheath: thenceforth this fortress was called the Fortress of the Holy Angel [the Castel Sant'Angelo]."[13] Based closely on the story, Zuccaro's scene depicts the small miraculous banner of the Virgin and Child as the focal point in the middle ground, while Christ, the Virgin, and saints in heaven appear to witness the procession in the city of Rome below. The Eternal City can be clearly identified because of the Castel Sant'Angelo (seen

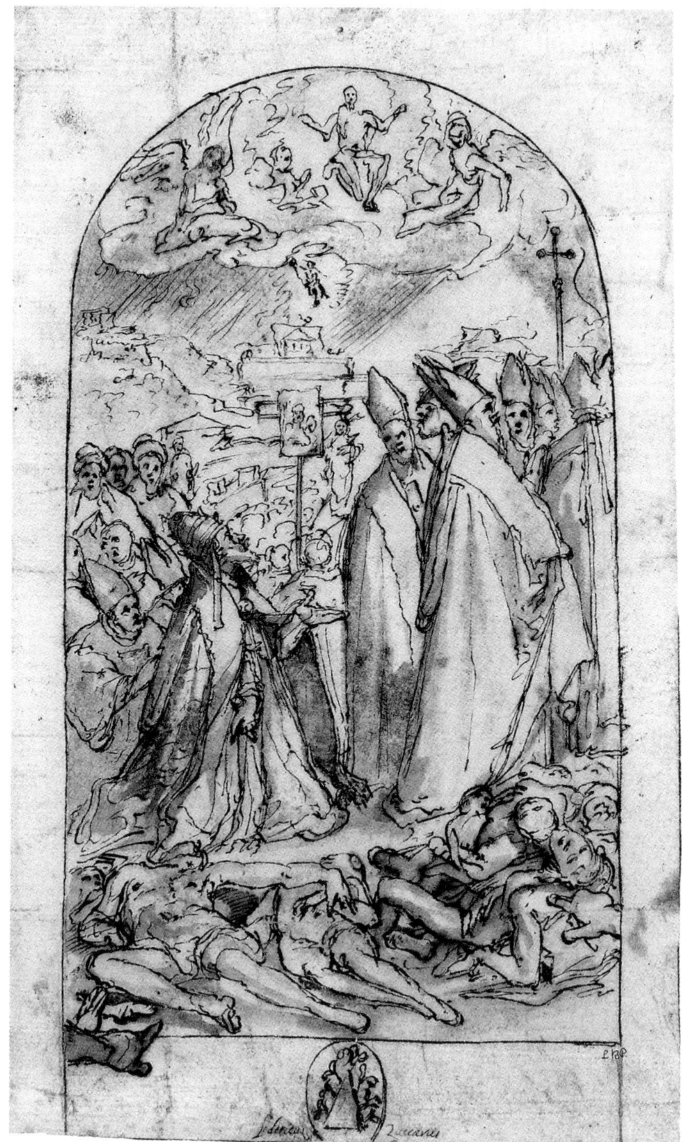

Fig. 28.3. Federico Zuccaro. *Sketch for the Votive Procession of Pope Saint Gregory against the Plague*, ca. 1580. Pen and brown ink, brush and brown wash. Staatliche Graphische Sammlung, Munich (1949:29 Z)

at center in the middle ground), and the tiny figure of the Archangel Michael stands with one foot on the fortress, which is dedicated to him. In the middle ground toward the left, the kneeling Pope Saint Gregory beckons the standing bishops at right, while pointing to the corpses of the victims of the plague strewn before him in the foreground.

CCB

1. For the historical details summarized here, see Acidini Luchinat 1999, vol. 2, pp. 127–32, no. 2.
2. Aliprando Caprioli's engraving was first discussed and illustrated in connection with Federico Zuccaro's lost altarpiece in Heikamp 1957, pp. 185–94, fig. 3.

A further engraving by an anonymous artist shows the composition in reverse (ibid., fig. 4).

3. An explanation of the *Porta Virtutis*, "Cartone d'un pittore per rappresentar la Virtù contra gl'Ignoranti," was probably written in 1582 by Federico Zuccaro himself (as discussed and transcribed in Acidini Luchinat 1999, vol. 2, pp. 127–32, 149–50 nn. 33–67, 281 [no. 6d]). See also Mundy 1989–90, pp. 252–55, no. 85.

4. Acidini Luchinat 1999, vol. 2, p. 132.

5. The picture was said to have been transferred to San Michele in Bosco, Bologna, but cannot be identified there or anywhere else (Supino 1938, pp. 443–46; Gere 1970, p. 130).

6. Discussed and illustrated in Acidini Luchinat 1999, vol. 2, p. 128, fig. 15.

7. See Gere 1970, p. 130, no. 17; Mundy 1989–90, pp. 252–55, under no. 85; and Acidini Luchinat 1999, vol. 2, p. 127.

8. As first noted in Gere 1970, p. 130, no. 17, but maintaining that the designs of the drawing and print were exactly alike, which is incorrect.

9. Birke and Kertész 1992–97, vol. 2, p. 1183, no. 2258.

10. Illustrated and discussed in Halm 1950, pp. 249–50, fig. 2.

11. Heikamp 1957, pp. 189–90, fig. 5, discusses and illustrates a drawing in the Emilio Santarelli collection of the Gabinetto Disegni e Stampe degli Uffizi, Florence, as by Aretusi for the altarpiece in Santa Maria del Baraccano.

12. Voragine ed. 1969, pp. 180–81.

13. Ibid.

ANDREA MICHIELI, IL VICENTINO

Vicenza, 1542(?)–Venice, 1617(?)

*Andrea Vicentino was a history painter and the author of altarpieces in an austere, Counter-Reformation style.
He trained in Vicenza and worked primarily in Venice, adopting the prevailing late sixteenth-century manner
that synthesized elements from Tintoretto, Veronese, and Palma Il Giovane. The art of Jacopo Bassano also played
a significant role in shaping his style. In the mid-1580s he assisted Tintoretto in some of the painted ceilings in
the Palazzo Ducale, Venice, and he later received an independent commission for a history painting there.*

29. *Pope Clement VIII on His Way from Bologna to Ferrara*, ca. 1598–1600

Pen and brown ink, brush and brown wash, over black chalk, 10⅜ x 15⁵⁄₁₆ in.
(26.3 x 39.5 cm)
Inscribed by the artist: *nostro S.re, caroci, gimilom / camarieri / del papy cavali cavali
ligieri chariagi leci.* Annotated on verso in red chalk: *12 50*
Watermark: a sort of device, partly illegible

Provenance: Pierre Crozat (Paris, 1665–1740); Pierre-Jean Mariette (Paris, 1694–
1774); F. Basan; sale, Paris, November 15, 1775, to January 30, 1776, lot 314 (sold as
Agostino Carracci, for 300 livres); Ian Woodner Family Collection; sale,
Christie's, London, July 2, 1991, lot 90; acquired in 1991

Reference: Christie's, London 1991, no. 90

Although the little-published drawing now in the Tobey
Collection was thought to be by the Bolognese painter
and draftsman Agostino Carracci (1557–1602), its subject
appeared correctly identified when it belonged to the famous
eighteenth-century collectors Pierre Crozat and Pierre-Jean
Mariette, as confirmed by the sales catalogue of 1775.[1] This

quickly sketched scene teems with iconographic notes by the
artist, which helps establish the historical details. It represents
the journey of Pope Clement VIII (r. 1592–1605), as he made
his formal entry into the city of Ferrara on May 8, 1598, information that provides a *post quem* date for the Tobey drawing.
The pope hailed from the Aldobrandini family—the arms
along with the papal tiara and the keys of Saint Peter are prominently displayed on the side of the litter at right of center in
the composition, and the whole motif is annotated above,
"*nostro S.re*" (Our Lord).

The abbreviated drawing style of the figures together with
the quick technique of outlines in pen and ink with wash is
typical of Vicentino (see figs. 29.1, 29.2), a rare and superbly
fluent draftsman who made a career as a prolific historical and
religious painter in the Veneto, employing a figural idiom that
was closely indebted to the luministic late styles of Jacopo
Tintoretto (1518–1594), Paolo Veronese (1528–1588), and

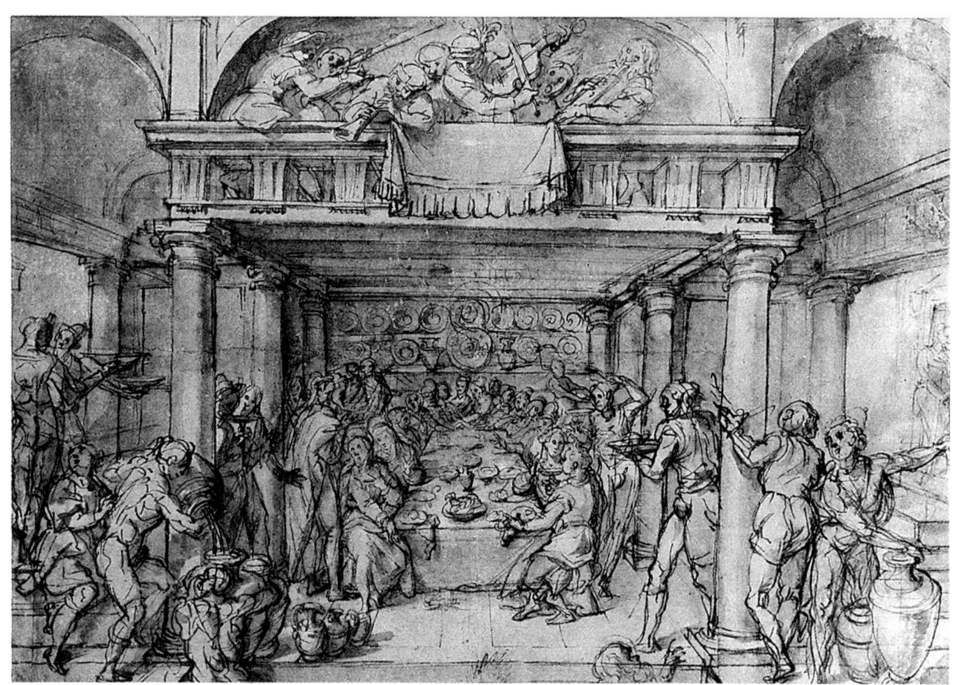

Fig. 29.1. Andrea Michieli, Il Vicentino.
Marriage at Cana, 1590s. Pen and brown
ink, brown wash, traces of black chalk,
13¹¹⁄₁₆ x 18¹³⁄₁₆ in. (34.8 x 47.8 cm).
Département des Arts Graphiques,
Musée du Louvre, Paris (5074)

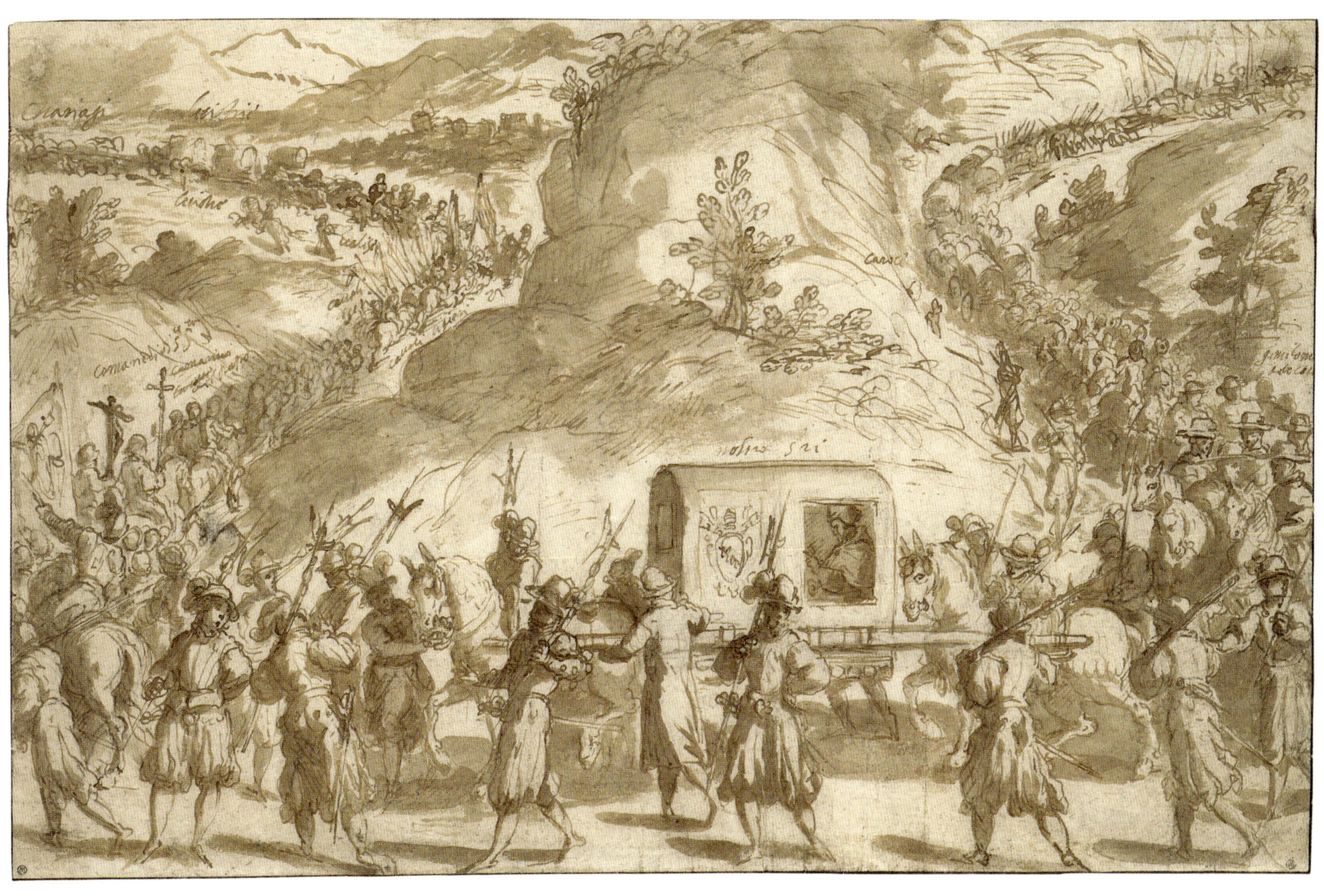

29

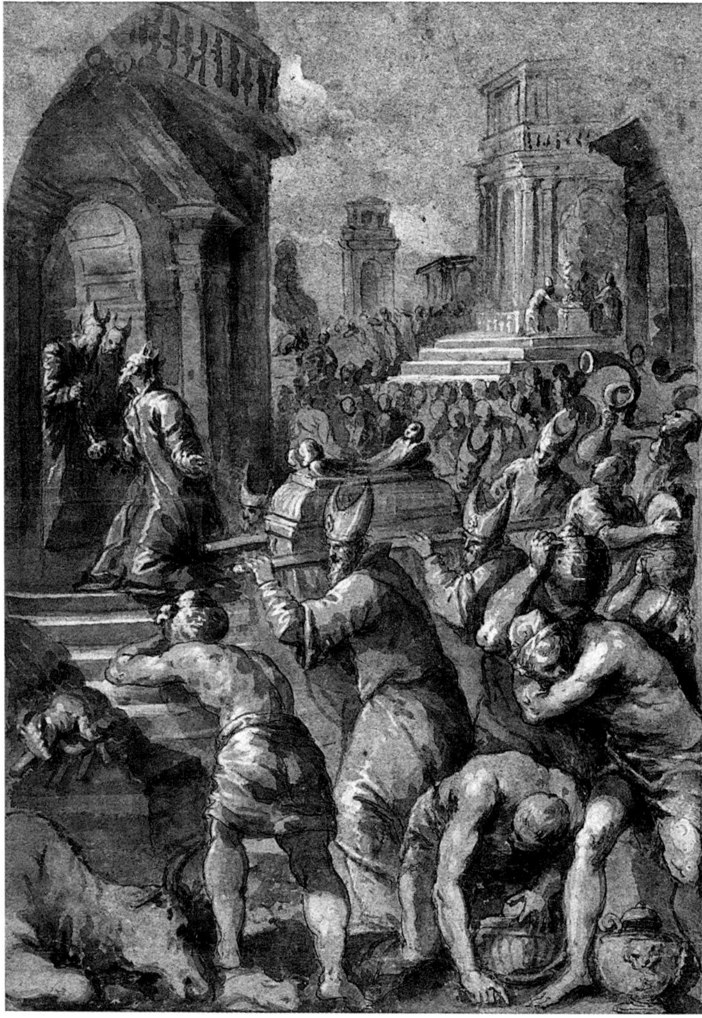

Fig. 29.2. Andrea Michieli, Il Vicentino. *King Solomon Beholds the Ark of the Covenant Being Brought to the Temple*, 1580s–90s. Pen and brown ink, brush and brown wash, highlighted with white gouache, over traces of black chalk, on blue paper, 18½ x 12¾ in. (47.2 x 32.7 cm). The Metropolitan Museum of Art, New York, Gift of William S. Lieberman, in memory of Jacob Bean, 1997 (1997.437)

Palma Il Giovane (ca. 1548–1628). He assimilated the Venetian tradition of drawing and painting from his training in the workshop of the local master, Alessandro Maganza (1556–after 1630), in his birthplace of Vicenza, and his roots in this northern tradition are especially palpable in the airy, endlessly roving space of the landscape depicted here. In addition to certain Venetian qualities of style, particularly those reminiscent of Palma Il Giovane's rapid, light-filled technique of pen and ink with wash modeling (see cat. no. 33), the present drawing also reveals close ties with the Mannerist vocabulary of central Italy, through the work of Federico Zuccaro (see cat. no. 28). The Zuccaresque touch is manifest here in the monumental foreground figures, with their dotlike facial features, elegant attenuation of bodily proportions, and the simplified, stainlike modeling with wash within contours that are continuous and somewhat curvy. During his stay in Venice in 1582, Zuccaro was entrusted to execute a fresco in the Sala del Maggior Consiglio of the Palazzo Ducale in Venice, portraying *Barbarossa Paying Homage to the Pope*, while Vicentino assisted Tintoretto at this time on another painting project in the Doge's palace.

Characteristic of many of his drawings, Vicentino quickly inscribed the Tobey sketch with the names of the various groups in the papal retinue—household servants, carriages, horses, and light cavalry. The composition was likely significantly cropped at right and in its complete state was probably relatively symmetrical with the nearly conical mount at center and the files of attendants at either side in mirroring S-shaped dispositions. When Alfonso II, duke of Ferrara, died childless on October 27, 1597, Pope Clement resolved to attach the stronghold of the Este family to the states of the Church. The papal army entered Ferrara almost unopposed, although Spain and the Holy Roman Empire had sided with Alfonso II's illegitimate cousin, Cesare d'Este. The Tobey drawing was once incorrectly attributed to Antonio Vassilacchi (called L'Aliense, 1556–1629), another artist, like Vicentino, whose drawings and paintings were influenced by Tintoretto and Veronese, and whose graphic style in pen and ink with wash is often similarly reductive.

CCB

1. Basan 1775, under no. 314, sold for 300 livres: "Le Pape Clément VIII, après avoir pris possession de Ferrare, en 1598, se met en marche pour se rendre à Bologne; il est précédé & suivi de tout son cortege, & porté dans une Litiere: Sujet capital, fait avec esprit, à la plume & au bistre, du Cabinet de M. Crozat." (The Pope Clement VIII, after having taken possession of Ferrara, in 1598, marched to seize Bologna; he was preceded and followed by a cortege being carried on a litter: an important subject-matter, done with verve, in pen and brown ink for the delegation of M. Crozat.)

JACOPO LIGOZZI

Verona, 1547–Florence, 1627

A native of Verona, Jacopo Ligozzi moved to Florence about 1577 to work for Francesco I de' Medici, who enlisted him as a scientific draftsman. In that capacity the artist produced many colored drawings of plants and animals. Upon the succession of Grand Duke Ferdinand in 1587, he became court artist to the Medici and was active as a designer of festival decorations, pietra dura, and glass. In the 1590s he also turned his energies to painting frescoes and altarpieces in Florence, and to carrying out commissions for the Gonzaga in Mantua. Ligozzi's numerous highly finished and meticulously executed drawings of religious, allegorical, literary, and historical subjects, often highlighted with gold, were executed as independent works of art and reflect his training as a miniature painter.

30. *Two Persian Grooms Holding a Sultan's Horse*, ca. 1580–85

Pen and brown ink, brush with watercolor and gouache, gold highlights, over traces of black chalk (background in pale green-blue gouache), 10¹⁵⁄₁₆ x 8¾ in. (27.8 x 22.3 cm)
Annotated on recto in pen and brown ink, over preliminary traces of black chalk: *PEICQ/Son[n]o gli staffieri, el Cauallo del Gran Turcho*
The Metropolitan Museum of Art, New York, Promised Gift of David M. Tobey

Provenance: Niccolò Gaddi (Florence, 1537–1591); Trinity Fine Art Ltd., London, 1998; acquired in 1998

References: Forlani 1982; London 1988, no. 19; London and New York 1991–92, no. 12; New York 1998b, pp. 16–17, no. 6; Conigliello 2007 (with reference to the series of drawings); Nathalie Strasser in New York and Edinburgh 2009, p. 48 n. 3, under no. 22

Books and travel accounts stimulated considerable interest in the Muslim East thoughout the Renaissance, and although culminating in the 1540s to 1560s, this fascination did not wane after the naval battle of Lepanto was won in 1571, in which the Ottoman fleet was defeated by the Holy League, a coalition formed by Spain, Venice, Genoa, and the papacy, among other western military powers. Dating to the later period in this history, the sheet in the Tobey Collection was part of a large suite of richly colored drawings depicting figures of the Ottoman court, executed by Jacopo Ligozzi sometime after his arrival in Florence in 1577 from his native town of Verona, most likely in 1580–85.

These drawings were inspired by the etchings illustrating a best-selling book of the period, *Les quatre premiers livres des navigations et pérégrinations orientales*, by the French geographer Nicolas de Nicolay (1517–1583), for Ligozzi himself never traveled to the East. Nicolay's book was first published in 1567 in a French edition (Lyon: Guillaume Rouille), which was illustrated with sixty etchings designed by the Fontainebleau engraver Léon Davent in 1555.[1] The second edition of the book in 1576 and the first Italian edition of 1577 were both published in Antwerp, the former titled *Les navigations pérégrina-*

tions et voyages, faits en la Turquie, and the latter, *Le navigationi et viaggi, fatti nella Turchia, di Nicolo de' Nicolai del Delfinato*. The source for Ligozzi's drawings was a Venetian edition of Nicolay's book published in 1580, illustrated with additional plates but representing the same text as the first Antwerp issue in Italian. Apparently versions of the book also exist with plates tinted with color.[2]

In contrast to his models, Ligozzi used a rich palette of color and invented the motifs of real and imaginary animals that accompany most of the figures in exotic dress. The project was a major accomplishment for Ligozzi and probably helped establish his reputation in the competitive Florentine art world of the 1580s. The drawings of this series were almost certainly part of an ensemble (possibly an album, binding, or even a book as in the editions of Nicolay's *Le navigazioni et viaggi nella Turchia*), which was later taken apart and dispersed. The sheets can be dated based on the relationship to the 1580 Venetian printed edition of Nicolay, during the period of Ligozzi's employment as court painter to Francesco I de' Medici (1541–1587), Grand Duke of Tuscany. It appears, however, that the actual patron of Ligozzi's project was the erudite Florentine art collector, Niccolò Gaddi (1537–1591).[3]

At least twenty-nine drawings from this series have been identified thus far. The largest number of them (twenty-one) is owned by the Gabinetto Disegni e Stampe degli Uffizi, Florence, and were given to the museum on February 7, 1867, by the Florentine sculptor Niccolò Bazzanti; the collection had a difficult history of loss and restitution in the 1940s.[4] Importantly, the backgrounds in the Uffizi sheets are not painted in colored gouache, perhaps an indication of the original state of the designs. Many of them are annotated with small numbers at upper right on the recto, and while the surface is well preserved, the Uffizi sheets are of slightly smaller dimensions than most of the other known works from the series. At least ten further related drawings are scattered among other public and

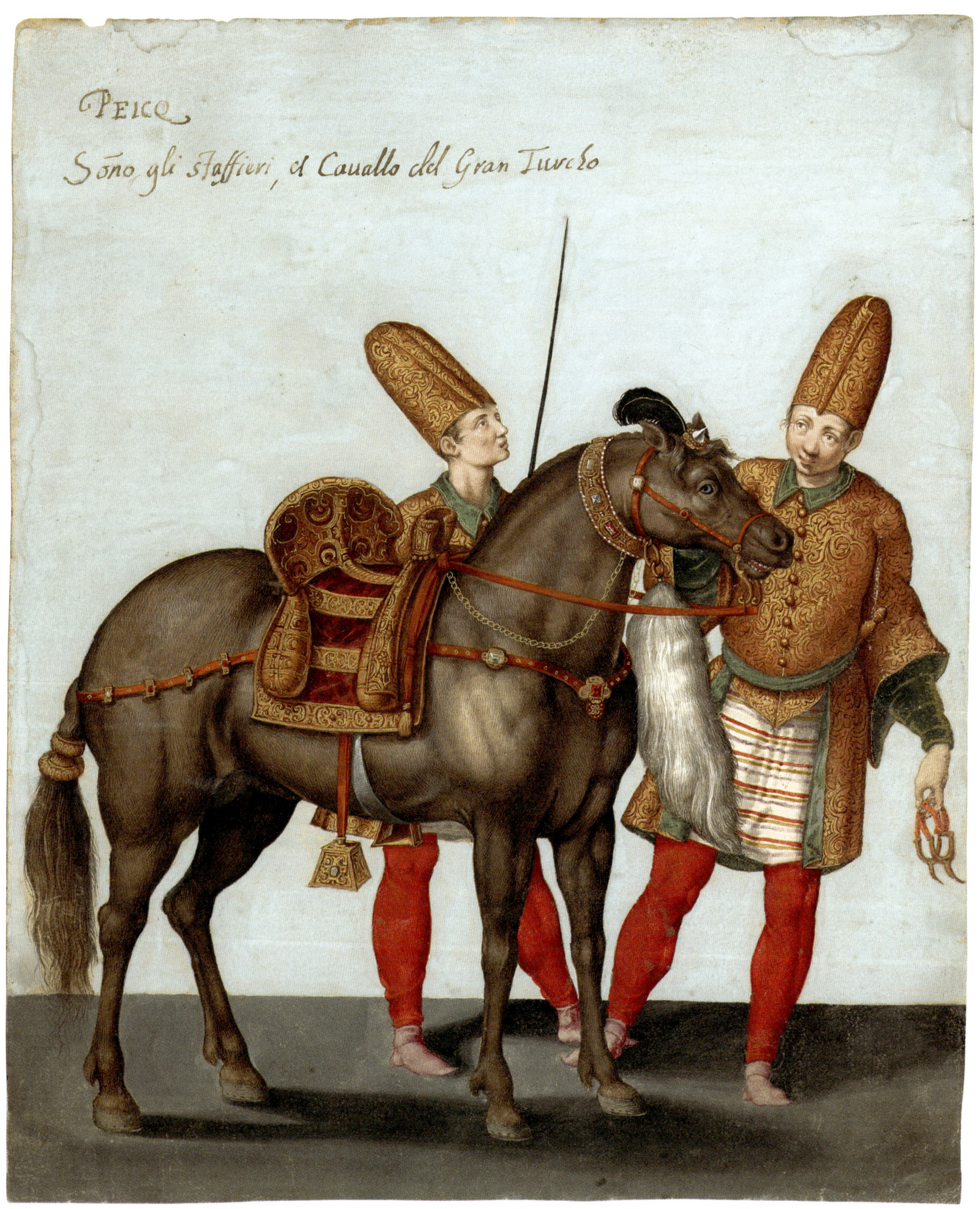

PEICO
Sono, gli staffieri, et Cauallo del Gran Turcho

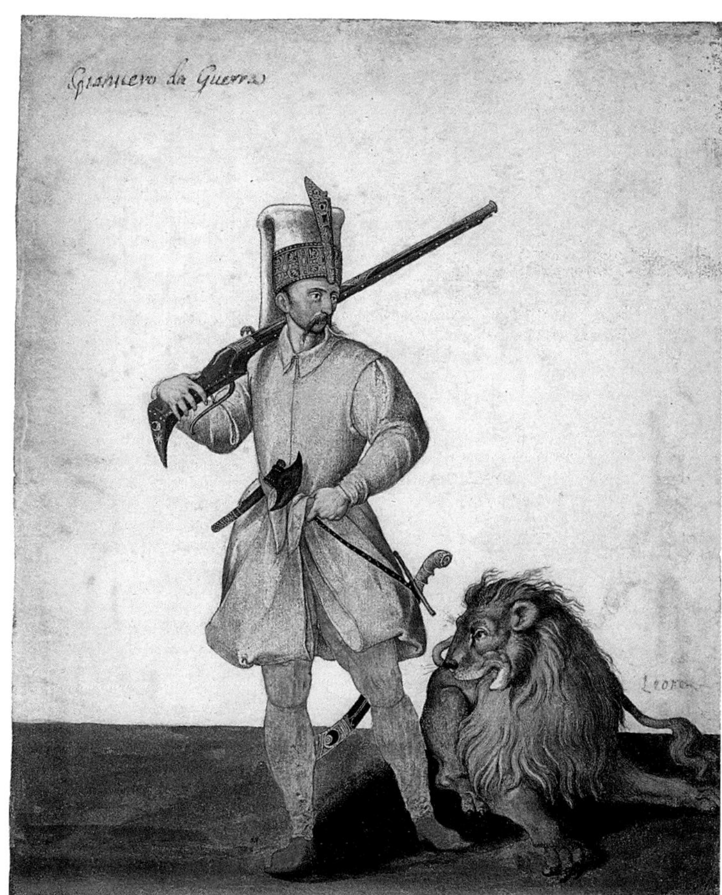

Fig. 30.1. Jacopo Ligozzi. *Janissary of War with a Lion*, ca. 1580–85. Brush with watercolor and gouache, pen and brown ink, gold highlights, over traces of black chalk (the background without color), 11⅛ x 8¹³⁄₁₆ in. (28.2 x 22.4 cm). The Metropolitan Museum of Art, New York, Harris Brisbane Dick Fund, 1997 (1997.21)

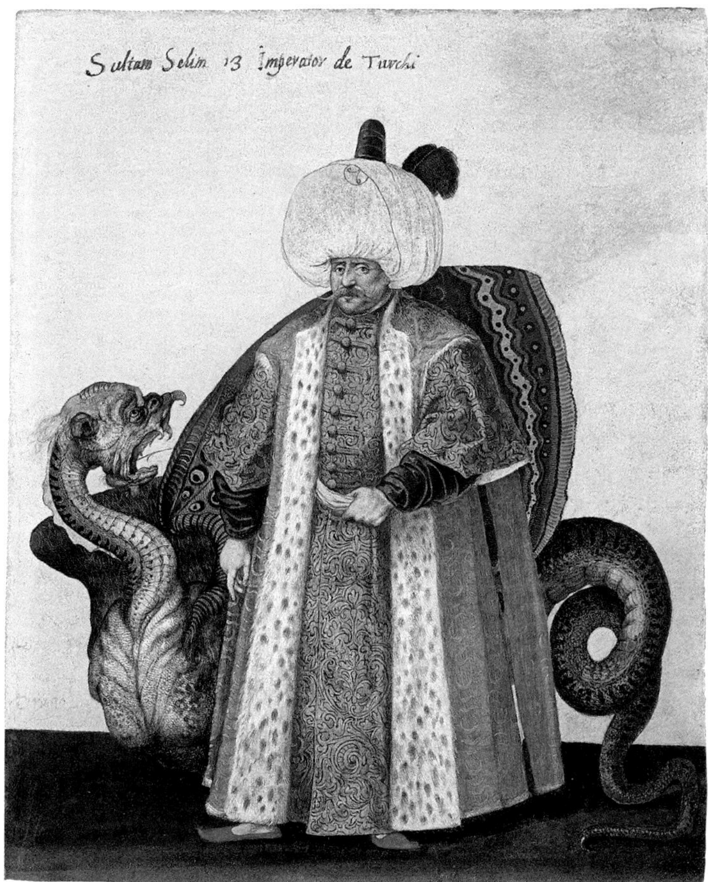

Fig. 30.2. Jacopo Ligozzi. *Sultan Selim II with a Dragon*, ca. 1580–85. Brush with watercolor and gouache, pen and brown ink, gold highlights, over traces of black chalk; the background colored light blue (by a later hand?), 10¹³⁄₁₆ x 8⁷⁄₁₆ in. (27.5 x 21.5 cm). Collection of Jean Bonna, Geneva

private collections (figs. 30.1, 30.2), most of which have been recent discoveries in the art market. As is the case with the present example, a number of them exhibit a uniform background in colored gouache,[5] ranging from light blue, as here, to pale green. While these areas may have been added by a later hand (the conventional explanation), the ductus of the script in pen and brown ink, which is seen in the present example along the upper left, is essentially the same as that in the inscriptions on the Uffizi sheets. This writing lies over the pale-blue gouache. It is therefore possible that the gouache backgrounds represent a partial reworking of traces of color that were already present, rather than being entirely a later addition.

The Tobey composition depicts two elaborately dressed adolescent grooms with tall hats who hold still a lavishly harnessed horse by the bridle. It is inscribed along the top: *PEICQ/Son[n]o gli staffieri, el Cauallo del Gran Turcho* (these are the pages and horse of the great Turk). The figural group is painted with an extraordinary delicacy of touch and precision, much like that

of a manuscript illumination, and the layer of densely applied pigments is fresh and well preserved. The design based on Davent's etching is plate 88 in the 1580 Venetian edition, but the conception of Ligozzi's figures is greatly more naturalistic, in keeping with the prevalent cultural taste in Florence and Bologna at the time for a learned understanding of exotic Eastern cultures and a scientific study of botanical and zoological species (see cat. no. 31). CCB

1. Much new historical data regarding Nicolay's *Les quatre premiers livres . . .* was published in Ilg 2008.
2. An example with the plates tinted in color (British Library, London, inv. no. 14.i.10) was cited in Turner, Hendrix, and Plazzotta 1997, p. 55, no. 23.
3. Conigliello 2007, p. 7.
4. Forlani 1982, p. 77, with citation of document. The twenty-one drawings in the Gabinetto Disegni e Stample degli Uffizi, Florence, are inv nos. 2946–2967 F. In this group, inv. no. 2955 F has reportedly been missing since the drawings were restituted to the museum after World War II, from Germany.
5. For the example at the J. Paul Getty Museum, Los Angeles (inv. no. 91.GG.53), in which the background was removed, see Turner, Hendrix, and Plazzotta 1997, pp. 55–57, no. 23.

31. *Botanical Specimen (Motherwort or* Leonurus cardiaca*)*, 1580–1600

Brush with watercolor and gouache on vellum; glued onto a mount, 21 x 13⅛ in. (53.3 x 33.3 cm)

The Metropolitan Museum of Art, New York, Promised Gift of David M. Tobey, and Purchase, Rogers Fund, 2004 (2004.435)

Provenance: Bernard Houthakker, Amsterdam; Private Collection, New York; Katrin Bellinger Kunsthandel, Munich; acquired by The Metropolitan Museum of Art, 2004

References: Bambach 2005; Nathalie Strasser in New York and Edinburgh 2009, pp. 50, 52 n. 9

A group of seventy-eight botanical drawings by Jacopo Ligozzi, now in the Gabinetto Disegni e Stampe degli Uffizi, Florence (inv. nos. 1894–1966 Ornati), represents the largest extant holding of his work in this genre, datable to about 1577–87, during the reign of Francesco I de' Medici (1541–1587) as Grand Duke of Tuscany. These entered the

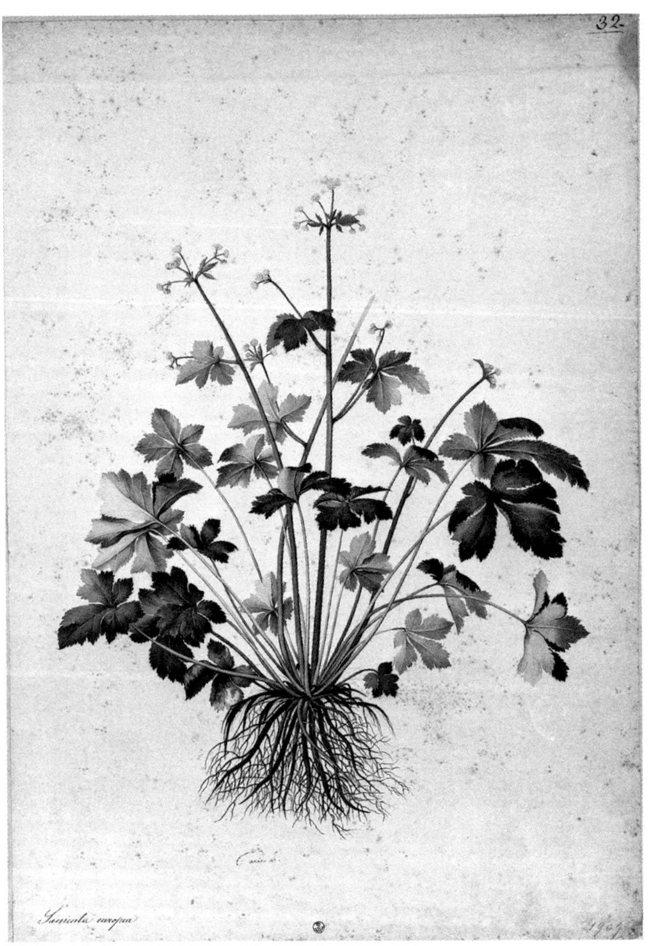

Fig. 31.1. Jacopo Ligozzi. *Sanicula Europea*, ca. 1577–91. Brush with gouache and watercolor, over traces of black chalk on off-white paper, 26⁹⁄₁₆ x 17⅞ in. (67.5 x 45.4 cm). Gabinetto Disegni e Stampe degli Uffizi, Florence (1909 Ornato)

grand-ducal collections that formed the Uffizi probably about the time that they were produced, in the late sixteenth century, or so (fig. 31.1).[1] Another large group of such drawings exists among the papers of the celebrated Bolognese naturalist Ulisse Aldrovandi (1522–1605), now at the Biblioteca Universitaria, Bologna. The present large drawing by Ligozzi is, therefore, among the very rare examples to be in a collection outside Italy (see fig. 31.2).[2] It is meticulously rendered in color on fine vellum, rather than on white paper (as are the Uffizi exemplars), and portrays a thoroughly detailed specimen of a motherwort (*Leonurus cardiaca*), a plant of the mint family that grows ubiquitously in Europe, Asia, and America (see fig. 31.3).[3] The important medicinal properties of motherwort in treating both cardiovascular and gynecological conditions were recognized since ancient Greek times. True to the primarily scientific purpose of describing the specimen, the artist portrayed it in a clear frontal view and in a monumental scale, in order to achieve the greatest amount of identifying detail possible. The image appears lifesize and is depicted in early bloom, with only a few small pale rose blossoms. The square shape of the stem, which is characteristic of all mint plants, is clearly discernible. The rendition of each of the ash-gray green leaves is precise, with careful attention given to the somewhat jagged profiles of the blades and the intricacies of the fanlike ribs of the interior veining. The representation of the secondary roots is wonderfully animated and atmospheric in its tonal delicacy; here, the strands seem almost like human hair. While the artist's mastery of perspective and pictorial effects of form placed in space is everywhere apparent, he nevertheless deliberately restrained his use of such devices so as not to compromise the overall scientific accuracy of the identifying details.

Ligozzi's early prowess as a draftsman and miniaturist of natural history subjects cemented his fifty-year career in Florence. Francesco I de' Medici had hired the young Ligozzi from Verona in 1577, three years after his ascension as Grand Duke of Tuscany, granting him a handsome salary of 25 *scudi* as court painter. The famous Aldrovandi highly praised Ligozzi as a scientific illustrator in 1577, while visiting Florence, and the artist's career specialty of recording the botanical specimens of the Medici gardens at Florence (the *Giardino dei Semplici*) and at Pisa (the *Orto Botanico*) developed during the following decade.[4] Documents suggest that Francesco I exchanged both specimens and drawings in color of plants, birds, and animals with Aldrovandi, who visited Florence again in 1586, to admire the great botanical rarities of the Medici gardens, and Ligozzi once more played a major role in these erudite exchanges.[5] The Tobey drawing was probably intended to form part of an

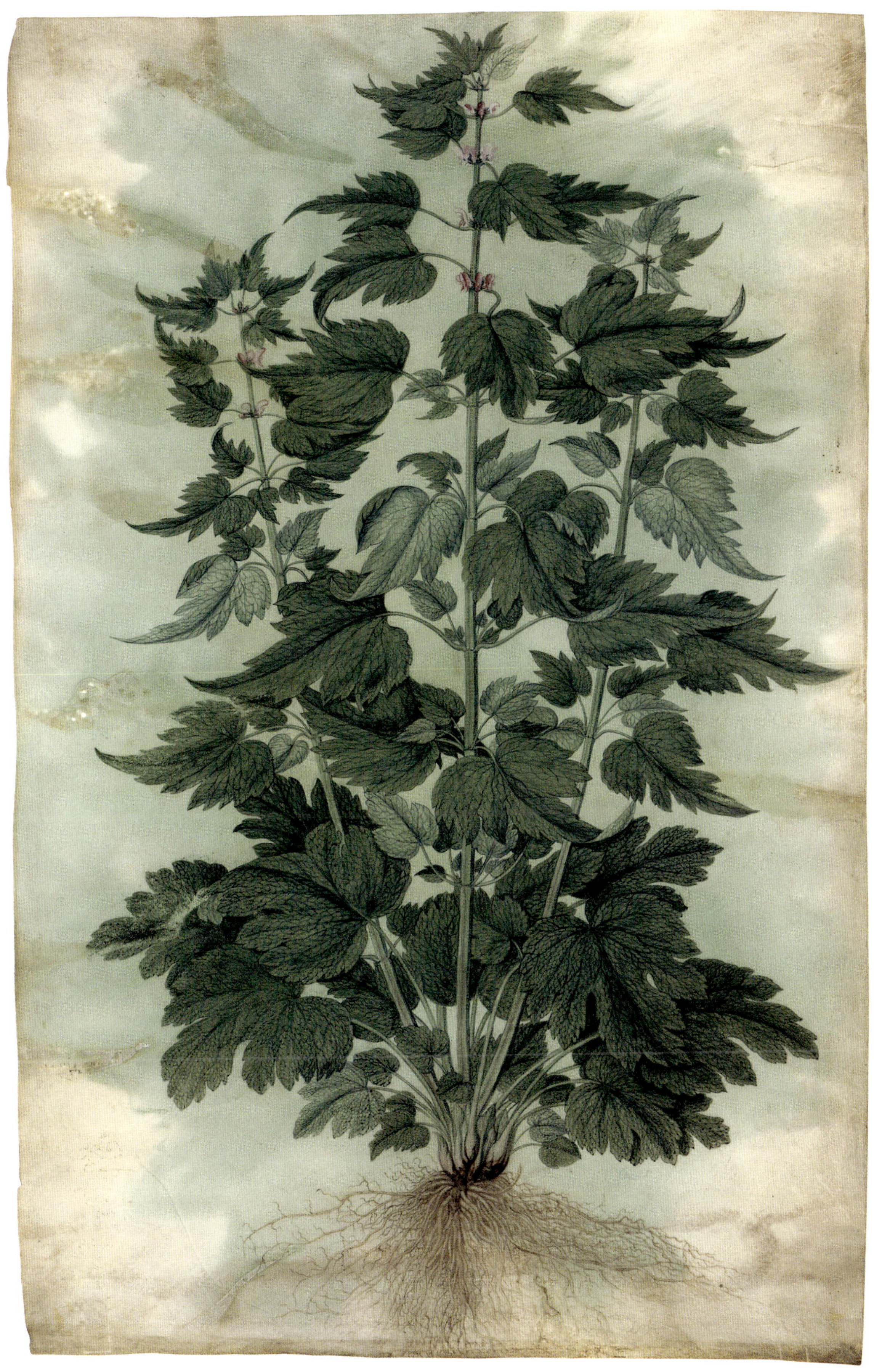

that are evident in Ligozzi's drawings—the atmospheric effects, tonal precision, or use of color.

The unusual condition of the present drawing merits some comment, for the design of the plant itself is fresh and relatively well preserved. The green wash background[8] seen here is not characteristic of Ligozzi's botanical studies from the grand-ducal collections at the Uffizi (see fig. 31.1), but a small group of closely related sheets drawn on vellum by the artist, such as the exemplar in the Collection of Jean Bonna, Geneva, also exhibit this quality (see fig. 31.2).[9] These works on vellum may have been pages from the same binding or album, and as they all display water stains in the background—not affecting the image of the plant—it seems likely that the green hue was the result of the accidental running of green water-based pigment. It may have occurred during the working process and may have caused the artist to refrain from finishing the drawing. In the present example, the lower portion of the plant, above the area of the root, is particularly detailed in the tonal articulations of the leaf blades, many of which are delicately defined with dark outlines, as well as with dark and light dots of pigment. By contrast, the upper portion of the plant seems unfinished, for it does not display a similarly detailed tonal calibration (it seems to lack the extent of dotted shadows and highlights and dark outlines in the veining of the leaf blades). The second blossom from the top also seems to omit completely a final outlining by the artist. Close comparisons to some of Ligozzi's botanical studies in the Uffizi suggest that a finishing upper layer of yellow and brown hues might have been added selectively by the artist as a final step. The water damage has somewhat diminished the sharpness of detail in the passage depicting the roots of the plant. There are small areas of abrasion on the drawing surface in the lower left quadrant.

The exquisitely observed botanical drawings of Ligozzi constitute milestones in the early modern history of scientific illustration (they were the most innovative in Italy since Leonardo da Vinci's plant studies, dating between ca. 1487 and ca. 1515) and were extremely influential for later generations of naturalists and scientific illustrators. Among Ligozzi's younger followers in this tradition were his cousin Francesco and grandson Bartolomeo (1630–1695),[10] as well as the accomplished specialist of still lifes, Giovanna Garzoni (1600–1670), but his virtuosity as a draftsman-illustrator of the natural world remained unsurpassed even by the teams of specialized graphic artists employed by the learned Cassiano dal Pozzo (1588–1657) in producing the celebrated works that he later described as the *Museo Cartaceo* (the Paper Museum of Natural History), begun soon after 1612.   CCB

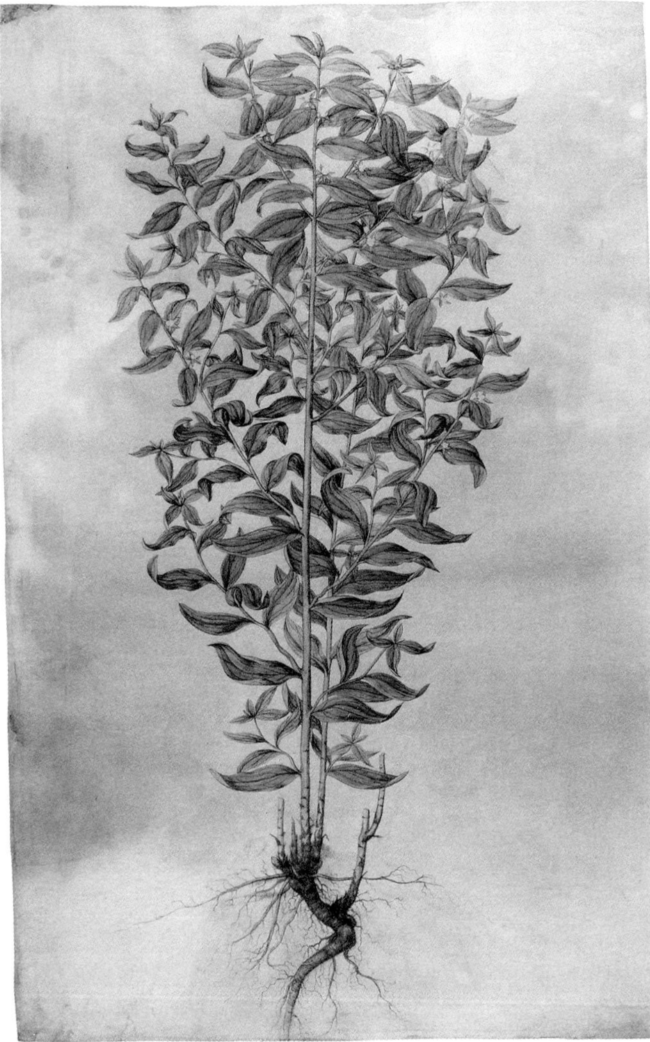

Fig. 31.2. Jacopo Ligozzi. *Plant Study*, ca. 1580–1600. Brush and gouache on vellum, 21½ x 13⁵⁄₁₆ in. (54.6 x 33.8 cm). Collection of Jean Bonna, Geneva

anthology and, based on its style, seems to date after Ligozzi's early activity as a botanical illustrator to Francesco I, who died in 1587. It was produced at a time when numerous herbals and botanical treatises were being printed in Italy,[6] that is, more than one hundred years after the first such treatise was published in 1470. While this and the drawings from the grand-ducal collections in the Uffizi were not published as prints, many of the artist's later botanical studies were reproduced in Tobia Aldini's book, *Exactissima descriptio rariorum quarundam plantarum . . . horto farnesiano* (Rome, 1625).[7] The medium of the printed book, however, whether done with woodcut or engraved illustrations, could hardly do justice to the subtleties

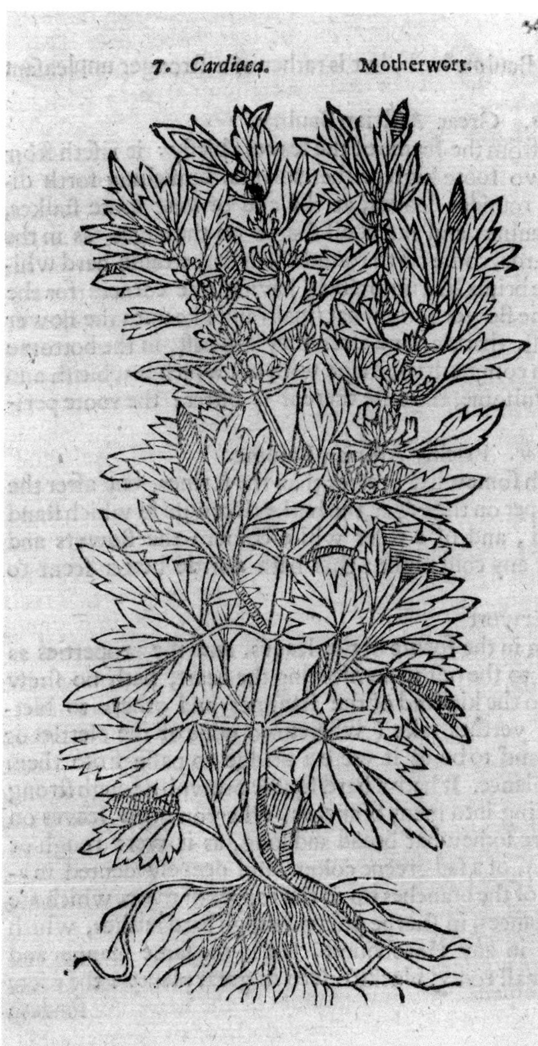

Fig. 31.3. John Parkinson. *Specimen of Motherwort*. Detail from *Theatrum Botanicum: The Theater of the Plants*, London, 1640, p. 42. Woodcut, 14³⁄₁₆ x 9⁷⁄₁₆ x 4⁵⁄₁₆ in. (36 x 24 x 11 cm). The Metropolitan Museum of Art, New York, Gift of Estate of Marie L. Russell, 1946 (46.117.3)

1. Compare Tongiorgi Tomasi and Tosi 1990, pp. 5–54, 77–85, nos. 48–64; Conigliello 1994.
2. The attribution of this drawing to Jacopo Ligozzi was confirmed by Federico Tognoni, specialist of Ligozzi's botanical drawings (written communication via email to dealer, August 6, 2004).
3. The identification of this specimen as Motherwort is due to Noelle O'Connor (written communication to the present author, March 29, 2005).
4. Compare Conigliello 1990a; Conigliello 1992, pp. 18–27.
5. Olmi 1977.
6. Many examples of these early printed botanical books are represented in the Department of Drawings and Prints, The Metropolitan Museum of Art, New York. See, for example, Arnoldo de Villanova's *Ortus Sanitatis* (Venice, 1511), Fabio Colonna's *Plantarum* (Naples, 1592), and Giovanni Battista Ferrari's *De Florum Cultura* (Rome, 1633).
7. Conigliello 1994.
8. This pigment is a copper green (hydrated copper sulfate); see the unpublished report by Marjorie N. Shelley, Sherman Fairchild Conservator in Charge, Department of Paper Conservation, The Metropolitan Museum of Art, New York (Archive of the Department of Drawings and Prints, The Metropolitan Museum of Art, New York, September 21, 2004).
9. On the drawing now in the Jean Bonna Collection, Geneva, which shares the points of technique described above, see Nathalie Strasser in New York and Edinburgh 2009, pp. 50–52. A third, closely related study of a plant on vellum, in the same scale, with the same issue of the green-wash background, and hence evidently belonging to this same group, was brought to my attention by Marjorie N. Shelley in March 2009, and is now in a private collection in New York.
10. Tongiorgi Tomasi and Tosi 1990, pp. 85–86, nos. 64–66.

32. *La Verna: Chapel of Saint Sebastian*, ca. 1607–12

Pen and brown ink, brush and brown wash; the lunette and the altarpiece of
Saint Sebastian are drawn on two separate sheets of paper inserted by the artist.
The outlines are indented with the stylus for transfer, and the verso is rubbed
with red chalk for transfer.
13½ x 9¾ in. (34.3 x 24.8 cm)

Provenance: Private Collection, Europe; Colnaghi, London, 1997; Private
Collection, Italy; Trinity Fine Art Ltd., London; acquired in 2002

Reference: Ongpin 1997, no. 21

In this late work by Jacopo Ligozzi, discovered in the London
art market in 1997, two male pilgrims kneel before an altarpiece framed by columns depicting Saint Sebastian within the
interior of a chapel dedicated to the martyr. A third pilgrim is
about to stride through the door at right. The lunette that sur-
mounts the main altarpiece panel, on the upper center, portrays
the Temptation of Saint Francis. The final designs for the motifs
depicting Saints Sebastian and Francis within the altarpiece
were drawn on two separate sheets of paper and pasted on to
the drawing, over the previous solutions.

This detailed composition forms part of a series of drawings
by Ligozzi, done to design the twenty-six reproductive prints
illustrating Fra Lino Moroni's guide to the monastery of La
Verna, titled *Descrizione del Sacro Monte della Vernia*, published
in Florence in 1612.[1] The prints in this book reproduce Ligozzi's
drawings in reverse design orientation; the engravings were
executed by Domenico Falcini, and the etchings by Raffaello
Schiaminossi. A complete bound volume with the prints
exists at the Gabinetto Disegni e Stampe degli Uffizi, Florence
(Stampe 4959-4981),[2] while an exemplar with one or two
missing plates is at The Metropolitan Museum of Art, New
York. The Tobey drawing corresponds to the engraving of the
plate marked "N" (fig. 32.1),[3] but here the design is cropped
along the bottom border, omitting the broad band with the
oval cartouche in the print. The inscriptions accompanying this
particular engraving clarify the more enigmatic details of the
composition. A tomb slab is seen on the floor, toward the deep
left corner of the interior, which was said to contain the trans-
ported remains of many Franciscan friars, while in the direct
foreground the four ovals and the small rectangle at center
represent the columns before the corridor and the main door
of the chapel.

Today called La Verna, the famous sanctuary marks the site
where Saint Francis of Assisi received the stigmata in 1224 and
is dramatically perched on Mount Penna in the Apennines, ris-
ing above the valley of the Casentino in southeastern Tuscany.
La Verna was donated to Saint Francis and his order in 1213 and
became a major center for the Franciscan faith. Ligozzi is known
to have accompanied Fra Lino Moroni, the Tuscan provincial

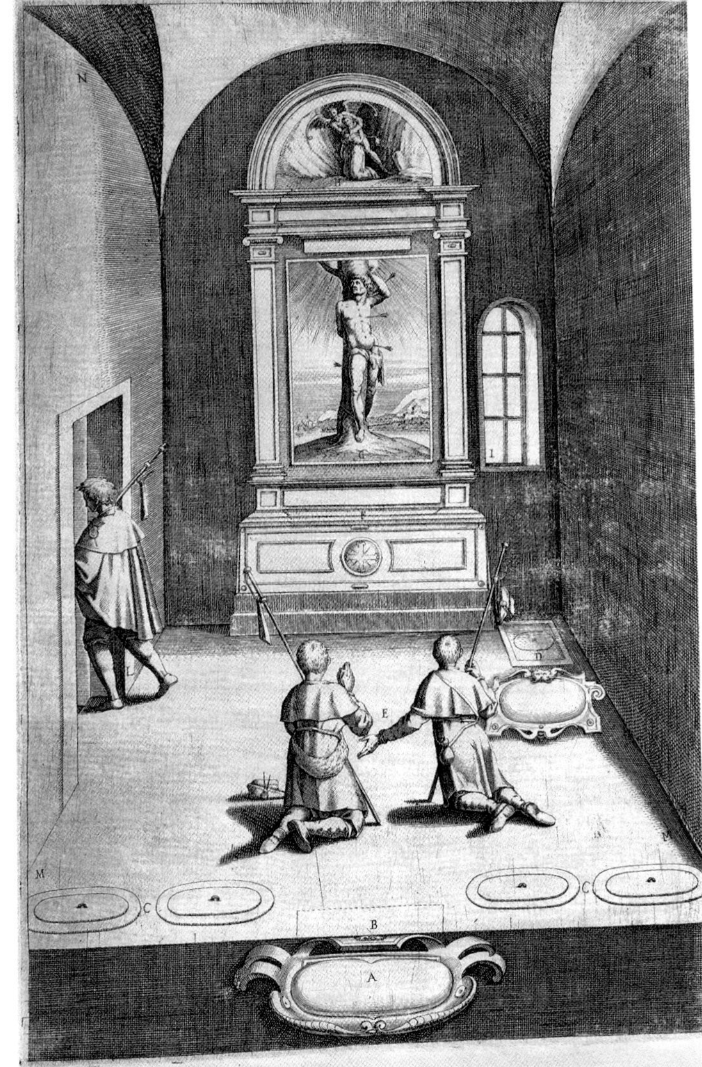

Fig. 32.1. After a design by Jacopo Ligozzi. *La Verna: Chapel of Saint
Sebastian*. Page from Fra Lino Moroni, *Descrizione del Sacro Monte della
Vernia*. Florence, 1612. Engraving. Plate marked "N," 18⅛ x 13⅜ x ¹¹⁄₁₆ in.
(46 x 34 x 1.8 cm). The Metropolitan Museum of Art, New York, The
Elisha Whittelsey Collection, The Elisha Whittelsey Fund, 1949 (49.62.11)

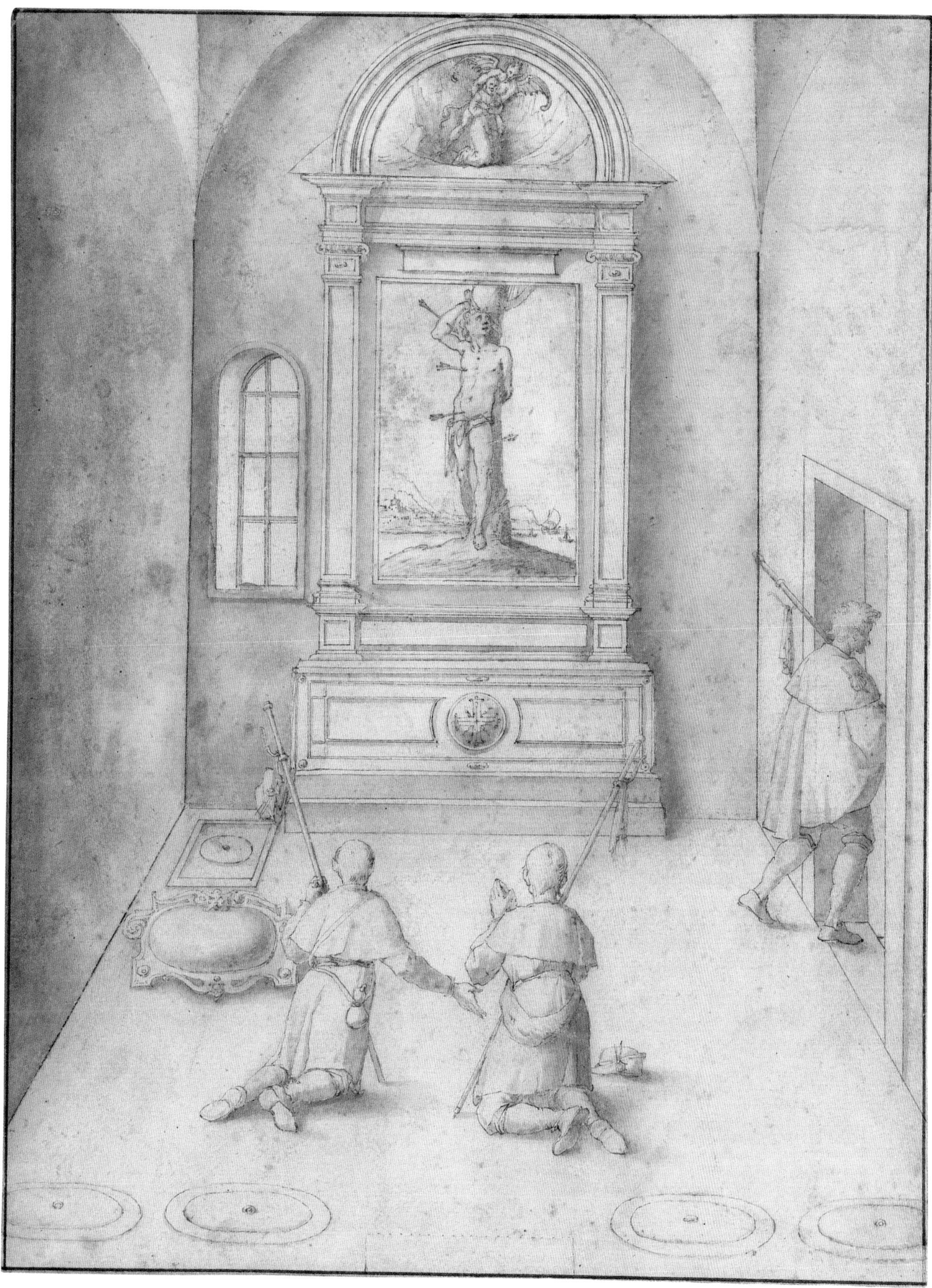

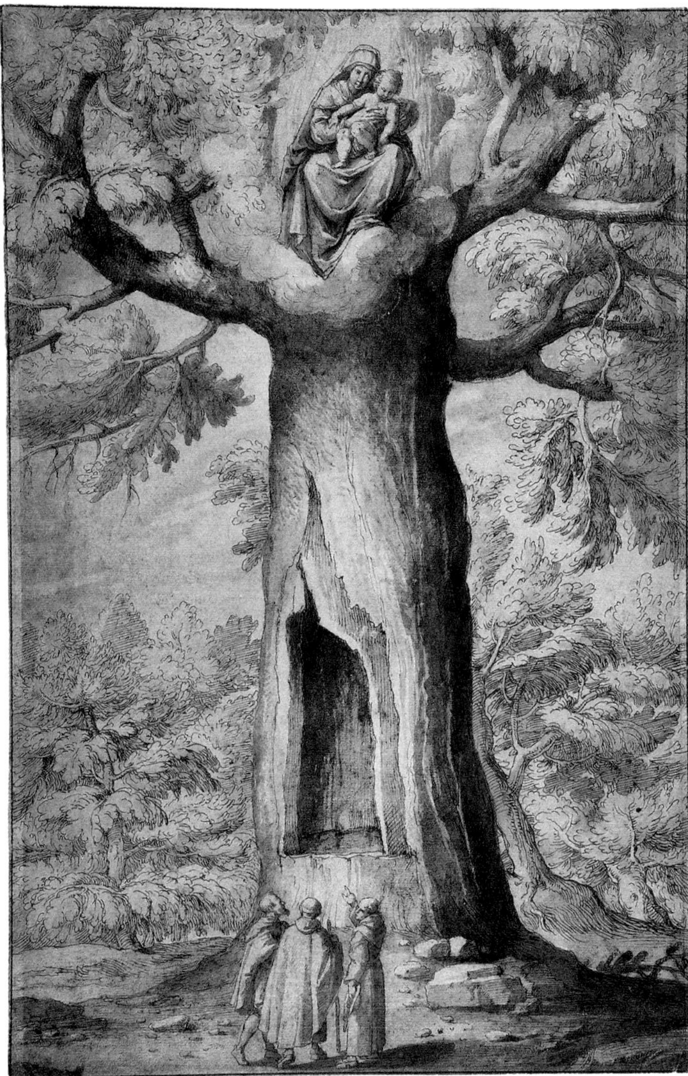

Fig. 32.2. Jacopo Ligozzi. *Beech of the Madonna at La Verna*, 1607–12. Pen and brown ink, brush with brown wash and traces of gray wash, over black chalk; the outlines stylus-indented for transfer, 15 ¹³⁄₁₆ x 10⅛ in. (40.2 x 25.7 cm). The Metropolitan Museum of Art, New York, Harry G. Sperling Fund, 1983 (1983.131.1)

of the Franciscan-Observant order, to La Verna in 1607, to portray the sites of the sanctuary in true-to-life detail, and this is probably also the date of this and the related drawings of the series for Fra Lino's *Descrizione del Sacro Monte della Vernia*. The text on the facing page at left, accompanying the engraving after Ligozzi's design, describes the scene here as "the Chapel of Saint Sebastian, which is located on top of the mount, where there is a cliff from which the enemy [the Devil] attempted to throw down Father Saint Francis, in which there are five graves, where many Blessed are buried and where the friars are buried" ("Cappella di San Bastiano situata sopra il Masso doue è il precipizio, doue il nimico volse precipitare il Padre San Francesco, nella quale sono cinque Sepolture, doue son sepolti molti Beati, e dove si seppelliscano i Frati"). This general description of the Chapel of Saint Sebastian had been mentioned already by Agostino Miglio in 1568, who added a number of details, and which had itself been the result of a previous written tradition.[4]

A number of Ligozzi's related preparatory drawings for this series dedicated to the monastery of La Verna have been identified; they are all done in the same drawing technique, in the full-scale of the corresponding print, but in reverse design orientation, and exhibit incised outlines. Three of the sheets have become well known since their publication in the 1980s; they are in The Metropolitan Museum of Art, New York (fig. 32.2);[5] the Louvre, Paris (fig. 32.3),[6] and the Collection Frits Lugt-Fondation Custodia, Paris (fig. 32.4).[7] A further drawing in an Italian private collection for a plate marked "Q," which depicts the *Chapel of the Watering Beech Tree*, was recorded in 1996.[8] The present sheet and five other of the associated drawings were discovered and exhibited at Colnaghi's, London, in 1997,[9] two of which were acquired by the Fitzwilliam Museum, Cambridge, England,[10] and another by the J. Paul Getty Museum, Los Angeles.[11] There is an excellent probability that more of Ligozzi's drawings for the La Verna series will eventually come to light.   CCB

1. Compare Bean 1990; William M. Griswold in Griswold and Wolk-Simon 1994, pp. 40–41, no. 35; Conigliello 1999; Lucilla Conigliello in Florence, Chicago, and Detroit 2002–3, pp. 319–20, no. 177.
2. Conigliello 1992, pp. 67–84, nos. 10–32.
3. Ibid., pp. 76–77, no. 22, pl. XXIII, without mention of the present drawing.
4. Text quoted from the impression of the book in The Metropolitan Museum of Art (49.62.11); see fig. 32.1.
5. This sheet was identified as a study for the plate marked "P" by Jacob Bean; see now William M. Griswold in Griswold and Wolk-Simon 1994, pp. 40–41, no. 35.
6. This sheet was identified as a study for the plate of the series marked "L"; see Viatte 1988, p. 144, no. 251; Conigliello 2005, p. 72, no. 21.
7. This sheet was identified as a study for the plate of the series marked "X"; see Byam Shaw 1983, vol. 1, pp. 43–44, no. 37, vol. 3, pl. 44.
8. The identification was made by Conigliello, as recorded in Ongpin 1997.
9. See Ongpin 1997, under nos. 18–23.
10. See ibid., nos. 18 and 19; Paris 2002, nos. 10–11.
11. See Ongpin 1997, no. 22; J. Paul Getty Museum, Los Angeles (97.GA.69).

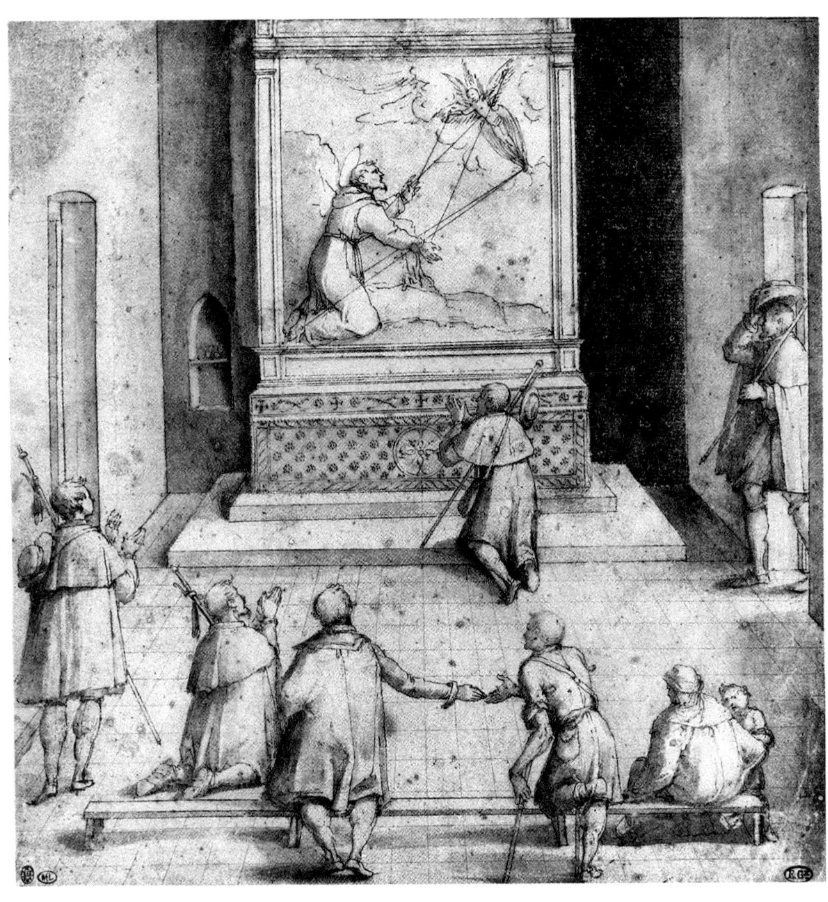

Fig. 32.3. Jacopo Ligozzi. *A Chapel's Sanctuary at La Verna*, 1607–12. Pen and brown ink, brush and brown wash, over black chalk; the outlines stylus-indented for transfer, 10⅗₁₆ x 9⁹⁄₁₆ in. (26.9 x 24.3 cm). Département des Arts Graphiques, Musée du Louvre, Paris (RF 77)

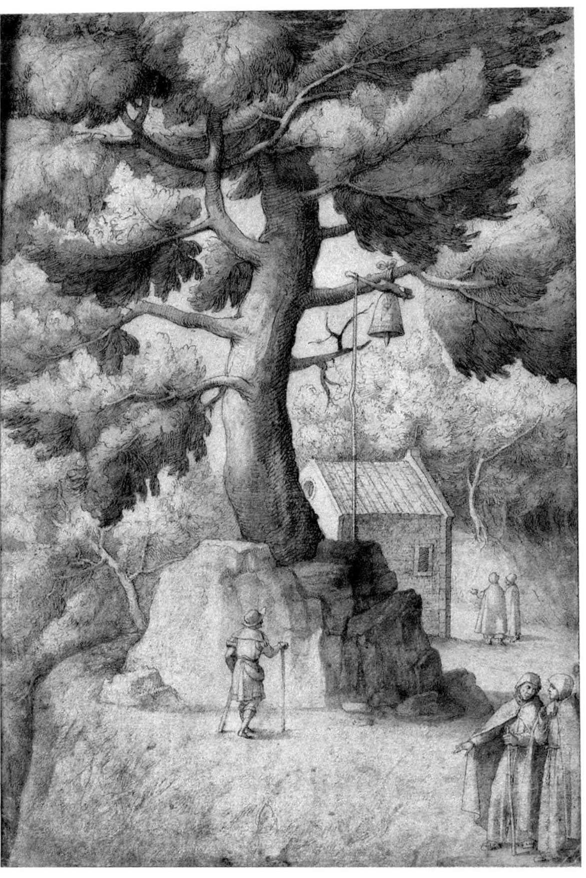

Fig. 32.4. Jacopo Ligozzi. *A Rocky Landscape with a Great Tree and a Hermit's Cell, Monks and a Pilgrim*, 1607–12. Pen and brown ink, brush and brown wash, over black chalk; the outlines stylus-indented for transfer, 14¹⁵⁄₁₆ x 9¹³⁄₁₆ in. (38 x 25 cm). Collection Frits Lugt–Fondation Custodia, Paris (5468)

PALMA IL GIOVANE

Venice, ca. 1548–Venice, 1628

Giacomo Palma, known as Palma Il Giovane, may have trained with Titian, but his style was most profoundly influenced by the elongated figures, dramatic chiaroscuro, effulgent landscapes, and painterly bravura of Tintoretto. After the latter's death in 1594, Palma became the most prominent artist in Venice, where, aside from an early period of study in Rome, he spent his entire long career. Among his most important works were the canvases he painted over a number of years in the Palazzo Ducale in the wake of the devastating fire of 1577, and the cycle in the Oratory of the Crociferi. He also executed portraits, altarpieces, and small mythological scenes, and frequently collaborated with the Venetian sculptor Alessandro Vittoria. His fame extended far beyond Venice, and in his later years he received commissions from the royal courts in Prague and Warsaw. Exceedingly prolific, Palma produced a vast oeuvre, of which over six hundred paintings and hundreds of drawings survive.

33. *Studies for a Scene of Christ's Descent into Limbo and the Raising of the Holy Fathers of the Church*, ca. 1620–28

Red chalk, pen and brown ink, brush with red and brown wash, 9¼ x 15½ in. (23.5 x 39.4 cm)
Annotated in pen and brown ink, along lower border toward left: *Palma*

Provenance: Sagredo-Borghese Album, annotated on verso in pen and dark brown ink: "G. P. No. 343"; Gaud Collection; sale, Sotheby's, Monaco, June 20, 1987, lot 57; acquired in 1987

Reference: Sotheby's, Monaco 1987, no. 57

A little published, late work by Palma Il Giovane, this energetic sheet of sketches was preparatory for a lunette canvas depicting *Christ's Descent into Limbo* at the church of San Zaccaria, Venice (fig. 33.1); the other two similarly shaped works represent *Christ Washing the Feet of the Apostles* and the *Martyrdom of Saint Ligerius*.[1] The prolific Palma, a painter of "soverchia speditezza" ("exceeding rapidity of execution," to quote his countryman Anton Maria Zanetti's judgment in 1771[2]), but possessing a greatly affable personality, decorated numerous churches and confraternities in Venice. His death in

1628 signaled the demise of "good taste in the Venetian style of painting" ("il buon gusto della maniera veneziana"), according to Carlo Ridolfi's biography of the artist in *Le meraviglie dell'arte*, published in 1648.[3] While the subject of the present composition and the final painting has at times been imprecisely described, the wording by Ridolfi, who is the artist's most direct reviewer, must be considered reliable; it depicts "how the Savior raised the Holy Fathers from Limbo" ("Saluatore . . . , e come egli trahe dal Limbo i Santi Padri").[4] Marco Boschini's 1674 guidebook of Venice, *Descrizione di tutte le pubbliche pitture della città di Venezia*, denoted it similarly.[5] The painting cycle was commissioned from Palma by the Confraternity of San Ligerio (or San Lizerio), which had its quarters at San Zaccaria and was located there by Ridolfi, but by the time of Boschini's writing, it had been placed in the "little church of the Holiest Sacrament on the grounds of San Zaccaria" ("Chiesuola del Santissimo nel recinto di

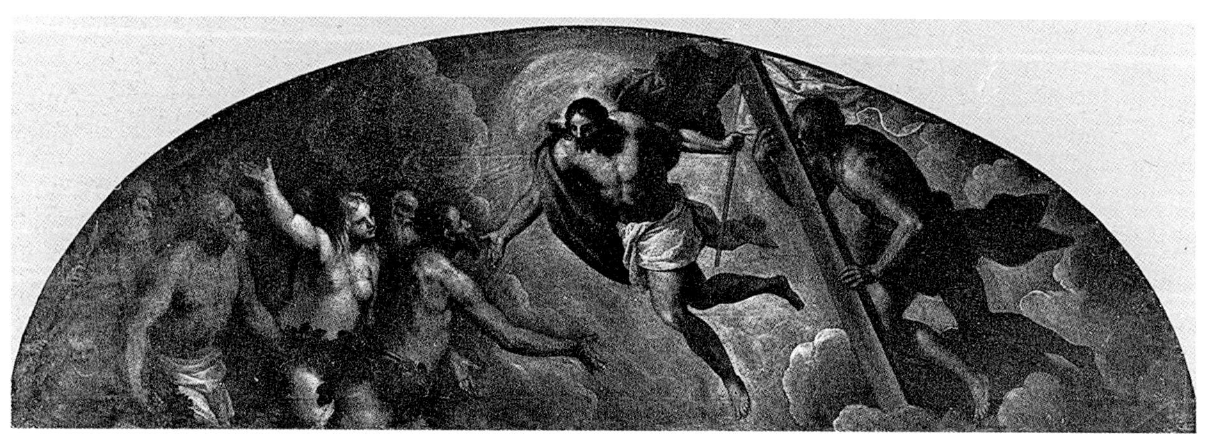

Fig. 33.1. Palma Il Giovane. *Christ's Descent into Limbo*, 1620–28. Oil on canvas. Church of San Zaccaria, Venice

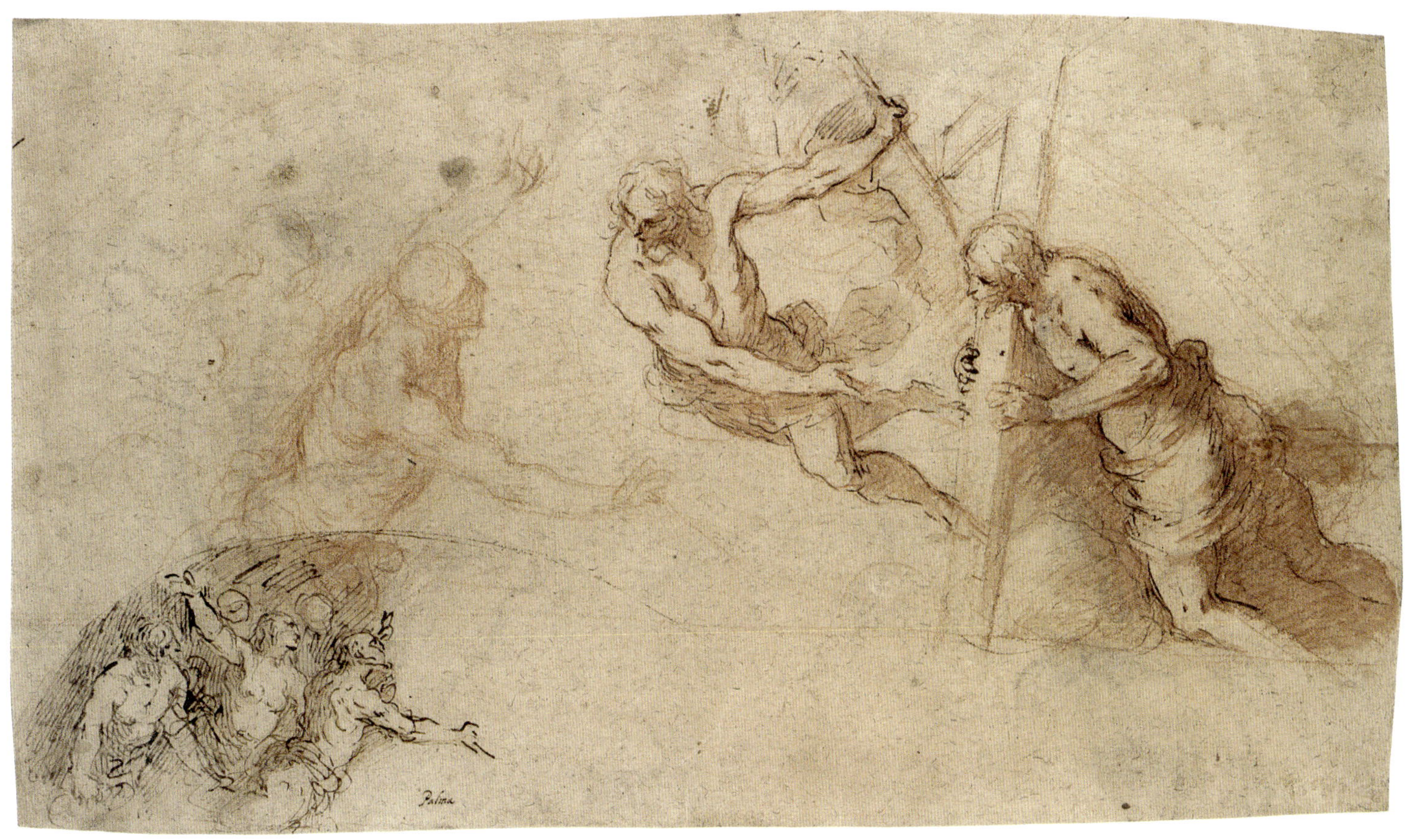

33

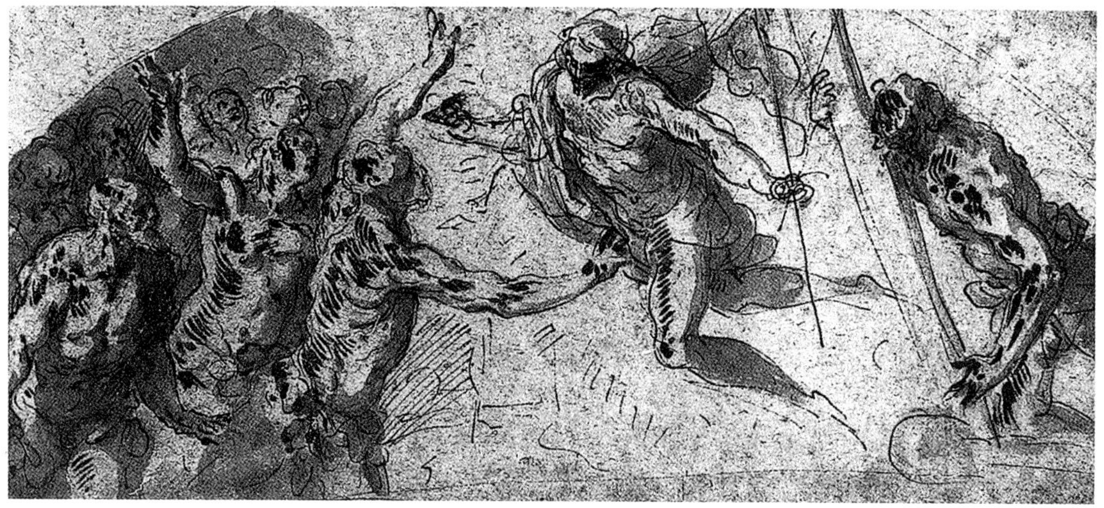

Fig. 33.2. Palma Il Giovane. *Studies for Christ's Descent into Limbo*, ca. 1620–28. Pen and brown ink, brush and brown wash, highlighted with white gouache (partly oxidized), on gray paper, 6⁵⁄₁₆ x 13¾ in. (16 x 35 cm). British Museum, London (Libro de' disegni, no. 130; 1862,0809.130)

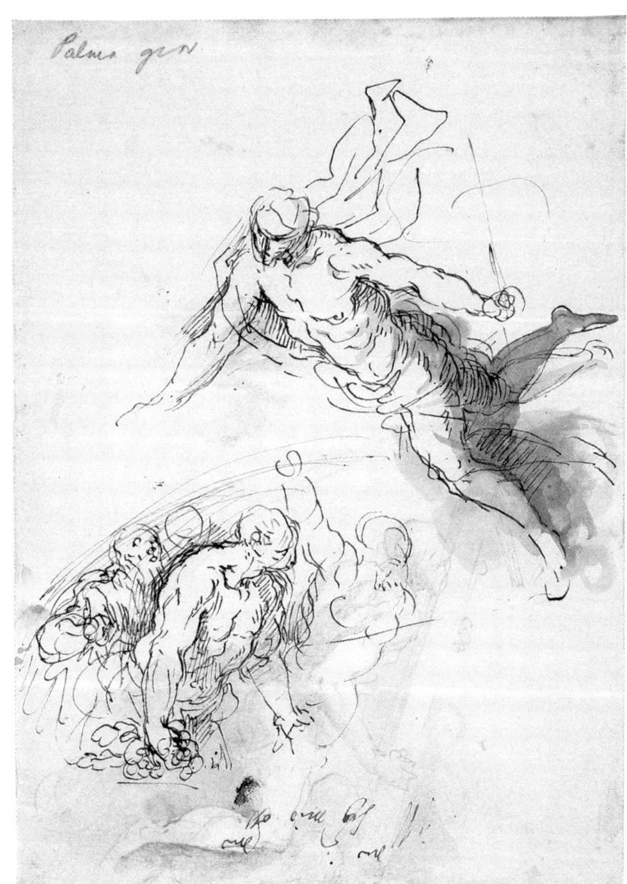

Fig. 33.3. Palma Il Giovane. *Christ's Descent into Limbo*, ca. 1620–28. Pen and brown ink, brush and brown wash, 11¾ x 8⅛ in. (29.8 x 20.7 cm). Statens Museum for Kunst, Kobberstiksamling, Copenhagen (1088)

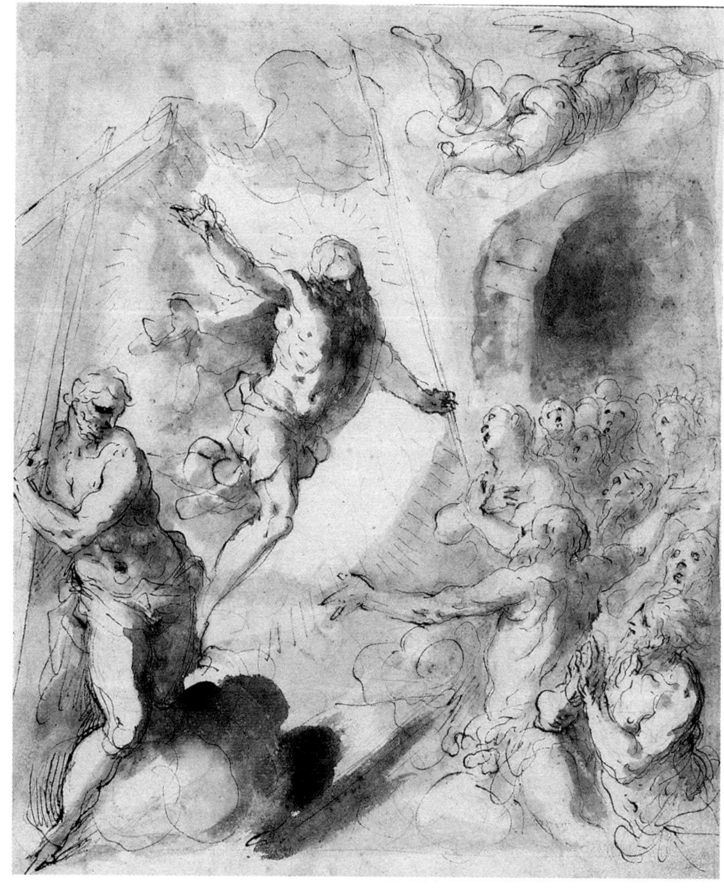

Fig. 33.4. Palma Il Giovane. *Christ in Limbo*, ca. 1620–28. Pen and and brown ink, brush with brown and gray wash, over black chalk, 11⅜ x 9⅛ in. (28.9 x 23.1 cm). British Museum, London (Libro de' disegni, no. 108; 1862,0809.108)

S. Zaccaria"), and so it is also mentioned in the 1733 edition of Boschini's guidebook by Zanetti.[6]

At least two other drawings are identified for this well-known composition, of which one is at the British Museum, London (fig. 33.2), and the other at the Statens Museum for Kunst, Copenhagen (fig. 33.3).[7] The Tobey sheet may be the most vigorous of the extant works, as well as the most varied in technique, as it represents motifs for the composition at three different stages of execution, clearly done in quick succession on the same paper. At upper left is the softly drawn, tentative sketch in red chalk for two figures of the Holy Fathers in Limbo, while at lower left a more comprehensive pen-and-ink sketch in small scale presents this group with additional figures, all situated within the arched space of the lunette. At center to the right, the large-scale sketch in pen and ink with wash over agitated red-chalk underdrawing depicts Christ pointing to the Cross, which is held by a kneeling saint. With respect to the final painting at San Zaccaria (fig. 33.1), the figure of Christ is the most changed from the Tobey sheet, given that He points with His right hand not to the Cross behind Him, but to the beckoning figures of the souls in Limbo to the left. The British Museum and Copenhagen studies also portray Christ with an outstretched hand. The gesture of Christ is that seen in the Tobey sheet, but the more exploratory quality of the sketches indicates that the Tobey sheet was probably the earliest of all the drawings done in the design process.

Palma produced a number of other drawings with variations on the theme of Christ's Descent into Limbo, executed in his typical sketching technique of pen and ink with wash, as is represented in a further sheet at the British Museum (fig. 33.4), in which the subject is explored in a vertical, rather than horizontal figural arrangement.

CCB

1. On Palma Il Giovane's painting at San Zaccaria, Venice, see Mason Rinaldi 1984, p. 134, nos. 492–94.
2. Quoted, with the present author's translation, from Zanetti 1771, p. 302.
3. See the biography of Palma Il Giovane in Ridolfi 1648, pp. 173–207 (quoted, with this author's translation, from ibid., p. 205).
4. Quoted, with this author's translation, from Ridolfi 1648, p. 199.
5. Boschini ed. 1733, p. 219 ("e la liberazione de' Santi Padri dal Limbo").
6. Compare Ridolfi 1648, p. 199; Boschini ed. 1733, p. 219; Zanetti 1771, p. 312.
7. On these two drawings (British Museum, London, *Libro de' disegni*, no. 130; Statens Museum for Kunst, Kobberstiksamling, Copenhagen, inv. no. 1088), see Mason Rinaldi 1984, pp. 154, 158, nos. D 26, D 95.

CRISTOFORO RONCALLI, IL POMARANCIO

Pomarance (Volterra), ca. 1553–Rome, 1626

Cristoforo Roncalli was one of the many Tuscan painters active in the years framing the turn of the seventeenth century who achieved considerable success in Rome, where he is first documented in early 1582. He carried out a number of frescoes in churches and oratories around the city, and received major commissions from Pope Clement VIII for work in Saint Peter's and San Giovanni in Laterano. His most important undertaking was the series of eight frescoes in the New Sacristy of the basilica of the Santa Casa at Loreto, begun in 1605. The chronicler and theorist Giulio Mancini, writing during Roncalli's lifetime, noted that the artist's manner synthesized power and grace—that is, elements of the new baroque style of Caravaggio and the Carracci with the late Mannerism of the Cavaliere d'Arpino.

34. *An Angel with a Crown of Laurel and a Palm Leaf*, 1604

Brown and gray oil paint on paper, 11⅝ x 8⅞ in. (29.5 x 22.5 cm)

Provenance: Pandora Old Masters, New York; acquired in 1998

Reference: New York 1998a, no. 4

In 1604, Orazio Rucellai commissioned Pomarancio to embellish his newly constructed family chapel in Sant' Andrea della Valle in Rome.[1] Work was probably completed about the time of the patron's death in the fall of 1605. Much of the decoration, which is mentioned in a number of seventeenth- and eighteenth-century guidebooks, no longer survives, and what remains is in ruinous condition.[2] Pomarancio's lost altarpiece depicted the Archangel Michael vanquishing the rebel angels; paintings on the lateral walls, also vanished, illustrated other scenes of angels; and the frescoes in the small dome, now illegible, represented a choir of celestial angels in paradise. A single angel filled each of the four pendentives; two are damaged, but the other two can still be discerned and are the best preserved elements of Pomarancio's original scheme.

The Tobey oil sketch is preparatory to one of the angel pendentives (fig. 34.1). It is one of the few such bozzetti in the artist's oeuvre. The five other extant examples are all connected with one of Pomarancio's most important commissions, the fresco cycle in the new sacristy of the basilica of Santa Maria in

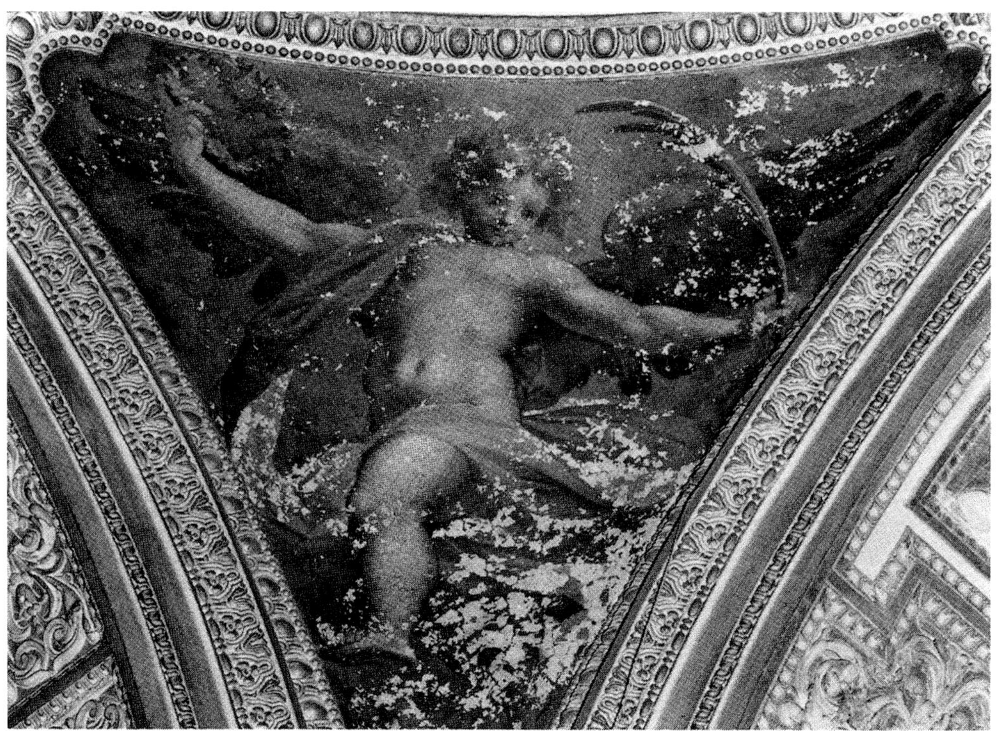

Fig. 34.1. Cristoforo Roncalli, Il Pomarancio. *Angel in Pendentive*, 1604–5. Fresco. Ruspoli (formerly Rucellai) Chapel, San Andrea della Valle, Rome

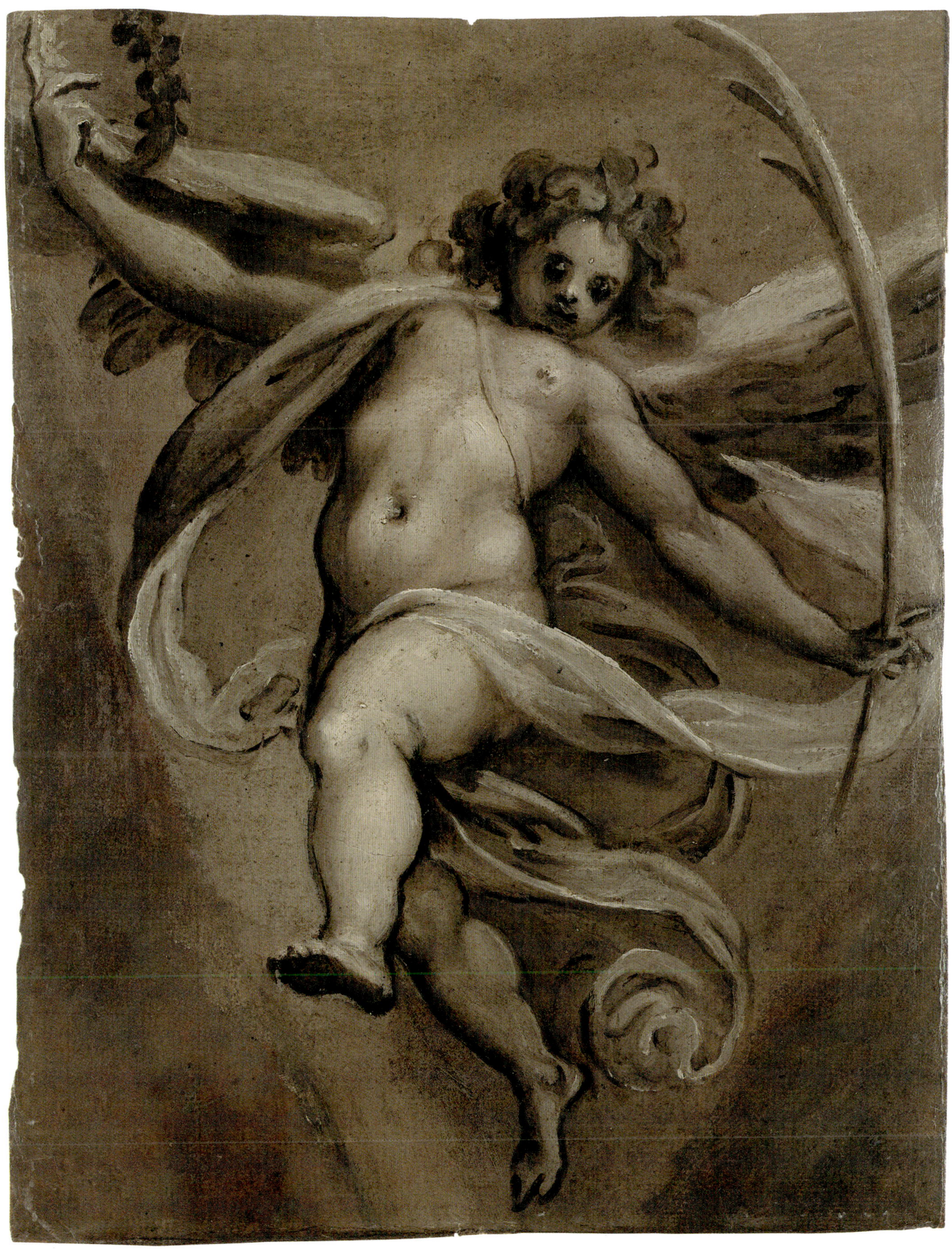

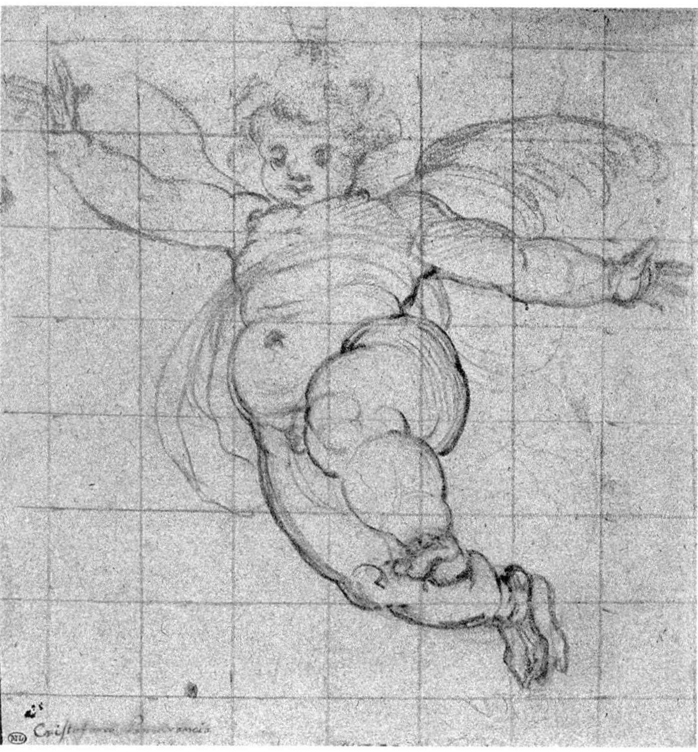

Fig. 34.2. Cristoforo Roncalli, Il Pomarancio. *Flying Putto.* Red chalk, with traces of black chalk on gray-green paper; with framing lines in red chalk, 8¹¹⁄₁₆ x 8³⁄₁₆ in. (22.1 x 20.8 cm). Département des Arts Graphiques, Musée du Louvre, Paris (11941)

Loreto, where he worked in the spring of 1605, immediately before undertaking the decoration of the Rucellai Chapel. In this confident oil sketch the artist established the pose of the exuberant angel and also described the fall of light on the celestial envoy's flesh and drapery. This expressive luminosity was obviously Pomarancio's preeminent concern. Even in its diminished state, the corresponding fresco preserves the compelling illusion of the angelic being emerging from darkness into a divine, celestial light—a light that signifies the promise of redemption and eternal salvation to the deceased entombed in the chapel.

Following the testimony of the contemporary biographer Giovanni Baglione, some scholars have suggested that the Ruccellai Chapel frescoes were executed by Pomarancio's pupil, Giovanni Battista Crescenzi.[3] Their poor condition makes efforts at attribution somewhat perilous, but the account of a well-informed contemporary observer cannot be lightly dismissed. Indeed, a decision to enlist a pupil as an executant would account for the production of this type of detailed and finished oil sketch by the master: such a work could have been used by the assistant as a model when carrying out the fresco. A squared drawing by Pomarancio or a follower of a flying angel whose pose is nearly identical to that in the Tobey sketch may be a hitherto unidentified preparatory study for the same decoration (fig. 34.2).[4]   LWS

1. Mentioned in Mancini ed. 1956, pp. 81–82, 286 (altarpiece).
2. See, for example, Titi 1674, p. 150, for a description of the original decorative program.
3. On the critical history see Chiappini di Sorio 1975, p. 113, no. 38.
4. Musée du Louvre, Paris (inv. no. 11941); see Viatte 1988, p. 196, no. 383, as Pomarancio (an attribution first advanced by Philip Pouncey). More recently the drawing has been catalogued as a copy after Pomarancio (see the online Inventaire du Département des Arts Graphiques, Museé du Louvre, http://arts-graphiques.louvre.fr/fo/visite?srv=home). The present author, who first observed the similarities with the Ruccellai Chapel frescoes, accepts it as an autograph work of the artist.

LUDOVICO CARRACCI

Bologna, 1555–Bologna, 1619

Ludovico Carracci spent virtually his entire career in his native Bologna, where, together with his cousins Agostino and Annibale Carracci, he founded the Accademia dei desiderosi, known as the Carracci academy, where young artists were schooled in life drawing, among other skills. A pupil of the Bolognese painter Prospero Fontana, he joined stylistic influences from late Mannerism and Correggio with the coloristic luminosity of Venetian painting to forge a naturalistic and affecting style of painting. That style was particularly suited to the many commissions that Ludovico received for altarpieces in numerous Bolognese churches and for private devotional images. While working together in Bologna, the three Carracci endeavored to formulate a unified style; consequently, the attribution of certain paintings, and of some of the red chalk drawings, that emanated from their studio continues to be a subject of dispute.

35. *Study of a Sleeping Nude Youth*, 1580s

Red chalk, 14 x 9⅞ in. (35.6 x 25.1 cm)
Annotated in pen and dark brown ink at lower right: *Academia Carracciò per la scola*

Provenance: Pandora Fine Arts, New York; acquired in 2009

Drawing from life was one of the foundational pillars of the Accademia dei desiderosi (later renamed the Accademia degli Incamminati), the academy that Ludovico Carracci and his cousins Agostino and Annibale established in Bologna in 1582 to promote their reform of painting and "teach students what they needed to learn in order to become artists."[1] A reflection of their advocacy of nature as a primary source of study and inspiration, this practice yielded a large corpus of red chalk figure drawings of male nudes by the Carracci (primarily Annibale and Ludovico) and their many pupils and followers. Most were executed strictly as studio exercises, although some were subsequently enlisted (and perhaps even deliberately formulated) as models for figures in painted compositions.[2] These academies, as this type of drawing came to be known, reflect both the didactic method of the Carracci academy as well as the theoretical ideas on which their artistic reform was founded.

This striking study of a youth sleeping on a draped stone slab suggestive of a bier or sarcophagus, his torso propped on a lightly outlined blanket or pillow, is a newly discovered example by Ludovico Carracci. It shares many affinities with his drawings of the 1580s, notably the ambitious and not entirely successful foreshortening of the figure; the rubbery, seemingly boneless fingers; the inflated, protruding torso; and the incisive reinforced contours that reiterate the initial, more tentative outlines (fig. 35.1).[3] The descriptive, portraitlike rendering of the face, with careful attention to hair, also finds parallels in Ludovico's life drawings (fig. 35.2).[4]

Such a study after a live model may well have been produced as a studio exercise, as the later annotation referring to

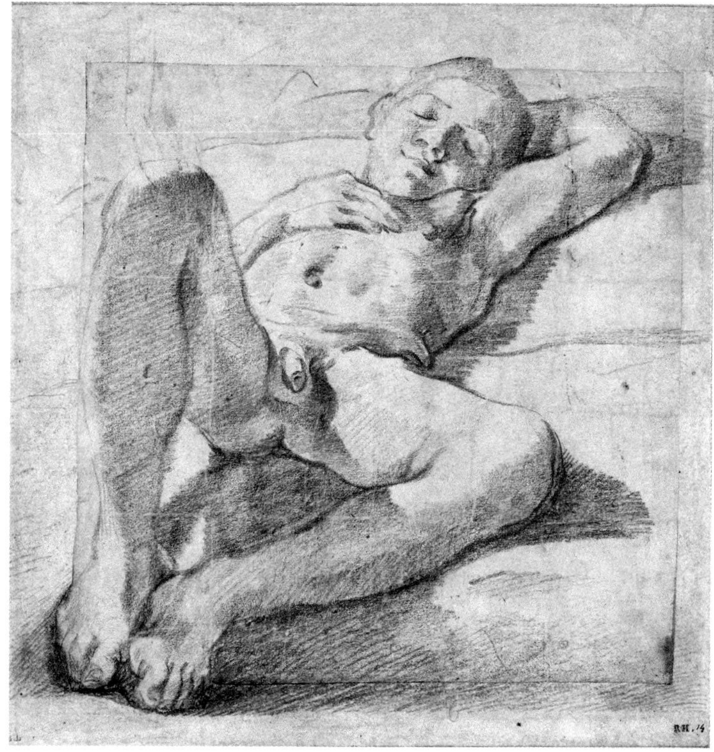

Fig. 35.1. Ludovico Carracci. *Study of a Nude Boy*, 1580s. Red chalk on cream paper, 9⅟₁₆ x 8¾ in. (23.7 x 22.3 cm). Ashmolean Museum of Art and Archaeology, Oxford (WA 1853.1.22)

the school of the Carracci academy seems to suggest. It is not impossible, however, that the Tobey sheet reflects the occasional practice of the Carracci to instruct the model to strike a pose that could be appropriated in a painting, allowing the life

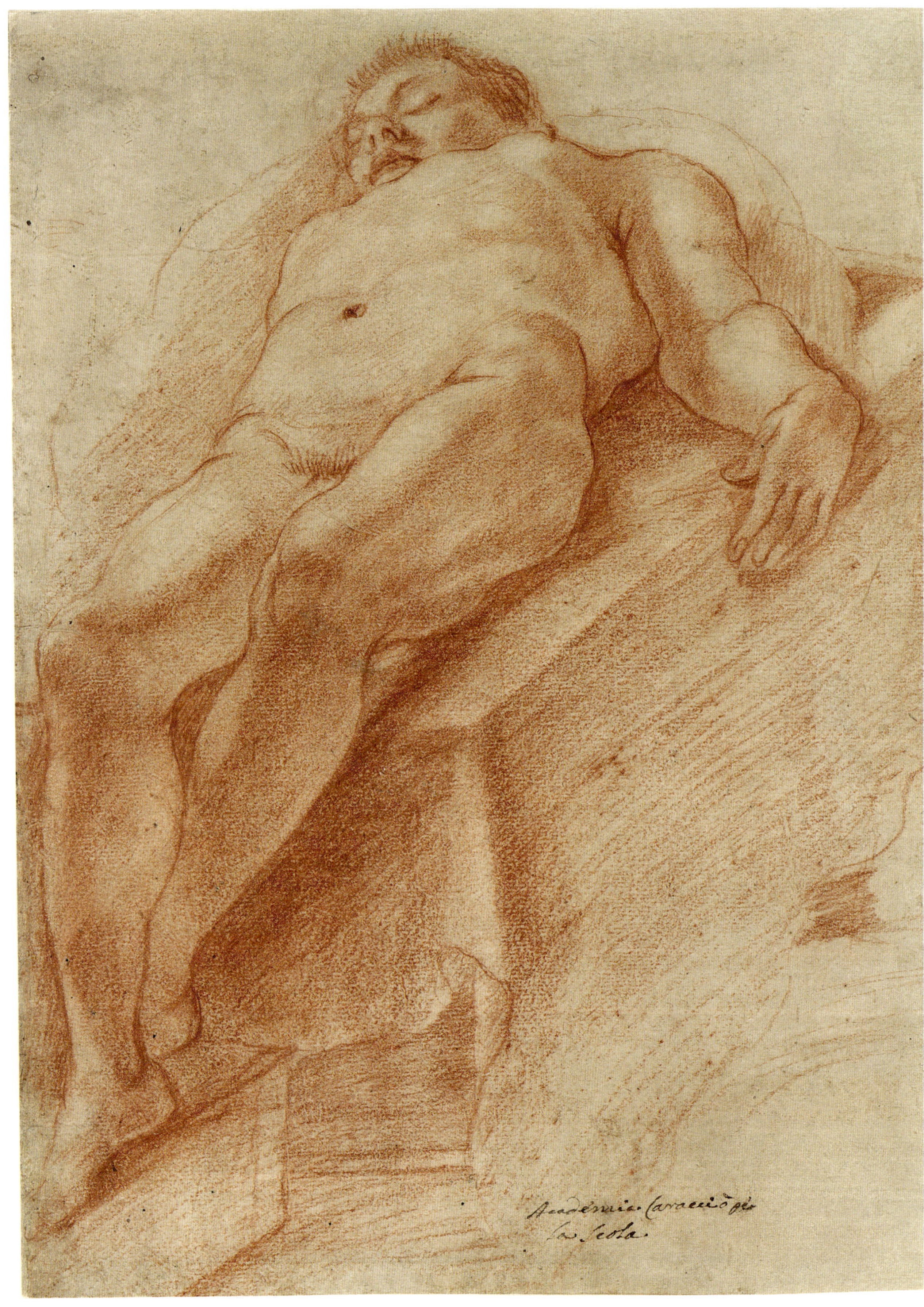

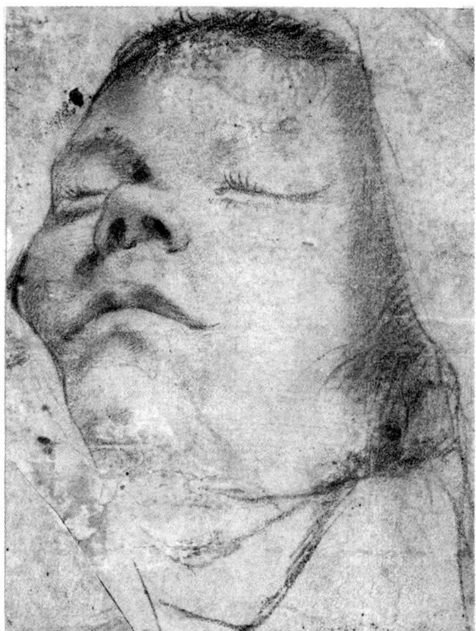

Fig. 35.2. Ludovico Carracci. *Study of the Head of a Sleeping Boy.* Red chalk on light brown paper, left corner made up, 7⅜ x 5⁷⁄₁₆ in. (18.7 x 13.8 cm). Kate Ganz Collection, London

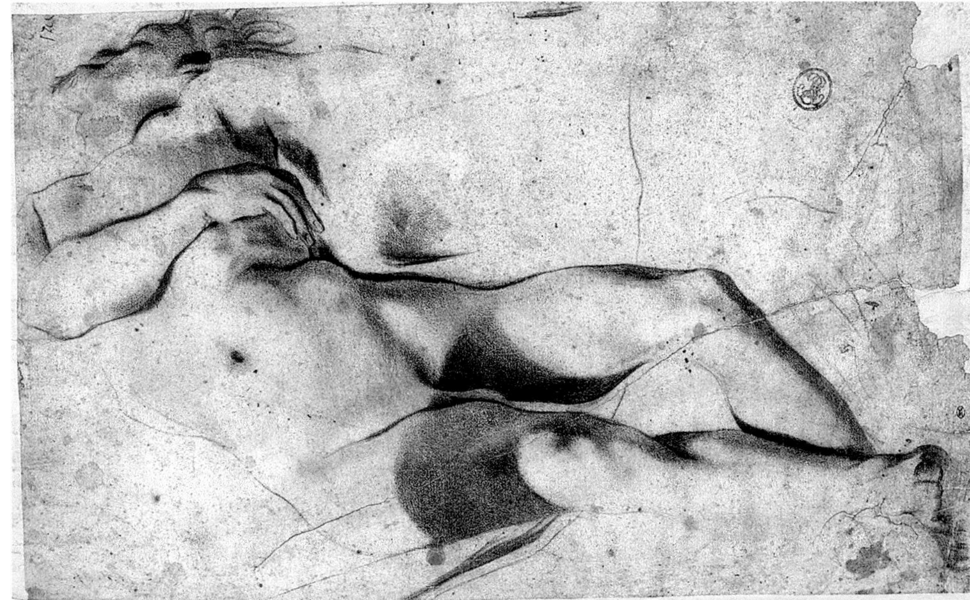

Fig. 35.3. Attributed to Ludovico Carracci. *Dead Christ,* 1580s. Red chalk; glued down on a sheet of an album, 10¹⁄₁₆ x 16¹⁄₁₆ in. (25.5 x 40.8 cm). Département des Arts Graphiques, Musée du Louvre, Paris (14730)

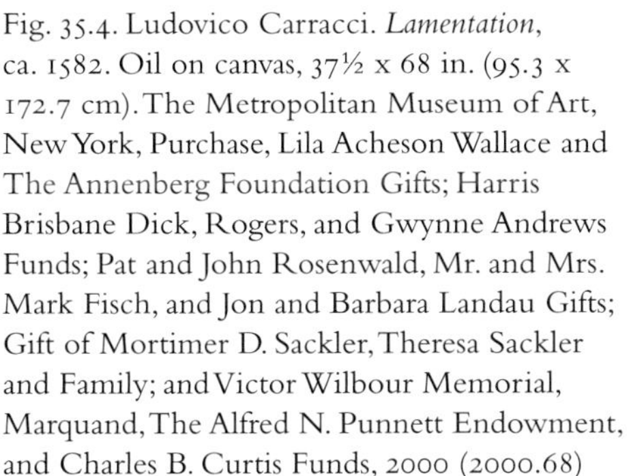

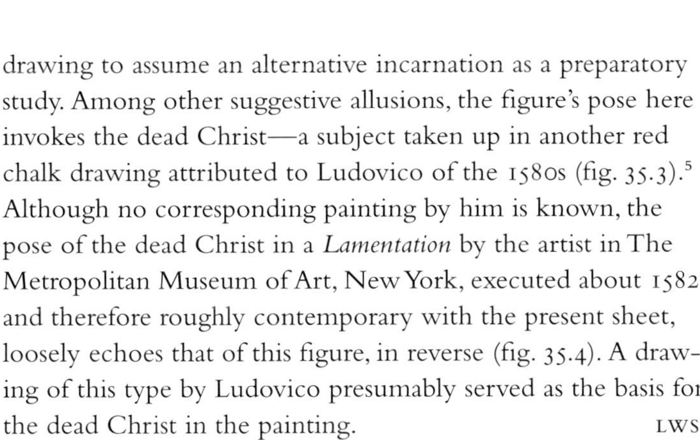

Fig. 35.4. Ludovico Carracci. *Lamentation,* ca. 1582. Oil on canvas, 37½ x 68 in. (95.3 x 172.7 cm). The Metropolitan Museum of Art, New York, Purchase, Lila Acheson Wallace and The Annenberg Foundation Gifts; Harris Brisbane Dick, Rogers, and Gwynne Andrews Funds; Pat and John Rosenwald, Mr. and Mrs. Mark Fisch, and Jon and Barbara Landau Gifts; Gift of Mortimer D. Sackler, Theresa Sackler and Family; and Victor Wilbour Memorial, Marquand, The Alfred N. Punnett Endowment, and Charles B. Curtis Funds, 2000 (2000.68)

drawing to assume an alternative incarnation as a preparatory study. Among other suggestive allusions, the figure's pose here invokes the dead Christ—a subject taken up in another red chalk drawing attributed to Ludovico of the 1580s (fig. 35.3).[5] Although no corresponding painting by him is known, the pose of the dead Christ in a *Lamentation* by the artist in The Metropolitan Museum of Art, New York, executed about 1582 and therefore roughly contemporary with the present sheet, loosely echoes that of this figure, in reverse (fig. 35.4). A drawing of this type by Ludovico presumably served as the basis for the dead Christ in the painting.   LWS

1. Feigenbaum 1993, p. 59.
2. The fluidity in the practice and function of life drawings produced in the Carracci academy has been discussed in Feigenbaum 1993.
3. These parallels with Ludovico's graphic style were noted by Babette Bohn (communication with the author), who kindly shared her stylistic analysis of the drawing and conveyed her endorsement of the attribution to Ludovico on the basis of having seen a photograph, and also pointed to the kinship with the *Study of the Head of a Sleeping Boy* illustrated here (see fig. 35.2 and note 4, below).
4. Bohn 2004, no. 51.
5. Loisel 2004, no. 5, as Ludovico. A very similar red chalk drawing of a supine nude boy by Annibale (which has also been attributed to Ludovico), perhaps of the same model and drawn at the same time as the Tobey study, is in the Nationalmuseum, Stockholm, inv. no. NM 769/1863; see Per Bjurström, *Drawings from the Age of the Carracci: Seventeenth Century Bolognese Drawings from the Nationalmuseum, Stockholm.* Ashmolean Museum, Oxford. Oxford, 2002, cat. no. 33

Andrea Boscoli was a pupil of Santi di Tito, one of the artists responsible for revitalizing late sixteenth-century Florentine art by eschewing the stylistic excesses and artifice of late Mannerism in favor of a new, more natural- istic and straightforward mode of expression. He was active as a fresco painter and portraitist but is today best known as a draftsman. His graphic oeuvre consists of fluid figure and composition studies in pen and ink with wash, and more finished drawings, often executed in a distinctive combination of red and black chalk.

36. *A Horse, Seen from Behind*, ca. 1587–88

Red and black chalk, 8⅞ x 5⅜ in. (22.6 x 13.6 cm)
Annotated in pen and brown ink at upper right: *M.4*

Provenance: Edward Bouverie (Lugt 325); sale, Sotheby's, London, December 5, 1977, lot 65; Jacques Petit-Hory, Paris; Private Collection, Los Angeles; Katrin Bellinger, Munich, 1991; Jak Katalan, New York; Katrin Bellinger, Munich, 1996; acquired in 1997

References: London 1991a, no. 20, ill.; Griswold and Wolk-Simon 1994, no. 40; Catherine Monbeig Goguel in Poughkeepsie and other cities 1995–96, no. 26; New York 1997, no. 15; Bellinger 2005, pp. 50–51, no. 22; Bastogi 2008, p. 334, no. 333

In its combination of red and black chalk, and its rather angu- lar, almost faceted forms, this study of a horse seen from behind is a paradigmatic example of Andrea Boscoli's graphic style. Here, as in numerous other drawings by this prolific late sixteenth-century Florentine draftsman, red chalk is employed for the subject (in this exceptional case, an animal, but in most of his drawings, human figures or details of heads and hands) and to describe shadows, and black is used to render the back- ground.[1] While some of these studies by Boscoli may have been drawn from life, others were conceivably based on statu- ettes, wax models, or lay figures.[2] Such a source is particularly plausible in the case of the Tobey drawing, as the equine sub- ject would have been incapable of sustaining the necessary immobility of a human model. Here, in an admirable display of artistic tour de force, the horse is portrayed in a complicated and steeply foreshortened pose, one foreleg gracefully raised. The obvious artifice is mitigated by certain details, notably the horse's loose forelock and swishing tail, meant to give the impression that the animal was studied *dal vero* (from life). Recourse to nature was one of the defining characteristics of late cinquecento Florentine draftsmanship (see cat. no. 40) and a lesson that Boscoli absorbed from his master Santi di Tito, who championed drawing from life and a naturalistic mode of expression.

Although many of Boscoli's chalk drawings were probably made as independent exercises, the artist seems on occasion to have reprised his own inventions in later designs. Such was evidently the case with the Tobey drawing: a similar horse appears in a fresco depicting the *Creation of the Universe* in the Montorsoli Chapel in Santissima Annunziata, Florence, com- pleted in 1588,[3] and at the right in a recently discovered pen- and-ink composition drawing by Boscoli illustrating a scene from Tasso's great epic poem, *Gerusalemme liberata* (fig. 36.1), part of a series executed about 1600–1605.[4]   LWS

1. As discussed by William Griswold in Griswold and Wolk-Simon 1994, under no. 40, who notes the existence of one other animal drawing, a study of a camel, by the artist (Galleria degli Uffizi, Florence; Bastogi 2008, no. 334). There is also a drawing by Boscoli of a cow (Princeton University Art Museum; Bastogi 2008, no. 336).
2. That Boscoli on occasion employed such models is suggested in an inscription on a drawing by him in the Biblioteca Reale, Turin, as noted in Griswold and Wolk-Simon 1994, under no. 40. Drawing from lay figures was an established practice in Florentine Renaissance workshops, the most notable example being that of Fra Bartolommeo, who is known to have had such a figure in his studio.
3. Bastogi 2008, p. 334, under no. 333.
4. New York 1996b, under no. 15, citing Julian Brooks.

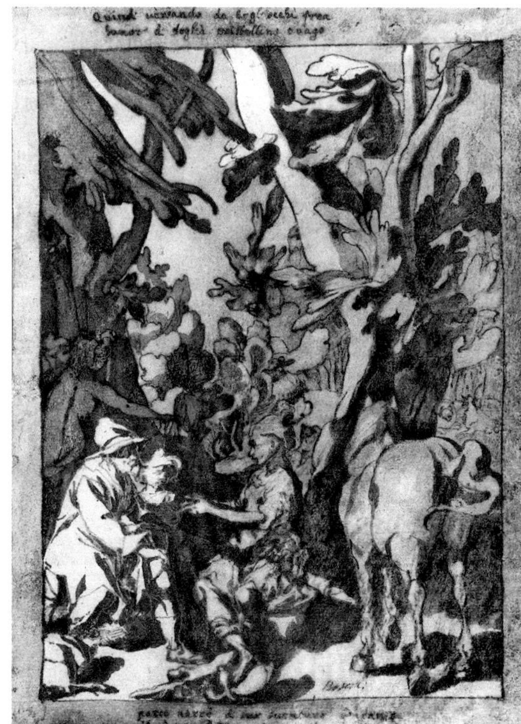

Fig. 36.1. Andrea Boscoli. *Erminia Tells Her Tale to the Shepherd; Scene from Tasso's* Gerusalemme liberata, ca. 1600– 1605. Pen and brown ink, brush and brown wash, over traces of black chalk, 10³⁄₁₆ x 6⅞ in. (25.9 x 17.5 cm). Whereabouts unknown

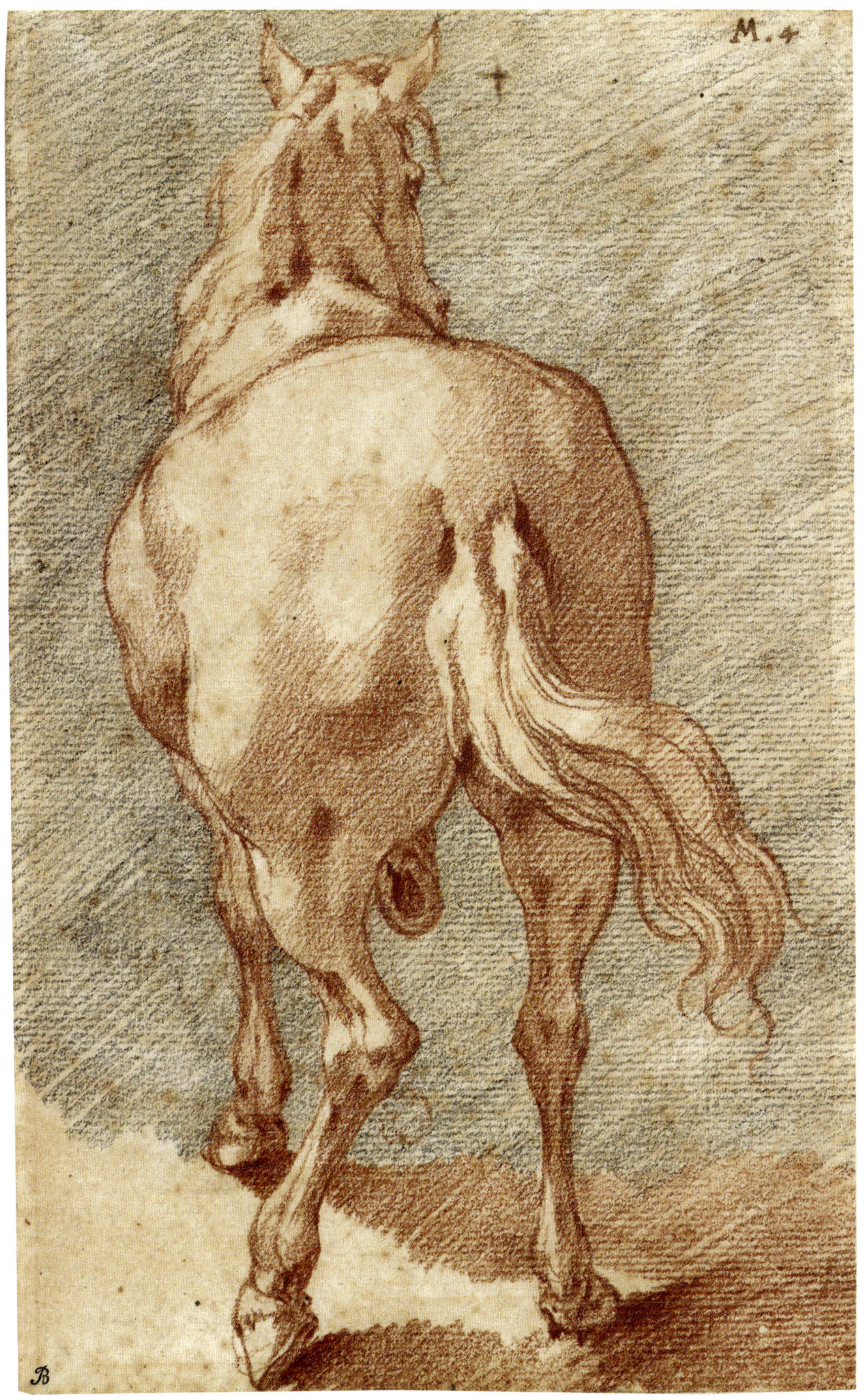

36

MASTER OF THE EGMONT ALBUMS
Netherlandish, active late 16th century

This Master's highly distinct and original style was recognized in 1958 by the British connoisseur Philip Pouncey, in drawings that had just entered the collection of the Yale University Art Gallery in New Haven with albums previously owned by John Percival, 1st Earl of Egmont (1683–1748). Several tens of drawings have been added to his oeuvre since, but so far they have failed to shed light on the Master's true identity. The obvious influence of Italian sixteenth-century art suggests he was active for some time in Italy.

37. *The Good Samaritan at the Inn*

Pen and brown ink, over a sketch in black chalk, 10¹¹⁄₁₆ x 13¹¹⁄₁₆ in. (27.1 x 34.8 cm)

Framing line in black chalk (?); laid down

Provenance: Nathan Chaikin, New York, in 1962;[1] P. & D. Colnaghi, London (?); sale London, Sotheby's, March 22, 1973, lot 28 (to Woodner); Ian Woodner (New York, 1903–1990); his sale, Christie's, London, July 7, 1992, lot 82; acquired in 1992

References: Haverkamp-Begemann and Logan 1970, vol. 1, p. 266, under no. 499; Taylor 1976, p. 28, under no. 6; Mielke 1980, p. 49; Goldner 1983–84, no. 47, ill.; George R. Goldner in Vienna and Munich 1986, no. 71, ill.; Starcky 1988, p. 87, under no. 93; Bevers 1989–90, p. 53, under no. 41; Dacos 1990, pp. 61–63, figs. 13–14; Boon 1992, vol. 1, p. 424 n. 6; Goldner, Hendrix, and Pask 1992, p. 234, under no. 100; Van der Sman 1999, p. 61; Caracciolo 2001, pp. 677 (mistakenly as belonging to the National Gallery of Art, Washington, D.C.), 683 n. 36

With the earlier Master of Liechtenstein, the Master of the Egmont Albums remains one of the most intriguing of Northern sixteenth-century draftsmen.[2] About fifty drawings have been associated with his name, but none of the attempts to identify him or to define his eclectic style have succeeded. Inscriptions on two of his sheets, which are difficult to read but are undoubtedly by a Netherlandish hand, prove that he hailed from the Low Countries.[3] Another inscription on a recently surfaced drawing, this time in ancient Greek, suggests that he must have been quite learned.[4] Although the drawings at Yale initially formed the basis for all attributions to the Master, it is the Louvre that preserves the largest and most varied group of his work.[5] There has been some discussion about whether all of these stylistically diverse sheets should be granted to the artist's oeuvre, but a few double-sided examples connect his different manners and help to prove that his style did indeed evolve considerably.[6]

The subjects of the Master's compositions are limited to battle scenes and episodes from the Bible. Depicted in the Tobey drawing is the Parable of the Good Samaritan, as told in the Gospel of Luke (10:25–37). At left, in the background, the man who "fell among thieves, which stripped him of his raiment, and wounded him, and departed, leaving him half dead," is being ignored by a priest and a Levite. At right, the

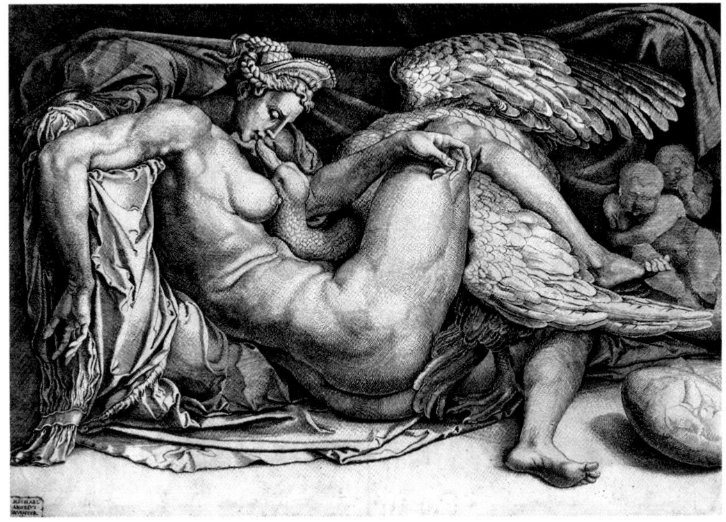

Fig. 37.1. Cornelis Bos, after Michelangelo. *Leda and the Swan*, 1530–56. Engraving, 12³⁄₁₆ x 16⁵⁄₁₆ in. (31 x 41.5 cm). British Museum, London (1878-7-13-161)

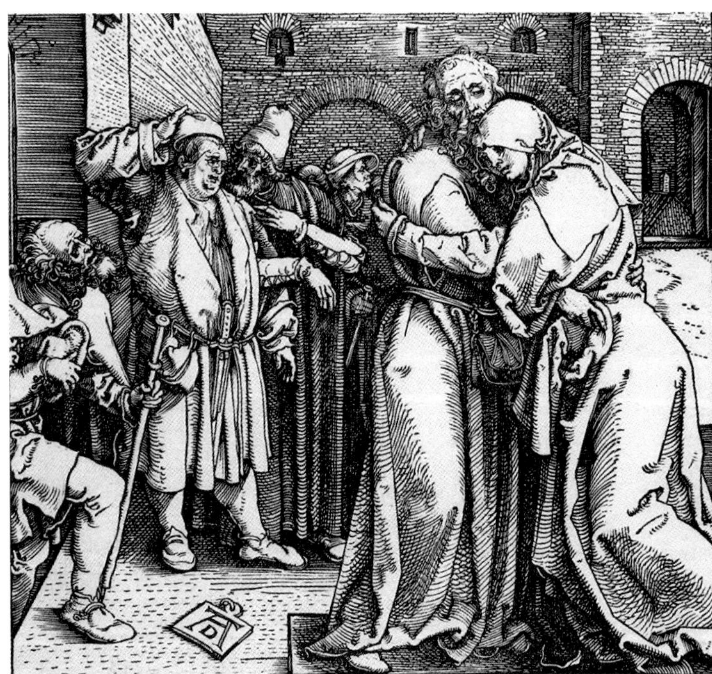

Fig. 37.2. Albrecht Dürer. Detail of *Joachim and Anna Meeting at the Golden Gate*, 1509. Woodcut, 11¹¹⁄₁₆ x 8³⁄₈ in. (29.7 x 21.3 cm). The Metropolitan Museum of Art, New York, Rogers Fund, 1918 (18.65.18)

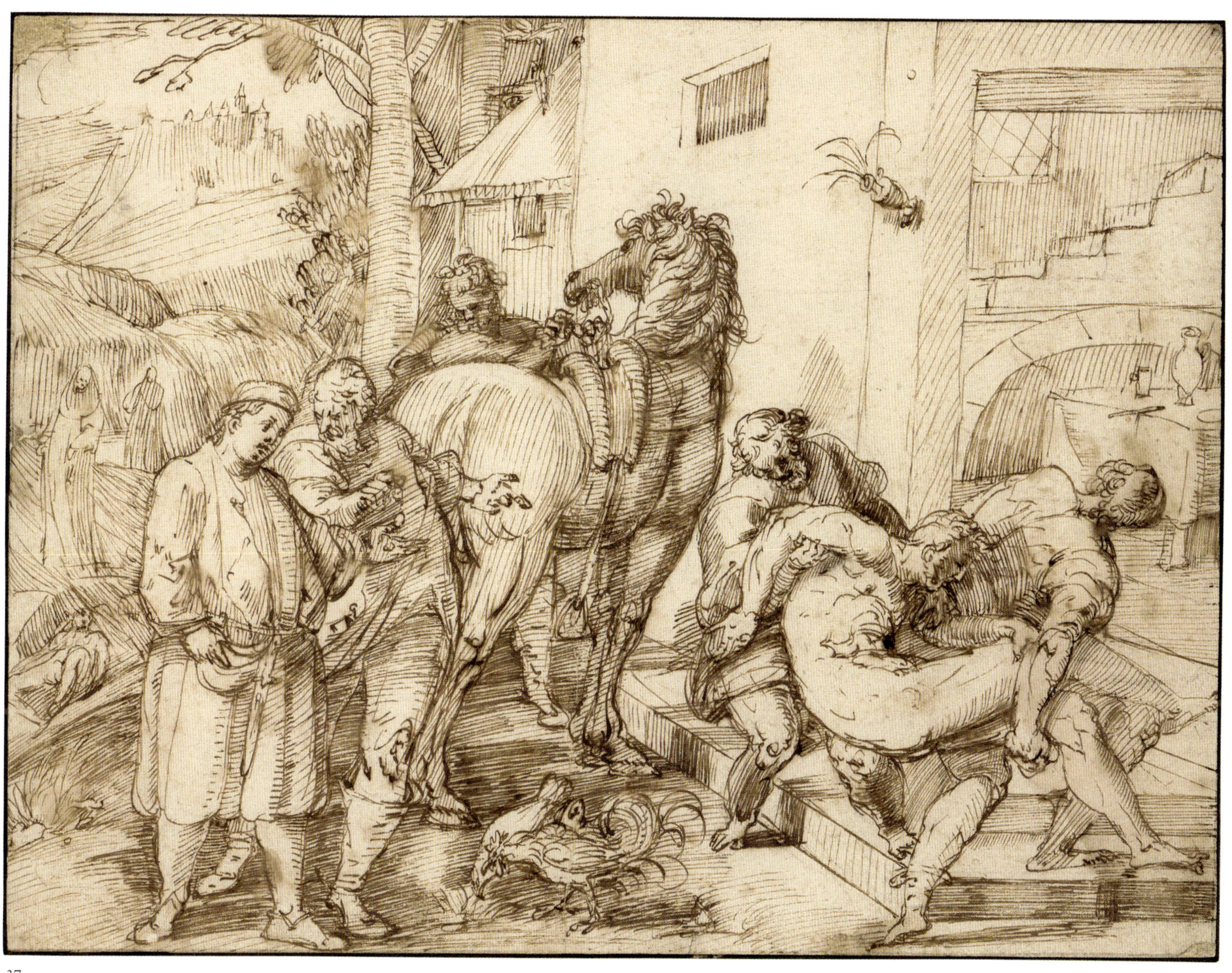

37

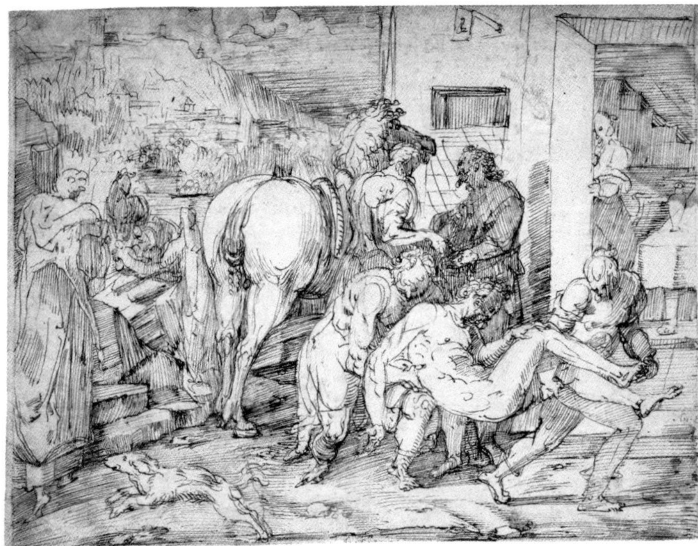

Fig. 37.3. Master of the Egmont Albums. *The Good Samaritan*, ca. 1580–90. Pen and brown ink, 10¾ x 13¾ in. (27.3 x 34 cm). J. Paul Getty Museum, Los Angeles (87.GG.29)

man is carried into an inn owing to the mercy shown by a Good Samaritan; the latter, meanwhile, standing next to his horse, is seen paying the innkeeper before going on his way. As first remarked by George R. Goldner,[7] the body of the man being carried is inspired by that of Leda in the well-known (but destroyed) painting by Michelangelo, which the Master may have been famililar with from a print in reverse by the Netherlandish engraver Cornelis Bos (fig. 37.1).[8] But he also counted Albrecht Dürer among his influences: Nicole Dacos noted that the innkeeper was taken from a woodcut that is part of Dürer's so-called Large Passion (fig. 37.2).[9]

The Master treated the same subject in a second drawing, now at the J. Paul Getty Museum (fig. 37.3).[10] Although it has been suggested that it was made shortly after the one in the Tobey Collection,[11] it seems that there is ground to suppose a reverse order. Certainly, the sheet in Los Angeles, which is more sketchily drawn, seems the less successful solution to the composition. The landscape is spatially both more complex and undefined; the imposing figure at far left plays no clear role apart from leading the eye toward the group in the background, where the Samaritan can be seen kneeling next to his horse, at the body of the thieves' victim; the arrangement of the two men carrying him, the Samaritan and the innkeeper, appears too crowded; and the inn is executed without much

care for perspectival correctness. The pentimento in the right leg of the figure carrying the upper part of the man's body has been followed in the Tobey drawing. It seems, thus, that the Getty sheet should be considered a first sketch of a composition that was only fully—and beautifully—resolved in the drawing presented here.

SA

1. Chaikin owned the drawing together with another sheet by the Master, formerly in a private collection in Montreal, its present whereabouts unknown, *Saint Cecilia and the Heavenly Chorus* (see Taylor 1976, no. 6, ill.).

2. For the Master of the Egmont Albums, see, among others, Dacos 1990; Boon 1992, vol. 1, pp. 422–26, under no. 245; Van der Sman 1997; Van der Sman 1999; and John Marciari in Sarasota, Austin, and New Haven 2006–8, pp. 104–6, under no. 26. To my knowledge, the Master was mentioned for the first time in the art historical literature in 1962 (Philip Pouncey in London, Birmingham, and Leeds 1962, no. 38, ill.). A catalogue of his drawings, announced in Dacos 1990, p. 67, has not yet been published. For the Master of Liechtenstein, see most recently New York and Edinburgh 2009, pp. 86–89, under no. 41.

3. The two inscribed drawings are in the Stichting Jean van Caloen, Loppem (Van der Sman 1997, ill.); and at the Universiteit Leiden, inv. no. PK-T-AW-564; (pen and brown ink, blue wash, 8¼ x 11½ in. [21 x 29.3 cm]).

4. The *Carrying of the Cross*, Private Collection, New York (pen and brown ink, 7⅞ x 11⅜ in. [20 x 28.8 cm]). The text was identified by Edward H. Wouk as taken from the Gospel of Luke (22:28).

5. For the drawings at the Yale University Art Gallery, New Haven, see Haverkamp-Begemann and Logan 1970, vol. 1, nos. 496–99, vol. 2, pls. 270–71; and John Marciari in Sarasota, Austin, and New Haven 2006–8, no. 26. For the sheets at the Département des Arts Graphiques, Musée du Louvre, Paris, see Starcky 1988, nos. 91–101, ill. One more drawing from Egmont's albums, which has never been connected with the Master, *Soldiers Gambling for the Robe of Christ* (Yale University Art Gallery, 1961.61.7), should be given to him (Haverkamp-Begemann and Logan 1970, vol. 1, no. 173, vol. 2, pl. 102, as attributed to Hans von Aachen); compare, for instance, one of the drawings by the Master, a *Resurrection of Lazarus*, at the Louvre (inv. no. 14091; Starcky 1988, no. 99, ill.).

6. See, most recently, Van der Sman 1997; and Van der Sman 1999.

7. Goldner 1983–84, p. 123, under no. 47. Nicole Dacos (1990, pp. 61, 68 n. 23) connects the horse in the Tobey drawing with works by Taddeo Zuccaro, but the similarities are almost certainly coincidental.

8. Schéle 1965, no. 59a, pl. 21. For Michelangelo's original, see Acidini Luchinat 2007, pp. 214–15. For other aspects of the Master's dependence on Italian sources, see Dacos 1990; Van der Sman 1999; and Caracciolo 2001.

9. Bartsch 1803–21, vol. 7, p. 131, no. 79; Schoch, Mende, and Scherbaum 2001–4, vol. 2, no. 169, ill. The connection was made in Dacos 1990, p. 61, where Dürer's print is mistakenly referred to as representing the Visitation; moreover, only the innkeeper, not the Samaritan, is associated with Dürer's print. Dacos (ibid., p. 68 n. 23) relates the prone man at left in the background with a figure at lower right in a woodcut of the Resurrection by Dürer (Bartsch 1803–21, vol. 7, p. 118, no. 15; Schoch, Mende, and Scherbaum 2001–4, vol. 2, no. 165, ill.), but the relationship does not seem entirely convincing, although there is evidence that the Master used the same figure in at least two other drawings (see Dacos 1990, p. 62; and Caracciolo 2001, pp. 677, 683). The running dog in the Master's other version of the Parable of the Good Samaritan, reproduced here as fig. 37.3, is clearly taken from that in Dürer's engraving *Knight, Death, and the Devil* (Bartsch 1803–21, vol. 7, pp. 106–8, no. 98; Schoch, Mende, and Scherbaum 2001–4, vol. 1, no. 69); the link was first noted in Dacos 1990, p. 63.

10. Lee Hendrix in Goldner, Hendrix, and Pask 1992, no. 100, ill.

11. See Dacos 1990, p. 63.

VENTURA SALIMBENI

Siena, 1568–Siena, 1613

Ventura Salimbeni was the son of the Sienese painter Arcangelo Salimbeni, from whom he received his artistic training. Beginning in 1588 he spent seven years in Rome, working at the Vatican Library, at the Gesù, and in Santa Maria Maggiore, and producing a small corpus of engravings. By 1595 he was back in Siena, where, together with his half brother Francesco Vanni, he was the leading painter of the transitional period between the late Renaissance and early Baroque. Salimbeni carried out numerous frescoes in churches and oratories in Siena and elsewhere in Tuscany, of which the most important are the two large Old Testament narratives in the apse of the cathedral of Siena, which reveal his skill at composing multifigured compositions in descriptively detailed landscape and architectural settings. As both a painter and a draftsman, Salimbeni, like Vanni, was profoundly influenced by the art of Federico Barocci.

38. *Saint Clare Repulsing the Saracens from Assisi*, ca. 1600

Red chalk, brush and reddish wash, 12⅝₆ x 8½ in. (31.2 x 21.6 cm)

Provenance: Sale, Sotheby's, New York, January 23, 2008, lot 118; acquired in 2008

Reference: Sotheby's, New York 2008, lot 118

Full of atmospheric light and agitated movement in the strong, broken-up contours, this masterful composition is drawn in red chalk with a highly pictorial treatment of the medium (the pale wash was created with red-chalk powder greatly diluted in water), an expansive quality of space, and a naturalistic conception of the figure in Ventura Salimbeni's typical proto-Baroque style. Although only discovered in 2008, the Tobey drawing is among Salimbeni's most accomplished, as it is exactly comparable to a number of composition studies in red chalk of his late years.[1] Here, the artist constructed the illustrative space along a diagonal to suggest a deep recession of planes, in which the main figures are seen in the foreground at left and bottom, deeply modeled in chiaroscuro, while the distant background landscape at right is reserved in an evenly pale red tone with the forms of buildings, soldiers, and trees only impressionistically sketched. He exploited the white of the paper to achieve vibrant highlights (shining like the cut facets on precious stones) that provide a dramatic foil for the thickly elaborated layers of red chalk in the modeling, which Salimbeni applied at first lightly with the side of the stick in diagonal parallel-hatching, then gradually worked up the tone and rubbed in the individual strokes. He articulated the darkest shadows and contours of the figures by wetting the tip of the chalk. This manner of drawing on the paper with very controlled, radiant effects and agitated, tonally inflected outlines closely resembles the style of Salimbeni's older half brother, Francesco Vanni (1563–1610), with whose hand drawings by Salimbeni are often confused, and the Sienese school of late sixteenth-century painters which they led—the "Barocceschi senesi"—artists who found their inspiration after 1580–85 in the work of Federico Barocci (ca. 1535–1612).[2] The *Head of an Infant in Three-Quarter View Facing Right* (cat. no. 27), a pastel study by Barocci, well illustrates his influential, painterly approach to form, in which color and the subtle plays of faceted light on surfaces create texture and dramatic interest. In contrast to Vanni's style of red-chalk drawing and that of other "Barocceschi senesi," Salimbeni's is more delicate in the rendering and more nervous in the outlines, the figures broader and more naturalistic, while displaying a more subtly faceted luminosity.

In the relatively worked-up Tobey composition, Saint Clare (1194–1253) is seen by the gates of San Damiano in Assisi at left, holding a ciborium with the Blessed Sacrament. She is accompanied by the sisters of her order, the Poor Clares, as she strides forward, to behold a pile of vanquished nude soldiers strewn in the foreground. A battle on horseback and foot rages in the middle distance of the field at right. The scene alludes to the miracle in 1234 or 1244, when Emperor Frederick II and his army, which included Saracens, besieged the valley of Spoleto and prepared to attack Assisi and Saint Clare's convent church of San Damiano, where she was abbess. Clare is said to have calmly risen from her sickbed and, taking a ciborium from the chapel by her cell, raised the Blessed Sacrament causing the retreat of the horrified soldiers.

The exquisitely rendered drawing is not securely connected to an extant final painting. In the present author's opinion, however, it seems closely related in iconography and compositional

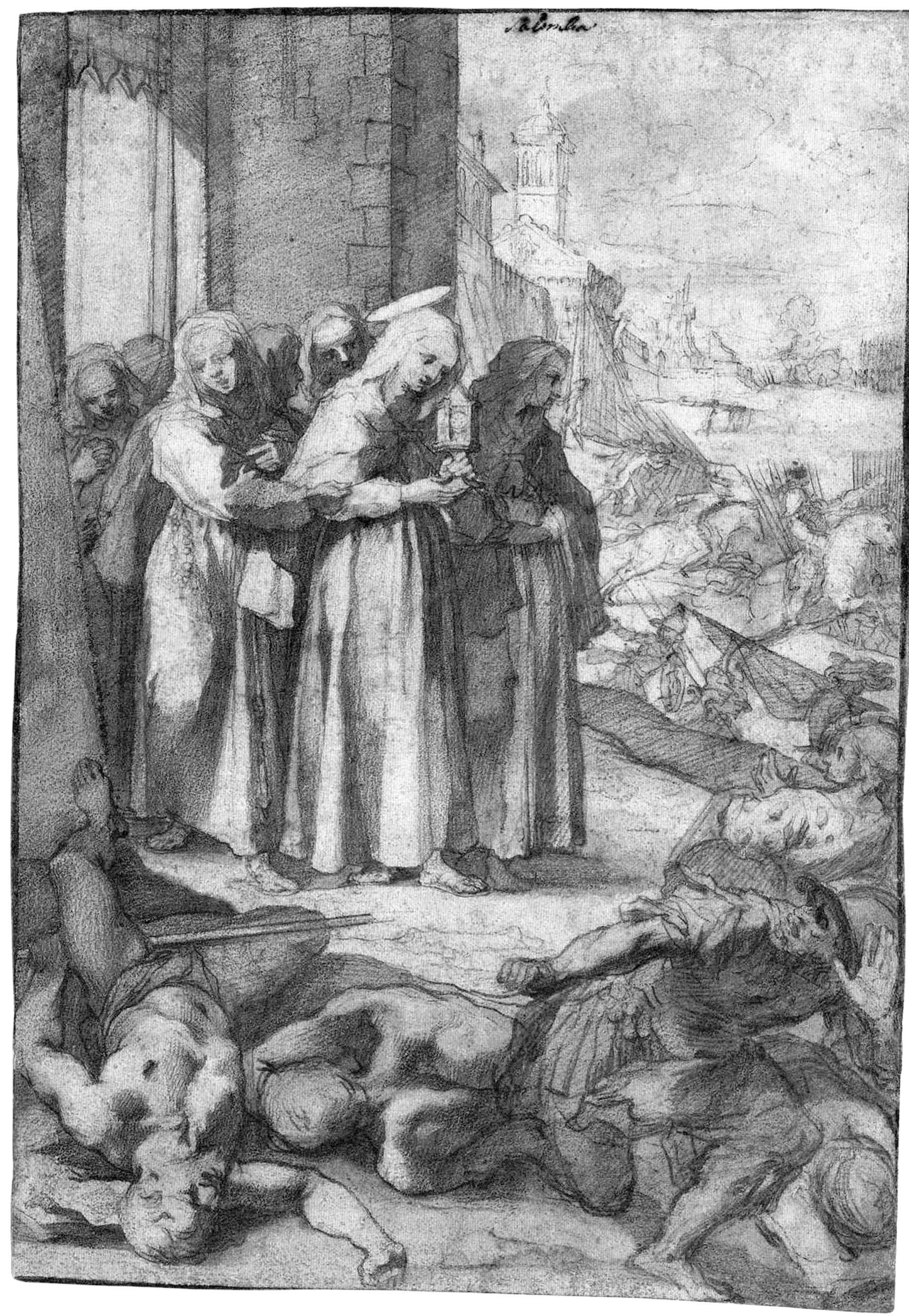

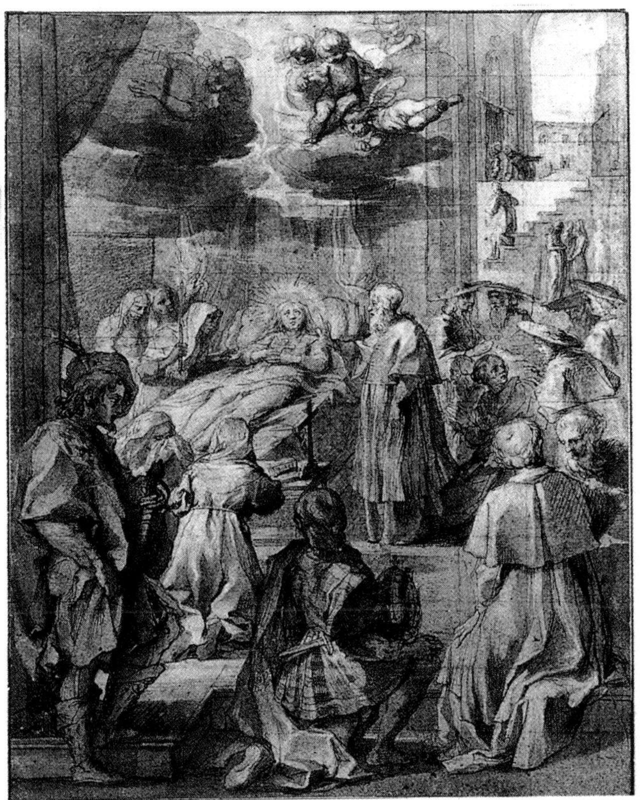

Fig. 38.1. Ventura Salimbeni. *Death of Saint Clare*, ca. 1600. Black chalk, brush and brown wash, 12⅜ x 9⁷⁄₁₆ in. (31.4 x 23.9 cm). Graphische Sammlung Albertina, Vienna (780)

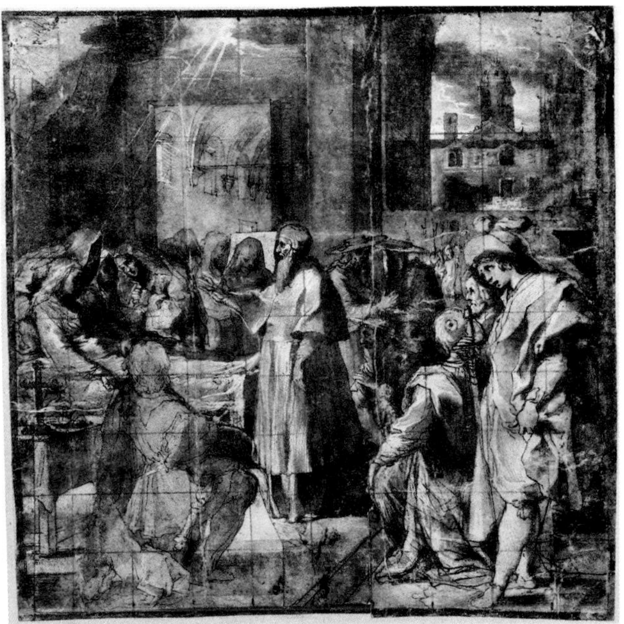

Fig. 38.2. Ventura Salimbeni. *Death of Saint Clare with Pope Innocent IV Blessing Her*, ca. 1600. Black chalk, pen and brown ink, brush and brown wash, highlighted with white gouache (partly oxidized), on light brown prepared paper, squared in red chalk, on four glued sheets of paper, 10³⁄₁₆ x 9¾ in. (25.8 x 24.8 cm). Formerly Collection of the Earl of Leicester, Holkham Hall

style to the frescoed scenes on the *Life of Saint Clare*, executed by Salimbeni at Santa Maria degli Angeli in Assisi, which were largely destroyed in 1832.[3] A drawing in black chalk with wash depicting the *Death of Saint Clare* (fig. 38.1), which was preparatory for the extant, though much repainted, fresco of this subject at Santa Maria degli Angeli, offers a similarly vertical format of design; the final painted scene is in a horizontal disposition and oriented in the opposite direction.[4] A more developed, squared *modello*, or demonstration drawing, by Salimbeni for the *Death of Saint Clare with Pope Innocent IV Blessing Her* (fig. 38.2) offers a similarly luminous style of composition and figures, as the Tobey drawing.[5] The subject of Saint Clare Repulsing the Saracens from Assisi also constitutes an iconographic pendant to the death scene of the saint. A closely related drawing at the Louvre (fig. 38.3), portrays two groups of figures much as in the Tobey composition, but without the setting; in the upper part of that sheet, Saint Clare is held by two sisters; at lower left are two nude dead soldiers.[6] The Louvre study must be preparatory for the same composition as the Tobey sheet, and both drawings can be dated to about 1600 based on style.[7]

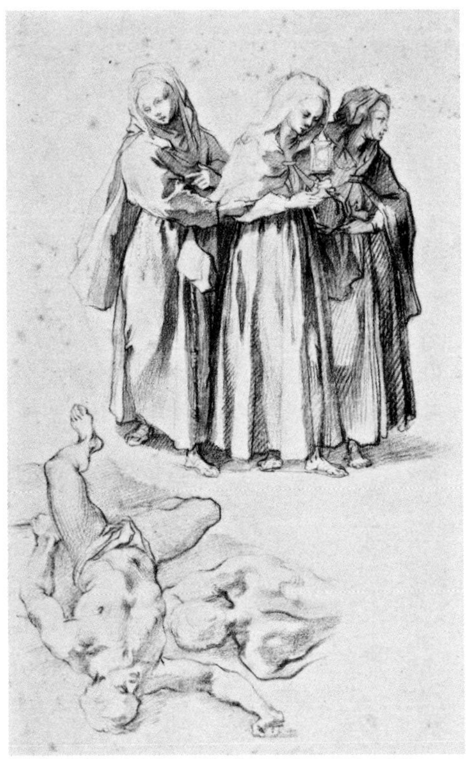

Fig. 38.3. Ventura Salimbeni. *Saint Clare and Two of Her Companions, and Two Male Figures Lying Down*, ca. 1600. Brush and gray wash, black chalk, 11¹¹⁄₁₆ x 7³⁄₁₆ in. (29.7 x 18.2 cm). Département des Arts Graphiques, Musée du Louvre, Paris (2025)

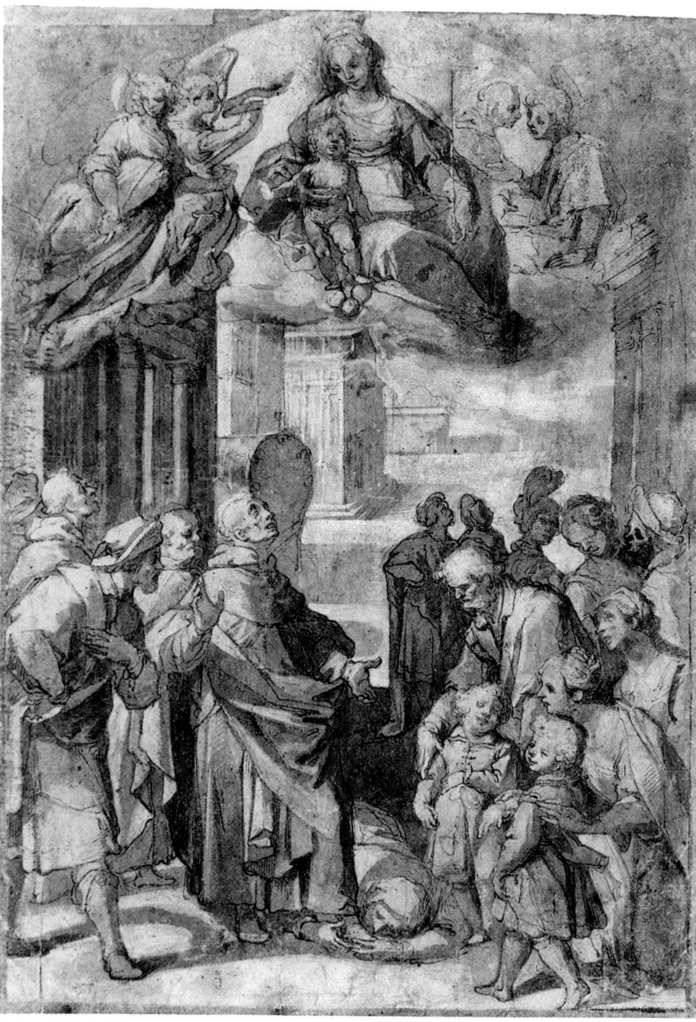

Fig. 38.4. Attributed to Ventura Salimbeni, or Francesco Rustici ("Il Rustichino"). *Saint Hyacinth Healing the Two Blind Boys.* Pen and brown ink, brush and brown wash, highlighted with white gouache, over black chalk, 15⁹⁄₁₆ x 10½ in. (39.6 x 26.7 cm). Ashmolean Museum of Art and Archaeology, Oxford (WA 1955.37)

Lastly, a similar type of composition occurs in a drawing in the Ashmolean Museum of Art and Archaeology, Oxford, *Saint Hyacinth Healing the Two Blind Boys* (fig. 38.4), which is connected to a signed altarpiece by Francesco Rustici ("Il Rustichino," active late 1590s, d. 1626), now in San Giacinto di Vita Eterna, Siena, and which is dated 1615. The stylistic resemblance indicates the extent to which Salimbeni's pictorial formulas influenced painting in Siena during the last years of the sixteenth century and the beginning of the seventeenth. The Ashmolean drawing has been published with alternative attributions, either to Rustichino, owing to the connection to the aforementioned altarpiece, or to Salimbeni, because of an early inscription on the verso and the comparability to some of his drawings and frescoes.[8] Both the Ashmolean composition and the Tobey sheet offer scenes arranged along a diagonal conception of space in which the figures are seen against an architectural setting of powerful upright lines at left and a deeply receding landscape toward the right of the center.   CCB

1. See, for example, the composition drawings in red chalk (Uffizi, Florence, inv. nos. 10854 F, 10868 F, 1284 F); illustrated and discussed in Riedl 1976, pp. 86–87, 90–91, 94–95, nos. 90, 94, 101; as well as the three sheets (Musée du Louvre, Paris, inv. no. 1976; École Nationale Supérieure des Beaux-Arts, Paris, inv. no. E.B.A. 347; Stadel Frankfurt, inv. no. 551) recorded in photographs, Archive of the Department of Drawings and Prints, The Metropolitan Museum of Art, New York.
2. On Salimbeni, Vanni, and the "Barocceschi senesi," see especially Riedl 1959; Riedl 1960; and Riedl 1976, pp. 9–13, and catalogue entries therein.
3. On this fresco cycle at Assisi see Peter Anselm Riedl's pioneering study (Riedl 1960), pp. 224–25 nn. 10–11, with the early bibliography, though it does not include the present drawing.
4. Although Riedl 1960, pp. 225–26, fig. 5, rightly attributed the Albertina drawing to Ventura Salimbeni, his article and attribution were ignored in Birke and Kertész 1992–97, vol. 1, p. 407, no. 780, where the drawing is mistakenly published as by Francesco Vanni. The related fresco, the *Death of Saint Clare*, at Santa Maria degli Angeli, Assisi, is illustrated and discussed in Riedl 1960, p. 225, fig. 4.
5. See sale, Christie's, London 1991, lot 14.
6. On this drawing (Musée du Louvre, Paris, inv. no. 2025), see the *Inventaire Ms. Morel d'Arleux*, no. 1316 ("Vanni"); Reiset 1866, p. 119, no. 361; Bacou 1981, p. 260; and Viatte 1988, p. 203, no. 401.
7. This is the opinion of Peter Anselm Riedl, which was quoted in the auction catalogue, Sotheby's, New York 2008, lot 118, although without allusion to the *Saint Clare* painting cycle at Santa Maria degli Angeli, Assisi.
8. On this drawing (Ashmolean Museum of Art and Archaeology, Oxford, WA 1955.37), see Parker 1956, vol. 2, pp. 564, no. 677*, as by Ventura Salimbeni. Macandrew 1980, pp. 65–66, no. 675-1, was the first to notice the connection of the Ashmolean drawing to Rustichino's painting at San Giacinto di Vita Eterna, Siena, prompting him to reattribute the drawing to him. The verso of the Ashmolean drawing is annotated "Solimbeni" [*sic*] by an eighteenth-century hand, which led Parker to propose the attribution of the recto to Salimbeni.

GUIDO RENI

Bologna, 1575–Bologna, 1642

Disregarding his father's wish that he become a musician, Guido Reni entered the studio of Denys Calvaert in Bologna about 1584, transferring a decade later to the Carracci academy, where he remained until a quarrel with Ludovico Carracci some four years later precipitated his exodus. He received commissions for several altarpieces in Bolognese churches and may also have been engaged as a sculptor before removing to Rome in 1601. Unlike his compatriots Domenichino and Albani, who joined Annibale Carracci's circle in Rome, Reni embarked on an independent course (while still maintaining ties to the community of Bolognese painters in Rome), aligning himself with the industrious Cavaliere d'Arpino and receiving a succession of fresco commissions from the Borghese family and other prominent patrons. He returned intermittently to Bologna, where his talents as a painter of altarpieces were much in demand, and settled there permanently by 1614, venturing once to Rome and twice to Naples in his later years. As he sought to achieve a heightened purity and simplicity in his religious imagery, Reni's devotional style became increasingly refined and idealized, his graceful figures—typically looking heavenward with expressions of pious supplication—acquired an attenuated, ethereal, almost otherworldly aspect, his palette lightened, and his style of execution grew more loose and painterly. The angelic nature of his religious iconography contrasted sharply with the painter's querulous and prickly personality. Dismissed by critics like John Ruskin as maudlin and cloying, Reni's work temporarily fell from favor in the nineteenth century, but his critical fortune has recovered from that nadir.

39. Recto: *Saint Benedict*, ca. 1604
Verso: *Youth Blowing a Trumpet*

Recto: Black and white chalk with slight traces of red chalk; verso: black chalk, on blue paper, 15⅜ x 9½ in. (39.1 x 24.2 cm)
Annotated on verso, on old mount: *192.*

Provenance: Private Collection, Switzerland, since at least 1930; Julien Stock; acquired in 2009

Between 1603 and 1605 Guido Reni received a number of payments for a mural in the cloister of San Michele in Bosco, the principal Olivetan monastic establishment in Bologna, representing *Saint Benedict Receiving Gifts from the Farmers*.[1] It was part of an extensive cycle illustrating the life of Saint Benedict overseen by Ludovico Carracci, who executed seven of the scenes and assigned others to his pupils and collaborators, although Reni received the commission independently from his former teacher and was paid more than Ludovico for his labors.[2] The work was painted in 1604 following the artist's brief return from Rome to his native Bologna, but because it was executed in oil rather than buon fresco it soon deteriorated. (In 1632 he was obliged to restore the already damaged mural at no charge.) Now lost, Reni's composition is recorded in a number of reproductive prints as well as a faithful copy by Giovanni Maria Viani (fig. 39.1).

This hitherto unknown, monumental drawing, an important new addition to Reni's graphic oeuvre, is connected with the lost San Michele in Bosco mural. The standing figure on the recto, tonsured and attired in a flowing monastic habit, is a

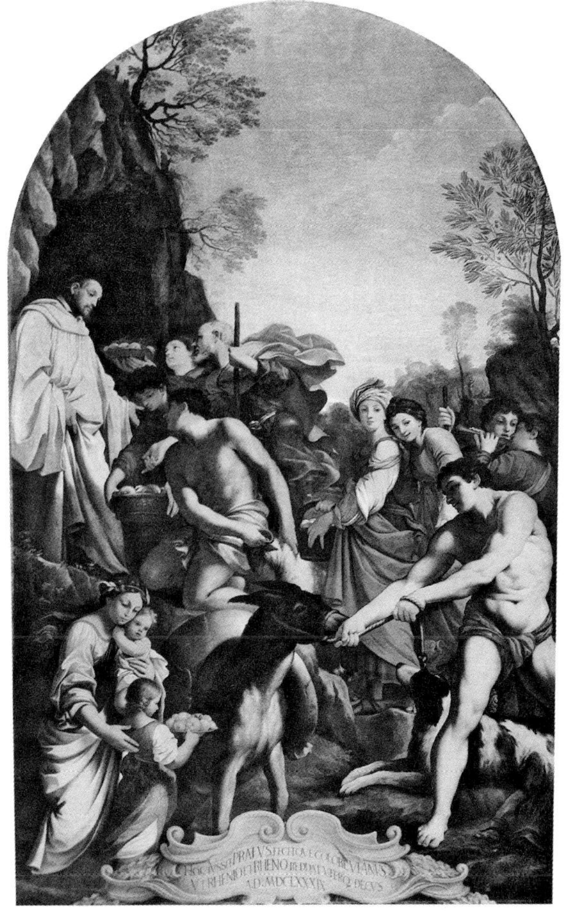

Fig. 39.1. Giovanni Maria Viani after Guido Reni. *Saint Benedict Receiving Gifts from the Farmers*. Oil on canvas, 16 ft. 4¹⁄₁₆ in. x 9 ft. 10⅛ in. (498 x 300 cm). San Michele in Bosco, Bologna

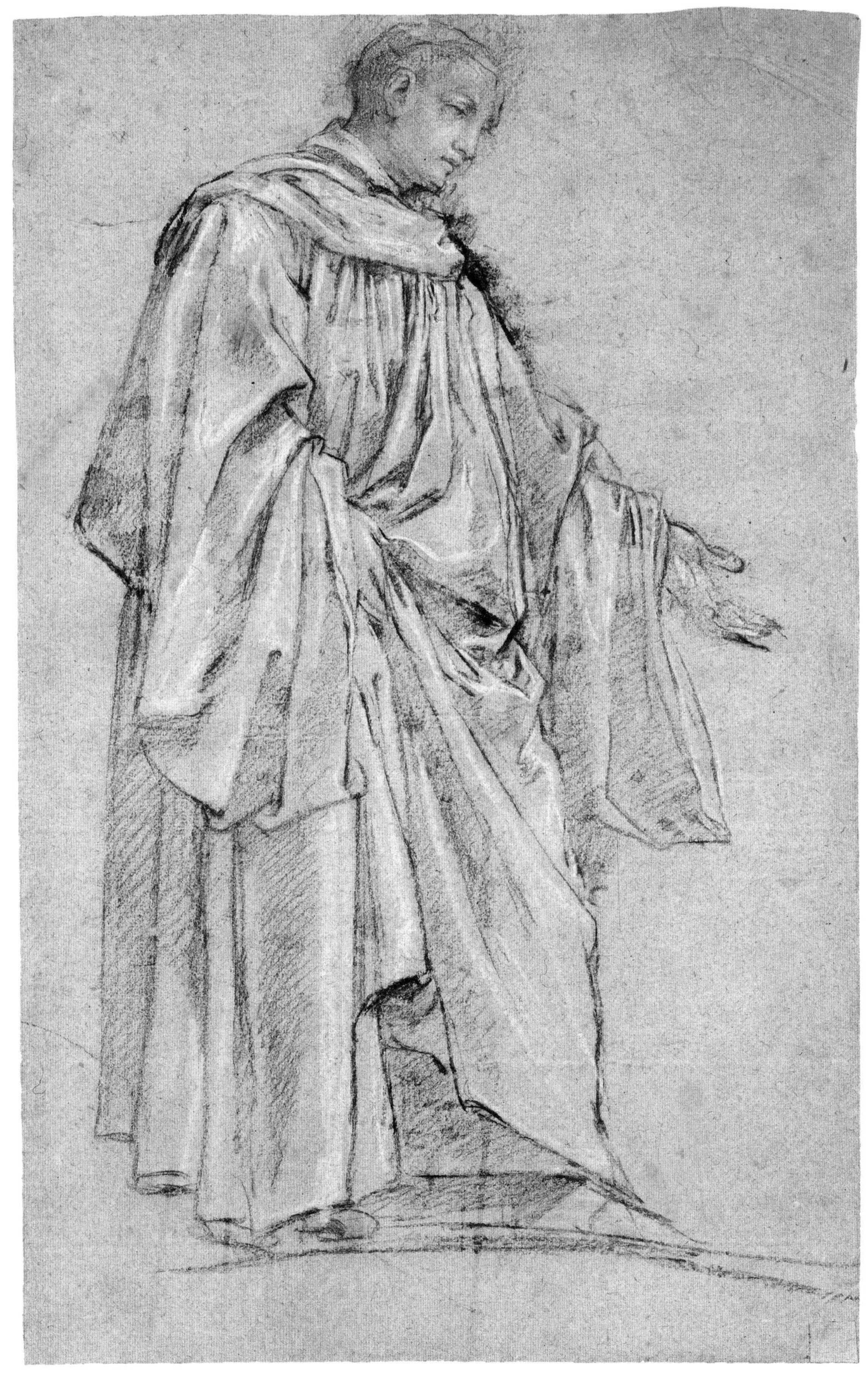

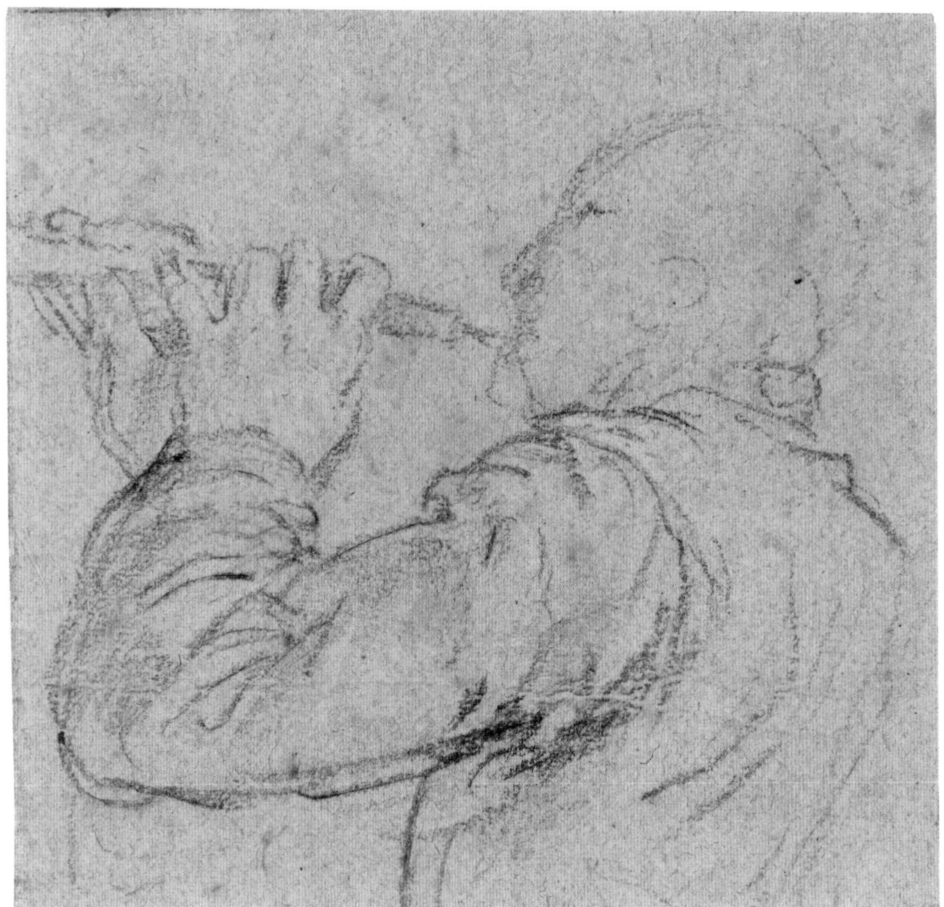

39 verso

study for Saint Benedict, who appeared in this precise manner at the left of the composition, extending his hand toward the humble citizens who greeted him bearing gifts of food. On the verso is a study for the boy blowing a pipe or small trumpet who was seen at the far right of Reni's painting, behind the muscular man wrestling with an intransigent mule. Both drawings are executed in soft black chalk employed in broad strokes, with (on the recto) touches of white chalk—a technique the artist frequently used in figure drawings. Relevant examples include a study of an angel playing a violin in the Uffizi (ca. 1602–3),[3] and another of Saint Etheldreda in the Royal Collection, Windsor Castle (ca. 1610);[4] like the Tobey sheet, both are fairly rare examples of studies of individual figures from this period of Reni's career that can be definitively linked with a specific painting.[5]

In addition to the *Saint Benedict* and the *Youth Blowing a Trumpet* in the Tobey Collection, there are two other drawings by Reni related to the lost San Michele in Bosco mural, a sheet of studies showing various figures including the youth pulling an ass in the foreground (Uffizi, Florence),[6] and another with two sketches of the animal alone, executed in the same technique as the present example (Pushkin State Museum, Moscow).[7] All show the artist's facility for naturalism that contemporaries admired in the lost painting.

LWS

1. For which see Hibbard 1965, p. 503.
2. See Garboli 1971, pp. 88–89, no. 30; and Pepper 1988, p. 219, no. 15, for a more extensive discussion including Ludovico's role in the overall cycle and an analysis of the payments to Reni. On Reni's lost work, see further the discussion by D. Stephen Pepper in Bologna, Los Angeles, and Fort Worth 1988–89, p. 169.
3. Uffizi, Florence (inv. no. 1584F); see Bohn 2008, no. 11. The drawing is a study for a *Coronation of the Virgin* now in the Prado, Madrid.
4. Royal Collection, Windsor Castle, inv. no. 3466; see Birke 1981, no. 39, ill. The drawing is a study for the corresponding figure in the Paoline Chapel in Santa Maria Maggiore, Rome.
5. This scarcity was remarked upon in Bohn 2008, p. 18, under no. 11.
6. Inv. no. 1587 F, black chalk and brown ink; cited in Pepper 1984, pp. 219–20, under no. 15; see Bologna 1954, no. 1.
7. Inv. no. 6211; see New York 1998–99, no. 28. The nude seen from the rear on the verso is a study for one of the figures framing the mural.

Cristofano Allori received his early training from his father, the late Florentine Mannerist painter Alessandro Allori, but soon adopted the new, more naturalistic, and emotionally accessible style promoted in Florence about 1600 by Ludovico Cigoli and other protagonists of the early Florentine Baroque. He was active as a portraitist and fresco painter and was also renowned for his landscapes and lyrical devotional images. His talents extended to poetry and music; parallels between his manner as a painter and the melodic purity of contemporary Florentine music have been observed.

40. *Study of the Head of a Boy Wearing a Hat*

Red chalk, 9⅞ x 7¼ in. (25 x 18.3 cm)
Annotated in brown ink at lower right: *A. Carracci*

Provenance: Sale, Sotheby's, London, July 3, 1996, lot 44, acquired in 1996

Reference: *Drawing* 1996, p. 56

The old attribution to Annibale Carracci, recorded in an early annotation at the lower right of this engaging study of the head of a boy, is a reflection of its appealing naturalism (see the discussion under cat. no. 35). The subject is undoubtedly drawn from life, as the individualized, portraitlike features, alert, focused gaze, and carefully observed cap confirm. Contrasting with the nuanced and plastic modeling of the boy's face is the sketchy rendering of his neck and shoulders, barely indicated by a few quick strokes of the chalk. A similar drawing of the head of a young boy by Cristofano Allori in the Louvre, executed in red and black chalk, may portray the same model (fig. 40.1).

The Tobey drawing, like the Louvre *Head of a Young Boy* and other similar studies,[1] signals Allori's place among the generation of artists active in Florence in the late sixteenth and early seventeenth centuries who embraced an affecting and straightforward naturalism. These artists, led by Ludovico Cigoli and Santi di Tito, eschewed contrived, artificial, overly stylized display and championed an artistic idiom that was grounded in the study of nature. As in Bologna, Rome, and elsewhere, drawing from life was a cornerstone of their artistic reform. Here, the use of red chalk—a medium that allows for the approximation of naturalistic flesh tones—is a reflection of that central tenet of early Florentine Baroque art, one of whose leading protagonists was Cristofano Allori.   LWS

1. Another relevant example is the *Head of a Boy* in the Gabinetto Disegni e Stampe degli Uffizi, Florence. See Petrioli Tofani 1991, no. 908F.

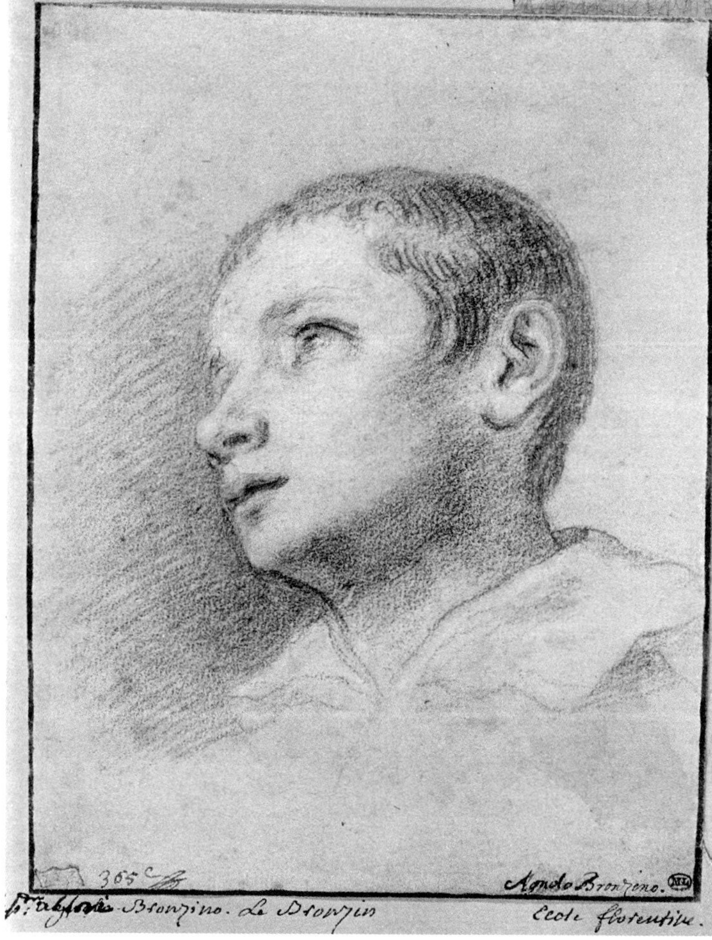

Fig. 40.1. Cristofano Allori. *Head of a Young Boy Turned toward the Left, Looking Upward*. Black chalk, red chalk, highlighted with white; with framing lines in pen and brown ink, 7⅝ x 5¹¹⁄₁₆ in. (19.4 x 14.4 cm). Département des Arts Graphiques, Musée du Louvre, Paris (12302)

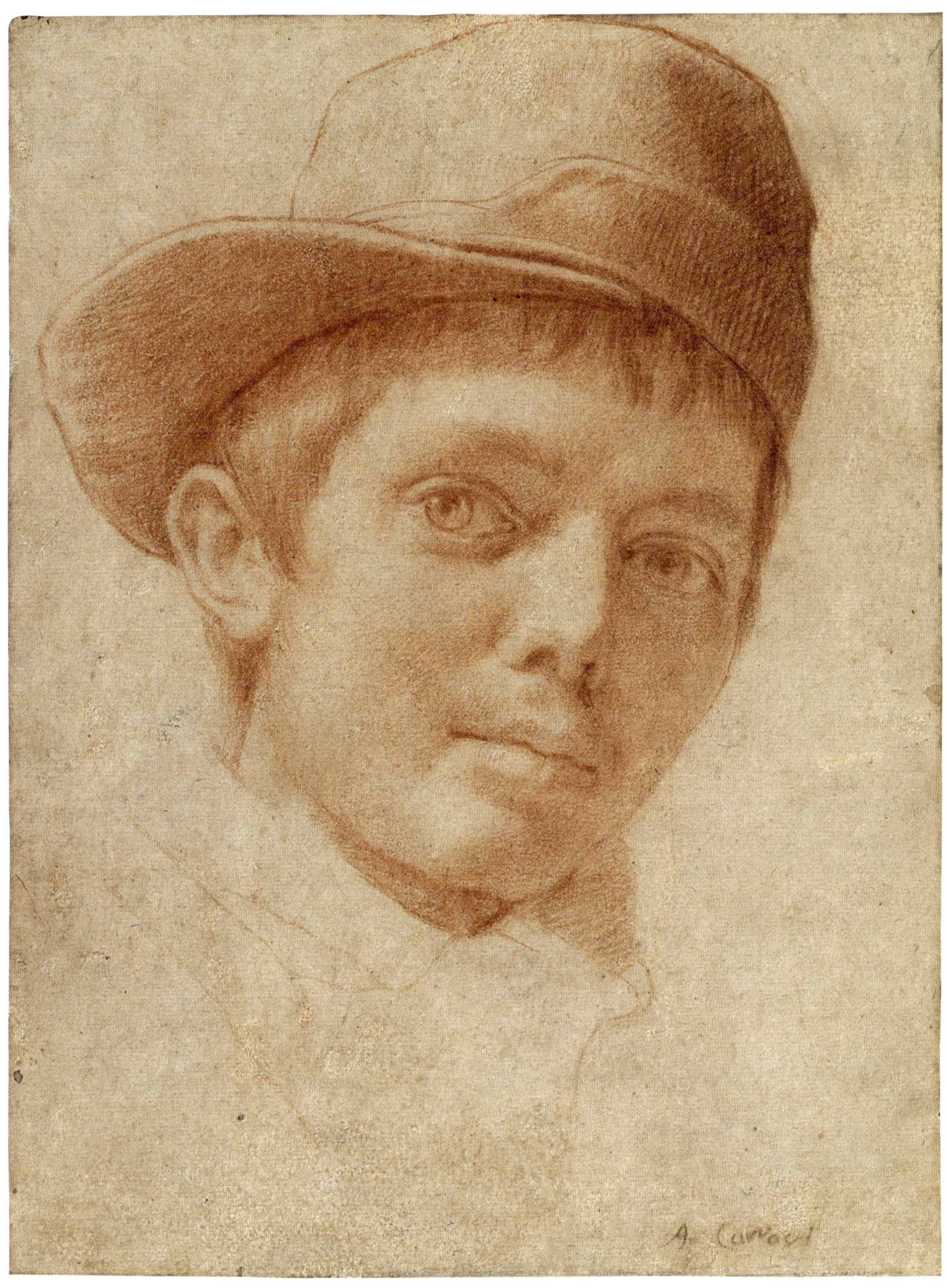

DOMENICHINO
Bologna, 1581–Naples, 1641

Following a period of training with Denys Calvaert, Domenichino entered the Carracci academy in Bologna about 1595. In 1602 he relocated to Rome in order to join Annibale Carracci, who was then engaged in the decorations of the Palazzo Farnese. Recommended by Annibale to a number of prominent patrons, he received important commissions for fresco cycles, both ecclesiastic and secular. He also painted small, refined mythological scenes, landscapes, altarpieces, and the occasional portrait. Besides long periods in Rome, Domenichino also worked in his native Bologna, in Fano, and in Naples, where he spent the last decade of his life. Indebted to the art of Raphael, his graceful figures; lucid, rigorously ordered, and spatially coherent compositions; expressive language of gesture; and restrained yet dramatic narrative content made Domenichino the paradigmatic exemplar of Baroque classicism.

41. *Head of a Bearded Old Man*, mid-1620s

Black and white chalk, 14⅛ x 8⅝ in. (36 x 22 cm)

The Metropolitan Museum of Art, New York, Promised Gift of David M. Tobey

Provenance: Earl of Plymouth; Katrin Bellinger Kunsthandel, Munich; acquired in 2000

Reference: Goldner 1993

This drawing was made as a preparatory study for the head of an old man standing prominently at the left side of Domenichino's *Presentation of the Virgin* in the Santuario di Nostra Signora della Misericordia, Savona, painted in the mid-1620s (figs. 41.1, 41.2), as was first recognized by the present author. It was executed well into the process of developing this figure: the head is tilted at the same angle as in the painting, and the deeper shadows on the left side of the face, right cheek, and eyelids already appear. However, the cloak worn by the corresponding figure in the painting is not shown here. The only other surviving drawing for this painting represents the standing man in lost profile seen at the right side (Royal Library, Windsor).[1]

The draftsmanship is entirely typical of Domenichino in its combination of economy of means and broad monumentality. He captures the grand form and expressive character of the face with relatively few black-chalk strokes, adding small highlights in white chalk very selectively.

G R G

1. Pope-Hennessy 1948, no. 1063 (recto).

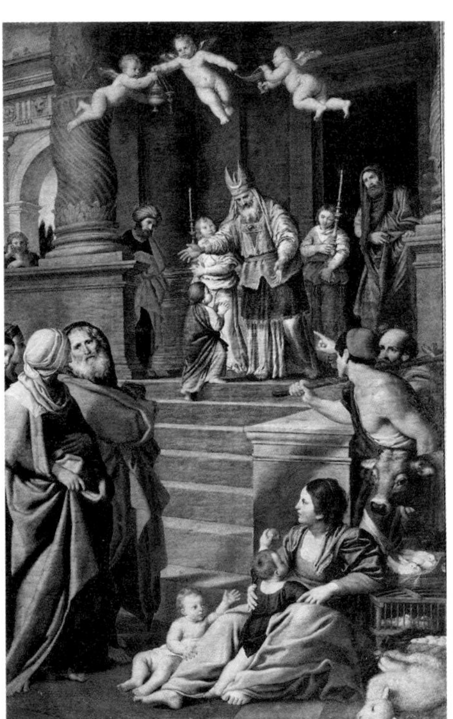

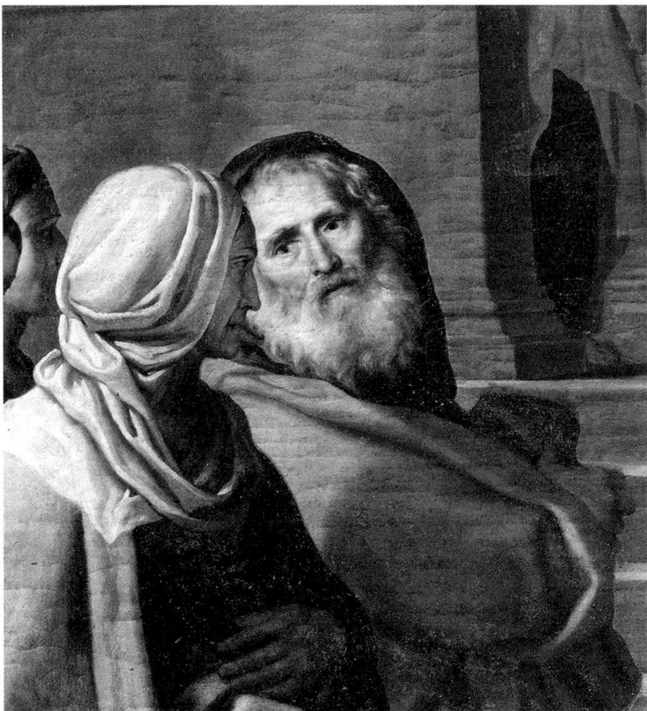

Fig. 41.1. Domenichino. *Presentation of the Virgin*, mid-1620s. Fresco. Santuario di Nostra Signora della Misericordia, Savona

Fig. 41.2. Domenichino. *Head of Bearded Man Standing to the Left*. Detail of fig. 41.1

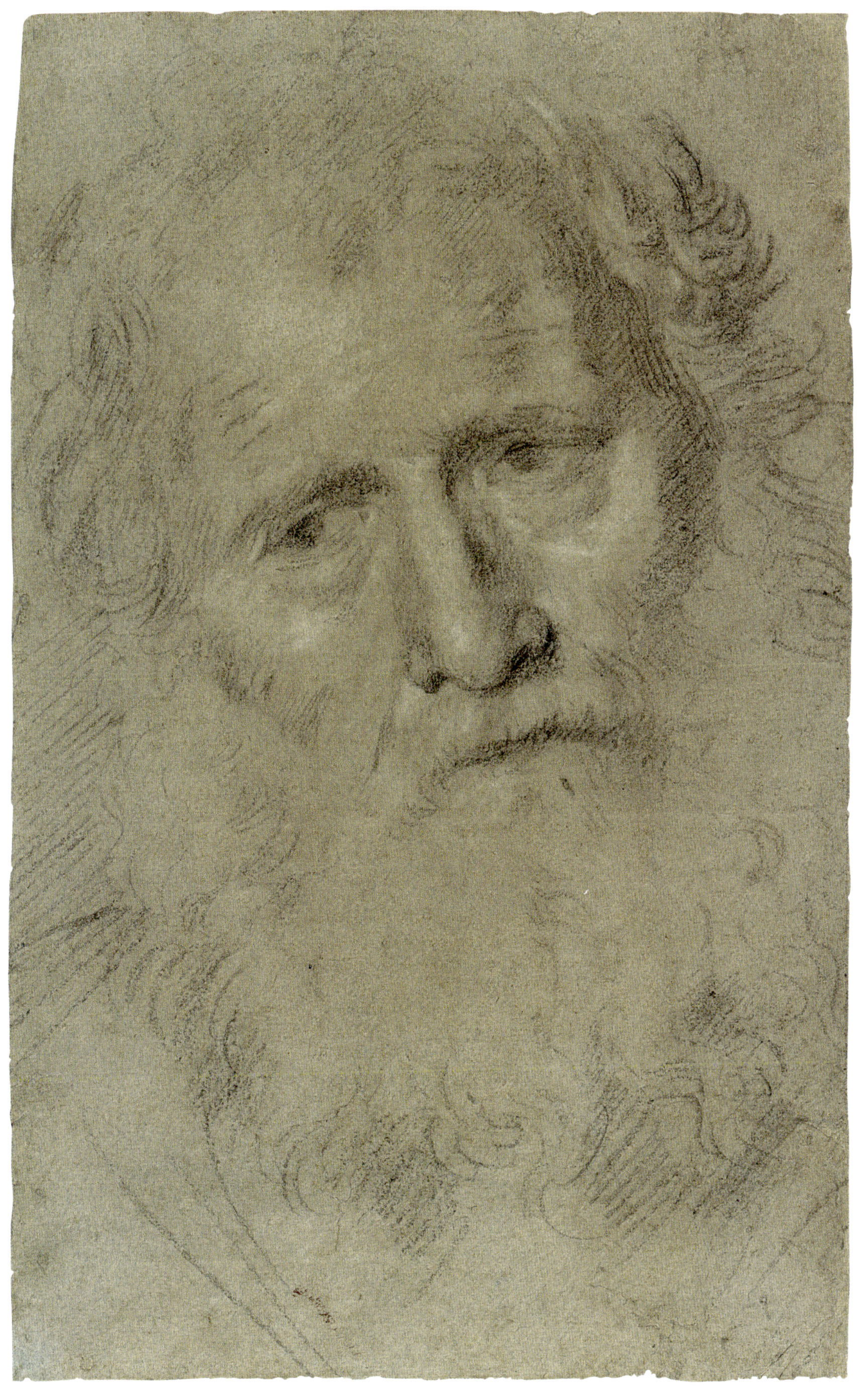

SIGISMONDO COCCAPANI

Florence, 1583–Florence, 1643

Sigismondo Coccapani was a pupil of Ludovico Cigoli, with whom he worked for a period in Rome. He also trained as an architect with Bernardo Buontalenti. His independent career was spent mostly in Florence, where he executed frescoes, private devotional images, and mythological paintings. His graphic style is indebted to the manner of Cigoli, to whom some of Coccapani's fluid, lively pen-and-ink studies were at one time attributed. Coccapani appears to have been an early collector of drawings, assembling a number of sheets by Cigoli and members of his circle.

42. *Diana and Actaeon*, ca. 1610–15

Black and red chalk, pen and brown ink, purple and blue wash, 10⅞ x 12¾ in. (27.6 x 32.3 cm)
Inscribed on old mount: *Del Cigoli*; on verso: *dell Albano*

Provenance: Sigismondo and Giovanni Coccapani (Lugt 2729); Sir John and Lady Witt, London; their sale, Sotheby's, London, February 19, 1987, no. 277 (as Cigoli); sale, Christie's, London, July 7, 1992, lot 153 (as Cigoli); sale, Christie's, London, July 2, 1996, lot 12 (as Coccapani); acquired in 1996

Reference: Chappell 1990, pp. 189–90

The mid-seventeenth-century Florentine art historian and biographer Filippo Baldinucci observed that Sigismondo Coccapani's manner as both a painter and a draftsman was shaped by the example of his master, Ludovico Cigoli.[1] A number of drawings now given to Coccapani were formerly ascribed to Cigoli, testifying to the acuity of Baldinucci's observation. One such work is this fluid study of *Diana and Actaeon*: long assigned to Cigoli, it was convincingly attributed in 1990 to Coccapani by Miles Chappell, who observed affinities with other drawings by the artist.[2] Chappell also identified a previously unrecognized blind stamp that occurs on a number of drawings by Cigoli and Florentine draftsmen from his circle, including the present example, as that of the Coccapani.[3] Its presence here is evidence that the Tobey sheet once formed part of the collection assembled by Sigismondo and augmented by his brother and fellow artist, Giovanni. The bulk of their collection, which was dispersed in the third quarter of the seventeenth century, was probably acquired by Cardinal Leopoldo de' Medici (1617–1675) and is now in the Uffizi, although a number of drawings with this provenance are also found in other public and private collections.[4] The Tobey sheet, and at least two others also attributed to Coccapani that have the identical stamp, must at one time have been in the same, later collection, as all three were attached to a mount inscribed in a large, florid script, "Del Cigoli."[5] A presumed inventory number, formerly visible at the lower edge of the present sheet, perhaps dates from the time that the drawing entered this unknown, later collection.[6]

This fluidly executed, multifigured composition represents Diana and Actaeon, a subject drawn from classical mythology and narrated, among other antique literary sources, by Ovid in the *Metamorphoses*. As punishment for the trespass of beholding the chaste goddess while she bathed, the hunter Actaeon was transformed into a stag and devoured by his own rapacious hounds. Identified by her crescent-moon crown, Diana appears at the upper left, peering down at the alarmed nymphs who flee to escape Actaeon's violating gaze. Standing at the center, he sprouts the horns of a stag, his fatal metamorphosis from hunter to prey at the command of the wrathful goddess already begun. The annotation on the verso may record an erroneous attribution to the seventeenth-century Bolognese artist Francesco Albani.

No painting of this subject by either Cigoli or Coccapani is known. As Chappell has noted, the composition and disposition of figures loosely recall Cigoli's ceiling fresco *Cupid and Psyche before Jupiter*. That late work, commissioned by Cardinal Scipione Borghese, was painted in Rome in 1611–13 when Coccapani was working as Cigoli's assistant.[7] The Tobey drawing conceivably dates from this period, when Coccapani most faithfully emulated his master's style.   LWS

1. "Questo artefice [i.e., Coccapani] . . . nel disegno e nella pittura appreso il Cigoli ebbe alti principi. . ." ("This artist learned the highest principles of drawing and painting from Cigoli"); in Baldinucci ed. 1845–47, p. 416.
2. Chappell 1990, pp. 189–90. The style of the Tobey drawing is particularly close to a pen-and-ink study by Coccapani of *Venus and the Dead Adonis* (Uffizi, Florence, inv. no. 8885F; ill. in Acanfora 1989, fig. 51a) not discussed by Chappell.
3. Ibid.
4. Chappell 1983, passim.
5. As observed by Chappell 1990, p. 189. The other two drawings that have the same mount, both attributed by Chappell to Coccapani and each now in a private collection, are a *Martyrdom of Saint Stephen* and a *Susanna and the Elders*.
6. The old mount is seen in the illustration of the drawing in the 1987 Witt Collection sale catalogue (Sotheby's, London 1987, no. 277), which shows it prior to a restoration that occurred sometime before its next appearance at auction in 1992.
7. Painted in the garden loggia of Cardinal Scipione Borghese's villa on the Quirinal, the detached frescoes are now in the Museo di Palazzo Braschi, Rome; see Faranda 1986, p. 171, no. 84.

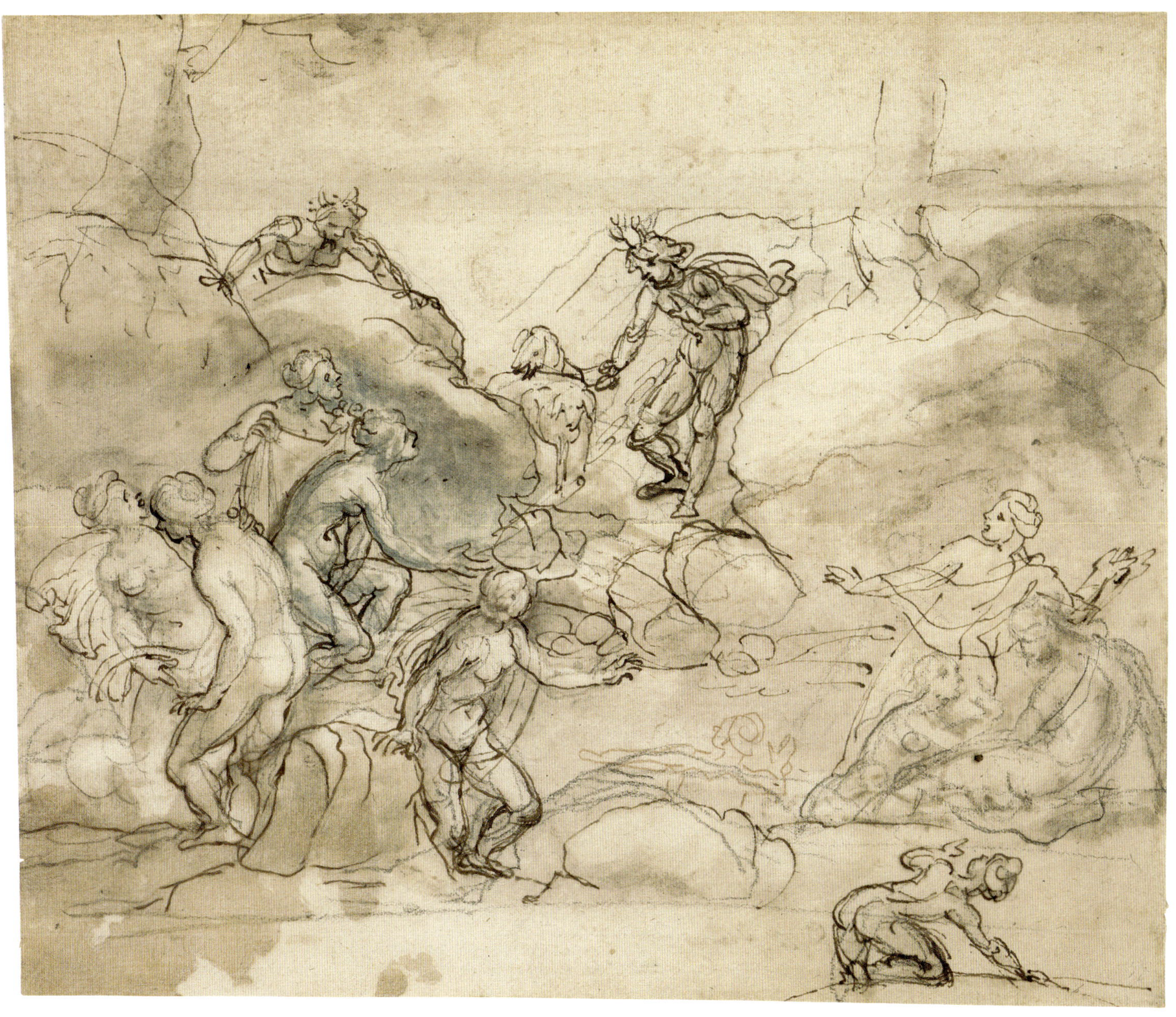

42

GUERCINO

Cento, 1591–Bologna, 1666

Guercino (Giovanni Francesco Barbieri), whose nickname means "the squinter," dominated Bolognese painting in the middle decades of the seventeenth century. Largely self-taught, he was deeply influenced by the art of Ludovico and Annibale Carracci and other local painters whose work he would have seen in Bologna and Ferrara. Although he lived in his native Cento until the death of his rival, Guido Reni, in 1642, Guercino received numerous significant commissions in Bologna and elsewhere beginning in the late 1610s. An important early patron was Cardinal Alessandro Ludovisi; upon his elevation to the papacy as Pope Gregory XV, Guercino journeyed to Rome in 1621. There, his exposure to the works of Reni and other painters caused a shift in his style, as the artist moved away from the dramatic chiaroscuro and foreshortenings of his early compositions in favor of lighter tonalities and a more classically balanced arrangement of figures. Following his return to Cento in 1623, Guercino received a stream of commissions for major altarpieces for churches across Emilia, and he also painted smaller devotional works, Old Testament and mythological subjects, and portraits. His mature style, which earned him widespread fame, is characterized by a rich, glowing, and subtle palette and a restrained yet highly expressive vocabulary of gestures and expressions. Guercino was among the most fluent and prolific draftsmen of the seventeenth century.

43. *The Young Bacchus Kneeling in a Landscape, Raising His Glass Aloft in His Left Hand While Looking Down at a Vat Filled with Grapes*, ca. 1625–30

Red chalk, with stumping, 16½ x 12 in. (41.9 x 30.5 cm)

Provenance: A. Normand (Lugt 153c); Artemis Fine Arts, Geneva; acquired in 2002

Reference: Nicholas Turner in New York 2003a, no. 13

Although this splendid, fully worked up, and highly finished red chalk composition study showing the young Bacchus beside a wine vat raising his glass would appear to be preparatory for a painting or a print, no such work by Guercino is known. Wine or wine-making, the implicit theme, was a subject taken up by the artist in a stylistically and chronologically coherent group of some six extant or lost drawings, none of which can be connected with an existing work or recorded commission. These include a study of a satyr holding a thyrsus seen from behind, reaching down with his right hand into a wine vat (whereabouts unknown), probably originally conceived as a pendant to the Tobey drawing;[1] a red and black chalk *Allegory of Wine-Making with Four Nude Putti* (Devonshire Collection, Chatsworth);[2] a red chalk study of putti making wine (Galleria Estense, Modena);[3] *Four Putti Making Wine, Two of Them Sitting in the Wooden Vat*, a drawing by Francesco Bartolozzi after a lost design by Guercino (Albertina, Vienna);[4] and an engraving by Bartolozzi, *Putto Drinking from a Carafe*, which likewise records a lost composition by Guercino.[5] Another drawing by Guercino (Victoria and Albert Museum, London) has been linked to this corpus;[6] its subject, four putti frolicking near a vat of grapes, is self-evidently related to the common theme shared by the above-cited studies, but its

sketchy, informal, and exploratory character, as well as the pen-and-ink medium, distinguish it from the others in the group. Nonetheless, the hasty sketch of a standing figure beside a mount facing right recalls the pose and disposition of Bacchus in the Tobey drawing, and it seems probable, as has been suggested, that this sheet, too, is in some way connected with the same unknown project.

That project may have been a single canvas illustrating an allegory of autumn (frequently represented by scenes of grape harvesting), or one of a series of images personifying the seasons, in this case, autumn. It is also possible that the Tobey drawing and its pendant were studies, or perhaps presentation drawings, not of seasonal allegories but of mythological themes of the type that appealed to cultivated patrons in Rome and elsewhere in the seventeenth century, of which Caravaggio's *Bacchus* (Uffizi, Florence) is the paradigmatic example. Like Caravaggio's fleshy, coyly nude god of wine, Guercino's Bacchus extends a glass goblet containing the elixir made from his grapes, although unlike that dissolute and vaguely inebriated deity he does not appear to have succumbed to its temptations.

The Tobey drawing has been dated to the second half of the 1620s on stylistic grounds. Some decades later Guercino executed a painting of *Lot and His Daughters* (Louvre, Paris). A recently identified red chalk preparatory study for that composition shows a youth holding a glass goblet and a carafe that are virtually identical to the same implements in the *Bacchus*

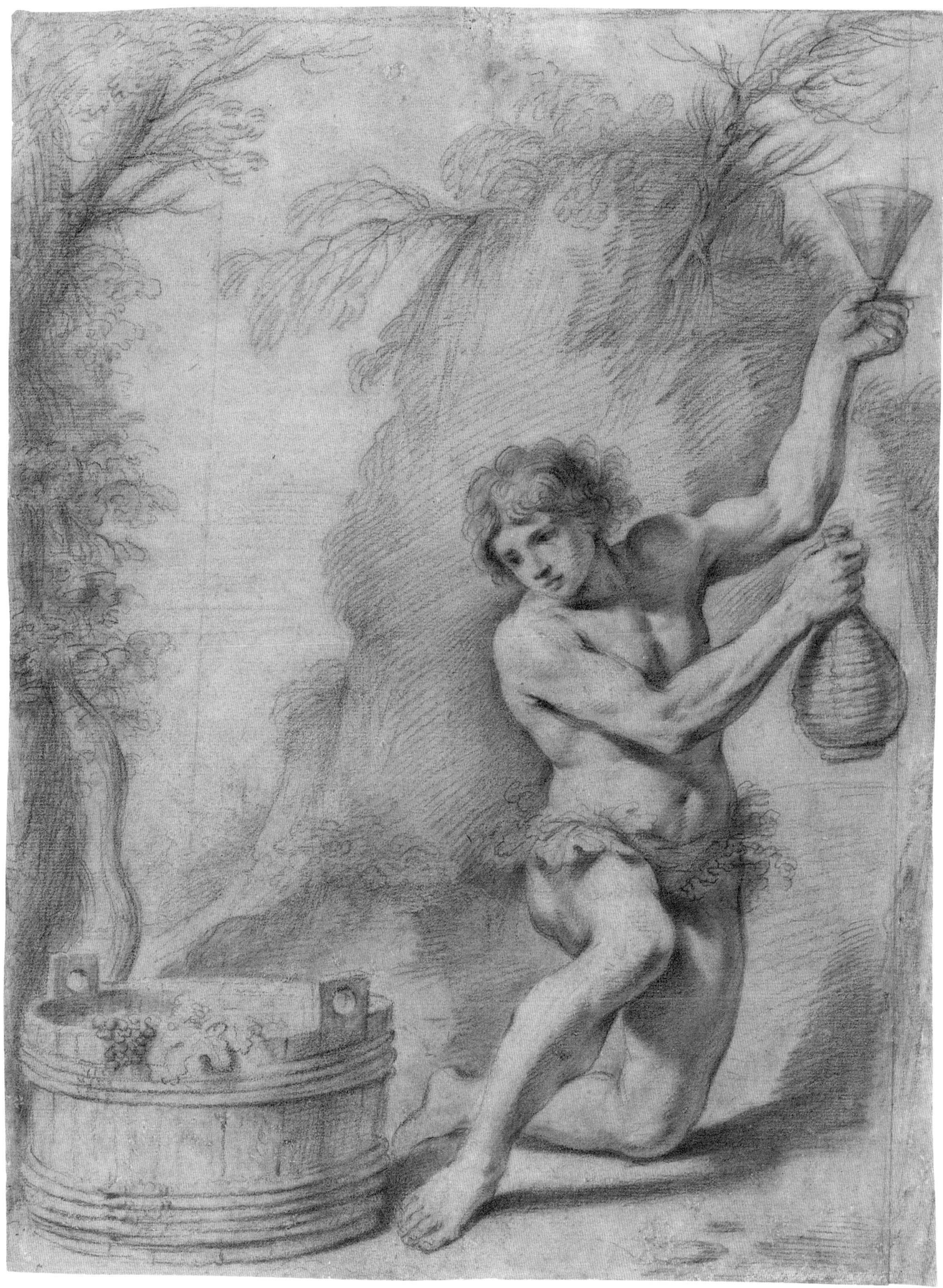

drawing, suggesting that these items may have been props the artist retained in his studio.[7]   LWS

1. Formerly in a private collection; see Nicholas Turner in New York 2003a, under no. 13, for this and the thematically related drawings by or after Guercino discussed here.
2. Inv. no. 550; Turner and Plazzotta 1991, no. 67.
3. Ibid., p. 96, under no. 67, p. 95, fig. 15.
4. Inv. no. 1399; see Birke and Kertész 1992–97, vol. 2, p. 751.
5. See Rome 1995, p. 111, no. 11, and p. 110, fig. 27-11.
6. Turner in New York 2003a, under no. 13. Inv. no. Dyce 321; see Ward-Jackson 1980, p. 59, no. 725.
7. The drawing, which was kindly brought to my attention by Eveline Baseggio, was sold at Bonhams, London, on April 23, 2008, lot 239.

44. *Sisyphus*, ca. 1636

Pen and brown ink, brown wash, 12 x 8⅛ in. (30.6 x 20.5 cm)

The Metropolitan Museum of Art, New York, Promised Gift of David M. Tobey

Provenance: Paul Prouté, Paris; Robert Laurent, Bloomington, Indiana; Lester Francis Avnet, New York; his sale, Sotheby's, London, March 27, 1969, lot 14; P. & D. Colnaghi, London, June 1970, no. 21; Private Collection; Katrin Bellinger Kunsthandel, Munich, 2001, no. 10

References: Indianapolis 1955, no. 25; Mahon and Turner 1989, p. 49; Bologna 1991, p. 144; Stone 1991, p. 92 n. 2; Llewellyn and Romalli 1992, p. 135, under no. 108

An entry in Guercino's account book, or *libro dei conti*, refers to a painting of "a figure of Sisyphus" (*una figura di un Sisifo*) for which the artist was paid 100 *ducati* on October 28, 1636, by the Bolognese count Girolamo Ranuzzi. That work is now lost, but the amount of the payment suggests that it portrayed a full-length figure.[1] A number of drawings by Guercino of this subject,[2] executed in both pen and ink and in chalk, are known, among them the Tobey sheet, which exhibits the tremulous and economic yet descriptive line typical of the artist's draftsmanship. These studies reveal that Guercino experimented with different poses for the figure of Sisyphus, the wicked and deceitful king of Corinth who was condemned by the gods to eternally push a boulder up a steep mountainside, only to have it tumble back down to the ground just before reaching the summit.

A double-sided sheet in the Teyler Museum, Haarlem, shows a beardless Sisyphus gazing upward as he supports the boulder against the side of the mountain.[3] An alternative pose is seen in a drawing in the Witt Collection at the Courtauld Institute of Art, London, in which the bearded figure hunches over the unwieldy boulder he struggles to transport.[4] In the Tobey drawing, the muscular Sisyphus does not push or carry the boulder, but rather bears it on his shoulders, straining beneath its massive weight—a formulation reiterated in a similar drawing in the Royal Collection, Windsor Castle, which shows the figure in reverse (fig. 44.1).[5] Two other sheets by Guercino that have been connected with the same composition, both formerly on the art market, similarly depict Sisyphus hauling the boulder on his back.[6]

The pose of Sisyphus in the Tobey sheet and in the closely linked drawings by Guercino is reminiscent of depictions of the mythological Atlas, a titan who is typically portrayed bearing the globe of the world or the heavens on his shoulders. Indeed, a painting of that precise subject was commissioned from Guercino by Don Lorenzo de' Medici a decade after he completed the lost *Sisyphus* (Museo Stefano Bardini, Florence; fig. 44.2).[7] The artist may well have referred to these drawings when executing that work.   LWS

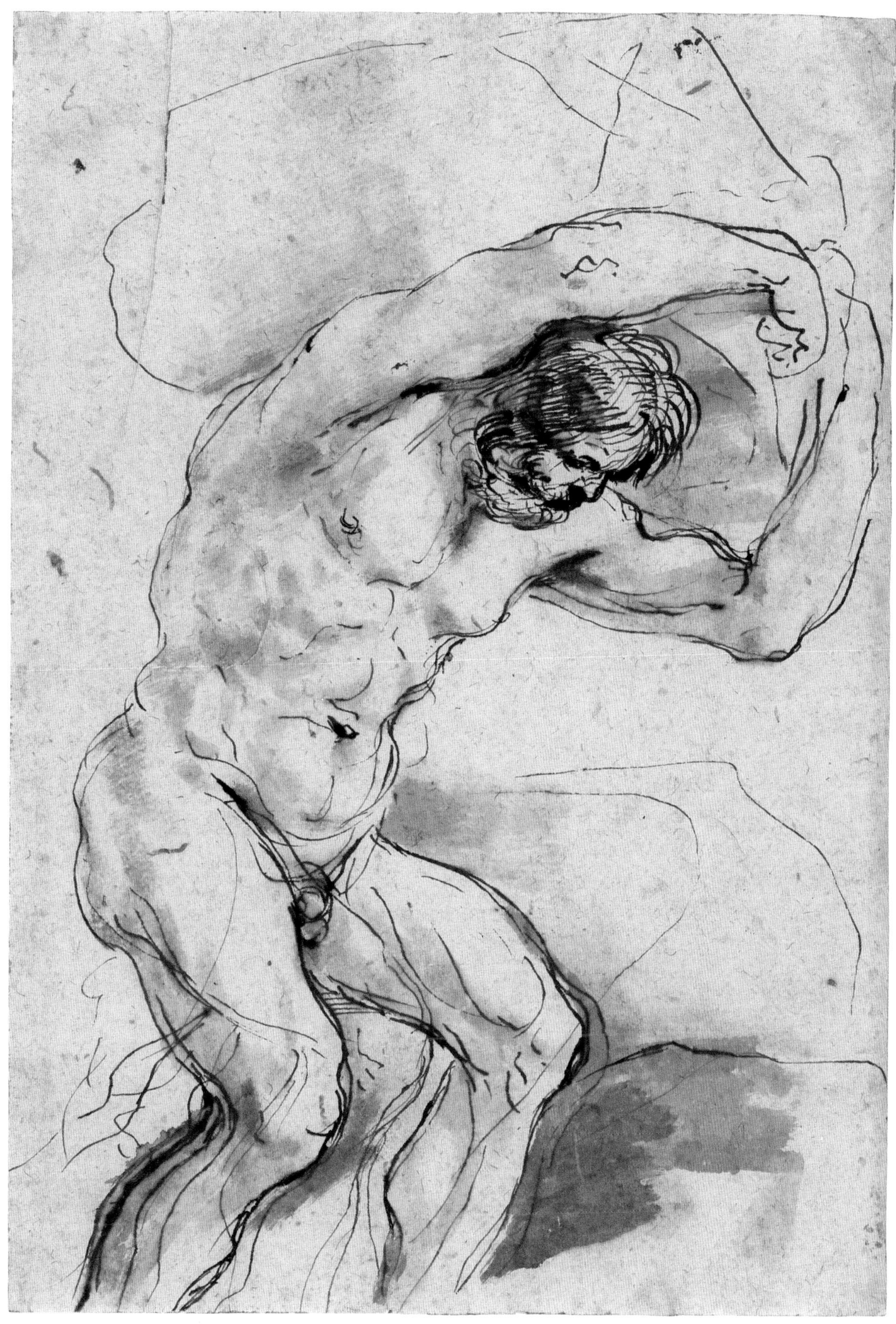

Guercino 149

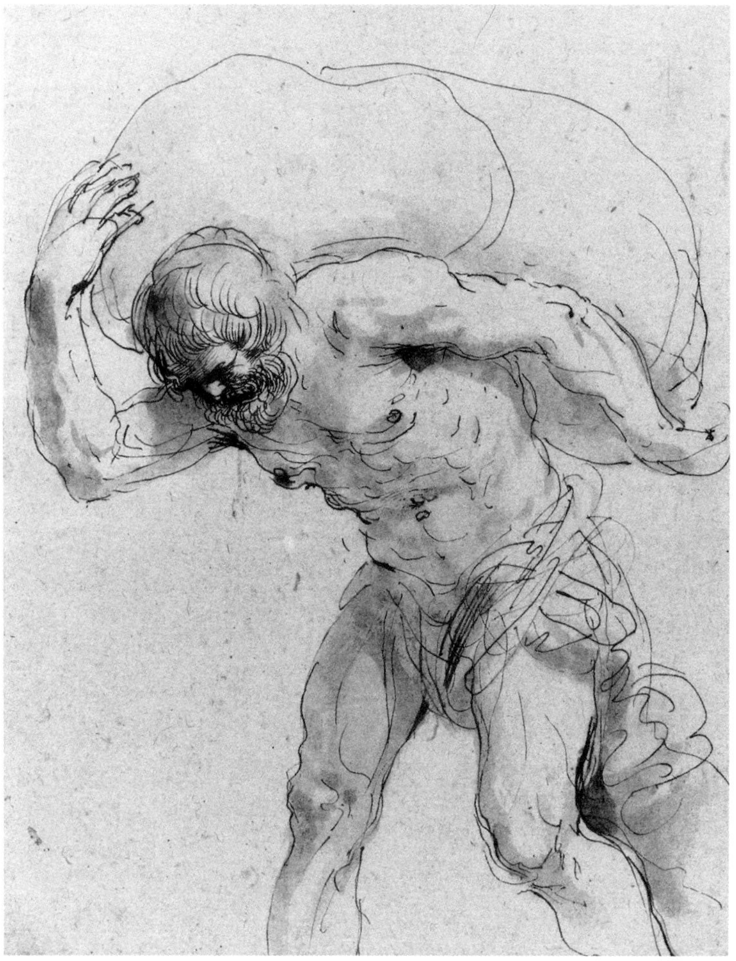

Fig. 44.1. Guercino. *Sisyphus*, 1636. Pen and ink, brush and grayish wash, on light-buff paper, 10½ x 7¹³⁄₁₆ in. (26.6 x 19.8 cm). The Royal Collection. © Her Majesty Queen Elizabeth II (2882)

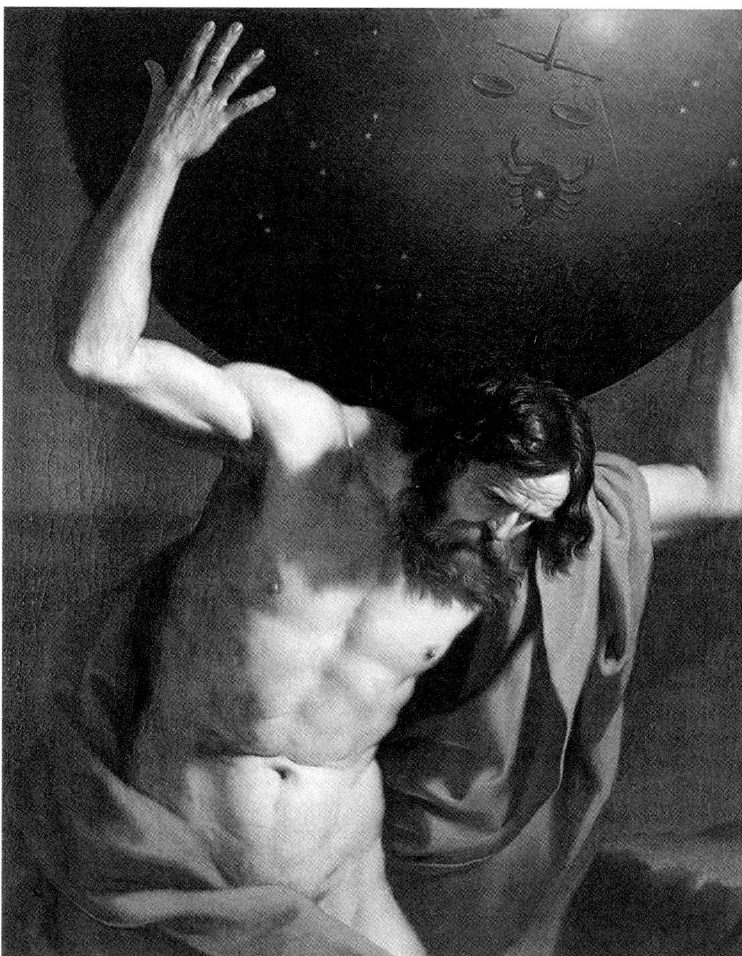

Fig. 44.2. Guercino. *Atlas*, 1645–46. Oil on canvas, 50 x 39¾ in. (127 x 101 cm) Museo Stefano Bardini, Florence

1. On the lost painting and the payment recorded in Guercino's account book, as well as the series of drawings related to the Sisyphus, see Mahon and Turner 1989, p. 49, under no. 84; Stone 1991, p. 92, under no. 38; Turner and Plazzotta 1991, nos. 107–8.
2. A sixth drawing of Sisyphus traditionally ascribed to Guercino and linked in the literature to the other sheets discussed here (Blanton Museum of Art, The University of Texas at Austin, The Suida-Manning Collection, 314.1999; see Stone 1991, no. 38) is probably by an eighteenth-century imitator of Guercino, according to Jonathan P. Bober, curator of European Art, who kindly shared his opinion with the present author.
3. Inv. no. H 29; Bologna 1991, pp. 142–43, no. 88.
4. Inv. no. 1366; Bologna 1991, no. 86.
5. Mahon and Turner 1989, p. 49, no. 84; Bologna 1991, no. 87; Turner and Plazzotta 1991, no. 108.
6. Ongpin 2003, no. 18; and Christie's, London, November 23, 1971, lot 72; ill. in Stone 1991, p. 92, fig. 38a. The latter is in a Casa Gennari mount.
7. Bologna, Frankfurt, and Washington, D.C., 1991–92, pp. 268–70, no. 41.

45. *A Wooded Landscape with Figures outside the Gate of a Castle*

Pen and brown ink, 9¼ x 15⅞ in. (23.5 x 40.4 cm)

Provenance: Thomas Coke, 1st Earl of Leicester, Holkham Hall; sale, Christie's, London, July 2, 1991, lot 24; acquired in 1991

Reference: Popham and Lloyd 1986, no. 147

Guercino's vast graphic corpus includes a number of engaging landscape drawings. Although landscapes occur in many of the artist's paintings, such studies were not made as preparatory designs—as far as has been ascertained none of the drawings corresponds to passages in any of his paintings—but rather as independent works. Almost none can be dated with any precision. Virtually all of Guercino's landscape drawings are

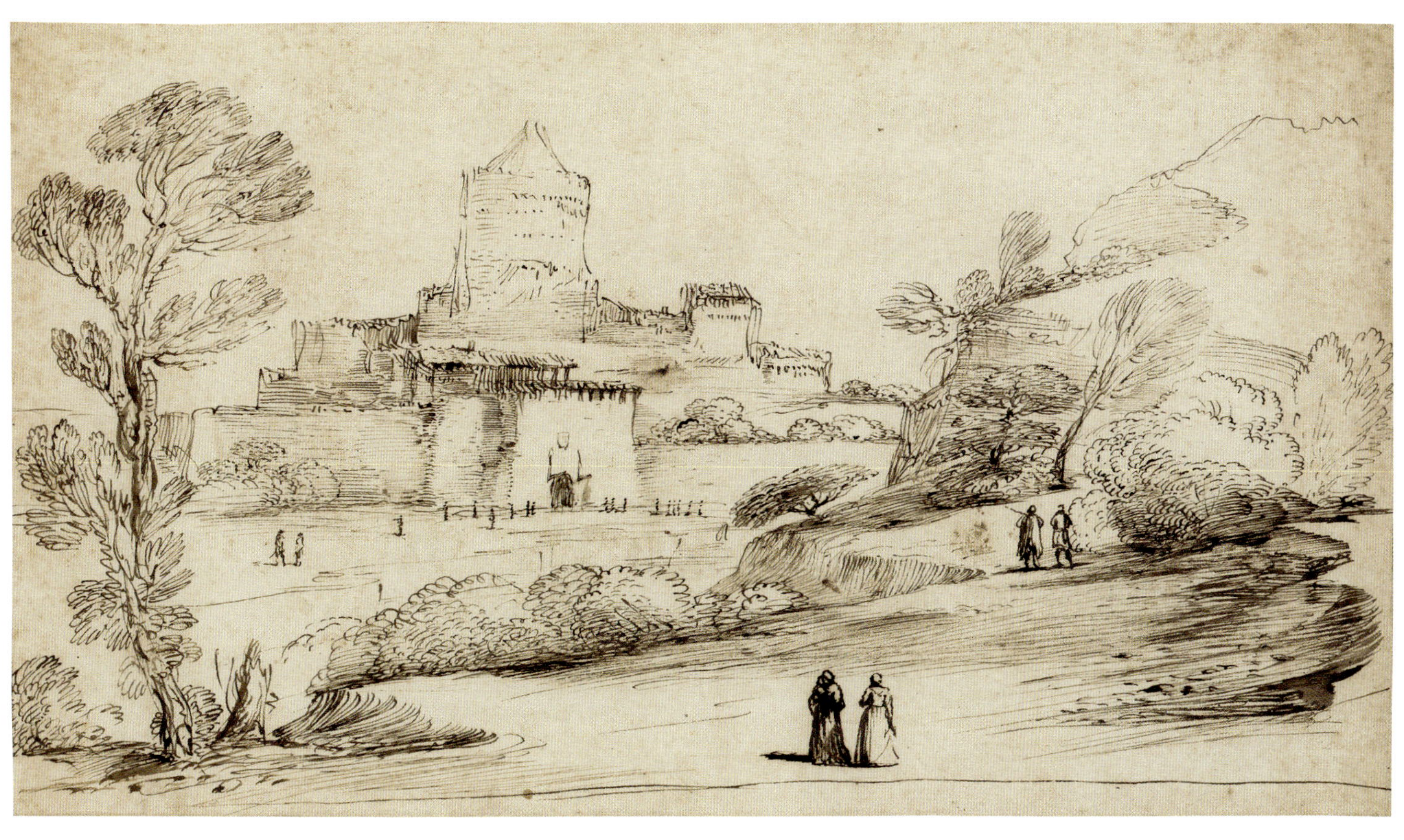

45

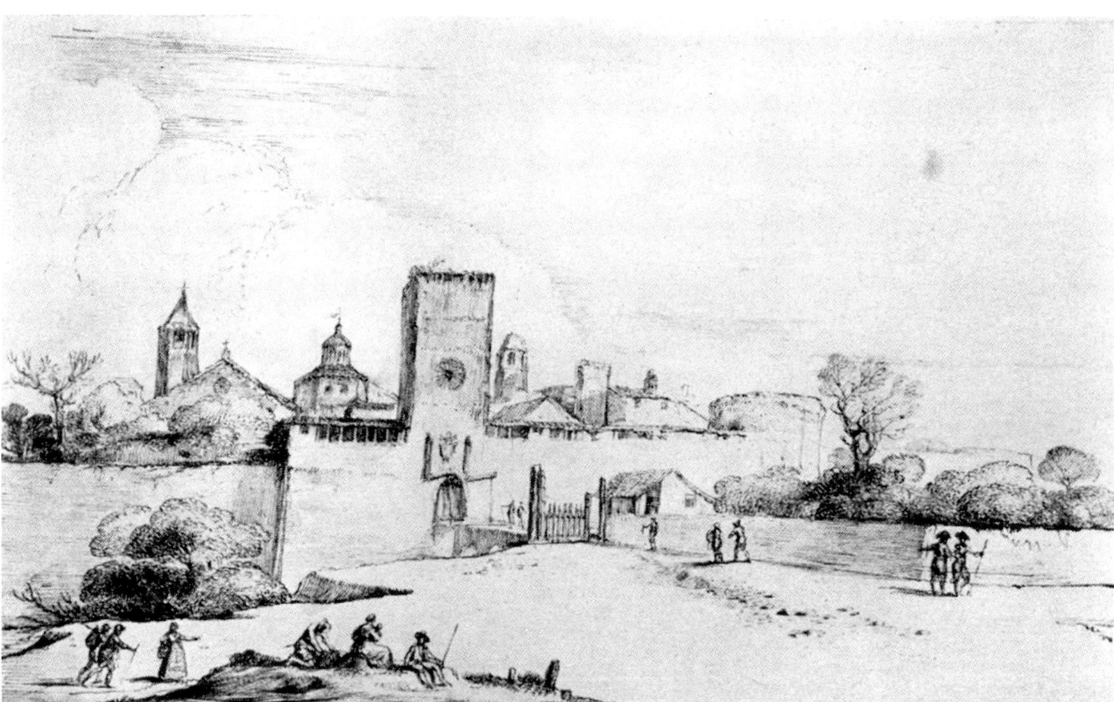

Fig. 45.1. Guercino. *Landscape with a Walled Town*. Pen and brown ink, 10¼ x 16³⁄₁₆ in. (26 x 41.5 cm). The Morgan Library and Museum, New York (I, 100)

executed in pen and ink and show detailed, finished compositions. Atmospheric vistas are punctuated by gently rolling hills, animated trees, rustic buildings, and walled towns. Diminutive people stroll languidly or pause in a moment of repose. Aptly characterized as having the aspect of a set piece, these idyllic, light-filled tableaux were probably not executed *en plein air*, but composed in the studio, the artist perhaps incorporating details of actual buildings and other motifs observed from nature.[1]

The Tobey sheet has an illustrious provenance, having formed part of the group of old master drawings assembled by the 1st Earl of Leicester at Holkham Hall. It was auctioned with other masterpieces from that collection in 1991. A quintessential example of Guercino's manner as a landscape

draftsman, its confident, sprightly, and assured line describes with equal facility and expressiveness the rolling foreground plane, dense shrubbery, willowy trees, and massing of medieval architectural forms, as well as the rural inhabitants on the countryside. Similar walled towns occur in other landscape drawings by Guercino, notably an example in the Morgan Library and Museum, New York (fig. 45.1), and another in the Royal Collection, Windsor Castle.[2]

LWS

1. This characterization follows that of Nicholas Turner in *Oxford Art Online* (Turner 2007–).
2. For the Morgan drawing, see Mahon 1968, no. 218, ill.; for the Windsor sheet, see Mahon and Turner 1989, no. 247 and pl. 231.

JUSEPE DE RIBERA

Jativa (Valencia), 1591–Naples, 1652

Spanish by birth, Jusepe de Ribera spent almost his entire career in Italy, working in Parma and Rome before settling in Naples in 1616. The deep chiaroscuro and unwavering, earthy realism of Caravaggio and his followers in Rome left a deep impression on Ribera, whose paintings typically show rough but dignified peasant-types in the guise of saints, philosophers, allegorical personifications, and the occasional mythological deity, set in murky shadow. He also explored an alternative stylistic mode, characterized by loose, painterly brushwork, a more coloristically rich palette, and an element of refinement and idealization in the figures. Enormously famous once he settled in Naples, Ribera received commissions from the Spanish ruling elite and the Grand Duke of Tuscany, and he achieved great renown as an engraver.

46. *Grotesque Man in Bust-Length*, ca. 1622–25

Red chalk over traces of black chalk, 7⅝ x 5³⁄₁₆ in. (19.4 x 13.2 cm), maximum, corners cropped
Annotated in pen and brown ink, at lower left by an early eighteenth-century hand: *Spagnoletto*

Provenance: Trinity Fine Art Ltd., London; acquired in 2000

Reference: New York 1995a, pp. 74–75, no. 32

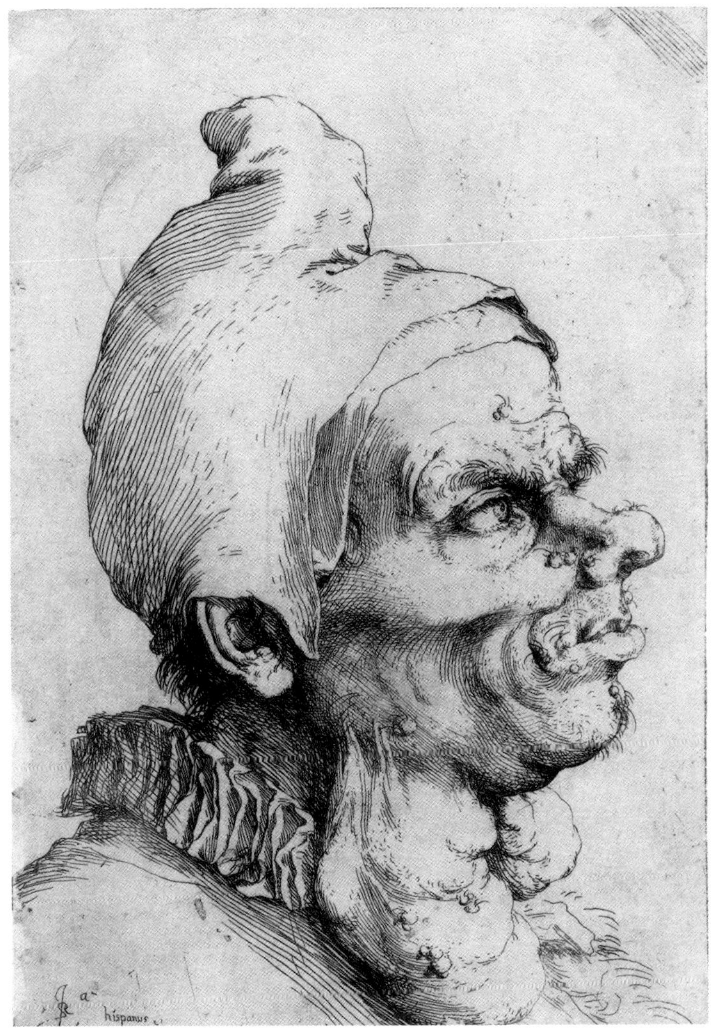

Fig. 46.1. Jusepe de Ribera. *The Large Grotesque Head*, ca. 1622. Etching, 8⁷⁄₁₆ x 5½ in. (21.4 x 13.9 cm). The Metropolitan Museum of Art, New York, Harris Brisbane Dick Fund, 1917 (17.3.1830)

The design of this lively drawing is the exact size and disposition, almost line for line, and in the same orientation facing right, as that of one of Jusepe de Ribera's most famous etchings, *The Large Grotesque Head*, which the artist produced about 1622 (fig. 46.1). The present author has been able to confirm this information by placing a tracing on transparent acetate done from the print, upon the drawing.[1] The Tobey sheet is executed with vigor and a great level of naturalistic detail. Its authorship by Ribera was accepted by Jonathan Brown in 1995 at the time of its exhibition at the Newhouse Gallery, New York, an opinion that he endorsed again in 2000;[2] this attribution had been stated by Alfonso E. Pérez Sánchez in 1994.[3]

Some minor differences of detail exist between the Tobey drawing and the etching, an indication, along with the significant evidence of abundant traces of black-chalk underdrawing on the sheet, that it was a study with a utilitarian purpose, not simply a copy after the print. In this author's view, the present drawing was most likely produced as a record of the design that the artist intended to etch, perhaps even to try out the final idea in the same direction before committing it to the printing plate. Although bolder, the expressive technique of the Tobey sheet is relatable to autograph drawings in red chalk by Ribera from the 1620s, especially those that served to prepare prints early in the decade and that manifest graphically precise modeling and finely detailed outlines. An example is

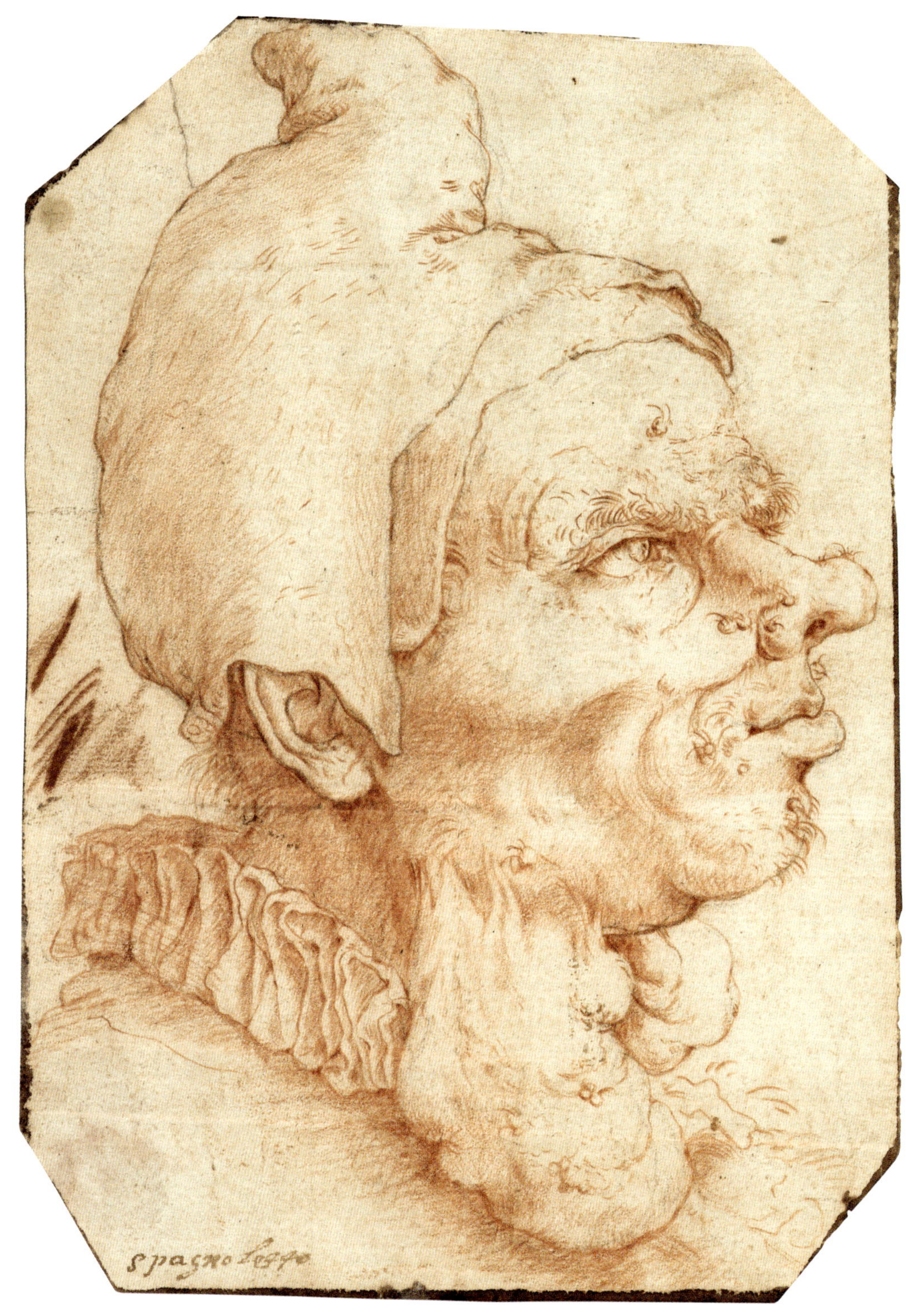

46

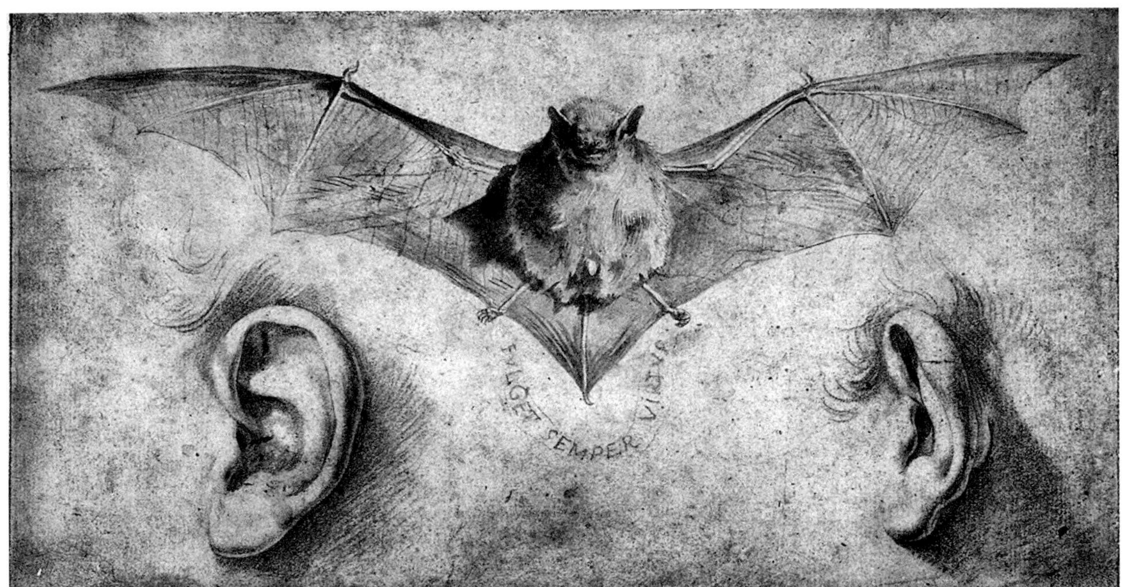

Fig. 46.2. Jusepe de Ribera. *Study of Two Human Ears and a Bat*; below, the motto: *FVLGET SEMPER VIRTVS*, ca. 1622. Red chalk, brush and red wash, on beige paper, 6¼ x 11 in. (15.9 x 27.9 cm). The Metropolitan Museum of Art, New York, Rogers Fund, 1972 (1972.77)

the delicate study of two human ears and a bat, inscribed by the artist "FVLGET SEMPER VIRTVS" (fig. 46.2), which is datable to about 1622, as it was likely partly preparatory for the etching of ears, signed with Ribera's monogram and inscribed by him with this date.[4] A closely comparable male grotesque head in profile in red chalk from this date, which relates to an etching by Ribera oriented in the same design direction, passed through the art market in 1980.[5] A study of a goiterous woman's head of about 1622, now in the Fitzwilliam Museum, Cambridge, England, is also similar.[6] The artist's red-chalk studies from the late 1620s to the 1650s gradually strove for an impressionistic, painterly handling of the medium.[7] What is in the present author's view a copy of the Tobey work exists at the Gabinetto dei Disegni e Stampe of the Museo e Gallerie Nazionali di Capodimonte, Naples (fig. 46.3).[8] With the discovery of the Tobey sheet in 1994–95, it has become clear by the comparison of the two sheets, that the Capodimonte copy is executed drily, smoothly, and relatively flatly, that the motif of the grotesque head is placed as if it were a floating form, and that the lower portions of the drawing abruptly terminate with a very even finish, rather than display suggestive sketchiness. In contrast to the Tobey sheet, it also lacks any pentimenti and black-chalk underdrawing.

As seen in the Tobey drawing and the related examples, the genre of grotesque head studies owes its origins to Leonardo da Vinci (1452–1519) and was much practiced throughout the late Renaissance into the seventeenth and eighteenth centuries.[9] Grotesques and "testes de caractere"—a term applied to Leonardo's drawings of deformed physiognomies by the Count of Caylus in 1730[10]—were produced by various Lombard

artists throughout the sixteenth century.[11] Ribera's knowledge of Lombard traditions almost certainly derived firsthand,[12] although the Leonardesque material was also widely disseminated through secondhand copies and prints, and particularly in the etching of the *Pagan Gods* by Martino Rota (ca. 1520–1583), which directly inspired our artist's *Large Grotesque Head* (fig. 46.1).[13] Giulio Mancini's biography of Ribera—written in manuscript about 1617–21—mentions his sojourn in Lombardy, an event that probably occurred between 1611, when the Spaniard is first documented in Parma, and 1615–16, toward the end of his stay in Rome.[14] By 1622, when Ribera had been well established in Naples for six years, his work as a printmaker and draftsman was already displaying a poignant interest in physiognomy. His earliest such exercises took two forms—studies of eyes, ears, noses, and mouths and deformed heads, as seen in the present sheet, the red-chalk study in the Metropolitan Museum's collection, and the related etching (see figs. 46.1, 46.2).[15] The depiction of individual physiognomic details is again a practice grounded in Leonardo's art theory.[16] Ribera's predilection for the disfigured is evident not only in his prints, but also in his drawings of heads in red chalk.

Writing less than a century after Ribera's death, his biographer Acisclo Antonio Palomino de Castro y Velasco praised his ability to portray the grotesquerie of old age ("cosas horrendas y asperas: quales son los cuerpos de los ancianos secos, arrugados y consumidos, con el rostro enjuto y macilento; todo hecho puntualmente por el natural").[17] The exactly contemporary account of Ribera's life by Bernardo de Dominici of 1749 commented especially on Ribera's drawings "most frequently done in red chalk from nature of some dried-up and decrepit old men" ("e per lo più lapis rosso . . . dipingeva quella figura col naturale presente, avendosi procacciato alcuni vecchi secchi, e decrepiti").[18] Dating from 1622 or thereabouts, the nearly caricatural etchings the *Large Grotesque Head* (see fig. 46.1) and the *Small Grotesque Head* apparently depict men with numerous tumors who suffer from multiple neurofibromatosis.[19] These, together with the tender portrayal of Magdalena Venturi in *The Bearded Woman*, seen with her husband and son (Palacio Lerma, Fundación Casa Ducal de Medinaceli, Toledo), painted in 1631,[20] represent the great extremes in Ribera's fascinating study of human deformity during the 1620s. It seemed to devolve between fantasy and utmost human reality.

Ribera is best known as a draftsman in pen and ink, with or without washes, and as an extremely prolific one at that, but he is yet to be entirely understood as an artist in red chalk, and very few drawings in that medium can be unquestionably attributed to him.[21]

CCB

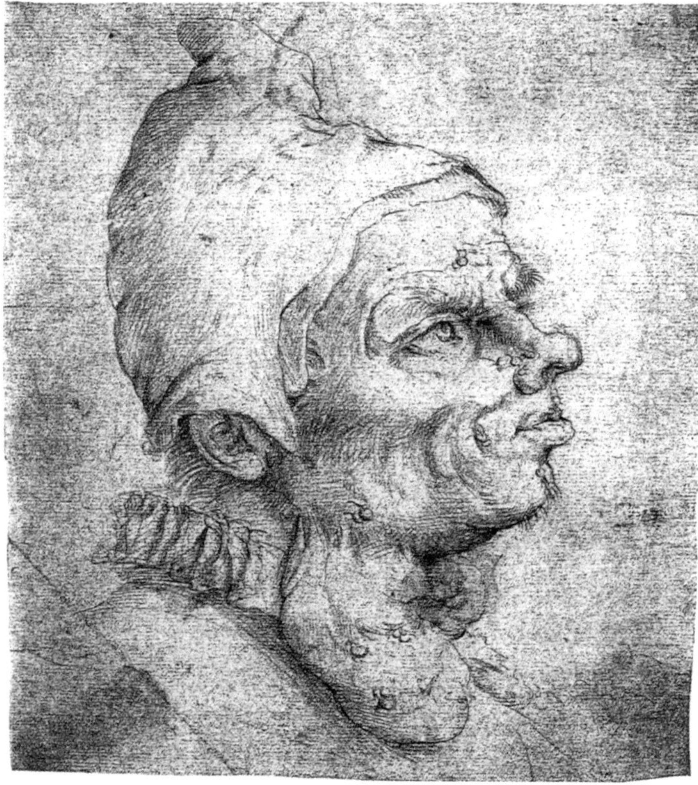

Fig. 46.3. Jusepe de Ribera. *Grotesque Head*, after 1622–25. Red chalk, 8⅞ x 7⁵⁄₁₆ in. (22.5 x 18.5 cm). Gabinetto dei Disegni e Stampe of the Museo e Gallerie Nazionali di Capodimonte, Naples (705)

1. As was confirmed on November 20, 2009. I am indebted to Marjorie N. Shelley, Sherman Fairchild Conservator in Charge, Department of Paper Conservation, The Metropolitan Museum of Art, New York, for her tracing from Ribera's etching, and to Andrea Bayer, curator, Department of European Paintings, The Metropolitan Museum of Art, New York, for fruitful discussions of Ribera as a printmaker. The impression of the etching, the *Large Grotesque Head*, is that of The Metropolitan Museum of Art, New York, 17.3.1830 (Bartsch XX.86.9), which is printed on paper with a late sixteenth- or early seventeenth-century watermark, a circle circumscribing a fleur-de-lis with two petals curving downward, and surmounted by a five-pointed crown (close to Briquet nos. 7111–7113). On other impressions, see Brown 1989, pp. 74–77, nos. 10, 11; Andrea Bayer in Madrid 1992, pp. 182–84, nos. 80, 81.

2. See the letter of February 2, 2000, to David and Julie Tobey.

3. As mentioned in a written communication to the owners (February 9, 2000), the quoted opinion by Alfonso E. Pérez Sánchez appears in a letter dated May 18, 1994.

4. On this drawing (The Metropolitan Museum of Art, New York, 1972.77), see Brown 1972, p. 7 n. 3; Brown 1973–74, no. 3, pl. 30; Manuela Mena Marqués in Madrid 1992, p. 412, no. D.3. On the impressions of the etching with studies of ears (Bartsch XX.86.17), see Brown 1989, pp. 68–69, no. 7; and Andrea Bayer in Madrid 1992, pp. 179–81, no. 77.

5. From the Calobrisi Collection, sale, Christie's, London 1980, lot 30 (ill.).

6. Inv. no. 26-1958. Discussed and illustrated by Mena Marqués in Madrid 1992, p. 413, no. D.4.

7. See Bambach 2009, for a detailed discussion of the evolution of Ribera's red-chalk drawing techniques.

8. This drawing was unconvincingly published as autograph in Madrid 1992, p. 415, no. D.6 (ill.); at that time the Tobey sheet was not widely known.

9. On Ribera and this Leonardesque tradition, see Bambach 2009, pp. 50–53. On Leonardo's own such designs, compare Carmen C. Bambach in Bambach et al. 2003, pp. 416–19, 451–67, 508–11, 640–48, nos. 59, 60, 69–76, 92, 120–23; and Varena Forcione in ibid., pp. 202–24, 678–722, nos. 136–38.

10. Varena Forcione in Bambach et al. 2003, pp. 702–5, no. 138.

11. For Giovanni Paolo Lomazzo, Aurelio Luini, the Accademia della Val di Blenio, and visual examples, see Manuela Kahn-Rossi, Giulio Bora, Francesco Porzio in Lugano 1998, pp. 111–341 (and p. 330, for the document of Lomazzo's election in August 1568).

12. Bambach 2009.

13. See Brown 1989, p. 26, fig. 4 (illustrating the impression at the Gabinetto Disegni e Stampe degli Uffizi, Florence).

14. See Mancini ed. 1956, p. 249. With regard to the secondary literature, compare Spinosa 2006, pp. 12–15; Milicua 1992; Finaldi 1992; and Papi 2007.

15. Brown 1982–83, pp. 71–75; Brown 1989, pp. 68–69, nos. 7–11.

16. Bambach 2009, pp. 53–55.

17. Palomino de Castro y Velasco 1742, p. 63.

18. De Dominici ed. 2008, vol. 1, p. 32.

19. Ribera's *Small Grotesque Head* etching is discussed and illustrated in Brown 1989, pp. 74–77, nos. 10, 11; Andrea Bayer in Madrid 1992, pp. 182–84, nos. 80, 81.

20. Discussed and illustrated by Alfonso Pérez Sánchez in Madrid 1992, pp. 93–94, no. 25; Spinosa 2006, p. 305, no. A120.

21. Compare Brown 1972, pp. 2, 7 n. 1; Brown 1973–74, no. 2, pl. 29; Brown 1974; Mena Marqués in Madrid 1992, pp. 115–29, 409–83; McDonald 1999; Finaldi 2005; Bambach 2009.

JACQUES CALLOT

Nancy, 1592–Nancy, 1635

Jacques Callot was a prolific and innovative printmaker active in the first half of the seventeenth century. Born in the duchy of Lorraine (today part of France), he spent his formative years at the Medici court in Florence. Returning to Nancy in 1621 following the death of Cosimo de' Medici, he produced a large corpus of etchings with subjects ranging from the pomp of court pageants to the miseries of war. The majority of his drawings were made in preparation for prints, although his technique in both chalk and pen and wash was considerably more expressive and abstract than his precise manner as an etcher.

47. Recto: *Study of a Horse*, ca. 1616
Verso: *Study of a Standing Horse*

Quill and reed pen and iron gall ink on off-white laid paper; evidence of lead point or graphite tracing of the hind legs of the standing horse on recto, 9¼ x 11¼ in. (23.5 x 28.6 cm)

Three collector's marks at the lower right corner: John Thane (Lugt 1544); Nathaniel Hone (Lugt 2793); an unidentified collector (Lugt 2736). The mark of John Thane also appears at the lower left corner on the verso

The Metropolitan Museum of Art, New York, Promised Gift of Mr. and Mrs. David M. Tobey, and Purchase, Mr. and Mrs. David M. Tobey Gift, 2000 (2000.253a, b)

Provenance: Unidentified collector, possibly a member of the Brandi family, Florence (Lugt 2736); Nathaniel Hone (London, 1718–1784) (Lugt 2793); John Thane (London, 1748–1818) (Lugt 1544); sale, Sotheby's, London, about 1950; acquired by Geoffrey Houghton-Brown; sold or given to John Fowler, London; left by him in 1977 to Hugh Street, London; Private Collection, London (per Ternois 1999, p. 21, no. S.1463); Richard Thune, New York; Spink-Leger Pictures, London; acquired by The Metropolitan Museum of Art, 2000

References: Ternois 1999, p. 21, no. S.1463, ill. p. 58; Stein 2001; Stein and Royalton-Kisch 2005–6, under no. 14, p. 219 n. 6

Following an apprenticeship with a medalist in his native Nancy in the duchy of Lorraine, Jacques Callot spent the better part of a decade in Florence where his artistic personality was forged. According to Baldinucci, Callot was the pupil of Giulio Parigi (1571–1635), architect and designer of court fetes. He also is documented as collaborating on prints with Antonio Tempesta (1555–1630) and Raffaello Schiaminossi (1572–1622). The Tobey sheet is part of a group of twenty studies that have been dated to about 1616, during his Florentine period, when he was on the payroll of the Medici court.

The group is largely concerned with equine anatomy and features many studies of horses inspired by Tempesta's series of etchings, *Cavalli di differenti paesi*, published in Rome in 1590.[1] The recto, *Study of a Horse*, is based on Tempesta's *A Horse Galloping to the Right* (fig. 47.1), and the verso, *Study of a Standing Horse*, on *A Horse Tethered to a Stump* (fig. 47.2). In both cases, Callot enlarged the scale of the horse and omitted the landscape background. Tempesta's horses were sometimes copied more than once by Callot as he experimented with style and scale. For instance, the motif of the galloping horse seen on the recto of the Tobey sheet, is also the subject of a full sheet in the Uffizi, while its head appears among fourteen sketches of

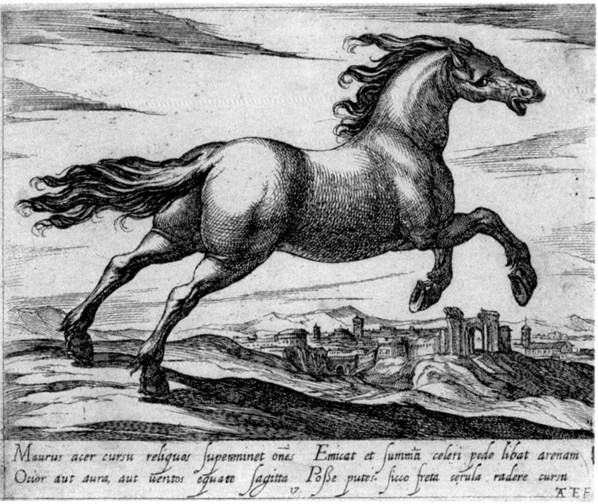

Fig. 47.1. Antonio Tempesta. *A Horse Galloping to the Right*, 1590. Etching, 5½ x 6⁷⁄₁₆ in. (14 x 16.4 cm). British Museum, London (1980,U.449-478; Bartsch XVII.161.957)

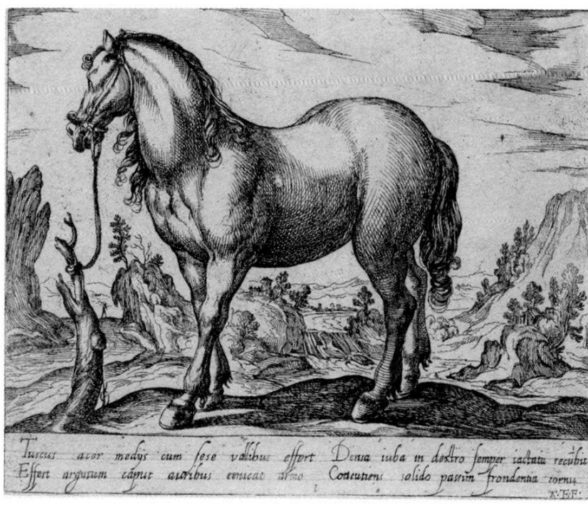

Fig. 47.1. Antonio Tempesta. *A Horse Galloping to the Right*, 1590. Etching, 5½ x 6⁷⁄₁₆ in. (14 x 16.4 cm). British Museum, London (1980,U.449-478; Bartsch XVII.161.957)

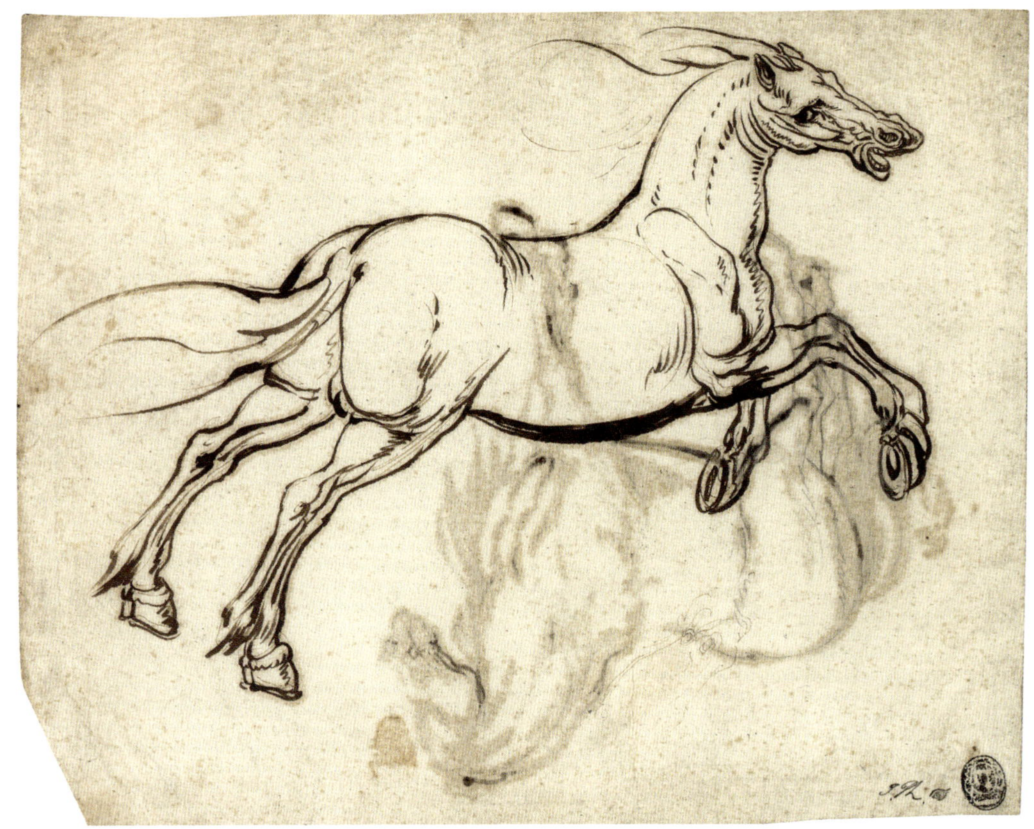

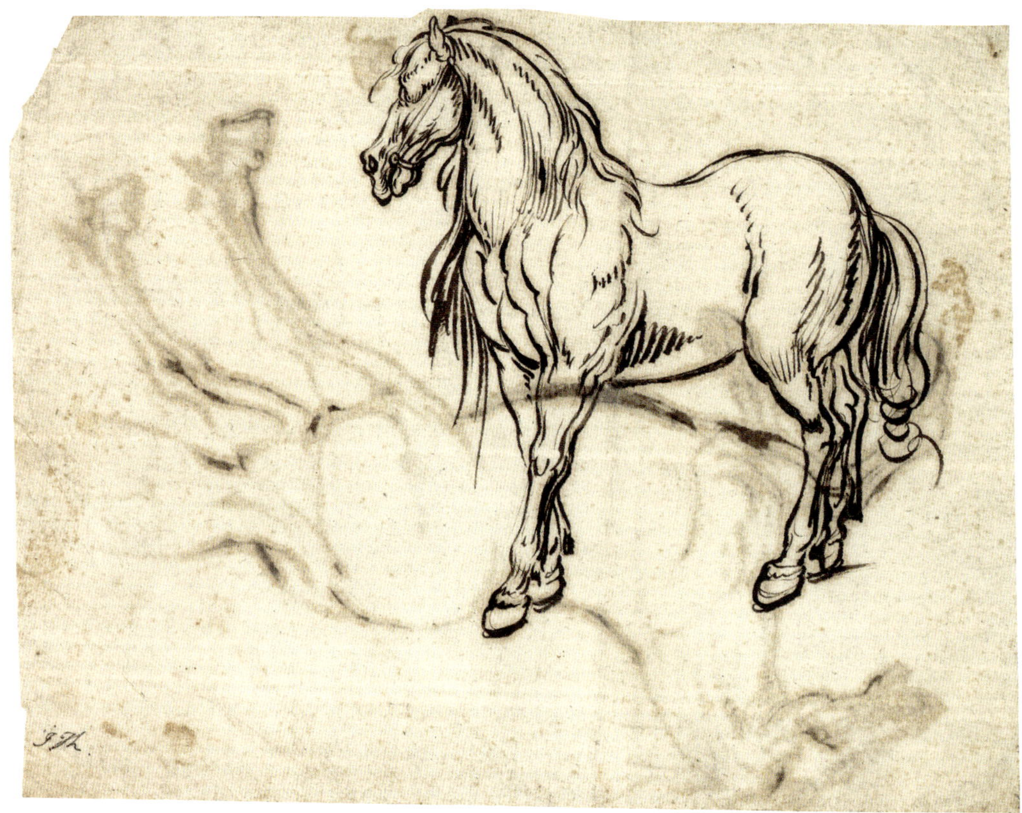

horses' heads, likewise in the Uffizi.[2] The figure of the standing horse—the verso of the Tobey sheet—is sketched a second time with great brio on the verso of yet another drawing in the Uffizi.[3]

Comparing Callot's drawings to their printed sources throws into relief the preoccupations of his draftsmanship. In addition to studying the musculature and movement of the horses, Callot explored the expressive potential of pen and ink to lend a sense of animation to his subjects. Instead of Tempesta's carefully modulated cross-hatching, Callot first used a quill pen to lightly sketch the forms and then reworked the sheet with the wider nib of a reed pen, operating with apparent speed to reinforce the contours. The natural swelling and tapering of the lines produced by the reed pen add to the overall calligraphic sensibility.

The early provenance of the group has generated some con-fusion. The Tobey drawing is one of five sheets that bear the marks of two eighteenth-century English collectors, Nathaniel Hone (1718–1784, Lugt 2793) and John Thane (1748–1818, Lugt 1544).[4] A third collector's mark (Lugt 2736), listed as "unidentified" by Lugt in 1956, was occasionally noted chrono-logically after Thane in the provenance of these drawings, despite the fact that it can also be found on four sheets that came to the British Museum as part of the William Fawkener bequest in 1769.[5] The same mark also appears on thirty Florentine school drawings at Christ Church, Oxford, that trace their provenance back to Filippo Baldinucci (1625–1697), and James Byam Shaw made a convincing argument in 1976, based on the physical evidence of the Christ Church drawings, that the anonymous collector who used the stamp Lugt 2736 predated Baldinucci.[6] Byam Shaw's theory has since found confirmation in Julian Brooks's observation that the heraldic device of Lugt 2736 corresponds to the coat of arms of the Brandi, a Florentine noble family.[7] This discovery implies that Callot must have sold, or given away, the drawings from this group of studies after Tempesta's *Cavalli* before he left Florence in 1621, rather than having kept them in his studio as one might have expected. PS

PS

1. Ternois 1962, nos. 25–36, pp. 46–48, and Ternois 1999, nos. S.1459–66, pp. 20–22; 54–61. Three horse studies in sanguine, two smaller in format than the sheets cited above, also took their inspiration from Tempesta. See Ternois 1962, pp. 48–49, nos. 37–39.
2. Ternois 1962, p. 48, nos. 35–36.
3. Ibid., p. 48, no. 33.
4. Ternois 1999, nos. 1459–60; 1463; and 1465–66, pp. 20–22. A number of these seem to have appeared on the art market in England in the 1950s and 1960s.
5. Lugt described mark 2736 as "probably 17th-century," adding that eighteen sheets bearing this mark were left to Christ Church, Oxford, in 1765. See Lugt 1956, p. 513.
6. Byam Shaw 1976, vol. 1, pp. 10–12. I thank Jon Whiteley for drawing my atten-tion to this reference.
7. See Ciabani 1992–93, vol. 2, p. 318. This information was supplied by Julian Brooks, who generously shared his unpublished research (email correspondence, August 28, 2009). For published references to Lugt 2736, see Whistler 2003–4, pp. 14, 20 n. 29; and Monbeig Goguel 2006, pp. 42, 60 n. 44.

NICOLAS POUSSIN

Les Andelys, 1594–Rome, 1665

One of the original masters of the French Grand Manner, Nicolas Poussin arrived in Rome in 1624 and spent the remainder of his career there, his paintings sought after by an illustrious and international clientele. His early painterly style influenced by Venetian art gradually gave way to an ever-increasing classicism enriched by a deep engagement with nature and the literature of antiquity. He employed neither assistants nor models, but worked alone, painstakingly constructing his complex compositions with the aid of small wax figures arranged in a box. His drawings document his search for compositional refinement and historical verisimilitude, but do not display a special facility with chalk or pen and ink; they are admired primarily as windows onto his artistic thought process.

48. *Studies of Warriors and Hippocamps, after Giovanni Battista Scultori,* ca. 1635

Pen and brown ink, brush and brown wash, over black chalk, 10⅞ x 8⅛ in. (27.5 x 20.7 cm)

Inscribed at lower right: *Nic Poussin*

The Metropolitan Museum of Art, New York, Promised Gift of David M. Tobey

Provenance: Private Collection; sale, Christie's, London, July 10, 2001, lot 94; acquired in 2001

References: Rosenberg and Prat 1994, vol. 2, p. 1016, under no. R899 (as a hypothetical lost original); Rosenberg 2001, p. 314, fig. 82; Stein 2002, pp. 173–74 n. 3; Rosenberg 2006, pp. 140, 162, fig. 42

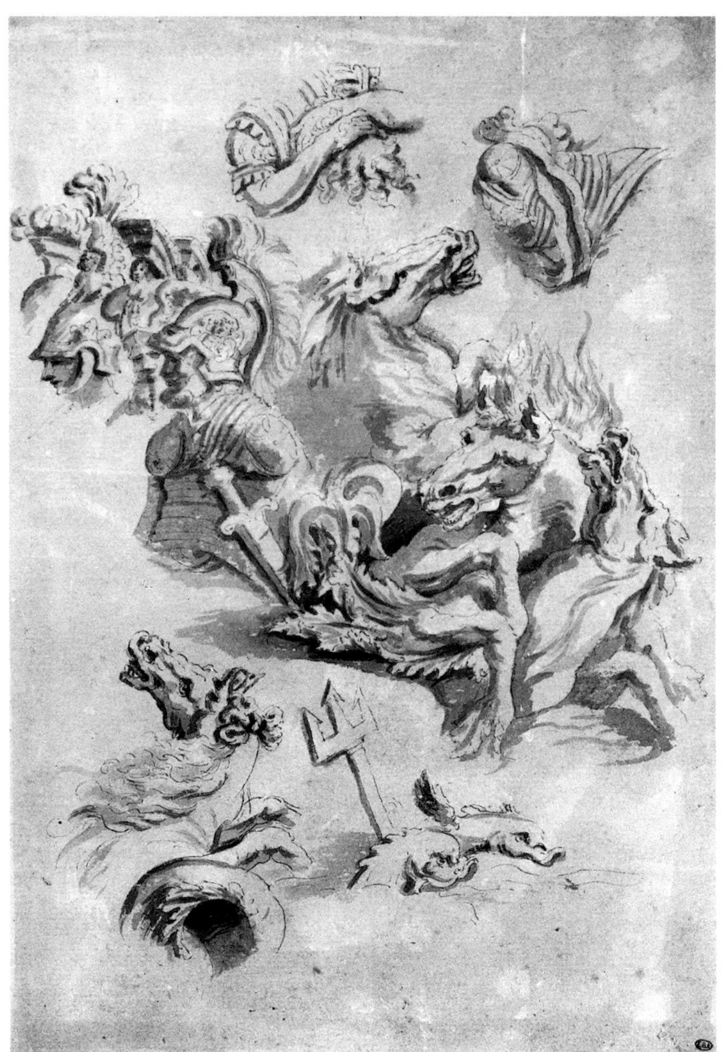

Fig. 48.1. After Nicolas Poussin. *Studies of Marine Soldiers and Horses*. Pen and brown ink, brush and brown wash, 12⅜ x 8⁵⁄₁₆ in. (31.5 x 21.1 cm). École nationale supérieure des Beaux-Arts, Paris (EBA 1453)

A founding figure of French classicism, Nicolas Poussin developed a mature style distinctly indebted to the art and literature of antiquity. Numerous surviving sheets reveal his assiduous study of ancient architecture, ornament, and costume. Curiously, the majority of these study sheets were made not after antique originals—examples of which abounded in seventeenth-century Rome—but after Renaissance prints. Moreover, Poussin seems rarely to have copied an entire composition, preferring instead to excerpt certain details and arrange them in a pleasing *mise-en-page*. Using prints as sources allowed him to work in a studio setting and facilitated his project of copying and collecting motifs.

When it appeared on the art market in 2001, the Tobey drawing confirmed the thesis put forward by Pierre Rosenberg and Louis-Antoine Prat in 1994 that a sheet in the École nationale supérieure des Beaux-Arts, Paris (fig. 48.1),[1] long held to be an autograph work by Poussin, was in fact a copy of a lost original. The motifs of the warriors and the hippocamps (mythological creatures combining the head and forefeet of a horse with the tail of a dolphin) were taken from *Naval Battle between Trojans and Greeks*, a 1538 engraving by Giovanni Battista Scultori (fig. 48.2). In the past, the composition was sometimes referred to as after Giulio Romano, although more recently scholars have viewed it as Scultori's own design.[2]

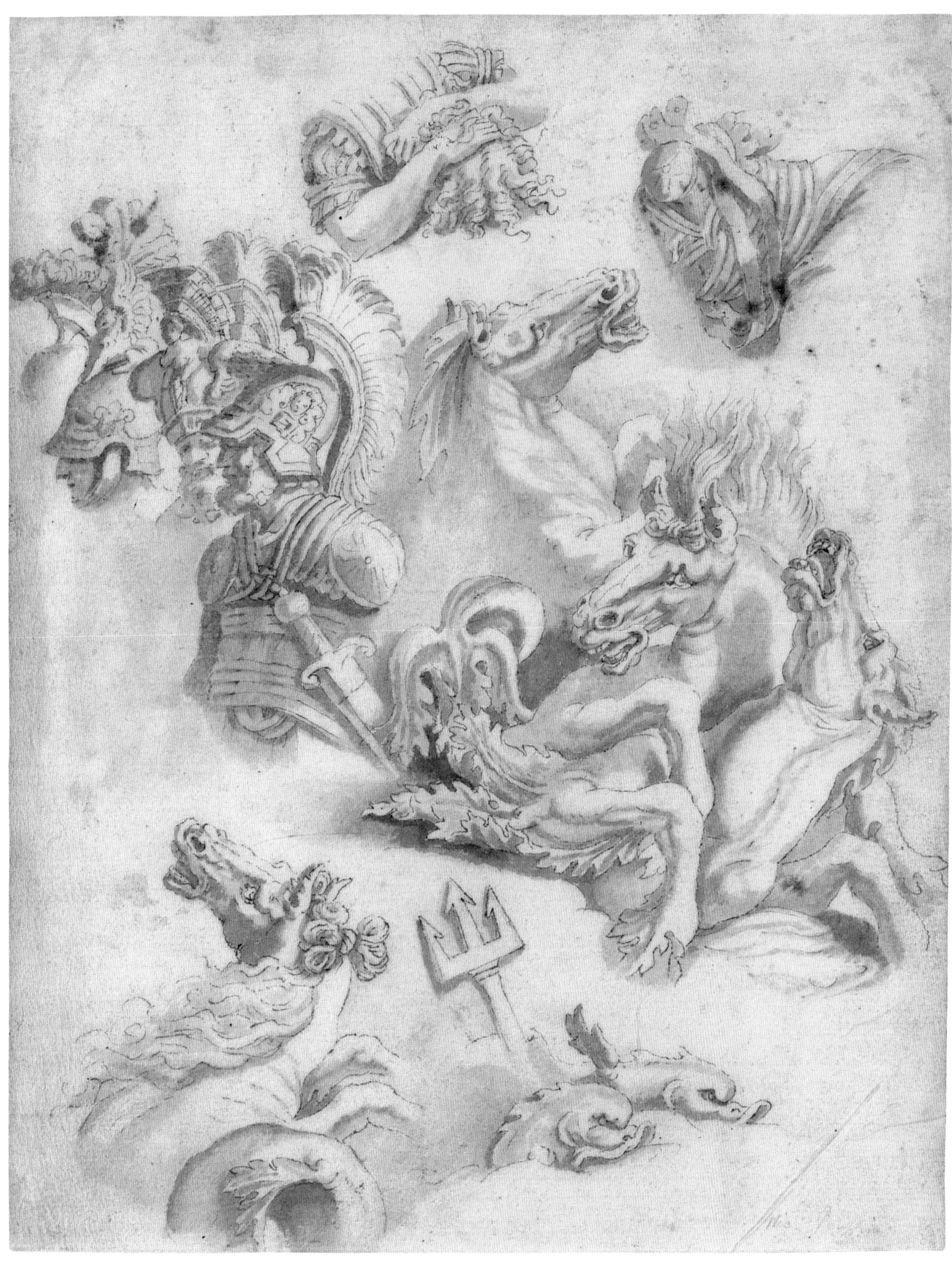

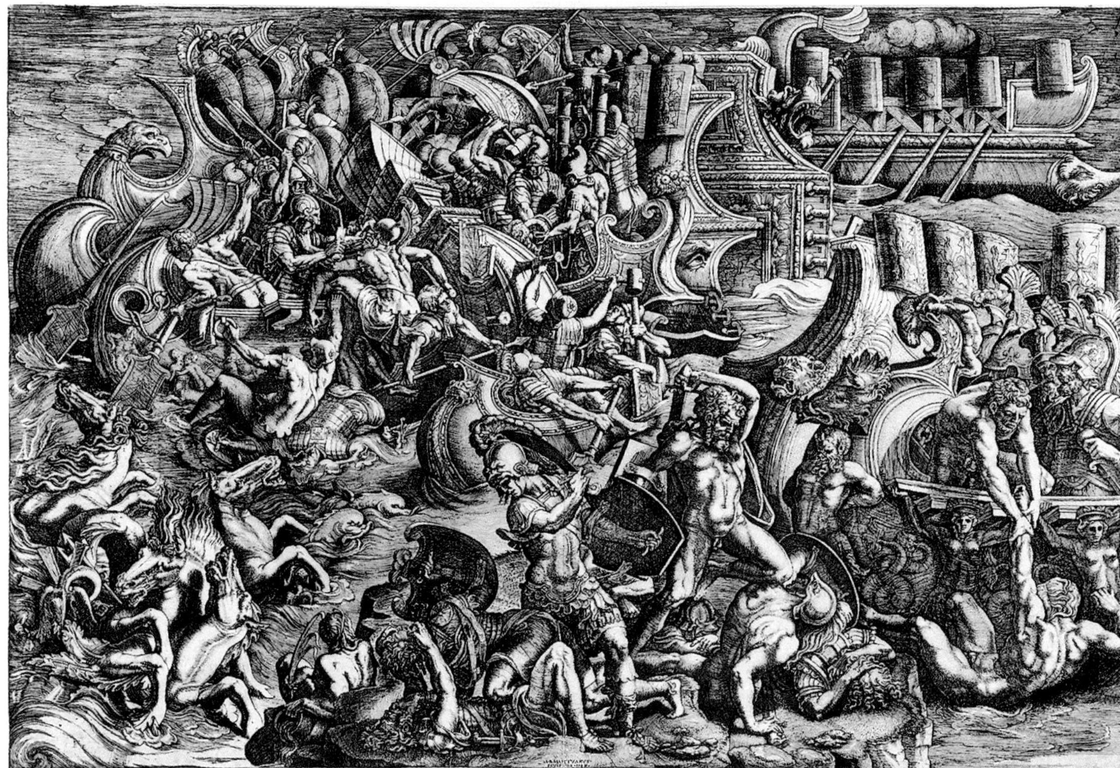

Fig. 48.2. Giovanni Battista
Scultori. *Naval Battle between
Trojans and Greeks*, 1538.
Engraving printed in brown
ink, 16 x 23 1/16 in. (40.6 x
58.5 cm). The Metropolitan
Museum of Art, New York,
Harris Brisbane Dick Fund,
1953 (53.600.996)

Details from the same print also appear in three other copy
drawings by Poussin.[3]

If Scultori's print suffered from horror vacui, Poussin used
an airy *mise-en-page* to invigorate his sheet of studies with a
baroque sense of movement. The motifs chosen for the Tobey
drawing reveal an interest in the twisting poses and windblown
manes of the muscular hippocamps as well as in the details of
ancient military costume. As is almost always the case in Poussin's
copy drawings, the placement of the design elements bears no
correlation to their location in the original composition. Small
changes can be noted in the form of the trident—which is
broken in the print, but whole in the drawing—and in the
half-length figure of a soldier just left of center, whose hand
is on the sword hilt in the print, but absent in the drawing.
Stylistically consistent with Poussin's other study drawings of
the mid-1630s, the elements are first indicated in pen and ink,
in this case occasionally allowed to skip over the rough surface

of the paper, lending a staccato quality to the line. Brown wash
of varying intensities is then delicately applied to model the
forms in shallow relief. The care with which the Tobey sheet is
executed reflects the important role such copy drawings played
in Poussin's working process. As has often been cited, an album
of 160 sheets drawn after antique and Renaissance sources was
recorded after the artist's death, in the possession of his brother-
in-law, Jean Dughet.[4]

PS

1. Rosenberg and Prat 1994, vol. 2, p. 1016, no. R899. Another anonymous copy
   has since come to light; see Rosenberg 2006, pp. 140, 162 (album de Louviers,
   feuillet 70).
2. Albricci 1976, pp. 46–48; and Massari 1980–81, pp. 22–23, no. 6, figs. 6a–6c.
3. Two are in the Musée Condé, Chantilly (inv. nos. AI 203; NI 247 and AI 204;
   NI 248), and one is in the Musée du Louvre, Paris (inv. no. R.F. 1165). See
   Rosenberg and Prat 1994, vol. 1, nos. 178, 182, and 183, pp. 338–39, 346–49.
4. The relevant section of the document, first published in 1858–60 by Anatole de
   Montaiglon, is reprinted in Rosenberg 2006 (see note 1, above), p. 134.

PIETRO DA CORTONA

Cortona, 1596–Rome, 1669

A painter and architect, Pietro da Cortona was one of the leading protagonists of the exuberant, high Baroque style. The patronage of the powerful Barberini family (who also lavished commissions on Gianlorenzo Bernini) placed him at the pinnacle of the art world in Rome in the mid-seventeenth century. He executed expansive allegorical frescoes, mythological scenes, classical landscapes, and biblical narratives, as well as portraits, altarpieces, and private devotional images, combining the grandeur and classicism of Raphael with the luminous palette of Venetian painting. His drawings reveal the same fluency and assurance as his paintings. Cortona had a number of talented followers, among them Ciro Ferri and Gianfrancesco Romanelli, who capabably emulated his style both as a draftsman and a painter.

49. *Study of an Angel,* ca. 1650

Black chalk with traces of white, 9¾ x 15 in. (24.7 x 38.1 cm)
Annotated in an early hand in black chalk at lower right: *solo* (?); in pen and brown ink at lower right: *scizzo visto* (?) *fare con hoggi* (?) *propere* (?) / *Pietro di Cortona in Roma per* (?) *quadro che faceva delli sedi papali* (?) / [ ]*tali per Papa Alessandro setti* [cropped] / *lanno 165*[ ] *(1651?)*; in graphite at lower right on mount: [ ] *da Cortona*

Provenance: Galerie de Bayser, Paris; acquired in 2009

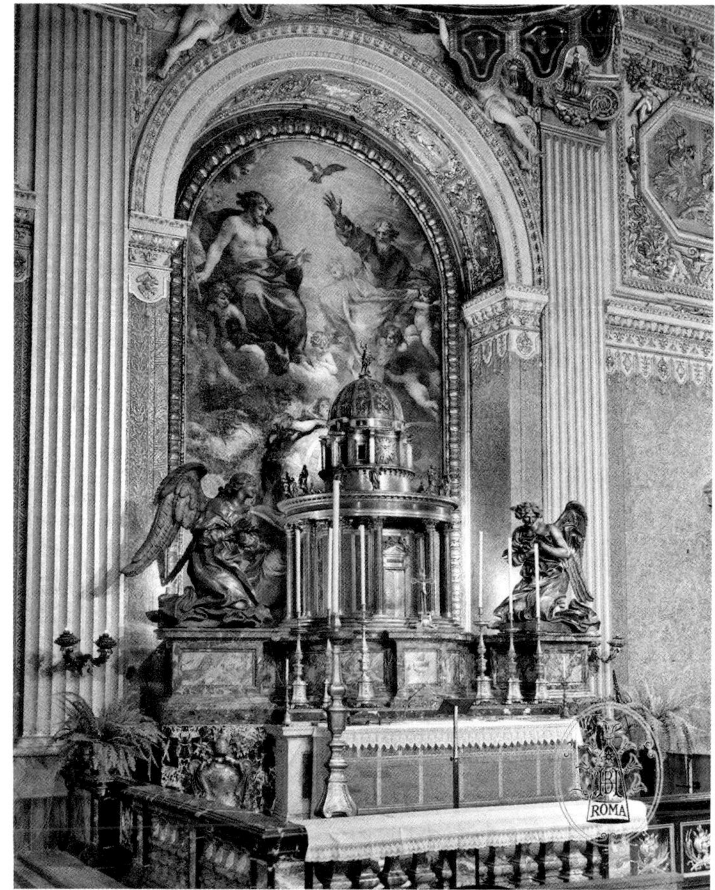

Fig. 49.1. Pietro da Cortona. *Holy Trinity*, 1632. Oil on slate. Chapel of the Sacrament, Saint Peter's Basilica, Vatican City

In the second half of the 1620s, the Congregazione per la Reverenda Fabbrica di San Pietro undertook to have altarpieces painted for the new basilica of Saint Peter's by various painters then active in Rome. After a long and heated discussion the prestigious commission for the imposing "tavola grande" for the Chapel of the Sacrament (at that time designated to be the new sacristy) was conferred on Guido Reni; his departure for Bologna before work was begun allowed Cardinal Francesco Barberini, nephew of Pope Innocent VIII (see cat. no. 50) and the most influential voice in these deliberations, to champion as a replacement Pietro da Cortona, who executed a monumental altarpiece on slate representing the Trinity (fig. 49.1).[1] Cortona reiterated the principal elements of the composition in a lost painting of Saint Michael slaying a dragon, executed about 1650 (and perhaps referred to in the somewhat illegible inscription at the lower right of the present sheet); like the *Trinity* altarpiece, it showed Christ and God the Father seated in the clouds in the upper zone with angels and cherubs below, as a *modello* in the Art Institute of Chicago records (fig. 49.2).[2] The composition of that later, now untraced work, was subsequently adapted for the frontispiece of the *Missale Romanum* of Alexander VII, published in Rome in 1662 (fig. 49.3).[3]

A recent discovery, the Tobey drawing is a study for the figure of the avenging Archangel Michael with outstretched wings who appears prominently in the Chicago *modello* at the

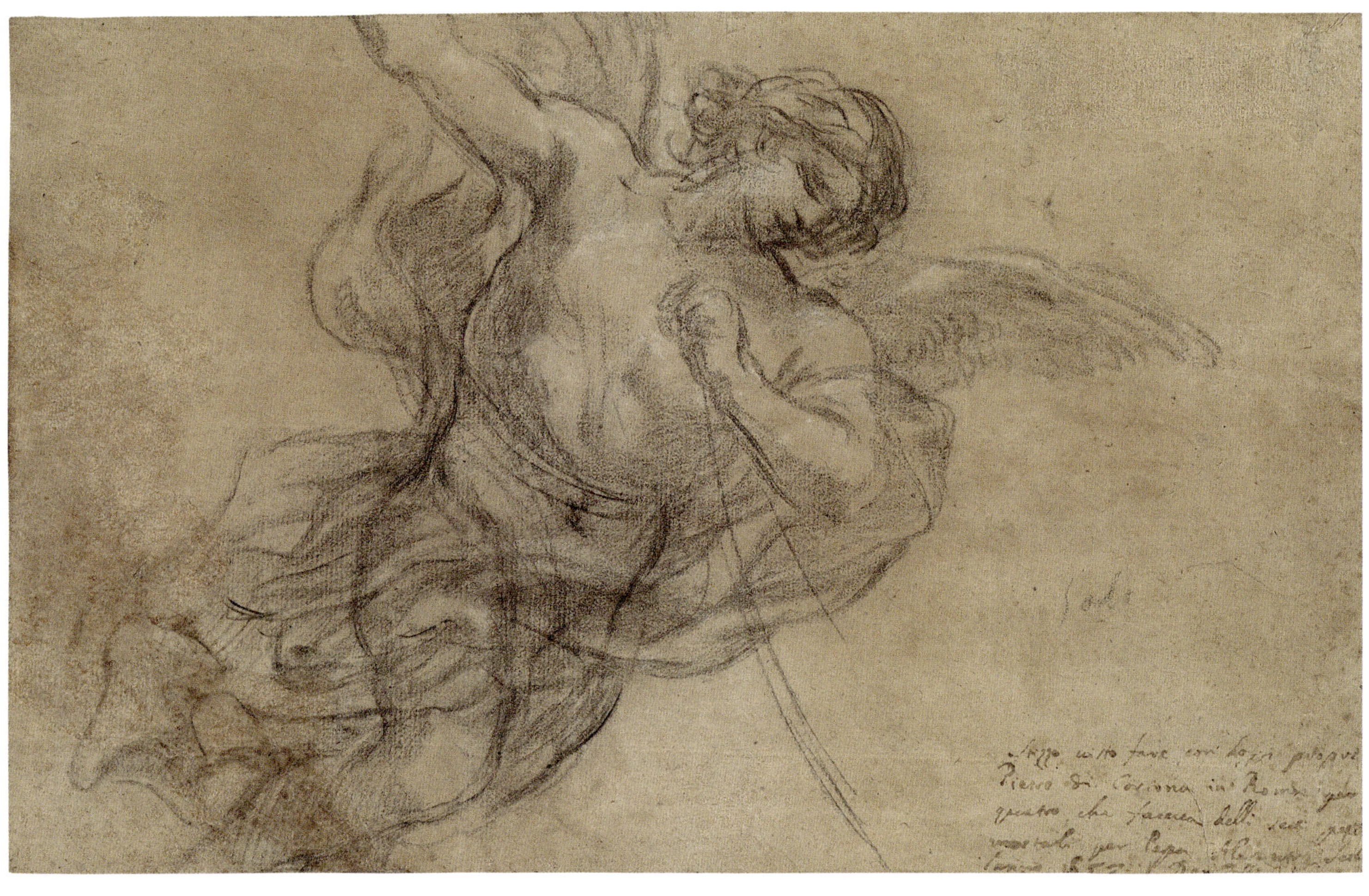

49

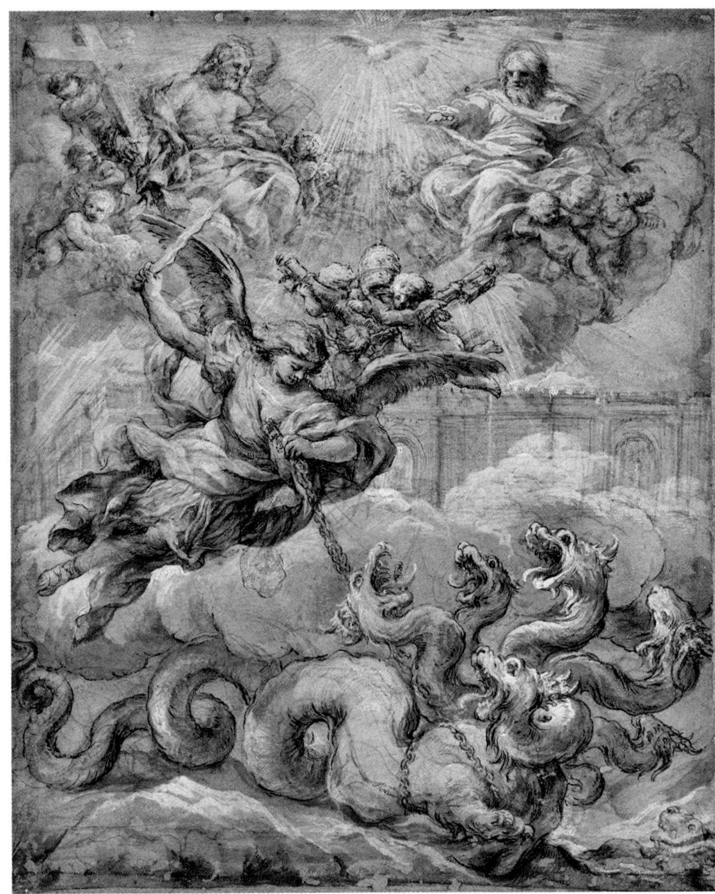

Fig. 49.2. Pietro da Cortona. *Holy Trinity with Saint Michael Conquering the Dragon*, ca. 1650. Pen and brown ink, with brush and brown and gray wash, heightened with lead white (discolored) and black chalk, on tan laid paper, 18½ x 14 1/16 in. (45.8 x 35.7 cm). Margaret Day Blake Collection, The Art Institute of Chicago (1965.860)

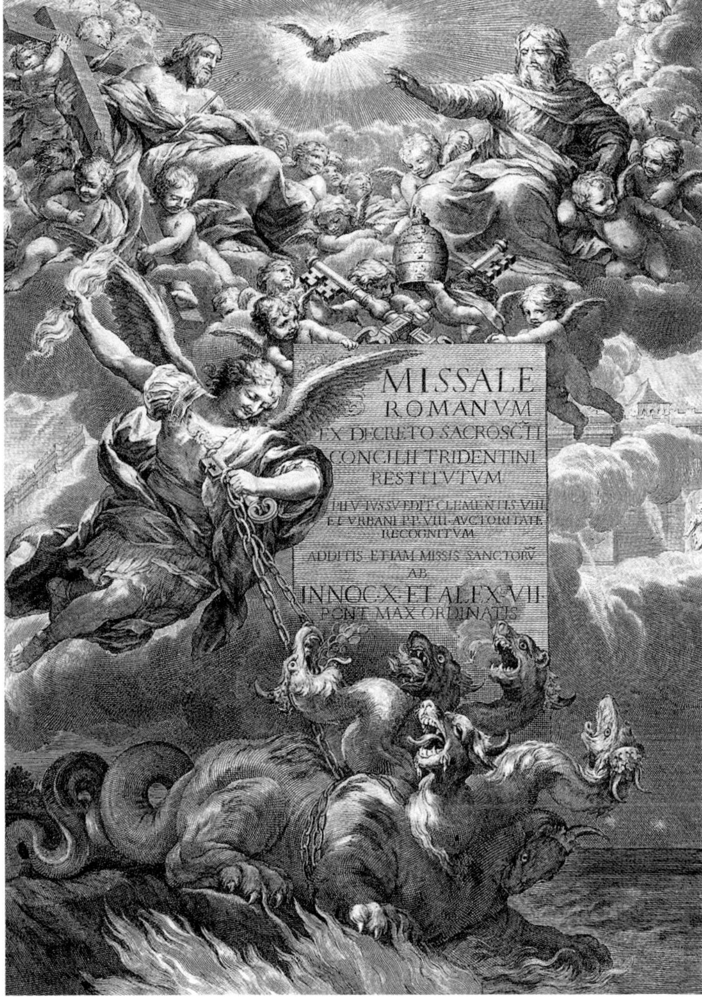

Fig. 49.3. François Spierre, after Pietro da Cortona. *Trinity with Saint Michael Vanquishing the Devil*, frontispiece to the *Missale Romanum*, 1662. Engraving, 13¾ x 9 9/16 in. (35 x 24.3 cm). The Metropolitan Museum of Art, New York, The Elisha Whittelsey Collection, The Elisha Whittelsey Fund, 1963 (63.616.8)

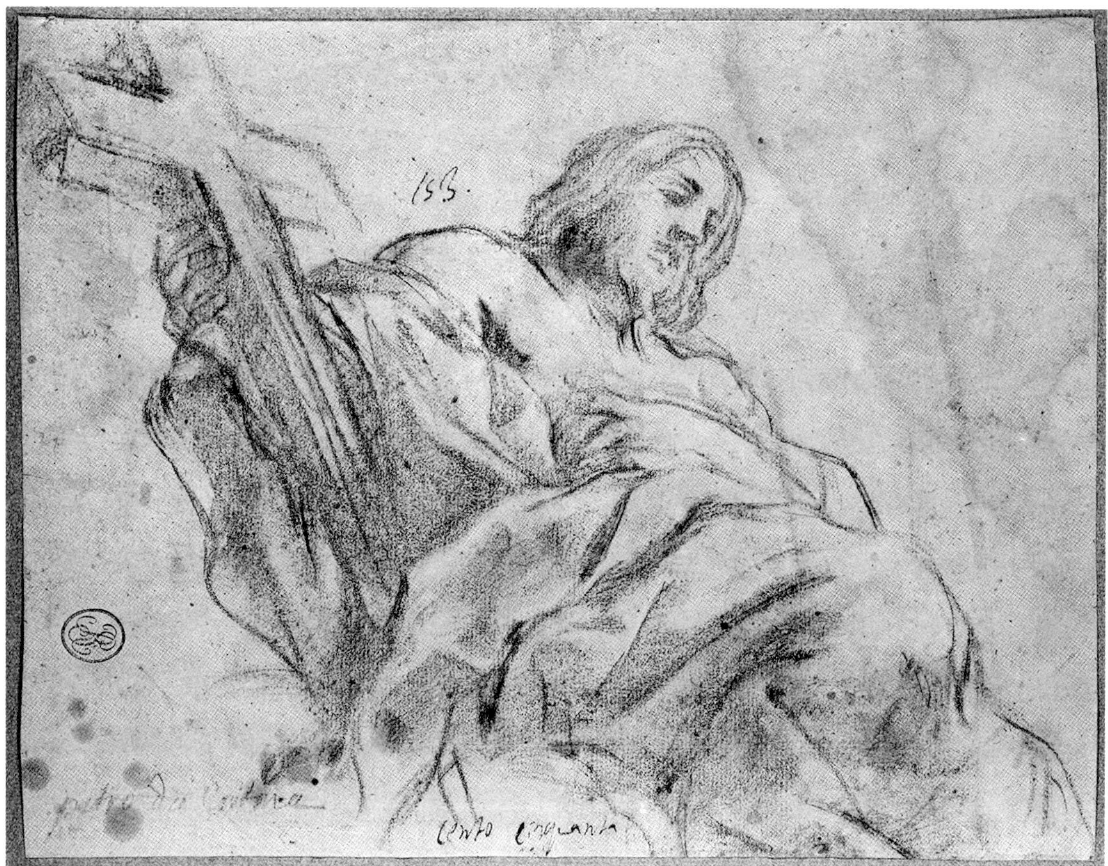

Fig. 49.4. Pietro da Cortona. *Christ Draped, Seated, Holding a Cross in His Right Hand*, ca. 1650. Black chalk with traces of white, on gray paper. Département des Arts Graphiques, Musée du Louvre, Paris (528r)

left center of the composition, beneath the seated figure of Christ. A comparison with that design explains the pose and attributes of the angel seen here: the nondescript lines emanating from his clenched left hand represent the chains or tethers with which he subdues the dragon, while his raised right hand, cropped at the top edge of the sheet, was meant to wield a sword or lightning bolt. Whether a comparable figure also appears in the closely related *Trinity* altarpiece of two decades earlier is difficult to ascertain, for the entire lower half of the painting is obscured by the ciborium designed by Bernini and installed on the altar of the chapel in 1673. The lower zone includes a host of angels; it is not inconceivable that, beneath the globe borne by a winged angel just glimpsed above the ciborium's concealing dome, Cortona depicted Saint Michael vanquishing a dragon or demon, symbol of sin and heresy— a confrontation between good and evil that contemporary viewers would have understood as a reference to the Church Triumphant.

Executed with soft, broad strokes of black chalk with some of the contours reinforced, the Tobey sheet is stylistically close to a drawing by Cortona in the Louvre representing Christ seated, holding a cross (fig. 49.4), which has also been connected with the lost *Trinity with Saint Michael*.[4] (As the Chicago *modello* reflects, this figure appeared at the upper left.) Not only is it an important new addition to the prolific Pietro da Cortona's graphic oeuvre, the *Study of an Angel* also preserves a detail of a composition that the artist himself must have particularly esteemed, given that he reprised it at different stages of his career and allowed it to be reproduced as his contribution to the *Missale Romanum*—one of the most splendid, elaborate, and ambitious illustrated books published in seventeenth-century Rome.

LWS

1. See Briganti 1982, pp. 187–90. The painting, for which the artist was paid the sizable sum of 1,000 *scudi*, was begun in July 1628 and completed in July 1632.
2. Art Institute of Chicago (inv. no. 1965.860); see Joachim and McCullagh 1979, pp. 54–55, no. 65. Graf 1998, pp. 203–4, proposed that the drawing is a *modello*

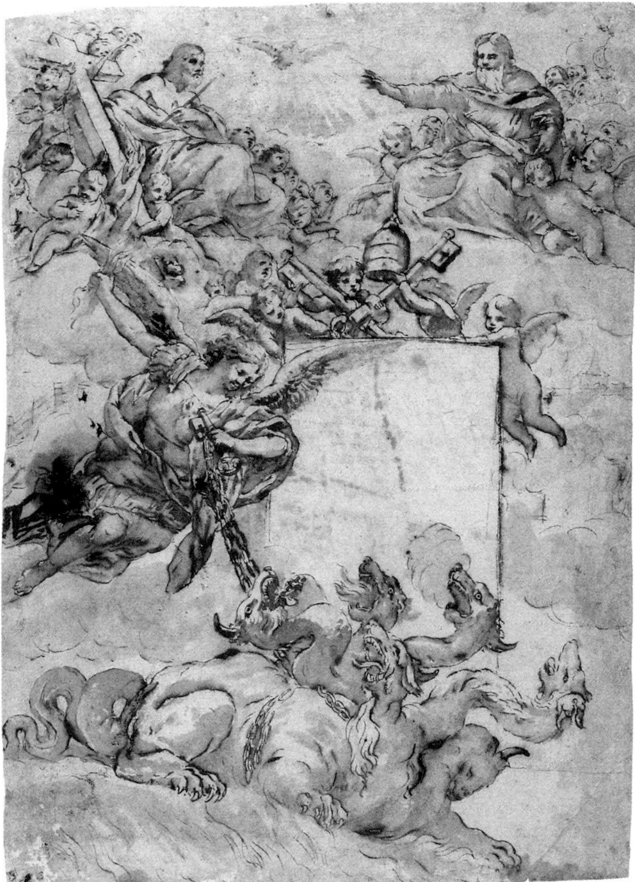

Fig, 49.5. Attributed to Pietro da Cortona or workshop. *Saint Michael Expurging Heresy*, ca. 1662. Pen and brown ink, brush and brown wash over traces of black chalk, 14¾ x 10⁵⁄₁₆ in. (37.4 x 26.2 cm). The Metropolitan Museum of Art, New York, The Elisha Whittelsey Collection, The Elisha Whittelsey Fund, 1949 (49.19.53)

for the lost painting (formerly in the Vatican) rather than for the corresponding image in the *Missal of Alexander VII*. If that argument is correct, the conventional dating of the Chicago sheet to the 1660s is erroneous, and it (and by extension the Tobey drawing and the study of Christ in the Louvre discussed here) instead should be dated about 1650.

3. This lavishly illustrated book containing twenty-eight illustrations ("almost a portable gallery in which the most significant painters of the Court of Alexander VII were reunited"; see Graf 1998, p. 203)—was conceived by Pope Innocent VIII, predecessor of Alexander VII. Graf, ibid., argues that the inscription on the frontispiece illustration, "pietro da cortona pinxit," indicates that this design, unlike all the others in the book save a second illustration based on a Cortona invention, reproduces a painting, and that the engraver, François Spierre, used Cortona's *modello* for the lost painting (fig. 49.2) as the source for the print (his fig. 4). A drawing of Saint Michael Expurging Heresy in The Metropolitan Museum of Art, New York, attributed to Pietro da Cortona (fig. 49.5), which previously has not been connected with this invention, includes a tablet beneath the papal tiara and crossed keys, but omits the inscription that appears in the frontispiece. It is probably a record copy documenting the adaptation of Cortona's design for the engraving.

4. Inv. no. 528; Graf 1998, p. 204.

ALESSANDRO ALGARDI

Bologna, 1598–Rome, 1654

Alessandro Algardi's artistic beginnings took place in his native Bologna, where he studied with Ludovico Carracci and a minor local sculptor. His early career brought him to Mantua and the court of the Gonzaga, through whose offices he was introduced to Cardinal Ludovico Ludovisi in Rome. Algardi's initial activity there focused on the restoration of antiquities, but he eventually rose to become, together with Gianlorenzo Bernini, the leading Roman sculptor of the mid-seventeenth century. The antithesis of Bernini's flamboyant, dramatic idiom, Algardi's restrained and refined style—given form in works of marble, stucco, silver, and bronze on both a monumental and more intimate scale—exemplifies the classical strain of Baroque sculpture.

50. *Design for the Prow of a Galley of Pope Urban VIII with Victories, Sea Gods, Angels, and Emblems of the Barberini Family*, ca. 1625–27 (?)

Pen and brown ink, over lead point and partial stylus incisions, 8½ x 16⅛ in. (21.6 x 41 cm)

The Metropolitan Museum of Art, New York, Partial and Promised Gift of Mr. and Mrs. David M. Tobey, 1997 (1997.346)

Provenance: Thomas Coke, 1st Earl of Leicester, Holkham Hall, his mount, thence by descent; sale, Christie's, London, July 2, 1991, lot 36; Duke Roberto Ferretti, Toronto; sale, Christie's, London, July 2, 1996, lot 55; Katrin Bellinger Kunsthandel, Munich; acquired in 1996

References: Vitzthum 1963, p. 84, fig. 19; Montagu 1985, vol. 1, p. 67, vol. 2, no. 83; Popham and Lloyd 1986, no. 37; Fusconi et al. 1992, p. 155, fig. 177; Birke and Kertész 1992–97, vol. 3, under inv. no. 2438; Edinburgh 1998, pp. 41–42, fig. 28

The elaborate, fanciful prow of a ship recorded in this splendid drawing and in a more detailed and finished study by Alessandro Algardi of the same subject in the Albertina, Vienna (fig. 50.1), has been identified as an idea for a papal galley to be christened *Urbano*.[1] That name, which appears above the figurehead of a winged victory holding a trophy at the upper right (in full in the Albertina drawing and slightly cropped here), refers to Urban VIII Barberini (r. 1623–44), whose heraldic bees and radiant sun are incorporated in the design. This hypothesis, admittedly attractive though it seems, is also somewhat problematic. For one thing, no such vessel is recorded in registries of the papal fleet.[2] In addition, if realized, Algardi's design—an excessive flight of fancy resplendent with elaborately carved and modeled figurative and ornamental details that constitute a "virtual pattern-book" of his decorative repertoire[3]—would have proved an exceptionally impractical and frivolous seafaring vessel. Perhaps the ship represented here was not a galley, then, but a pleasure craft or an ephemeral apparatus in the form of a ship to be constructed for a ceremonial occasion or celebration. If more plausible, that theory, too, is not fully convincing, however, primarily because unlike Bernini, who was constantly employed by Urban VIII on myriad projects and grandiose commissions during his long

pontificate, Algardi never worked for the Barberini pope. (He only succeeded in procuring papal patronage under Urban's successor, Innocent X Pamphilj.) It is therefore doubtful that he would have had occasion to design such a ship, be it a real galley or an inventive temporary confection.[4]

An alternative conjecture concerning the function of Algardi's ambitious design advanced here, should be considered. As a pictorial allusion to the *navicula Sancti Petri* (the Bark of Saint Peter), the ship was a ubiquitous metaphor for the Catholic Church and a frequent image in works of art resulting from papal commissions. (A notable and influential paradigm is Giotto's destroyed and reconstructed *Navicella* mosaic from Old Saint Peter's basilica; another is Raphael's *Calling of Peter and Andrew*, one of the *Acts of the Apostles* tapestries he designed for the Sistine Chapel.) As an appropriately aqueous motif, ships were also a commonplace component of Roman Renaissance and Baroque fountains, particularly in examples commissioned by popes. When present in that context, a ship adhered to prevailing theoretical ideas about decorum and the suitability of certain kinds of subject matter to a specific setting, while also carrying widely recognized allusions to a pontifical patron, successor to Saint Peter the fisherman and the helmsman who guides the ship of the Church. Notable examples include the Navicella Fountain erected by Pope Leo X (r. 1513–21) outside the titular church of his cardinalate, Santa Maria in Domnica (also known as Santa Maria in Navicula or in Navicella);[5] the fountain and decorations of the Casino of Pius IV (r. 1559–65) in the Vatican Gardens;[6] and the Barcaccia Fountain in the Piazza di Spagna (fig. 50.2).[7]

Commissioned by Pope Urban VIII, the Barcaccia Fountain was designed by Bernini, perhaps in collaboration with his father, Pietro, and completed about 1627. Shaped like a large, partly sunken ship, it is embellished with the pope's coat of arms and the Barberini sun. Perhaps Algardi's ship design, which reprises the fountain's central element and is likewise

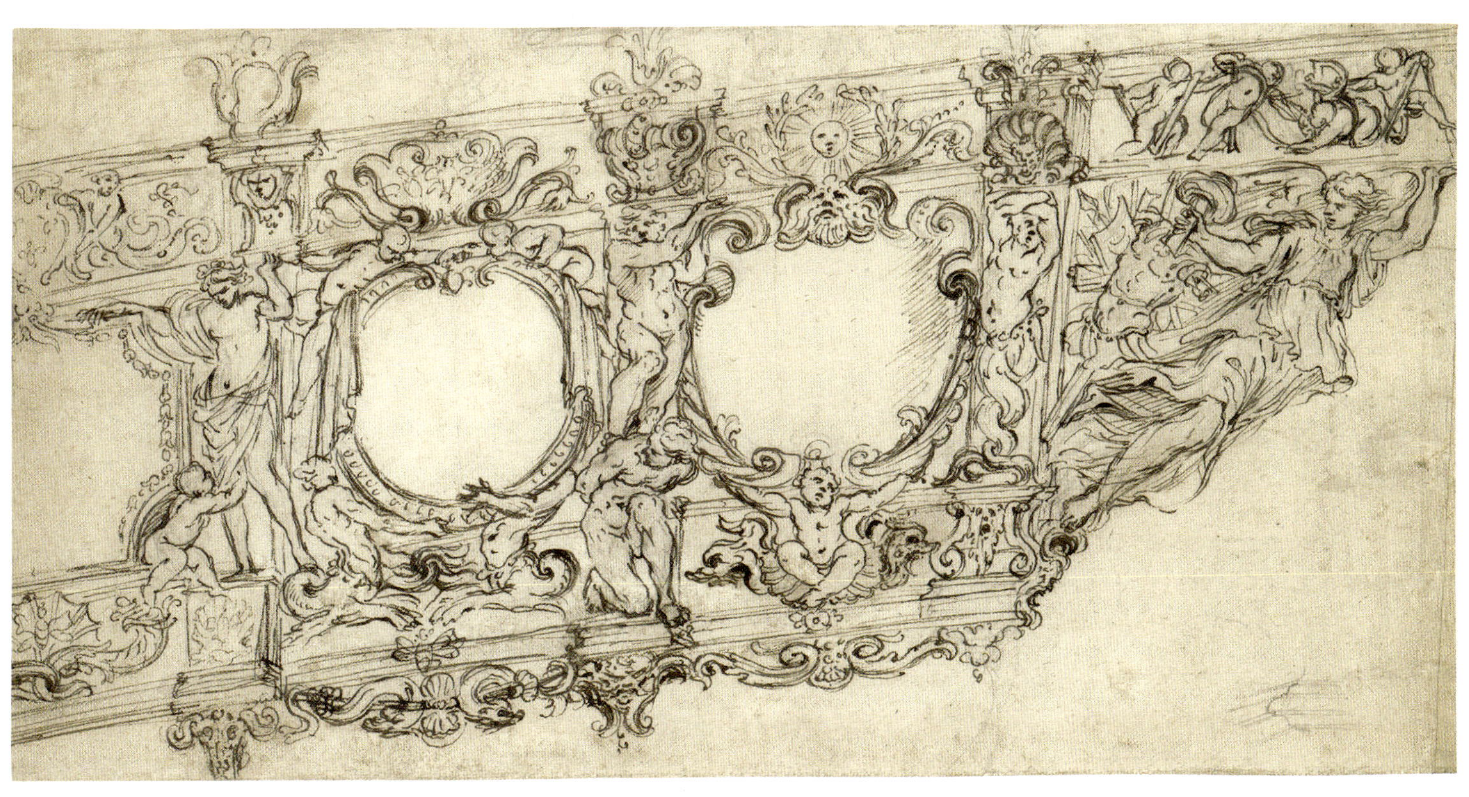

50

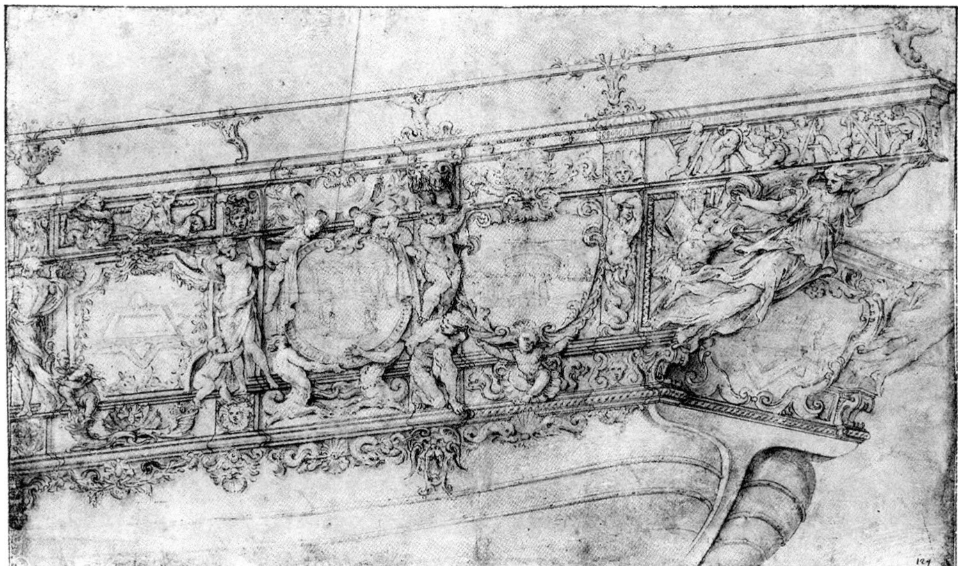

Fig. 50.1. Alessandro Algardi. *Study for the Prow of a Ship*, ca. 1625–27. Pen and ink, 12¹³⁄₁₆ x 13½ in. (32.5 x 34.3 cm). Graphische Sammlung, Albertina, Vienna (2438)

replete with an iconographic vocabulary celebrating Urban and the Barberini, represents an idea for this fountain. (Such an interpretation of the drawing would account for the presence of the lightly sketched architectural detail at the lower right of the sheet, which could be for a supporting element or part of a surrounding basin.) If so, it was executed shortly after the Bolognese sculptor's arrival in Rome in 1625, and represents an early, if evidently futile, effort by this newcomer to the Eternal City to garner a papal commission.   LWS

1. Discussed by Montagu 1985, vol. 1, p. 67.
2. Ibid., p. 246 n. 3, citing the documents published in the nineteenth century by Guglielmotti, "La squadra permanente della marina romana" (1886–93).
3. Ibid., p. 67.
4. Montagu, ibid., suggests that the design may have been commissioned by Alessandro Zambeccaro, lieutenant general of the papal fleet from 1643 until his death in 1646, in an attempt to win papal patronage for Algardi, while concluding that such a presumed attempt to arouse the interest of Urban VIII (if indeed it occurred) "must be regarded as a failure, for we know of no commissions from the Pope or his agents" to the sculptor. Given that the elaborate structure visualized in Algardi's drawing would be an impractical ship in utilitarian terms, this idea is tenuous.
5. For which see Wolk 1987, pp. 104–5.
6. On the water imagery of the iconographic program of the Casino of Pius IV, see Fagiolo and Madonna 1972, especially pp. 242ff.
7. See Hibbard and Jaffe 1964; see also Avery 1997, pp. 182–84.

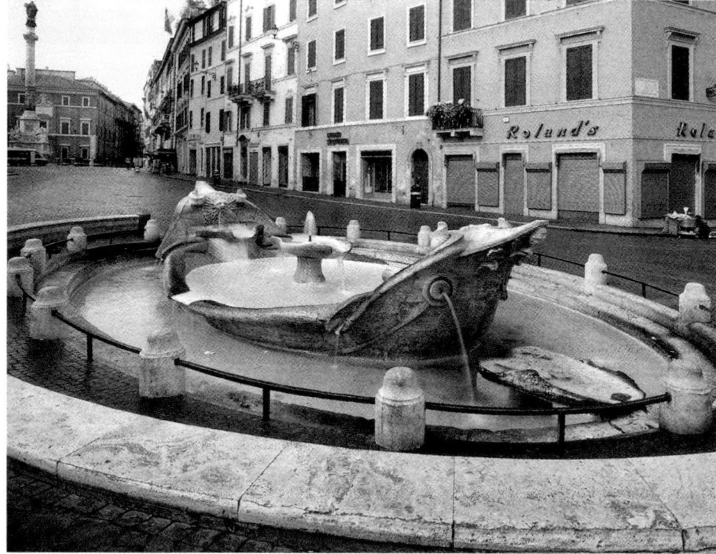

Fig. 50.2. Gianlorenzo Bernini and Pietro Bernini. Barcaccia Fountain, ca. 1627. Piazza di Spagna, Rome

GIANLORENZO BERNINI

Naples, 1598–Rome, 1680

Son of the capable but less gifted sculptor Pietro Bernini, Gianlorenzo Bernini was the towering artistic genius of Baroque Rome and the greatest sculptor of the seventeenth century. His imprint on the interior and exterior fabric of the Eternal City is found in the myriad tombs, fountains, chapels, and architectural monuments he designed and erected. Bernini enjoyed papal favor and patronage for much of his long career, and was significantly responsible for transforming Saint Peter's basilica into a dynamic, theatrical visual spectacle expressing the power, grandeur, and immutable authority of the papacy. In addition to his activity as a sculptor and architect, in which his astonishing virtuosity is ever present, the versatile and talented Bernini also produced portrait paintings and drawings; like some of his portrait busts, these reveal a more personal and intimate side to his personality.

51. *Seated Male Nude Seen from the Right*

Two shades of red chalk, heightened with white chalk, 15⅜ x 21¼ in. (39 x 54 cm)
Annotated in pen on old label at right on recto: *Gio = / Cas . . .*

The Metropolitan Museum of Art, New York, Promised Gift of David M. Tobey

Provenance: Trinity Fine Art Ltd., London; acquired in 1999

Reference: Edinburgh 1998, no. 39

Anumber of academies by Gianlorenzo Bernini are known.[1] These monumental chalk studies of male nudes drawn from life were admired by the biographer Filippo Baldinucci for their *franchezza di tocco* (freshness of touch).[2] Four of the drawings in question, all executed in red chalk and evidently representing the same muscular model, constitute a stylistically and chronologically cohesive group: two sheets in the Royal Collection, Windsor Castle, showing a seated male nude seen from behind (fig. 51.1) and a seated male nude in profile (fig. 51.2); a third study of a male nude with windswept drapery in the Uffizi (fig. 51.3); and the example in the Tobey Collection.[3] Although the pose of the model in the Uffizi drawing calls to mind one of the figures in Bernini's Four Rivers Fountain in the Piazza Navona in Rome, as many scholars have remarked, none of these academies was made as a preparatory study; rather they were conceived as "demonstration pieces," independent works in which the artist displayed his skill as a draftsman—his mastery of the human form deployed in a variety of complex postures and poses, and his facility with red chalk. The Uffizi drawing has been aptly characterized as a "variation" by Bernini of Michelangelo's Sistine Chapel *ignudi*;[4] an analogous evocation of his great cinquecento predecessor is perhaps also to be discerned in the powerful reclining nude in the Tobey drawing, whose pose recalls the drunken Noah in the Sistine Chapel ceiling (fig. 51.4).

The date of these figure studies is a matter of discussion. A terminus ante quem of 1650 is suggested by the fact that Bernini rarely used red chalk after that year. It is conceivable that the drawings were executed considerably earlier, during the period of the sculptor's closest association with the Accademia di San Luca in Rome (in 1630, at the urging of the group's patron, Cardinal Francesco Barberini, he grudgingly served as *Principe*)—a reasonable supposition given that instruction and practice in life drawing were among the principal undertakings of its members. Another possibility is that they were produced in one of the life drawing classes held in various private academies and artists' studios around Rome—including that of

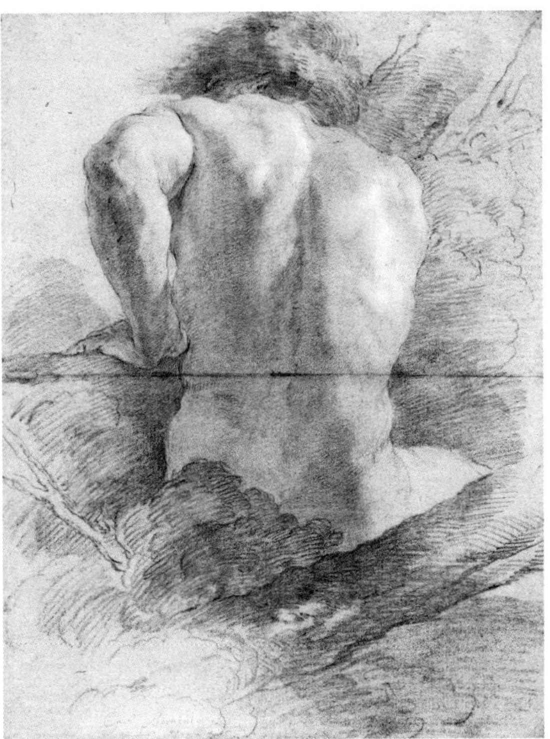

Fig. 51.1. Gianlorenzo Bernini. *Seated Male Nude Seen from Behind*. Two shades of red chalk, heightened with white chalk, on buff paper, 22⅛ x 16⅝ in. (56.2 x 42.2 cm). The Royal Collection. © Her Majesty Queen Elizabeth II (RL 5537)

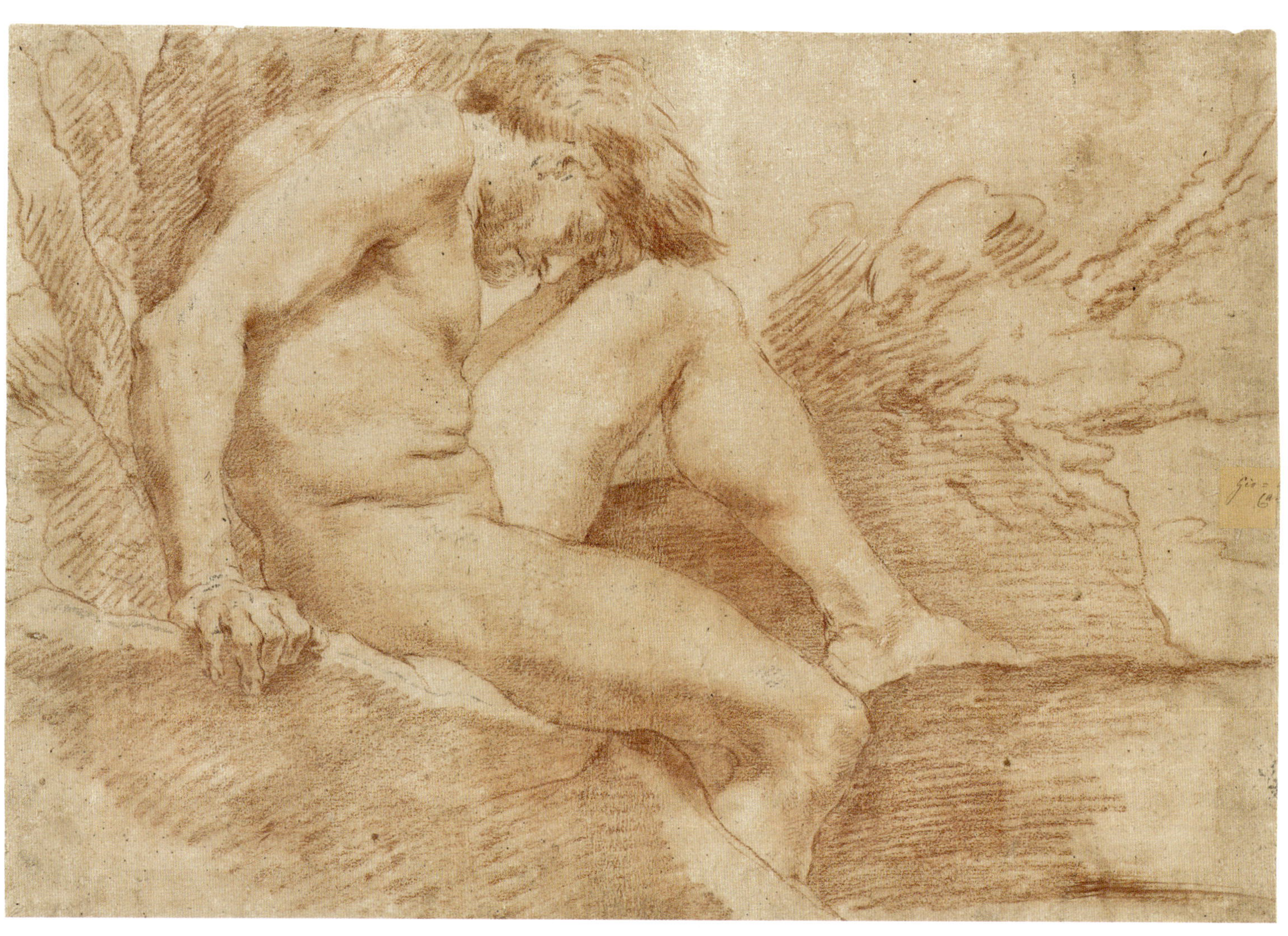

51

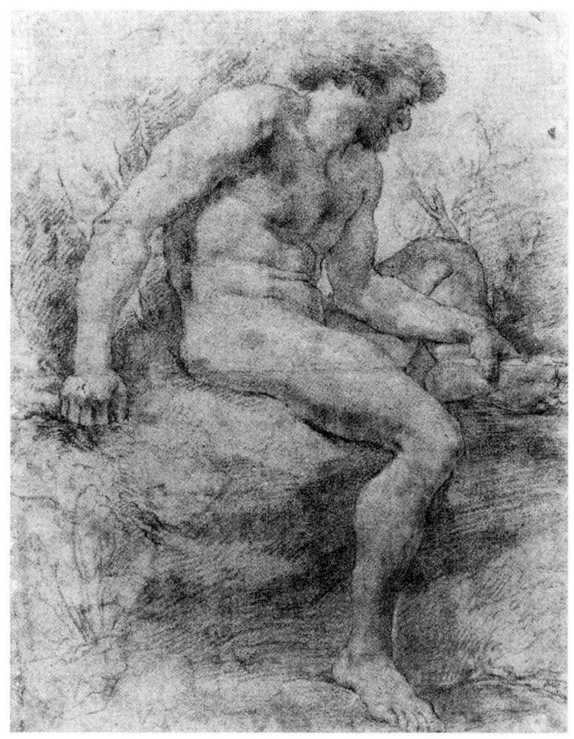

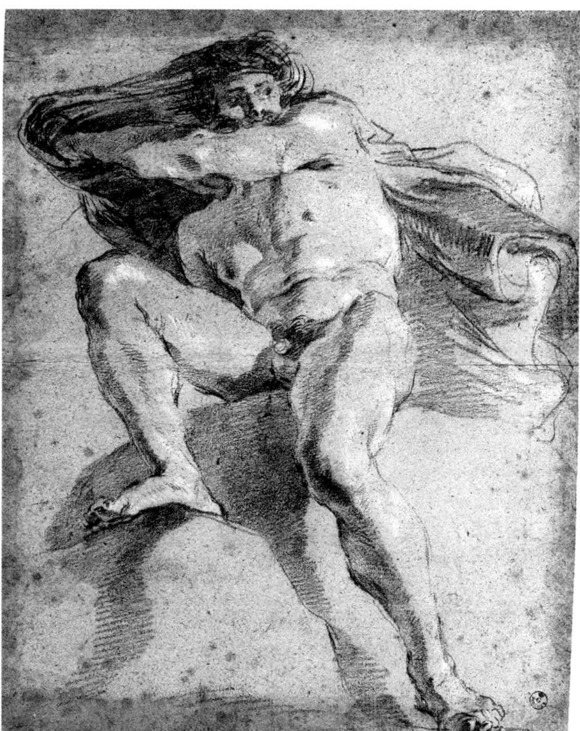

Fig. 51.2. Gianlorenzo Bernini. *Seated Male Nude.* Two shades of red chalk, heightened with white chalk, on buff paper, 22 x 16⅝ in. (55.9 x 42.3 cm). The Royal Collection. © Her Majesty Queen Elizabeth II (RL 5538)

Fig. 51.3. Gianlorenzo Bernini. *Male Nude.* Red chalk, 20⁹⁄₁₆ x 16 in. (52.2 x 40.6 cm). Gabinetto Disegni e Stampe degli Uffizi, Florence (11922F)

Bernini himself.[5] Neither the Tobey sheet nor the three related figure drawings are pure "academies," however: none of the models holds or is supported by obvious studio props, and in both this example and the two Windsor studies a broadly sketched landscape setting has been added around the figure, transforming the academic life drawings into pictorial ruminations on the theme of the heroic male nude.　　　　LWS

1. See Harris 1977, pp. vii, xiii–xiv; and Harris 2003.
2. Baldinucci ed. 2006, p. 73.
3. As discussed by Aidan Weston-Lewis in Edinburgh 1998, p. 85.
4. Fischer Pace 1997, p. 177, under no. 114, who notes that Bernini depicts the Michelangelesque form "almost as a prelude to [its] 'pietrification.'"
5. Weston-Lewis in Edinburgh 1998, pp. 85–87. In his diary of Bernini's sojourn in France, Paul Fréart, Sieur de Chantelou, recorded the sculptor's boyhood reminiscence of having encountered Annibale Carracci in Rome en route to such a private drawing academy, and the painter's explanation of how the models were posed (ibid., p. 87).

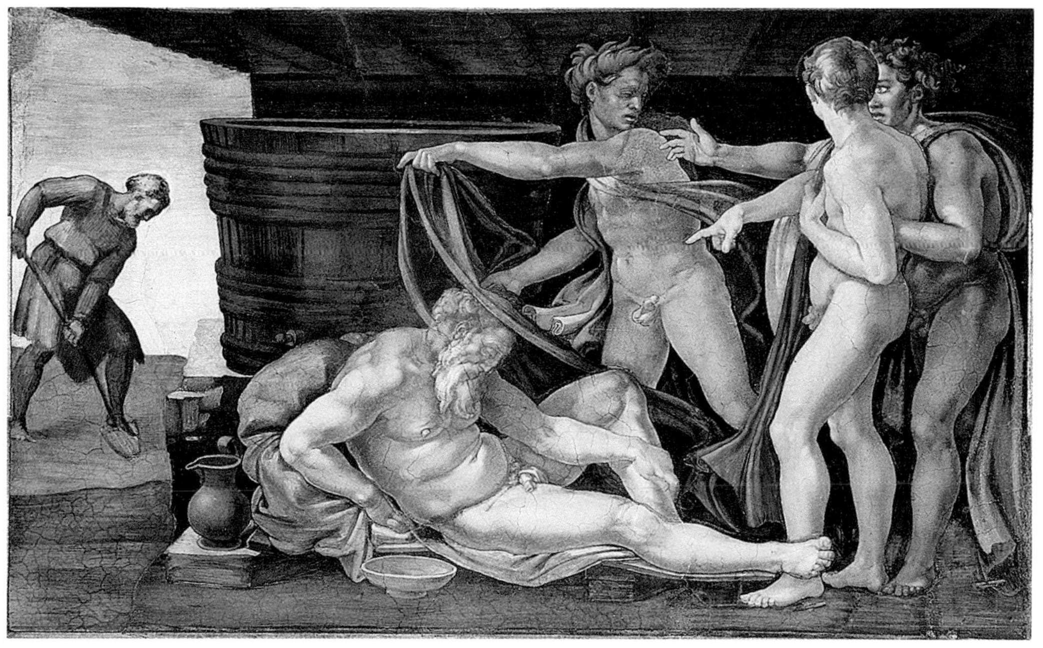

Fig. 51.4. Michelangelo. *Drunkenness of Noah,* 1509. Fresco. Sistine Chapel, Vatican City

CECCO BRAVO

Florence, 1601–Innsbruck, 1661

Cecco Bravo, who worked primarily as a fresco painter, was one of the most inventive Florentine artists of the seventeenth century. Following an early affiliation with Giovanni Bilivert, he was associated with the painters Sigismondo Coccapani and Matteo Rosselli, but left Florence in 1660 to work for Archduke Ferdinand Charles of Austria in Innsbruck. A prolific and energetic draftsman, Cecco Bravo favored red chalk, occasionally combined with black chalk, describing figures with a quivering, searching, and exploratory line.

52. Recto: *The Head of a Devil*, ca. 1653
Verso: *Study of a Flower*

Red and white chalk, 5¼ x 6⅛ in. (13.4 x 15.5 cm)
Annotated on recto at lower left, in brown ink: *Ceccho Bravo*; on verso: *Papuero Colori Uariati*
Verso not reproduced

Provenance: Cosimo de' Noferi, Florence(?); Filippo Baldinucci, Florence (Lugt 1886); Nicolo Gabburi(?) (his mount and inscription); Seiferheld and Co., New York; Hans Calmann, London; Private New England Trust; sale, Christie's, New York, January 24, 2001, lot 45; acquired in 2001

Reference: Florence 1999, under no. 45

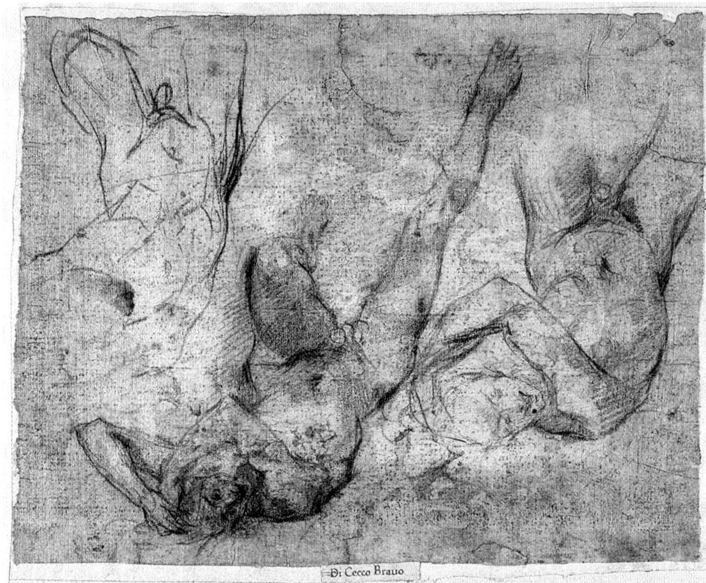

Fig. 52.1. Cecco Bravo. *Three Studies of a Fallen Nude Figure*, ca. 1653. Red chalk, 10¾ x 13⅛ in. (27.2 x 33.5 cm). Département des Arts Graphiques, Musée du Louvre, Paris (1338r)

It has long been recognized that this wild-eyed, demonic head is a study for one of the fallen angels in Cecco Bravo's lost fresco, *Saint Michael Vanquishing the Rebel Angels*, formerly above the organ on the interior facade of the church of San Michele e Gaetano in Florence.[1] Executed in 1653, the work— one of the artist's most celebrated inventions—was at least partly destroyed during a renovation of the church in 1786, although it is recorded as surviving in some form as late as 1820. Numerous drawings by Cecco Bravo for this composition are known, most if not all of which may have belonged to a little-known Florentine collector, Cosimo de' Noferi, before being acquired by the seventeenth-century biographer and collector Filippo Baldinucci.

A large group of thirteen preparatory studies, one for the avenging Archangel Michael wielding a sword, the others for fallen angels, is preserved in the Louvre.[2] All are drawn from life and are executed in red chalk; like the Tobey sheet, some also have white heightening. In one of the Louvre drawings the upside-down form of a rebellious angel is reiterated three times, the artist fixing the collapsed pose of the figure as it is hurled to the ground (fig. 52.1). The sketch in the center is the most fully worked up, showing the transformed demon in full, as well as his grotesquely exaggerated facial features. The physiognomy is so close to the more detailed and descriptive, horrific visage captured in the Tobey drawing as to make it conceivable that both are studies for the same vanquished figure in the lost fresco.

LWS

1. Recorded on a label on the old backing. For this lost work, see Florence 1999, p. 116, under nos. 45–46.
2. Monbeig Goguel and Viatte 1981–82, nos. 81–82. Others are in the Uffizi and the Biblioteca Marucelliana in Florence, and in the National Gallery of Scotland, Edinburgh; see Bigongiari and Cantelli 1970, pp. 18–19, under no. 7; Florence 1999, p. 116, nos. 45–46.

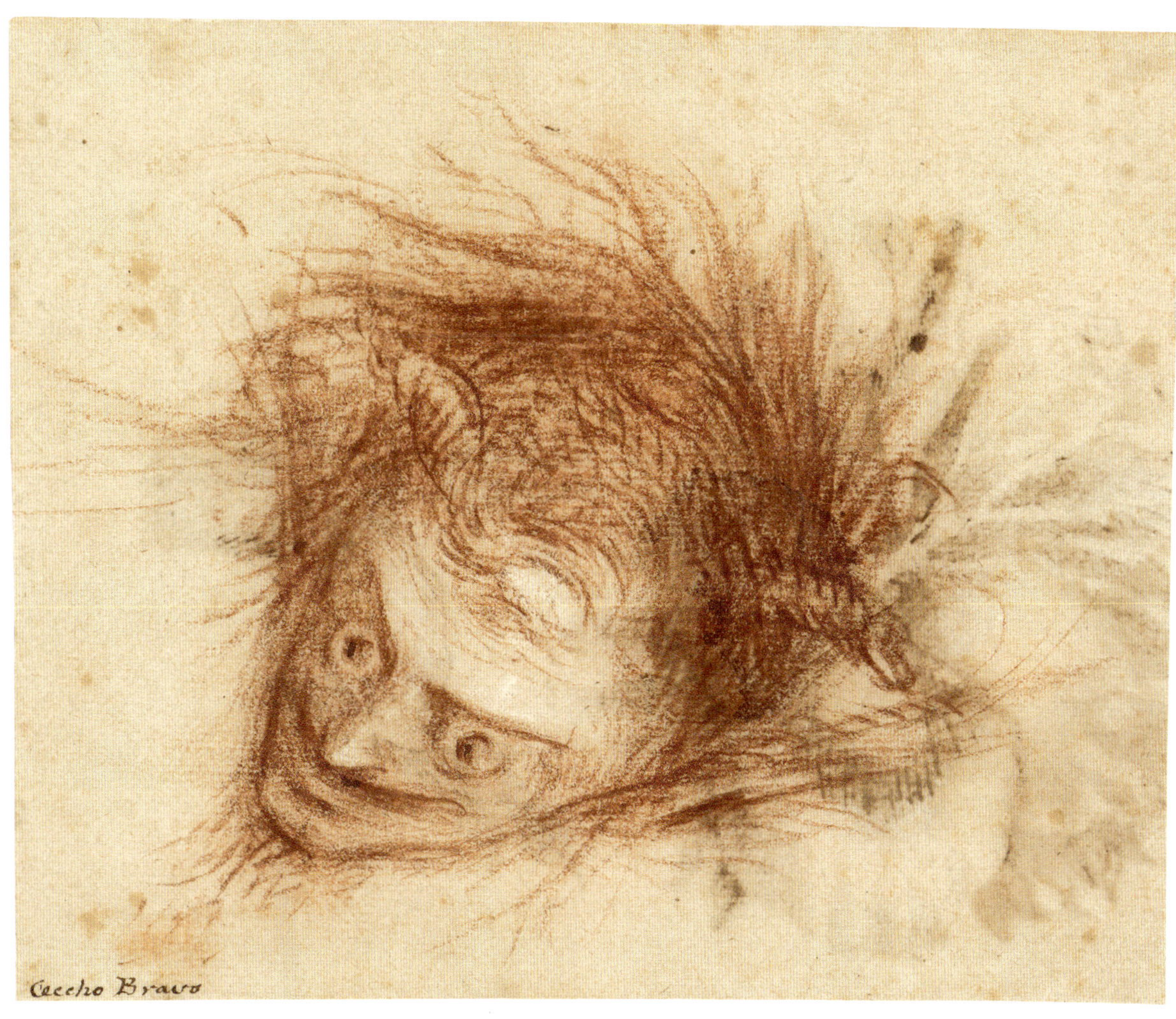

52

GIOVANNI BENEDETTO CASTIGLIONE

Genoa, 1609–Mantua, 1664

Castiglione specialized in paintings and drawings representing journeys of the patriarchs, particularly Jacob—pastoral scenes showing rustic figures and their herds traversing an arcadian landscape, the ostensible religious subject matter of which is often barely discerned. His style was shaped by a number of disparate sources and influences absorbed in his native Genoa, from the lingering mannerist tendencies of his teacher, Giovanni Battista Paggi, to the luminious oil sketches of Rubens and van Dyck, to the animal prints of seventeenth-century northern artists. Castiglione was particularly innovative as a graphic artist, creating signature drawings in which chalk and oil paint applied with a dry brush are combined, and inventing the monotype—a print medium that yields only a single, unique impression.

53. *Shepherds with Their Flock*

Red paint on paper, 16⅜ x 22¾ in. (41.7 x 57.9 cm)

The Metropolitan Museum of Art, New York, Promised Gift of David M. Tobey

Provenance: Katrin Bellinger Kunsthandel, Munich; acquired in 1998

Reference: Munich 1999, no. 20

In this pictorial eclogue Giovanni Benedetto Castiglione evokes the innocent age of a pastoral arcadia. A group of shepherds, aided by the hound at the right who lifts his muzzle to sniff the air, drive their herd of sheep and a single cow toward a wood at left. Enacting two opposing modes of coercion, one of the shepherds wields a lash and prepares to strike the cow's flank; another sounds a small horn. The horn-blower's short tunic transports the scene from the quotidien contemporary world to an imagined, idyllic classical past.

Castiglione specialized in such pastoral scenes—the subject matter of many of his canvases, etchings, and drawings. (His other favorite theme, the journeys of biblical patriarchs, particularly Jacob—the source of his appellation in a legal document of 1635 as "He who often paints Jacob's journeys"[1]— shares the aesthetic of his bucolic scenes in showing rustic figures and animals in a landscape setting.) Like the Tobey sheet, these do not represent specific literary, historical, or mythological subjects but are instead poetic evocations. An analagous example depicting a journey with flocks and herds at a stream is in The Metropolitan Museum of Art, New York (fig. 53.1);[2] that drawing, like the Tobey sheet and others by Castiglione in the same vein were not produced as preparatory designs for paintings or prints, but rather as independent works.

In addition to the subject matter, the distinctive technique employed here, in which red paint, possibly mixed with oil, is applied to unprepared paper with a dry brush, is also typical of the artist. The resulting fluid and painterly quality and atmospheric effect is midway between a drawing and an oil sketch. This manner of execution may have been influenced by the

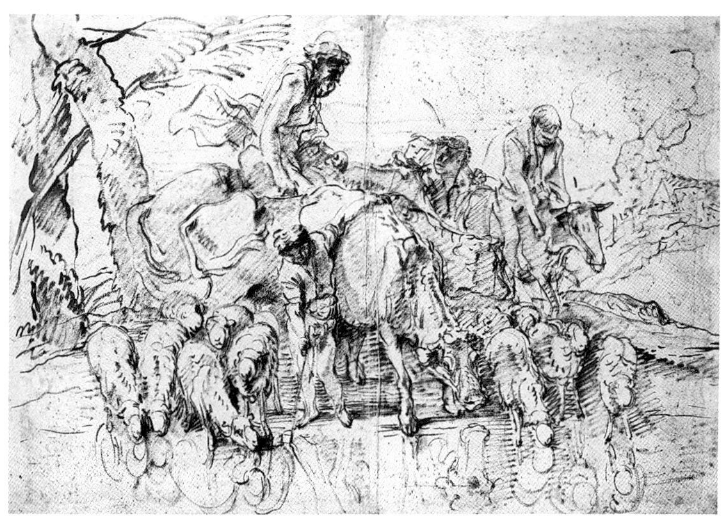

Fig. 53.1. Giovanni Benedetto Castiglione. *Pastoral Journey with Flocks and Herds at a Stream*, 1660–64. Brush with red and brown oil paint, 16 x 22¾ in. (40.6 x 57.8 cm). The Metropolitan Museum of Art, New York, Bequest of Walter C. Baker, 1971 (1972.118.246)

oil sketches of Peter Paul Rubens and especially Anthony Van Dyck, works that Castiglione would have seen in Genoa. The naturalistic vocabulary of these pastoral essays, with their cast of shepherds, sheep, and lumbering bovines, also suggests a Flemish influence, reflecting the artist's familiarity with the animal and landscape prints of Johann Roos and Nicolaes Berchem,[3] among other sources—material that Castiglione may have known from the time of his affiliation in 1626–27 with the Genoese painter Giovanni Battista Paggi, who owned a large print collection. LWS

1. As discussed in Newcome Schleier 1985, under no. 68; Standring 2007– .
2. See Bean 1979, no. 117.
3. The latter as a possible source was kindly suggested by Nadine M. Orenstein.

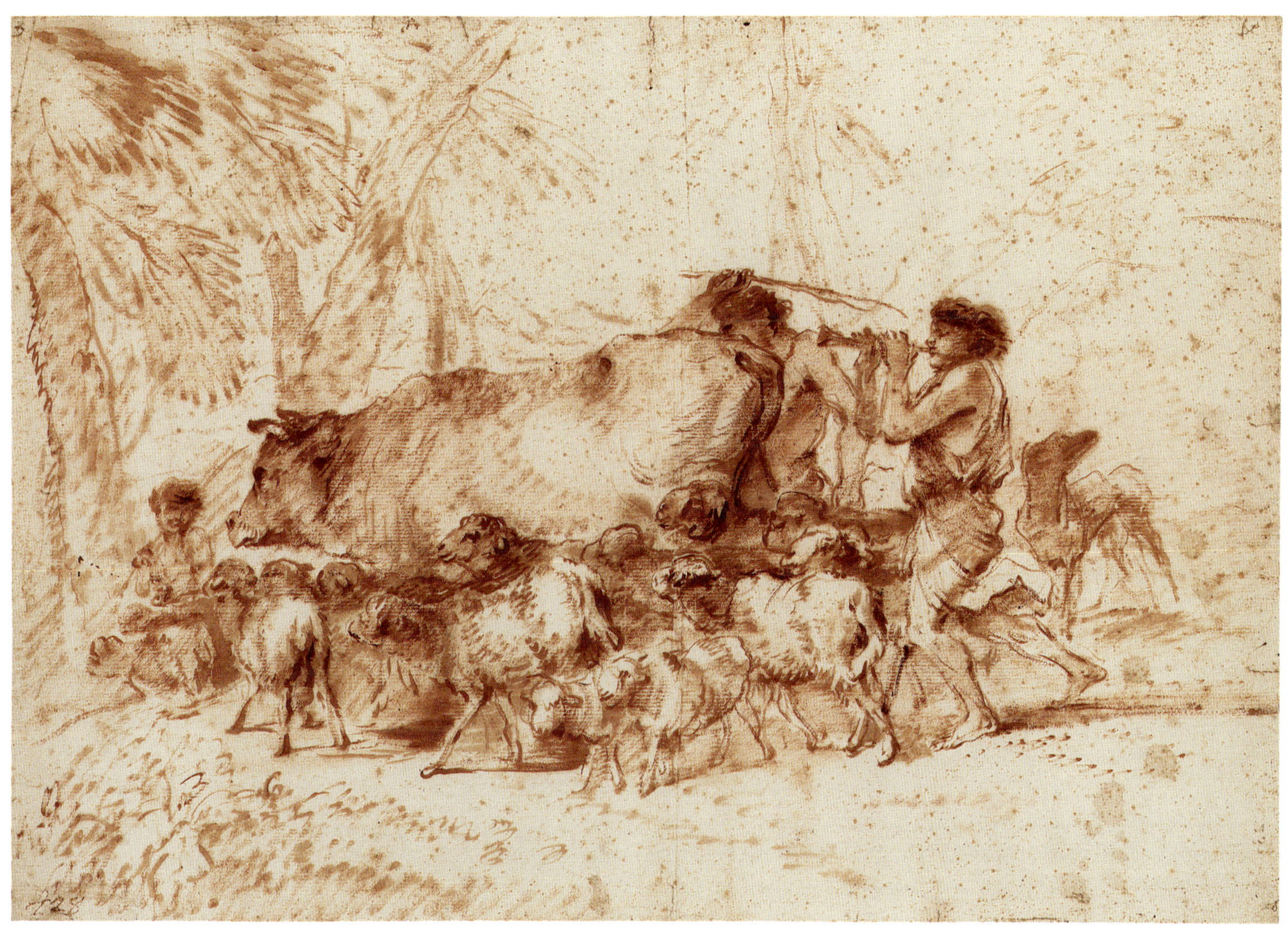

53

Over the course of his long career Franceschini distinguished himself as a fresco painter, receiving a succession of prestigious commissions to decorate chapels in Florentine churches, the palaces of the city's aristocrats, and one of the villas belonging to Prince Don Lorenzo de' Medici. A trip to Rome introduced him to the baroque exuberance of Bernini and Pietro da Cortona, some measure of which he injected into his Florentine fresco decorations. A graceful and refined draftsman, Franceschini often employed red chalk. His many figure drawings combine a softness of modeling and contour reminiscent of Correggio with a monumentality and sense of volume that derive from Michelangelo and other sixteenth-century Florentine predecessors.

54. *Study for the Figure of The New Law*, ca. 1642

Red chalk, with traces of white heightening, 15 x 10⅝ in. (38 x 27 cm)
Inscribed in open book: *I N P R / C*

Provenance: Private Collection; sale, Finarte, Milan, March 22, 1999, lot 42
(as Matteo Rosselli); Katrin Bellinger Kunsthandel, Munich, 1999, no. 18
(as Volterrano); acquired in 1999

References: McCorquodale 1983, p. 65, fig. 43 (as Volterrano); *Il Giornale dell'arte*,
no. 177, May 1999, pp. 92–93, fig. 9 (as Matteo Rosselli)

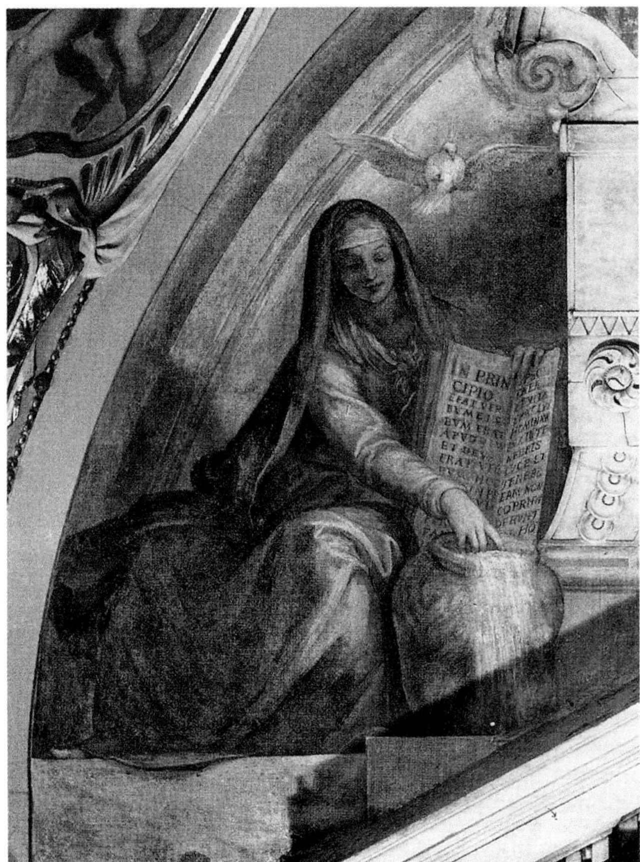

Fig. 54.1. Baldassare Franceschini, Il Volterrano. *The New Law*,
ca. 1642. Fresco. Orlandini Chapel, Santa Maria Maggiore, Florence

About 1642, the wealthy Florentine merchant and newly elected senator Francesco di Orlandino di Giovanni (1592–1662) commissioned Baldassare Franceschini, Il Volterrano, to embellish his family's funerary chapel in Santa Maria Maggiore in Florence. Reflecting the chapel's recent rededication to the Madonna del Carmine, Volterrano's fresco and stucco decoration in the vault emphasized the Madonna's role as divine intercessor and vehicle of salvation, central tenets of the Carmelite devotion.[1] For the altarpiece, Giovanni Bilivert painted the founders of the Carmelite Order (now lost) to surround a venerated medieval image of the Madonna and Child Enthroned, then housed in the chapel.

The biographer Filippo Baldinucci, in his *Notizie dei professori del disegno da Cimabue in quà*, refers to Volterrano's work in the Orlandini Chapel.[2] Among the details he describes is a personification of The New Law in one of the lunettes (fig. 54.1). Portrayed as a veiled female figure holding a book, symbol of the era *sub grazia* (Age of Grace), and a large amphora from which purifying water spills, she is paired with a personification of The Old Law, whose attribute is a tablet, symbol of the era *sub lege*, the Age of Law, or Age before Christ—the Old Testament—which was eclipsed by The New Law. The two other allegorical figures in the lunettes represent Humility and Chastity or Purity, virtues associated with the Virgin Mary to whom the chapel was dedicated.

As Charles McCorquodale first realized, the Tobey sheet is a study by Volterrano for the personification of The New Law.[3] The figure seen here appears in identical form in the fresco, suggesting that the drawing represents a late stage of the preparatory process. The artist has taken into account the architectural setting, indicating the pediment beneath the painted figure with a rapidly sketched diagonal line at her feet. The figure's left hand, which supports the book, is redrawn at the lower right. In the drawing, only a few letters are legible in its open pages,

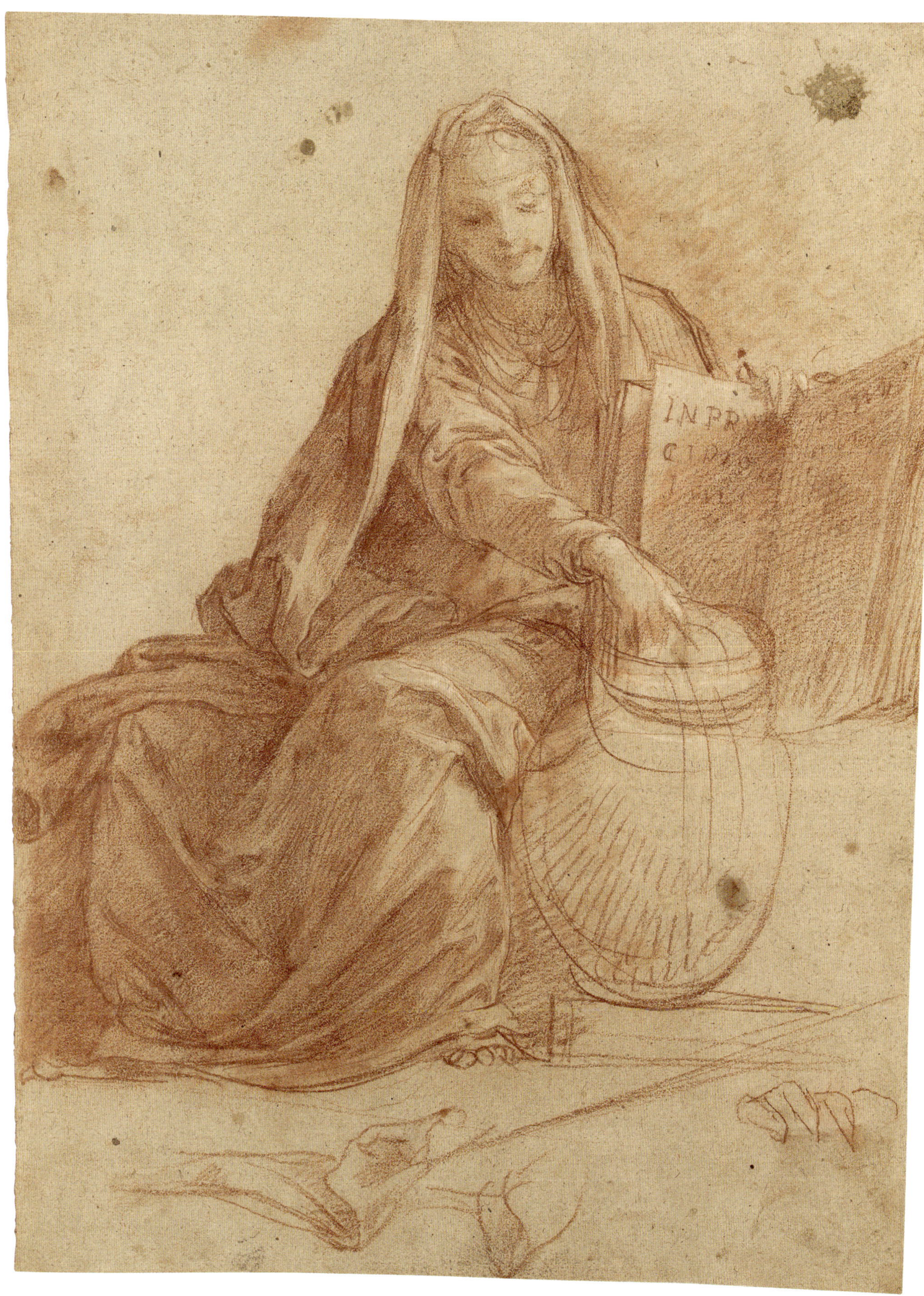

BALDASSARE FRANCESCHINI, IL VOLTERRANO   179

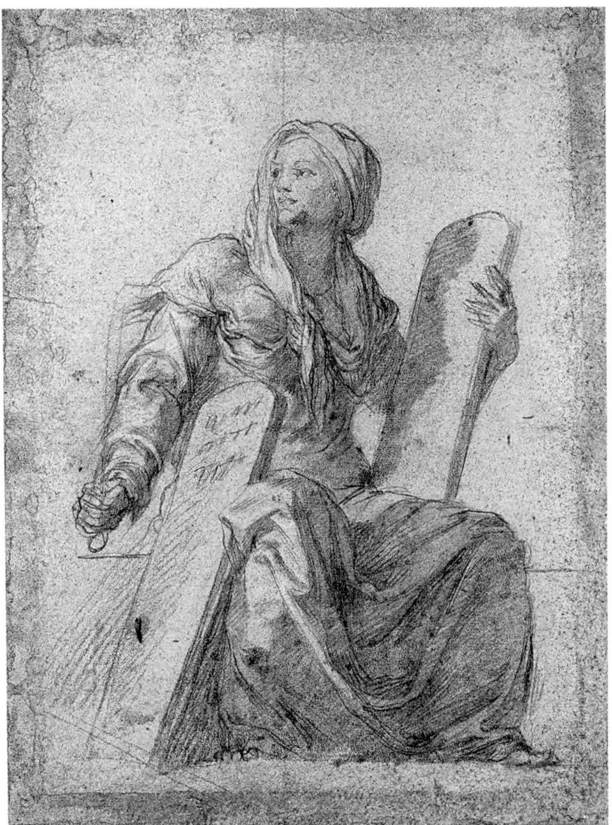

Fig. 54.2. Baldassare Franceschini, Il Volterrano. *The Old Law*, ca. 1642. Red chalk, partly washed, heightened with a little white, on pale buff paper, 14⅝ x 10⁹⁄₁₆ in. (37.2 x 26.9 cm). Ashmolean Museum of Art and Archaeology, Oxford (WA 1958.13)

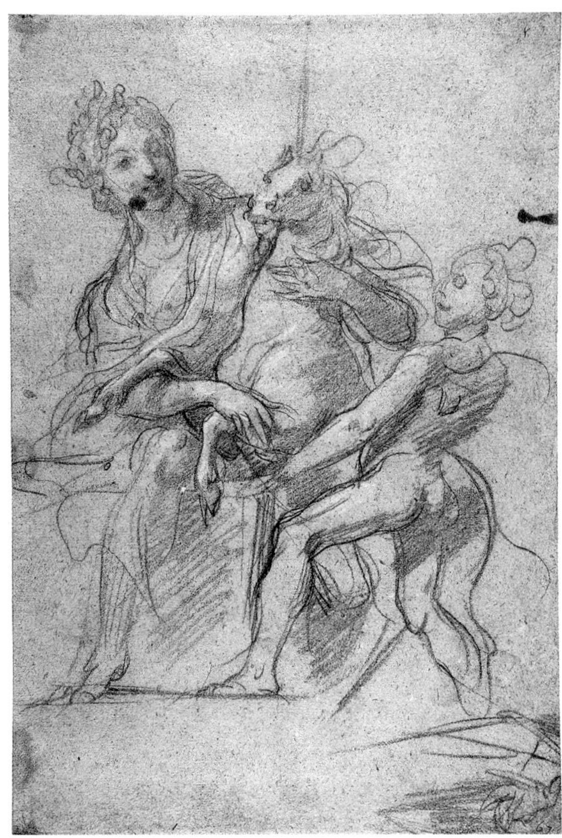

Fig. 54.3. Baldassare Franceschini, Il Volterrano. *Allegorical Figure of Purity with a Unicorn and Putto*, ca. 1642. Red chalk on beige paper, 15⅝ x 10⁵⁄₁₆ in. (39.7 x 26.2 cm). The Metropolitan Museum of Art, New York, Rogers Fund, 1969 (69.172)

sufficient, however, to allow the passage to be recognized as the opening verses of the Gospel of John, which are fully inscribed in the fresco:

> *In principio erat Verbum et Verbum erat apud Deum et Deus erat Verbum; hoc erat in principio apud Deum; omnia per ipsum facta sunt et sine ipso factum est nihil quod factum est; in ipso vita erat et vita erat lux hominum.* (In the beginning was the Word, and the Word was with God, and the Word was God. The same was in the beginning with God. All things were made by him; and without him was not any thing made that was made. In him was life; and the life was the light of men, John 1:1–4)

Volterrano worked in Santa Maria Maggiore immediately following a trip to northern Italy and Rome in 1640. His study of Correggio's frescoes in the dome of Parma Cathedral (see cat. no. 5), and of Michelangelo's and Raphael's frescoes in the Vatican, is reflected in the monumentality and volumetric forms of the Orlandini Chapel allegorical personifications and in the dramatic illusionism of the *Elijah in His Fiery Chariot* in the vault. Both the Tobey drawing, *Study for the Figure of*

The New Law, and a similar sheet in the Ashmolean Museum of Art and Archaeology, Oxford, for the pendant figure of *The Old Law* (fig. 54.2), with their sculptural yet softly modeled forms, also reflect this dual influence from Correggio and Michelangelo.

In addition to the Tobey and Ashmolean sheets, numerous other preparatory drawings by Volterrano for the Orlandini Chapel decorations survive. These include a sketch for the right hand of the personification of The Old Law (formerly London art market); studies for the figure of Elijah, an angel, Purity, and for the design of the entire vault, in the Uffizi; two further depictions of Purity in The Metropolitan Museum of Art, New York (fig. 54.3), and a third in the Louvre; and two additional drawings for the *Elijah* fresco in the National Gallery of Scotland, Edinburgh.[4]   LWS

1. On the Orlandini Chapel, see Baldassari 1990.
2. Baldinucci ed. 1845–47, pp. 143–44.
3. McCorquodale 1983, fig. 43 and p. 65.
4. Volterrano's preparatory studies for the Orlandini Chapel are discussed in Cooney 1974; Thiem 1977, pp. 405–6, no. 216, figs. 216, 305; Bean 1979, pp. 181–83, under nos. 182–83; McCorquodale 1983; Baldassari 1990, p. 40 and figs. 13, 17–21.

PIER FRANCESCO MOLA

Coldrerio, Switzerland, 1612–Rome, 1666

With the exception of two periods in northern Italy, Pier Francesco Mola worked in Rome for his entire career. A versatile painter, he created small, luminous landscapes populated with figures from the Bible, classical mythology, and Renaissance poetry, as well as monumental frescoes and altarpieces, combining the rich palette and dramatic light and shadow of Venetian art with the imposing grandeur and expressive drama of the Roman High Baroque. Mola greatly admired the art of Guercino, whose influence may be discerned in both his paintings and his drawings, the latter typically executed in pen and brown ink with pools of brown wash. In addition to figure and composition studies, he produced a number of witty and satirical caricatures.

55. Recto: *Onlookers Peering over a Balustrade, and Caricatures of a Man in Profile to the Left and a Lady in Court Dress*, ca. 1656
Verso: *Two Putti and an Archway*

Recto: Pen and brown ink, brown wash; verso: red chalk and red wash, 7 x 9⅞ in. (17.9 x 25.1 cm)
Annotated on recto at lower right: *=f. mola fecit 48*, beside unidentified collector's mark

Provenance: Pierre Crozat (?); Yvonne Tan Bunzl, London, 1987; Private Collection, Belgium; sale, Christie's, New York, January 30, 1997, lot 62; acquired in 1997

References: Lugano and Rome 1989–90, pp. 236–37, no. III.26; Brussels 1993, no. 75

Pier Francesco Mola's fresco *Joseph Making Himself Known to His Brethren* in the Palazzo Quirinale was singled out for particular praise by the seventeenth-century biographer Giuseppe Passeri and is regarded by modern critics as the masterpiece of his Roman career (fig. 55.1).[1] Executed in 1656–57, as records of payment to the artist document, it is part of a grand decorative cycle commissioned by Pope Alexander VII Chigi shortly after his elevation to the papacy in 1655. The artistic campaign was overseen by Pietro da Cortona, who assigned to Mola one of the two principal scenes (the other, representing the Adoration of the Shepherds, was executed by Carlo Maratta); other painters who participated in the project included Ciro Ferri, Giovanni Franceso Grimaldi, and Gaspard Dughet. No fewer than ten drawings by Mola for this fresco, as well as a cartoon for one of Joseph's brothers,[2] survive, attesting to the great importance he attached to this prestigious commission and the considerable care he devoted to formulating the composition. Interestingly, none of the drawings—a series of figure and composition studies—conforms precisely to the corresponding details in the fresco.[3]

Mola's fresco in the Palazzo Quirinale takes its subject from the Old Testament (Genesis 45:1–16). Joseph, the most beloved son of the patriarch Jacob, who had endured a long series of tribulations before becoming the powerful confidant of the Egyptian pharaoh, reveals his true identity to his brothers years after they had cruelly sold him into slavery. (In a typological pairing, this disclosure of his true identity was thought to prefigure the Epiphany, the revelation of Christ's divinity at the time of the Nativity—the subject painted by Maratta in the pendant fresco.) Gathered before a classical landscape reminiscent of Pietro da Cortona, Mola's figures react with suitable astonishment to Joseph's announcement, enacting a range of rhetorically expressive poses and gestures that communicate their surprise and reverence. In the background at the left diminutive figures congregate beneath a monumental arcade. Some observe the drama transpiring in the foreground while others appear to be unaware of the momentous confrontation.

Since it entered the literature the Tobey drawing has been considered a study for the background figures in the *Joseph* fresco. Like Mola's other preparatory drawings for this composition, the correspondence is not exact, but the presence and placement of the laterally receding arcade at the left, the disposition of figures around a parapet, and the way in which their attention is directed by the pointing youth in the center to some unseen action, are all consistent with the background vignette in the painting. That such a detail was always part of the artist's conception even when he was experimenting with an alternative design is attested in a study in a private collection showing the composition in reverse, with two sketchily rendered figures—witnesses to the dramatic event—standing under an arcade behind a parapet.[4]

Mola was one of the first Italian draftsmen to execute caricatures.[5] That more informal and amusing aspect of his artistic production is represented in the two rapid sketches at the lower right of the Tobey sheet, one of a shaggy-haired, vaguely

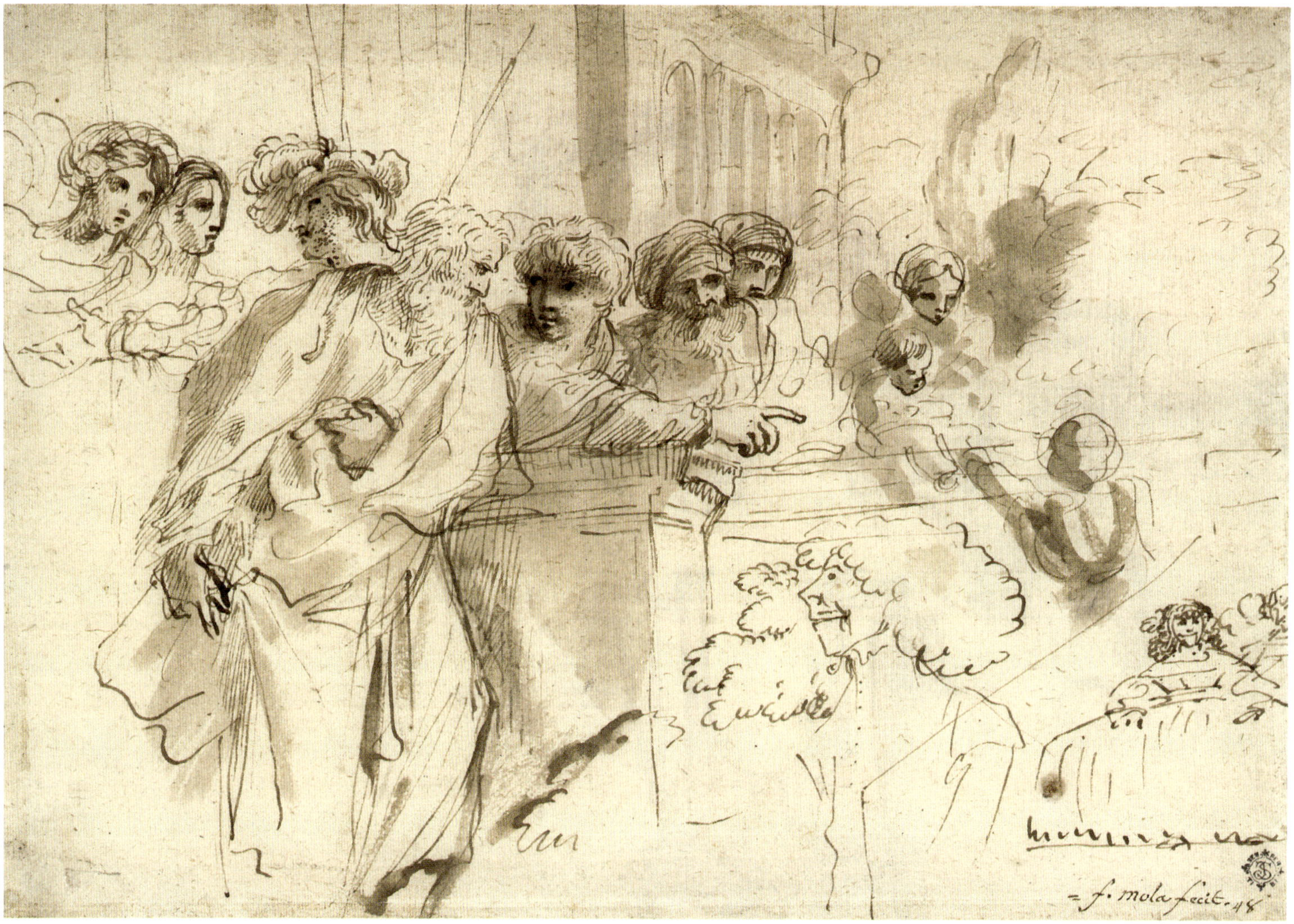

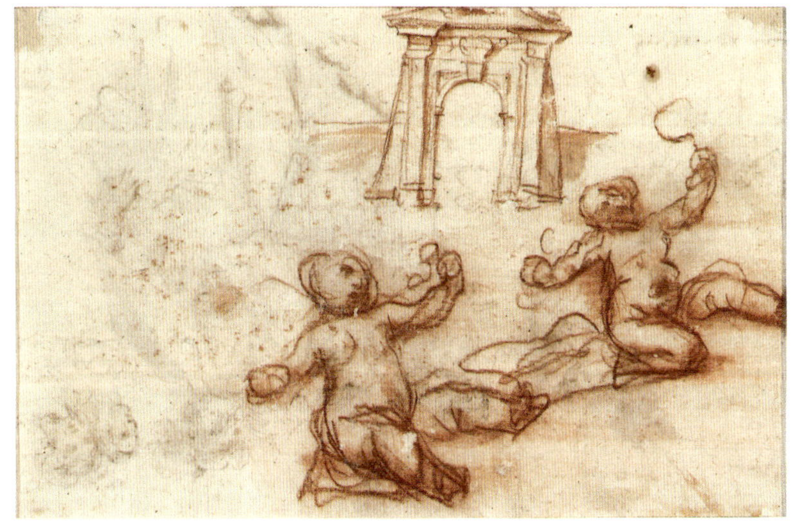

55

55 verso

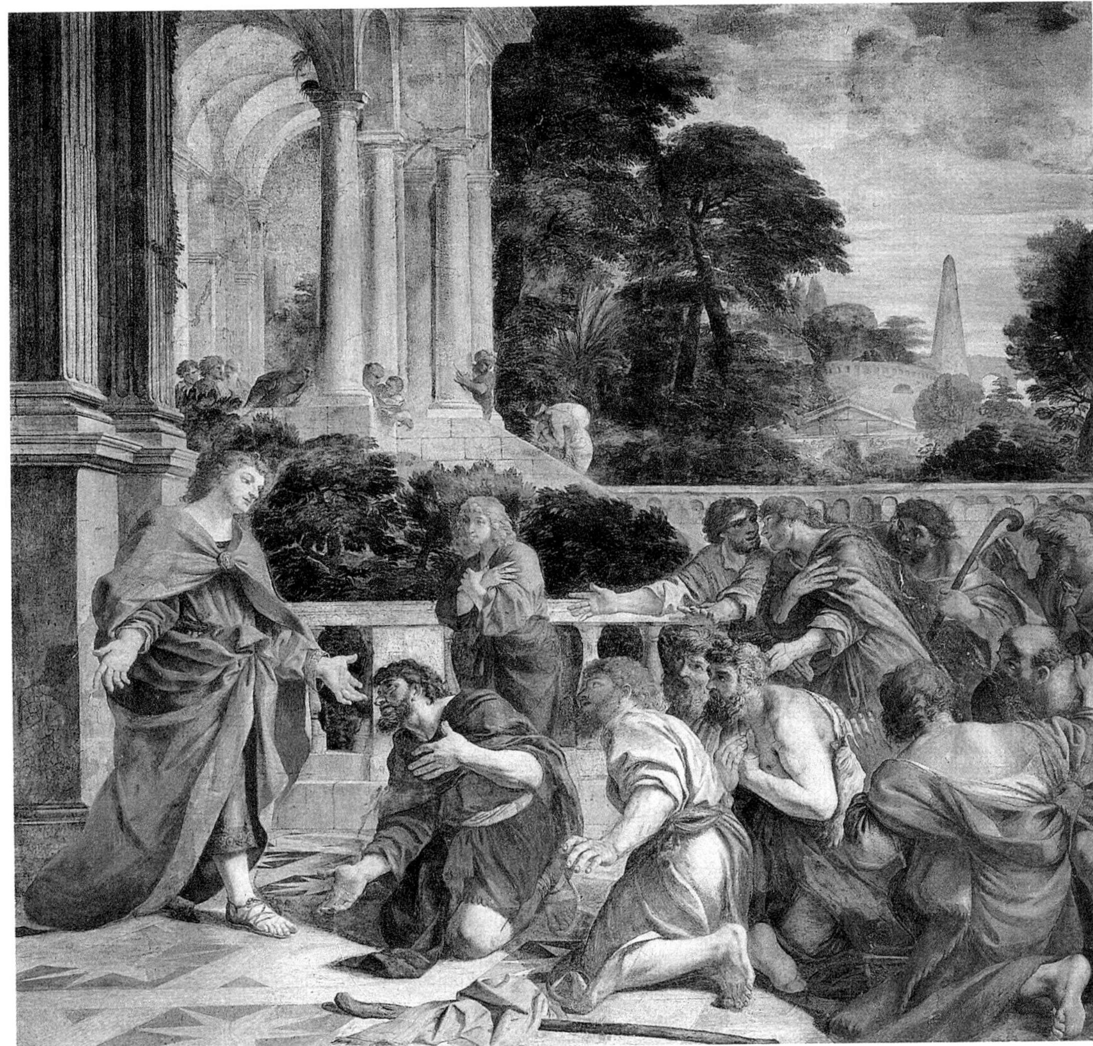

foppish courtier-type and the other of a young woman, attended, perhaps, by her maid and attired in an elegant gown with a comically prodigious hoopskirt reminiscent of the Spanish court style.

The studies of putti on the verso have been loosely related to another, more finished drawing by Mola of two putti in the British Museum.[6] Squared for transfer, that sheet is a *modello* for a detail of the ceiling in the Palazzo Pamphilj in Nettuno where Mola worked in 1651–52. It is unlikely, however, that the putti and the architectural sketch on the verso of the Tobey sheet relate to that commission, given the disparity in date with the later Quirinale fresco.

An etching by Mola reproduces in reverse, with slight revisions, the composition of the *Joseph* fresco in the Palazzo Quirinale.[7] It was undoubtedly made to record and disseminate this important invention.　　　　　　　　　　　LWS

1. See Cocke 1972, pp. 26–28; Lugano and Rome 1989–90, pp. 213–15, no. II.6.
2. Sold at Christie's, London, July 3, 1990, lot 56.
3. As noted in Lugano and Rome 1989–90, p. 215, under no. II.6. The sequence of drawings is discussed in Cocke 1972, pp. 27–28. See also Harris 1969.
4. Harris 1969, p. 83, fig. 2.
5. See Kahn-Rossi 1989–90.
6. Inv. no. 1952-1-21-46; Lugano and Rome 1989–90, no. III.5. The connection with the verso of the Tobey sheet was made in ibid., p. 236, under no. III.26.
7. Bartsch XIX.1; Cocke 1972, p. 26; Lugano and Rome 1989–90, p. 298, no. III.127.

SALVATOR ROSA

Arenella (Sicily), 1615–Rome, 1673

Painter, draftsman, etcher, poet, actor, wit, satirist, and philosopher Salvator Rosa was one of the most brilliant and tempestuous personalities of the seventeenth century. He worked in Naples, Florence, and Rome, often outside the contractual framework of the patronage system, which he vociferously denounced. Famous and influential as the author of moody, darkly poetic landscapes and energetic battle scenes, he also painted portraits, biblical narratives and parables, hagiographic subjects, allegories, and macabre scenes of witchcraft and necromancy. A gifted, inventive, and prolific draftsman and etcher, Rosa explored many of the same themes in his graphic art as in his paintings.

56. *Allegory*, 1649

Pen and brown ink, brownish-gray wash, 11½ x 16¹⁵⁄₁₆ in. (29.2 x 43 cm)
Inscribed on recto in pen and brown ink in tablet at upper center: *Sormonta l'Arte a vincer La Natura*; in pen and brown ink on curtain at lower center: *Chi non fatica ben Gloria si perde*; on verso in pen and brown ink: *Ad 24 Agosto 1649*

Provenance: Pandora Fine Arts, New York; acquired in 2005

The autograph inscription on the verso of this fascinating drawing establishes that it was executed within months of Salvator Rosa's return from Florence to Rome early in 1649, the artist having abandoned the city nearly a decade earlier after imprudently insulting the all-powerful Gianlorenzo Bernini in one of his satirical performances. Its subject, an allegory of the practice of painting, takes up a theme that Rosa explored in a number of drawings and paintings,[1] and in his satirical poem *Painting*, which was composed within a year of this dated sheet.[2] Like Rosa's other satires, that literary work was meant to be delivered as a theatrical recitation performed by the artist himself, who was renowned for his comic brilliance, uncanny ability to throw his voice, and pitch-perfect rendition of regional accents.[3] In Rome, these recitals were performed in a specially furnished room in his own house, the simple chairs and benches of which presented a "deliberately Spartan, or rather, Stoic [air], in keeping with the high moral tone of the poems"[4] and Rosa's own philosophical bent.

In most of his allegorical ruminations on the theme of Painting, Rosa bemoaned the corrupt state of that once noble practice—the ignorance and indolence of artists; the paucity of taste and discernment shown by contemporary collectors; the corrupting stranglehold of papal patronage; and the lack of acclaim accorded the few worthy practitioners (himself, implicitly, foremost among them). Such is the lament that informs the *Allegory of Painting* in the Bonna Collection, which depicts a ragged personification of Painting swishing away flies from the stack of unwanted canvases representing all different genres that litter an impoverished artist's studio (fig. 56.1). Graffiti on the wall showing a crowned ass receiving a bulging bag of coins makes it clear that the deserving painter's just but unattained rewards went instead to a most unworthy, literally asinine, rival.

Contemporary with the Bonna drawing, the Tobey sheet is informed by the same topos. It is not a satirical diatribe, however, but a Stoic exhortation—a road map of the noble if arduous path that the worthy painter must follow if he is to achieve glory.[5] Represented here is another painter's studio, its inventory neatly hung in two skied rows flanking a curtained portal suggestive of a Roman triumphal arch. Resisting the cloying grasp of a contingent of demons—personifications of the myriad, corrupting temptations to which the undisciplined and unskilled practitioners of art fall prey—a man makes his way to a gentleman standing in the center, his slightly bowed posture and doffed hat signaling his respectful demeanor. The taller man gestures to the curtain behind him, where the painter's attributes, a palette and brushes, are encircled in a giant laurel wreath, a pictorial conceit illustrating the Triumph of Painting. That the road to glory is difficult is made evident by the rocks and thorns littering the ground, while the admonition inscribed on the curtain— "he who does not create good work loses glory"—serves as a reminder that only the truly worthy will achieve eternal fame. Ultimately, art will triumph, as the inscription in the cartouche above the curtain (a loose paraphrase of a humanist trope concerning the power of art to rival and surpass Nature) proclaims.

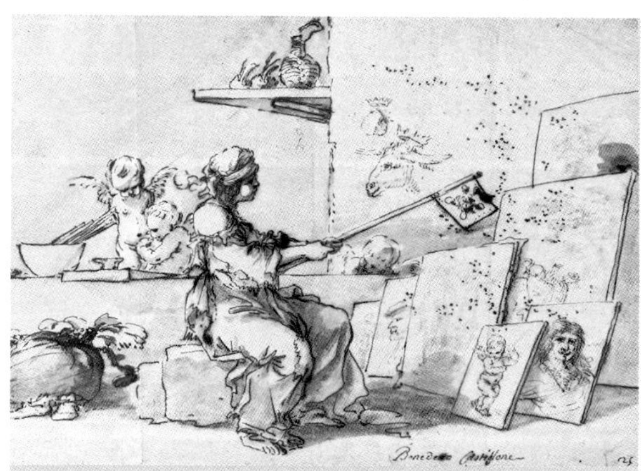

Fig. 56.1. Salvator Rosa. *Allegory of Painting*, ca. 1650. Pen and brown ink, brush and brown wash, 8¾ x 12¹⁄₁₆ in. (22.2 x 30.6 cm). Collection of Jean Bonna, Geneva

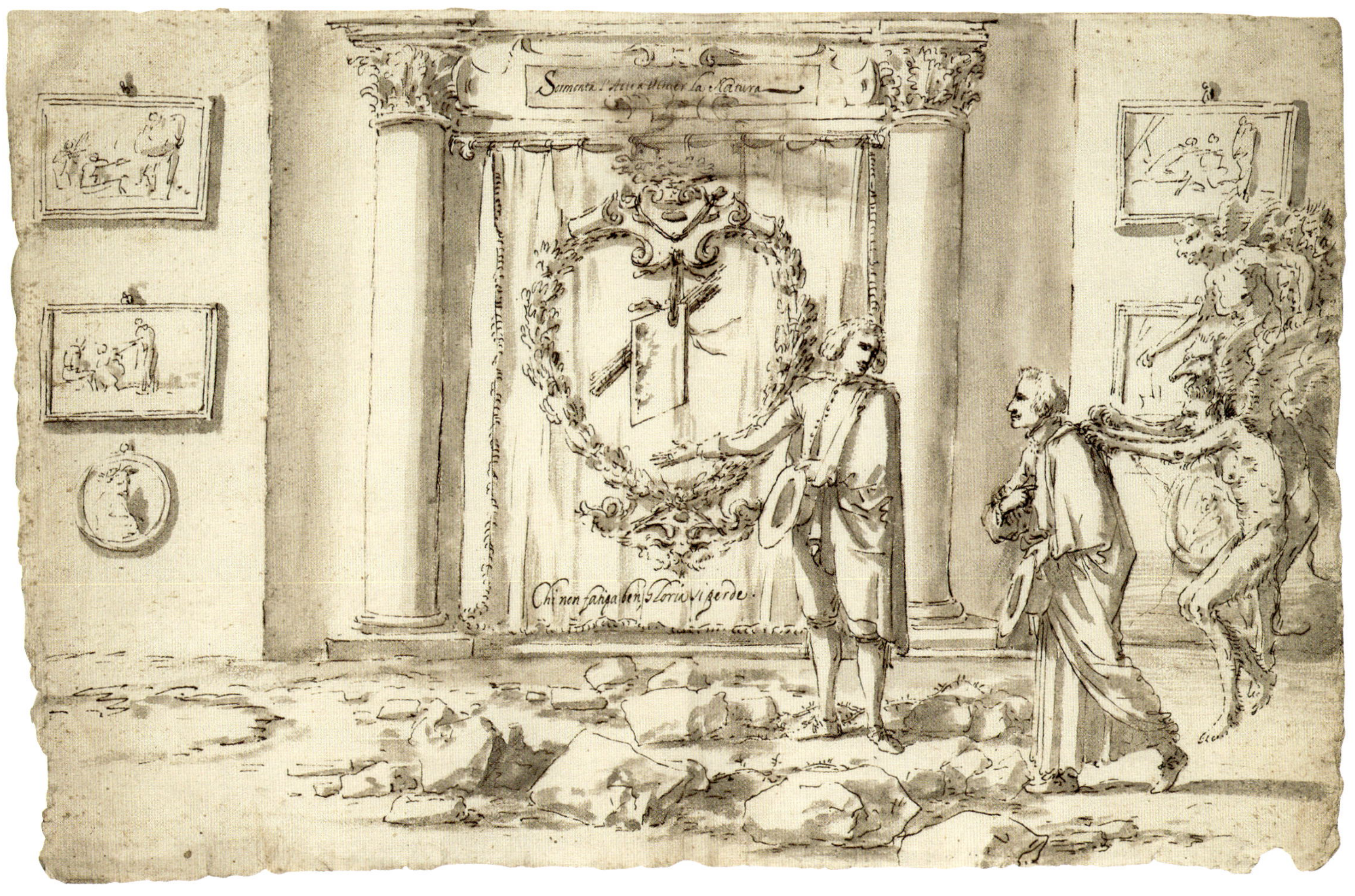

Sementa l'Arte et tinci la Natura
Chi non fatiga ben, Gloria vi perde.

56

It is tempting to see in the mustachioed protagonist with chin-length hair a self-portrait of Rosa, his arm extravagantly extended in a declarative gesture drawn from the repertoire of the theater (where he was as much at home as in the painter's studio), and to recognize as the setting of this morally instructive tableau the private stage he constructed for performances of his recitations, most notably *Painting*—a satire composed at the very time he executed this drawing, and which provides an interpretative key for understanding its complex imagery.   LWS

1. The drawings include an allegory of *Painting Begging for Charity* (Royal Library, Windsor, inv. no. 6124); a *Satire on Painting* (Staatliche Graphische Sammlung, Munich, inv. no. 34923r); and an *Allegory of Painting* (Private Collection; see Mahoney 1977, vol. 1, nos. 24.5 and 25.20; and the entry by Nathalie Strasser in New York and Edinburgh 2009, p. 68, no. 32, respectively). Relevant paintings are Rosa's *Self-Portrait as an Artist* (Uffizi, Florence), in which he portrays himself holding the painter's brushes and the satirist's dart, and the *Allegory of Fortune* (J. Paul Getty Museum, Los Angeles); see Scott 1995, pp. 61, and 121–24, respectively.

2. On the dating of the poem to the period June–December 1650, see Roworth 1981, p. 613; Scott 1995, pp. 86, 242 n. 16. Like Rosa's other satires, *Painting* was only published posthumously, but it was performed, as well as circulated in manuscript form, during his lifetime.

3. Scott 1995, p. 90.

4. Ibid.

5. A similar artistic-philosophical formulation was articulated, though in a more dense and complex composition, by Rosa's contemporary Pietro Testa in his etching *The Triumph of the Virtuous Artist on Parnassus* (ca. 1644–46), which shows a heroic nude artist guided along a difficult, rocky terrain illuminated by Divine Wisdom as he is crowned by Fame. A poetic meditation on the triumph of ignorance over vice, the arcane pictorial tableau also expresses the conceit that pursuit of virtue, and the mastery of that true art inspired by the Muses, promises to the worthy the reward of eternal fame—themes likewise taken up by Rosa.

57. *Six Men in a Landscape (Study for* Diogenes Throwing Away His Cup), ca. 1652

Pen and brown ink, brown wash, 9 x 7¾ in. (22.8 x 19.7 cm)

Provenance: Queen Christina of Sweden, Rome; then by inheritance to Cardinal Decio Azzolini and to Marchese Pompeo Azzolini, Rome; Prince Livio Odescalchi; Prince Ladislao Odescalchi, Rome, by descent; Pandora Old Masters, New York; acquired in 2007

Reference: Mahoney 1977, vol. 1, no. 33.1

Two of Salvator Rosa's preferred pictorial themes, landscapes and philosophers, coalesce in this poetic drawing of classically robed figures in a dark, vaguely mysterious wood. Representing a spectrum from youth to old age, three pairs of men engage in discourse. Rhetorical gestures signaling speech identify the speakers among the interlocutors. To the left, lying on its side is a large urn or other vessel. Rosa's characteristic dark wash imparts a moodiness to the scene. The sheet boasts an illustrious provenance, having once belonged to the voracious and discerning Queen Christina of Sweden, whose vast collection included a sizable number of drawings by the artist.[1]

The present composition shares many similarities with Rosa's painting *Diogenes Throwing Away His Cup* (fig. 57.1).[2] That work was conceived as a pendant to the slightly earlier *Democritus in Meditation*, which portrays a melancholic philosopher brooding in a dark and rather menacing landscape, a classical urn at his side and an array of animal skulls scattered at his feet, and which had caused quite a sensation when it was shown at the Pantheon in Rome in 1651.[3] Exhibited there the following year, the *Diogenes* also depicts a philosopher—in this case the ancient Cynic who renounced all his worldly goods and lived in a barrel—in a similar moonlit setting. Standing at the center in a short robe, Diogenes gestures to a peasant boy drinking from a stream with his bare hands—the simple act that, once witnessed, led him to cast off the crude cup that was his only remaining material possession, as he explains to the disciples gathered around him. Both the arrangement of the figures and the particular setting are close enough to the Tobey drawing to support the long-standing suggestion that this sheet is an early idea for the painting, in which case the large object seen here at the left may be meant to evoke Diogenes' barrel.   LWS

1. See Mahoney 1965.

2. As proposed in Mahoney 1977, vol. 1, pp. 371–72, no. 33.1. The painting is in the Statens Museum for Kunst, Copenhagen; see Scott 1995, pp. 98–100. Rosa had treated this subject in a painting executed earlier in the 1640s, when he was still in Florence, known as *The Philosophers' Grove* (Palazzo Pitti, Florence), for which see ibid., p. 46. The ordering of the figures in the landscape into three discrete pairs, two standing and one seated, in this painting is reprised in the Tobey drawing.

3. Statens Museum for Kunst, Copenhagen; see Scott 1995, pp. 96–98, fig. 101.

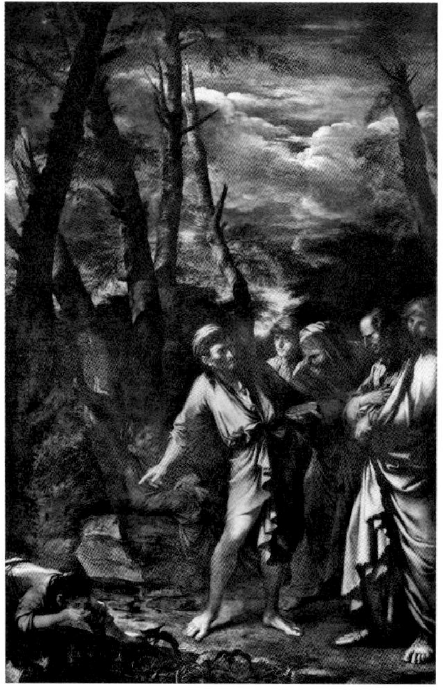

Fig. 57.1. Salvator Rosa. *Diogenes Throwing Away His Cup*, 1652. Oil on canvas. Statens Museum for Kunst, Copenhagen (KMS 4113)

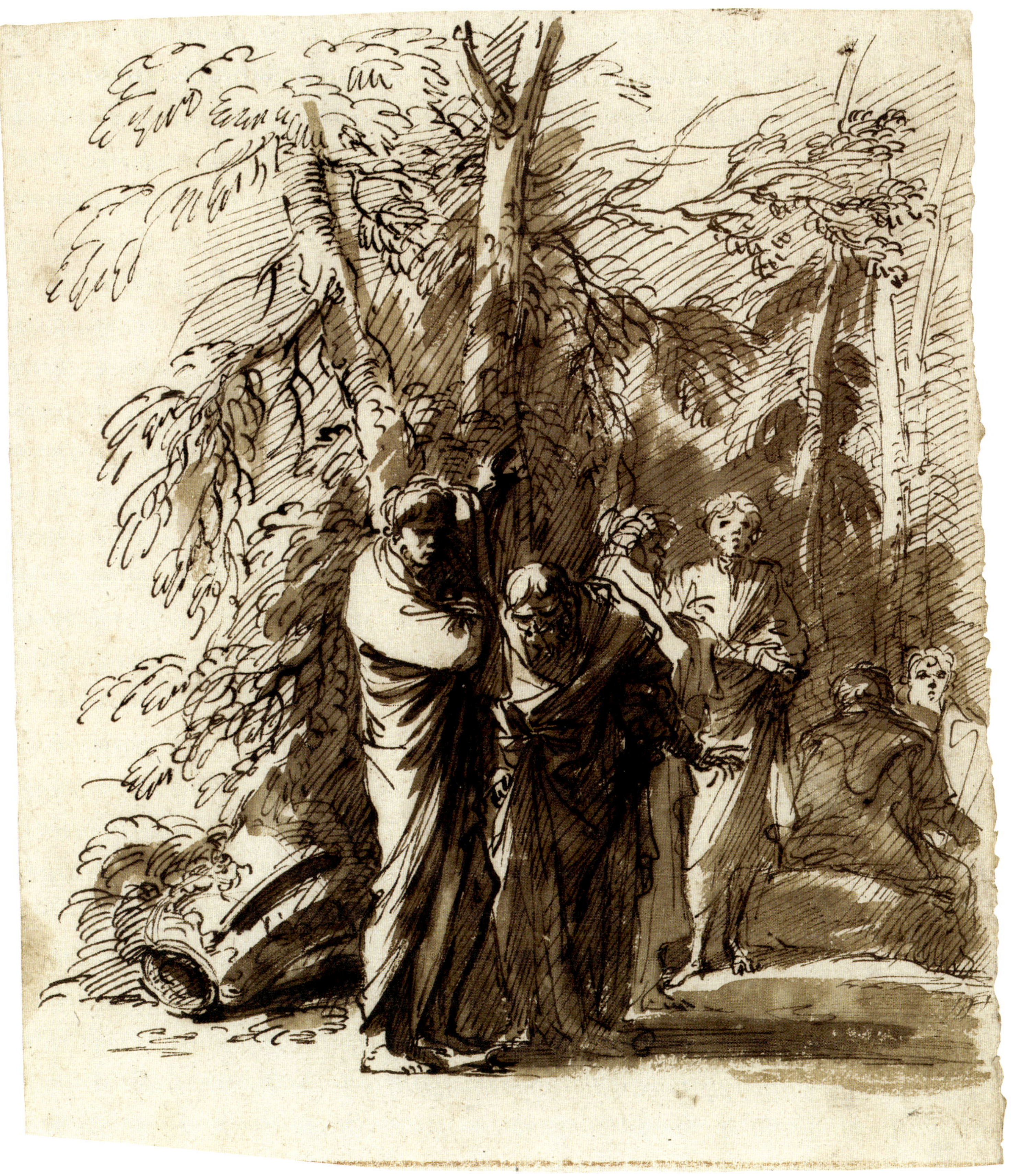

57

CARLO DOLCI
Florence, 1616–Florence, 1687

The preeminent Florentine painter of the seventeenth century, Carlo Dolci is best known for his intimate, pious, at times even mystical, representations of Christ, the Madonna, and female saints, executed with a highly polished surface and a deep, jewel-tone palette. He also worked as a portrait painter, lavishing attention not only on his subject's features, but on inanimate details such as gems, fabric, and still-life elements. A number of portrait drawings by the artist exist, some of which depict members of his family. Typically executed in a combination of red and black chalk (a technique also employed by his master, Jacopo Vignali, and other Florentine draftsmen of the period), these reveal his affinity for naturalistic, compellingly lifelike portrayals of his subject. According to the biographer Filippo Baldinucci, Dolci suffered from depression and mental torment.

58. *Portrait of a Young Woman, Possibly Teresa Bucarelli, the Artist's Wife, or Agnese Dolci, the Artist's Daughter,* ca. 1670

Black and red chalk, 11⅛ x 7⅜ in. (28.2 x 18.8 cm)

Provenance: Jules Dupan, Paris (Lugt 1440); Private Collection, France; Thomas Le Claire Kunsthandel, Hamburg; acquired in 2006

A notable aspect of Carlo Dolci's graphic oeuvre is the corpus of refined, intimate portrait drawings of the artist's family members, many identified on the basis of early inscriptions. Some are executed in red chalk, while in others, including an example in The Metropolitan Museum of Art, New York (fig. 58.1), red and black chalk are used together—a combination favored by many seventeenth-century Florentine draftsmen for its enhanced naturalism and rich coloristic effect. An impressive new addition to this group is this bust-length study of a young woman in the Tobey Collection. Casting an unwavering gaze at the viewer, she exudes the solemnity and vague melancholy that run through much of Dolci's work, both his religious paintings and his portraits.

At the time of the drawing's recent appearance on the market, the sitter was identified as Dolci's wife, Teresa Bucarelli (d. 1683), whom he married in 1654. The artist recorded her comely features in a number of images, including two portrait drawings now in the Louvre and the Lugt Collection, both of which belonged to the seventeenth-century Florentine biographer and collector Filippo Baldinucci,[1] and in a painted portrait formerly in the Cowper Collection but now lost.[2] Teresa also served as a model for many of the religious and devotional images in which Dolci specialized. Comparison with the Louvre and Lugt drawings, which undoubtedly show the same person, does not unequivocally support the proposal that the subject here is also Teresa, however. While those certain portrayals of the artist's wife present a round-faced young woman with a short, slightly upturned nose and notably small mouth, the sitter in the present drawing displays a longer, narrower

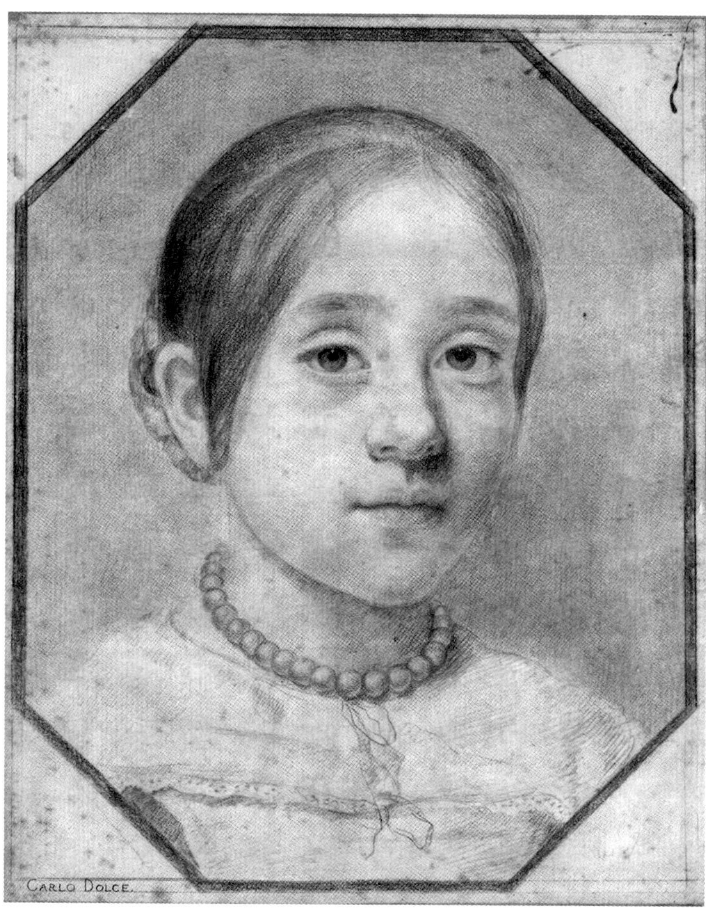

Fig. 58.1. Carlo Dolci. *Portrait of Agata Dolci*. Red and black chalk on pale gray paper, 10³⁄₁₆ x 7¹⁵⁄₁₆ in. (25.8 x 20.2 cm). The Metropolitan Museum of Art, New York, Rogers Fund, 1994 (1994.383)

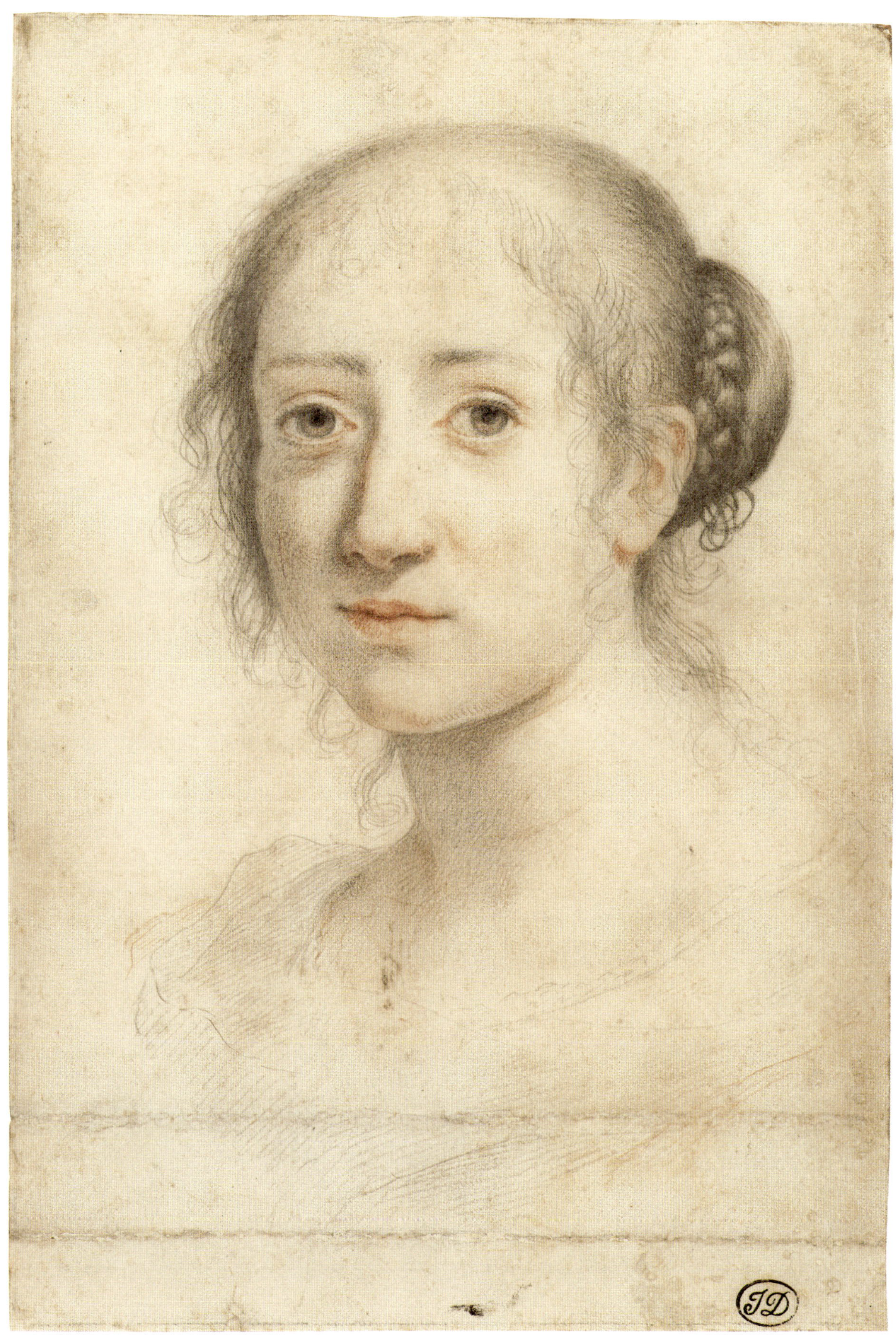

58

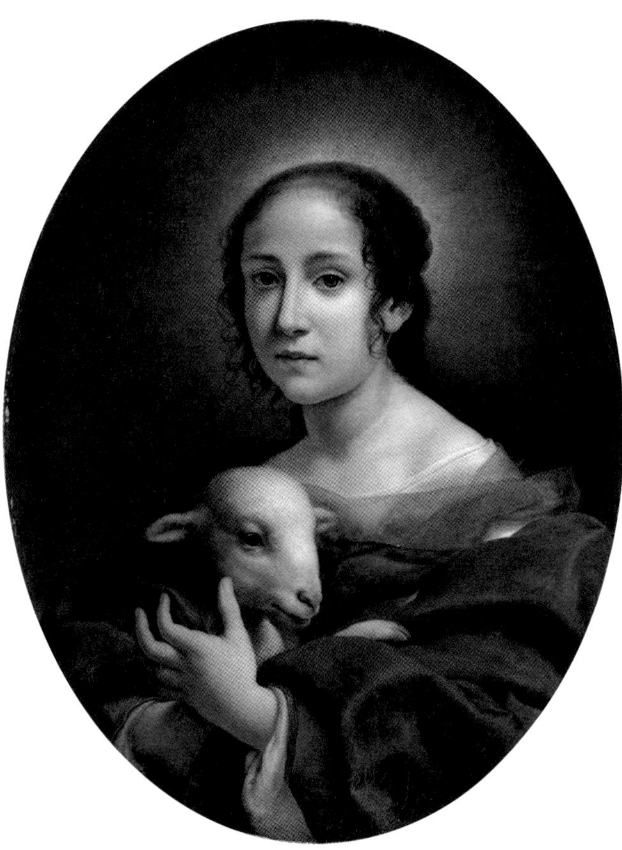

Fig. 58.2. Carlo Dolci. *Saint Agnes*, ca. 1670. Oil on canvas, 28¹⁵⁄₁₆ x 21⅞ in. (73.5 x 55.5 cm). Collection of Sir Mark Fehrs Haukohl and the Haukohl Family, Houston

face, aristocratic nose, and somewhat fuller and wider lips. And unlike the woman in those portrait drawings, she has sparsely curling bangs falling over her forehead. Even allowing for advancing years and changing styles, the physiognomic differences are pronounced enough as to make it unlikely that this young woman is Teresa Bucarelli.

An alternative conjecture advanced here is that the Tobey drawing represents not Dolci's wife, but one of his seven daughters, possibly Agnese (d. 1689), who was trained in the art of painting by her father.[3] A half-length oval painting of Saint Agnes by Dolci of about 1670—one of his numerous renditions of this hagiographic subject—self-evidently shows the same sitter (fig. 58.2), and may be based on the contemporaneous Tobey drawing. Like many of Dolci's depictions of female saints, that work has been identified as a portrait of the artist's wife,[4] though it, too, may instead represent his daughter Agnese, an apt model for portraying her honomastic saint.

LWS

1. Musée du Louvre, Paris, inv. no. 1140; Fondation Custodia, Frits Lugt Collection, Institut Néerlandais, Paris, inv. no. 7880; see, respectively, Monbeig Goguel and Viatte 1981–82, no. 114; and Thiem 1977, p. 410, no. 222. Other portrait drawings by Dolci of Teresa Bucarelli are mentioned in McCorquodale 2007– .
2. McCorquodale 1973, p. 479, with reference to Waagen 1838, vol. 3, p. 10.
3. Many of the drawings in a sketchbook in the Fitzwilliam Museum, Cambridge, England, are attributed to Agnese; see McCorquodale 1976, p. 320.
4. See Baldassari 1995, no. 133.

<h1 style="text-align:center">GIOVANNI BATTISTA BEINASCHI</h1>

Fossano (near Turin), 1636–Naples, 1688

A painter, engraver, and draftsman, Giovanni Battista Beinaschi began his career in Turin but soon moved to Rome, where he studied with the printmaker Pietro del Pò. He was deeply influenced by the illusionistic ceiling paintings of Annibale Carracci and Giovanni Lanfranco. In 1664 he relocated to Naples, where he executed frescoes and altarpieces for a number of churches, adopting aspects of the grand manner of Luca Giordano. Following a brief return to Rome in 1678, Beinaschi spent the rest of his career in Naples, where he continued to paint elaborate decorative cycles in a dramatic Baroque style and oversaw a large and industrious workshop.

59. *Studies of Angels and of a Hand*, late 1670s

Black chalk, heightened with white chalk, on blue paper, 20⅜ x 15⅛ in. (51.8 x 38.4 cm)

Provenance: Private Collection ("property of a lady"); sale, Sotheby's, New York, January 13, 1988, lot 13; sale, Sotheby's, London, July 5, 1993, lot 13

References: Nicodemi 1993, pp. 39, 42, fig. 13; Cristiana Romalli in Naples 2009–10, vol. 2, p. 99, no. 3.63, ill.

This sheet of studies depicting an angel with a lily, an extended right arm, and a figure holding a book and gazing upward belongs to a group of sixty-two drawings, many by Giovanni Battista Beinaschi, which formed part of an album believed to have been assembled in Rome in the middle of the eighteenth century. Several are academies and were probably made as studio exercises, but at least some appear to be related to paintings by the artist. Four of the figure studies show close affinities with Beinaschi's fresco *God the Father and the Virgin in Glory* in Santa Maria del Suffragio, Rome, as was noted at the time they came up at auction in 1988,[1] although it is unclear if the drawings were created with that specific composition in mind or were adapted for that purpose.

Rather exceptionally, the Tobey drawing is among the few from this group that can be directly connected with a painting by Beinaschi: it is a study for the *Annunciation* in San Bonaventura al Palatino in Rome (fig. 59.1).[2] The muscular angel with coiled curls seen in left profile extending a lily in his outstretched left hand, and the pointing right hand at the upper left, are preparatory to the figure of Gabriel, and the nude youth gazing upward to the right and holding an open book is a study for the angel supporting God the Father at the upper right of the painting.

One of three altarpieces that Beinaschi painted for San Bonaventura, the *Annunciation* was commissioned by Pellegrino Peri, a Genoese merchant who resided in Rome. The impetus for this campaign to re-outfit the interior was the acquisition of the church and adjoining convent by the Zoccalanti, a congregation of friars minor of the Franciscan order, in 1677.

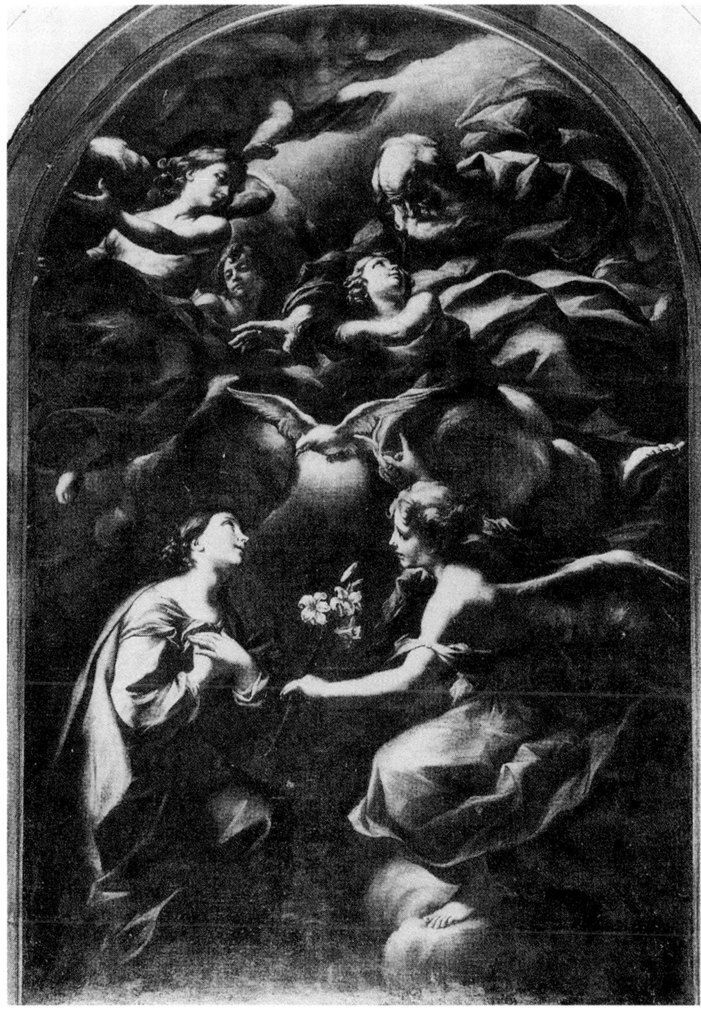

Fig. 59.1. Giovanni Battista Beinaschi. *Annunciation*, ca. 1680. Oil on canvas. San Bonaventura al Palatino, Rome

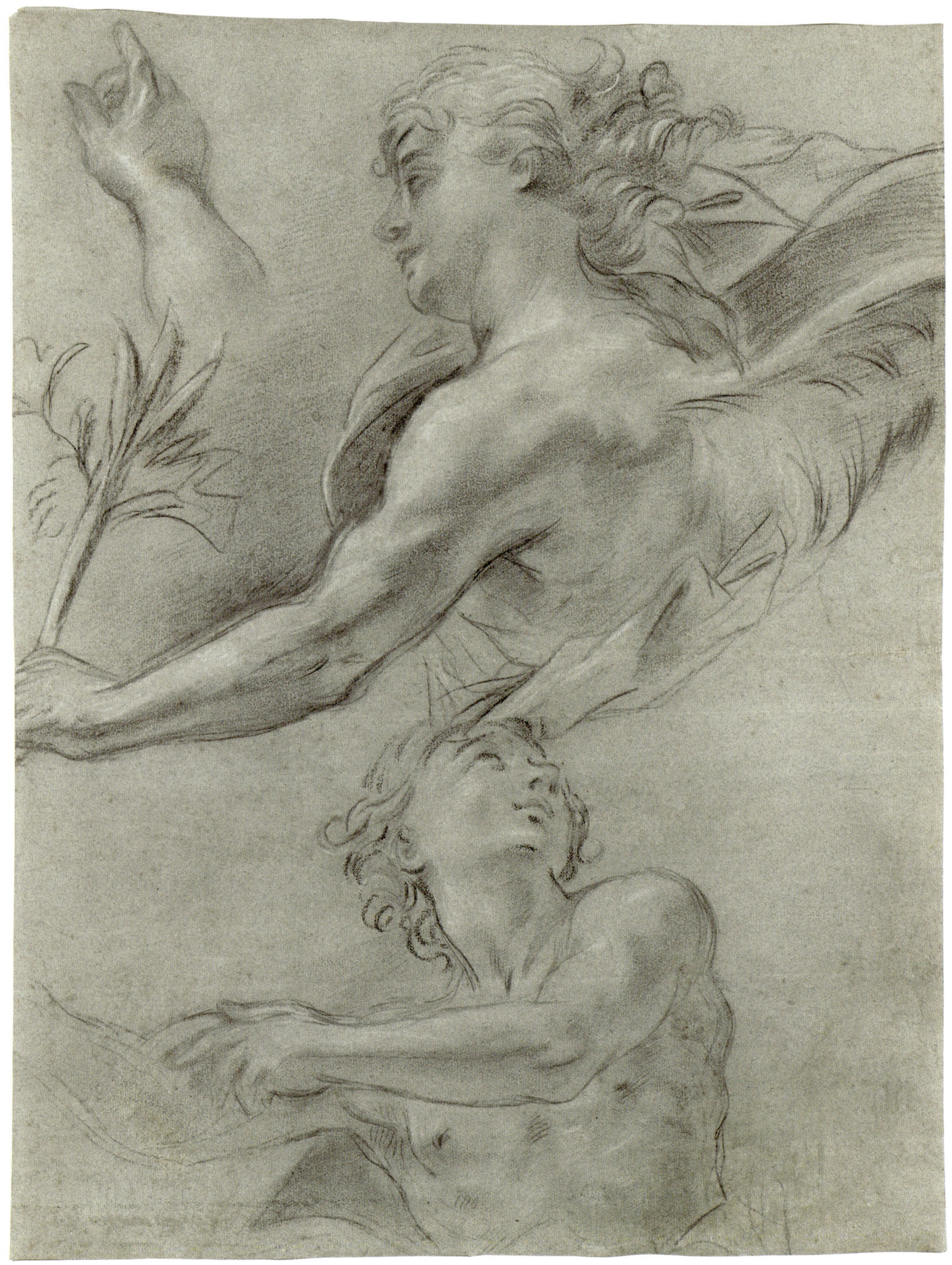

Its exact date is unknown, but the painting was begun shortly after Beinaschi's appearance in Rome the following year. The first published reference to it occurs in the 1686 edition of Filippo Titi's *Studio di pittura, scoltura, et architettura, nelle chiese di Roma*, establishing that it was completed and in place by that date. In any event, the *Annunciation*, which may be the product of a collaboration between Beinaschi and his daughter Angela,[3] was almost certainly the last work the artist executed before his departure for Naples. In Beinaschi's relatively brief second Roman period, the Tobey drawing may therefore be assigned to the late 1670s or early 1680s.

LWS

1. Sotheby's, New York, January 13, 1988, lots 8–11; illustrated in Salerno, Spezzaferro, and Tafuri 1973, fig. 244.
2. As first recognized by Nicodemi 1993, p. 39.
3. Ibid.

GIOVANNI FRANCESCO CASTIGLIONE

Genoa, 1641–Genoa, 1710

Giovanni Francesco Castiglione was the son of Giovanni Benedetto Castiglione, whose style and subject matter he thoroughly adopted as his own. Most of his paintings and drawings are pastoral scenes recalling his father's works. He also executed hunting scenes.

60. *A Rest during a Hunt*

Pen, brown ink, brown-gray and gray wash, with watercolor, 8⅛ x 12 in. (20.6 x 30.6 cm)
Annotated at lower left, in brownish-gray ink: *21*; on verso in brown ink: *Bazani di Mantova*

Provenance: Unidentified collector's mark (coat of arms) at lower left corner; Art Counselling, Ticino, Switzerland, 2000

Only a handful of drawings by Giovanni Francesco Castiglione are known, among them two examples in The Metropolitan Museum of Art, New York (figs. 60.1, 60.2); another in the Philadelphia Museum of Art; and a sheet in the Crocker Art Museum in Sacramento, California.[1] A manifold debt to the art of his father, Giovanni Benedetto Castiglione, is evident in their technique and also in the choice of pastoral scenes populated by dogs, mules, birds, and the occasional shepherd. One of the drawings in the Metropolitan, however, includes a panoply of more exotic beasts—among them, a peacock, leopard, ostrich, and lion—which has led to the suggestion that this composition, and perhaps its pendant in the same collection, may illustrate a scene from *Aesop's Fables* (fig. 60.2)[2] Inscriptions in the reliable Venetian hand on those two examples record the attribution to Francesco Castiglione; similar in style, technique, subject matter, and scale, the Tobey sheet can be securely assigned to the artist as well.

Francesco Castiglione's small painted oeuvre includes hunting scenes. The thematically related subject here is the rest during a hunt. (The hunt itself is relegated to the left background, where lightly sketched, diminutive hunters, one astride a horse, and their hounds are in fast pursuit of unseen prey.) In an amusing ironic inversion, most of the composition is given over to the gathering of mangy hounds, dead hares, and a pair of vaguely comic servants or peasants, each sporting a prodigious, floppy hat. The elderly, seemingly toothless old man is perched atop a mule, while his younger, sneering companion stands beside him, collaring an emaciated hound that nearly dwarfs him. The latter exemplifies Francesco's predilection for exaggerated, almost caricatural facial expressions.[3] It is unclear if this inelegant pair is guarding the day's catch or—seizing advantage of the unsuspecting hunters' temporary absence—preparing to make off with it in the old man's saddlebags, a plan that might account for the younger perpetrator's conspiratorial smirk.

The influence of Dutch and Flemish paintings, drawings, and prints of animals and hunting scenes—works that were readily accessible in the artist's native Genoa—has been discerned in Francesco's choice of subject matter,[4] including the present sheet. Its finished composition and the discrete application of watercolor (a favorite medium of the artist) to highlight certain details and impart a pictorial quality to the design suggest that *A Rest during a Hunt*, like other painterly drawings by both Franceso and Giovanni Benedetto, were made as independent works of art.

An annotation on the verso, *Bazani di Mantova*, presumably refers to the obscure eighteenth-century painter Giuseppe Bazzani (1690–1769), who spent extended periods in Mantua in the service of the Gonzaga and other patrons. It is possible that Bazzani was the original owner of the Tobey sheet and that the unidentified stamp at the lower left is in some way connected with him or with the Accademia di Belle Arti of Mantua, where he was a faculty member and, later, director.

LWS

1. On these and other drawings attributed to the artist, see Percy 1971, nos. 118–30.
2. Ibid., pp. 129–30, no. 121.
3. As discussed in ibid., p. 45.
4. New York 1996, under nos. 26–27.

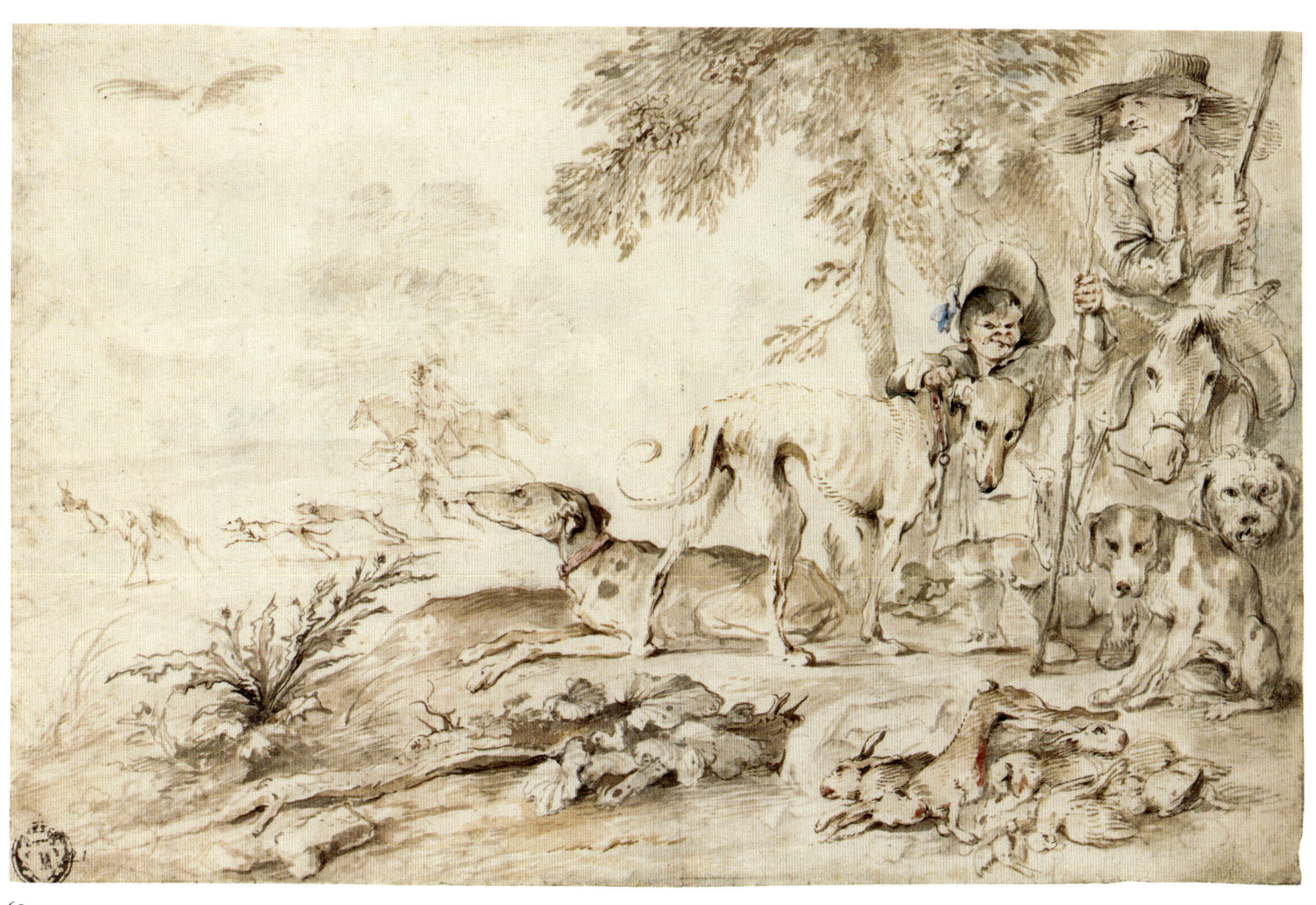

60

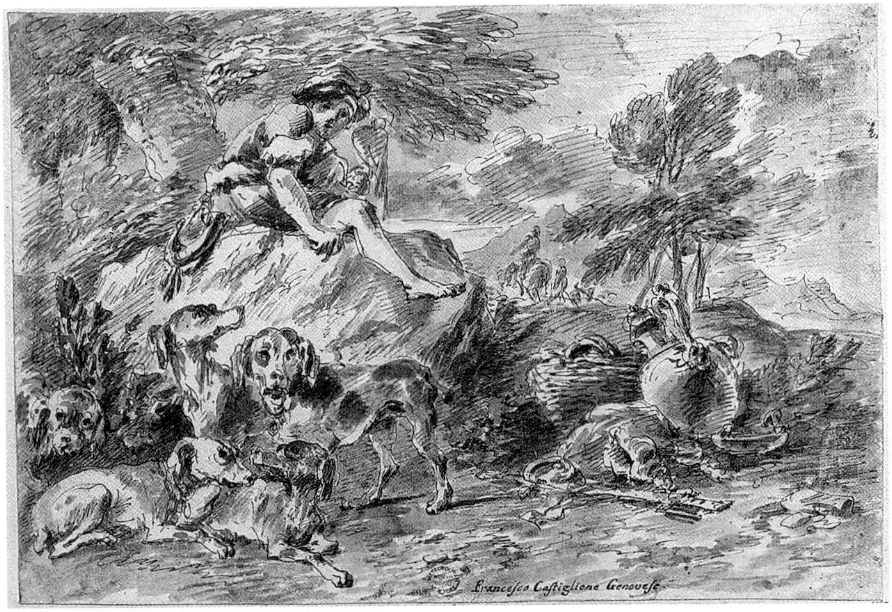

Fig. 60.1. Giovanni Francesco Castiglione. *Young Hunter with His Dogs in a Landscape*. Pen and brown ink, brush and watercolor, $8\frac{5}{16}$ x $12\frac{1}{16}$ in. (21.1 x 30.6 cm). The Metropolitan Museum of Art, New York, Rogers Fund, 1908 (08.227.24)

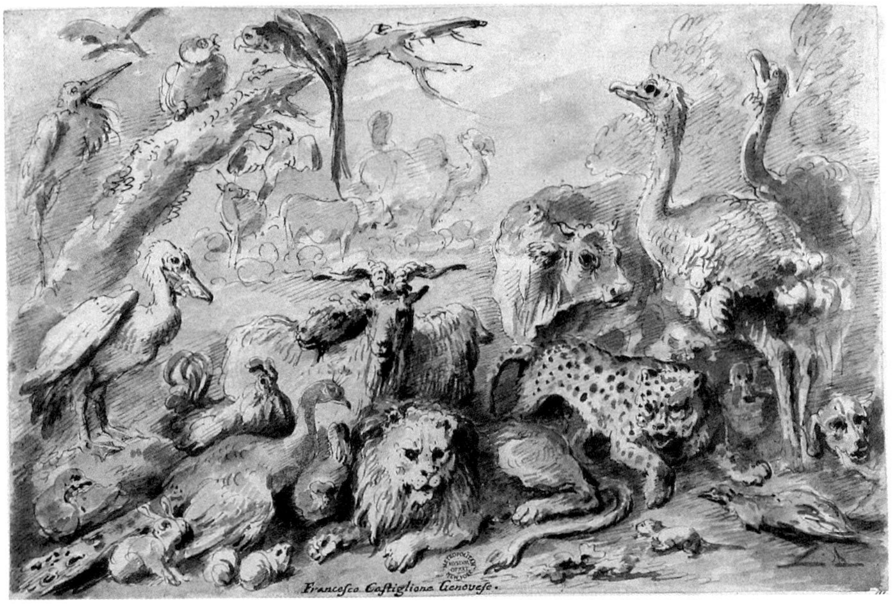

Fig. 60.2. Giovanni Francesco Castiglione. *A Congress of Animals*. Pen and brown ink, brush and watercolor, over traces of black chalk, $8\frac{1}{8}$ x $12\frac{1}{8}$ in. (20.7 x 30.8 cm). The Metropolitan Museum of Art, New York, Rogers Fund, 1908 (08.227.25)

GASPARE VANVITELLI (GASPAR VAN WITTEL)

Amersfoort, 1652/53–Rome, 1736

Dutch by birth, Gaspare Vanvitelli spent virtually his entire career in Rome, where he is first documented in 1675. He was one of the earliest vedutisti *(view painters), anticipating such eighteenth-century practitioners of the genre as Carlevarijs and Canaletto. Vanvitelli specialized in panoramic, perspectival depictions of the modern urban fabric of the city and its suburban environs rather than the evocative ruins of ancient Rome, and frequently adopted a ground-level, as opposed to bird's-eye, view, thereby approximating a spectator's real vantage point. In addition to his many depictions of Rome he also painted views of Venice, Naples, and locales in Lombardy—places he visited during his brief travels. It was Vanvitelli's practice to employ drawings he sketched on site and completed or reiterated in expanded fashion in his studio as models for painted compositions. A number of his* vedute *drawings survive. Vanvitelli was the father of the eighteenth-century architect Luigi Vanvitelli.*

61. Recto: *A View of the Roman Campagna,* ca. 1710–15
Verso: *A Partial View of the Left Side of the Farnese Palace of Caprarola*

Pen and brown ink, over black chalk; verso squared in black chalk and numbered from one to seven, and inscribed in the windows of the upper stories, 9½ x 14⅝ in. (24 x 37 cm)

Provenance: Sale, Sotheby's, London, July 8, 2004, lot 92; acquired in 2004

Designed in the mid-sixteenth century by the celebrated late Renaissance architect Jacopo Vignola and embellished with frescoes by Taddeo and Federico Zuccaro, Jacopo Bertoia, and others, the Palazzo Farnese at Caprarola stands as an enduring monument to the prestige of the Farnese family at the height of its power.[1] The building's distinctive pentagonal shape, which proceeded from its function as a *rocca*, or fortified palace; its rigorously ordered, classical architectural lexicon; and its beautiful gardens, made Caprarola a much-admired site on the road from Florence to Rome. Vanvitelli portrayed one of its facades and the surrounding landscape in a number of works, both drawings and paintings, executed in the 1710s, in each case adopting the particular view recorded on the verso of this important double-sided sheet.

This study of Caprarola was presumably made on the site, as the careful measurements and notations in the artist's hand confirm. It almost certainly served as the model for Vanvitelli's painted depictions of the villa, and perhaps also for the more pictorial, finished drawing of the same subject at Chatsworth (fig. 61.1); signed and dated 1713, the latter would have been worked up in the studio on the basis of this more perfunctory design, or one of the painted iterations of this particular *veduta*.[2]

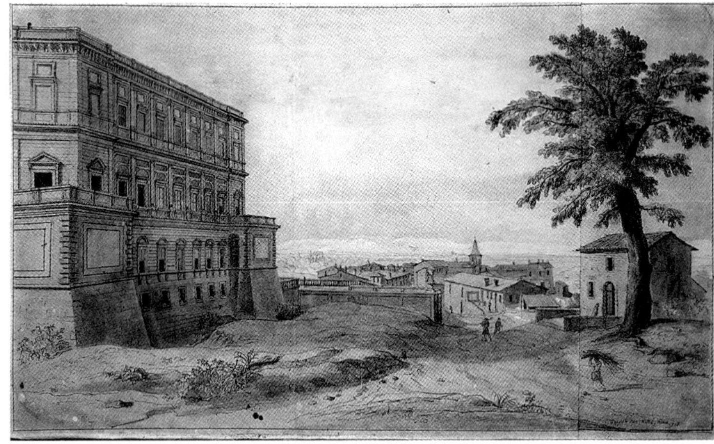

Fig. 61.1. Gaspare Vanvitelli (Gaspar van Wittel). *View of Caprarola*, 1713. Pen and brown ink, brown wash. Devonshire Collection, Chatsworth (114)

The charming landscape on the recto, in which the gently rolling hills, graceful trees, and typical rustic edifice of the Roman *campagna* are rendered with confident and fluent strokes of the pen, was probably inspired by the rural countryside around Caprarola. LWS

1. On Caprarola, see Jestaz 1994, pp. 35–48. Caprarola provided the model for the Pentagon in Washington, D.C., while its harmonious garden loggia spawned numerous offspring, among them the William L. Clements Library of the University of Michigan in Ann Arbor.
2. For Vanvitelli's *vedute* of Caprarola, see Briganti 1996, pp. 216–17, nos. 232–37 (four canvases and two gouaches); and pp. 325–26, no. D110.

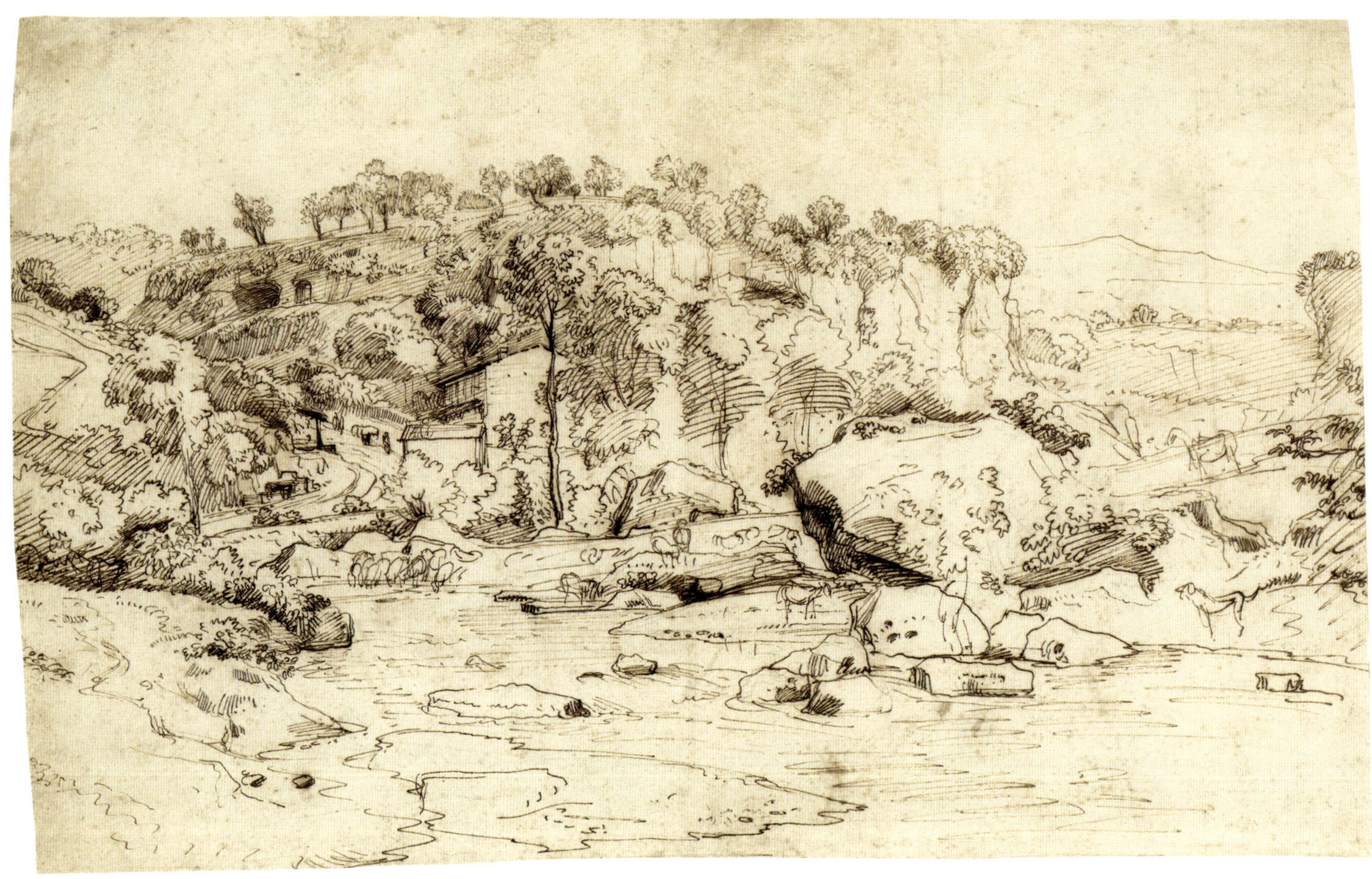

61

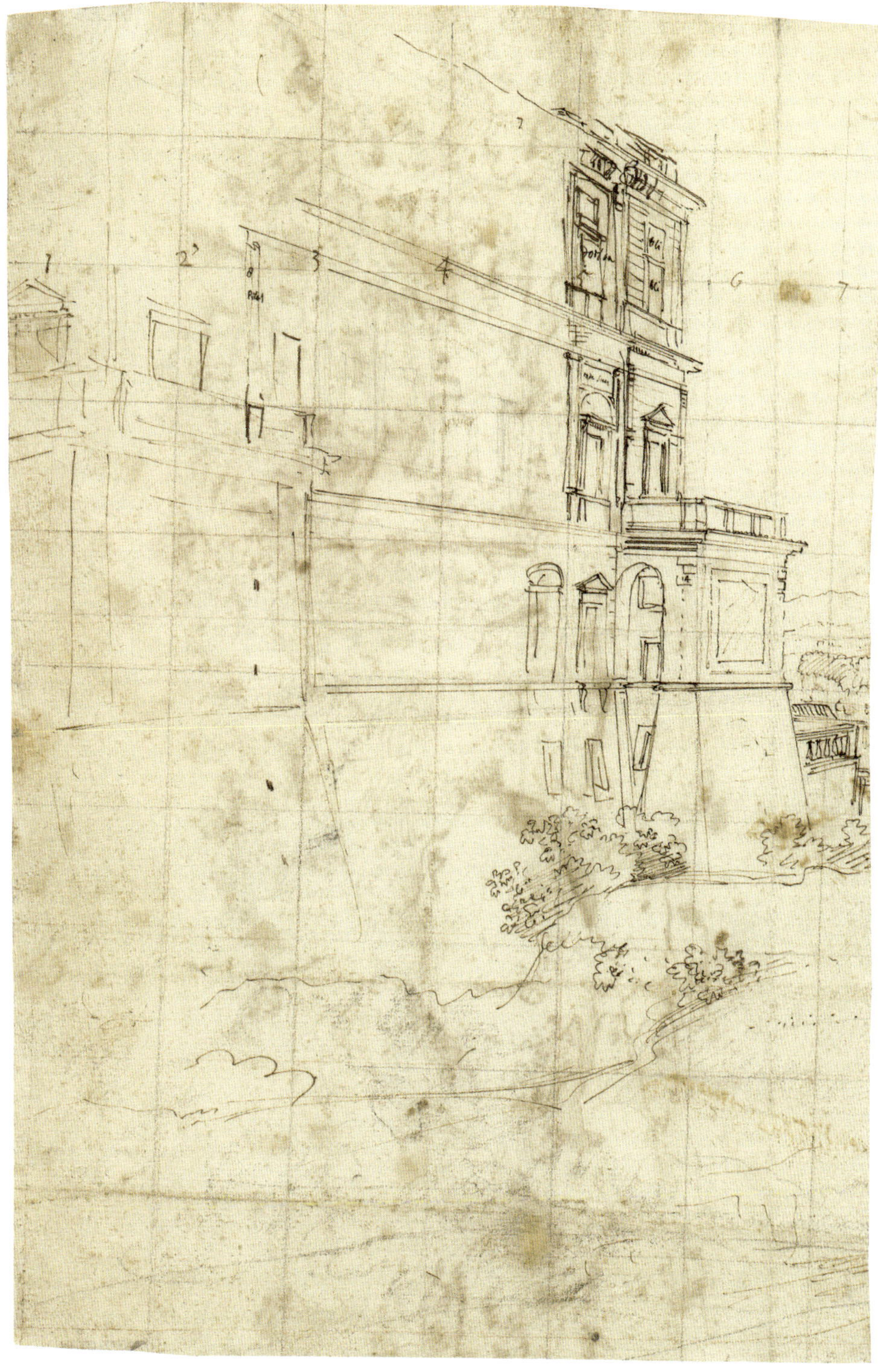

61 verso

Luca Carlevarijs was the innovator of the tradition of vedute *painting in eighteenth-century Venice. Like Canaletto—for whom Carlevarijs's paintings and prints were of singular significance—he produced both paintings and prints recording the urban topography of Venice and its inhabitants. His important series of engravings,* Le fabriche e vedute di Venetia, *consisting of 104 views of Venice, the most extensive visual record of the city undertaken before the advent of photography, was upheld as a model for later* vedutisti.

62. *The Palazzo Grimani on the Grand Canal, Venice,* ca. 1700–1702

Pen and brown ink, black chalk, gray wash, the outlines incised for transfer, 7⅜ x 7½ in. (18.6 x 19 cm)

Provenance: John Strange (d. 1799), Venice(?); sale, Christie's, London, March 1800(?); sale, Christie's, New York, January 30, 1998, lot 122

John Strange, the British Resident (envoy) in Venice from 1773 to 1788, pronounced Luca Carlevarijs "the first of any note who painted views of Venice."[1] One of his earliest efforts as a *vedutista* was a series of 104 etchings of the principal edifices of Venice, *Le fabriche e vedute di Venetia*, dedicated to Doge Alvise Mocenigo and published in 1703. Inspired by the Roman printmaker Giovanni Battista Falda's vastly influential *Nuovo teatro delle fabriche et edificii . . . di Roma moderna* published four decades earlier, Carlevarijs's *Fabriche* was intended primarily as a visual record and testimonial for foreigners of the architectural magnificence of the Serenissima. Like the artist's painted *vedute*, this ambitious undertaking—a descriptive, detailed, and panoramic compilation of the urban topography of Venice that has been described as the "Magna Carta of Venetian View Painting"[2]—became the model for the eighteenth-century Venetian printmakers who followed in Carlevarijs's path, among them Canaletto, Antonio Visentini, author of a series of etched views of Venice after paintings by Canaletto, and Michele Marieschi, who, like Carlevarijs, recorded the architectural fabric of the lagoon city in both paintings and prints.[3]

Preparatory to one of the etchings in the *Fabriche* (fig. 62.1), the Tobey drawing shows the Palazzo Grimani (later known as the Palazzo Vendramin-Calergi) on the Grand Canal (fig. 62.2).

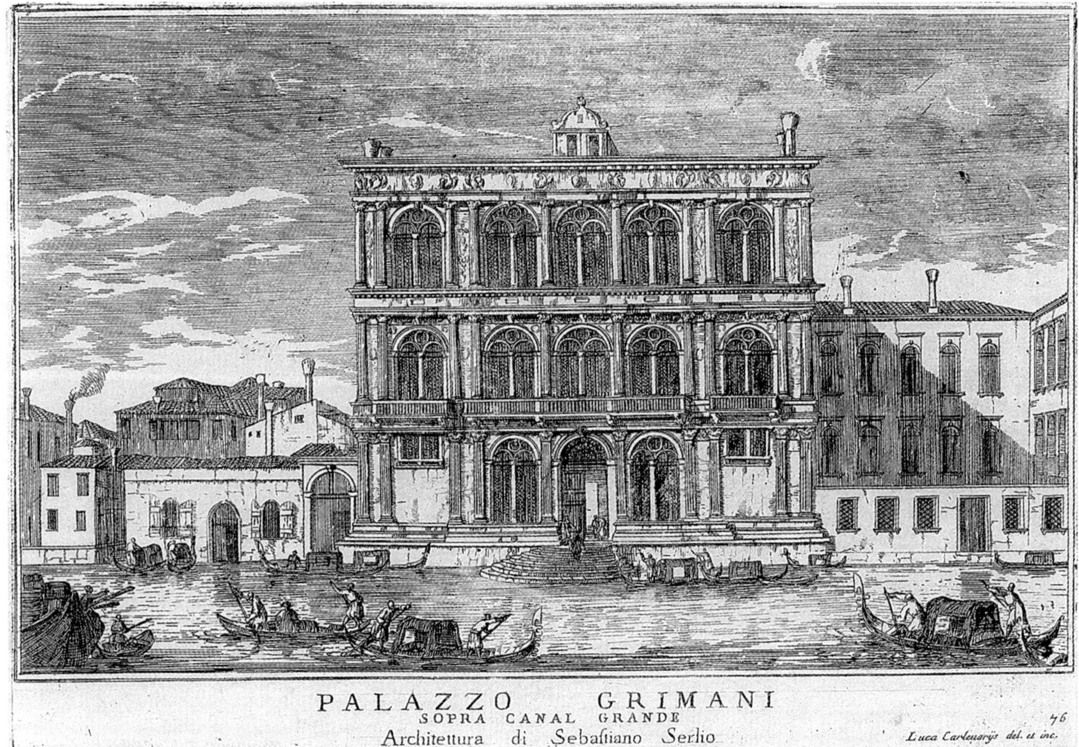

Fig. 62.1. Luca Carlevarijs. *Palazzo Grimani*, from *Le fabriche e vedute di Venetia*, 1703. Etching, 10¾ x 15½ in. (27.3 x 39.4 cm). The Metropolitan Museum of Art, New York, The Elisha Whittelsey Collection, The Elisha Whittelsey Fund, 1957 (57.618)

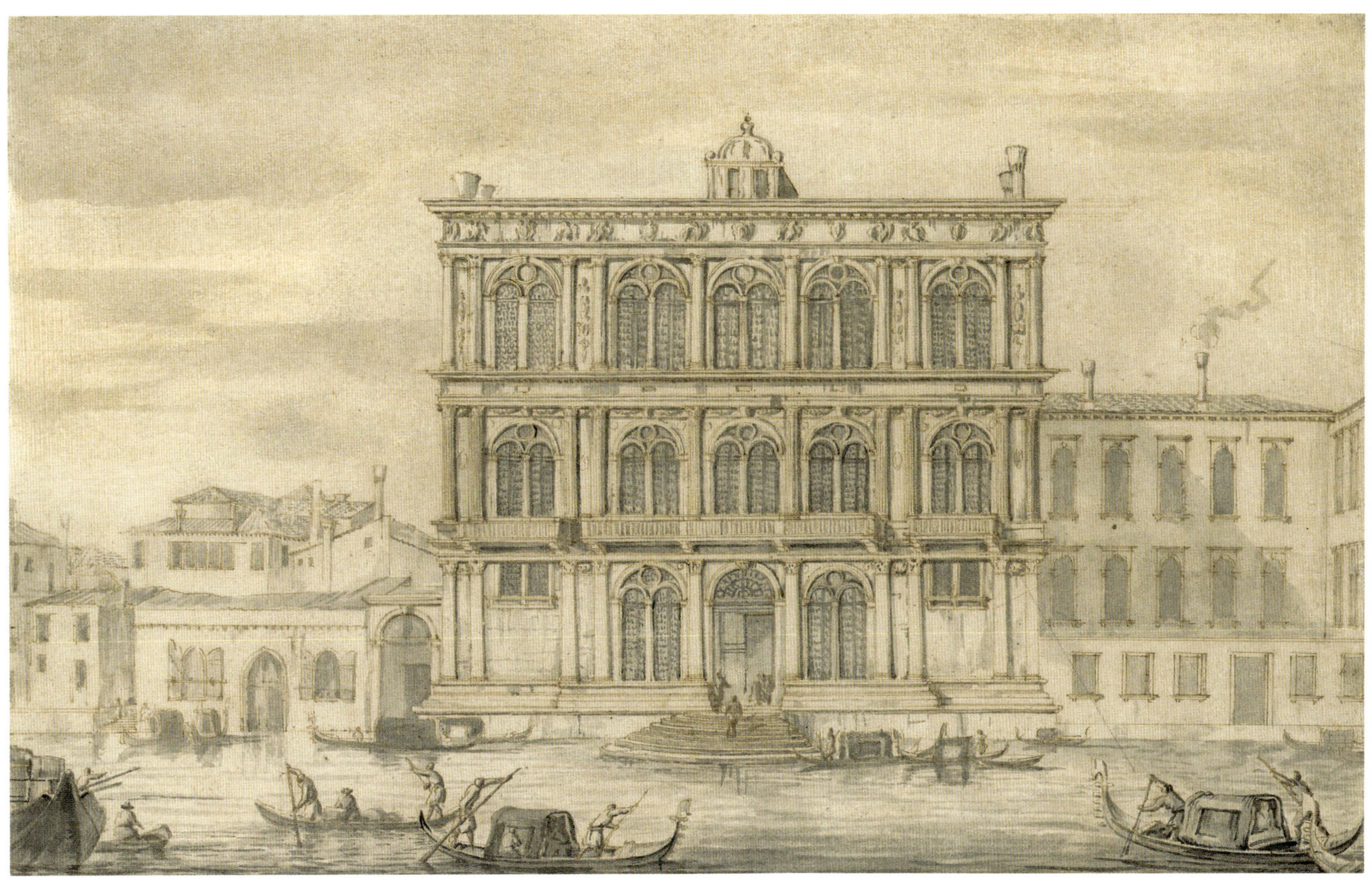

62

This elegant, imposing, and widely admired Renaissance palace, commissioned by Andrea Loredan in the late fifteenth century, was designed by the Venetian architect Mauro Codussi (and not by Sebastiano Serlio, as the inscription on the print erroneously states). The German composer Richard Wagner occupied the piano nobile of the Palazzo Grimani in 1882 and died there the following year, a historical event commemorated in a poetic verse by Gabriele D'Annunzio:

> *In questo palagio / l'ultimo spiro di Riccardo Wagner / odono le anime perpetuarsi come la marea / che lambe i marmi.* (In this palace / the souls hear / the last breath of Richard Wagner / perpetuating itself like the tide / which washes the marble beneath.)[4]

As the frontispiece of the *Fabriche* and the inscription at the lower right of each plate indicate, Carlevarijs both designed the compositions and made the etchings. The outlines of the Tobey drawing are incised, indicating that he used this sheet, which corresponds in size to the print, as the model for etching the plate (number 76 in the series). Virtually every detail of the meticulously rendered architecture and staffage of gondolas and diminutive figures recorded in the drawing is faithfully translated, the print differing only in the addition of the cast shadow that falls across the facade of the Palazzo Grimani to the viewer's right and the plume of smoke issuing from the chimney at the far left.

A number of Carlevarijs's drawings for *Le fabriche e vedute di Venetia* are preserved in the British Museum, London, having been acquired in 1886 (as the work of Canaletto) from the collection of a Lord de Mauley.[5] These had earlier belonged to John Strange, who must have acquired them during his residency in Venice, and were sold at auction in London in 1800 following his death the previous year. The present drawing was presumably separated from this group sometime before 1866. Listed as a "dessin manqué" in Aldo Rizzi's 1967 monograph on Carlevarijs, it resurfaced at auction a dozen years ago.[6]

LWS

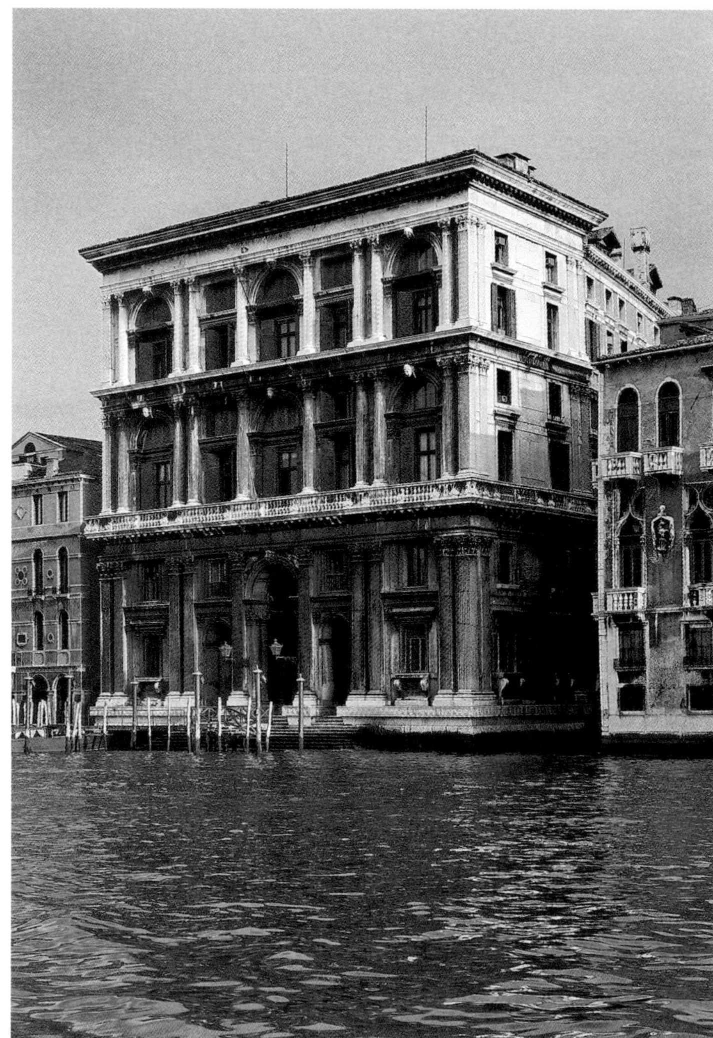

Fig. 62.2. Palazzo Grimani on the Grand Canal, Venice

1. The artist is so described in *A Descriptive Catalogue of a Genuine and Capital Collection of Italian Pictures, . . . particularly of the Venetian and Lombard Schools* (London 1789, p. 14, lot 30 [Carlevarijs, *La Piazza de' Signori, Padua*]).
2. Pallucchini, R. 1967, pp. 537–38.
3. See Succi 1994; London and Washington, D.C., 1994–95, p. 444, no. 24; Concina and Reale 1995–96; and Beddington 2001, pp. 13–16.
4. Quoted and translated in Grimbert 1995, p. 401.
5. Inv. no. 1886.1012.596. The drawings are bound in an album containing eighty-six leaves, titled VEDUTE / DI / VENEZIA. DISEGNI / ORIGINALI.
6. Rizzi 1967, p. 99.

ALESSANDRO MAGNASCO

Genoa, 1667–Genoa, 1749

Alessandro Magnasco worked in Milan, employed by some of the city's most prominent and culturally sophisticated aristocratic families, and in Florence before returning to his native Genoa in 1735. He often collaborated with other artists, painting figures into landscapes and architectural scenes. Although he executed a few altarpieces, his favorite subjects were monks, nuns, witches, hunters, and woodsmen, set in nocturnal, vaguely ominous, mysteriously illuminated landscapes or interiors. Such works were appreciated by private collectors and reflect Magnasco's engagement with some of the intellectual debates of his day. His graphic oeuvre consists almost entirely of figure studies, with many of the same types who populate his paintings recurring in his drawings.

63. *Three Men Lifting a Tree and One Man Stripping the Bark Off a Log,* ca. 1710s

Black chalk, brush and brown wash, heightened with white, 8⅛ x 16⅝ in. (20.6 x 42.3 cm)
Inscribed at upper left, in brown ink, presumably in the artist's hand: *26.*

Provenance: Stephen Spector, New York; sale, Christie's, New York, January 30, 1997, lot 68

Alessandro Magnasco created a "varied dictionary of *macchiette*"[1]—sketches of humble figures, often portrayed in groups of three or four, akin to those who populate some of his paintings. Among the stock characters are brigands, woodsmen, hunters, washerwomen, monks, and fishermen. A typical example of this type of drawing is the Tobey sheet, which depicts four men frenetically felling and hauling trees, executed in the artist's nervous, quivering graphic style. Woodsmen provided the subject matter of a number of similar drawings by Magnasco, among them a sheet in the Istituto Nazionale per la Grafica, Rome;[2] another in the Civico Gabinetto dei Disegni di Castello Sforzesco, Milan;[3] and two further examples in the Gabinetto Disegni e Stampe di Palazzo Rosso, Genoa.[4] One of the latter pair, a similar study of four woodsmen (fig. 63.2), has been assigned to the first decade of the eighteenth century. Executed in pen and brown ink with brown wash and white heightening, with the same thick contour lines, it is stylistically close to the Tobey drawing, which probably dates from roughly the same moment.

Several of Magnasco's *macchiette* are inscribed with a number, typically at the upper left of the sheet, as here. The same number appears on more than one drawing; both the Tobey sheet and the thematically related sketch of a man carrying a tree in the Castello Sforzesco in Milan, cited above, bear the identifying numeration *26,* as does another sheet that appeared at auction at the same time as this study of woodsmen.[5] A plausible explanation for this repetition is that Magnasco grouped the *macchiette* by subject matter, often (if not always) assigning the same number to drawings depicting similar types of figures and activities.[6]

Many of Magnasco's poetic, often enigmatic and vaguely tempestuous landscapes are the domain of lively figures engaged in the same activities recorded in the *macchiette,* for example, a canvas in the Muzeum Narodowe, Cracow, in which laundresses and woodsmen energetically carry out their respective, unrelated labors (fig. 63.1).[7] The assemblage of *macchiette* probably functioned in the artist's workshop as a repertoire of stock figures and vignettes that could be incorporated into such painted compositions.   LWS

1. Franchini Guelfi 1999, p. 98, under no. 7.
2. Inv. no. F.N. 12409; see Milan 1996, pp. 300–301, no. 100.
3. Inv. no. 4159; Franchini Guelfi 1999, no. 20.
4. Inv. nos. 2462, 2459; Franchini Guelfi 1999, nos. 7–8. The first, a study of four woodsmen that Franchini Guelfi dates to the 1710s, is stylistically and thematically close to the Tobey drawing, as noted here.
5. Christie's, New York, January 30, 1997, lot 69.
6. As proposed by Mary Newcome in Milan 1996, p. 300, under no. 100.
7. Milan 1996, pp. 212–14, no. 56.

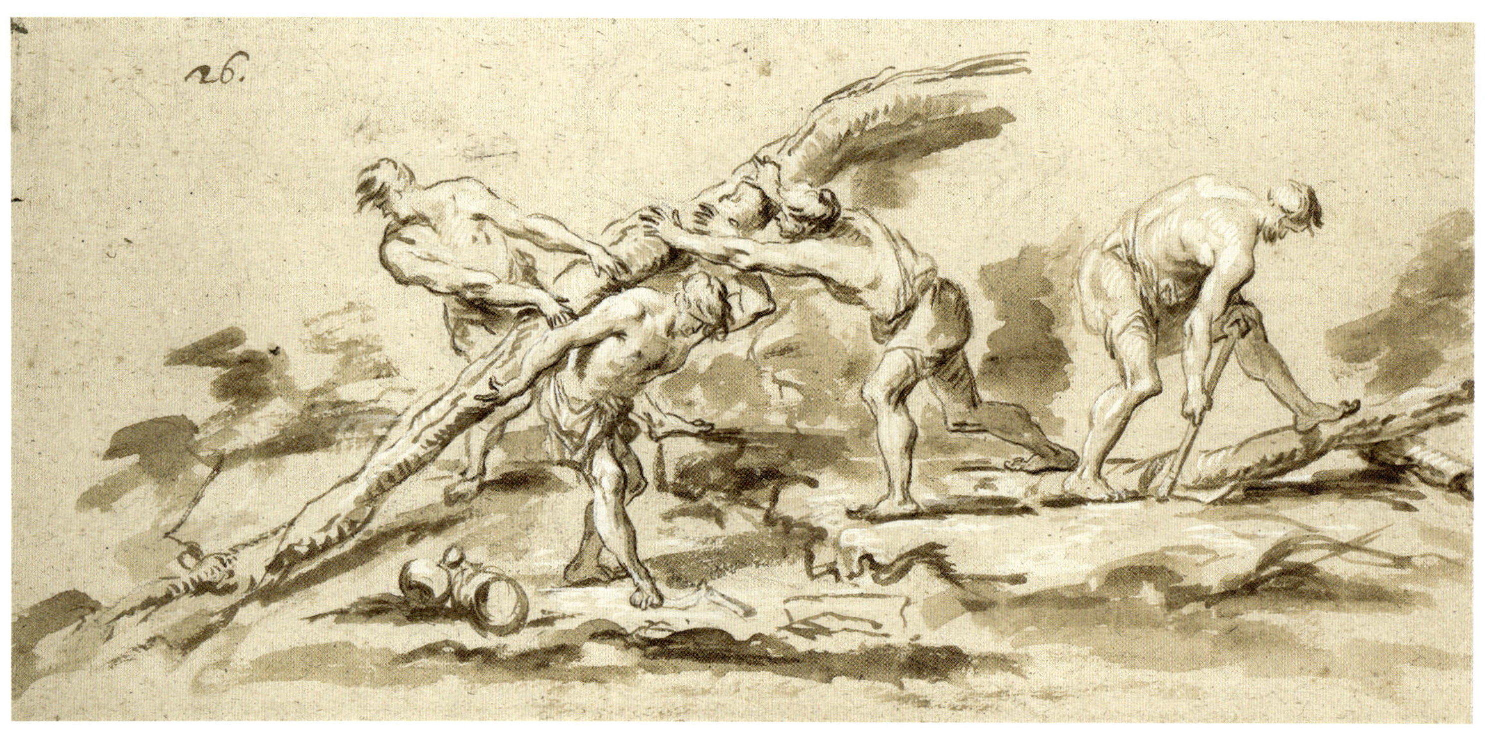

63

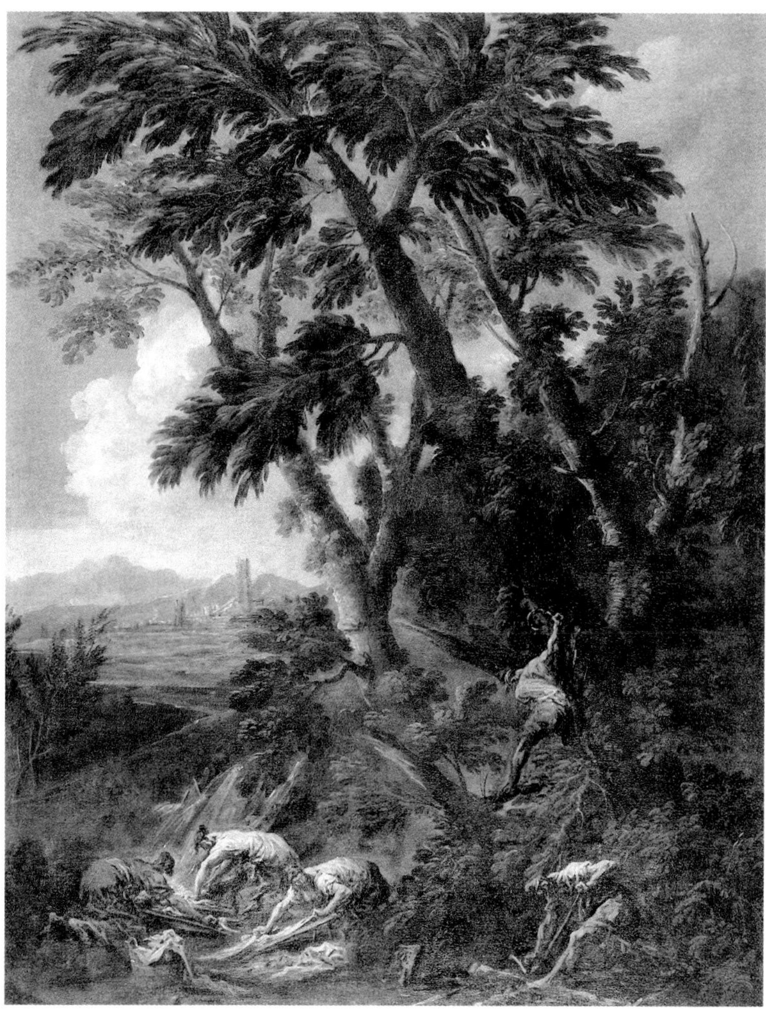

Fig. 63.1. Alessandro Magnasco. *Landscape with Washerwomen and Woodsmen*. Oil on canvas, 6 ft. 4⅞ in. x 4 ft. 5¾ in. (195 x 144 cm). Muzeum Narodowe, Cracow (XIIa 116)

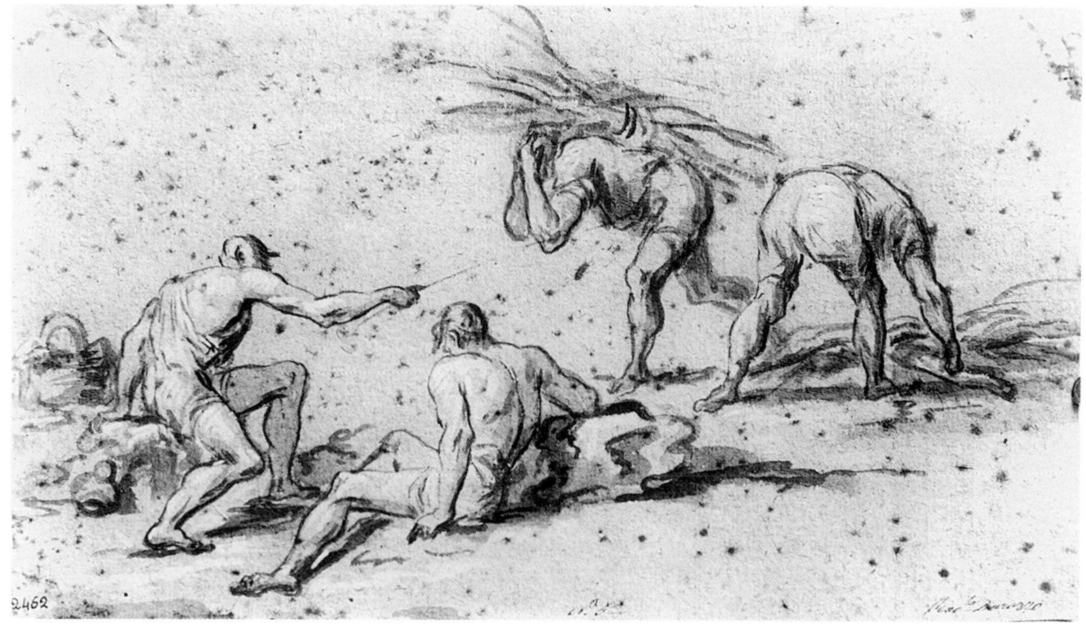

Fig. 63.2. Alessandro Magnasco. *Four Woodsmen*, ca. 1710s. Brush and brown wash, 7½ x 12⅝ in. (19 x 32 cm). Gabinetto Disegni e Stampe di Palazzo Rosso, Genoa (D 2462)

GIOVANNI BATTISTA TIEPOLO

Venice, 1696–Madrid, 1770

Giovanni Battista Tiepolo was the most celebrated Italian painter of the eighteenth century. His sparkling, light-drenched, allegorical and narrative frescoes covering vast expanses of walls and ceilings and populated by elaborate casts of expressively gesturing protagonists and attentively watchful bystanders—elegantly attired and coiffed, bearded, turbaned, bejeweled—represent the culmination of the Venetian Grand Manner of Titian and Veronese. His art was admired across Europe, prompting invitations to the artist from royal patrons to work in Wurzburg and Madrid, in addition to the many commissions he received for frescoes and altarpieces in churches and palaces around the Veneto and Lombardy. Tiepolo also painted mythological scenes, subjects drawn from epic poetry, and devotional images representing the Virgin and Child, the Holy Family, and saints, and was a master of the oil sketch, creating small-scale, painterly studies as a preliminary step preceding the execution of a finished work of art. His prodigious powers of invention are equally manifest in his two brilliant series of etchings, the Scherzi di Fantasia *and the* Capricci, *and in his drawings in both chalk and pen and ink, which take up the same range of subject matter as his immense painted oeuvre.*

64. *Caesar Shown the Severed Head of Pompey*, ca. 1743–45

Pen and brown ink, brown wash, over black chalk, 8⅛ x 11⅝ in. (20.6 x 29.4 cm)

Provenance: Sale, Sotheby's, New York, January 16, 1986, lot 147; Dr. Carlo Croce; sale, Christie's, London, July 6, 1993, lot 91

References: Barcham 1992, p. 86, under no. 20; Weber 1996, pp. 183–84; Wurzburg 1996, vol. 1, no. 94

In 1743, the cultivated, erudite, and well-traveled Venetian diplomat Francesco Algarotti commissioned a painting from Giovanni Battista Tiepolo for Augustus III, king of Poland and elector of Saxony. Algarotti had been charged with acquiring

art for the royal collection in Dresden and set about assembling works representing a variety of genres—history scenes, animal paintings, *vedute*—by the premier modern artists of the day. Foremost among the history painters he commended was Tiepolo, who was asked to represent a gory scene from Roman antiquity: Caesar presented with the head of his decapitated rival Pompey. The literary source of the unusual and rarely portrayed subject was Plutarch's *Lives*:

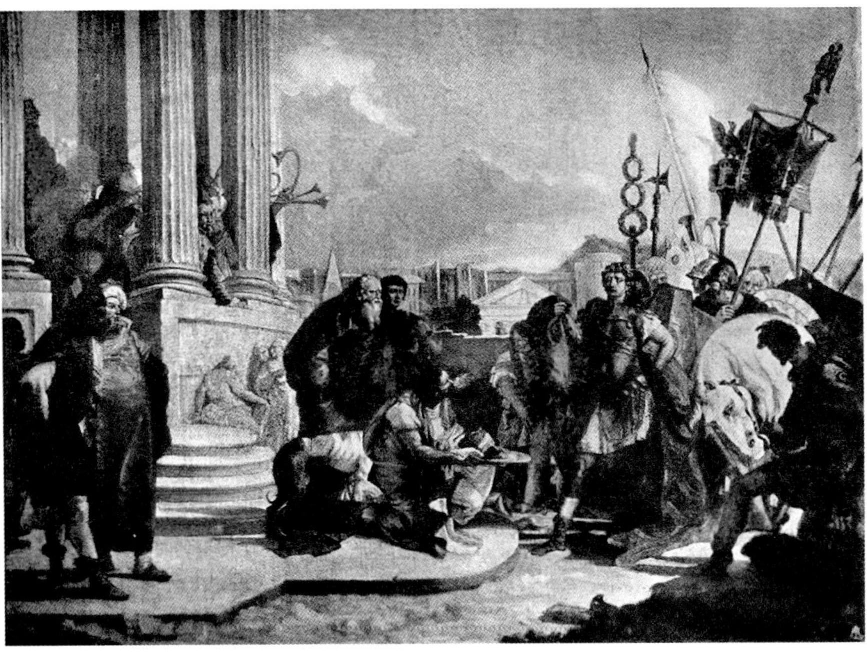

Fig. 64.1. Giovanni Battista Tiepolo. *Caesar Contemplates the Severed Head of Pompey*, 1744. Oil on canvas, 21⅝ x 28⅜ in. (55 x 72 cm). Formerly Giusti Collection, Modena

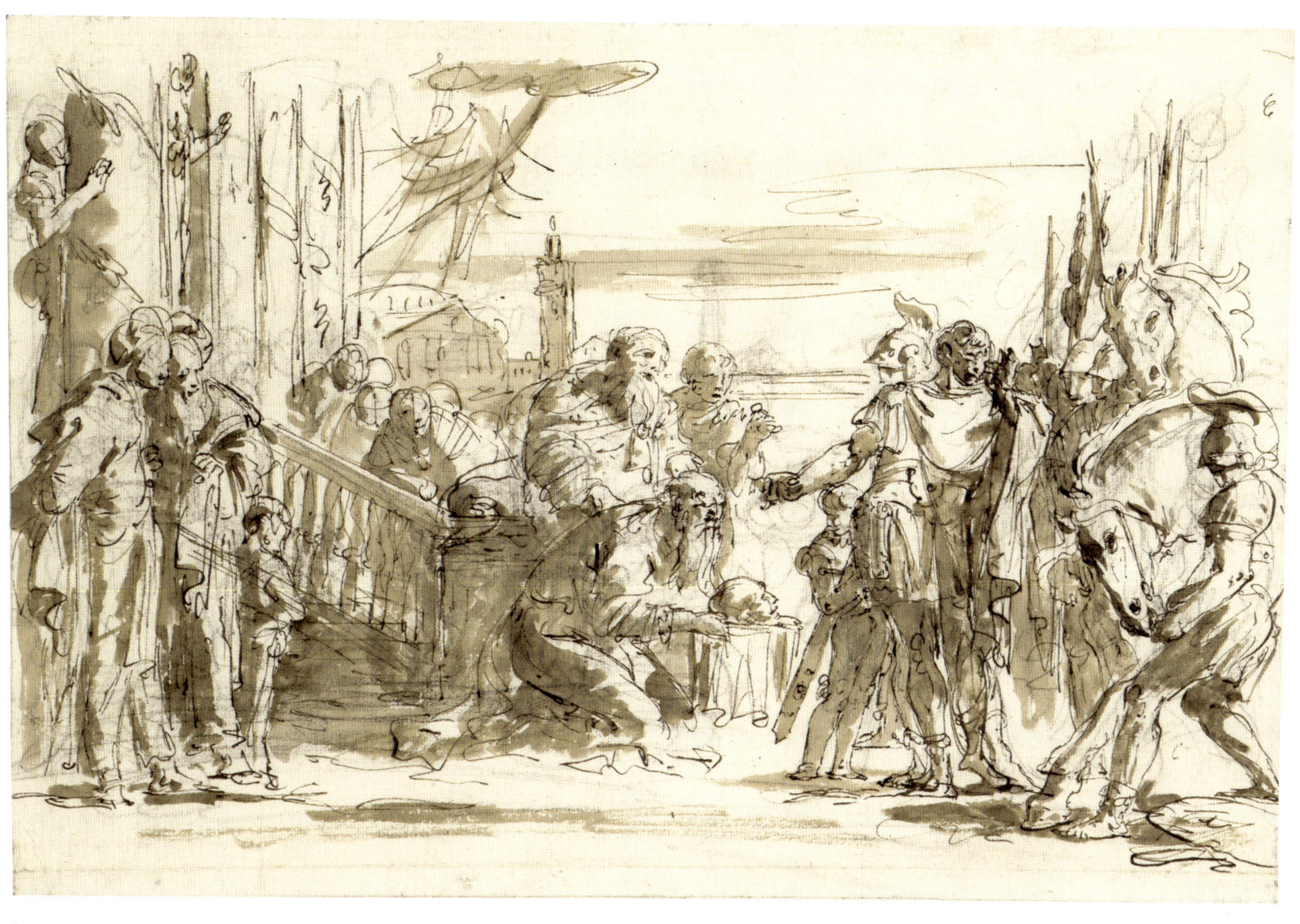

64

Arriving at Alexandria just after Pompey's death, [Caesar] turned away in horror from Theodotus as he presented the head of Pompey, but he accepted Pompey's seal-ring, and shed tears over it. Moreover, all the companions and intimates of Pompey who had been captured by the king as they wandered over the country, he treated with kindness and attached them to himself. And to his friends in Rome he wrote that this was the greatest and sweetest pleasure that he derived from his victory, namely, from time to time to save the lives of fellow citizens who had fought against him (Book VII, chapter 48: 2–4).[1]

Now lost, the painting was delivered in 1746.[2] An untraced *modello* by the artist, completed in 1744 and also lost, is known through an old photograph (fig. 64.1).[3] The Tobey sheet, which records the same composition as the lost sketch with minor differences, is the only surviving record of Tiepolo's invention. A rare type of drawing in his graphic oeuvre (few full composition studies by Tiepolo exist), it was unknown before it appeared at auction in 1986.

The events recounted by Plutarch took place in Alexandria in Egypt; accordingly, Algarotti specified that Tiepolo's scene was to be set in "una piazza di Alessandria."[4] That locus is vaguely invoked by the hastily sketched, arch-topped structure with a minaret seen in the distant left background, which recalls the mosque in Gentile Bellini's monumental canvas,

Saint Mark Preaching in Alexandria—an authoritative if somewhat fanciful portrayal of an exotic Oriental setting. (The artist had traveled to Constantinople in 1479.) That nod to historical geography aside, the balustrade and colonnade at the left instead recall the familiar, Veronese-inspired architectural settings of Tiepolo's many ancient history scenes. Also typical of Tiepolo is the chorus of onlookers and bystanders, who in this case may represent the members of Pompey's retinue whom the victorious Caesar, according to Plutarch, befriended. That laudable display of princely magnanimity occurred after he was presented with his rival's severed head—the moment captured here by Tiepolo. Averting his eyes as he turns away, and shielding his gaze with his upraised hand, Caesar recoils in horror at the sight of the gruesome offering, his expressive gesture providing the formal and dramatic fulcrum of the composition. While the opportunity to portray a moment of high drama undoubtedly appealed to both Tiepolo and Algarotti, this particular episode from the life of Caesar may well have been chosen as a worthy ancient exemplum for the modern-day Augustus Caesar for whom it was commissioned.   LWS

1. Plutarch ed. 1919, pp. 555–57.
2. On the commission and the lost canvas, which measured approximately 53⅛ x 72⅞ in. (135 x 185 cm), see Precerutti Garberi 1958. See also Levey 1986, pp. 127–28.
3. Formerly Giusti Collection, Modena; see Precerutti Garberi 1958, fig. 1; and Gemin and Pedrocco 1993, p. 362, no. 299.
4. Quoted in Levey 1986, p. 128.

65. *Family Group*, late 1750s

Pen and brown ink, brown wash, over black chalk, 9½ x 13½ in. (24.1 x 34.3 cm)

The Metropolitan Museum of Art, New York, Promised Gift of David M. Tobey

Provenance: Private Collection; Wildenstein, New York; acquired in 1999

References: Byam Shaw 1962, under no. 70; Rizzi and Morassi 1965, under no. 116; Knox 1970, no. 95; Morassi 1970, p. 299; Bean and Stampfle 1971, p. 64, under no. 149; Pallucchini, A. 1971, under no. 64; Stampfle and Denison 1973, p. 48, under no. 77; Knox 1975, p. 54, under no. 85; Gealt 1986, p. 182 n. 2, under no. 83; Aikema and Dreyer 1996–97, under no. 72; Knox 1996–97, p. 34, ill., and p. 39

Giovanni Battista Tiepolo produced three studies of this unidentified family group in a villa garden—the Tobey drawing; a sheet formerly in the Heinemann Collection and now in the Morgan Library and Museum, New York (fig. 65.1),[1] and a third drawing in the Museo della Fondazione Horne, Florence, on deposit in the Uffizi.[2] It has been suggested that the sitters are members of the Pisani family.[3] In 1760, Tiepolo was commissioned to execute frescoes at their villa in Strà, work on which he was engaged from 1761 to 1762. His allegorical ceiling fresco includes likenesses of several family members, among them Alvise Pisani and his wife.

The Tobey drawing and the two similar sheets do not relate to that particular decoration, but it is possible that Tiepolo intended to paint a group portrait of the Pisani family comparable to that executed by Pietro Longhi in 1759.[4] It is probably not a coincidence that Tiepolo's designs (which are

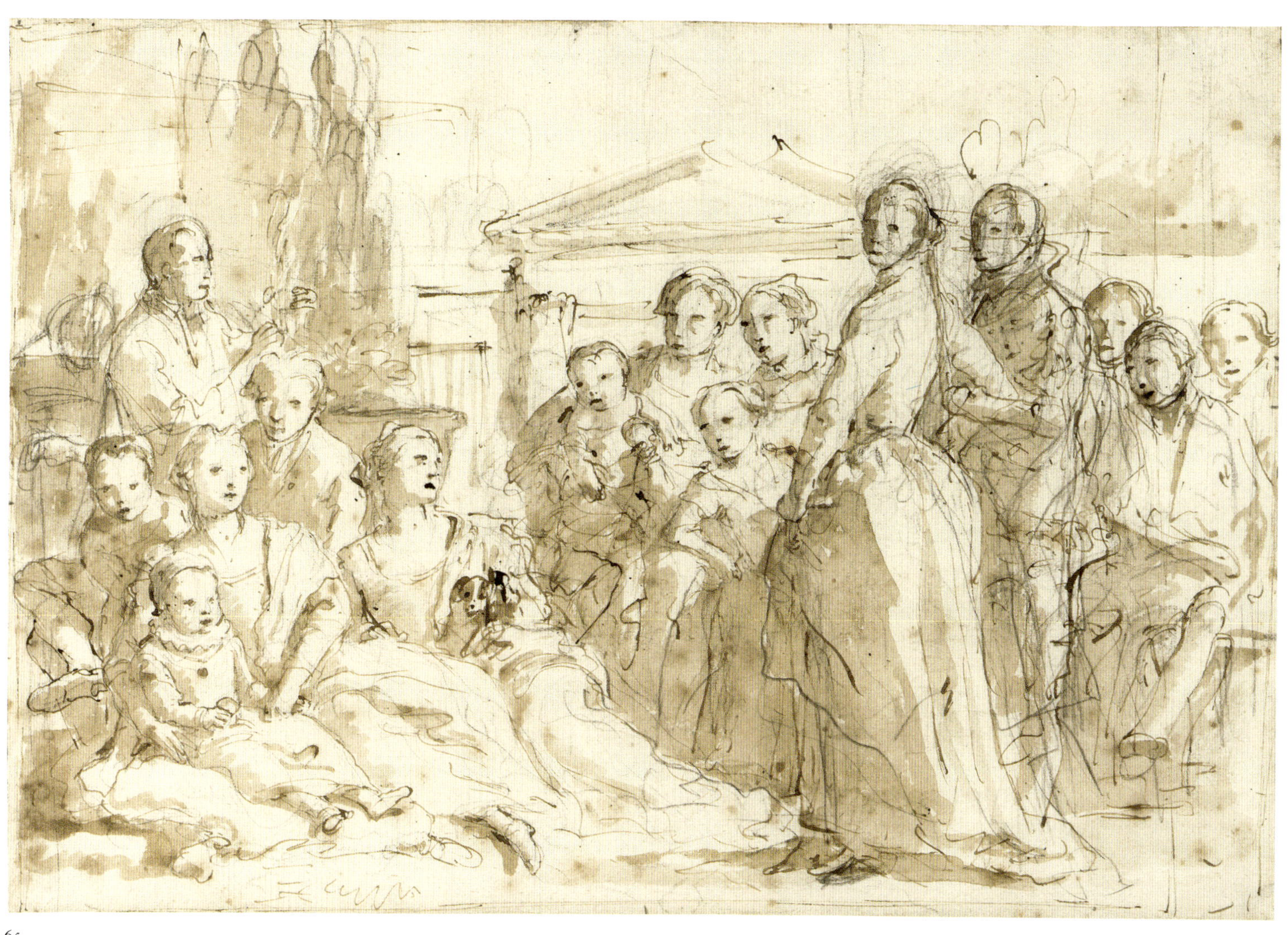

65

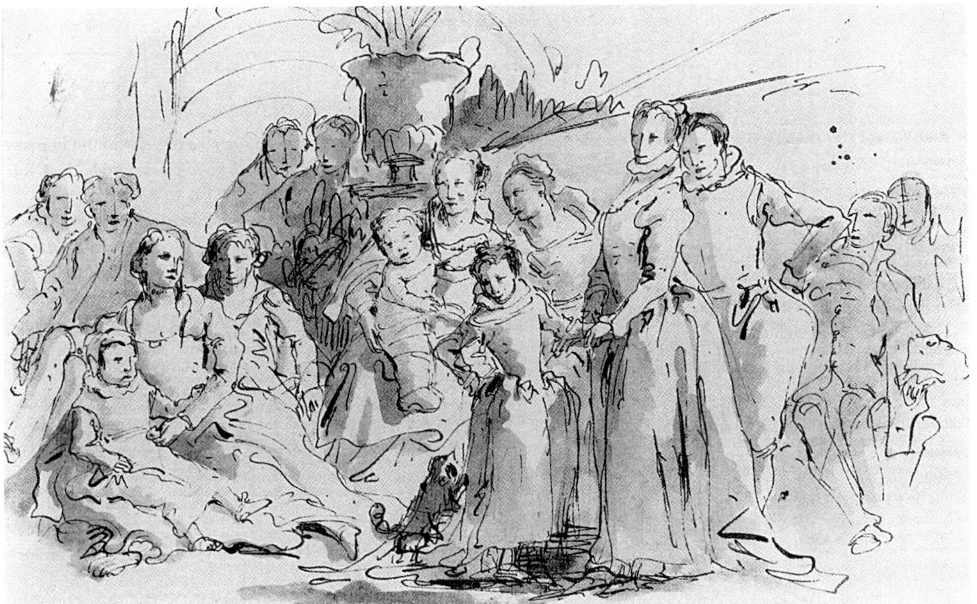

Fig. 65.1. Giovanni Battista Tiepolo. *Family Group*, late 1750s. Pen and brown ink, gray and brown wash, over black chalk, 10⅞ x 16½ in. (27.7 x 41.8 cm). The Morgan Library and Museum, New York (1997.23)

set in elegant gardens such as those that likely existed at the Villa Pisani[5]) have been dated to precisely the time of Longhi's painting, and significant for this conjecture that they are also roughly contemporaneous with the date of the Pisani project. Perhaps both artists received simultaneous commissions from members of the Pisani family for group portraits. Alternatively, Longhi may have succeeded to a commission that Tiepolo failed to fulfill after executing a series of preparatory studies. In any event, Tiepolo left Strà for Madrid two years before his work was scheduled to end. If he, indeed, contemplated such an ambitious portrait for his Pisani patrons, it was conceivably interrupted by his premature and unanticipated departure.

As was his frequent practice, Tiepolo's son Domenico reprised this composition of his father's in a drawing of a family group in a villa garden.[6]

LWS

1. See Aikema and Dreyer 1996–97, no. 72.
2. Inv. no. 6317; see Rizzi and Morassi 1965, pp. 116–17, no. 116; and Brussels 1983, no. 32.
3. Rizzi and Morassi 1965, under no. 116.
4. Rizzi and Morassi 1965; Knox 1970. Bernard Aikema (Aikema and Dreyer 1996–97, p. 188) has refuted this suggestion on the grounds that Longhi's portrait shows a different assembly of sitters and that some of the men in his portrait wear wigs while none of Tiepolo's subjects are so outfitted. It is possible, however, that Alvise Pisani commissioned more than one portrait and that Tiepolo's composition, with its expanded cast, simply shows a more extended family gathering than Longhi's, with the sitters less formally attired. Given that the drawings can be roughly dated to the period of Tiepolo's activity at the Villa Pisani, the hypothesis cannot be completely dismissed.
5. This topographically descriptive setting finds analogies in Tiepolo's landscape drawings that are thought to be based on actual buildings, as noted in Knox 1996–97, p. 39.
6. Ex-Beurdeley collection; sold at Sotheby's, London, July 6, 1967, lot 45.

CANALETTO

Venice, 1697–Venice, 1768

The greatest vedutista *of the eighteenth century, Canaletto was a painter, draftsman, and etcher. He began his career working in the company of his father and uncle as a painter of stage sets for Vivaldi operas, and burnished his formative experience with a trip to Rome. He later spent a decade in London. His panoramic, sparkling, light-suffused views of the Grand Canal and other paradigmatic or evocative vistas of the Venetian lagoon and mainland—some real, others (known as* capricci*) imagined—found an enthusiastic audience in the legions of foreign visitors who flocked to Italy on the Grand Tour. Many of Canaletto's* vedute *and* capricci *drawings were made as autonomous works rather than as studies for paintings or prints, and his etchings rank among the most beautiful and technically accomplished examples of that medium.*

66. *The Grand Canal, Venice, Looking North from near the Rialto Bridge,* ca. 1725

Pen and brown ink, upper left hand corner made up, 6⅞ x 11¾ in. (17.5 x 30 cm)

Inscribed at upper right in brown [black?] ink: *16*; at upper right in brown ink, obscured by hatching: a column of mathematical computations; inscribed at lower right in brown ink in the artist's hand: *Fondamenta*

Provenance: Sale, Sotheby, Parke, Bernet, & Co., London, July 2, 1984, lot 119; Dr. Carlo M. Croce, Philadelphia; Christie's, London, July 6, 1993, lot 86; acquired in 1993

References: Constable and Links 1989, vol. 2, p. 743, no. 592*; New York 1989–90, p. 90, under no. 9, and no. 87, pp. 282–83; Links 1998, p. 50, no. 592*; Venice 2001, no. 22

When this previously unknown study by Canaletto for an important early painting of the identical subject (fig. 66.1) first appeared in the mid-1980s, its fortuitous survival was hailed as a "remarkable coincidence."[1] That picture and its pendant were commissioned in 1725 by Stefano Conti, a Lucchese cloth merchant, whose agent in Venice had advised him to procure the view paintings he desired from Canaletto rather than from the older *vedutista* Luca Carlevarijs.[2] Upon completing the two canvases late that year Canaletto penned a letter to his patron in which he narrated the topography of the respective scenes. His description of the second picture explicates the vista recorded here: ". . . the same Canal looking down to the Fish market the Palazzo Pesaro and in the distance the Campanile de S. Marcola, on the other side of the Canal but near is the Palazzo de Casa Grimani and in succession other Palaces, as Rezonico, Sagrado and many more."[3]

The Tobey drawing was initially presumed to be a preparatory study for a painting showing a slightly expanded version of this composition (Royal Collection).[4] That work originally

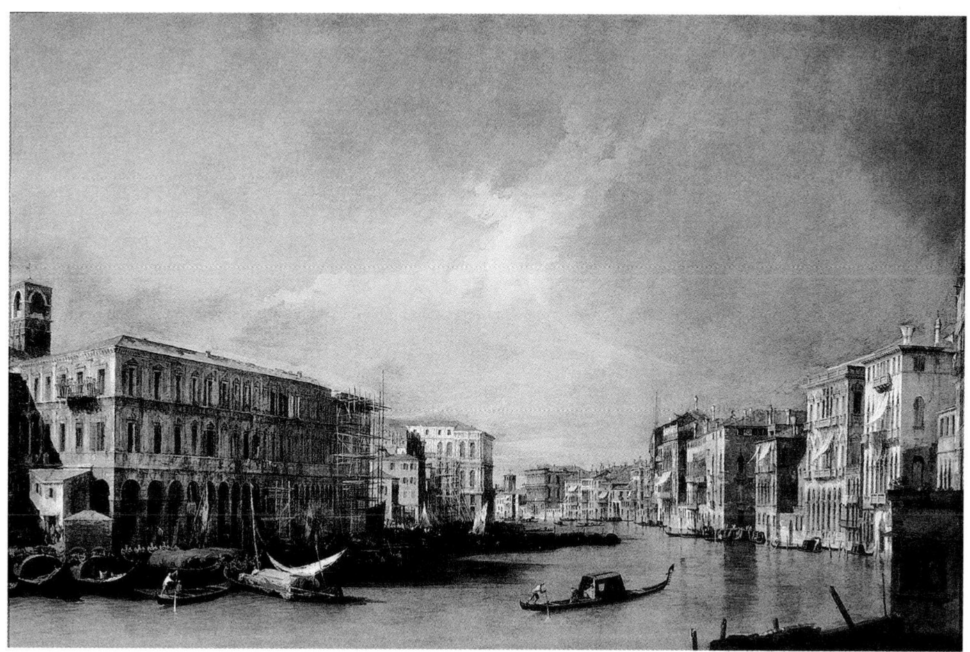

Fig. 66.1. Canaletto. *The Grand Canal, Venice, Looking North from near the Rialto Bridge*, 1725. Oil on canvas, 35¼ x 51¾ in. (89.5 x 131.4 cm). Pinacoteca del Lingotto Giovanni e Marella Agnelli, Turin (C/L 230)

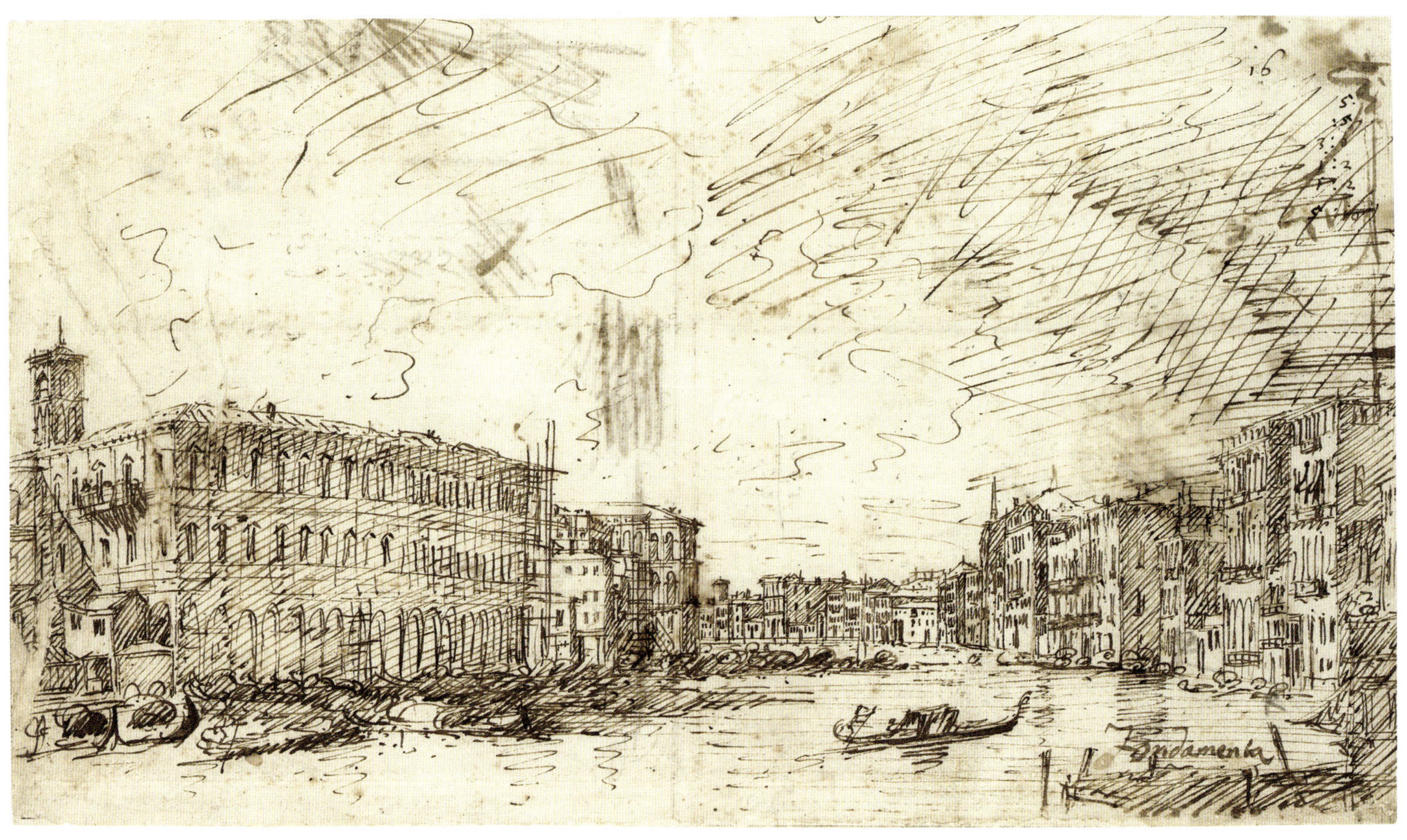

66

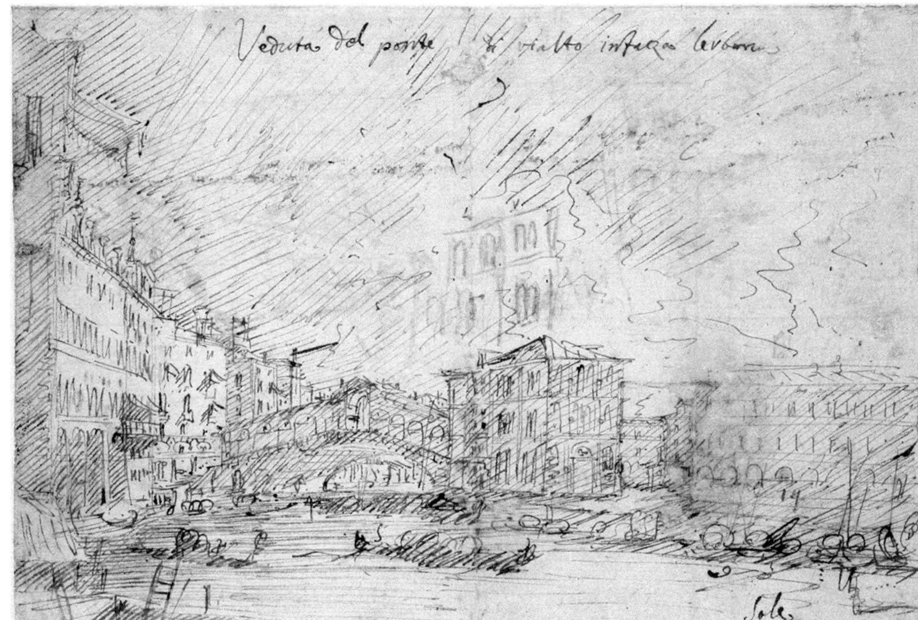

Fig. 66.2. Canaletto. *Grand Canal: the Rialto Bridge from the North*, ca. 1725. Pen and brown ink with red and black chalk, 5½ x 8 in. (14 x 20.2 cm). Ashmolean Museum of Art and Archaeology, Oxford (C/L 593)

belonged to Canaletto's great patron Joseph Smith, British Consul in Venice, and was the source of Antonio Visentini's engraving after Canaletto of this scene.[5] However, the presence of scaffolding at the corner of the Palazzo Corner della Regina at left, which was erected during a construction campaign in 1724, indicates unequivocally that this can only be a study for the painting commissioned by Stefano Conti—the sole version of this composition in which Canaletto included that particular detail.[6]

It has been suggested that Canaletto's preparatory study for the pendant *veduta*, *Grand Canal: the Rialto Bridge from the North* (fig. 66.2), was probably drawn on-site rather than in the studio.[7] The same is conceivably also true of the Tobey drawing, which—although larger, somewhat less sketchy, and more descriptively detailed in comparison—shares something of the same rapid, free, and confident handling of the pen.　　　　LWS

1. So described in New York 1989–90, p. 90, under no. 9. The drawing was unknown before it appeared at auction in 1984.
2. On the commission from Stefano Conti, see ibid., p. 87.
3. New York 1989–90, p. 90, no. 9; p. 364. What Canaletto in this letter called the Palazzo Grimani is better known as the Palazzo Vendramin-Calergi; the German composer Richard Wagner died there in 1883 (see ibid., p. 90, under no. 9); see cat. 62.
4. Constable and Links 1989, vol. 2, Supplementary Index, no. 592*, describe the present sheet as "almost certainly preparatory . . . for [their] no. 233," the *Grand Canal, looking North from near the Rialto Bridge* now in the Royal Collection, Windsor Castle. That opinion is revised in Links 1998, p. 50, no. 592*, where the drawing is correctly connected with the Conti version; see also note 6 below.
5. Constable and Links 1989, vol. 2, p. 299, no. 233.
6. As first observed in New York 1989–90, p. 282, no. 87.
7. Constable and Links 1989, vol. 2, p. 510, no. 593, who suggest that the drawing "was probably made on the ground."

FRANCESCO FONTEBASSO

Venice, 1707–Venice, 1769

Francesco Fontebasso trained with the Venetian painter Sebastiano Ricci and, like his much-admired near-contemporary and compatriot Tiepolo, specialized in grand, large-scale frescoes, decorative cycles, and monumental altarpieces. An appealing draftsman, he produced many finished, pictorially rich drawings as autonomous works, some of which were created as a series. His pen-and-ink drawings reflect a consuming ambition to emulate Tiepolo. Fontebasso was also a designer of book illustrations and an engraver. Although he was active primarily in Venice, Fontebasso studied in Rome and Bologna early in his career, and later worked in Trent and St. Petersburg.

67. *God Confronting Cain after He Slew Abel*

Pen and brown ink, brown and brownish-rose wash over black chalk, heightened with white (partly oxidized), on pink prepared paper, 17⅞ x 12½ in. (45.5 x 31.7 cm)

Provenance: Sale, Christie's, New York, January 25, 2005, lot 91; acquired in 2005

Francesco Fontebasso was a prolific draftsman and painter, yet relatively few of his drawings can be connected with his frescoes or canvases.[1] His graphic oeuvre includes a series of large-scale, finished drawings representing biblical subjects from both the Old and New Testaments, many of which are preserved in an album in the Museo Correr, Venice.[2] Another album illustrating scenes from ancient history is now dispersed among several public and private collections. All these drawings by Fontebasso are distinguished by a rich combination of media and pictorial character, and a number of the compositions derive from Sebastiano Ricci and Giovanni Battista Tiepolo. Finished works of art in their own right, they have been aptly described as "pictures in themselves."[3]

Depicting a scene from the Old Testament, God appearing to Cain after the slaying of his brother, Abel, the Tobey drawing belongs stylistically and iconographically to the group of biblical drawings, most of which have roughly comparable dimensions and a similar combination of black chalk, white heightening, and pinkish or gray wash.[4] Fontebasso's predilection for theatrical, rhetorically expressive gestures and postures is evident in Cain's dramatic, spiraling pose. Flung upward in fear or self-defense, his hand is isolated against the sky, answered by the open-palm acclamation of God the Father who appears before him, levitating on a cloud above the lifeless body of Abel. In the background an altar displays the smoldering remains of a sacrifice—an allusion to the narration in the book of Genesis (4:1–16), the source of Fontebasso's design, which recounts that God rejected the offering of Cain, a farmer, but accepted that of his brother, Abel, a shepherd, thereby precipitating the first fratricide.

Probably intended for the album of an amateur—a mode of display preserved in the Correr album—this sheet belongs to the Venetian tradition of "presentation" drawings of biblical and hagiographic subjects that culminates in the elaborate series of New Testament and Apocryphal subjects by Domenico Tiepolo.[5]   LWS

1. As remarked in Byam Shaw 1954, p. 318.
2. Byam Shaw 1954, pp. 320–25; Magrini 1990, pp. 192–96, nos. 170–200.
3. Byam Shaw 1954, p. 321.
4. See, for example, *The Sacrifice of Isaac* (Albertina, Vienna, inv. no. 32422; Magrini 1990, no. 209, fig. 98).
5. Gealt and Knox 2006–2007; Udine and Bloomington 1996–97, pp. 159–84, nos. 88–113.

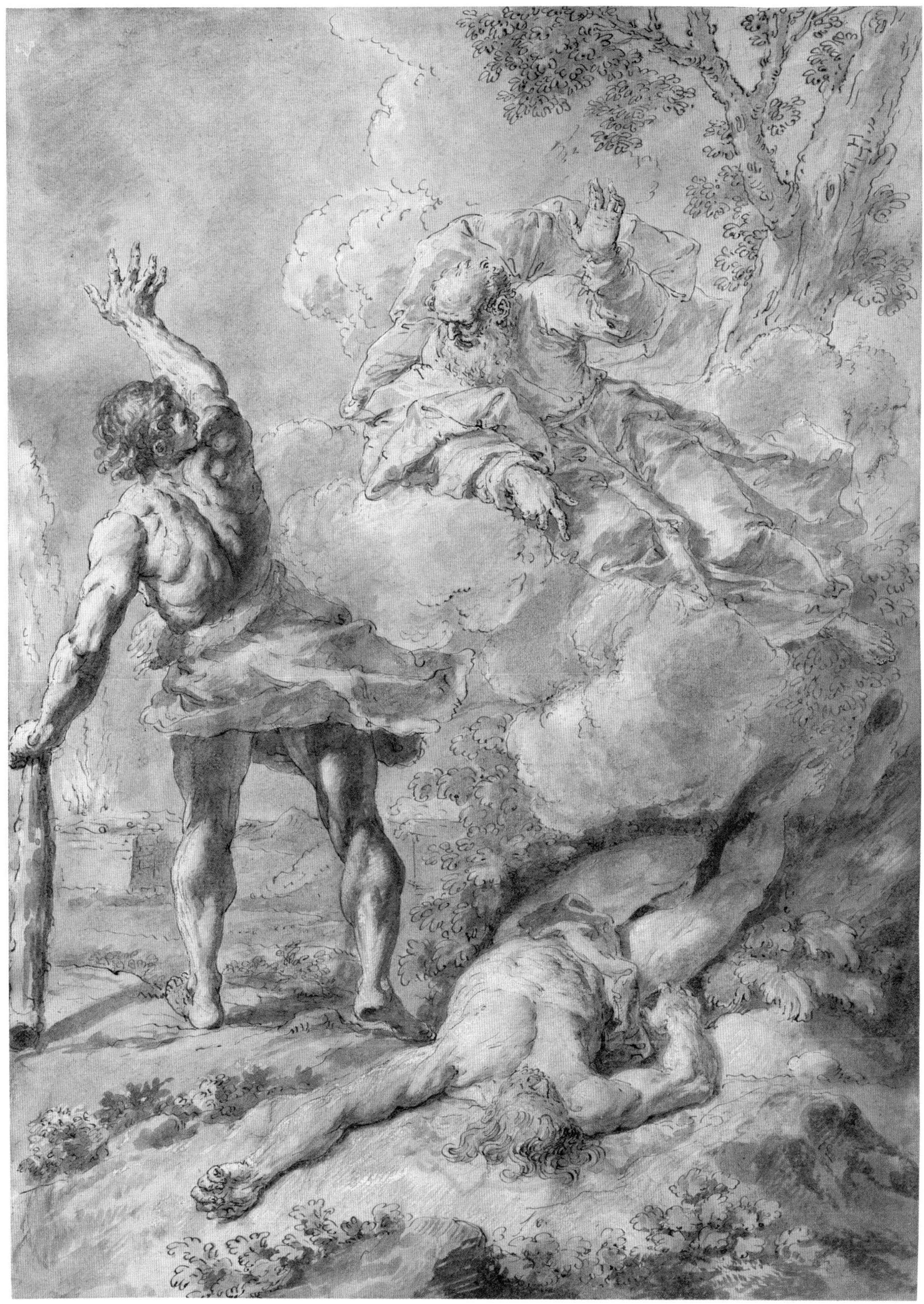

FRANCESCO GUARDI

Venice, 1712–Venice, 1793

Francesco Guardi belonged to a family of artists that included his brother Gian Antonio and his son Giacomo, and was related by marriage to Giovanni Battista Tiepolo, husband of his sister Cecilia. He is one of the most celebrated Venetian vedutisti *(view painters) of the eighteenth century, and was greatly influenced by Canaletto, the genre's greatest exponent, in whose studio he may have spent some time as an already independent artist. Canaletto's etched views, like those of Michele Marieschi, provided compositional models for some of Guardi's inventions, which comprise paintings and drawings of both real and imagined views of Venice, executed with an increasing looseness and fluidity. He frequently populated his compositions with diminutive, anonymous figures executed with rapid stabs of the brush or flamelike strokes of the pen, delineating such human staffage in a number of drawings known as* macchiette.

68. *Arcade with a Campiello in the Background*

Pen and brown ink, brown and gray wash, 15 x 11¾ in. (38 x 30 cm)
Inscribed in brown ink at lower center: *Franciscus Guardi inv. del. et pin.*

Provenance: F. Colonna, Turin; Crespi Collection, Milan; Compagnie des Beaux-Arts Ltd., Lugano; acquired in 2000

Reference: Morassi 1975, no. 577, fig. 569

The use of an arch to frame a view on to a more distant vista was a pictorial device frequently employed by Francesco Guardi in his *vedute* of both real and imagined topography. Here, the pointed arches of an arcade beneath which an elegant couple strolls open on to a *campiello*, or small Venetian piazza. Beyond its walls rise three cypress trees and the spire of a tall campanile attached to a church, its apse or narthex punctured by thermal windows of the type favored by the great Venetian architect Andrea Palladio. The realistic and descriptive aspect of the carefully transcribed and detailed architecture suggests that the drawing records an actual arcade and church in Venice, although neither of the structures has been identified.

Antonio Morassi linked the Tobey sheet with three other architectural *vedute* drawings by Francesco Guardi and noted that the artist also executed a painting of the same composition (fig. 68.1).[1] The unusual inscription below the framing line, which refers to the latter work (it records that the artist invented, drew, and painted the design), suggests that the drawing may be a *ricordo*, or record copy, after the canvas rather than a preparatory study for it, or an autonomous invention reiterating the composition of the painting. The hard, precise character of the line, which lacks Guardi's quivering spontaneity, would support this conjecture. More typical of his draftsmanship are the flamelike silhouettes of the figures and their rather amorphous forms. This distinctive aspect of Guardi's manner was emulated

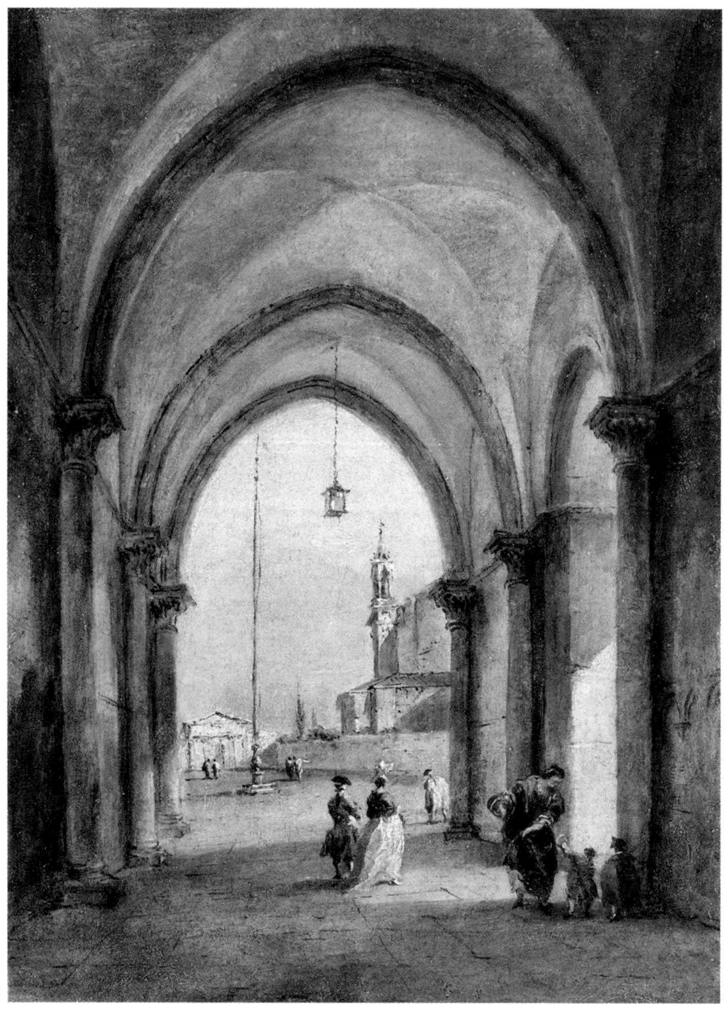

Fig. 68.1. Francesco Guardi. *Arcade with a View onto a Campiello.* Oil on canvas, 9⁷⁄₁₆ x 6¹¹⁄₁₆ in. (24 x 17 cm). Gulbenkian Foundation, Lisbon (93A)

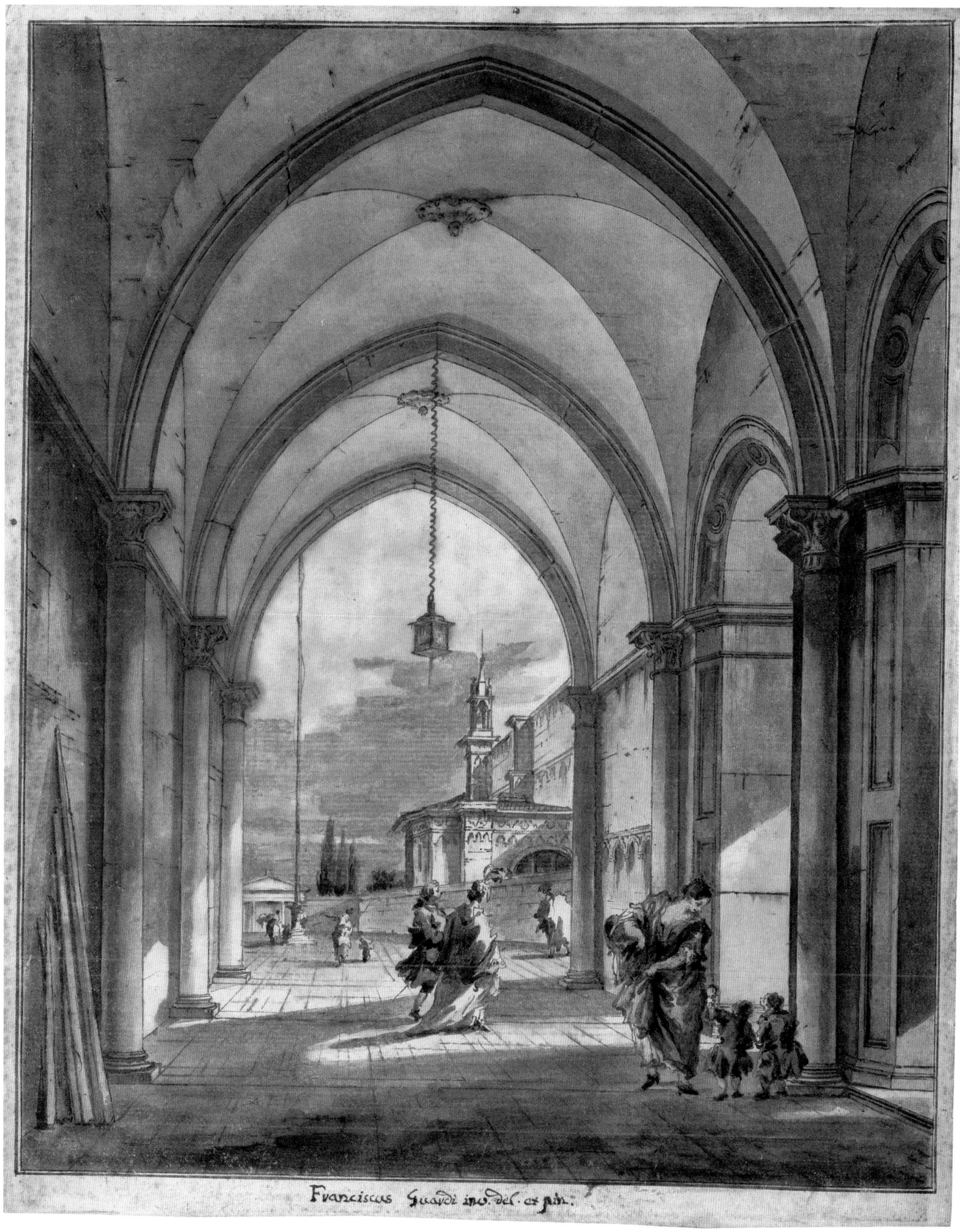
Franciscus Guardi inv. del. et pin.

by his son, Giacomo (1764–1835), whose graphic style was purely derivative of his father's; indeed, as Morassi long ago observed, the present sheet is in some respects close to Giacomo's draftsmanship. However, it also finds parallels among Francesco's autograph drawings, such as a view of the arcade of the Palazzo Ducale, formerly in the Crespi Collection in Milan,[2] which originally constituted part of a series to which the Tobey drawing also belongs; and a view under an arcade with a palace in the background in the Kupferstichkabinett, Berlin.[3] Here it is relevant to note that all three drawings were reproduced, in the same direction, in engravings.[4] Their precise, careful draftsmanship is perhaps accounted for by the fact that they served as models for prints—a rather exceptional circumstance in the case of Francesco Guardi, for unlike other Venetian *vedutisti* such as Carlevarijs (see cat. no. 62), Canaletto (see cat. no. 66), Bellotto, and Michele Marieschi, he was not actively involved in designing prints or making etchings of his compositions.

LWS

1. According to Morassi 1975, under no. 577, the present drawing belongs to a series comprising three additional sheets (Morassi 1975, nos. 514, 522, and 534), all four of which share the same dimensions and provenance. For the Gulbenkian painting, see Morassi 1973, vol. 1, p. 459, no. 803, vol. 2, fig. 730.
2. Morassi 1975, no. 534, fig. 526.
3. Ibid., no. 549, fig. 538.
4. Ibid., under no. 577, fig. 568. The engraving of the present composition, by Teodoro Viero, is dedicated to the Venetian nobleman Angelo Querini. The two other drawings cited in this connection were engraved by Dionigi Valesi; ibid., figs. 527 and 539. Impressions of all three are in the Museo Correr, Venice.

GIOVANNI BATTISTA PIRANESI

Mogliano di Mestre (Venice), 1720–Rome, 1778

A native of Venice, Giovanni Battista Piranesi was a printmaker, draftsman, architect, archaeologist, designer, and theorist. His technically brilliant and exceedingly influential etchings of the monuments of ancient Rome—an undertaking that occupied him for much of his career—reflect his deep antiquarian interests and his affinity for the decaying yet heroic and resonant ruins of antiquity. Widely circulated and avidly collected, Piranesi's views provide a rich and visually descriptive record, at once poetic and archaeological, of the glories of ancient Rome, while his haunting and vaguely sinister etchings of carceri *(prisons) reveal a bizarre inventive fantasy akin to that which imbues the etched* capricci *of his compatriot Giovanni Battista Tiepolo.*

69. *Study of a Kneeling Man*, early to mid-1760s

Pen and brown ink, 7½ x 11¾ in. (19 x 30 cm)

Provenance: Lamberto Vitali, Milan; Compagnie des Beaux-Arts Ltd., Lugano; acquired in 2000

References: Rome 1959, no. 461a; Salamon 1961–62, no. 233 (as attributed to Piranesi); Bologna 1963, no. 171 (as attributed to Piranesi); Bettagno 1978, no. 56 (as Piranesi)

This rapid, informal sketch of a kneeling man in a waistcoat relates to a group of similar figure studies by Giovanni Battista Piranesi, all of which exhibit a comparable heavy, scratchy pen-work and analogous thick contour lines.[1] In some of the drawings in question the subjects are seated or standing; in others they energetically perform assorted nondescript activities.[2] A similar study of two seated figures is in the National Gallery of Canada, Ottawa.[3] Even more closely related to the Tobey sheet is a drawing formerly in the collection of Jacques Petit-Hory, Paris, showing a man seen from behind: as in the present example, the figure is supported on a generic platform economically described by a series of rapid vertical strokes of the pen, and the surrounding space is filled with a spirited diagonal hatching (fig. 69.1).[4]

Dated to the later 1750s and 1760s, these engaging figures studies are believed to have been done from life. Most if not all were probably created to form "an anthology of pictorial motifs"[5]—a repertoire of human staffage—rather than as preparatory studies for specific compositions. Myriad diminutive figure populate Piranesi's views of ancient and modern Rome, the fanciful *Carceri*, and his other *vedute*, although few if any of his relatively rare figure drawings have been directly connected with his etchings.

LWS

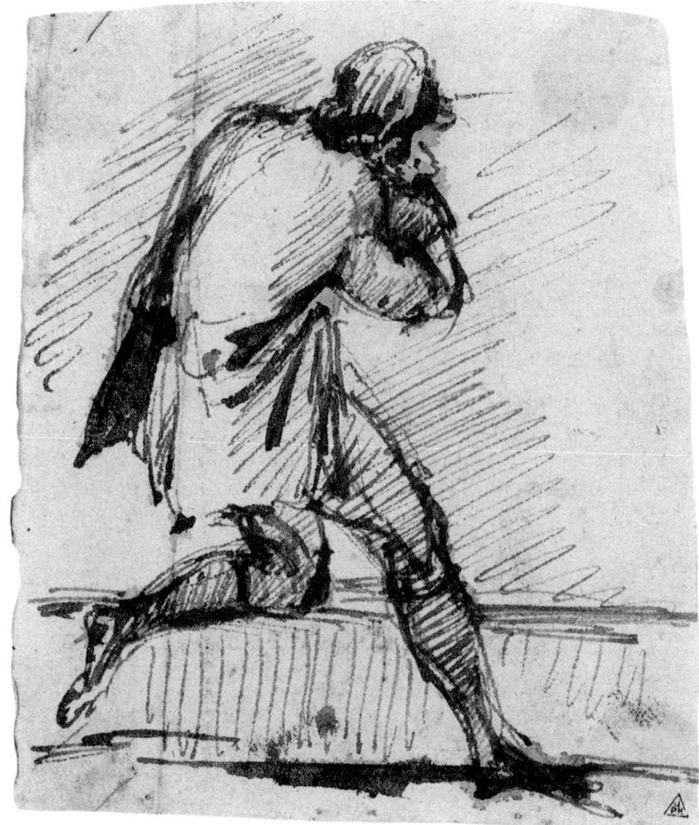

Fig. 69.1. Giovanni Battista Piranesi. *Study of a Man Leaning Seen from Behind*, early to mid-1760s. Pen and dark brown ink with a few lines drawn in red chalk. Formerly Collection of Jacques Petit-Hory, Paris; whereabouts unknown

1. See Thomas 1954, nos. 67–79; Bettagno 1978, nos. 55–59; Wilton-Ely 1978, pp. 40–41. According to Bettagno 1978 (no. 56), who dates the drawing to the early to mid-1760s, the man portrayed in the Tobey drawing is smoking a pipe. However, the line to the left of his face does not appear to be a pipe, nor is it between his lips.

2. See, for example, a drawing in the École des Beaux-Arts, Paris, in Bettagno 1978, no. 58; and in Wilton-Ely 1978, p. 41, fig. 58.

3. Bettagno 1978, no. 55.

4. See New York 1994a, no. 26. The drawing, which was kindly brought to my attention by Eveline Baseggio, was last on the art market in 2003 (sale, Piasa, Paris, June 19, 2003, lot 24), present whereabouts unknown. I am grateful to Andrew Robison for information on its most recent provenance.

5. Wilton-Ely 1978, p. 40.

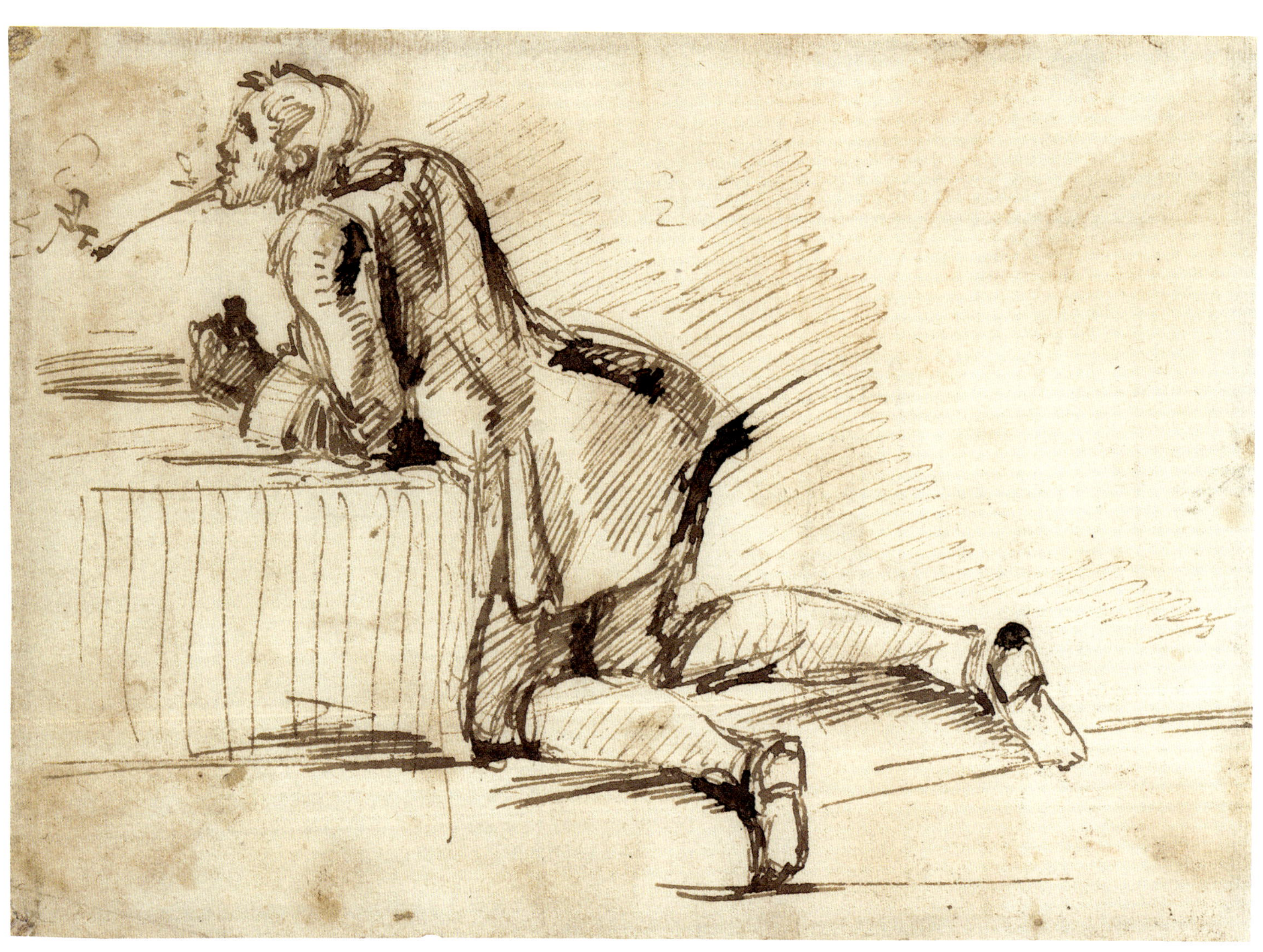

69

BERNARDO BELLOTTO

Venice, 1721–Warsaw, 1780

Bernardo Bellotto was the nephew and pupil of Canaletto. Like Canaletto he was a vedutista *(view painter), creating topographically descriptive yet poetically evocative paintings and etchings of Venice and the mainland, as well as imaginary views inspired by the lagoon city. Bellotto traveled to Rome, Florence, and Lombardy, and eventually relocated permanently to northern Europe, where he depicted the distinctive architecture and urban spaces of Dresden, Vienna, Munich, and Warsaw. His early works, both paintings and drawings, were in the past often confused with those of Canaletto, whose manner he capably emulated.*

70. *A Church and Campanile beside a Road on the Venetian Terra Firma*, ca. 1741–43

Pen and brown ink, black chalk, 7½ x 10⅝ in. (19 x 27 cm)

Provenance: The artist's family, Vilnius; Ludwig Heinrich Bojanus (1776–1827), Vilnius and later Darmstadt, until 1827; Court Advocate R. K. R. Eigenbrodt, Darmstadt; Kupferstichkabinett des Hessisches Landesmuseum, Darmstadt, 1829–1933 (Lugt 1257e); New York Art Market, 1948; Kurt Meissner, Zurich; sale, Christie's, London, June 1990, lot 79; acquired in 1990

Selected References: Parker 1948, under no. 96; Sumowski 1967, no. 124; Kozakiewicz 1972, vol. 2, no. 49; Constable and Links 1989, vol. 1, under no. 698

At one time ascribed to Canaletto, this engaging study has long been recognized as the work of his gifted pupil and nephew, Bernardo Bellotto.[1] The single-nave church with a classicizing facade and medieval bell tower depicted here has not been identified, but the carriage at the left and the screen of trees behind it suggest a location on the Venetian mainland.

In the early 1740s Bellotto, in the company of Canaletto, traveled along the Brenta Canal to Padua.[2] Both artists produced a number of drawings recording different sights along the way—among them, presumably, this example by Bellotto. Some fifty sheets by him from this corpus are preserved in the Hessisches Landesmuseum, Darmstadt, a provenance shared by the present work.[3] These were part of a collection of some eighty drawings by Canaletto and Bellotto, purportedly acquired directly from the latter's heirs, which had been in the possession of the family of Professor Ludwig Heinrich Bojanus, a celebrated German scientist and expert in animal diseases and pharmaceuticals, and were purchased for the collection of the Grand Duke of Hesse in 1829.

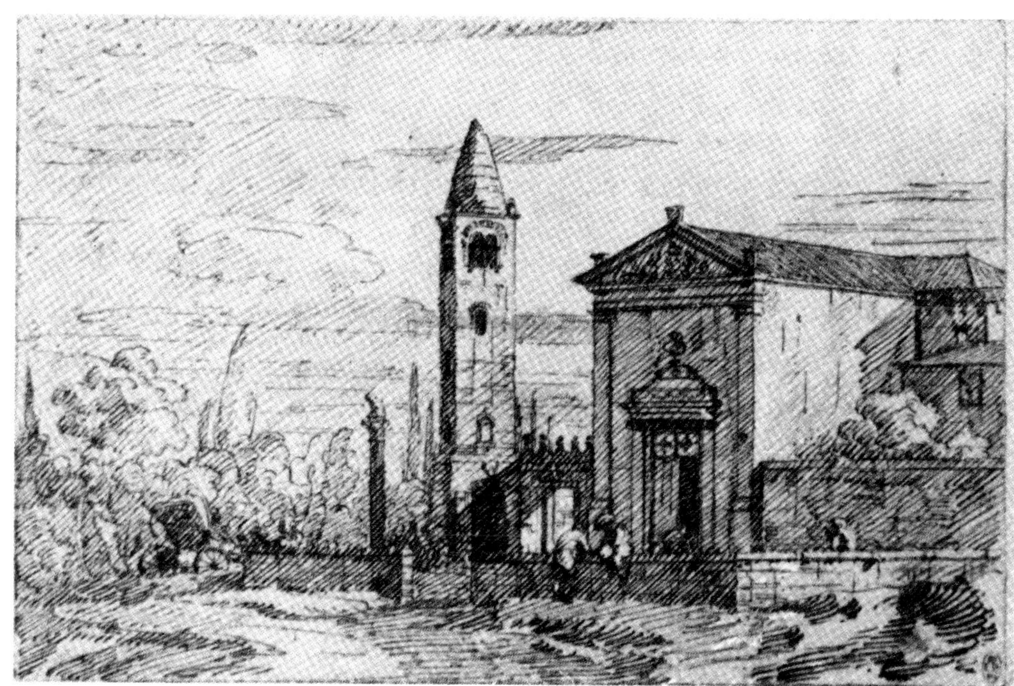

Fig. 70.1. Canaletto. *A Church, Presumably on the Venetian Terraferma*, ca. 1741–43. Pen and black/grayish-black ink over pencil (freehand and ruled), 7⁷⁄₁₆ x 10¹¹⁄₁₆ in. (18.9 x 27.2 cm). The Royal Collection. © Her Majesty Queen Elizabeth II (RL 7512)

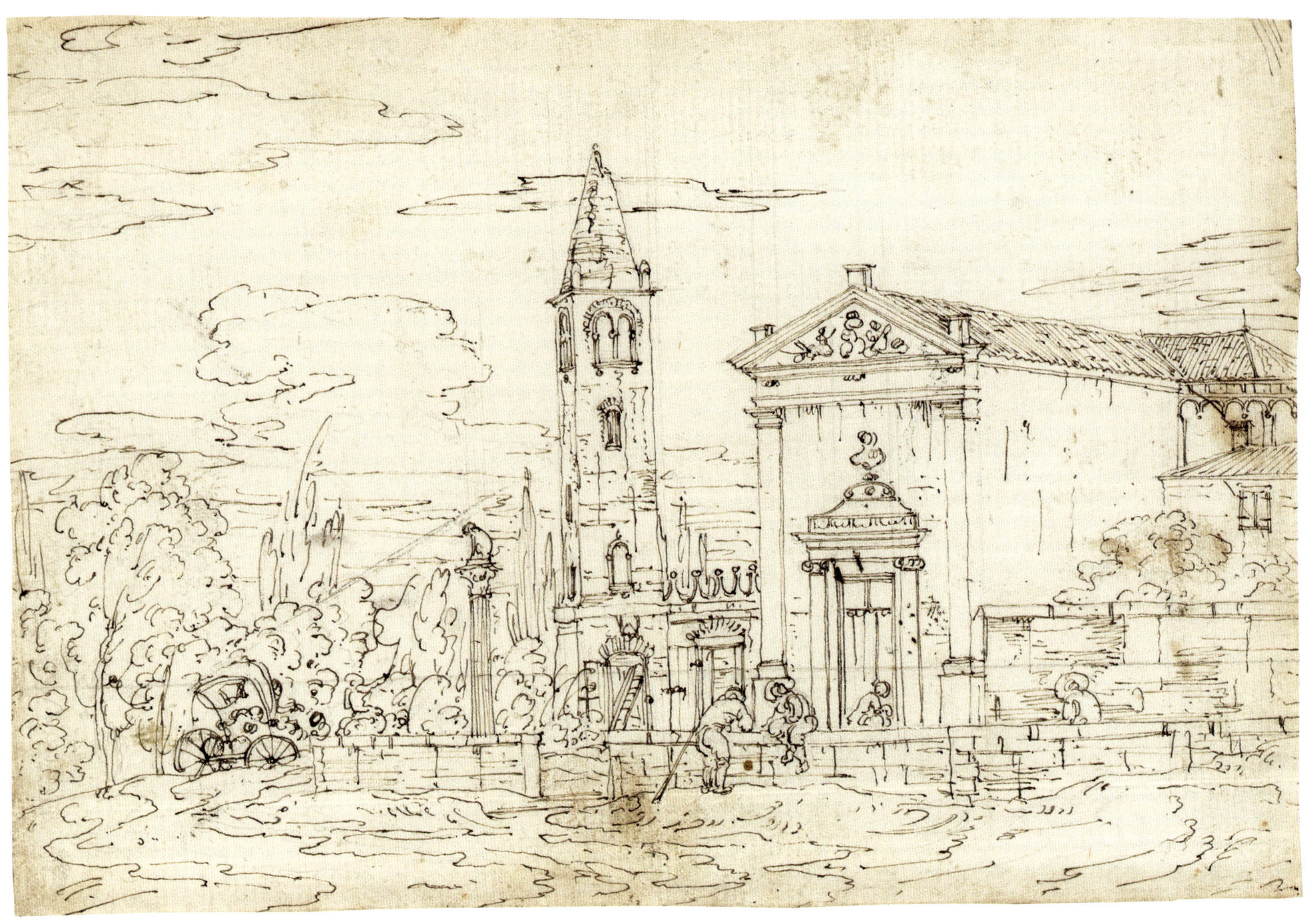

70

Bellotto here reprised a view that Canaletto recorded in a pen-and-ink drawing of virtually the same dimensions in the Royal Collection, Windsor Castle (fig. 70.1). Not only does the Tobey drawing depict the identical, prominent architectural structures viewed from precisely the same angle and vantage point; it also includes the same staffage, identically deployed— the diminutive figures lolling around the wall in the foreground; the tall column beside the campanile on which a beast (probably the Venetian *marzocco*, or lion) is perched; and the carriage seen in profile at the left. Even the backdrop of trees shows the same contours and variety of species as the comparable, though more detailed, passage in Canaletto's scene. The unwavering parallels led both Parker and Constable to consider Bellotto's drawing a copy of Canaletto's; this proposition was all but rejected by Kozakiewicz, who, while acknowledging the myriad similarities, mysteriously opined that "there are probably not sufficient grounds for accepting this verdict."[4] Whatever the case, Bellotto's drawing is no mere slavish imitation, exhibiting a freer handling and a looser, abbreviated manner of articulating forms in comparison with Canaletto's more finished design, and eschewing the older artist's careful attention to the descriptive play of light and shadow.[5] This pairing highlights the approach of Bellotto in his early career to the venerable example of Canaletto, whose inventions he assiduously studied and emulated but also subtly recast, thereby imprinting his Venetian *vedute* with his own stamp of individuality.

LWS

1. Sumowski 1967, no. 124.
2. Links 1989–90, p. 9.
3. The Tobey *veduta* was among a group of eighteenth-century drawings selected from the collection of the Hessisches Landesmuseum for exchange for works by German artists sometime between 1933 or 1936 and 1945 (Lugt 1956, p. 182; Bleyl 1981, p. 40, under no. 29). On the Bellotto drawings in Darmstadt, many of which are copies of paintings or drawings by Canaletto, see Bleyl 1981.
4. Kozakiewicz 1972, vol. 2, p. 38, under no. 49.
5. Another Paduan view, one of the group preserved in the Hessisches Landesmuseum, Darmstadt (inv. no. AE2226; see Bleyl 1981, no. 31), is stylistically analogous to the Tobey drawing.

DOMENICO TIEPOLO

Venice, 1727–Venice, 1804

Domenico Tiepolo was the talented son and assistant of Giovanni Battista Tiepolo. He fully mastered his father's style of painting, as attested by his earliest independent work—a series of paintings in San Polo in Venice, completed in 1749—as much as by his last major public commission, a ceiling fresco in the ducal palace in Genoa, executed in 1785. His greater affinity was for genre subjects and incidental, anecdotal detail, as his many charming paintings and drawings illustrating scenes from contemporary Venetian life reveal. Like Giovanni Battista, Domenico was also a talented etcher; his series of twenty variations on the theme of the Flight into Egypt is one of the masterpieces of eighteenth-century printmaking. It is in his many series of drawings reiterating, in large number and with endless variety, a range of themes and subjects that his independent artistic personality comes most to the fore. In addition to his vignettes of daily life, these include animals, garden sculptures, the Baptism of Christ, Saint Anthony of Padua, the New Testament and Apocrypha, satyrs and centaurs, Oriental horsemen, and—most famously—the Venetian commedia dell'arte comic hero Punchinello.

71. *A Peasant Family on Its Way to Church,* ca. 1790–91

Black chalk, pen and brown ink, brown wash, 14⅞ x 20 in. (37.9 x 50.7 cm)
Signed in dark brown ink on rock at lower right: *Dom. Tiepolo f*; inscribed in ink at upper left: *67* or *47*

Provenance: Sale, Sotheby's, London, November 11, 1965, lot 24; Agnew's, London; Private Collection; sale, Christie's, London, December 8, 1987, lot 136; sale, Christie's, New York, January 10, 1990, lot 88; Peter Jay Sharp, New York; sale, Christie's, London, July 8, 2008, lot 64;[1] acquired in 2008

References: Knox 1974, p. 82, no. 69; New York 1994b, no. 29; Knox 1996–97, p. 40, fig. 13; Udine and Bloomington 1996–97, no. 137; Gealt et al. 2005, no. 6

In the early 1790s, Domenico Tiepolo created an engaging series of drawings depicting scenes of contemporary life. Aristocrats, petits bourgeois, shopkeepers, schoolteachers, tradesmen, peasants, Gypsies, charlatans, and street entertainers—not to mention a vast menagerie of dogs, turkeys, cattle, monkeys, horses, and more exotic beasts—are among the colorful protagonists of these charming tableaux. The mostly idle amusements and frivolous pastimes recorded by Domenico's witty pen take place in elegant drawing rooms and boudoirs, in makeshift theaters and circuses, under the arcades of a piazza and around gondolas in a canal, in the gardens of elegant villas, and across the rural countryside.[2] Like Pietro Longhi's "conversation pieces" (paintings of the leisured, vaguely claustrophobic world of Venetian private life), and the bourgeois realism of the playwright Carlo Goldoni, Domenico's drawings of contemporary life offer a diverting kaleidoscope of reflections of eighteenth-century Venice.

The Tobey sheet depicts a peasant family (so characterized by their humble dress and bare feet) walking toward a church. The figures are seen from the rear, a vantage point the artist employed in many of his drawings and paintings. Although Domenico frequently exploited the comic and caricatural possibilities of that particular angle, exaggerating the wide derrieres and unfortunate coiffures and millinery of his unknowing subjects, there is nothing undignified about the humble faithful portrayed here. The architecture—brick wall at left and open loggia at right—is a virtuoso display of one-point perspective, with the dramatically receding diagonal lines of the wall and the roof that converge at a single vanishing point at the back of the man who is about to mount the steps of the church. This group of buildings, which Domenico is believed to have based on a now lost drawing by his father, Giovanni Battista Tiepolo, has been identified as the church and convent of the Madonna delle Grazie in Udine, near Venice, where both worked in the summer of 1759. The same structures recur in at least four other drawings by Domenico.[3]   LWS

1. According to the drawing's published provenance of record, owners prior to the 1965 Sotheby's sale included, possibly, Alfred Beurdeley, Paris, and T. L. de Gara; however, the first certain provenance is the 1965 sale (as per Stephen Geiger; correspondence with author).
2. On Domenico Tiepolo's *Scenes from Contemporary Life* drawings, see Byam Shaw 1962, pp. 46–51; Udine and Bloomington 1996–97, pp. 196–215, nos. 135–54; Wolk-Simon 1997, pp. 55–58; Wolk-Simon 1996–97.
3. One drawing is in the Morgan Library and Museum, New York; two are in the Fitzwilliam Museum, Cambridge, England; and a fourth is in the Los Angeles County Museum of Art; see Gealt et al. 2005, under no. 6.

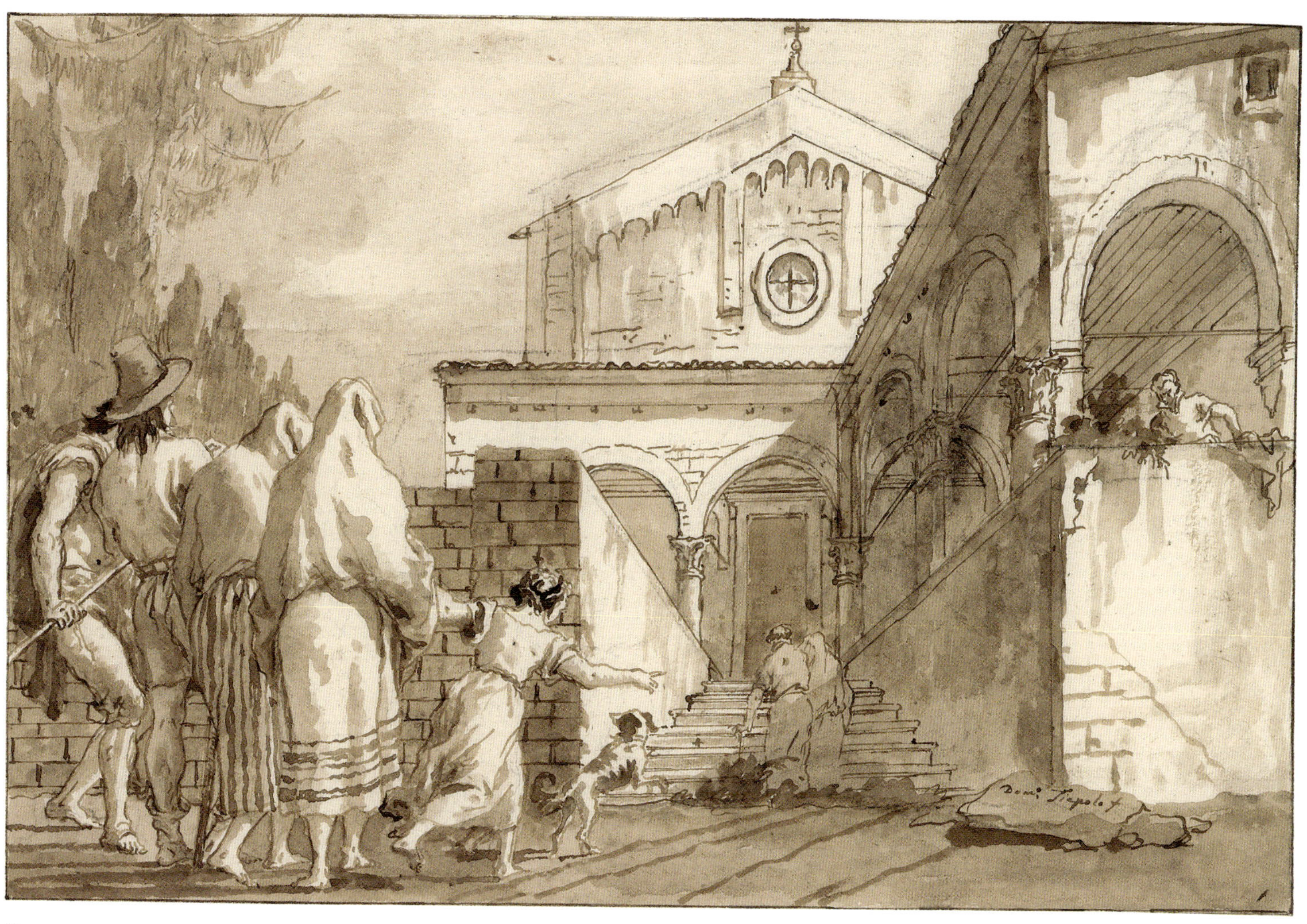

71

GIOVANNI DAVID

Cabella Ligure, 1743–Genoa, 1790

The well-traveled Giovanni David spent time in Venice, Rome, England, the Netherlands, and France but was active primarily in Genoa, where he painted altarpieces as well as large canvases depicting historical and allegorical themes. He also worked as an engraver. For much of his career he benefited from the patronage of the Durazzo, one of Genoa's most prominent aristocratic families. David stands at the end of the Genoese tradition of grand decorative cycles, characterized by dramatic foreshortenings and light effects; some of his drawings are studies for such works, while others show him working in a more intimate mode.

72. *An Allegory of the Wool Guild with Minerva and the Fates, the Coat of Arms of Giacomo Durazzo Below,* ca. 1777

Black chalk, gray wash, white and yellow bodycolor, over black chalk, on washed brown paper, 16⅛ x 9¾ in. (40.9 x 24.9 cm)
Inscribed in gray ink on tablet at upper center: *ET NOVA LANIFICA/SVB TEXUNT/FILA SOL*; in black chalk at lower left: *La Societa de Lanifici*

The Metropolitan Museum of Art, New York, Promised Gift of David M. Tobey

Provenance: Private Collection, Maine; Christie's, London, July 5, 1994; Colnaghi, New York, 1995, no. 34; acquired in 1995

References: Griswold 1995, p. 204; Ongpin 1995, no. 34; New York 1996, no. 61; Cera 2002, vol. 1, n.p. [Giovanni David] no. 6; Newcome Schleier and Grasso 2003, p. 32, no. D10

A dense allegorical invention, the scene conjured in this design takes place in a monumental classical interior with a coffered dome reminiscent of the Pantheon, and perhaps inspired by Piranesi's etching of a fanciful ancient temple in the *Prima parte di architetture, e prospettive* of 1743 (fig. 72.1). At the left is Minerva, vigilant goddess of wisdom, perched on a pedestal throne and extending a distaff with the thread of life toward one of the three Fates, Lachesis, who measures a length of thread with her rod. Seated at the base of the throne is another of the Fates, Clotho, who spins the thread on to a spindle, while the third, Atropos, the naked, enchained hag, sprawls at the lower right, restrained by a putto and vanquished by a personification of Painting before her deadly scissors can sever the thread of life: *ars vincit omnia* (Art conquers all). Behind Painting, in the center of the composition, appears an artist executing a drawing—presumably a self-portrait of Giovanni David—surrounded by great painters of the past, among them Raphael, Dürer, Michelangelo, and Titian.[1] In the background a chaste robed female, possibly Virtue, holds a crown, while a figure of Fame wielding a trumpet flies overhead, gesturing toward a tablet with a Latin inscription that, loosely translated, reads "they weave the new wool."[2] Not integral to the design, another inscription at the lower right refers to the Società dei Lanifici, or wool-workers' guild, of

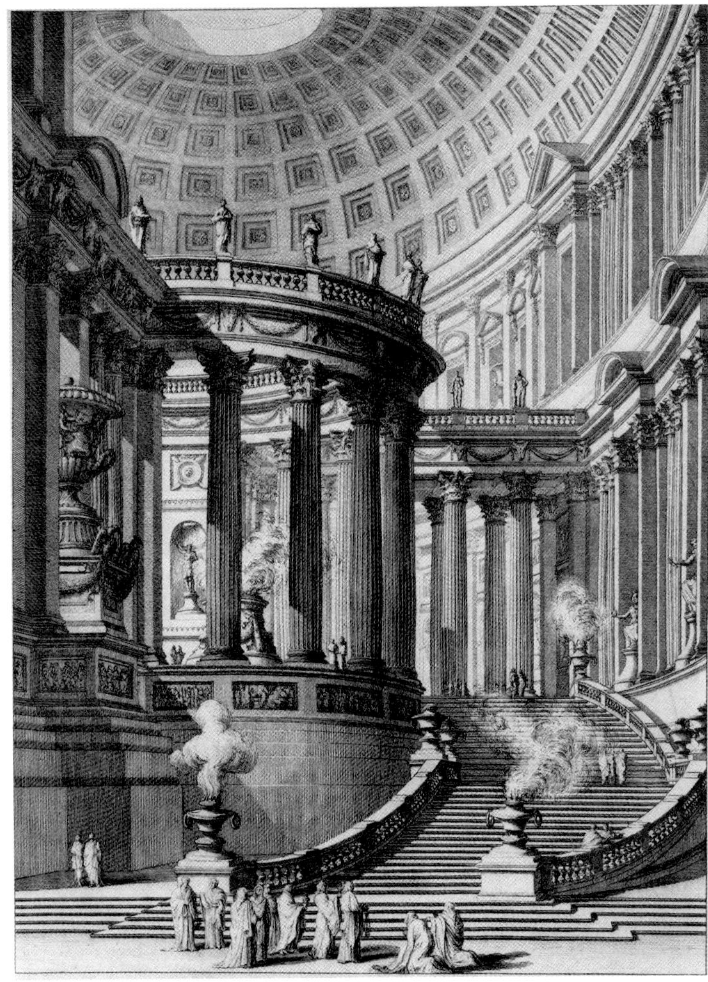

Fig. 72.1. Giovanni Battista Piranesi. *Tempio Antico*, from the *Prima parte di architetture, e prospettive*, 1743. Etching. National Gallery of Art, Washington, D.C. (1974.66.1)

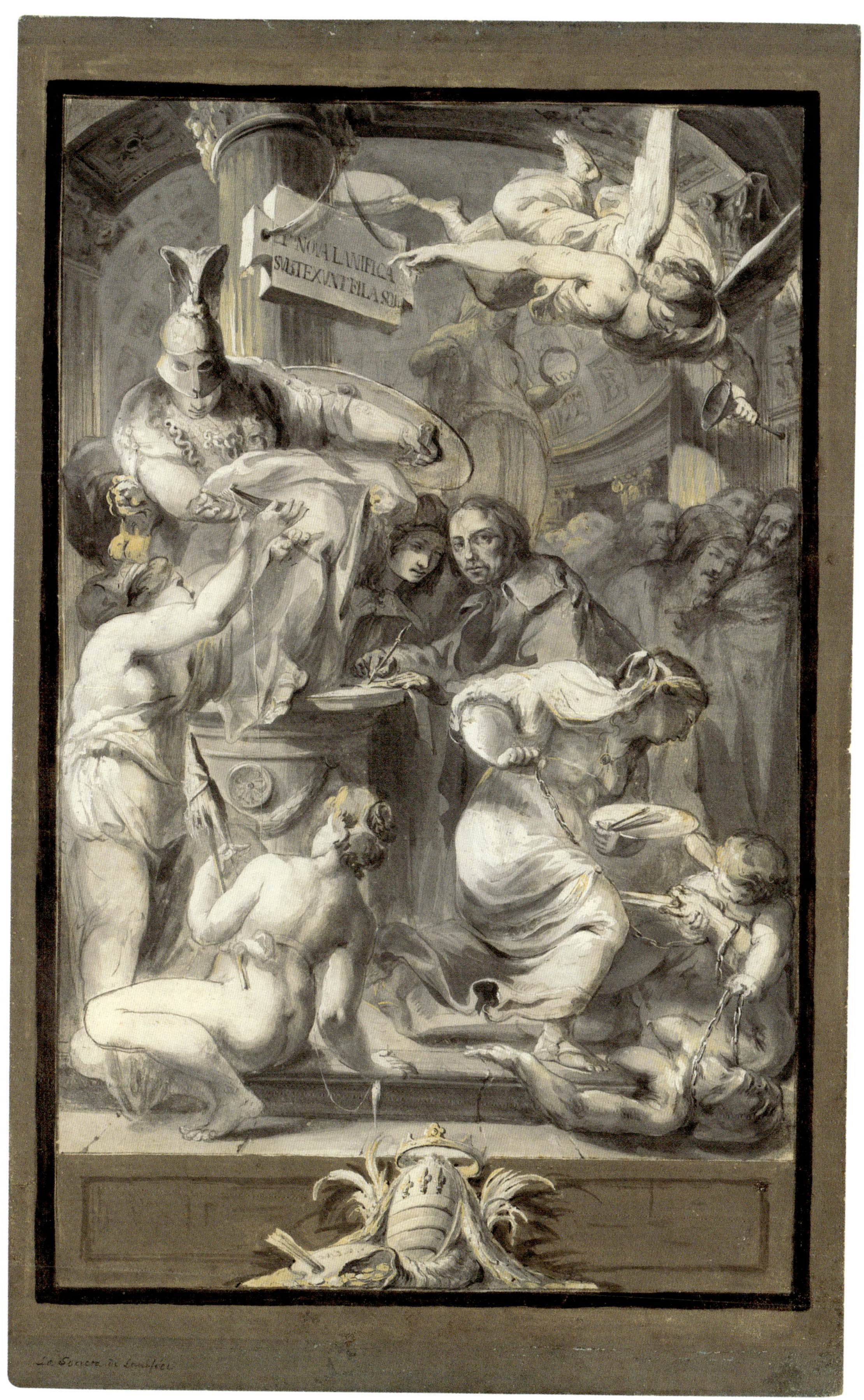

72

Genoa. What connection, if any, the artist had to the Lanifici is unknown, but David's father, a fabric designer, was involved in the textile manufacturing industry in Genoa, so the unusual imagery presumably carried some autobiographical import.[3]

At the lower edge of the sheet is the coat of arms of the Durazzo, one of the most prominent aristocratic families of Genoa, surmounted by a circlet crown and accompanied by a cornucopia of gold coins and a painter's palette and brushes. Giacomo Durazzo, a diplomat and ambassador to Vienna, was David's preeminent patron;[4] his brother Marcello Durazzo was a senator and doge of Genoa from 1767 to 1769. The presence here of the Durazzo stemma has led to the repeated suggestion that Giacomo Durazzo commissioned this ambitious design, which links the success and fame of the artist to the protection and patronage of the Durazzo. David's allegorical tableau also apotheosizes the activities of the wool-workers' guild (which perhaps also benefited from Durazzo protection and beneficence); its industry, a traditional engine of Genoa's prosperity, is here cloaked in the language of classical myth, while the fruit of its labor is likened to the very thread of life itself. Such a propagandistic message must have resonated with a heightened urgency as well as nostalgia when David devised this design: by the eighteenth century the Genoese wool-workers' guild saw its numbers and importance dwindling in the face of foreign competition and diminished demand.[5]

The function of the Tobey drawing remains a matter of conjecture. The vertical format suggests that it may have been created as a model for a book illustration or, as Mary Newcome Schleier and Giovanni Grasso suggest, a commemorative print,[6] although no such reproductive iteration is known. Alternatively, the drawing may have been executed as a *modello* for a monochrome painting for the guild hall of the Lanifici, celebrating their vital role in Genoese civic life under Durazzo patronage. Finally, its pictorially rich combination of media and fluid, bravura technique point to the possibility that this fully formulated and finished invention was conceived as an independent work.[7] Whatever the case, this impressive design, like a number of prints by the artist, attests to "David's capacity for describing complex themes as well as his early ties with [Giacomo] Durazzo."[8]

LWS

1. As first noted in Griswold 1995, p. 204.
2. Kindly translated by Frank Dabell.
3. Newcome Schleier and Grasso 2003, p. 32.
4. See Newcome 1993, p. 469.
5. For which see Massa 1998, pp. 250–51.
6. Newcome Schleier and Grasso 2003, p. 32, note that the field around the coat of arms was perhaps meant to receive an inscription.
7. Note that both Giacomo and Marcello Durazzo were important collectors of drawings; see Newcome 1993, pp. 474–75 n. 4.
8. Ibid., p. 470. As observed in New York 1996, under no. 61. The technique and style of the Tobey sheet are identical to David's *modello* for an altarpiece representing the Stoning of Saint Stephen, which is exactly contemporaneous with the *Allegory of the Wool Guild* and was commissioned by Giacomo Durazzo.

Bibliography
Index of Artists
Photograph Credits

BIBLIOGRAPHY

Acanfora 1989
Acanfora, Elisa. "Sigismondo Coccapani disegnatore e trattatista."
Paragone 40, no. 477 (November 1989), pp. 71–99, pls. 43–66.

Acidini Luchinat 1999
Acidini Luchinat, Cristina. *Taddeo e Federico Zuccari fratelli pittori del Cinquecento.* 2 vols. Milan and Rome, 1999.

Acidini Luchinat 2007
Acidini Luchinat, Cristina. *Michelangelo pittore.* Milan, 2007.

Adelson 1990
Adelson, Candace. "The Tapestry Patronage of Cosimo I de' Medici: 1545–1553." PhD diss., New York University, Graduate School of Arts and Science, New York, 1990.

Aikema and Dreyer 1996–97
Tiepolo and His Circle: Drawings in American Collections. Exhibition, Fogg Art Museum, Harvard University, Cambridge, Mass., October 12–December 15, 1996; The Pierpont Morgan Library, New York, January 17–April 13, 1997. Catalogue by Bernard Aikema and Peter Dreyer. Cambridge, Mass., 1996.

Albricci 1976
Albricci, Gioconda. "Le incisioni di G. Battista Scultori." *Print Collector/Il conoscitore di stampe,* nos. 33–34 (September–December 1976), pp. 10–63.

Angelelli and De Marchi 1991
Angelelli, Walter, and Andrea G. De Marchi. *Pittura dal Duecento al primo Cinquecento nelle fotografie di Girolamo Bombelli.* Milan, 1991.

Antwerp 1993
Rubens Cantoor: Een verzameling tekeningen ontstaan in Rubens' atelier. Exhibition, Rubenshuis, Antwerp, May 15–June 27, 1993. Catalogue by Paul Huvenne, Iris Kockelbergh, and others. Antwerp, 1993.

Avery 1997
Avery, Charles. *Bernini, Genius of the Baroque.* London, 1997.

Bacou 1981
Bacou, Roseline. *The Famous Italian Drawings from the Mariette Collection at the Louvre in Paris.* Milan, 1981.

Baglione 1642
Baglione, Giovanni. *Le vite de' pittori, scultori, architetti, dal pontificato di Gregorio XIII. del 1572 fino a' tempi di papa Urbano VIII. nel 1642.* Rome, 1642.

Baldassari 1990
Baldassari, Francesca. "Cappella Orlandini in Santa Maria Maggiore." In *Cappelle Barocche a Firenze,* edited by Mina Gregori, pp. 31–54. Cinisello Balsamo, Milan, 1990.

Baldassari 1995
Baldassari, Francesca. *Carlo Dolci.* Turin, 1995.

Baldinucci ed. 1845–47
Baldinucci, Filippo. *Notizie dei professori del disegno da Cimabue in quà, per le quali si dimostra come, e per chi le belle arti di pittura, scultura e architettura, lasciata la rozzezza delle maniere greca e gotica, si siano in questi secoli ridotte all'antica loro perfezione con nuove annotazioni e supplementi.* Edited by F[erdinando] Ranalli. 5 vols. 1681–1728. Florence, 1845–47.

Baldinucci ed. 2006
Baldinucci, Filippo. *The Life of Bernini.* Translated by Catherine Enggass; introduction by Maarten Delbeke, Evonne Levy, and Steven F. Ostrow. New ed. 1966. University Park, Pa., 2006.

Bambach 1999
Bambach, Carmen C. *Drawing and Painting in the Italian Renaissance Workshop: Theory and Practice, 1300–1600.* Cambridge and New York, 1999.

Bambach 2005
Bambach, Carmen C. "Jacopo Ligozzi: *Botanical Specimen (Motherwort or Leonurus cardiaca).*" In "Recent Acquisitions, A Selection: 2004–2005." *The Metropolitan Museum of Art Bulletin* 63, no. 2 (Fall 2005), p. 16.

Bambach 2007
Bambach, Carmen C. "Agnolo Bronzino: *Study of a Left Leg and Drapery.*" In "Recent Acquisitions, A Selection: 2006–2007." *The Metropolitan Museum of Art Bulletin* 65, no. 2 (Fall 2007), p. 21.

Bambach 2009
Bambach, Carmen C. "A New Ribera Drawing Among Michelangelos." *Apollo* 170, no. 568 (September 2009), pp. 50–55.

Bambach et al. 2003
Leonardo da Vinci, Master Draftsman. Exhibition, The Metropolitan
Museum of Art, New York, January 22–March 30, 2003. Catalogue by
Carmen C. Bambach and others. New York, 2003.

Baratte 1993
Baratte, Sophie. *Léonard Limosin au Musée du Louvre.* Paris, 1993.

Barcham 1992
Barcham, William L. *Giambattista Tiepolo.* New York, 1992.

Baroni Vannucci 1997
Baroni Vannucci, Alessandra. *Jan Van Der Straet detto Giovanni Stradano:
Flandrus pictor et inventor.* Milan and Rome, 1997.

Bartolini 1987
Bartolini, Elio. *Giovanni da Udine: La vita.* [Udine], 1987.

Bartsch 1803–21
Bartsch, Adam von. *Le peintre graveur.* 21 vols. Vienna, 1803–21.

Basan 1775
Basan, [Pierre] F[rançois]. *Catalogue raisonné des différens objets de curiosités
dans les sciences et arts, qui composoient le cabinet de feu Mr[.] Mariette,
Contrôleur général de la Grande Chancellerie de France, Honoraire Amateur
de l'Académie Rle. de Peinture, et de celle de Florence. Par F. Basan, graveur.*
Paris, 1775.

Bastogi 2008
Bastogi, Nadia. *Andrea Boscoli.* Florence, 2008.

Bean 1960
Bean, Jacob. *Les dessins italiens de la collection Bonnat.* Inventaire général
des dessins des musées de province, 4, Bayonne, Musée Bonnat. Paris,
1960.

Bean 1979
Bean, Jacob. *17th Century Italian Drawings in The Metropolitan Museum
of Art.* New York, 1979.

Bean 1990
Bean, Jacob. "Two Drawings by Jacopo Ligozzi." In *Festschrift to
Erik Fischer: European Drawings from Six Centuries,* edited by Villads
Villadsen et al., pp. 211–16. Copenhagen, 1990.

Bean and Stampfle 1965–66
The Italian Renaissance. Exhibition, The Metropolitan Museum of Art,
New York, November 8, 1965–January 9, 1966. Catalogue by Jacob
Bean and Felice Stampfle. Drawings from New York Collections, 1.
New York, 1965.

Bean and Stampfle 1971
The Eighteenth Century in Italy. Exhibition, The Metropolitan Museum
of Art, New York, January 30–March 21, 1971. Catalogue by Jacob
Bean and Felice Stampfle. Drawings from New York Collections, 3.
New York, 1971.

Bean and Turčić 1982
Bean, Jacob, and Lawrence Turčić. *15th and 16th Century Italian
Drawings in The Metropolitan Museum of Art.* New York, 1982.

Beddington 2001
Luca Carlevarijs: Views of Venice. Exhibition, Timken Museum of Art,
San Diego, April 27–August 31, 2001. Catalogue by Charles
Beddington. San Diego, 2001.

Béguin 1983–84
Béguin, Sylvie. "Disegni inediti di Nicolò dell'Abate per Palazzo
Torfanini e un pezzo d'archivio dimenticato." *Prospettiva,* no. 33–36
(April 1983–January 1984), pp. 183–90.

Béguin 2001
Béguin, Sylvie. "A proposito di due disegni di Nicolò dell'Abate." In
L'intelligenza della passione: Scritti per Andrea Emiliani, edited by
Michela Scolaro and Francesco P. Di Teodoro, pp. 73–84. Bologna,
2001.

Béguin, Di Giampaolo, and Vaccaro 2000
Béguin, Sylvie, Mario Di Giampaolo, and Mary Vaccaro. *Parmigianino:
The Drawings.* Turin and London, 2000.

Belkin 2009
Belkin, Kristin Lohse. *Rubens Copies and Adaptations from Renaissance
and Later Artists: German and Netherlandish Artists.* Corpus Rubenianum
Ludwig Burchard, part 26 (1). 2 vols. London and Turnhout, 2009.

Bellinger 2005
Bellinger, Katrin. *Master Drawings, 1985–2005.* London, 2005.

Bellori ed. 1976
Bellori, Giovanni Pietro. *Le vite de' pittori, scultori e architetti moderni.*
Edited by Evelina Borea. 1672. Turin, 1976.

Berenson ed. 1968
Berenson, Bernard. *Italian Pictures of the Renaissance: Central Italian and
North Italian Schools.* 3 vols. London and New York, 1968.

Berkeley 1996–97. *See* **Steward and Knox 1996–97.**

Bettagno 1978
Disegni di Giambattista Piranesi. Exhibition, Fondazione Giorgio Cini,
Venice, 1978. Catalogue by Alessandro Bettagno. Vicenza, 1978.

Bevers 1989–90
*Niederländische Zeichnungen des 16. Jahrhunderts in der Staatlichen graphi-
schen Sammlung München.* Exhibition, Staatliche Graphische Sammlung
München, November 22, 1989–January 21, 1990. Catalogue by Holm
Bevers. Munich, 1989.

Bigongiari and Cantelli 1970
Disegni di Cecco Bravo. Exhibition, Palazzo Strozzi, 1970. Catalogue by
Piero Bigongiari and Giuseppe Cantelli. Quaderni della Biennale
Internazionale della Grafica, 2. Florence, 1970.

Birke 1981
Guido Reni: Zeichnungen. Exhibition, Graphische Sammlung Albertina, Vienna, May 14–July 5, 1981. Catalogue by Veronika Birke. [Vienna], 1981.

Birke and Kertész 1992–97
Birke, Veronika, and Janine Kertész. *Die Italienischen Zeichnungen der Albertina, Generalverzeichnis.* Veröffentlichungen der Albertina, 33–36. 4 vols. Vienna, 1992–97.

Blanc 1870
Blanc, Charles. *Histoire des peintres de toutes les écoles: École ombrienne et romaine.* Paris, 1870.

Bleyl 1981
Bleyl, Matthias. *Bernardo Bellotto genannt Canaletto: Zeichnungen aus dem Hessischen Landesmuseum Darmstadt.* Kataloge des Hessischen Landesmuseums Darmstadt, 11. Darmstadt, 1981.

Bober and Rubinstein 1986
Bober, Phyllis Pray, and Ruth Rubinstein. *Renaissance Artists and Antique Sculpture: A Handbook of Sources.* London and Oxford, 1986.

Bohn 1988
Bohn, Babette. "Bartolommeo Passarotti and Reproductive Etching in Sixteenth-Century Italy." *Print Quarterly* 5, no. 2 (June 1988), pp. 114–27.

Bohn 1994
Bohn, Babette. Review of *Bartolomeo Passerotti* [sic] *pittore (1529–1592): Catalogo generale,* by Angela Ghirardi. *Master Drawings* 32, no. 2 (Summer 1994), pp. 163–68.

Bohn 1996
Bohn, Babette. *Italian Masters of the Sixteenth Century: Bartolommeo Passarotti, Domenico Tibaldi, Camillo Procaccini, Ludovico Carracci, and Annibale Carracci.* The Illustrated Bartsch, 39, Commentary Part 2 (*Le peintre-graveur,* 18 [Part 1]). New York, 1996.

Bohn 2004
Bohn, Babette. *Ludovico Carracci and the Art of Drawing.* Turnhout, Belgium, 2004.

Bohn 2008
Le "Stanze" di Guido Reni: Disegni del maestro e della scuola. Exhibition, Gabinetto Disegni e Stampe, Galleria degli Uffizi, Florence, March 27–June 1, 2008. Catalogue by Babette Bohn. Gabinetto Disegni e Stampe degli Uffizi, Cataloghi, 95. Florence, 2008.

Bok-van Kammen 1977
Bok-van Kammen, Welmoet. "Stradanus and the Hunt." PhD diss., Johns Hopkins University, Baltimore, 1977.

Bologna 1954
Mostra di Guido Reni. Exhibition, Palazzo dell'Archiginnasio, Bologna, September 1–October 31, 1954. Catalogue by Gian Carlo Cavalli, Andrea Emiliani, and Lidia Puglioli Mandelli. Bologna, 1954.

Bologna 1963
Mostra di incisioni di G. B. Piranesi. Exhibition, Palazzo di Re Enzo, Bologna, January 27–February 24, 1963. Catalogue by Maria Catelli Isola, Amalia Mezzetti, and Silla Zamboni. Bologna, 1963.

Bologna 1968. *See* **Mahon 1968.**

Bologna 1988
Bologna e l'umanesimo, 1490–1510. Exhibition, Pinacoteca Nazionale, Bologna, March 6–April 24, 1988. Catalogue by Marzia Faietti, Konrad Oberhuber, and others. Bologna, 1988.

Bologna 1991
Giovanni Francesco Barbieri il Guercino, 1591–1666: Disegni. Exhibition, Museo Civico Archeologico, Bologna, September 6–November 10, 1991. Catalogue by Denis Mahon and others. Bologna, 1992.

Bologna 2005
Primaticcio: Un bolognese alla corte di Francia. Exhibition, Palazzo di Re Enzo e del Podestà, Bologna, January 30–April 10, 2005. Catalogue by Dominique Cordellier and others. Milan, 2005.

Bologna 2008–9
Amico Aspertini, 1474–1552: Artista bizzarro nell'età di Dürer e Raffaello. Exhibition, Pinacoteca Nazionale, Bologna, September 27, 2008–January 11, 2009. Catalogue by Andrea Emiliani, Daniela Scaglietti Kelescian, and others. Cinisello Balsamo, Milan, 2008.

Bologna, Frankfurt, and Washington, D.C., 1991–92
Guercino: Master Painter of the Baroque. Exhibition, Pinacoteca Nazionale, Bologna, July 6–November 10, 1991; Schirn Kunsthalle, Frankfurt, December 2, 1991–February 9, 1992; National Gallery of Art, Washington, D.C., March 15–May 17, 1992. Catalogue by Denis Mahon and others. Washington, D.C., 1991.

Bologna, Los Angeles, and Fort Worth 1988–89
Guido Reni, 1575–1642. Exhibition, Pinacoteca Nazionale, Bologna, September 5–November 10, 1988; Los Angeles County Museum of Art, December 11, 1988–February 14, 1989; Kimbell Art Museum, Fort Worth, March 10–May 10, 1989. Catalogue by D. Stephen Pepper and others. Bologna, 1988.

Bologna, Washington, D.C., and New York 1986–87
The Age of Correggio and the Carracci: Emilian Painting of the Sixteenth and Seventeenth Centuries. Exhibition, Pinacoteca Nazionale, Bologna, September 10–November 10, 1986; National Gallery of Art, Washington, D.C., December 19, 1986–February 16, 1987; The Metropolitan Museum of Art, New York, March 26–May 24, 1987. Catalogue by Giuliano Briganti and others. Washington, D.C., 1986.

Bonger-van der Borch van Verwolde 1941
Bonger-van der Borch van Verwolde, F. "De invloed van den Theagenes- en Chariclea roman op de beeldende kunsten." *Maandblad voor beeldende kunsten* 18, no. 4 (April 1941), pp. 114–24.

Boon 1992
Boon, Karel G. *The Netherlandish and German Drawings of the XVth and XVIth Centuries of the Frits Lugt Collection.* 3 vols. Paris, 1992.

Boschini ed. 1733
Boschini, Marco. *Descrizione di tutte le pubbliche pitture della città di Venezia e isole circonvicine: o sia rinnovazione delle* Ricche minere *di Marco Boschini, colla aggiunta di tutte le opera, che uscirono da 1674 sino al presente 1733: con un compendio della vite e maniere de' principali pittori.* Edited by Antonio Maria Zanetti. 1674. Venice, 1733.

Bremen and Zurich 1967. *See* **Sumowski 1967.**

Briganti 1982
Briganti, Giuliano. *Pietro da Cortona o della pittura barocca.* 2nd ed. 1962. Florence, 1982.

Briganti 1996
Briganti, Giuliano. *Gaspar van Wittel.* Edited by Laura Laureati and Ludovica Trezzani. New ed. 1966. Milan, 1996.

Briquet 1923
Briquet, C[harles]-M[oïse]. *Les filigranes: Dictionnaire historique des marques du papier dès leur apparition vers 1282 jusqu'en 1600.* Leipzig, 1923.

Briquet 1968
Briquet, C[harles]-M[oïse]. *Les filigranes: Dictionnaire historique des marques du papier dès leur apparition vers 1282 jusqu'en 1600.* Edited by Allan Stevenson. Rev. ed. 4 vols. 1923. Amsterdam, 1968.

Brown 1972
Brown, Jonathan. "Notes on Princeton Drawings 6: Jusepe de Ribera." *Record of The Art Museum, Princeton University* 31, no. 2 (1972), pp. 2–7.

Brown 1973–74
Jusepe de Ribera: Prints and Drawings. Exhibition, The Art Museum, Princeton University, Princeton, N.J., October–November 1973; Fogg Art Museum, Harvard University, Cambridge, Mass., December 1973–January 1974. Catalogue by Jonathan Brown. Princeton, N.J., 1973.

Brown 1974
Brown, Jonathan. "More Drawings by Jusepe de Ribera." *Master Drawings* 12, no. 4 (Winter 1974), pp. 367–72, pls. 25–36.

Brown 1982–83
Brown, Jonathan. "The Prints and Drawings of Ribera." In *Jusepe de Ribera Lo Spagnoletto, 1591–1652,* pp. 70–90. Exhibition, Kimbell Art Museum, Fort Worth, Texas, December 4, 1982–February 6, 1983. Catalogue by Craig Felton, William B. Jordan, and others. Fort Worth, 1982.

Brown 1989
Jusepe de Ribera, Grabador, 1591–1652. Exhibition, Sala de Exposiciones de la Fundación Caja de Pensiones, Valencia, January 13–February 12, 1989; Calcografía Nacional, Real Academia de Bellas Artes de San Fernando, Alcalá, February 23–March 28, 1989. Catalogue by Jonathan Brown. Valencia, 1989.

Brown and Delmarcel 1996
Brown, Clifford M., and Guy Delmarcel. *Tapestries for the Courts of Federico II, Ercole, and Ferrante Gonzaga, 1522–63.* Seattle and London, 1996.

Brugerolles and Guillet 1994–95
The Renaissance in France: Drawings from the École des Beaux-Arts, Paris. Exhibition, École nationale supérieure des Beaux-Arts, Paris, September 23–November 6, 1994; Fogg Art Museum, Harvard University Art Museums, Cambridge, Mass., February 4–April 9, 1995; The Metropolitan Museum of Art, New York, September 12–November 12, 1995. Catalogue by Emmanuelle Brugerolles and David Guillet. New York, 1994.

Bruges 2008–9
Stradanus (1523–1605): Court Artist of the Medici. Exhibition, Groeningemuseum, Bruges, October 9, 2008–January 4, 2009. Catalogue by Manfred Sellink and others. Turnhout, Belgium, forthcoming.

Brussels 1983
Dessins venitiens du XVIIIe siècle. Exhibition, Palais des Beaux-Arts, Brussels, April 15–June 5, 1983. Catalogue by Giandomenico Romanelli and others. Brussels, 1983.

Brussels 1993
De Giorgione à Tiepolo: Dessins italiens du 15e au 18e siècle dans les collections privées et publiques de Belgique. Exhibition, Musée communal d'Ixelles, Brussels, October 8–December 12, 1993. Catalogue by Benoît Boëlens van Waesberghe and others. Brussels, 1993.

Brussels and Rome 1995 (Dutch ed.)
Fiamminghi a Roma 1508–1608: Kunstenaars uit de Nederlanden en het prinsbisdom Luik te Rome tijdens de Renaissance. Exhibition, Paleis voor Schone Kunsten, Brussels, February 24–May 21, 1995; Palazzo delle esposizioni, Rome, June 16–September 10, 1995. Catalogue by Piet Coessens, Nicole Dacos, and others. Brussels, 1995.

Brussels and Rome 1995 (Italian ed.)
Fiamminghi a Roma 1508–1608: Artisti dei Paesi Bassi e del Principato di Liegi a Roma durante il Rinascimento. Exhibition, Palais des Beaux-Arts, Brussels, February 24–May 21, 1995; Palazzo delle esposizioni, Rome, June 16–September 10, 1995. Catalogue by Piet Coessens, Nicole Dacos, and others. Brussels, 1995.

Buffa 1982
Buffa, Sebastian. *Italian Artists of the Sixteenth Century.* The Illustrated Bartsch, 34; formerly Vol. 17 (Part 1). New York, 1982.

***Burlington Magazine* 1985**
"London Calendar." *The Burlington Magazine* 127, no. 985 (April 1985), p. 271.

Buschmann 1916
Buschmann, Paul. "Drawings by Cornelis Bos and Cornelis Floris." *The Burlington Magazine* 29, no. 164 (November 1916), pp. 325–26, pl. 1.

Byam Shaw 1954
Byam Shaw, J[ames]. "The Drawings of Francesco Fontebasso." *Arte veneta* 8 (1954), pp. 317–25.

Byam Shaw 1962
Byam Shaw, James. *The Drawings of Domenico Tiepolo.* London, 1962.

Byam Shaw 1976
Byam Shaw, James. *Drawings by Old Masters at Christ Church, Oxford.* 2 vols. Oxford, 1976.

Byam Shaw 1983
Byam Shaw, James. *The Italian Drawings of the Frits Lugt Collection.* 3 vols. Paris, 1983.

Cambridge 1988. *See* **Ward 1988.**

Cambridge, Mass., 1970. *See* **Knox 1970.**

Cambridge, Mass., and New York 1996–97. *See* **Aikema and Dreyer 1996–97.**

Cambridge, Mass., Ottawa, and Cleveland 1991. *See* **Stone 1991.**

Campbell et al. 2002
Tapestry in the Renaissance: Art and Magnificence. Exhibition, The Metropolitan Museum of Art, New York, March 14–June 19, 2002. Catalogue by Thomas P. Campbell and others. New York, 2002.

Caracciolo 2001
Caracciolo, Maria Teresa. "Pour le Maître des albums Egmont et ses sources." In *Francesco Salviati et la Bella Maniera: Actes des colloques de Rome et de Paris (1998),* edited by Catherine Monbeig Goguel, Philippe Costamagna, and Michel Hochmann, pp. 667–89. Collection de L'École Française de Rome, 284. Rome, 2001.

Cargnelutti, ed. 1987
Cargnelutti, Liliana, ed. *Giovanni da Udine: I Libri dei conti.* Udine, 1987.

Cera 2002
Cera, Adriano. *Disegni, acquarelli, tempere di artisti italiani dal 1770 ca. al 1830 ca.* 2 vols. Bologna, 2002.

Chappell 1983
Chappell, Miles L. "On the Identification of a Collector's Mark (Lugt 2729)." *Master Drawings* 21, no. 1 (Spring 1983), pp. 36–58.

Chappell 1990
Chappell, Miles [L]. "Proposals for Coccapani." *Paradigma* [*Firenze*] 9 (1990), pp. 183–90.

Chiappini di Sorio 1975
Chiappini di Sorio, Ileana. *Cristoforo Roncalli detto il Pomarancio.* I pittori Bergamaschi dal XIII al XIX secolo, il Seicento, 1. Bergamo, 1975.

Christie's, London 1971
Fine Old Master Drawings. Sale catalogue, Christie's, London, November 23, 1971. London, 1971.

Christie's, London 1980
Important Old Master Drawings. Sale catalogue, Christie's, London, April 15, 1980. London, 1980.

Christie's, London 1990
Old Master Drawings. Sale catalogue, Christie's, London, July 3, 1990. London, 1990.

Christie's, London 1991
Old Master Drawings from Holkham. Sale catalogue, Christie's, London, July 2, 1991. London, 1991.

Christie's, London 1995
Old Master Drawings. Sale catalogue, Christie's, London, July 4, 1995. London, 1995.

Christie's, London 1998
Old Master Drawings. Sale catalogue, Christie's, London, July 3, 1998. London, 1998.

Christie's, London 1999
Old Master Drawings. Sale catalogue, Christie's, London, July 6, 1999. London, 1999.

Christie's, London 2007
Old Master and 19th Century Drawings. Sale catalogue, Christie's, London, July 3, 2007. London, 2007.

Christie's, Monaco 1994
Dessins de maîtres anciens et du XIXème siècle: Dessins de la collection de M. Alfred Normand. Sale catalogue, Christie's, London, at Hôtel Métropole Palace, Monte Carlo, Monaco, June 20, 1994. Monte Carlo, 1994.

Christie's, New York 1997
Old Master Drawings. Sale catalogue, Christie's, New York, January 30, 1997. New York, 1997.

Christie's, New York 1999
Important Old Master Drawings. Sale catalogue, Christie's, New York, January 28, 1999. New York, 1999.

Ciabani 1992–93
Ciabani, Roberto. *Le famiglie di Firenze.* 4 vols. Florence, 1992–93.

Cocke 1972
Cocke, Richard. *Pier Francesco Mola.* Oxford Studies in the History of Art and Architecture. Oxford, 1972.

Concina and Reale 1995–96
Luca Carlevarijs: Le fabriche, e vedute di Venetia. Exhibition, Soprintendenza BAAAAS, Friuli-Venezia Giulia, Udine, December 4, 1995–January 20, 1996. Catalogue by Ennio Concina and Isabella Reale. Venice, 1995.

Conigliello 1990a
Conigliello, Lucilla. "Alcune note su Jacopo Ligozzi e sui dipinti del 1594." *Paragone* 41, no. 485 (July 1990), pp. 21–42, pls. 16–25.

Conigliello 1990b
Conigliello, Lucilla. "L'intervento di Jacopo Ligozzi e il completamento del ciclo." In *Il chiostro di Ognissanti a Firenze: Restauro e restituzione degli affreschi del ciclo francescano,* pp. 31–37. Quaderni dell'Ufficio Restauri della Soprintendenza per i Beni Artistici e Storici di Firenze e Pistoia, 2. Florence, 1990.

Conigliello 1992
Jacopo Ligozzi: Le Vedute del Sacro Monte della Verna; I dipiniti di Poppi e Bibbiena. Exhibition, Castello dei Conti Guidi, Poppi, July 4–September 30, 1992. Catalogue by Lucilla Conigliello. Poppi, 1992.

Conigliello 1994
Conigliello, Lucilla. "Francesco di Jacopo Ligozzi." *Paragone* 45, no. 527 (January 1994), pp. 41–52, pls. 28–40.

Conigliello 1999
Conigliello, Lucilla. *Le Vedute del Sacro Monte della Verna: Jacopo Ligozzi, pellegrino nei luoghi di Francesco.* Florence, 1999.

Conigliello 2005
Ligozzi. Exhibition, Musée du Louvre, Paris, January 26–June 25, 2005. Catalogue by Lucilla Conigliello. Paris and Milan, 2005.

Conigliello 2007
Conigliello, Lucilla. "Four Sheets from Jacopo Ligozzi's Album of Figures of the Ottoman Empire: Old Master Drawings to Be Included as Lots 48–51 in the Old Master Paintings Sale, January 25, 2007." In *Old Master Drawings,* pp. 6–15. Sale catalogue, Sotheby's, New York, January 24, 2007. New York, 2007.

Constable and Links 1989
Constable, W[illiam] G. *Canaletto: Giovanni Antonio Canal, 1697–1768.* 2nd ed., revised by J. G. Links. 2 vols. 1962. Oxford, 1989.

Cooney 1974
Cooney, J. Patrick. "Drawings by Il Volterrano for Three Decorative Projects." *Master Drawings* 12, no. 4 (Winter 1974), pp. 372–76, pls. 37–45.

Cosmo 1984
Cosmo, Giulia. "Aspertini e la scultura antica." *Antologia di belle arti,* nos. 21–22 (1984), pp. 24–39.

Cox-Rearick et al. 1999
Giulio Romano, Master Designer: An Exhibition of Drawings in Celebration of the Five Hundredth Anniversary of His Birth. Exhibition, The Bertha and Karl Leubsdorf Art Gallery, Hunter College, New York, September 16–November 27, 1999. Catalogue by Janet Cox-Rearick and others. New York, 1999.

Dacos 1987
Dacos, Nicole. "Raphaël et les Pays-Bas: L'École de Bruxelles." In *Studi su Raffaello: Atti del Congresso Internazionale di Studi (Urbino-Firenze, 6–14 aprile 1984),* edited by Micaela Sambucco Hamoud and Maria Letizia Strocchi, vol. 1, pp. 611–23, vol. 2, figs. 304–9b. 2 vols. Urbino, 1987.

Dacos 1990
Dacos, Nicole. "Le Maître des albums Egmont: Dirck Hendricksz Centen." *Oud Holland* 104, no. 2 (1990), pp. 49–68.

Dacos and Furlan 1987
Dacos, Nicole, and Caterina Furlan. *Giovanni da Udine, 1487–1561.* [Udine], 1987.

Dacos et al. 1980
Dacos, Nicole, et al. *Il tesoro di Lorenzo il Magnifico: Repertorio delle gemme e dei vasi.* Florence, 1980.

Davidson 1959
Davidson, Bernice. "Drawings by Perino del Vaga for the Palazzo Doria, Genoa." *The Art Bulletin* 41, no. 4 (December 1959), pp. 315–26.

De Dominici ed. 2008
De Dominici, Bernardo. *Vite de' pittori, scultori ed architetti napoletani.* Edited by Fiorella Sricchia Santoro and Andrea Zezza. 2 vols. 1742. Naples, 2008.

De Grazia 2003
De Grazia, Diane. Review of *Parmigianino: The Drawings,* by Sylvie Béguin, Mario Di Giampaolo, and Mary Vaccaro. *Master Drawings* 41, no. 4 (Winter 2003), pp. 388–91.

DeGrazia Bohlin 1980
DeGrazia Bohlin, Diane. *Italian Masters of the Sixteenth Century.* The Illustrated Bartsch, 39; formerly Vol. 18 (Part 1). New York, 1980.

DeGrazia et al. 1984
Correggio e il suo lascito: Disegni del Cinquecento emiliano. Exhibition, Palazzo della Pilotta, Parma, June 6–July 15, 1984. Catalogue by Diane DeGrazia and others. Parma, 1984.

Delmarcel 1997
Delmarcel, Guy. "Giulio Romano and Tapestry at the Court of Mantua." In *La corte di Mantova nell'età di Andrea Mantegna, 1450–1550: Atti del convegno, Londra, 6–8 marzo 1992, Mantua, 28 marzo 1992 / The Court of the Gonzaga in the Age of Mantegna, 1450–1550,* edited by Cesare Mozzarelli, Robert Oresko, and Leandro Ventura, pp. 383–92, figs. 1–7. Rome, 1997.

Delmarcel and Brown 1988
Delmarcel, Guy, and Clifford M. Brown. "Les Jeux d'Enfants: Tapisseries italiennes et flamandes pour les Gonzague." *RACAR: Revue d'art canadienne/Canadian Art Review* 15, no. 2 (1988), pp. 109–21, 170–77.

De Tolnay 1948
De Tolnay, Charles. *Michelangelo.* Vol. 3, *The Medici Chapel.* Princeton, N.J., 1948.

Di Giampaolo 1997
Di Giampaolo, Mario. *Girolamo Bedoli, 1500–1569.* Florence, 1997.

Di Giampaolo 2001
Di Giampaolo, Mario. *Correggio disegnatore/Correggio as Draughtsman.* Cinisello Balsamo, Milan, 2001.

Di Giampaolo et al. 1989
Di Giampaolo, Mario, et al. *Disegni emiliani del Rinascimento.* Milan, 1989.

Drawing 1996
"International Auction Review." *Drawing* 18, no. 2 (Fall 1996), pp. 56–61.

Edinburgh 1998
Effigies and Ecstasies: Roman Baroque Sculpture and Design in the Age of Bernini. Exhibition, National Gallery of Scotland, Edinburgh, June 25–September 20, 1998. Catalogue by Aidan Weston-Lewis and others. Edinburgh, 1998.

Ekserdjian 1997
Ekserdjian, David. *Correggio.* New Haven and London, 1997.

Ekserdjian 1999
Ekserdjian, David. "Unpublished Drawings by Parmigianino: Towards a Supplement to Popham's *catalogue raisonné.*" *Apollo* 150, no. 450 (August 1999), pp. 3–41.

Ekserdjian 2001
Ekserdjian, David. "Parmigianino and the Antique." *Apollo* 154, no. 473 (July 2001), pp. 42–50.

Ekserdjian 2006
Ekserdjian, David. *Parmigianino.* New Haven and London, 2006.

Emiliani 1985
Emiliani, Andrea. *Federico Barocci (Urbino 1535–1612).* 2 vols. Bologna, 1985.

Fagiolo and Madonna 1972
Fagiolo, Marcello, and Maria Luisa Madonna. "La Casina di Pio IV in Vaticano: Pirro Ligorio e l'architettura come geroglifico." *Storia dell'arte,* nos. 15/16 (July–December 1972), pp. 237–81.

Faietti and Scaglietti Kelescian 1995
Faietti, Marzia, and Daniela Scaglietti Kelescian. *Amico Aspertini.* Modena, 1995.

Faranda 1986
Faranda, Franco. *Ludovico Cardi detto il Cigoli.* Rome, 1986.

Feigenbaum 1993
Feigenbaum, Gail. "Practice in the Carracci Academy." In *The Artist's Workshop* [Proceedings of the symposium . . . sponsored by the Center for Advanced Study in the Visual Arts and Johns Hopkins University Department of the History of Art, Washington, D.C., March 10–11, 1989], edited by Peter M. Lukehart. *Studies in the History of Art* 38 (1993), pp. 58–76.

Fermor 1996
Fermor, Sharon. *The Raphael Tapestry Cartoons: Narrative, Decoration, Design.* London, 1996.

Finaldi 1992
Finaldi, Gabriele. "Apéndice documental de la vida y la obra de José de Ribera." In **Madrid 1992,** pp. 485–504.

Finaldi 2005
Finaldi, Gabriele. "Dibujos inéditos y otros poco conocidos de Jusepe de Ribera." *Boletín del Museo del Prado* 23, no. 41 (2005), pp. 24–44.

Fischel 1912
Fischel, Oskar. "Letters to the Editors: Some Lost Drawings by or near to Raphael." *The Burlington Magazine* 20, no. 107 (February 1912), pp. 294–301.

Fischer Pace 1997
Disegni del Seicento romano. Exhibition, Gabinetto disegni e stampe, Galleria degli Uffizi, Florence, 1997. Catalogue by Ursula Verena Fischer Pace. Gabinetto Disegni e Stampe degli Uffizi, [Cataloghi,] 80. Florence, 1997.

Florence 1970. *See* **Bigongiari and Cantelli 1970.**

Florence 1976. *See* **Rearick 1976.**

Florence 1986–87
Il Seicento fiorentino: Arte a Firenze da Ferdinando I a Cosimo III. Exhibition, Palazzo Strozzi, Florence, December 21, 1986–May 4, 1987. 3 vols. Catalogue by Piero Bigongiari, Mina Gregori, and others. Florence, 1986.

Florence 1997. *See* **Fischer Pace 1997.**

Florence 1997–98
Magnificenza alla corte dei Medici: Arte a Firenze alla fine del Cinquecento. Exhibition, Palazzo Pitti, Museo degli Argenti, Florence, September 24, 1997–January 6, 1998. Catalogue by Detlef Heikamp and others. Milan, 1997.

Florence 1999
Cecco Bravo: Pittore senza regola, Firenze 1601–Innsbruck 1661. Exhibition, Casa Buonarroti, Florence, June 23–September 30, 1999. Catalogue by Anna Barsanti, Roberto Contini, and Luigi Baldacci. Milan, 1999.

Florence 2008. *See* **Bohn 2008.**

Florence and Rome 1983–84. *See* **Meijer and van Tuyll 1983–84.**

Florence, Chicago, and Detroit 2002–3
The Medici, Michelangelo, and the Art of Late Renaissance Florence. Exhibition, Palazzo Strozzi, Florence, June 6–September 29, 2002; The Art Institute of Chicago, November 9, 2002–February 2, 2003; The Detroit Institute of Arts, March 16–June 8, 2003. Catalogue by Cristina Acidini Luchinat and others. New Haven and London, 2002.

Forlani 1982
Forlani, Anna. "Jacopo Ligozzi nel Gran Serraglio." *FMR* (Milan), no. 1 (March 1982), pp. 72–103.

Fornari Schianchi 2008
Fornari Schianchi, Lucia. "Gerolamo Bedoli:'Invenzioni' pittoriche e interpretazione del modello parmigianinesco negli arconi e nei catini nord e sud." In *Santa Maria della Steccata a Parma: Da chiesa "civica" a basilica magistrale dell'Ordine costantiniano,* edited by Bruno Adorni, pp. 215–34. Milan, 2008.

Fortunati Pietrantonio et al. 1986
Fortunati Pietrantonio, Vera, et al. *Pittura bolognese del +500.* 2 vols. Bologna, 1986.

Franchini Guelfi 1999
Franchini Guelfi, Fausta. *Alessandro Magnasco: I disegni.* Genoa, 1999.

Franklin and Ekserdjian 2003–4
The Art of Parmigianino. Exhibition, National Gallery of Canada, Ottawa, October 3, 2003–January 4, 2004; The Frick Collection, New York, January 27–April 18, 2004. Catalogue by David Franklin and David Ekserdjian. Ottawa, 2003.

Franklin et al. 2005
Leonardo da Vinci, Michelangelo, and the Renaissance in Florence. Exhibition, National Gallery of Canada, Ottawa, May 29–September 5, 2005. Catalogue by David Franklin, Louis A. Waldman, and Andrew Butterfield. Ottawa, 2005.

Frey 1923–30
Frey, Karl, ed. and annot. *Der literarische Nachlass Giorgio Vasaris.* 2 vols. Munich, 1923–30.

Fuhring 1989
Fuhring, Peter. *Design into Art, Drawings for Architecture and Ornament: The Lodewijk Houthakker Collection.* 2 vols. London, 1989.

Fusconi et al. 1992
Fusconi, Giulia, et al. *Drawing.* Vol. 2, *The Great Collectors.* Turin and Cinisello Balsamo, Milan, 1992.

Gainesville and other cities 1991–93. *See* **Wolk-Simon 1991–93.**

Garboli 1971
Garboli, Cesare. *L'opera completa di Guido Reni.* Classici dell'arte, 48. Milan, 1971.

Gealt 1986
Gealt, Adelheid [M]. *Domenico Tiepolo: The Punchinello Drawings.* New York, 1986.

Gealt and Knox 2006–7
Domenico Tiepolo: A New Testament. Exhibition, The Frick Collection, New York, October 24, 2006–January 7, 2007. Catalogue by Adelheid M. Gealt and George Knox. Bloomington, Ind., 2006.

Gealt et al. 2005
Gealt, Adelheid M., et al. *Giandomenico Tiepolo: Scene di vita quotidiana a Venezia e nella terraferma.* [Venice], 2005.

Gemin and Pedrocco 1993
Gemin, Massimo, and Filippo Pedrocco. *Giambattista Tiepolo, I dipinti: Opera completa.* Venice, 1993.

Gentili di Giuseppe 1933
Gentili di Giuseppe, Federico. "Una lettera autografa inedita di Raffaello e un disegno di lui ritenuto smarrito." *L'arte* 36, no. 1 (January 1933), pp. 30–37.

Gere 1960
Gere, J[ohn] A. "Two Late Fresco Cycles by Perino del Vaga: The Massimi Chapel and the Sala Paolina." *The Burlington Magazine* 102, no. 682 (January 1960), pp. 8–19.

Gere 1969
Gere, J[ohn] A. *Taddeo Zuccaro: His Development Studied in His Drawings.* London, 1969.

Gere 1970
Gere, J[ohn] A. "The Lawrence-Phillipps-Rosenbach 'Zuccaro Album.'" *Master Drawings* 8, no. 2 (Summer 1970), pp. 123–40, pls. 1–27.

Gere 1971
Gere, J[ohn] A. "Some Early Drawings by Pirro Ligorio." *Master Drawings* 9, no. 3 (Autumn 1971), pp. 239–50, pls. 1–24.

Gerszi 2005
Gerszi, Teréz. *17th-Century Dutch and Flemish Drawings in the Budapest Museum of Fine Arts: A Complete Catalogue.* Budapest, 2005.

Ghirardi 1990
Ghirardi, Angela. *Bartolomeo Passerotti, pittore (1529–1592): Catalogo generale / Painter (1529–1592): General Catalogue.* Rimini, 1990.

Gnann 2007
Gnann, Achim. *Parmigianino: Die Zeichnungen.* Studien zur internationalen Architektur- und Kunstgeschichte, 58. 2 vols. Petersberg, Germany, 2007.

Goldner 1983–84
Master Drawings from the Woodner Collection. Exhibition, The J. Paul Getty Museum, Malibu, May 28–August 12, 1983; Kimbell Art Museum, Fort Worth, September 10–November 13, 1983; National Gallery of Art, Washington, D.C., December 18, 1983–February 26, 1984. Catalogue by George R. Goldner. Malibu, 1983.

Goldner 1993
Goldner, George R. "A New Domenichino Drawing." In *Essays in Memory of Jacob Bean (1923–1992),* edited by Linda Wolk-Simon and William M. Griswold. *Master Drawings* 31, no. 4 (Winter 1993), pp. 426–27.

Goldner, Hendrix, and Pask 1992
Goldner, George R., Lee Hendrix, and Kelly Pask. *European Drawings 2: Catalogue of the Collections.* [The J. Paul Getty Museum.] Malibu, 1992.

Graf 1998
Graf, Dieter. "Disegni di Pietro da Cortona e della sua scuola per il Missale Romanum del 1662." In *Pietro da Cortona: Atti del convegno internazionale Roma-Firenze, 12–15 novembre 1997,* edited by Christoph Luitpold Frommel and Sebastian Schütze, pp. 201–14. [Milan], 1998.

Grimbert 1995
Grimbert, Joan Tasker. *Tristan and Isolde: A Casebook.* New York and London, 1995.

Griswold 1995
Griswold, William M. "New York: Old-Master Paintings and Drawings." *The Burlington Magazine* 137, no. 1104 (March 1995), pp. 203–5.

Griswold and Wolk-Simon 1994
Sixteenth-Century Italian Drawings in New York Collections. Exhibition, The Metropolitan Museum of Art, New York, January 11–March 27, 1994. Catalogue by William M. Griswold and Linda Wolk-Simon. New York, 1994.

Guicciardini ed. 1984
Guicciardini, Francesco. *The History of Italy.* Translated, edited, and annotated by Sidney Alexander. 1969. Princeton, N.J., 1984.

Gunn 1831
Gunn, W[illiam]. *Cartonensia, or, An historical and critical account of the tapestries in the palace of the Vatican: copied from the designs of Raphael of Urbino, and of such of the cartoons whence they were woven as are now in preservation.* London, 1831.

Halm 1950
Halm, Peter. "Staatliche Graphische Sammlung." In "Berichte der Staatlichen Kunstsammlungen: Neuerwerbungen 1945–1949." *Münchner Jahrbuch der bildenden Kunst,* ser. 3, 1 (1950), pp. 247–50.

Harris 1969
Harris, Ann Sutherland. "Trois nouvelles études de Pier Francesco Mola pour la fresque du Quirinal 'Joseph et ses frères.'" *Revue de l'art,* no. 6 (1969), pp. 82–87.

Harris 1977
Harris, Ann Sutherland. *Selected Drawings of Gian Lorenzo Bernini.* New York, 1977.

Harris 2003
Harris, Ann Sutherland. "Three Proposals for Gian Lorenzo Bernini." *Master Drawings* 41, no. 2 (Summer 2003), pp. 119–27.

Hartt 1958
Hartt, Frederick. *Giulio Romano.* 2 vols. New Haven, 1958.

Haskell and Penny 1981
Haskell, Francis, and Nicholas Penny. *Taste and the Antique: The Lure of Classical Sculpture, 1500–1900.* New Haven and London, 1981.

Haverkamp-Begemann and Logan 1970
Haverkamp-Begemann, E[gbert], and Anne-Marie S. Logan. *European Drawings and Watercolors in the Yale University Art Gallery, 1500–1900.* 2 vols. New Haven and London, 1970.

Heikamp 1957
Heikamp, Detlef. "Vicende di Federigo Zuccari." *Rivista d'arte* 32, ser. 3, 7 (1957), pp. 175–232.

Held 1980
Held, Julius S. *The Oil Sketches of Peter Paul Rubens. A Critical Catalogue.* 2 vols. Princeton, N.J., 1980.

Heliodorus ed. 1957
Heliodorus. *An Ethiopian Romance.* Translated by Moses Hadas. Ann Arbor, Mich., 1957.

Heliodorus ed. 1960
Héliodore [Heliodorus]. *Les éthiopiques: Théagène et Chariclée.* Edited by R[obert] M. Rattenbury and T[homas] W. Lumb; translated by J[ean Claude] Maillon. Collection des universités de France. 2nd ed. 3 vols. 1935–43. Paris, 1960.

Hibbard 1965
Hibbard, Howard. "Notes on Reni's Chronology." *The Burlington Magazine* 107, no. 751 (October 1965), pp. 502–10.

Hibbard and Jaffe 1964
Hibbard, Howard, and Irma Jaffe. "Bernini's Barcaccia." *The Burlington Magazine* 106, no. 733 (April 1964), pp. 159–71.

Hollstein 1980
Hollstein, F[riedrich] W[ilhelm] H[einrich]. *Dutch and Flemish Etchings, Engravings, and Woodcuts, ca. 1450–1700.* Vol. 21, *Aegidius Sadeler to Raphael Sadeler II.* Text compiled by Dieuwke de Hoop Scheffer; edited by K[arel] G. Boon. Amsterdam, 1980.

Höper 1987
Höper, Corinna. *Bartolomeo Passarotti (1529–1592).* Manuskripte zur
Kunstwissenschaft in der Wernerschen Verlagsgesellschaft, 12. 2 vols.
Worms, 1987.

D'Hulst and Vandenven 1989
D'Hulst, R[oger]-A[dolf], and M[arc] Vandenven. *Rubens: The Old
Testament.* London, 1989.

Ilchman and Saywell 2007
Ilchman, Frederick, and Edward Saywell. "Michelangelo and
Tintoretto: *Disegno* and Drawing." In **Madrid 2007,** pp. 385–415.

Ilg 2008
Ilg, Ulrike. "Vom Reisebericht zum ethnographischen Kompendium:
Zur Rezeptionsgeschichte von Nicolas de Nicolays *Quatre premiers
livres des navigations et pérégrinations orientales (1567)."* In *Text und Bild
in Reiseberichten des 16. Jahrhunderts: Westlische Zeugnisse über Amerika
und das Osmanische Reich,* edited by Ulrike Ilg, pp. 161–92, 298–308.
Kunsthistorisches Institut in Florenz Max-Planck-Institut, Studi e
ricerche, 3. Venice, 2008.

Il Giornale dell'arte 1999
Il Giornale dell'arte, no. 177 (May 1999), pp. 92–93.

Indianapolis 1955
European Old Master Drawings from Indiana Collections. Exhibition,
John Herron Art Museum, Indianapolis, March 6–April 10, 1955.
Indianapolis, 1955.

Jaffé 1956
Jaffé, Michael. "Cornelius Bos en Peter Paul Rubens." *Bulletin Museum
Boymans* 7, no. 1 (1956), pp. 6–10.

Jaffé 1989
Jaffé, Michael. *Rubens: Catalogo completo.* Milan, 1989.

Jaffé 1994
Jaffé, Michael. *The Devonshire Collection of Italian Drawings.* [Vol. 2],
Roman and Neapolitan Schools. London, 1994.

Jerusalem 1977
*Old Master Drawings: A Loan from the Collection of the Duke of
Devonshire.* Exhibition, The Israel Museum, Jerusalem, April–July 1977.
Jerusalem, 1977.

Jestaz 1994
Jestaz, Bertrand. "Il Palazzo Farnese di Caprarola." In *Casa Farnese:
Caprarola, Roma, Piacenza, Parma,* by Ingeborg Walter et al., pp. 35–71.
Milan, 1994.

Joachim and McCullagh 1979
Joachim, Harold, and Suzanne Folds McCullagh. *Italian Drawings in
the Art Institute of Chicago.* Chicago and London, 1979.

Kahn-Rossi 1989–90
Kahn-Rossi, Manuela. "Pier Francesco Mola e la caricatura." In
Lugano and Rome 1989–90, pp. 121–33.

Knox 1970
*Tiepolo, A Bicentenary Exhibition, 1770–1970: Drawings, Mainly from
American Collections, by Giambattista Tiepolo and the Members of His
Circle.* Exhibition, Fogg Art Museum, Harvard University, Cambridge,
Mass., March 14–May 3, 1970. Catalogue by George Knox.
Cambridge, Mass., 1970.

Knox 1974
Knox, George. *Un quaderno di vedute di Giambattista e Domenico Tiepolo.*
[Milan, 1974].

Knox 1975
Knox, George. *Catalogue of the Tiepolo Drawings in the Victoria and Albert
Museum.* 2nd ed. 1960. London, 1975.

Knox 1996–97
Knox, George. "The Private Art of the Tiepolos." In **Steward and
Knox 1996–97,** pp. 34–48.

Kozakiewicz 1972
Kozakiewicz, Stefan. *Bernardo Bellotto.* 2 vols. Greenwich, Conn., 1972.

Kügelgen 1992
Kügelgen, H. von. "Aspertini, Amico." In *Saur Allgemeines Künstler-
Lexikon: Die Bildenden Künstler aller Zeiten und Völker,* vol. 5,
pp. 441–44. Munich and Leipzig, 1992.

Leesberg 2008
Leesberg, Marjolein. *Johannes Stradanus.* Edited by Huigen Leeflang.
3 vols. The New Hollstein Dutch and Flemish Etchings, Engravings
and Woodcuts, 1450–1700, [18]. Ouderkerk aan den IJssel, 2008.

Leone de Castris 1994
Leone de Castris, Pierluigi. "Marco Pino: Il ventennio oscuro."
Bollettino d'arte 79, nos. 84–85 (March–June 1994), pp. 71–86.

Leone de Castris 1996
Leone de Castris, Pierluigi. *Pittura del Cinquecento a Napoli, 1540–1573:
Fasto e devozione.* Naples, 1996.

Leone de Castris 2001
Leone de Castris, Pierluigi. *Polidoro da Caravaggio: L'opera completa.*
Naples, 2001.

Levey 1986
Levey, Michael. *Giambattista Tiepolo: His Life and Art.* New Haven and
London, 1986.

Links 1989–90
Links, J[oseph] G. "Canaletto: A Biographical Sketch." In **New York
1989–90,** pp. 2–15.

Links 1998
Links, J[oseph] G. *A Supplement to W. G. Constable's Canaletto: Giovanni Antonio Canal, 1697–1768*. London, 1998.

Linz 1991. *See* **Widauer 1991.**

Llewellyn and Romalli 1992
Drawing in Bologna, 1500–1600. Exhibition, Courtauld Institute Galleries, University of London, June 18–August 31, 1992. Catalogue by Elizabeth Llewellyn and Cristiana Romalli. London, 1992.

Łódź and Warsaw 2007
Między teorią a praktyką. Rysunek włoski xvi wieku ze zbiorów Gabinetu Rycin Biblioteki Uniwersyteckiej w Warszawie/Between Theory and Practice: 16th Century Italian Drawings from the Print Room Collection of the University of Warsaw Library. Exhibition, Pałac Herbsta, Muzeum Sztuki w Łódźi, Łódź; Gabinet Rycin Biblioteki Uniwersyteckiej w Warszawie, 2007. Catalogue by Jerzy Wojciechowski and others. Warsaw, 2007.

Loisel 2004
Loisel, Catherine. *Ludovico, Agostino, Annibale Carracci.* Musée du Louvre, Département des Arts Graphiques. Inventaire général des dessins italiens, 7. Paris, 2004.

London n.d.
Catalogue of Old Master Drawings of the 16th to 19th Centuries. Exhibition, London, [1955 or 1956?]. Catalogue by W[ynne] R[ice] Jeudwine. London, n.d.

London 1789
A Descriptive Catalogue of a Genuine and Capital Collection of Italian Pictures, Never before seen in this Country, And by the most celebrated Masters, particularly of the Venetian and Lombard Schools, from the Earliest Era of Painting to the Present Times, being the sole and Genuine property of A Gentleman[John Strange], Long resident in Italy, and a great Lover of the Art, who has left off Collecting. . . . The whole lately imported from Italy. Sale catalogue, No. 125, Pall Mall, London, December 10, 1789. London, 1789.

London 1836
One Hundred Original Drawings by Zucchero, Andrea del Sarto, Polidore da Caravaggio, and Fra Bartolomeo, Collected by Sir Thomas Lawrence. Exhibition, The Lawrence Gallery, London, April 1836. London, 1836.

London 1875
A Brief Chronological Description of a Collection of Original Drawings and Sketches by the Old Masters of the Different Schools of Europe, From the Revival of Art in Italy in the XIIIth to the XIXth Century; Formed by the Late Mr. William Mayor . . . Sale catalogue. London, 1875.

London 1953
Drawings by Old Masters. Exhibition, Royal Academy of Arts, Diploma Gallery, London, August 13–October 25, 1953. Catalogue by K[arl] T[heodore] Parker, James Byam Shaw, and Gerald Kelly. London, 1953.

London 1956a
Exhibition of Old Master Drawings. Exhibition, Wilton Gallery, London, April 18–May 9, 1956. Catalogue by W[ynne] R[ice] Jeudwine. London, 1956.

London 1956b
Exhibition of Old Master Drawings. Exhibition, P. and D. Colnaghi, London, May 10–June 14, 1956. London, 1956.

London 1960
Italian Art and Britain. Exhibition, Royal Academy of Arts, London, January 2–March 6, 1960. London, 1960.

London 1962
Exhibition of Old Master Drawings. Exhibition, P. and D. Colnaghi, London, June 19–July 21, 1962. London, 1962.

London 1963
The John Witt Collection. Part 1, European Schools. Exhibition, Courtauld Institute Galleries, London, January–March 1963. London, 1963.

London 1969. *See* **Popham 1969.**

London 1970. *See* **Van Regteren Altena and Ward-Jackson 1970.**

London 1981–82
Splendours of the Gonzaga. Exhibition, Victoria and Albert Museum, London, November 4, 1981–January 31, 1982. Catalogue by David Chambers, Jane Martineau, and others. London, 1981.

London 1988
European Drawings: Recent Acquisitions. Exhibition, Hazlitt, Gooden and Fox, London, November 23–December 9, 1988. London, 1988.

London 1991a
Die Zeichnung in Florenz/Drawing in Florence, 1500–1650. Exhibition, Katrin Bellinger Kunsthandel, at Harari and Johns, London, June 25–July 12, 1991. [Munich], 1991.

London 1991b. *See* **Turner and Plazzotta 1991.**

London 1992a
Drawings Related to Sculpture, 1520–1620. Exhibition, Katrin Bellinger Kunsthandel, at Harari and Johns, London, June 24–July 10, 1992. London, 1992.

London 1992b. *See* **Llewellyn and Romalli 1992.**

London 2001
Master Drawings. Exhibition, Katrin Bellinger Kunsthandel, London, 2001. Catalogue by Christine Deininger and others. Munich, 2001.

London and New York 1991–92
Italian Drawings. Exhibition, Hazlitt, Gooden and Fox, London, November–December 1991; Hazlitt, Gooden and Fox, New York, January 1992. [London], 1991.

London and New York 1992
Andrea Mantegna. Exhibition, Royal Academy of Arts, London, January 17–April 5, 1992; The Metropolitan Museum of Art, New York, May 5–July 12, 1992. Catalogue edited by Jane Martineau. Milan, 1992.

London and New York 2000–2001
Correggio and Parmigianino: Master Draughtsmen of the Renaissance. Exhibition, The British Museum, London, October 6, 2000–January 7, 2001; The Metropolitan Museum of Art, New York, February 5–May 6, 2001. Catalogue by Carmen Bambach, Hugo Chapman, Martin Clayton, and George R. Goldner. London, 2000.

London and Washington, D.C., 1994–95
The Glory of Venice: Art in the Eighteenth Century. Exhibition, Royal Academy of Arts, London, September 15–December 14, 1994; National Gallery of Art, Washington, D.C., January 29–April 23, 1995. Catalogue by Jane Martineau, Andrew Robison, and others. New Haven and London, 1994.

London, Birmingham, and Leeds 1962
Old Master Drawings from the Collection of Mr. C. R. Rudolf. Exhibition, The Arts Council Gallery, London, January 5–February 3, 1962; City Museum and Art Gallery, Birmingham, February 17–March 11, 1962; Leeds City Art Gallery, March 17–April 7, 1962. Catalogue by Paul Hulton, Philip Pouncey, and Christopher White. [London], 1962.

Los Angeles 2007–8
Taddeo and Federico Zuccaro: Artist-Brothers in Renaissance Rome. Exhibition, The J. Paul Getty Museum, Los Angeles, October 2, 2007–January 6, 2008. Catalogue by Julian Brooks, Peter M. Lukehart, Christina Strunck, and others. Los Angeles, 2007.

Lugano 1998
Rabisch: Il grottesco nell'arte del Cinquecento: L'Accademia della Val di Blenio, Lomazzo e l'ambiente milanese. Exhibition, Museo Cantonale d'Arte, Lugano, March 28–June 21, 1998. Catalogue by Manuela Kahn-Rossi, Francesco Porzio, Giulio Bora, and others. Lugano and Milan, 1998.

Lugano and Rome 1989–90
Pier Francesco Mola, 1612–1666. Exhibition, Museo Cantonale d'Arte, Lugano, September 23–November 19, 1989; Musei Capitolini, Rome, December 3, 1989–January 31, 1990. Catalogue by Manuela Kahn-Rossi and others. Milan, 1989.

Lugt 1921
Lugt, Frits. *Les marques de collections de dessins & d'estampes: Marques estampillées et écrites de collections particulières et publiques; Marques de marchands, de monteurs et d'imprimeurs; Cachets de vente d'artistes décédés; Marques de graveurs apposées après le tirage des planches; Timbres d'édition, etc., avec des notices historiques sur les collectionneurs, les collections, les ventes, les marchands et éditeurs, etc.* Amsterdam, 1921.

Lugt 1956
Lugt, Frits. *Les marques de collections de dessins and d'estampes . . . avec des notices historiques sur les collectionneurs, les collections, les ventes, les marchands et éditeurs, etc., Supplément.* The Hague, 1956.

Maastricht and Bruges 2002–3. *See* **Van der Sman and Sellink 2002–3.**

Macandrew 1980
Macandrew, Hugh. *Catalogue of the Collection of Drawings.* Vol. 3, *Italian Schools: Supplement.* Ashmolean Museum, Oxford. Oxford, 1980.

Madrid 1992
Ribera, 1591–1652. Exhibition, Museo del Prado, Madrid, June 2–August 16, 1992. Catalogue by Alfonso E. Pérez Sánchez, Nicola Spinosa, and others. Madrid, 1992.

Madrid 2007
Tintoretto. Exhibition, Museo Nacional del Prado, Madrid, January 30–May 13, 2007. Catalogue by Miguel Falomir and others. Madrid, 2007.

Magrini 1988
Magrini, Marina. *Francesco Fontebasso (1707–1769).* Vicenza, 1988.

Magrini 1990
Magrini, Marina. "Francesco Fontebasso: I disegni." *Saggi e memorie di storia dell'arte* 17 (1990), pp. 165–385.

Mahon 1968
Il Guercino (Giovanni Francesco Barbieri, 1591–1666): Catalogo critico dei disegni. Exhibition, Palazzo dell'Archiginnasio, Bologna, September 1–November 18, 1968. Catalogue by Denis Mahon. Bologna, 1968.

Mahon and Turner 1989
Mahon, Denis, and Nicholas Turner. *The Drawings of Guercino in the Collection of Her Majesty the Queen at Windsor Castle.* Cambridge and New York, 1989.

Mahoney 1965
Mahoney, Michael. "Salvator Rosa Provenance Studies: Prince Livio Odescalchi and Queen Christina." *Master Drawings* 3, no. 4 (Winter 1965), pp. 383–89.

Mahoney 1977
Mahoney, Michael. *The Drawings of Salvator Rosa.* [Garland] Outstanding Dissertations in the Fine Arts. 2 vols. 1965. New York and London, 1977.

Malibu, Fort Worth, and Washington, D.C., 1983–84. *See* **Goldner 1983–84.**

Mancini ed. 1956
Mancini, Giulio. *Considerazioni sulla pittura.* Vol. 1, *Considerazioni sulla pittura; viaggio per Roma; appendici.* Edited by Adriana Marucchi. Accademia Nazionale dei Lincei. Fonti e documenti inediti per la storia dell'arte, 1. Rome, 1956.

Mantua 1989
Giulio Romano. Exhibition, Palazzo Te and Palazzo Ducale, Mantua, September 1–November 12, 1989. Catalogue by Ernst H. Gombrich, Manfredo Tafuri, and others. Milan, 1989.

Mantua 2001
Perino del Vaga: Tra Raffaello e Michelangelo. Exhibition, Palazzo Te, Mantua, March 18–June 10, 2001. Catalogue by Elena Parma and others. Milan, 2001.

Masetti Zannini 1974
Masetti Zannini, Gian Ludovico. *Pittori della seconda metà del Cinquecento in Roma (documenti e regesti).* Raccolta di fonti per la storia dell'arte, ser. 2, vol. 2. Rome, 1974.

Mason Rinaldi 1984
Mason Rinaldi, Stefania. *Palma il Giovane: L'opera completa.* Milan, 1984.

Massa 1998
Massa, Paola. "The Genoese Guilds in the Sixteenth and Seventeenth Centuries: The Food Administration Offices and the Food Sector Guilds in Genoa; Organisation and Conflict." In *Guilds, Markets and Work Regulations in Italy, 16th–19th Centuries,* edited by Alberto Guenzi, Paola Massa, and Fausto Piola Caselli, pp. 246–65. Aldershot, U.K., 1998.

Massari 1980–81
Incisori Mantovani del '500: Giovan Battista, Adamo, Diana Scultori e Giorgio Ghisi dalle collezioni del Gabinetto Nazionale delle Stampe e della Calcografia Nazionale. Exhibition, Istituto Nazionale per la Grafica, Rome, December 18, 1980–January 31, 1981. Catalogue by Stefania Massari. Rome, 1980.

Massari 1993
Giulio Romano pinxit et delineavit: Opere grafiche autografe di collaborazione e bottega. Exhibition, Istituto Nazionale per la Grafica, Rome, 1993. Catalogue by Stefania Massari. Rome, 1993.

McCorquodale 1973
McCorquodale, Charles P. "A Fresh Look at Carlo Dolci." *Apollo* 97, no. 135 (May 1973), pp. 477–88.

McCorquodale 1976
McCorquodale, Charles P. "Some Paintings and Drawings by Carlo Dolci in British Collections." In *Kunst des Barock in der Toskana: Studien zur Kunst unter den letzten Medici,* pp. 313–20. Italienische Forschungen, ser. 3, vol. 9. Munich, 1976.

McCorquodale 1983
McCorquodale, C[harles P]. "Some Unpublished Works by Baldassare Franceschini, il Volterrano." *Paradigma Firenze* 5 (1983), pp. 63–71.

McCorquodale 2007–
McCorquodale, Charles P. "Carlo Dolci." In *Oxford Art Online.* [Oxford and New York], 2007– .

McDonald 1999
McDonald, Mark P. "Ribera's Earliest Drawing?" *Master Drawings* 37, no. 4 (Winter 1999), pp. 368–72.

Meijer and van Tuyll 1983–84
Disegni italiani del Teylers Museum Haarlem provenienti dalle collezioni di Cristina di Svezia e dei principi Odescalchi. Exhibition, Istituto Universitario Ollandese di Storia dell'Arte, Florence, October 29–December 18, 1983; Istituto Nazionale per la Grafica, Gabinetto Nazionale delle Stampe, Rome, January 10–February 20, 1984. Catalogue by Bert W. Meijer and Carel van Tuyll. Florence, 1983.

Mielke 1980
Mielke, Hans. Review of *Netherlandish Drawings of the Fifteenth and Sixteenth Centuries* (Catalogue of Dutch and Flemish Drawings in the Rijksmuseum, vol. 2), by K[arel] G. Boon. *Simiolus* 11, no. 1 (1980), pp. 39–50.

Milan 1996
Alessandro Magnasco, 1667–1749. Exhibition, Palazzo Reale, Milan, March 21–July 7, 1996. Catalogue by Ettore Camesasca, Marco Bona Castellotti, and others. Milan, 1996.

Milanesi 1973
Milanesi, G[aetano], comp. and ed. *Nuovi documenti per la storia dell'arte toscana dal XII al XV secolo, per servire d'aggiunta all'edizione del Vasari edita da Sansoni nel 1885.* Soest, 1973.

Milicua 1992
Milicua, José. "De Játiva a Nápoles (1591–1616)." In **Madrid 1992,** pp. 18–33.

Milstein 1978
Milstein, Ann Rebecca. *The Paintings of Girolamo Mazzola Bedoli.* [Garland] Outstanding Dissertations in the Fine Arts. 1977. New York and London, 1978.

Milwaukee and New York 1989–90. *See* **Mundy 1989–90.**

Modena 2005
Nicolò dell'Abate: Storie dipinte nella pittura del Cinquecento tra Modena e Fontainebleau. Exhibition, Foro Boario, Modena, March 20–June 19, 2005. Catalogue by Sylvie Béguin, Francesca Piccinini, and others. Cinisello Balsamo, Milan, 2005.

Monbeig Goguel 2005
Monbeig Goguel, Catherine. *Dessins toscans XVIe–XVIIIe siècles.* Vol. 2, *1620–1800.* Musée du Louvre, Département des Arts Graphiques. Paris, 2005.

Monbeig Goguel 2006
Monbeig Goguel, Catherine. "Les artistes florentins collectionneurs de dessins de Giorgio Vasari à Emilio Santarelli." In *L'artiste collectionneur de dessin, de Giorgio Vasari à aujourd'hui: Rencontres internationales du Salon du Dessin, 22 et 23 mars 2006,* edited by Catherine Monbeig Goguel, vol. 1, pp. 35–65, 182–94. 2 vols. Milan and Paris, 2006.

Monbeig Goguel and Viatte 1981–82
Dessins baroques florentins du Musée du Louvre. Exhibition, Cabinet des Dessins, Musée du Louvre, Paris, October 2, 1981–January 18, 1982. Catalogue by Catherine Monbeig Goguel and Françoise Viatte. Paris, 1981.

Montagu 1985
Montagu, Jennifer. *Alessandro Algardi.* 2 vols. New Haven and London, 1985.

Morassi 1970
Morassi, Antonio. "Sui disegni del Tiepolo nelle recenti mostre di Cambridge, Mass., e di Stoccarda." *Arte veneta* 24 (1970), pp. 294–304.

Morassi 1973
Morassi, Antonio. *Guardi: [L'opera completa di] Antonio e Francesco Guardi.* Venice, [1973].

Morassi 1975
Morassi, Antonio. *Guardi: Tutti i disegni di Antonio, Francesco e Giacomo Guardi.* Venice, 1975.

Mundy 1989–90
Renaissance into Baroque: Italian Master Drawings by the Zuccari, 1550–1600. Exhibition, Milwaukee Art Museum, November 17, 1989–January 14, 1990; National Academy of Design, New York, March 13–April 29, 1990. Catalogue by E. James Mundy, with Elizabeth Ourusoff de Fernandez-Gimenez. Milwaukee, 1989.

Munich 1989–90. *See* **Bevers 1989–90.**

Munich 1999
Italian Drawings, 1500–1800. Exhibition, Katrin Bellinger Kunsthandel, Munich, 1999. Munich, 1999.

Naples 2009–10
Ritorno al Barocco: Da Caravaggio a Vanvitelli, scultura e arti decorative. Exhibition, Museo di Capodimonte, Certosa e Museo di S. Martino, Castel S. Elmo, Museo Duca di Martina, Museo Pignatelli, Palazzo Reale, Naples, December 12, 2009–April 11, 2010. Catalogue by Nicola Spinosa and others. 2 vols. Naples, 2009.

Nesselrath 1989
Nesselrath, Arnold. "Giovanni da Udine disegnatore." *Bollettino dei monumenti, musei e gallerie pontificie* 9, no. 2 (1989), pp. 237–91.

Newcome 1993
Newcome, Mary. "Drawings by Giovanni David." In *Essays in Memory of Jacob Bean (1923–1992),* edited by Linda Wolk-Simon and William M. Griswold. *Master Drawings* 31, no. 4 (Winter 1993), pp. 469–79.

Newcome Schleier and Grasso 2003
Newcome Schleier, Mary, and Giovanni Grasso. *Giovanni David: Pittore e incisore della famiglia Durazzo.* Turin, 2003.

Newcome Schleier and Monbeig Goguel 1985
Le dessin à Gênes du XVIe au XVIIIe siècle. Exhibition, Cabinet des Dessins, Musée du Louvre, Paris, May 30–September 9, 1985. Catalogue by Mary Newcome Schleier and Catherine Monbeig Goguel. Paris, 1985.

New York 1965–66. *See* **Bean and Stampfle 1965–66.**

New York 1971. *See* **Bean and Stampfle 1971.**

New York 1973. *See* **Stampfle and Denison 1973.**

New York 1989–90
Canaletto. Exhibition, The Metropolitan Museum of Art, New York, October 30, 1989–January 21, 1990. Catalogue by Katharine Baetjer, J. G. Links, and others. New York, 1989.

New York 1990
Master Drawings. Exhibition, Colnaghi, New York, May 9–June 1, 1990. Catalogue by Jean-Luc Baroni. New York, 1990.

New York 1992
Master Drawings, 1500–1900. Exhibition, Thomas le Claire Kunsthandel, Hamburg, at W. M. Brady and Co., New York, January 15–February 1, 1992. Hamburg, 1992.

New York 1994a
An Exhibition of Old Master Drawings and European Works of Art. Exhibition, Trinity Fine Art Ltd., London, at Newhouse Galleries, New York, May 5–17, 1994. London, 1994.

New York 1994b
European Master Drawings from the Collection of Peter Jay Sharp. Exhibition, National Academy of Design, New York, May 25–August 28, 1994. Catalogue by William L. Barcham and others. New York, 1994.

New York 1994c. *See* **Griswold and Wolk-Simon 1994.**

New York 1995a
An Exhibition of Old Master Drawings and European Works of Art. Exhibition, Trinity Fine Art Ltd., London, at Newhouse Galleries, New York, May 4–18, 1995. London, 1995.

New York 1995b. *See* **Ongpin 1995.**

New York 1996
Genoa: Drawings and Prints, 1530–1800. Exhibition, The Metropolitan Museum of Art, New York, April 23–July 10, 1996. Catalogue by Carmen C. Bambach, Nadine M. Orenstein, and William M. Griswold. New York, 1996.

New York 1997a
Disegno: Italian Renaissance Designs for the Decorative Arts. Exhibition, Cooper-Hewitt National Design Museum, Smithsonian Institution,

New York, February 11–May 18, 1997. Catalogue by Beth L. Holman and others. New York, 1997.

New York 1997b
Old Master Drawings. Exhibition, Katrin Bellinger Kunsthandel, at W. M. Brady and Co., New York, May 8–31, 1997. New York, 1997.

New York 1997c. *See* **Wolk-Simon 1997.**

New York 1998a
An Exhibition of Italian Old Master Drawings and Oil Sketches. Exhibition, Pandora Old Masters, New York, January 27–February 14, 1998. New York, 1998.

New York 1998b
An Exhibition of Old Master Drawings, Prints, and Paintings. Exhibition, Trinity Fine Art Ltd., London, at Newhouse Galleries, New York, May 6–15, 1998. London, 1998.

New York 1998–99
Master Drawings from the Hermitage and Pushkin Museums. Exhibition, The Pierpont Morgan Library, New York, September 25, 1998– January 10, 1999. Catalogue by Marina Bessonova and others. New York, 1998.

New York 1999. *See* **Cox-Rearick et al. 1999.**

New York 2002. *See* **Campbell et al. 2002.**

New York 2003a
Old Master Drawings. Exhibition, C. G. Boerner, New York, January 22– February 8, 2003. New York, 2003.

New York 2003b. *See* **Bambach et al. 2003.**

New York 2006–7. *See* **Gealt and Knox 2006–7.**

New York 2008–9
The Philippe de Montebello Years: Curators Celebrate Three Decades of Acquisitions; Online Catalogue. Exhibition, The Metropolitan Museum of Art, New York, October 24, 2008–February 1, 2009. Catalogue edited by Helen C. Evans. New York, 2008. http://www.metmuseum.org/ special/philippe_de_montebello_years/index.aspx.

New York 2010
The Drawings of Bronzino. Exhibition, The Metropolitan Museum of Art, New York, January 20–April 18, 2010. Catalogue by Carmen C. Bambach, Janet Cox-Rearick, George R. Goldner, and others. New York, 2010.

New York and Edinburgh 2009
Raphael to Renoir: Drawings from the Collection of Jean Bonna. Exhibition, The Metropolitan Museum of Art, New York, January 21–April 26, 2009; National Gallery of Scotland, Edinburgh, June 5–September 6, 2009. Catalogue by Stijn Alsteens, Carmen C. Bambach, and others. New York, 2009.

New York and London 1997. *See* **Ongpin 1997.**

New York and London 2003. *See* **Ongpin 2003.**

New York and London 2005–6. *See* **Stein and Royalton-Kisch 2005–6.**

Nichols 1996
Nichols, Thomas. "Tintoretto." In *The [Grove] Dictionary of Art,* edited by Jane Turner, vol. 31, pp. 5–19. 34 vols. New York, 1996.

Nichols 2000
Nichols, Thomas. "Tintoretto [Robusti]." In *Grove Art Online,* in *Oxford Art Online.* [Oxford and New York], 2007– .

Nickel in progress
Nickel, Tobias. "The Drawings of Domenico Campagnola (1500–1564)." PhD diss., Universität Wien, Institut für Kunstgeschichte, Vienna, in progress.

Nicodemi 1993
Nicodemi, Gabriella. "Disegni di Giovanni Battista Beinaschi." *Arte cristiana* 81, no. 754 (January–February 1993), pp. 35–44.

Olmi 1977
Olmi, Giuseppe. "Osservazione della natura e raffigurazione in Ulisse Aldrovandi (1522–1605)." *Annali dell'Istituto Storico Italo-Germanico in Trento* 3 (1977), pp. 105–81.

Ongpin 1995
An Exhibition of Old Master and 19th Century Drawings. Exhibition, Colnaghi Gallery, New York, January 10–28, 1995. Catalogue by Stephen Ongpin. New York, 1995.

Ongpin 1997
An Exhibition of Master Drawings. Exhibition, Otto Naumann Ltd., New York, May 7–24, 1997; Colnaghi, London, June 12–July 11, 1997. Catalogue by Stephen Ongpin. London, 1997.

Ongpin 2003
An Exhibition of Old Master Drawings. Exhibition, Jean-Luc Baroni Ltd., at Adam Williams Fine Art Ltd., New York, May 1–30, 2003; Jean-Luc Baroni Ltd., London, July 3–26, 2003. Catalogue by Stephen Ongpin. London, 2003.

Ottawa 2005. *See* **Franklin et al. 2005.**

Ottawa 2009
From Raphael to Carracci: The Art of Papal Rome. Exhibition, The National Gallery of Canada, Ottawa, May 29–September 7, 2009. Catalogue by David Franklin and others. Ottawa, 2009.

Ottawa and New York 2003–4. *See* **Franklin and Ekserdjian 2003–4.**

Ottawa, Vancouver, and Halifax 1976. *See* **Taylor 1976.**

Ovid ed. 1916
Ovid. *Metamorphoses.* Translated by Frank Justus Miller. The Loeb Classical Library. 2 vols. Cambridge, Mass., 1916.

Oxford, London, and Nottingham 2003–4. *See* **Whistler 2003–4.**

Pallucchini, A. 1971
Pallucchini, Anna. *Giambattista Tiepolo.* Collana disegnatori italiani. Milan, 1971.

Pallucchini, R. 1967
Pallucchini, Rodolfo. "Francesco Guardi, ultima voce del Rococò veneziano." In *Sensibilità e razionalità nel Settecento,* edited by Vittore Branca, vol. 2, pp. 529–48. Civiltà europea e civiltà veneziana. Aspetti e problemi, 5. 2 vols. Florence, 1967.

Palomino de Castro y Velasco ed. 1742
Palomino de Castro y Velasco, [Acisclo] Antonio. *Las vidas de los pintores y estatuarios eminentes españoles, que con sus heroycas obras, han ilustrado la nación . . . 1724.* London, 1742.

Papi 2007
Papi, Gianni. *Ribera a Roma.* Soncino, 2007.

Paris 1971
Dessins du XVIe et du XVII siècle dans les collections privées françaises. Exhibition, Galerie Claude Aubry, Paris, December 1971. Paris, 1971.

Paris 1981–82. *See* **Monbeig Goguel and Viatte 1981–82.**

Paris 1985. *See* **Newcome Schleier and Monbeig Goguel 1985.**

Paris 1993
Le siècle de Titien: L'âge d'or de la peinture à Venise. Exhibition, Grand Palais, Paris, March 9–June 14, 1993. Catalogue by Michel Laclotte, Alessandro Ballarin, and others. Paris, 1993.

Paris 2002
Chefs-d'oeuvre du Fitzwilliam Museum de Cambridge: Dix ans d'acquisitions de dessins de maîtres anciens. Exhibition, Artemis–C. G. Boerner, Paris, March 19–25, 2002. Paris, 2002.

Paris 2004–5
Primatice: Maître de Fontainebleau. Exhibition, Musée du Louvre, Paris, September 22, 2004–January 3, 2005. Catalogue by Dominique Cordellier and others. Paris, 2004.

Paris 2005. *See* **Conigliello 2005.**

Paris, Cambridge, Mass., and New York 1994–95. *See* **Brugerolles and Guillet 1994–95.**

Parker 1948
Parker, K[arl] T[heodore]. *The Drawings of Antonio Canaletto in the Collection of His Majesty the King at Windsor Castle.* The Italian Drawings at Windsor Castle, edited by A[nthony] F. Blunt. Oxford and London, 1948.

Parker 1956
Parker, K[arl] T[heodore]. *Catalogue of the Collection of Drawings in the Ashmolean Museum.* Vol. 2, *Italian Schools.* Oxford, 1956.

Parma 1984. *See* **DeGrazia et al. 1984.**

Parma and Vienna 2003
Parmigianino e il manierismo europeo. Exhibition, Galleria Nazionale, Parma, February 8–May 15, 2003; Kunsthistorisches Museum, Vienna, June 4–September 14, 2003. Catalogue by Lucia Fornari Schianchi, Sylvia Ferino-Pagden, and others. Cinisello Balsamo, Milan, 2003.

Parma Armani 1986
Parma Armani, Elena. *Perin del Vaga: L'anello mancante; studi sul Manierismo.* Genoa, 1986.

Pepper 1984
Pepper, D. Stephen. *Guido Reni: A Complete Catalogue of His Works with an Introductory Text.* New York, 1984.

Pepper 1988
Pepper, [D.] Stephen. *Guido Reni: L'opera completa.* 2nd ed. 1984. Novara, 1988.

Percy 1971
Giovanni Benedetto Castiglione, Master Draughtsman of the Italian Baroque. Exhibition, Philadelphia Museum of Art, September 17–November 28, 1971. Catalogue by Ann Percy; foreword by Anthony Blunt. Philadelphia, 1971.

Petrioli Tofani 1991
Petrioli Tofani, Annamaria. *Inventario: Disegni di figura.* Gabinetto Disegni e Stampe degli Uffizi, 1. Florence, 1991.

Philadelphia 1971. *See* **Percy 1971.**

Pigler 1974
Pigler, A[ndor]. *Barockthemen: Eine Auswahl von Verzeichnissen zur Ikonographie des 17. und 18. Jahrhunderts.* 2nd ed. 3 vols. 1956. Budapest, 1974.

Pliny ed. 1938–63
Pliny. *Natural History.* Translated by H[arris] Rackham, W. H. S. Jones, and D. E. Eichholz. The Loeb Classical Library. 10 vols. Cambridge, Mass., and London, 1938–63.

Plutarch ed. 1919
Plutarch. *Plutarch's Lives.* Vol. 7, *Demosthenes and Cicero; Alexander and Caesar.* Translated by Bernadotte Perrin. The Loeb Classical Library. London and Cambridge, Mass., 1919.

Pope-Hennessy 1948
Pope-Hennessy, John. *The Drawings of Domenichino in the Collection of*

His Majesty the King at Windsor Castle. The Italian Drawings at Windsor Castle. London, 1948.

Pope-Hennessy and Radcliffe 1970
Pope-Hennessy, John, and Anthony F. Radcliffe. *The Frick Collection: An Illustrated Catalogue.* Vol. 3, *Sculpture, Italian.* New York, 1970.

Popham 1962–63
Old Master Drawings from Chatsworth: A Loan Exhibition from the Devonshire Collection, Circulated by the Smithsonian Institution, 1962–1963. Exhibition, National Gallery of Art, Washington, D.C., and traveled, 1962–63. Catalogue by A[rthur] E[wart] Popham. Washington, D.C., 1962.

Popham 1969
Old Master Drawings from Chatsworth: A Loan Exhibition from the Devonshire Collection. Exhibition, Diploma Galleries, Royal Academy of Arts, London, July 5–August 31, 1969. Catalogue by A[rthur] E[wart] Popham. London, 1969.

Popham 1971
Popham, A[rthur] E[wart]. *Catalogue of the Drawings of Parmigianino.* 3 vols. New Haven and London, 1971.

Popham and Lloyd 1986
Popham, A[rthur] E[wart], and Christopher Lloyd. *Old Master Drawings at Holkham Hall.* Chicago, 1986.

Poppi 1992. *See* **Conigliello 1992.**

Poughkeepsie 1963
Italian Drawings from the Collection of Mrs. Richard Krautheimer. Exhibition, Vassar College Art Gallery, Poughkeepsie, N.Y., April 3–30, 1963. Poughkeepsie, N.Y., 1963.

Poughkeepsie and other cities 1995–96
The Katalan Collection of Italian Drawings. Exhibition, The Frances Lehman Loeb Art Center, Vassar College, Poughkeepsie, N.Y., April 14–June 18, 1995, and other cities through June 16, 1996. Catalogue by [E.] James Mundy and others. Poughkeepsie, N.Y., 1995.

Pouncey and Gere 1962
Pouncey, Philip, and J[ohn] A. Gere. *Raphael and His Circle: Giulio Romano, G. F. Penni, Perino del Vaga, Giovanni da Udine, Tommaso Vincidor, Polidoro da Caravaggio, Baldassare Peruzzi, Timoteo Viti and Girolamo Genga, also Sebastiano del Piombo.* Italian Drawings in the Department of Prints and Drawings in the British Museum. 2 vols. London, 1962.

Precerutti Garberi 1958
Precerutti Garberi, Mercedes. "Di alcuni dipinti perduti del Tiepolo." *Commentari: Rivista di critica e storia dell'arte* 9 (1958), pp. 110–23, pls. 46–50.

Princeton and Cambridge, Mass., 1973–74. *See* **Brown 1973–74.**

Rearick 1976
Tiziano e il disegno veneziano del suo tempo. Exhibition, Gabinetto Disegni e Stampe degli Uffizi, Florence, 1976. Catalogue by W[illiam] R. Rearick. Gabinetto Disegni e Stampe degli Uffizi, Cataloghi, 45. Florence, 1976.

Van Regteren Altena and Ward-Jackson 1970
Drawings from the Teyler Museum, Haarlem. Exhibition, Victoria and Albert Museum, London, 1970. Catalogue by I. Q. van Regteren Altena and Peter Ward-Jackson. London, 1970.

Reiset 1866
Reiset, M[arie] Frédéric. *Notice des dessins, cartons, pastels, miniatures et émaux exposés dans les salles du 1er étage au Musée impérial du Louvre.* Vol. 1, *Écoles d'Italie, écoles allemande, flamande et hollandaise.* Paris, 1866.

Reitlinger 1922
Reitlinger, Henry Scipio. *Old Master Drawings: A Handbook for Amateurs and Collectors.* London, Bombay, and Sydney, 1922.

Ridolfi 1648
Ridolfi, Carlo. *Le maraviglie dell'arte, ouero, Le vite de gl'illustri pittori veneti, e dello stato: Oue sono raccolte le opere insigni, i costumi, e i ritratti loro: Con la narratione delle historie, delle fauole, e delle moralità da quelli dipinte.* 2 vols. in 1. Venice, 1648.

Riedl 1959
Riedl, Peter Anselm. "Zu Francesco Vanni und Ventura Salimbeni." *Mitteilungen des Kunsthistorischen Institutes in Florenz* 9, no. 1 (August 1959), pp. 60–70.

Riedl 1960
Riedl, Peter Anselm. "Zum Oeuvre des Ventura Salimbeni." *Mitteilungen des Kunsthistorischen Institutes in Florenz* 9, nos. 3–4 (November 1960), pp. 221–48.

Riedl 1976
Riedl, Peter Anselm. *Disegni dei Barocceschi senesi: Francesco Vanni e Ventura Salimbeni.* Gabinetto Disegni e Stampe degli Uffizi, Cataloghi, 46. Florence, 1976.

Ripa 1603
Ripa, Cesare. *Iconologia, overo, Descrittione di diverse imagini cauate dall'antichità, & di propria inuentione.* 1593. Rome, 1603.

Ripa ed. 1976
Ripa, Cesare. *Iconologia, Padua, 1611.* 1611. Reprint, [Garland] Renaissance and the Gods. New York and London, 1976.

Rizzi 1967
Rizzi, Aldo. *Luca Carlevarijs.* Profili e saggi di arte veneta, 5. Venice, 1967.

Rizzi and Morassi 1965
Disegni del Tiepolo. Exhibition, Loggia del Lionello, Udine, October 10–November 14, 1965. Catalogue by Aldo Rizzi and Antonio Morassi. Udine, 1965.

Rome 1959
Il Settecento a Roma. Exhibition, Istituto di Studi Romani; Palazzo delle Esposizioni, Rome, March 19–May 31, 1959. Catalogue by Emilio Lavagnino and others. Rome, 1959.

Rome 1980–81. *See* **Massari 1980–81.**

Rome 1984
Quando gli dei si spogliano: Il bagno di Clemente VII a Castel Sant'Angelo e le altre stufe romane del primo Cinquecento. Exhibition, Museo Nazionale di Castel Sant'Angelo, Rome, 1984. Catalogue by Bruno Contardi, Henrik Lilius, and others. Rome, 1984.

Rome 1991
Il segno del genio: Cento disegni di grandi maestri del passato dall'Ashmolean Museum di Oxford. Exhibition, Palazzo Ruspoli, Rome, May 13–July 28, 1991. Catalogue by Christopher White, Catherine Whistler, and Colin Harrison. Rome, 1991.

Rome 1993. *See* **Massari 1993.**

Rome 1995
Francesco Bartolozzi, incisore delle Grazie. Exhibition, Istituto Nazionale per la Grafica, Villa Farnesina, Rome, October 27–December 17, 1995. Catalogue by Barbara Jatta and others. Rome, 1995.

Rome and Paris 1998
Francesco Salviati (1510–1563) o la Bella Maniera. Exhibition, Villa Medici, Rome, January 29–March 29, 1998; Musée du Louvre, Paris, April 30–June 29, 1998. Catalogue by Catherine Monbeig Goguel and others. Paris and Milan, 1998.

Rosand and Muraro 1976–77
Titian and the Venetian Woodcut. Exhibition, National Gallery of Art, Washington, D.C.; Dallas Museum of Fine Arts; The Detroit Institute of Arts. Catalogue by David Rosand and Michelangelo Muraro. Washington, D.C., 1976.

Rosenberg 2001
Rosenberg, Pierre. "Paris: Seventeenth-Century French Drawings." *The Burlington Magazine* 143, no. 1178 (May 2001), pp. 313–14.

Rosenberg 2006
Rosenberg, Pierre. "Un ensemble de copies de dessins d'après l'Antique de Poussin." *Studiolo: Revue d'histoire de l'art de l'Académie de France à Rome* 4 (2006), pp. 129–66.

Rosenberg and Prat 1994
Rosenberg, Pierre, and Louis-Antoine Prat. *Nicolas Poussin, 1594–1665: Catalogue raisonné des dessins.* 2 vols. Milan, 1994.

Roworth 1981
Roworth, Wendy Wassyng. "A Date for Salvator Rosa's *Satire on Painting* and the Bamboccianti in Rome." *The Art Bulletin* 63, no. 4 (December 1981), pp. 611–17.

Rubin 2007
Rubin, Patricia Lee. *Portraits by the Artist as a Young Man: Parmigianino ca. 1524.* Groningen, 2007.

Ruland 1876
Ruland, C[arl]. *The Works of Raphael Santi da Urbino as Represented in the Raphael Collection in the Royal Library at Windsor Castle, formed by H. R. H. the Prince Consort, 1853–1861, and completed by Her Majesty Queen Victoria.* Weimar, 1876.

Saccomani 1991
Saccomani, Elisabetta. "Apports et précisions au catalogue des dessins de Domenico Campagnola." *Disegno: Actes du Colloque du Musée des Beaux-Arts de Rennes, 9 et 10 novembre, 1990,* pp. 31–36. Rennes, 1991.

Salamon 1961–62
G. B. Piranesi: Acqueforti e disegni. Exhibition, Galleria Civico d'Arte Moderna, Turin, December 1, 1961–January 21, 1962. Catalogue by Ferdinando Salamon. Turin, 1961.

Salerno, Spezzaferro, and Tafuri 1973
Salerno, Luigi, Luigi Spezzaferro, and Manfredo Tafuri. *Via Giulia: Una utopia urbanistica del 500.* Rome, 1973.

Sambin 1973–74
Sambin, Paolo. "Spigolature d'archivio: 1, La tonsura di Giulio Campagnola, ragazzo prodigio, e un nuovo documento per Domenico Campagnola." *Atti e Memorie dell'Accademia Patavina di Scienze, Lettere ed Arti* 86 (1973–74), pp. 381–88.

San Diego 2001. *See* **Beddington 2001.**

Sarasota, Austin, and New Haven 2006–8
Master Drawings from the Yale University Art Gallery. Exhibition, The John and Mable Ringling Museum of Art, Sarasota, October 19, 2006–January 7, 2007; The Blanton Museum of Art, Austin, June 1–August 12, 2007; Yale University Art Gallery, New Haven, February 12–June 8, 2008. Catalogue by Suzanne Boorsch, John Marciari, and others. New Haven, 2006.

Van Sasse van Ysselt 2003
Van Sasse van Ysselt, Dorine. "Een jacht van Johannes Stradanus thuisgebracht: Indianen in Mexico roken wild uit." *Delineavit et sculpsit,* no. 26 (November 2003), pp. 1–9.

Van Sasse van Ysselt 2009
Van Sasse van Ysselt, Dorine. "Johannes Stradanus." *Delineavit et sculpsit,* no. 32 (July 200[9]), pp. 56–61.

Scaglietti 1963–64
Scaglietti, Daniela. "Amico Aspertini." PhD diss., Università degli Studi di Bologna, 1963–64.

Schapelhouman 1998
Schapelhouman, Marijn. "Tekeningen uit de verzameling Lodewijk Houthakker." *Bulletin van het Rijksmuseum* 46, no. 4 (1998), pp. 367–90.

Schéle 1965
Schéle, Sune. *Cornelis Bos: A Study of the Origins of the Netherland Grotesque.* Stockholm, 1965.

Schoch, Mende, and Scherbaum 2001–4
Schoch, Rainer, Matthias Mende, and Anna Scherbaum. *Albrecht Dürer: Das druckgraphische Werk.* 3 vols. Munich, London, and New York, 2001–4.

Schweikhart 1986
Schweikhart, Günter. *Der Codex Wolfegg: Zeichnungen nach der Antike von Amico Aspertini.* Studies of the Warburg Institute, 38. London, 1986.

Scott 1995
Scott, Jonathan. *Salvator Rosa, His Life and Times.* New Haven and London, 1995.

Shearman 1965
Shearman, John. *Andrea del Sarto.* 2 vols. Oxford, 1965.

Shearman 1972
Shearman, John. *Raphael's Cartoons in the Collection of Her Majesty the Queen, and the Tapestries for the Sistine Chapel.* London and New York, 1972.

Shearman 2003
Shearman, John. *Raphael in Early Modern Sources, 1483–1602.* 2 vols. New Haven, London, and Rome, 2003.

Van der Sman 1997
Van der Sman, Gert Jan. "Meester van de Egmont Albums." *Delineavit et sculpsit*, no. 18 (November 1997), pp. 7–10.

Van der Sman 1999
Van der Sman, Gert Jan. "Observations on the Master of the Egmont Albums." In *Fiamminghi a Roma 1508–1608: Proceedings of the Symposium held at Museum Catharijneconvent, Utrecht, 13 March 1995*, edited by Sabine Eiche, Gert Jan van der Sman, and Jeanne van Waadenoijen, pp. 45–65. [Florence], 1999.

Van der Sman and Sellink 2002–3
Le siècle de Titien: Gravures vénitiennes de la Renaissance. Exhibition, Bonnefantenmuseum, Maastricht, November 17, 2002–February 16, 2003; Groeningemuseum, Arentshuis, Bruges, March 1–May 26, 2003. Catalogue by Gert Jan van der Sman and Manfred Sellink. Zwolle, 2002.

Smyth 1997
Smyth, Carolyn. *Correggio's Frescoes in Parma Cathedral.* Princeton, N.J., 1997.

Sotheby's, London 1954
Catalogue of Old Master Drawings of the Dutch and Flemish Schools: The H. S. Reitlinger Collection, Part VII. Sale catalogue, Sotheby's, London, June 22–23, 1954. London, 1954.

Sotheby's, London 1967
Catalogue of Important Old Master Drawings. Sale catalogue, Sotheby's, London, July 6, 1967. London, 1967.

Sotheby's, London 1987
Drawings, Watercolours and Paintings from the Collection of the Late Sir John and Lady Witt. Sale catalogue, Sotheby's, London, February 19, 1987. London, 1987.

Sotheby's, London 1993
Old Master Paintings. Sale catalogue, Sotheby's, London, April 21, 1993. London, 1993.

Sotheby's, Monaco 1987
Dessins italiens du XIVe au XVIIe siècle: Collection Michael Gaud. Sale catalogue, Sotheby's, Monte Carlo, Monaco, June 20, 1987. Monte Carlo, 1987.

Sotheby's, New York 1986
Old Master Drawings. Sale catalogue, Sotheby's, New York, January 16, 1986. New York, 1986.

Sotheby's, New York 1988
Old Master Drawings. Sale catalogue, Sotheby's, New York, January 13, 1988. New York, 1988.

Sotheby's, New York 2002
Old Master Drawings, Including Works on Paper from the Collection of Charles Ryskamp. Sale catalogue, Sotheby's, New York, January 25, 2002. New York, 2002.

Sotheby's, New York 2008
Old Master Drawings: Lots 110–230. Sale catalogue, Sotheby's, New York, January 23, 2008. New York, 2008.

Spinosa 2006
Spinosa, Nicola. *Ribera.* 2nd ed. 2003. [Naples], 2006.

Stampfle and Denison 1973
Drawings from the Collection of Lore and Rudolf Heinemann. Exhibition, The Pierpont Morgan Library, New York, 1973. Catalogue by Felice Stampfle and Cara D. Denison. New York, 1973.

Standring 2007–
Standring, Timothy. "Giovanni Benedetto Castiglione." In *Oxford Art Online.* [Oxford and New York], 2007– .

Starcky 1988
Starcky, Emmanuel. *Inventaire général des dessins des écoles du Nord: Écoles allemande, des Anciens Pays-Bas, flamande, hollandaise et suisse,*

XVe–XVIIIe siècles. Supplément aux inventaires publiés par Frits Lugt et Louis Demonts. Musée du Louvre, Cabinet des dessins. Paris, 1988.

Stechow 1953
Stechow, Wolfgang. "Heliodorus' *Aethiopica* in Art." *Journal of the Warburg and Courtauld Institutes* 16, nos. 1–2 (1953), pp. 144–52.

Stein 2001
Stein, Perrin. "Jacques Callot: *Study of a Horse.*" In "Recent Acquisitions, A Selection: 2000–2001." *The Metropolitan Museum of Art Bulletin* 59, no. 2 (Fall 2001), p. 28.

Stein 2002
Stein, Perrin. Review of *From Drawing to Painting: Poussin, Watteau, Fragonard, David, and Ingres,* by Pierre Rosenberg. *Master Drawings* 40, no. 2 (Summer 2002), pp. 173–74.

Stein and Royalton-Kisch 2005–6
French Drawings from the British Museum, Clouet to Seurat. Exhibition, The Metropolitan Museum of Art, New York, November 8, 2005–January 29, 2006; The British Museum, London, June 29–November 26, 2006. Catalogue by Perrin Stein and Martin Royalton-Kisch. London, 2005.

Steward and Knox 1996–97
The Mask of Venice: Masking, Theater, and Identity in the Art of Tiepolo and His Time. Exhibition, Berkeley Art Museum, University of California, December 11, 1996–March 4, 1997. Catalogue by James Christen Steward and George Knox. Berkeley, 1996.

Stone 1991
Guercino, Master Draftsman: Works from North American Collections. Exhibition, Arthur M. Sackler Museum, Harvard University, Cambridge, Mass., February 15–March 31, 1991; National Gallery of Canada, Ottawa, May 3–June 16, 1991; Cleveland Museum of Art, August 27–October 13, 1991. Catalogue by David M. Stone. Cambridge, Mass., 1991.

Succi 1994
Succi, Dario. "Venezia incisa: Le fabriche, e vedute." In *Luca Carlevarijs e la veduta veneziana del Settecento,* pp. 295–98. Exhibition, Palazzo della Ragione, Padua, September 25–December 26, 1994. Catalogue by Isabella Reale, Dario Succi, and others. Milan, 1994.

Sumowski 1967
Handzeichnungen alter Meister aus Schweizer Privatbesitz. Exhibition, Kunsthalle, Bremen, April 16–May 21, 1967; Kunsthaus, Zurich, October–December 1967. Catalogue by Werner Sumowski. Bremen, 1967.

Supino 1938
Supino, I[gino] B[envenuto]. *L'arte nelle chiese di Bologna, secoli XV–XVI.* Bologna, 1938.

Taylor 1976
European Drawings from Canadian Collections, 1500–1900 / Dessins européens des collections canadiennes, 1500–1900. Exhibition, National Gallery of Canada, Ottawa; Vancouver Art Gallery; Dalhousie Art Gallery, Dalhousie University, Halifax, 1976. Catalogue by Mary Cazort Taylor. Ottawa, 1976.

Ternois 1962
Ternois, Daniel. *Jacques Callot: Catalogue complet de son oeuvre dessiné.* Paris, 1962.

Ternois 1999
Ternois, Daniel. *Jacques Callot: Catalogue de son oeuvre dessiné; Supplément (1962–1998).* Paris, 1999.

Thiem 1977
Thiem, Christel. *Florentiner Zeichner des Frühbarock.* Italienische Forschungen, ser. 3, vol. 10. Munich, 1977.

Thomas 1954
Thomas, Hylton. *The Drawings of Giovanni Battista Piranesi.* New York, 1954.

Tietze and Tietze-Conrat 1944
Tietze, Hans, and E[rika] Tietze-Conrat. *The Drawings of the Venetian Painters in the 15th and 16th Centuries.* New York, 1944.

Titi 1674
Titi, Filippo. *Stvdio di pittvra, scoltvra, et architettvra, nelle chiese di Roma: nel quale si hà notitia di tutti gl'artefici, che hanno iui operato: con vna breue introduttione delle fondationi e ristori delle medesime chiese, e strada facile per ritrouarle.* Rome, 1674.

Tokyo 1975
Devonshā Kōshaku shozō Yōroppa shbyō meisakuten: Chattsuwāsu korekushon / Old Master Drawings from Chatsworth: A Loan Exhibition from the Devonshire Collection. Exhibition, Kokuritsu Seiyō Bijutsukan [National Museum of Western Art], Tokyo, January 25–March 23, 1975. Catalogue by A[rthur] E[wart] Popham and others. Tokyo, 1975.

Tongiorgi Tomasi and Tosi 1990
Tongiorgi Tomasi, Lucia, and Alessandro Tosi. *"Flora e Pomona": L'orticoltura nei disegni e nelle incisioni dei secoli XVI–XIX.* Florence, 1990.

Turin 1961–62. *See* **Salamon 1961–62.**

Turner 2000
Turner, Nicholas. *Federico Barocci.* Paris, 2000.

Turner 2002
Turner, Nicholas. "Le periferie del *corpus graphicum* del Parmigianino: Problemi di attribuzioni incerte fra gli specialisti." In *Parmigianino e il manierismo europeo: Atti del Convegno internazionale di studi—Parma, 13–15 giugno 2002,* edited by Lucia Fornari Schianchi, pp. 227–32. Cinisello Balsamo, Milan, 2002.

Turner 2007–
Turner, Nicholas. "Guercino." In *Oxford Art Online*. [Oxford and New York], 2007– .

Turner and Plazzotta 1991
Drawings by Guercino from British Collections. Exhibition, The British Museum, London, May 17–August 18, 1991. Catalogue by Nicholas Turner and Carol Plazzotta. London, 1991.

Turner, Hendrix, and Plazzotta 1997
Turner, Nicholas, Lee Hendrix, and Carol Plazzotta. *European Drawings 3: Catalogue of the Collections.* [The J. Paul Getty Museum.] Los Angeles, 1997.

Van Tuyll van Serooskerken 2000
Van Tuyll van Serooskerken, Carel. *The Italian Drawings of the Fifteenth and Sixteenth Centuries in the Teyler Museum.* Haarlem, Ghent, and Doornspijk, 2000.

Van Tuyll van Serooskerken 2008
Van Tuyll van Serooskerken, Carel. *Baccio Bandinelli.* Musée du Louvre, Cabinet des dessins, 16. Milan and Paris, 2008.

Udine 1965. *See* **Rizzi and Morassi 1965.**

Udine 1995–96. *See* **Concina and Reale 1995–96.**

Udine and Bloomington 1996–97
Domenico Tiepolo, Master Draftsman. Exhibition, Castello di Udine, September 14–December 31, 1996; Indiana University Art Museum, Bloomington, January 15–March 9, 1997. Catalogue by Adelheid M. Gealt, George Knox, and others. Bloomington, Ind., 1996.

Vaccaro 2001
Vaccaro, Mary. "Parmigianino and Andrea Baiardi: Figuring Petrarchan Beauty in Renaissance Parma." *Word & Image* 17, no. 3 (July–September 2001), pp. 243–58.

Vaccaro 2005
Vaccaro, Mary. "Parmigianino's Virgins in Santa Maria della Steccata: Wise or Foolish?" *Belle arti: Saggi di storia e di stile* 1 (2005), pp. 40–47.

Valencia and Alcalá 1989. *See* **Brown 1989.**

Vasari ed. 1966–87
Vasari, Giorgio. *Le vite de' più eccellenti pittori, scultori e architettori nelle redazioni del 1550 e 1568.* Edited by Rosanna Bettarini; commentary by Paola Barocchi. 6 vols. 1550; 1568. Florence, 1966–87.

Vasari–Milanesi ed. 1906
Vasari, Giorgio. *Le vite de' più eccellenti pittori, scultori ed architettori scritte da Giorgio Vasari, pittore aretino, con nuove annotazioni e commenti di Gaetano Milanesi.* 2nd ed. 9 vols. 1878–85. Florence, 1906.

Venice 1978. *See* **Bettagno 1978.**

Venice 2001
Canaletto: Prima maniera. Exhibition, Fondazione Giorgio Cini, Venice, March 18–June 10, 2001. Catalogue by Alessandro Bettagno, Bożena Anna Kowalczyk, and others. Milan, 2001.

Viale Ferrero 1963
Viale Ferrero, Mercedes. *Arazzi italiani del Cinquecento.* 2nd ed. 1961. Milan, 1963.

Viatte 1988
Viatte, Françoise. *Dessins toscans XVIe–XVIIIe siècles.* Vol. 1, *1560–1640.* Musée du Louvre, Cabinet des Dessins. Inventaire général des dessins italiens, 3. Paris, 1988.

Vienna 1981. *See* **Birke 1981.**

Vienna and Munich 1986
Meisterzeichnungen aus sechs Jahrhunderten: Die Sammlung Ian Woodner. Exhibition, Graphische Sammlung Albertina, Vienna, January 25–March 2, 1986; Haus der Kunst, Munich, March 25–May 25, 1986. Catalogue by Veronika Birke, Friedrich Piel, and others. Cologne, 1986.

Vitzthum 1963
Vitzthum, Walter. "Disegni di Alessandro Algardi." *Bollettino d'arte* 48, nos. 1–2 (January–June 1963), pp. 75–98.

Volpi et al. 1994
Volpi, Caterina, et al. *Il Libro dei disegni di Pirro Ligorio all'Archivio di Stato di Torino.* Rome, 1994.

Voragine ed. 1969
Voragine, Jacobus de. *The Golden Legend of Jacobus de Voragine.* Translated by William Granger Ryan and Helmut Ripperger. 1941. New York, 1969.

Voragine ed. 1993
Voragine, Jacobus de. *The Golden Legend: Readings on the Saints.* Translated by William Granger Ryan. 2 vols. Princeton, N.J., 1993.

Waagen 1838
Waagen, G[ustave] F[riedrich]. *Works of Art and Artists in England.* 3 vols. London, 1838.

Waldman 2004
Waldman, Louis A. *Baccio Bandinelli and Art at the Medici Court: A Corpus of Early Modern Sources.* Memoirs of the American Philosophical Society, 251. Philadelphia, 2004.

Ward 1988
Baccio Bandinelli, 1493–1560: Drawings from British Collections. Exhibition, Fitzwilliam Museum, Cambridge, May 3–July 3, 1988. Catalogue by Roger Ward. Cambridge, 1988.

Ward-Jackson 1980
Ward-Jackson, Peter. *Italian Drawings.* Vol. 2, *17th–18th Century.*
Victoria and Albert Museum Catalogues. London, 1980.

Washington, D.C., 1962–63. *See* **Popham 1962–63.**

Washington, D.C., Dallas, and Detroit 1976–77. *See* **Rosand
and Muraro 1976–77.**

Weber 1996
Weber, Gregor J. M. "Die Auftragsarbeiten Giovanni Battista Tiepolos
für König August III." *Dresdener Kunstblätter* 40, no. 6 (1996), pp. 181–90.

Wethey 1987
Wethey, Harold E. *Titian and His Drawings: With Reference to Giorgione
and Some Close Contemporaries.* Princeton, N.J., 1987.

Whistler 2003–4
Whistler, Catherine. "Artists, Collectors and the Appreciation of
Florentine Drawings of the Early Seventeenth Century." In *Graceful
and True: Drawing in Florence c.1600,* pp. 10–21. Exhibition, Ashmolean
Museum, Oxford, October 15, 2003–January 18, 2004; P. & D.
Colnaghi, London, January 30–March 2, 2004; The Djanogly Art
Gallery, Nottingham, March 12–May 9, 2004. Catalogue by Julian
Brooks and Catherine Whistler. Oxford, 2003.

Widauer 1991
*Italienische Zeichnungen des 16. Jahrhunderts: Die Graphische Sammlung des
Linzer Stadtmuseums Nordico.* Exhibition, Stadtmuseum Linz-Nordico,
Linz, January 11–February 24, 1991. Catalogue by Heinz Widauer. Linz,
1991.

Widauer 1997
Widauer, Heinz. *Italienische Zeichnungen des 16. bis 19. Jahrhunderts.*
Kataloge der Graphischen Sammlung des Stadtmuseums Linz-Nordico,
9. Linz, 1997.

Wilton-Ely 1978
Wilton-Ely, John. *The Mind and Art of Giovanni Battista Piranesi.*
London, 1978.

Wolk 1987
Wolk, Linda Jane. "Studies in Perino del Vaga's Early Career." PhD
diss., University of Michigan, Ann Arbor, 1987.

Wolk-Simon 1987
Wolk-Simon, Linda. "A Drawing by Perino del Vaga for the *Loggia
degli Eroi* of the Villa Doria and a Document from the Genoese
Period." *Master Drawings* 25, no. 4 (Winter 1987), pp. 410–14, pl. 45.

Wolk-Simon 1991–93
Italian Old Master Drawings from the Collection of Jeffrey E. Horvitz.
Exhibition, Samuel P. Harn Museum of Art, University of Florida,

Gainesville, July 12–September 8, 1991; then Spencer Museum of
Art, The University of Kansas, Lawrence; The Minneapolis Institute
of Arts; Fogg Art Museum, Harvard University, Cambridge, Mass.;
The Taft Museum, Cincinnati; The Montreal Museum of Fine
Arts, 1991–93. Catalogue by Linda Wolk-Simon. Gainsville, Fla.,
1991.

Wolk-Simon 1992
Wolk-Simon, Linda. "The 'Pala Doria' and Andrea Doria's Mortuary
Chapel: A Newly Discovered Project by Perino del Vaga." *Artibus et
historiae* 13, no. 25 (1992), pp. 163–75.

Wolk-Simon 1996–97
Wolk-Simon, Linda. "People Watching in the Piazza: Love, Marriage,
and Divorce in Tiepolo's Scenes of Contemporary Life." *Drawing* 18,
no. 3 (Winter 1996–97), pp. 65–70.

Wolk-Simon 1997
*Domenico Tiepolo: Drawings, Prints, and Paintings in The Metropolitan
Museum of Art.* Exhibition, The Metropolitan Museum of Art, New
York, January–April 1997. Catalogue by Linda Wolk-Simon. New
York, 1997. Also published as *The Metropolitan Museum of Art Bulletin*
54, no. 3 (Winter 1996–97).

Wolk-Simon 2002
Wolk-Simon, Linda. "Two Early Fresco Cycles by Perino del Vaga:
The Palazzo Baldassini and the Pucci Chapel." *Apollo* 155, no. 481
(March 2002), pp. 11–21.

Würzburg 1996
Der Himmel auf Erden: Tiepolo in Würzburg. Exhibition, Der Bayerischen
Verwaltung der staatlichen Schlösser, Gärten und Seen in der
Residenz Würzburg, February 15–May 19, 1996. Catalogue by Peter
O. Krückmann and others. 2 vols. Munich, 1996.

Zanetti 1771
Zanetti, Antonio Maria. *Della pittura veneziana e delle opere pubbliche de
veneziani maestri, libri V.* Venice, 1771.

Zezza 1994
Zezza, Andrea. "Tra Perino del Vaga e Daniele da Volterra: Alcune
proposte, e qualche conferma, per Marco Pino a Roma." *Prospettiva,*
no. 73–74 (January–April 1994), pp. 144–58.

Zezza 1995
Zezza, Andrea. "Precisazioni su Marco Pino al Gesù Vecchio." *Dialoghi
di storia dell'arte,* no. 1 (1995), pp. 104–25.

Zezza 2003
Zezza, Andrea. *Marco Pino: L'opera completa.* Naples, 2003.

Tiepolo, Giovanni Battista, **206–10**, *206, 207, 209, 210,* 214, 216,
219, 224
Tintoretto, Jacopo, **74–76**, *75, 76,* 104, 106, 118
Titian, 34, *34,* 74, 118, 206, 226
Tito, Santi di, 128, 140

van Dyck, Anthony, 176
Vanni, Francesco, 133
Vanvitelli, Gaspare (Gaspar van Wittel), **197–99**, *197, 198, 199*
Vanvitelli, Luigi, 197
Vasari, Giorgio, 2, 6, 10, 13, 18, 21, 24, 25, 26, 28, 29, 30, 63, **68–70**,
69, 80
Vassilacchi, Antonio, 106

Veronese, Paolo, 104, 106, 206
Viani, Giovanni Maria, 137, *137*
Vicentino, Andrea Michieli, Il, **104–6**, *104, 105, 106*
Vignali, Jacopo, 188
Vincidor, Tommaso, **26–29**
Visentini, Antonio, 200, 213
Volterrano, Baldassare Franceschini, Il, **178–80**, *178, 179, 180*

Wijngaarde, Frans van den, 67, *67*
Wittel, Gaspar van. *See* Vanvitelli, Gaspare (Gaspar van Wittel)

Zuccaro, Federico, 84, **99–103**, *99, 100, 101, 102,* 106, 197
Zuccaro, Taddeo, 77, *77,* 78, **92–94**, *93, 94,* 95, 99, 197

PHOTOGRAPH CREDITS

Unless otherwise specified, all photographs were supplied by the owners of the works of art, who hold the copyright thereto, and are reproduced with permission. We have made every effort to obtain permissions for all copyright-protected images. If you have copyright-protected work in this publication and you have not given us permission, please contact the Metropolitan Museum's Editorial Department. Photographs of works in the Metropolitan Museum's collection are by the Photograph Studio, The Metropolitan Museum of Art; new photography is by Mark Morosse. Additional photograph credits:

Albertina, Vienna: figs. 20.2, 28.1, 28.2, 38.1, 50.1

Alinari / Art Resource, NY: figs. 10.2, 22.1, 26.1, 50.2

Photography © The Art Institute of Chicago: fig. 49.2

Ashmolean Museum of Art and Archaeology, Oxford: figs. 18.1, 35.1, 38.4, 66.2

Baldassari 1990, p. 48, fig. 24: fig. 54.1

Biblioteca Marucelliana, Florence: photographs Donato Pineider: figs. 17.1, 17.2, 17.3, 17.4

Bohn 2004, cat. no. 51, p. 163: fig. 35.2

Boijmans Van Beuningen Museum, Rotterdam: fig. 9.2

Bologna, Los Angeles, and Fort Worth 1988–89, cat. no. 9, pp. 26–7: fig. 39.1

Collection of Jean Bonna, Geneva: figs. 30.2, 31.2

Professor Paolo Brandinelli: figs. 3.1, 3.2

© The Trustees of the British Museum: figs. 3.4, 9.1, 9.4, 18.5, 18.6, 33.2, 33.4, 37.1, 47.1, 47.2

© The Trustees of the British Museum / Art Resource, NY: figs. 2.3, 5.2

Campbell et al. 2002: fig. 7.3

Chiappini di Sorio 1975, no. 38, p. 113: fig. 34.1

© By permission of the Governing Body of Christ Church, Oxford: figs. 1.1, 18.4, 27.3

Christie's, London 1991, lot 14: fig. 38.2

Cooper-Hewitt, National Design Museum, Smithsonian Institution, New York / Art Resource, NY: fig. 23.2

Crocker Art Museum, E. B. Crocker Art Collection, Sacramento: fig. 4.1

© DeA Picture Library / Art Resource, NY: photograph G. Nimatallah: figs. 41.1, 41.2

© The Devonshire Collection, Chatsworth. Reproduced by permission of The Chatsworth Settlement Trustees: fig. 61.1

Di Giampaolo 1997, p. 181, fig. 99: fig. 16.3

École nationale supérieure des Beaux-Arts, Paris: fig. 48.1

Emiliani 1985, p. 115, fig. 204: fig. 27.2

Foto Marburg / Art Resource, NY: fig. 24.1

John R. Freeman & Co. Ltd., London: fig. 1.2

Gemin and Pedrocco 1993, no. 299: fig. 64.1

J. Paul Getty Museum, Los Angeles: fig. 37.3

Gulbenkian Foundation, Lisbon: fig. 68.1

Collection of Sir Mark Fehrs Haukohl and the Haukohl Family, Houston, Texas: fig. 58.2

Höper 1987: fig. 25.1

Erich Lessing / Art Resource, NY: fig. 51.4

Mason Rinaldi 1984, cat. no. 493, fig. 767: fig. 33.1; cat. no. D 95, fig. 768: fig. 33.2